Interpreting Law and Literature

D0777667

Interpreting Law and Literature

A Hermeneutic Reader

Edited by
Sanford Levinson
and
Steven Mailloux

Northwestern University Press
Evanston, IL

Northwestern University Press
Evanston, Illinois 60201

Copyright © 1988 by Northwestern University Press.
First published 1988. All rights reserved.

Printed in the United States of America.
95 94 93 92 91 90   6 5 4 3 2

Library of Congress Cataloging-in-Publication Data

Interpreting law and literature: a hermeneutic reader/edited by
    Sanford Levinson and Steven Mailloux.
            p.   cm.
        Bibliography: p.
        Includes index.
        ISBN 0-8101-0770-8   ISBN 0-8101-0793-7 (pbk.)
        1. United States—Constitutional law—Interpretation and
    construction. 2. Hermeneutics. 3. Law and literature.
    I. Levinson, Sanford, 1941-   . II. Mailloux, Steven.
    KF4550.A2I53 1988
    342.73—dc19
    [347.302]   88-22402
                                                       CIP

For Stanley Fish,
whatever the consequences

Contents

Preface

Hermeneutics is "the theory or art of explication, of interpretation."[1] Its lineage goes back to ancient attempts to construct general rules for understanding religious texts such as the Bible. Interest in biblical interpretation, however, was scarcely neutral and detached: the Sacred Text defined itself as normatively binding, and debates about textual meaning necessarily became debates about how lives should be lived. Legal texts are similarly normative for cultures recognizing their authority, so it is not surprising that similar controversies have developed in regard to methods of legal interpretation.[2] As E. D. Hirsch has written, traditional "hermeneutical theorizing was confined almost exclusively to two domains where correct interpretation was a matter of life and death (or Heaven and Hell)—the study of scripture and the study of law."[3]

Almost all aspects of a mature legal system—and "maturity" has been present at least since the Roman law system of some two thousand years ago—involve recourse to written documents, ranging from the wills of discrete individuals to the constitution of a modern nation-state. Of course, legal events more often require the reading of texts such as wills, custody decrees, business contracts, and the like than scrutiny of administrative regulations, statutes, or constitutions. But what all such events do have in common is the necessity of interpretation, of giving meaning to the black ink on the white page. Though some argue that methods of interpretation may differ depending on whether a will or a constitution is being analyzed, few disagree that ascertaining the meaning of texts is a central reality of any legal system.

The word *hermeneutics* entered American legal discourse almost 150 years ago, when Francis Lieber, a German immigrant, in 1839 published *Legal and Political Hermeneutics or Principles of Interpretation and Construction in Law and Politics with Remarks on Precedents and Authorities*.[4] Lieber defined hermeneutics as "[t]hat branch of science which establishes the principles and rules of interpretation and construction."[5] He also expressed the anxiety sometimes attached to recognizing the inevitability of interpretation: "[C]onstruction endeavors to arrive at conclusions beyond the absolute sense of the text, and . . . it is dangerous on this account." Thus, he says, "we must strive the more anxiously to find out safe rules, to guide us on the dangerous path."[6] The debate, then as now, concerns what count as "safe rules," whether they can be "scientifically" established, and their independence from political or other "interested" perspectives.

The nineteenth century also saw the development of interest in what might be called "general" or "philosophical hermeneutics." This approach, associated with the work of Friedrich Schliermacher and Wilhelm Dilthey, attempted, in Roy Howard's words, to find "a theory of knowledge for the data with which the cultural [as opposed to the natural] scientist works—such things as texts, signs and symbols of various sorts, rituals, images, examples of the fine and useful arts—in short, for such products as are the result rather of man's deliberate ingenuity than of nature's blind working."[7] In this way, *all* texts, including literary ones, came within the purview of the hermeneutic theorist. During the twentieth century, and increasingly within the last forty years, literary studies as a discipline has devoted more and more attention to the problematics of interpretive theory, and it is fair to say that the sophistication of the analyses has far surpassed anything that had previously occurred within the legal academy.

Recent literary theory has emphasized the ubiquity of interpretation in the process of reading every text—even where it seems to us as readers that no active interpretation is taking place at all. This claim implies that not even the simplest text is immune to interpretive controversy. The constitutional requirement that the president be at least thirty-five, for example, is "clear" only so long as one assumes a consensus, which now exists, about which calendar to use, in our case the so-called Gregorian, solar calendar. But some cultures, including Judaism, Islam, and China, compute dates on the basis of a lunar calendar, and someone who is thirty-five under one system might well not be thirty-five under the other. Identifying someone's age turns out to be a delicate question of interpretation.

One of the most influential contemporary approaches to literary analysis is "deconstruction," which is most often linked with the name of the French philosopher Jacques Derrida. Commenting on deconstruction as a strategy of reading, Derrida states that "the writer writes *in* a language and *in* a logic whose proper system, laws, and life his discourse by definition cannot dominate absolutely. He uses them only by letting himself, after a fashion and up to a point, be governed by the system. And the reading must always aim at a certain relationship, unperceived by the writer, between what he commands and what he does not command of the patterns of the language that he uses."[8] More recently, Derrida has explained that "deconstruction used as a French word, means not 'destroying' but 'undoing,' while analyzing the different layers of a structure to know how it has been built. Everything which is not natural has a structure, and has been built; and deconstruction is, to some extent, a way of analyzing the structure. . . . Deconstruction . . . emphasizes the history of the construction and the different layers which have built this construction."[9]

What are some of the implications of such an approach? Barbara Johnson, a leading American deconstructionist theorist, notes the traditional emphasis on looking for what she calls the "bottom line" of determinate meaning. "[W]hat deconstruction does," she says, "is to teach you to ask: 'What does the construction of the bottom line leave out? What does it repress? What does it disregard? What does it consider unimportant? What does it put in the margins?'"[10] Deconstructionist critics, including Derrida, Johnson, and the late Paul de Man of Yale, seek to show that the repression of certain questions from a discourse is not merely an occasional fact about it—and a signal of some kind of "imperfection" of the discourse—but rather a *structuring principle* that makes possible the discourse itself.

"Disciplines," whether we call them law, literary criticism, medicine, or whatever, make very strong claims to unity, self-sufficiency, and determinacy, at least on the part of those who have adequately learned their modes of speaking. What a deconstructionist does is to point to repressed elements within a particular discourse and therefore to disrupt these claims and, beyond this, to challenge established boundaries and disciplinary demarcations. Indeed, it has been argued by recent theorists that the separation of one discipline from another—literature from philosophy, literary criticism from law—exemplifies the way the purported unity and coherence of a discipline are constituted by the repression of some set of issues and questions which become designated as alien or "other." To learn to "think like a lawyer" is, among other things, to learn what kinds of questions *not* to ask at pain of appearing "nonlawyerly." As Brook Thomas notes in his recent *Cross-Examinations of Law and Literature*, "one result of the specialization and professionalization of knowledge" that developed in the late nineteenth century was to break up an earlier "law-and-letters configuration" that had bound creative writers and lawyers together both in their personal relationships and professional concerns.[11] As Thomas adds, "[A]lthough professional specialization led to important advances in knowledge, it also led to the production of categories that excluded certain types of questions." Almost inevitably, this kind of observation leads one to ask whether the acknowledged benefits of "advances in knowledge" might have been mixed, to whatever extent, with the less acknowledged costs of excluding "certain types of questions" from the self-confident discourse of the discipline or profession.

It is such exclusions that recent literary theory has been most concerned to reveal (and to criticize), and one result has been the confluence of legal and literary interpretation that has resulted in this anthology. Contemporary theory has usefully analyzed how alternative modes of interpretation produce different meanings, how reading itself is constituted by the variable perspectives of readers, and how these perspectives are in turn defined by prejudices, ideologies, interests, and so forth. Some theorists have argued persuasively that textual meaning, in literature and in literary interpretation, is structured by repression and forgetting, by what the literary or critical text does *not* say as much as by what it does. All these claims are directly relevant to legal hermeneutics, and thus it is no surprise that legal theorists have recently been turning to literary theory for potential insight into the interpretation of law. This collection of essays is designed to represent the especially rich interaction that has taken place between legal and literary hermeneutics during the past ten years.

We hope that the gathering together of these cross-disciplinary essays will prove useful to specialists in both literary and legal studies. We do not, however, imagine specialists to be our only audience, and we hope that readers outside these professional disciplines, including students, will find the essays to be as informative as they are challenging. With these nonspecialists in mind, we begin by providing the larger political context for recent controversies over legal hermeneutics. Thus, section I, on Politics and Interpretive Theory, illustrates the passionate debate over constitutional interpretation. Certainly one reason for such passion is the widespread belief that large political stakes rest on the answers chosen to questions of legal method and interpretive theory.

Section II, on The Question of Method, then presents a broad range of perspectives, from "originalism" through "critical legal studies" and "deconstruction," positions which focus on the main theoretical problems in legal and literary hermeneutics. Here the selections dramatize the current controversies over such issues as intention, formalism, and the possibility of objective interpretation. All of these controversies involve the key question of whether an interpreter can remain separate from an external text and ultimately submit to the reading demanded by the text. In what sense, if at all, do texts exert control over what their readers make of them? Apparently simple at first sight, this question proves surprisingly complex when pursued.

Practically everyone now admits that texts can be interpreted only in some "context."[12] The obvious question then becomes how such contextual reading takes place, and how we decide what the relevant contexts are. The question is inconsequential only so long as everyone reads a text, whether a sonnet or a constitution, in the same way. Interpretive disputes most often arise precisely when there is no such common reading. The easy resolution of conflict by arguing that "everyone knows what *x* means" is made impossible by the very fact that a litigant or a literary critic is challenging the asserted commonality. In law, the structure of litigation, of course, involves turning to an outsider called a judge who presumably provides a disinterested account of what the law requires. A central issue within law is therefore the ability to maintain a separation between disinterested legal analysis and interest-saturated political decision-making. Only such a separation allows the litigants to believe that well-trained judges will reach their verdicts without any taint of their personal political views. The decline of a belief in judicially produced right answers derived from techniques of right reading has recently led some analysts, especially those identified with critical legal studies (represented in this collection especially by Mark Tushnet and Clare Dalton), to assert that legal rules are determined by political and historical contingencies. Given these ambiguities of interpretation, many legal theorists have substituted for the hermeneutics of objective interpretation what Gerald Graff has termed a "hermeneutics of power,"[13] where one emphasizes the political and social determinants of reading texts one way as opposed to another. Indeed, it is often suggested that the major reason for preferring a reading lies in the political consequences occasioned by it.

This brings us to the final section, Rhetorical Politics. This section presents a group of essays that respond to the dilemmas at issue in the earlier debates by insisting that the terms in which the questions are posed be redefined. In particular, the reader will discover in this section a shift in emphasis from the search for a sound hermeneutical method to the elaboration of the rhetorical underpinnings of all interpretive arguments. The focus of attention here becomes the individual legal opinion, which is analyzed less for the abstract interpretive theories it may purport to incarnate than for the particular context in which it was written and the audience to which it was addressed.

It will remain for the reader, of course, to decide whether the interaction between law and literary theory is a productive one or, just as importantly, whether the move from hermeneutics to rhetoric illustrated here resolves any of the anxieties that called forth the concern about interpretation in the first place. We can only hope that this collection of essays will foster a more general understanding and a deeper exploration of the issues and stakes involved in contemporary theories of reading cultural texts, whether legal or literary.

Acknowledgments

Steve Mailloux would like to thank the University of Miami and Syracuse University for financial assistance and the Stanford Humanities Center for a year-long fellowship that helped support some of his work on this volume, and he is grateful to Dee Marquez and Susan Sebbard for assistance in typing the section introductions. Sanford Levinson would like to thank the National Endowment for the Humanities and the University of Texas Research Institute, who provided the funding by which he could be a member of the Institute for Advanced Study in Princeton, New Jersey, during 1986–87, where he completed his editorial contributions to this book.

Both editors owe their greatest debt to Jerry Graff, who came up with the idea for the volume, drafted the editors, and then helped at every stage in the development of the project. Without his encouragement and advice, *Interpreting Law and Literature* would never have been completed.

Politics and Interpretive Theory

Introduction

The more general topics of hermeneutics concern *all* legal documents. Yet our introduction—and a large number of readings throughout the collection—focuses on one particular text—the Constitution of the United States. This emphasis reflects the concentration on constitutional interpretation by many of the theorists who have written in the past decade about legal hermeneutics. Surely one reason for this concentration is the high degree of public controversy surrounding the Constitution. Given the linkage between constitutional interpretation and politically urgent issues such as busing, abortion, or affirmative action, more rides on how the Constitution is interpreted than on, say, how a particular state statute is construed. "What the Constitution means" takes on importance when the interpretation directly affects public policy toward social problems and political conflicts.

These effects derive, in part, from the coercive power of the state that can, in the name of the Constitution, be brought to bear against recalcitrants. But another, more subtle but no less real, effect involves the respect, indeed some would say veneration, accorded the Constitution within American political rhetoric (even if not necessarily practice). Insofar as people believe that the Constitution is a repository of wisdom on which the vision of social order and justice contained in the Preamble depends, any statement that the Constitution "requires" or "prohibits" certain conduct is viewed not only as a factual assertion about the law but as a normative principle with moral weight. To be able to invoke the Constitution in the defense of one's position is thought to be no small matter.

Invocations of the Constitution—and disputes about rules for its interpretation—are likely to be made with greatest intensity in times of political conflict. As Michael Kammen has said, "Ultimately, . . . for better and for worse, it is ideological conflict that most meaningfully calls attention to the Constitution."[1] The recent burst of interest in constitutional interpretation certainly corroborates Kammen's claim.

American politics in the Reagan era is probably more self-consciously ideological than at any time in living memory. A focus on consensus and only marginal differences between the two major political parties have been replaced by a choice between sharply contrasting visions of political life. Surely no recent president has come to office in such ostensible commitment to a "revolutionary" approach to government. Part of this revolution involves an attack on, and reordering of, the judicial branch of the national government, which has been accused of collaborating with (and at times leading) an illegitimate deviation from the ideal government established by the Constitution. For example, William Bradford Reynolds, the assistant attorney general in charge of the Civil Rights Division of the Justice Department, has specifically attacked Supreme Court Justice William Brennan for his alleged vision of "a radically egalitarian society." Indeed, according to Mr. Reynolds, "Nothing threatens our civil rights and political liberties more."[2] It is not surprising that an administration with such views has attempted to change the direction of the judiciary as new judges are appointed.

Most presidents have chosen judges from their own political party, but no other administration in modern times has so self-consciously emphasized constitutional ideology in choosing judicial nominees. This phenomenon became especially visible with the nominations of William Rehnquist to succeed Warren Burger as chief justice of the Supreme Court and of Antonin Scalia and Robert Bork to join the Court as associate justices. All three nominees were chosen in significant measure because of their perceived devotion to achieving conservative political results through judicial interpretation of legal texts. But that, of course, is a tendentious way of putting it. These justices and their supporters would argue instead that the political consequences of their interpretations are simply a function of required modes of construction that are independent of the political results they generate. Indeed, many supporters of Justice Brennan would make the same sort of defense against those critics who viewed him as inappropriately seeking liberal reforms through his legal decisions. In precisely this way, debates between political conservatives and liberals now often take place, not in direct encounters over specific solutions to social problems, but through clashes over differing approaches to constitutional interpretation.

The emergence in the past decade of a vigorous right-wing conservatism has served, among other things, to move what had appeared to be merely esoteric debates about constitutional interpretation from the pages of the law reviews to the headlines of the nation's newspapers and magazines. Ten years ago, speaking at the University of Texas Law School, then-Justice Rehnquist, already recognized as the leading intellectual proponent of a conservative turn by the Supreme Court, described his role as consisting only of the enforcement of the understandings and values that "may be derived from the language and intent of the framers" of the Constitution. He presented in invidious contrast the proponents of a so-called living Constitution, who, he alleged, wish to substitute "some other set of values" in place of the original ones. He denounced this theory as a "formula for an end run around popular government" insofar as it legitimizes the imposition by appointed federal judges of "a rule of conduct that the popularly elected branches of government would not have enacted and the voters have not and would not have embodied in the Constitution."[3]

Robert Bork, while a law professor at Yale, had made similar arguments in the early 1970s. Appointed by President Reagan to the Court of Appeals for the District of Columbia in 1981, Bork stated in a 1984 lecture that "[i]t is necessary to establish the proposition that the framers' intentions . . . are the sole legitimate premise from which constitutional analysis may proceed."[4] Justice Rehnquist's and Judge Bork's remarks were short and to the point, yet few nonreaders of law reviews became aware of them. Things are different now, in large part because of the dramatic public support given to similar views by Attorney General Edwin Meese, who made headlines when he raised the question of constitutional interpretation in a 1985 speech before the American Bar Association.[5] The attorney general is no philosopher and his remarks were scarcely systematic, but they nonetheless triggered an important public debate whose ground had been laid by such writers as Rehnquist and Bork.

Meese invoked the writtenness of our Constitution and the consequent authority this writtenness presumably engenders. "The preservation of liberty required a document of clear and common language that created limited powers. . . . A *written* constitution was to serve as an external tangible check on any arbitrary exercise of governmental power," including the arbitrariness of which judges could themselves be capable. Judges were thus to remain faithful to the boundaries of the written text, a text which was itself the repository of specific ideas held by the eighteenth-century authors of the initial 1787 document.

For Meese, the oath of office, where judges pledge to be faithful to the Constitution, entailed a promise to enforce only the original meaning of the founding document. Any danger of judicial arbitrariness would be obviated by adherence to "strict rules" by which "they would be hedged in by the common law regard for precedent." Regrettably, says Meese, this promise has not been observed: "[T]oo many courts have become more policy planners than interpreters of the law."[6] The contemporary Supreme Court, not to mention myriads of lower-court judges, have exhibited "a greater allegiance to what the Court thinks a constitutionally sound public policy than a deference to what the Constitution—its text and intention—may demand." Meese complains that modern judges tend to view the Constitution as "a transitional document that takes its meaning from the circumstances of each age. It is argued—and taught—and decreed—that in order to keep the Constitution viable its language and original meaning must often be ignored or blatantly changed by judicial opinion." Meese calls on the public to join him in opposing such revisionism.

The attorney general goes on to offer a new standard by which to test judges (and judicial nominees): a "Jurisprudence of Original Intention" to guarantee that constitutional "meaning [is] not to be changed by ordinary interpretation." This approach would require judges to ascertain the intentions of the initial authors of the relevant constitutional text, whether the Founding Fathers of 1787 in regard to the body of the Constitution or the 1868 framers of the Fourteenth Amendment. He assumes both that we can discover, through diligent historical research, what these authors intended their words to mean and that subsequent generations are bound by these intentions. According to the attorney general, such a jurisprudence "would produce defensible principles of government that would not be tainted by ideological predilection," for all judges would be constrained by the presumptively similar lessons to be learned from study of the background of the constitutional text.

* * *

Meese's talk focuses on several specific constitutional problems that exemplify his concern for historical fidelity and suspicion of judicial innovation. Part of the reason his talk received much more attention than the similar speeches of Rehnquist and Bork is that the attorney general offered a particularly volatile illustration of what consequences the acceptance of his theory might entail. He seemed to call into serious question the judicial application of the protections associated with the Bill of Rights[7]—including such basic notions as freedom of speech, free exercise of religion, and the prohibition of an established church—against action by the states. Lawyers refer to this application as the "incorporation" of the Bill of Rights into the Fourteenth Amendment, a twentieth-century development with a complicated genealogy.

Chief Justice Marshall had ruled in 1833 for a unanimous Court that the first eight amendments apply only to the *national* government. States were therefore presumably free to establish religions, infringe speech, and engage in a variety of behaviors forbidden to Congress. These were not mere hypothetical possibilities: Massachusetts, for example, had an established church until 1833, and southern states regularly prohibited the distribution of abolitionist tracts even to whites, let alone to slaves.

Probably the most important legal consequence of the Civil War was the passage and ratification of the Fourteenth Amendment in 1868, which among other things prohibited the states from abridging the "privileges and immunities of United States citizenship." Some commentators argued that the framers of the Fourteenth Amendment intended this clause to apply the Bill of Rights to the states, thus overruling Marshall's earlier decision, just as the very first clause of the amendment, establishing citizenship by birth, overturned the *Dred Scott* decision, which had held that blacks were constitutionally barred from being treated as United States citizens. There has been little serious debate about the first clause, and many would say that the reason is the clarity of both the language and the intentions underlying the language. Were the language and intentions as clear in supporting the application of the Bill of Rights to the states, then Meese's own argument would presumably have to support such an application. The language, however, is notoriously unclear, and there is no agreement about the probable meanings intended by its drafters.

The Supreme Court first interpreted this clause in the 1873 *Slaughter-House* cases.[8] The majority opinion has traditionally been read as rejecting the view, articulated in the dissenting opinions of four justices, that the clause applied the Bill of Rights to the states. Furthermore, the Supreme Court engaged in a full-scale debate about the original intentions behind the Fourteenth Amendment in a 1947 case, and the majority firmly rejected Justice Black's argument that the Fourteenth Amendment was intended by its drafters to include the substantive protections of the Bill of Rights.[9]

One might think that this background, however complex, had settled the issue of the application of the Bill of Rights to the states, but that is not at all the case. The Supreme Court may have decided that the authors of the Fourteenth Amendment had no intention of applying the Bill of Rights to the states; nonetheless, the Court has held almost all of the provisions of the Bill of Rights applicable to the states by "incorporating" them as part of the "due process" that the Fourteenth Amendment also requires from the states. Although particular theories differed, many different judges over this time found that the preservation of central conceptions of American liberty required that states be held to the same limits as the national government.

The history of this development covers almost a hundred years, beginning in 1886 with the incorporation of the right to just compensation when the state takes private property. In 1925 came the application of the free speech provisions of the First Amendment; the prohibition of state establishment of religion followed two decades later, in 1947. This decision was probably the first to generate widespread public discussion (and dissension), especially when, in 1948, the Court invalidated a policy of an Illinois school board that had allowed children to be "released" from school during the day in order to study religion. The 1947 decision also served as the ultimate basis for the extremely volatile decisions in 1961 and 1962 striking down school prayer laws in New York and Pennsylvania (and, inferentially, in all the other states that had adopted similar policies). Perhaps the most controversial of all, though, were a spate of decisions involving the rights of criminal defendants. In 1962, for example, the Court held that the Constitution prohibited the use in trial of evidence that had been seized by the police in violation of the Fourth Amendment. Similarly, in 1966, the Court promulgated the famous *Miranda* warnings, which had among their consequences the exclusion of confessions by defendants who had not been suitably advised of their right to remain silent. Although little public opposition is heard to the requirement, announced in 1963, that the state provide a lawyer to an indigent defendant, there is widespread antagonism to the exclusionary rule, which is often perceived, in Justice Cardozo's vivid phrase, as letting the burglar go free because the constable blundered.

The Reagan administration has publicly called for a constitutional amendment allowing at least some kinds of prayer in the public schools and for an overruling of the *Miranda* decision. Part of what lies behind the attorney general's argument, then, is an animus against the results achieved by the decisions of the 1960s. The argument focuses, however, not so much on the particular results as on the method of incorporation by which they were justified, in particular the seeming willingness of the Court to ignore the presumably limited intentions of the Fourteenth Amendment's authors in regard to applying the Bill of Rights to the states. "[N]othing can be done," wrote Meese, "to shore up the intellectually shaky foundation upon which the doctrine rests. And nowhere else has the principle of federalism been dealt so politically violent and constitutionally suspect a blow as by the theory of incorporation."

What generated headlines, of course, was the context of the attorney general's speech. Not simply abstract remarks, they announce a perception that many contemporary judges are illegitimately imposing idiosyncratic political values when they attempt to prevent states from engaging in behavior that would be clearly unconstitutional if attempted by the national government. Moreover, the attorney general implicitly promises that something can and will be done about this infringement of state power, including the appointment of judges willing to reconsider the legitimacy of the incorporation doctrine itself. This would, among other things, put in seeming jeopardy the duty of states to respect the freedom of speech. For obvious reasons, opponents of the attorney general wish to defend the legitimacy of the current understanding.

Meese's speech was not only widely reported, but also vigorously scrutinized and attacked. In the *Los Angeles Times*, for example, the distinguished historian Henry Steele Commager argued that "Meese Fails Course in Constitutional History,"[10] inasmuch as his argument called into question the legitimacy of much of the handiwork of the Supreme Court going well beyond simply contemporary decisions. A writer in the *Baltimore Sun* attacked "The Radical Jurisprudence of Mr. Meese."[11]

Perhaps most notable was the response, both direct and indirect, delivered by two sitting justices of the United States Supreme Court. Criticizing Meese's comments about the incorporation of the Bill of Rights, Justice John Paul Stevens accused the attorney general of insensitivity to the "profound importance of the Civil War and the post-war amendments on the structure of our government." In addition, Justice Stevens indirectly pointed to one important feature of Meese's argument that is true of all "intentionalist" positions—the potential for a sharp clash between attempts to follow original intentions and the traditional legal respect for previous judicial decisions. To be sure, Meese had invoked the authority of precedent and criticized judges for contemporary deviations from it. Yet Justice Stevens noted "that no Justice who has sat on the Supreme Court during the past sixty years" has questioned the legitimacy of incorporating as limits on state action the prohibitions on regulating speech that have been deemed part of the First Amendment.[12] An anti-incorporationist argument has the potential for massive instability in what has come to be settled law.

Ironically turning the methodology of intentionalism on the attorney general himself, Justice Stevens raised the possibility that he had "misconstrued the speech" given by Meese "and that [the attorney general] did not actually intend his recommended 'Jurisprudence of Original Intention' as a rejection of the proposition that the Fourteenth Amendment has made the First Amendment applicable to the States." However, says Stevens, "if there is ambiguity in the message that was conveyed by an articulate contemporary lawyer last July, is it not possible that some uncertainty may attend an effort to identify the precise messages that equally articulate lawyers were attempting to convey almost two hundred years ago?" And the justice goes on to dispute Meese's specific reconstruction of late eighteenth-century attitudes concerning the intersection of religion and state, about which Meese had criticized the Court regarding its pronouncements on the issue.

Perhaps the most significant attack on Meese's views was that delivered by Supreme Court Justice William Brennan, the first selection reprinted below. No judge more clearly incarnates what Meese opposes, and Justice Brennan took little time to prepare a full-scale answer, which he delivered as part of a symposium at Georgetown University on "Text and Teaching."[13] It is relatively unusual for a justice to speak publicly about contemporary controversies, and Justice Brennan's talk, though without overt reference to the attorney general, also generated headlines. In addition to headlines came scrutiny and, in some cases, criticism as vigorous as that directed at Meese. The *Wall Street Journal*, describing Justice Brennan as a "Voice from the Past," viewed his remarks as "the death-rattle of respectability for judicial activism."[14] In turn the attorney general further responded to Justice Brennan and other critics in a speech before the Federalist Society, the second selection reprinted below.

The *Wall Street Journal* assumes that there is an identifiable mode of behavior called "judicial activism," though almost no judges have ever described themselves as "activists." But in addition the *Journal* implies that one's propensity to be a "judicial activist" depends on the approach to constitutional interpretation that one adopts. In particular, there may be a tendency to identify intentionalism with political conservatism, given the extent to which Meese and the Reagan administration have carried the banner for that position; concomitantly, anti-intentionalism would presumably be identified with the political Left. Though there might be a modicum of truth to this identification if one focuses exclusively on some of the debates occurring in the mid 1980s, it is surely false as a general proposition.

Recall, for example, that Justice Black, in the 1947 debates about the meaning of the Fourteenth Amendment, had based his argument on the intentions of the framers of the amendment. Indeed, Justice Black, who was one of the major forces behind the Court's increased willingness to protect controversial speech against state interference, based his jurisprudence on the premise that the intentions of Madison and Jefferson, the ostensible authors of the First Amendment, determined its meaning and that they intended speech to be "absolutely" protected. "It is my belief that there *are* 'absolutes' in our Bill of Rights, and that they were put there on purpose by men who knew what words meant, and meant their prohibitions to be 'absolutes.' "[15] Thus, the admonition of the First Amendment that Congress pass "no law" abridging freedom of speech served as the basis for striking down what many regarded as reasonable regulation of speech.

* * *

As already suggested, few of the participants in the contemporary debates about constitutional interpretation, regardless of their place on the political spectrum, unequivocally deny that judges have a duty to respect the constitutional text. Indeed, the debate tends to take a highly stylized form, dictated by the conventions of American legal and political rhetoric. There are three standard questions (and their standard affirmative answers): First, ought we to expect judges to stay within the confines of the Constitution that they are appointed to interpret? Second, do there exist particular *methods* of approaching the constitutional text that allow us to distinguish between legitimate interpretation and sheer fabrication? It is as difficult to give a negative answer here as to the first question, unless we seemingly wish to commit ourselves to a radically relativist posture that could not tell the difference between interpretation and invention or, indeed, sanity and lunacy. The third part of this standard triad involves showing that a given judge has violated the interpretive standards whose existence we have presumably validated by our answer to the second question. The judge would thus be exposed as behaving illegitimately and as worthy of censure.

One aim of this book is to turn the questions sketched above into genuine interrogatories. Are we really saying anything of substance when we register an expectation that judges stay "within" the constraints provided by the constitutional text? Can one speak meaningfully of a "method" (much less a "science") of interpretation or, at most, are there only looser "modes" or "approaches"? Is there only *one* legitimate mode of interpretation, such as original intent? If there is more than one (and Philip Bobbitt's important contribution was to specify six modes of interpretation), is there any principled way of choosing among them? As will be clear, many of the legal theorists asking such questions have been much influenced by similar controversies going on within literary criticism and theory.

Whatever the theoretical connection, if any, between politics and theories of constitutional interpretation, the lively debate continues. We begin with Meese and Brennan because their essays are the most accessible to the general lay reader. Later selections in this anthology, written by members of various academies, whether legal or literary, are more systematic and probing, even if more difficult. Whether the technical arguments developed here resolve (or dissolve) the concerns expressed by the attorney general and the justice will be determined by their rhetorical success in the more public arena of cultural politics and judicial practice.

The Constitution of the United States: Contemporary Ratification

William J. Brennan, Jr.

I am deeply grateful for the invitation to participate in the "Text and Teaching" symposium. This rare opportunity to explore classic texts with participants of such wisdom, acumen, and insight as those who have preceded and will follow me to this podium is indeed exhilarating. But it is also humbling. Even to approximate the standards of excellence of these vigorous and graceful intellects is a daunting task. I am honored that you have afforded me this opportunity to try.

It will perhaps not surprise you that the text I have chosen for exploration is the amended Constitution of the United States, which, of course, entrenches the Bill of Rights and the Civil War amendments, and draws sustenance from the bedrock principles of another great text, the Magna Carta. So fashioned, the Constitution embodies the aspiration to social justice, brotherhood, and human dignity that brought this nation into being. The Declaration of Independence, the Constitution, and the Bill of Rights solemnly committed the United States to be a country where the dignity and rights of all persons were equal before all authority. In all candor we must concede that part of this egalitarianism in America has been more pretension than realized fact. But we are an aspiring people, a people with faith in progress. Our amended Constitution is the lodestar for our aspirations. Like every text worth reading, it is not crystalline. The phrasing is broad and the limitations of its provisions are not clearly marked. Its majestic generalities and ennobling pronouncements are both luminous and obscure. This ambiguity of course calls forth interpretation, the interaction of reader and text. The encounter with the constitutional text has been, in many senses, my life's work.

My approach to this text may differ from the approach of other participants in this symposium to their texts. Yet such differences may themselves stimulate reflection about what it is we do when we "interpret" a text. Thus I will attempt to elucidate my approach to the text as well as my substantive interpretation.

Perhaps the foremost difference is the fact that my encounters with the constitutional text are not purely or even primarily introspective; the Constitution cannot be for me simply a contemplative haven for private moral reflection. My relation to this great text is inescapably public. This is not to say that my reading of the text is not a personal reading, only that the personal reading perforce occurs in a public context, and is open to critical scrutiny from all quarters.

The Constitution is fundamentally a public text—the monumental charter of a government and a people—and a justice of the Supreme Court must apply it to resolve public controversies. For, from our beginnings, a most important consequence of the constitutionally created separation of powers has been the American habit, extraordinary to other democracies, of casting social, economic, philosophical, and political questions in the form of law suits, in an attempt to secure ultimate resolution by the Supreme Court. In this way, important aspects of the most fundamental issues confronting our democracy may finally arrive in the Supreme Court for judicial determination. Not infrequently, these are the issues upon which contemporary society is most deeply divided. They arouse our deepest emotions. The main burden of my twenty-nine terms on the Supreme Court has thus been to wrestle with the Constitution in this heightened public context, to draw meaning from the text in order to resolve public controversies.

Two other aspects of my relation to this text warrant mention. First, constitutional interpretation for a federal judge is, for the most part, obligatory. When litigants approach the bar of court to adjudicate a constitutional dispute, they may justifiably demand an answer. Judges cannot avoid a definitive interpretation because they feel unable to, or would prefer not to, penetrate to the full meaning of the Constitution's provisions. Unlike literary critics, judges cannot merely savor the tensions or revel in the ambiguities inhering in the text—judges must resolve them.

Second, consequences flow from a justice's interpretation in a direct and immediate way. A judicial decision respecting the incompatibility of Jim Crow with a constitutional guarantee of equality is not simply a contemplative exercise in defining the shape of a just society. It is an order—supported by the full coercive power of the state—that the present society change in a fundamental aspect. Under such circumstances the process of deciding can be a lonely, troubling experience for fallible human beings conscious that their best may not be adequate to the challenge. We justices are certainly aware that we are not final because we are infallible; we know that we are infallible only because we are final. One does not forget how much may depend on the decision. More than the litigants may be affected. The course of vital social, economic, and political currents may be directed.

These three defining characteristics of my relation to the constitutional text—its public nature, obligatory character, and consequentialist aspect—cannot help but influence the way I read that text. When justices interpret the Constitution they speak for their community, not for themselves alone. The act of interpretation must be undertaken with full consciousness that it is, in a very real sense, the community's interpretation that is sought. Justices are not Platonic guardians appointed to wield authority according to their personal moral predilections. Precisely because coercive force must attend any judicial decision to countermand the will of a contemporary majority, the justices must render constitutional interpretations that are received as legitimate. The source of legitimacy is, of course, a wellspring of controversy in legal and political circles. At the core of the debate is what the late Yale Law School professor Alexander Bickel labeled "the counter-majoritarian difficulty." Our commitment to self-governance in a representative democracy must be reconciled with vesting in electorally unaccountable justices the power to invalidate the expressed desires of representative bodies on the ground of inconsistency with higher law. Because judicial power resides in the authority to give meaning to the Constitution, the debate is really a debate about how to read the text, about constraints on what is legitimate interpretation.

There are those who find legitimacy in fidelity to what they call "the intentions of the Framers." In its most doctrinaire incarnation, this view demands that justices discern exactly what the Framers thought about the question under consideration and simply follow that intention in resolving the case before them. It is a view that feigns self-effacing deference to the specific judgments of those who forged our original social compact. But in truth it is little more than arrogance cloaked as humility. It is arrogant to pretend that from our vantage we can gauge accurately the intent of the Framers on application of principle to specific, contemporary questions. All too often, sources of potential enlightenment such as records of the ratification debates provide sparse or ambiguous evidence of the original intention. Typically, all that can be gleaned is that the Framers themselves did not agree about the application or meaning of particular constitutional provisions, and hid their differences in cloaks of generality. Indeed, it is far from clear whose intention is relevant—that of the drafters, the congressional disputants, or the ratifiers in the states—or even whether the idea of an original intention is a coherent way of thinking about a jointly drafted document drawing its authority from a general assent of the states. And apart from the problematic nature of the sources, our distance of two centuries cannot but work as a prism refracting all we perceive. One cannot help but speculate that the chorus of lamentations calling for interpretation faithful to "original intention"—and proposing nullification of interpretations that fail this quick litmus test—must inevitably come from persons who have no familiarity with the historical record.

Perhaps most importantly, while proponents of this facile historicism justify it as a depoliticization of the judiciary, the political underpinnings of such a choice should not escape notice. A position that upholds constitutional claims only if they were within the specific contemplation of the Framers in effect establishes a presumption of resolving textual ambiguities against the claim of constitutional right. It is far from clear what justifies such a presumption against claims of right. Nothing intrinsic in the nature of interpretation—if there is such a thing as the "nature" of interpretation—commands such a passive approach to ambiguity. This is a choice no less political than any other; it expresses antipathy to claims of the minority to rights against the majority. Those who would restrict claims of right to the values of 1789 specifically articulated in the Constitution turn a blind eye to social progress and eschew adaptation of overarching principles to changes of social circumstance.

Another, perhaps more sophisticated, response to the potential power of judicial interpretation stresses democratic theory: because ours is a government of the people's elected representatives, substantive value choices should by and large be left to them. This view emphasizes not the transcendent historical authority of the Framers but the predominant contemporary authority of the elected branches of government. Yet it has similar consequences for the nature of proper judicial interpretation. Faith in the majoritarian process counsels restraint. Even under more expansive formulations of this approach, judicial review is appropriate only to the extent of ensuring that our democratic process functions smoothly. Thus, for example, we would protect freedom of speech merely to ensure that the people are heard by their representatives, rather than as a separate, substantive value. When, by contrast, society tosses up to the Supreme Court a dispute that would require invalidation of a legislature's substantive policy choice, the Court generally would stay its hand because the Constitution was meant as a plan of government and not as an embodiment of fundamental substantive values.

The view that all matters of substantive policy should be resolved through the majoritarian process has appeal under some circumstances, but I think it ultimately will not do. Unabashed enshrinement of majority will would permit the imposition of a social caste system or wholesale confiscation of property so long as a majority of the authorized legislative body, fairly elected, approved. Our Constitution could not abide such a situation. It is the very purpose of a Constitution—and particularly of the Bill of Rights—to declare certain values transcendent, beyond the reach of temporary political majorities. The majoritarian process cannot be expected to rectify claims of minority right that arise as a response to the outcomes of that very majoritarian process. As James Madison put it: "The prescriptions in favor of liberty ought to be levelled against that quarter where the greatest danger lies, namely, that which possesses the highest prerogative of power. But this is not found in either the Executive or Legislative departments of Government, but in the body of the people, operating by the majority against the minority" (I *Annals* 437). Faith in democracy is one thing, blind faith quite another. Those who drafted our Constitution understood the difference. One cannot read the text without admitting that it embodies substantive value choices; it places certain values beyond the power of any legislature. Obvious are the separation of powers; the privilege of the writ of habeas corpus; prohibition of bills of attainder and ex post facto laws; prohibition of cruel and unusual punishments; the requirement of just compensation for official taking of property; the prohibition of laws tending to establish religion or enjoining the free exercise of religion; and, since the Civil War, the banishment of slavery and official race discrimination. With respect to at least such principles, we simply have not constituted ourselves as strict utilitarians. While the Constitution may be amended, such amendments require an immense effort by the people as a whole.

To remain faithful to the content of the Constitution, therefore, an approach to interpreting the text must account for the existence of these substantive value choices, and must accept the ambiguity inherent in the effort to apply them to modern circumstances. The Framers discerned fundamental principles through struggles against particular malefactions of the crown; the struggle shapes the particular contours of the articulated principles. But our acceptance of the fundamental principles has not and should not bind us to those precise, at times anachronistic, contours. Successive generations of Americans have continued to respect these fundamental choices and adopt them as their own guide to evaluating quite different historical practices. Each generation has the choice to overrule or add to the fundamental principles enunciated by the Framers; the Constitution can be amended or it can be ignored. Yet with respect to its fundamental principles, the text has suffered neither fate. Thus, if I may borrow the words of an esteemed predecessor, Justice Robert Jackson, the burden of judicial interpretation is to translate "the majestic generalities of the Bill of Rights, conceived as part of the pattern of liberal government in the eighteenth century, into concrete restraints on officials dealing with the problems of the twentieth century" (Barnette, 319 U.S., at 639).

We current justices read the Constitution in the only way that we can: as twentieth-century Americans. We look to the history of the time of framing and to the intervening history of interpretation. But the ultimate question must be, What do the words of the text mean in our time? For the genius of the Constitution rests not in any static meaning it might have had in a world that is dead and gone, but in the adaptability of its great principles to cope with current problems and current needs. What the constitutional fundamentals meant to the wisdom of other times cannot be their measure to the vision of our time. Similarly, what those fundamentals mean for us, our descendants will learn, cannot be the measure to the vision of their time. This realization is not, I assure you, a novel one of my own creation. Permit me to quote from one of the opinions of our Court, *Weems* v. *United States*, 217 U. S. 349, written nearly a century ago:

> Time works changes, brings into existence new conditions and purposes. Therefore, a principle to be vital must be capable of wider application than the mischief which gave it birth. This is peculiarly true of constitutions. They are not ephemeral enactments, designed to meet passing occasions. They are, to use the words of Chief Justice John Marshall, "designed to approach immortality as nearly as human institutions can approach it." The future is their care and provision for events of good and bad tendencies of which no prophesy can be made. In the application of a constitution, therefore, our contemplation cannot be only of what has been, but of what may be.

Interpretation must account for the transformative purpose of the text. Our Constitution was not intended to preserve a preexisting society but to make a new one, to put in place new principles that the prior political community had not sufficiently recognized. Thus, for example, when we interpret the Civil War amendments to the charter—abolishing slavery, guaranteeing blacks equality under law, and guaranteeing blacks the right to vote—we must remember that those who put them in place had no desire to enshrine the status quo. Their goal was to make over their world, to eliminate all vestige of slave caste.

Having discussed at some length how I, as a Supreme Court justice, interact with this text, I think it time to turn to the fruits of this discourse. For the Constitution is a sublime oration on the dignity of man, a bold commitment by a people to the ideal of libertarian dignity protected through law. Some reflection is perhaps required before this can be seen.

The Constitution on its face is, in large measure, a structuring text, a blueprint for government. And when the text is not prescribing the form of government it is limiting the powers of that government. The original document, before addition of any of the amendments, does not speak primarily of the rights of man, but of the abilities and disabilities of government. When one reflects upon the text's preoccupation with the scope of government as well as its shape, however, one comes to understand that what this text is about is the relationship of the individual and the state. The text marks the metes and bounds of official authority and individual autonomy. When one studies the boundary that the text marks out, one gets a sense of the vision of the individual embodied in the Constitution.

As augmented by the Bill of Rights and the Civil War amendments, this text is a sparkling vision of the supremacy of the human dignity of every individual. This vision is reflected in the very choice of democratic self-governance: the supreme value of a democracy is the presumed worth of each individual. And this vision manifests itself most dramatically in the specific prohibitions of the Bill of Rights, a term which I henceforth will apply to describe not only the original first eight amendments, but the Civil War amendments as well. It is a vision that has guided us as a people throughout our history, although the precise rules by which we have protected fundamental human dignity have been transformed over time in response to both transformations of social conditions and evolution of our concepts of human dignity.

Until the end of the nineteenth century, freedom and dignity in our country found meaningful protection in the institution of real property. In a society still largely agricultural, a piece of land provided men not just with sustenance but with the means of economic independence, a necessary precondition of political independence and expression. Not surprisingly, property relationships formed the heart of litigation and of legal practice, and lawyers and judges tended to think stable property relationships the highest aim of the law.

But the days when common-law property relationships dominated litigation and legal practice are past. To a growing extent economic existence now depends on less certain relationships with government— licenses, employment, contracts, subsidies, unemployment benefits, tax exemptions, welfare, and the like. Government participation in the economic existence of individuals is pervasive and deep. Administrative matters and other dealings with government are at the epicenter of the exploding law. We turn to government and to the law for controls which would never have been expected or tolerated before this century, when a man's answer to economic oppression or difficulty was to move two hundred miles west. Now hundreds of thousands of Americans live entire lives without any real prospect of the dignity and autonomy that ownership of real property could confer. Protection of the human dignity of such citizens requires a much modified view of the proper relationship of individual and state.

In general, problems of the relationship of the citizen with government have multiplied and thus have engendered some of the most important constitutional issues of the day. As government acts ever more deeply upon those areas of our lives once marked Private, there is an even greater need to see that individual rights are not curtailed or cheapened in the interest of what may temporarily appear to be the "public good." And as government continues in its role of provider for so many of our disadvantaged citizens, there is an even greater need to ensure that government act with integrity and consistency in its dealings with these citizens. To put this another way, the possibilities for collision between government activity and individual rights will increase as the power and authority of government itself expands, and this growth, in turn, heightens the need for constant vigilance at the collision points. If our free society is to endure, those who govern must recognize human dignity and accept the enforcement of constitutional limitations on their power conceived by the Framers to be necessary to preserve that dignity and the air of freedom which is our proudest heritage. Such recognition will not come from a technical understanding of the organs of government, or the new forms of wealth they administer. It requires something different, something deeper—a personal confrontation with the wellsprings of our society. Solutions of constitutional questions from that perspective have become the great challenge of the modern era. All the talk in the last half-decade about shrinking the government does not alter this reality or the challenge it imposes. The modern activist state is a concomitant of the complexity of modern society; it is inevitably with us. We must meet the challenge rather than wish it were not before us.

The challenge is essentially, of course, one to the capacity of our constitutional structure to foster and protect the freedom, the dignity, and the rights of all persons within our borders, which it is the great design of the Constitution to secure. During the time of my public service this challenge has largely taken shape within the confines of the interpretive question whether the specific guarantees of the Bill of Rights operate as restraints on the power of state government. We recognize the Bill of Rights as the primary source of express information as to what is meant by constitutional liberty. The safeguards enshrined in it are deeply etched in the foundation of America's freedoms. Each is a protection with centuries of history behind it, often dearly bought with the blood and lives of people determined to prevent oppression by their rulers. The first eight amendments, however, were added to the Constitution to operate solely against federal power. It was not until the Thirteenth and Fourteenth amendments were added, in 1865 and 1868, in response to a demand for national protection against abuses of state power, that the Constitution could be interpreted to require application of the first eight amendments to the states.

It was in particular the Fourteenth Amendment's guarantee that no person be deprived of life, liberty, or property without process of law that led us to apply many of the specific guarantees of the Bill of Rights to the states. In my judgment, Justice Cardozo best captured the reasoning that brought us to such decisions when he described what the Court has done as a process by which the guarantees "have been taken over from the earlier articles of the federal bill of rights and brought within the

Fourteenth Amendment by a process of absorption . . . [that] has had its source in the belief that neither liberty nor justice would exist if [those guarantees] . . . were sacrificed" (Palko, 302 U. S., at 326). But this process of absorption was neither swift nor steady. As late as 1922 only the Fifth Amendment guarantee of just compensation for official taking of property had been given force against the states. Between then and 1956 only the First Amendment guarantees of speech and conscience and the Fourth Amendment ban of unreasonable searches and seizures had been incorporated—the latter, however, without the exclusionary rule to give it force. As late as 1961, I could stand before a distinguished assemblage of the bar at New York University's James Madison Lecture and list the following as guarantees that had not been thought to be sufficiently fundamental to the protection of human dignity so as to be enforced against the states: the prohibition of cruel and unusual punishments, the right against self-incrimination, the right to assistance of counsel in a criminal trial, the right to confront witnesses, the right to compulsory process, the right not to be placed in jeopardy of life or limb more than once upon accusation of a crime, the right not to have illegally obtained evidence introduced at a criminal trial, and the right to a jury of one's peers.

The history of the quarter century following that Madison Lecture need not be told in great detail. Suffice it to say that each of the guarantees listed above has been recognized as a fundamental aspect of ordered liberty. Of course, the above catalog encompasses only the rights of the criminally accused, those caught, rightly or wrongly, in the maw of the criminal justice system. But it has been well said that there is no better test of a society than how it treats those accused of transgressing against it. Indeed, it is because we recognize that incarceration strips a man of his dignity that we demand strict adherence to fair procedure and proof of guilt beyond a reasonable doubt before taking such a drastic step. These requirements are, as Justice Harlan once said, "bottomed on a fundamental value determination of our society that it is far worse to convict an innocent man than to let a guilty man go free" (Winship, 397 U. S., at 372). There is no worse injustice than wrongly to strip a man of his dignity. And our adherence to the constitutional vision of human dignity is so strict that even after convicting a person according to these stringent standards, we demand that his dignity be infringed only to the extent appropriate to the crime and never by means of wanton infliction of pain or deprivation. I interpret the Constitution plainly to embody these fundamental values.

Of course the constitutional vision of human dignity has, in this past quarter century, infused far more than our decisions about the criminal process. Recognition of the principle of "one person, one vote" as a constitutional one redeems the promise of self-governance by affirming the essential dignity of every citizen in the right to equal participation in the democratic process. Recognition of so-called new property rights in those receiving government entitlements affirms the essential dignity of the least fortunate among us by demanding that government treat with decency, integrity, and consistency those dependent on its benefits for their very survival. After all, a legislative majority initially decides to create governmental entitlements; the Constitution's due process clause merely provides protection for entitlements thought necessary by society as a whole. Such due process rights prohibit government from imposing the devil's bargain of bartering away human dignity in exchange for human sustenance. Likewise, recognition of full equality for women—equal protection of the laws—ensures that gender has no bearing on claims to human dignity.

Recognition of broad and deep rights of expression and of conscience reaffirms the vision of human dignity in many ways. They too redeem the promise of self-governance by facilitating—indeed demanding—robust, uninhibited, and wide-open debate on issues of public importance. Such public debate is of course vital to the development and dissemination of political ideas. As importantly, robust public discussion is the crucible in which personal political convictions are forged. In our democracy, such discussion is a political duty; it is the essence of self-government. The constitutional vision of human dignity rejects the possibility of political orthodoxy imposed from above; it respects the right of each individual to form and to express political judgments, however far they may deviate from the mainstream and however unsettling they might be to the powerful or the elite. Recognition of these rights of expression and conscience also frees up the private space for both intellectual and spiritual development free of government dominance, either blatant or subtle. Justice Brandeis put it so well sixty years ago when he wrote, "Those who won our independence believed that the final end of the State was to make men free to develop their faculties; and that in its government the deliberative forces should prevail over the arbitrary. They valued liberty both as an end and as a means" (Whitney, 274 U. S., at 375).

I do not mean to suggest that we have in the last quarter century achieved a comprehensive definition of the constitutional ideal of human dignity. We are still striving toward that goal, and doubtless it will be an eternal quest. For if the interaction of this justice and the constitutional text over the years confirms any single proposition, it is that the demands of human dignity will never cease to evolve.

Indeed, I cannot in good conscience refrain from mention of one grave and crucial respect in which we continue, in my judgment, to fall short of the constitutional vision of human dignity. It is in our continued tolerance of state-administered execution as a form of punishment. I make it a practice not to comment on the constitutional issues that come before the

Court, but my position on this issue, of course, has been for some time fixed and immutable. I think I can venture some thoughts on this particular subject without transgressing my usual guideline too severely.

As I interpret the Constitution, capital punishment is under all circumstances cruel and unusual punishment prohibited by the Eighth and Fourteenth amendments. This is a position of which I imagine you are not unaware. Much discussion of the merits of capital punishment has in recent years focused on the potential arbitrariness that attends its administration, and I have no doubt that such arbitrariness is a grave wrong. But for me, the wrong of capital punishment transcends such procedural issues. As I have said in my opinions, I view the Eighth Amendment's prohibition of cruel and unusual punishments as embodying to a unique degree moral principles that substantively restrain the punishments our civilized society may impose on those persons who transgress its laws. Foremost among the moral principles recognized in our cases and inherent in the prohibition is the primary principle that the state, even as it punishes, must treat its citizens in a manner consistent with their intrinsic worth as human beings. A punishment must not be so severe as to be utterly and irreversibly degrading to the very essence of human dignity. Death for whatever crime and under all circumstances is a truly awesome punishment. The calculated killing of a human being by the state involves, by its very nature, an absolute denial of the executed person's humanity. The most vile murder does not, in my view, release the state from constitutional restraints on the destruction of human dignity. Yet an executed person has lost the very right to have rights, now or ever. For me, then, the fatal constitutional infirmity of capital punishment is that it treats members of the human race as nonhumans, as objects to be toyed with and discarded. It is, indeed, "cruel and unusual." It is thus inconsistent with the fundamental premise of the clause that even the most base criminal remains a human being possessed of some potential, at least, for common human dignity.

This is an interpretation to which a majority of my fellow justices—not to mention, it would seem, a majority of my fellow countrymen—does not subscribe. Perhaps you find my adherence to it, and my recurrent publication of it, simply contrary, tiresome, or quixotic. Or perhaps you see in it a refusal to abide by the judicial principle of stare decisis, obedience to precedent. In my judgment, however, the unique interpretive role of the Supreme Court with respect to the Constitution demands some flexibility with respect to the call of stare decisis. Because we are the last word on the meaning of the Constitution, our views must be subject to revision over time or the Constitution falls captive, again, to the anachronistic views of long-gone generations. I mentioned earlier the judge's role in seeking out the community's interpretation of the constitutional text. Yet, again in my judgment, when a justice perceives an interpretation of the text to have departed so far from its essential meaning, that justice is bound, by a larger constitutional duty to the community, to expose the departure and point toward a different path. On this issue, the death penalty, I hope to embody a community striving for human dignity for all, although perhaps not yet arrived.

You have doubtless observed that this description of my personal encounter with the constitutional text has in large portion been a discussion of public developments in constitutional doctrine over the last quarter century. That, as I suggested at the outset, is inevitable because my interpretive career has demanded a public reading of the text. This public encounter with the text, however, has been a profound source of personal inspiration. The vision of human dignity embodied there is deeply moving. It is timeless. It has inspired Americans for two centuries and it will continue to inspire as it continues to evolve. That evolutionary process is inevitable and, indeed, it is the true interpretive genius of the text.

If we are to be as a shining city upon a hill, it will be because of our ceaseless pursuit of the constitutional ideal of human dignity. For the political and legal ideals that form the foundation of much that is best in American institutions—ideals jealously preserved and guarded throughout our history—still form the vital force in creative political thought and activity within the nation today. As we adapt our institutions to the ever-changing conditions of national and international life, those ideals of human dignity—liberty and justice for all individuals—will continue to inspire and guide us because they are entrenched in our Constitution. The Constitution with its Bill of Rights thus has a bright future, as well as a glorious past, for its spirit is inherent in the aspirations of our people.

Address before the D.C. Chapter of the Federalist Society Lawyers Division

Edwin Meese III

A large part of American history has been the history of constitutional debate. From the Federalists and the anti-Federalists, to Webster and Calhoun, to Lincoln and Douglas, we find many examples. Now, as we approach the Bicentennial of the framing of the Constitution, we are witnessing another debate concerning our fundamental law. It is not simply a ceremonial debate, but one that promises to have a profound effect on the future of our Republic.

The current debate is a sign of a healthy nation. Unlike people of many other countries, we are free both to discover the defects of our laws and our government through open discussion and to correct them through our political system.

This debate on the Constitution involves great and fundamental issues. It invites the participation of the best minds the bar, the academy, and the bench have to offer. In recent weeks there have been important new contributions to this debate from some of the most distinguished scholars and jurists in the land. Representatives of the three branches of the federal government have entered the debate, journalistic commentators too.

A great deal has already been said, much of it of merit and on point. But occasionally there has been confusion and in some cases even distortion. Caricatures and straw men, as one customarily finds even in the greatest debates, have made appearances. I've been surprised at some of the hysterical shrillness that we've seen in editorials and other commentary. Perhaps this response is explained by the fact that what we've said defies liberal dogma.

Still, whatever the differences, most participants are agreed about the same high objective: fidelity to our fundamental law.

Today I would like to discuss further the meaning of constitutional fidelity. In particular, I would like to describe in more detail this administration's approach.

Before doing so, I would like to make a few commonplace observations about the original document itself.

It is easy to forget what a young country America really is. The bicentennial of our independence was just a few years ago, that of the Constitution still two years off.

The period surrounding the creation of the Constitution is not a dark and mythical realm. The young America of the 1780s and 90s was a vibrant place, alive with pamphlets, newspapers, and books chronicling and commenting upon the great issues of the day. We know how the Founding Fathers lived, and much of what they read, thought, and believed. The disputes and compromises of the Constitutional Convention were carefully recorded. The minutes of the convention are a matter of public record. Several of the most important participants—including James Madison, the "father" of the Constitution—wrote comprehensive accounts of the convention. Others, Federalists and anti-Federalists alike, committed their arguments for and against ratification, as well as their understandings of the Constitution, to paper, so that their ideas and conclusions could be widely circulated, read, and understood.

In short, the Constitution is not buried in the mists of time. We know a tremendous amount of the history of its genesis. The Bicentennial is encouraging even more scholarship about its origins. We know who did what, and many times why. One can talk intelligently about a "founding generation."

With these thoughts in mind, I would like to discuss the administration's approach to constitutional interpretation which has been led by President Reagan and which we at the Department of Justice and my colleagues in other agencies have advanced. But to begin, it may be useful to say what is not.

Our approach does not view the Constitution as some kind of super municipal code, designed to address merely the problem of a particular era—whether those of 1787, 1789, or 1868. There is no question that the Constitutional Convention grew out of widespread dissatisfaction with the Articles of Confederation. But the delegates at Philadelphia moved beyond the job of patching that document to write a *Constitution*. Their intention was to write a document not just for their times but for posterity.

The language they employed clearly reflects this. For example, they addressed *commerce*, not simply shipping or barter. Later the Bill of Rights spoke, through the Fourth Amendment, to "unreasonable searches and seizures," not merely the regulation of specific law enforcement practices of 1789. Still later, the Framers of the Fourteenth Amendment were concerned not simply about the rights of black citizens to personal security, but also about the equal protection of the law for all persons within the states.

The Constitution is not a legislative code bound to the time in which it was written. Neither, however, is it a mirror that simply reflects the thoughts and ideas of those who stand before it.

Our approach to constitutional interpretation begins with the document itself. The plain fact is, it exists. It is something that has been written down. Walter Berns of the American Enterprise Institute has noted that the central object of American constitutionalism was "the effort" of the Founders "to express fundamental governmental arrangements in a legal document—to 'get it in writing.' "

Indeed, judicial review has been grounded in the fact that the Constitution is a written, as opposed to an unwritten, document. In *Marbury* v. *Madison* John Marshall rested his rationale for judicial review on the fact that we have a written constitution with meaning that is binding upon judges. "[I]t is apparent," he wrote, "that the framers of the constitution contemplated that instrument as a rule for the government of *courts*, as well as of the legislature. Why otherwise does it direct the judges to take an oath to support it?"

The presumption of a written document is that it conveys meaning. As Thomas Grey of the Stanford Law School has said, it makes "relatively definite and explicit what otherwise would be relatively indefinite and tacit."

We know that those who framed the Constitution chose their words carefully. They debated at great length the most minute points. The language they chose meant something. They proposed, they substituted, they edited, and they carefully revised. Their words were studied with equal care by state ratifying conventions.

This is not to suggest that there was unanimity among the Framers and ratifiers on all points. The Constitution and the Bill of Rights, and some of the subsequent amendments, emerged after protracted debate. Nobody got everything they wanted. What's more, the Framers were not clairvoyants—they could not foresee every issue that would be submitted for judicial review. Nor could they predict how all foreseeable disputes would be resolved under the Constitution. But the point is, the meaning of the Constitution can be known.

What does this written Constitution mean? In places it is exactingly specific. Where it says that presidents of the United States must be at least thirty-five years of age it means exactly that. (I have not heard of any claim that thirty-five means thirty or twenty-five or twenty.) Where it specifies how the House and Senate are to be organized, it means what it says.

The Constitution, including its twenty-six amendments, also expresses particular principles. One is the right to be free of an unreasonable search or seizure. Another concerns religious liberty. Another is the right to equal protection of the laws.

Those who framed these principles meant something by them. And the meanings can be found, understood, and applied.

The Constitution itself is also an expression of certain general principles. These principles reflect the deepest purpose of the Constitution— that of establishing a political system through which Americans can best govern themselves consistent with the goal of securing liberty.

The text and structure of the Constitution are instructive. It contains very little in the way of specific political solutions. It speaks volumes on how problems should be approached, and by *whom*. For example, the first three articles set out clearly the scope and limits of three distinct branches of national government, the powers of each being carefully and specifically enumerated. In this scheme it is no accident to find the legislative branch described first, as the Framers had fought and sacrificed to secure the right of democratic self-governance. Naturally, this faith in republicanism was not unbounded, as the next two articles make clear.

Yet the Constitution remains a document of powers and principles. And its undergirding premise remains that democratic self-government is subject only to the limits of certain constitutional principles. This respect for the political process was made explicit early on. When John Marshall upheld the act of Congress chartering a national bank in *McCulloch* v. *Maryland* he wrote, "The Constitution [was] intended to endure for ages to come, and, consequently, to be adapted to the various crises of human affairs." But to use *McCulloch,* as some have tried, as support for the idea that the Constitution is a protean, changeable thing is to stand history on its head. Marshall was keeping faith with the original intention that Congress be free to elaborate and apply constitutional powers and principles. He was not saying that the Court must invent some new constitutional value in order to keep pace with the times. In Walter Berns's words, "Marshall's meaning is not that the Constitution may be adapted to the 'various crises of human affairs,' but that the legislative powers granted by the Constitution are adaptable to meet these crises."

The approach this administration advocates is rooted in the text of the Constitution as illuminated by those who drafted, proposed, and ratified it. In his famous "Commentary on the Constitution of the United States" Justice Joseph Story explained that "[t]he first and fundamental rule in the interpretation of all instruments is, to construe them according to the sense of the terms, and the intention of the parties."

Our approach understands the significance of a written document and seeks to discern the particular and general principles it expresses. It recognizes that there may be debate at times over the application of these principles. But it does not mean these principles cannot be identified.

Constitutional adjudication is obviously not a mechanical process. It requires an appeal to reason and discretion. The text and intention of the Constitution must be understood to constitute the banks within which constitutional interpretation must flow. As James Madison said, if "the sense in which the Constitution was accepted and ratified by the nation . . . be not the guide in expounding it, there can be no security for a consistent and stable, more than for a faithful exercise of its powers."

Thomas Jefferson, so often cited incorrectly as a framer of the Constitution, in fact shared Madison's view: "Our peculiar security is in the possession of a written Constitution. Let us not make it a blank paper by construction."

Jefferson was even more explicit in his personal correspondence: "On every question of construction [we should] carry ourselves back to the time, when the constitution was adopted; recollect the spirit manifested in the debates; and instead of trying [to find] what meaning may be squeezed out of the text, or invented against it, conform to the probable one, in which it was passed."

In the main a jurisprudence that seeks to be faithful to our Constitution—a jurisprudence of original intention, as I have called it—is not difficult to describe. Where the language of the Constitution is specific, it must be obeyed. Where there is a demonstrable consensus among the Framers and ratifiers as to a principle stated or implied by the Constitution, it should be followed. Where there is ambiguity as to the precise meaning or reach of a constitutional provision, it should be interpreted and applied in a manner so as to at least not contradict the text of the Constitution itself.

Sadly, while almost everyone participating in the current constitutional debate would give assent to these propositions, the techniques and conclusions of some of the debaters do violence to them. What is the source of this violence? In large part I believe that it is the misuse of history stemming from the neglect of the idea of a written constitution.

There is a frank proclamation by some judges and commentators that what matters most about the Constitution is not its words but its so-called spirit. These individuals focus less on the language of specific provisions than on what they describe as the "vision" or "concepts of human dignity" they find embodied in the Constitution. This approach to our jurisprudence has led to some remarkable and tragic conclusions.

In the 1850s, the Supreme Court under Chief Justice Roger B. Taney read blacks out of the Constitution in order to invalidate Congress's attempt to limit the spread of slavery. The *Dred Scott* decision, famously described as a judicial "self-inflicted wound," helped bring on the Civil War. There is a lesson in such history. There is danger in seeing the Constitution as an empty vessel into which each generation may pour its passion and prejudice.

Our own time has its own fashions and passions. In recent decades many have come to view the Constitution—more accurately, part of the Constitution, provisions of the Bill of Rights and the Fourteenth Amendment—as a charter for judicial activism on behalf of various constituencies. Those who hold this view often have lacked demonstrable textual or historical support for their conclusions. Instead they have "grounded" their rulings in appeals to social theories, to moral philosophies or personal notions of human dignity, or to "penumbras," somehow emanating ghostlike from various provisions—identified and not identified—in the Bill of Rights. The problem with this approach, as John Hart Ely, Dean of Stanford Law School, has observed with respect to one such decision, is not that it is bad constitutional law, but that it is not constitutional law in any meaningful sense at all.

Despite this fact, the perceived popularity of some results in particular cases has encouraged some observers to believe that any critique of the methodology of those decisions is an attack on the results. This perception is sufficiently widespread that it deserves an answer. My answer is to look at history.

When the Supreme Court, in *Brown* v. *Board of Education,* sounded the death knell for official segregation in the country, it earned all the plaudits it received. But the Supreme Court in that case was not giving new life to old words, or adapting a "living," "flexible" Constitution to new reality. It was restoring the original principle of the Constitution to constitutional law. The *Brown* Court was correcting the damage done fifty years earlier, when in *Plessy* v. *Ferguson* an earlier Supreme Court had disregarded the clear intent of the framers of the Civil War amendments to eliminate the legal degradation of blacks, and had contrived a theory of the Constitution to support the charade of "separate but equal" discrimination.

It is amazing how so much of what passes for social and political progress is really the undoing of old judicial mistakes.

Mistakes occur when the principles of specific constitutional provisions—such as those contained in the Bill of Rights—are taken by some as invitations to read into the Constitution values that contradict the clear language of other provisions.

Acceptances to this illusory invitation have proliferated in recent decades. One Supreme Court justice identified the proper judicial standard as asking "what's best for this country." Another said it is important to "keep the Court out in front" of the general society. Various academic commentators have poured rhetorical gasoline on this judicial fire, suggesting that constitutional interpretation appropriately be guided by such standards as whether a public policy "personifies justice" or "comports with the notion of moral evolution" or confers "an identity" upon our society or was consistent with "natural ethical law" or was consistent with some "right of equal citizenship." These amorphous concepts, as opposed to the written Constitution, form a very poor base for judicial interpretation.

Unfortunately, as I've noted, navigation by such lodestars has in the past given us questionable economics, governmental disorder, and racism—all in the guise of constitutional law. Recently one of the distinguished judges of one of our federal appeals courts got it about right when he wrote, "The truth is that the judge who looks outside the Constitution always looks inside himself and nowhere else." Or, as we recently put it before the Supreme Court in an important brief: "The further afield interpretation travels from its point of departure in the text, the greater the danger that constitutional adjudication will be like a picnic to which the framers bring the words and the judges the meaning."

In the *Osborne* v. *Bank of United States* decision twenty-one years after *Marbury*, Chief Justice Marshall further elaborated his view of the relationship between the judge and the law, be it statutory or constitutional: "Judicial power, as contradistinguished from the power of the laws, has no existence. Courts are the mere instruments of the law, and can will nothing. When they are said to exercise a discretion, it is a mere legal discretion, a discretion to be exercised in discerning the course prescribed by law; and, when that is discerned, it is the duty of the Court to follow it."

Any true approach to constitutional interpretation must respect the document in all its parts and be faithful to the Constitution in its entirety.

What must be remembered in the current interpretation does not imply results. The Framers were not trying to anticipate every answer. They were trying to create a tripartite national government, within a federal system, that would have the flexibility to adapt to face new exigencies—as it did, for example, in chartering a national bank. Their great interest was in the distribution of power and responsibility in order to secure the great goal of liberty for all.

A jurisprudence that seeks fidelity to the Constitution—a jurisprudence of original intention—is not a jurisprudence of political results. It is very much concerned with process, and it is a jurisprudence that in our day seeks to depoliticize the law. The great genius of the constitutional blueprint is found in its creation and respect for spheres of authority and the limits it places on governmental power. In this scheme the Framers did not see the courts as the exclusive custodians of the Constitution. Indeed, because the document posits so few conclusions, it leaves to the more political branches the matter of adapting and vivifying its principles in each generation. It also leaves to the people of the states, in the Tenth Amendment, those responsibilities and rights not committed to federal care. The power to declare acts of Congress and laws of the states null and void is truly awesome. This power must be used when the

Constitution clearly speaks. It should not be used when the Constitution does not.

In *Marbury* v. *Madison,* at the same time he vindicated the concept of judicial review, Marshall wrote that the "principles" of the Constitution "are deemed fundamental and permanent," and except for formal amendment, "unchangeable." If we want a change in our Constitution or in our laws we must seek it through the formal mechanisms presented in that organizing document of our government.

In summary, I would emphasize that what is at issue here is not an agenda of issues or a menu of results. At issue is a way of government. A jurisprudence based on first principles is neither conservative nor liberal, neither right nor left. It is a jurisprudence that cares about committing and limiting to each organ of government the proper ambit of its responsibilities. It is a jurisprudence faithful to our Constitution.

By the same token, an activist jurisprudence, one which anchors the Constitution only in the consciences of jurists, is a chameleon jurisprudence, changing color and form in each era. The same activism hailed today may threaten the capacity for decision through democratic consensus tomorrow, as it has in many yesterdays. Ultimately, as the early democrats wrote into the Massachusetts state constitution, the best defense of our liberties is a government of laws and not men.

On this point it is helpful to recall the words of the late Justice Frankfurter. As he wrote, "There is not under our Constitution a judicial remedy for every political mischief, for every undesirable exercise of legislative power. The Framers carefully and with deliberate forethought refused so to enthrone the judiciary. In this situation, as in others of like nature, appeal for relief does not belong here. Appeal must be to an informed, civically militant electorate."

I am afraid that I have gone on somewhat too long. I realize that these occasions of your society are usually reserved for brief remarks. But if I have imposed on your patience, I hope it has been for a good end. Given the timeliness of this issue, and the interest of this distinguished organization, it has seemed an appropriate forum to share these thoughts.

I close, unsurprisingly, by returning a last time to the period of the Constitution's birth.

As students of the Constitution are aware, the struggle for ratification was protracted and bitter. Essential to the success of the campaign was the outcome of the debate in the two most significant states: Virginia and New York. In New York that battle between Federalist and anti-Federalist forces was particularly hard. Both sides eagerly awaited the outcome in Virginia, which was sure to have profound effect on the struggle in the Empire State. When news that Virginia had voted to ratify came, it was a particularly bitter blow to the anti-Federalist side. Yet on the evening the message reached New York an event took place that speaks volumes about the character of early America. The losing side, instead of grousing, feted the Federalist leaders in the taverns and inns of the city. There followed a night of good fellowship and mutual toasting. When the effects of the good cheer wore off, the two sides returned to their inkwells and presses, and the debate resumed.

There is a great temptation among those who view this debate from the outside to see in it a clash of personalities, a bitter exchange. But you and I, and I hope the other participants in this dialogue, know better. We and our distinguished opponents carry on the old tradition, of free, uninhibited, and vigorous debate. Out of such arguments come no losers, only truth.

It's the American way. And the Founders wouldn't want it any other way.

SECTION II

The Question of Method

Introduction

As the previous section demonstrates, hermeneutic theory has been at the center of recent controversies over legal interpretation. Theoretical models and normative rules are constantly being invoked to establish acceptable interpretive procedures. Such hermeneutic foundation-building takes various forms within legal studies, forms that resemble normative theorizing in other interpretive disciplines, especially literary criticism. The following essays illustrate the most widely debated concepts in legal and literary hermeneutics: intention, formalism, and objectivity. These concepts are at issue in the most important recent attempts to establish or criticize principles for correctly interpreting statutes, poems, wills, novels, and other such texts. Some brief definitions are thus in order.

In one of its senses, the term *formalism* refers to a theory of interpretation that sees the meaning of a text as inherent in the words on the page, independent of authorial intent, reader response, and historical context. *Intentionalism* defines itself against this kind of formalism by asserting that textual meaning is inseparable from authorial intention, usually going on to argue that evidence outside the text is crucial to any correct interpretation of meaning as intention. Thus, formalists and intentionalists differ over the nature of the interpreted object—textual meaning—and on the method of objectively interpreting—through internal or external evidence.

The intentionalist-formalist debate has a long history in both the legal and literary disciplines, but histories of the debates in the two arenas have run on independent tracks that rarely intersected. In 1930 Max Radin put forth the most famous anti-intentionalist argument in statutory interpretation, while during the next decade Monroe Beardsley and W. K. Wimsatt did the same for literary interpretation in their article "The Intentional Fallacy." In their very different institutional contexts, these two essays attacked the dominant intentionalist assumptions in their respective disciplines and set the stage for more recent arguments over the hermeneutical role of intention. A brief analysis of one of these seminal essays with a few passing comparisons to the other will highlight the contexts of current debates over interpretive theory.

"The Intentional Fallacy" and its companion piece, Wimsatt and Beardsley's "The Affective Fallacy," are two of the most influential American essays on literary hermeneutics. In these widely reprinted articles first published in the late forties, the authors attack "the psychological fallacies" that lead away from "objective criticism" of literary texts. "The Affective Fallacy is a confusion between the poem and its results. . . . It begins by deriving the standard of criticism from the psychological effects of the poem and ends in impressionism and relativism." The problem of relativism also plays a part in their attack on the intentional fallacy, "a confusion between the poem and its origins." Charging that the intentionalist "derives the standard of criticism from the psychological *causes* of the poem," Wimsatt and Beardsley argue that intentionalism leads away from legitimate textual exegesis toward literary biography, from objective criticism toward interpretive relativism.[1]

The charge of relativism is crucial to the theoretical debate between intentionalists and formalists, but it is not always clear what is meant by the charge. In "The Affective Fallacy," Wimsatt and Beardsley describe exactly how a critical focus on different readers' interpretations results in idiosyncratic impressionism and infinitely multiple meanings. But in "The Intentional Fallacy," the authors do not explain why they see similar relativistic dangers in intentionalism. We can, however, infer an explanation from a later article, "Genesis: A Fallacy Revisited," in which Wimsatt responds to attacks on the earlier essay.[2]

At one point, Wimsatt claims that in "The Intentional Fallacy" he had "tried to delineate one of the principles by which [the objective] critic will have to discipline his efforts unless he wishes to surrender to the flux, the gossip, the muddle and the 'motley' for which [intentionalists] seem so earnestly to yearn" ("Genesis," p. 222). The formalist argument here seems to be that intentionalism leads to relativism because it encourages critics to go outside the text to find its meaning in biographical and historical facts, facts that are potentially infinite in number. Once the intentionalist allows an extratextual fact to determine an interpretation, Wimsatt suggests, there is no closing the hermeneutical door. When the text itself can be overruled or ignored in an account of authorial intention based on external evidence, what extratextual fact can be excluded as irrelevant? The intentionalist critic becomes lost in the unbounded "flux" and "muddle" of biography and history. The text "as an object of specifically critical judgement, tends to disappear" (*VI*, p. 21), and we are left once again, as with the affective fallacy, in unconstrained relativism.

As important as it obviously was to Wimsatt and Beardsley, their fight against relativism was not the battle most important to the explicit argument of "The Intentional Fallacy." That argument focuses more on the danger of error and distortion than it does on the fear of infinite meanings and unconstrained interpretation. In *The Verbal Icon: Studies in the Meaning of Poetry*, the collection which reprints both essays on the psychological fallacies, Wimsatt defines a poem "as a wholeness of meaning established through internally differentiated form, the reconciliation of diverse parts" (*VI*, p. 236). He distinguishes poetry from "practical messages, which are successful if and only if we correctly infer the intention" (*VI*, p. 5). In contrast, though it can exist only through the meaning of its words, a poem "*is*, simply is, in the sense that we have no excuse for inquiring what point is intended or meant. Poetry is a feat of style by which a complex of meaning is handled all at once" (*VI*, p. 4). Thus, a poem is a "verbal icon": "Through its meaning or meanings the poem is. It has an iconic validity. . . . The poem has, not an abstractly meant or intended meaning, but a fullness of actually presented meaning" (*VI*, p. 231).

The hermeneutic consequences of such a definition are made clear throughout the explicit argument of "The Intentional Fallacy." Since poetry consists not of "intended meaning" but "actually presented meaning," not what an author planned or wanted to write but what he did write, the author's intention is irrelevant as an interpretive category. But even if such an intention were relevant, Wimsatt and Beardsley ask, how could a critic determine what it is: "How is he to find out what the poet tried to do? If the poet succeeded in doing it, then the poem itself shows what he was trying to do. And if the poet did not succeed, then the poem is not adequate evidence, and the critic must go outside the poem—for evidence of an intention that did not become effective in the poem" (*VI*, p. 4). That is, if the poet was successful in fulfilling his design in writing his poem, then he has embodied his intention in the text, and looking for intention outside the text is unnecessary. Only interpreting the text itself matters. On the other hand, if the poet did not fulfill his design, if he did not embody his intention in his text, then looking for that intention elsewhere has nothing to do with interpreting the text actually written. It is the text actually written that alone should concern—and constrain—interpretations.

One way of responding to Wimsatt and Beardsley would be to take seriously their distinction between poetry and other forms of writing. That is, one might agree with their implication that poetry demands a "special" interpretive method that excludes intentionalist evidence, but still maintain that other forms of writing, including law, require a different hermeneutic approach that makes reference to authors and their intentions. Indeed, several of the selections below can be read as making a case for a distinction between "specialized" and "general" hermeneutics: these essays distinguish poems from novels, literature from law, and wills from statutes or constitutions. Others, however, suggest that these separations do not work and that the problems relevant to explicating a poem are fundamentally similar to those involved in interpreting legal and other kinds of texts.

A legal theorist belonging to the formalist camp was Max Radin, who in 1930 presented an argument closely related to that of "The Intentional Fallacy." In "Statutory Interpretation," he, too, tests an interpretive method by its capacity to "effectively lessen the dangers of arbitrary action on the part of the courts," and he goes on to mount a concerted attack on the confused legal theories that "impute imaginary intentions to fictitious entities."[3] Radin's anti-intentionalist critique develops along lines very similar to the arguments we have just examined. "The courts in England and America," he writes,

> have generally qualified the "golden rule" that intent governs the meaning of a statute, by saying that it must be the intent "as expressed in the statute." In that case, it would obviously be better to use the expression alone, without reference to the intent at all, since if the intent is not in the expression, it is nowhere. If the doctrine means anything, it means that, once the expression is before the court, the intent becomes irrelevant. ["SI", p. 872]

Radin argues further that even if it were relevant to interpreting a law, the intention of a legislature is multiple and conflicted: "A legislature certainly has no intention whatever in connection with words which some two or three men drafted, which a considerable number rejected, and in regard to which many of the approving majority might have had, and often demonstrably did have, different ideas and beliefs" ("SI", p. 870). Indeed, the legislative intention behind any statute always turns out to be either radically indeterminate or ultimately undiscoverable.

Focusing on statutes, Radin does not indicate whether his anti-intentionalism extends to those particular legal texts called wills. A major part of his argument concerns the genesis of statutes in collective decisions and the difficulty, if not impossibility, of ascertaining collective "intent." A will, in contrast, is usually attributed to a single author. Does this make a difference? Once again we are presented with the problem of "specialized" versus "general" hermeneutic approaches.

Still, if intention does not determine interpretation, what does? Wimsatt and Beardsley argue that the poem is neither the author's nor the critic's. "The poem belongs to the public. It is embodied in language's, the peculiar possession of the public, and it is about the human being, an object of public knowledge" (VI, p. 5). This emphasis on public knowledge allows Wimsatt and Beardsley to make a further methodological distinction: the difference between internal and external evidence for interpreting the meaning of a literary text. External evidence is "private or idiosyncratic; not a part of the work or a linguistic fact." Instead, it consists of authorial "revelation" outside the text being interpreted. Internal evidence, on the other hand, is public not private: "it is discovered through . . . our habitual knowledge of the language . . . in general through all that makes a language and culture" (VI, p. 10). Though Wimsatt and Beardsley admit that a person aware of extratextual information may appreciate a poem better than someone without this awareness, they are more concerned that such a preoccupation with external evidence "could distort a critic's view of a poem." In such cases of interpretive distortion, critics allow external evidence to override internal evidence from the text itself; they "disregard the implicit language" and "prefer private evidence to public" (*VI*, pp. 13–14). Thus, intentionalism leads to interpretive distortion of public meaning and ends in a privatized critical impressionism. Wimsatt and Beardsley sum up their anti-intentionalist position by calling for a return to the text, not to the author: "Critical inquiries are not settled by consulting the oracle" (*VI*, p. 18).

In trying to clarify their view of intention, Wimsatt and Beardsley make the literary scholar E. E. Stoll's rhetorical question into a real one: "Is not a critic a judge, who does not explore his own consciousness, but determines the author's meaning or intention, as if the poem were a will, a contract or the constitution?"[4] Wimsatt and Beardsley answer in the negative and in so doing restate an opposition found in Radin's essay on statutory interpretation. Both articles completely reject the analogy between literary and legal texts, but for quite different reasons. Radin claims that laws are unlike literature, because in literary interpretation we try to "enter into the mind of an artist" ("SI", p. 867) to seek his intention, whereas in legal interpretation intention is irrelevant and only the statute itself counts. Conversely, Wimsatt and Beardsley claim that literature differs from law, because in legal interpretation we try to get at the "practical message" the author intended, whereas in literary interpretation intention is irrelevant and only the poem itself counts. The legal and literary theorists each make intention the province of the *other* discipline, not their own.

Arguing from different premises about the texts to be interpreted, these two seminal essays arrive at the same conclusion: literary and legal interpretation have little in common. Even though all the following essays reject this conclusion, they continue to share common areas of concern with Radin, Wimsatt, and Beardsley: the danger of relativism, misreading, public knowledge, and external evidence. Though the essays are grouped around three topics—intentionalism, formalism, and objectivity—it will soon become clear that several pieces could have appeared in any of the three groupings. This is due to the fact that debates over intention are often debates over formalism, and both intentionalist and anti-intentionalist arguments are usually arguments about interpretive objectivity.

Indeed, in a certain sense, *objectivity* constitutes both the end and means of foundationalist theory, which claims that objective descriptions can lead to objective methods applied objectively to reach objective conclusions. Thus, hermeneutic foundationalism proposes detailed descriptions of the interpretive process leading to neutral procedures to be applied disinterestedly to reach correct interpretations. Both formalism and intentionalism lay claim to this sort of objectivity. Both provide foundationalist descriptions and prescriptions, accounts of where meaning resides and how it can be derived in correct interpretation. Formalism defines meaning in the text and advocates intrinsic criticism, while intentionalism focuses on authorial meaning and argues for extrinsic criticism as a supplement to close reading.

We saw how the formalism of Wimsatt and Beardsley attempted to avoid relativism and misreading by proposing an "objective criticism" that interpreted the text in and of itself. In the most rigorous case made for intentionalism in literary theory, E. D. Hirsch rejects this New Critical formalism because its supposed objectivity results in the very relativism it wished to avoid. Hirsch then goes on to argue that objective interpretation can only be grounded in the intentions of authors.

In *Validity in Interpretation* (1967) Hirsch defines "verbal meaning" as "whatever someone has willed to convey by a particular sequence of linguistic signs and which can be conveyed (shared) by means of those linguistic signs."[5] Both the author's willed meaning and the sharability of that meaning are indispensable aspects of Hirsch's definition. Linguistic norms enable an intended meaning to be shared, Hirsch argues, but they are not sufficient by themselves to guarantee that a text's meaning will be determinate and reproducible. Reference only to a speech community's potential system of norms without reference to the choices authors make within the system "opens the door to subjectivism and relativism, since linguistic norms may be invoked to support any verbally possible meaning" (p. 226).

For Hirsch, "the author's meaning, as represented by his text, is unchanging and reproducible" (p. 216), and only by reconstructing this intended meaning can objective interpretation become truly possible. He summarizes his thesis with "the paradox that objectivity in textual interpretation requires explicit reference to the speaker's subjectivity" (p. 237). From these premises, Hirsch derives methods for correct interpretation: though "extrinsic data" should not be "read into the text," it can be "used to verify that which we read out of it." And "even though the text itself should be the primary source of clues and must always be the final authority, the interpreter should make an effort to go beyond his text wherever possible" (p. 241). Distinguishing the "speaking subject" from the "actual historical person," Hirsch argues that the "interpreter's primary task is to reproduce in himself the author's 'logic,' his attitudes, his cultural givens, in short, his world" (p. 242). These suggestions constitute Hirsch's intentionalist form of foundationalism, his attempt to establish "normative principles in interpretation" (p. 212). It is precisely this foundationalist question of method that all of the following essays take up: can hermeneutic theory provide specific constraints on interpretive procedures?

(A)

Intentionalism

Sonnet LXV and the "Black Ink" of the Framers' Intention

Charles Fried

I

At the very core of the rule of law is the conviction—perhaps it is only a hope—that legal texts have meaning. As a teacher and a scholar I have tried to show how the meaning of legal texts persists through time and controls the outcomes of concrete cases; as a latecomer to practice I have tried to make that idea central to the positions the government takes in court. Because anniversaries permit, if not demand, personal reflection, or at least reflection in a different and more personal voice than has been usual in these pages, I shall address this central concern—the rule of law and the meaning of laws—in that special way.

My work as a scholar and now as a practitioner suggests to me that respect for the rule of law has been somewhat abraded by a generation or more of skepticism about the discipline and definiteness of law. The attitude is abroad that rules and principles simply cannot control concrete cases at all, that they thus cannot be applied in adjudication, and indeed that they are not even worth seeking to establish in the first place.[1] My indictment runs against adjudication that seeks to escape the discipline of texts and doctrine, and substitutes the judge's own authority for the authority of the law—his only just source of power. When we cut ourselves off from text and doctrine on the premise that they cannot constrain judgment, great damage is done; this is true whether the impulse causes us to strike down politically uncongenial legislation or to produce an emotionally congenial result in a particular case.

This skeptical stance toward the law evidences itself through a skein of more particular dispositions, the manifestations and motivations of which are various and sometimes elusive. In recent years, this substitution of will for the exercise of reason may be moved by a project to redistribute power and wealth to less favored segments of the population;[2] at another time, it had the effect—if not the purpose—of entrenching privileges and advantages against legislative attack.[3] And judges with no systematic ideological agendas may play fast and loose with rules and doctrines to produce the results they favor in particular cases, without regard for systematic implications.[4]

Something like cynicism infects what is on occasion celebrated as judicial statesmanship: where a court, perhaps quite rightly, concludes that the time has come to modify or overrule precedent but shrinks from doing so candidly, it shrinks from encountering the discipline of explicit justification.[5] Some early examples of this stance seem benign enough. Who might not be seduced by the sonorous if somewhat impenetrable passages of *Allegheny College* v. *National Chautauqua County Bank*,[6] in which Judge Benjamin Cardozo sought to persuade us that Allegheny College really had given bargained-for consideration in exchange for, and thus could enforce in an action for breach of contract, a straightforward charitable subscription.[7] The result strikes me as a just one, but one better reached by a frank revision of doctrine. I also once thought the American Law Institute's *Restatement of Contracts* was right to use promissory estoppel to hold subcontractors to the unbargained-for unilateral offers that they supply to general contractors putting together bids on large projects.[8] I am beginning, however, to see the wisdom of Judge Learned Hand's remark in *James Baird Co.* v. *Gimbel Brothers, Inc.*[9] that "in commercial transactions it does not in the end promote justice to seek strained interpretations in aid of those who do not protect themselves."[10]

Similarly, there is cause for wonder that a doctrine like the tort law duty to warn, which initially appeared so reasonable, should take the grotesque turn it did in *Tarasoff* v. *Board of Regents*,[11] in which a murder victim's parents were allowed a cause of action against her killer's psychiatrist for failing to warn them of the killer's threats expressed in therapy—even though the psychiatrist had alerted the police.[12] This absurdity was followed by *Henderson* v. *United States*,[13] in which the court held the government could be liable for the accidental electrocution of adult persons who had trespassed upon government land and scaled electrical towers to steal cable.[14] The fabric of the law is abraded just as surely when courts indulge their yearning to do "substantive justice" by ignoring clearly defined procedural constraints, such as those limiting judicial review by requiring deference to agency discretion,[15] or those precluding such review when the statute of limitations has run[16] or the plaintiff has not exhausted his administrative remedies.[17]

I could address these issues by discussing aspects of the work of the Department of Justice, in which I have been involved, that can be seen as an attempt to "ravel up" the sometimes ragged edges of the fabric of law. I think of the department's tort initiative,[18] its recent guidelines on consent decrees and special masters,[19] and I hope not a few amicus briefs filed by my office.[20] I am apprised, however, of the rest of the contents of this celebratory issue and so have contrived to make my point by indirection, through poetry. If my legal message is controversial, at least the poetry I invite you to consider is lovely.

I propose to confront indirectly the notion that legal rules and doctrines cannot control particular cases or even coerce our judgment, and that such rules are a sham, merely invoked after the fact to justify results reached on other grounds. Of course, this attitude is expressed most dramatically and prominently in the current debate about constitutional interpretation. This debate, I believe, centers on whether the Constitution should be taken seriously as law—that is, as a deliberately produced, deliberated legal text—or rather should be regarded as nothing more than a set of improving slogans chiseled on the walls of our public consciousness—"our legend and hope."[21] This essay is my contribution to the debate between those who go forward under the banner of "original intent" and those who believe that constitutional interpretation must express a free response to contemporary conditions, mores, and temperaments.[22]

II

This dispute over the interpretation of texts breaks out not only in our profession but in literary theory as well. And so, keeping true to my promise to lighten the batter out of which this birthday cake is baked, I will take as my text Shakespeare's Sonnet LXV. I start with the poem:

> Since brass, nor stone, nor earth, nor boundless sea,
> But sad mortality o'ersways their power,
> How with this rage shall beauty hold a plea,
> Whose action is no stronger than a flower?
> O! how shall summer's honey breath hold out
> Against the wrackful seige of batt'ring days,
> When rocks impregnable are not so stout,
> Nor gates of steel so strong, but Time decays?
> O fearful meditation! where, alack,
> Shall Time's best jewel from Time's chest lie hid?
> Or what strong hand can hold his swift foot back?
> Or who his spoil of beauty can forbid?
> O! none, unless this miracle have might,
> That in black ink my love may still shine bright.[23]

Let us attempt first to understand what this poem is saying on a literal level. It begins by contrasting the solid and powerful with the extremely transitory; brass, stone, sea, "rocks impregnable," and "gates of steel" are contrasted to beauty,[24] the strength of a flower, honey breath, and finally, love—"Time's best jewel." Next, we have an apostrophe of a thing that is so powerful that it is to brass, stone, and steel as they are to flowers and honey breath; that powerful thing is time's rage, the "wrackful siege of batt'ring days." All of this is intended to give a sense of the implacable potency of time, of change, and of decay. Time's chest is not a place of safety and safekeeping, but an engulfing active force, a black hole that devours everything.[25]

However, this seemingly unstoppable force may be overcome by a miraculous force: "black ink"—no more substantial than a flower, and certainly far less substantial than "rocks impregnable" or "gates of steel." Black ink can triumph over the terrible power of time: its strength and cunning can give permanence to that most flimsy and impermanent of things, love, and cause it to shine bright. For how long? In the case of this sonnet, almost four hundred years.

Now, the impermanence of things is a standard poet's theme; it is, perhaps, the great theme of the human condition. Our sense of time and of continuity is what makes us human; in psychoanalytical jargon, it is the basis of our ego, our sense of self. It also is what permits us to make plans for the future. However, this sense of time comes at a price: our awareness that "time decays," and our knowledge that "sad mortality o'ersways" even the best-laid plans which our sense of time makes possible. Indeed, this may be the sense in which love, "Time's best jewel," is also described as time's prey.

But all this is clear. I am now prepared to return to my original subject: the claim that the attempt to understand the Constitution according to the intention of those who conceived it is so hopelessly unavailing that advocating such an attempt must be either foolishness or subterfuge. As I have stated, this claim is just a special version of the notion that such an attempt is generally in vain because it is impossible to treat any legal text—or indeed any legal rule or principle—as a real constraint upon judgment.

Those who object to consideration of the Framers' intention in constitutional interpretation claim that we cannot know the intention of people so distant from us in time and circumstance.[26] This objection, I take it, is not just that it would be inconvenient or even bad policy to act on that original intention but that the "wrackful siege of batt'ring days" has made that very enterprise devoid of sense. Words, surrounded by new contexts, do not mean now what they did then; they may seem comprehensible, even familiar, but a proper historical sense reveals them to be mere homonyms of their present counterparts. Meaning cannot survive this process "When rocks impregnable are not so stout, / Nor gates of steel so strong, but Time decays." Still, these critics argue, this "fearful meditation" may not be so fearful after all. Perhaps our impotence gives us potency, freeing us of past meanings and allowing us to be marvelously creative. We can accord new meanings to words and texts to serve our present needs, our present visions, and even our present whims.

Should we accept this line of argument? Is it true? Is it even plausible? Recall my exegesis of the transparent meaning of Sonnet LXV. Put aside for a moment the content of the exegesis and recall just the fact of it. In following along with me in my exegesis, whether you agreed with it or not, you at least agreed in my unstated premise that the poem had a meaning and that we could understand it; so you surely also agreed that respect for human intelligence demands that we attempt to understand the sonnet's meaning rather than make it up.

What is this poem really about? It is, I submit, about writing. More generally, it is about words: the miracle that black ink can make even what is most fragile and evanescent shine brightly through time. Why should we believe this? Is this not just a naked assertion? No, the poem proves itself. For in understanding its claim, we prove its claim. In treating the enterprise of reading and understanding Shakespeare's poem as a normal, compassable exercise of human intelligence, we prove Shakespeare's claim that black ink can perform the miracle of causing meaning to shine brightly between persons and across years. Similarly, the enterprise of discoursing about the Constitution, and about the possibility of understanding it, proves that such a discourse is possible, and by extension, it suggests that it is also possible to understand the subject of the discourse—the constitutional text itself.

Sonnet LXV also speaks to the miracle of human intelligence, which is coextensive with the miracle of human language. Language, words, fix meaning. Words create meaning as a bond or a channel between persons, a common and identical possession—identical because only then can it be common, offering an escape from solipsism. To doubt the reality of this common possession is to doubt other minds and thus to doubt community and humanity. So, black ink is indeed a miracle; more than just love "shines bright," but any product of the human spirit—including intention. Indeed, language, black ink, is the very condition of intention, and intention is the vehicle of meaning.

We can respond now to the fallacious notion that if we only cut ourselves loose from past meanings, we will be wonderfully free to create and innovate. Surely innovation in law or in poetry or in any other human enterprise depends on our ability to create something new and distinct like a poem, for instance, or a constitution. Without the ability to fix and transmit the intention of framers—and we are all framers—across the void of time and between persons, we are powerless to create and innovate at all.

This observation is not undercut by the argument that the Framers of the Constitution, or indeed those who establish any legal rules, no more envisaged every application of their general terms than Shakespeare envisaged the use I am making here of his sonnet. This claim ignores the miracle of language, and the miracle of general terms. For it is the very essence of general terms that they are capable of governing particular cases not envisaged by their authors.[27] General terms are not mere compendia of the specific instances imagined by those individuals who first enunciated them. What the miracle of language requires is that words, ideas, and concepts reach new instances. Those who deny that general terms can reach new cases, and those who claim that they can reach new cases but without imposing constraints or limits, are really in the same camp; they are the enemies of meaning and, therefore, the enemies of the very conditions of human creativity.

Ronald Dworkin's splendid new book, *Law's Empire*,[28] is concerned with just these themes. Dworkin is scornful, and I think properly so, of the notion that in interpreting poetry or the Constitution we should seek to discern authorial intent as a mental fact of some sort.[29] As to poetry, his argument rightly holds that we would not consider an account of Shakespeare's mental state at the time he wrote a sonnet to be a more complete or better account of the sonnet than the sonnet itself.[30] Dworkin would certainly disagree, as would I, with the notion that when we consider the Constitution we are really interested in the mental state of each of the persons who drew it up and ratified it.[31] In this view, which we both reject, the texts of a sonnet or of the Constitution would be a kind of second-best; we would prefer to take the top off the heads of authors and Framers—like soft-boiled eggs—to look inside for the truest account of their brain states at the moment that the texts were created.

The argument placing paramount importance upon an author's mental state ignores the fact that authors writing a sonnet or a constitution seek to take their intention and embody it in specific words. I insist that words and text are chosen to embody intentions and thus replace inquiries into subjective mental states. In short, the text *is* the intention of the authors or of the Framers. That is why readers interpreting such texts have a special duty to the cause of rationality and to the determinacy of meaning to take them seriously.

It may be said, with some justice, that to make a point I have caricatured a more nuanced position—that rules and texts are not always definite, that where indeterminate they leave room for choice, and that sometimes they give out altogether, leaving us wholly adrift. There is some truth to this claim, but not nearly enough. Indeed, my point can be taken too far; certainly I do not mean by it that any gibberish at all has determinate meaning, or that even sensible texts must be applicable to all possible new cases. The real issue is what we make of this acknowledgment that our language, like our reason and will, is fallen and imperfect. Do we give up, or do we make the effort to understand and interpret in good faith, assuming the good faith and competence both of our language and of our interlocutors? Do we take the frequent lack of unanimity about the correctness of an interpretation as a spur to further discourse or as a sign that we should give up altogether?

III

A great deal is at stake here: the whole notion of the integrity of the means of human communication—whether it be in poetry or in law—and more specifically, the whole notion of the integrity of the tools of legal and political discourse. The possibility of understanding rules and texts means that law need not be just a matter of power. The "miracle" that has "might" is thus not just a transmission of fleeting sentiments, but the might to constrain with words—that is, with reasons. This is what law is: a constraint, not of force, but of reason—the reasons that one man can offer to another for his judgment and for his actions, the reasons that one age offers to another for its judgments and its actions.

Accordingly, I affirm the possibility of the enterprise that the Framers embarked on in Philadelphia two hundred years ago: the establishment as a foundation for government of a structure for relations of power embodied in a written constitution—that is, in black ink. As we can understand Shakespeare's meaning, so can we understand the Framers' meaning in the Constitution. Although such understanding may not necessarily be achieved without difficulty, that should not be an objection in principle to making the effort. Indeed, we owe such an effort to the texts of both the sonnet and the Constitution.

There is this difference between the sonnet and the Constitution: the sonnet addresses understanding only, whereas the Constitution addresses action, seeking to structure and constrain great action. The striking thing, of course, is that the courts can ignore the provisions of the Constitution, just as the president—or anyone who is bound to follow the law—can ignore the law. That is because the law operates through reason and understanding rather than physical constraint; whatever coercion takes place, if it is lawful, is guided by reason and understanding. It is for this reason that I find so disturbing the suggestion that we cannot understand the intention of the framers of laws, whether of the Constitution or of law in its more humble manifestations, whether twenty years or two hundred have passed. Shakespeare refutes this suggestion in Sonnet LXV; it is Shakespeare's miracle of black ink that we, as free persons whose freedom is underwritten by the rule of law, should celebrate.

["On Sonnet LXV"]

Philip Martin

Since brasse, nor stone, nor earth, nor boundlesse sea,
But sad mortallity ore-swaies their power,
How with this rage shall beautie hold a plea,
Whose action is no stronger then a flower?
O how shall summers hunny breath hold out,
Against the wrackfull siedge of battring dayes,
When rocks impregnable are not so stoute,
Nor gates of steele so strong but time decayes?
O fearefull meditation, where alack,
Shall times best Jewell from times chest lie hid?
Or what strong hand can hold his swift foote back,
Or who his spoile of beautie can forbid?
   O none, unlesse this miracle have might,
   That in black inck my love may still shine bright.

The tremendous strength of the first twelve lines is obvious; one may come more slowly to accept the final couplet. Indeed I once thought it one of the disappointing couplets, but I no longer think so. For what the poem exists to say is that amid such universal ruin as it contemplates, beauty can have no chance of preservation unless a miracle occurs: most of the imaginative weight must fall, then, on the "rage," the "wrackfull siedge" of mortality, and on the defenselessness of beauty's "flower" and "summers hunny breath"; the poem's ending is therefore deliberately and properly tentative. There is nothing here of the facile optimism we have seen elsewhere. Instead, full recognition is given to the spectacle described; the exclamation, "O fearefull meditation," dominates the rest of the poem's thought. Nothing is *asserted* in the couplet, except a possibility ("O none, unlesse. . ."), and even that, the poem admits, will require a miracle. Perhaps there is *something* more than this: the insinuation that the poem itself may be "this miracle," may have the "might" spoken of; but it is nothing like an explicit claim. A backward glance at Sonnet LX will show this by contrast: "And yet to times in hope, my verse shall stand." The end of LXV is stronger precisely because it *is* so tentative. Further, it should be clear how much more *intelligent* this poem is than Sonnet LX and some others: it accepts its own logic, without trying at the end to ignore the disturbing realities it has faced earlier.

Counterfactuals in Interpretation

E. D. Hirsch, Jr.

In this chapter I shall suggest that we will get a clearer insight into some recalcitrant problems of literary and legal interpretation if we face up to the need for counterfactuals in interpreting texts. Counterfactual conditionals are if-then statements, as in the song "If I were a rich man," or in the claim of the young lad from Hahant: "I would if I could but I can't." These contrary-to-fact speculations are just the sorts of statements that tough-minded thinkers and skeptical historians try to avoid. Historians (as opposed to modal logicians who have recently done path-breaking work on the subject) do not like to make conjectures about who Hitler or Napoleon would have been *if* they had had different upbringings, or *if* they were born in different times.[1] And popular attitudes to counterfactuals are sometimes more contemptuous than scholarly ones: "Yeah, if pigs had wings they could fly."

But people who concern themselves with the interpretation of texts should probably not be intimidated by these disdainful attitudes to counterfactual conditionals. Interpreters sometimes need to imagine what a text from the past *would* mean if it were being reauthored in the present. If they could not conceive such a possibility, they could not conduct responsible interpretations of texts. By "responsible" interpretations I mean ones that remain true both to the spirit of older texts, and to the realities of the present time as well. If you removed the counterfactual conditional from our intellectual repertoire, our understanding of texts would be confined entirely to the present. Responsible interpretation exists in two worlds at once, the world of the past and the world of the present, the world of the writer and the world of the reader. The problematics of textual interpretation arise chiefly from this counterfactual yoking of historical moments that do not in reality coexist. The only way we can bridge these two historical moments is through counterfactual thinking. All interpreters know this implicitly. Perhaps we have omitted to make this truth explicit because we share in the contemptuous attitudes, learned and popular, toward the counterfactual conditional.

As an example of learned contempt, consider this remark of Quine's in *Word and Object:*

> What traits of the real world to suppose preserved in the feigned world of the contrary-to-fact antecedent can be guessed only from a sympathetic sense of the fabulist's likely purpose in spinning his fable. Thus consider the pair . . . :
>
> If Caesar were in command, he would use the atom bomb;
> If Caesar were in command, he would use catapults.
>
> We are likelier to hear the former, but only because that one is likelier to fit a lesson that a speaker would try to dramatize. The subjective conditional is an idiom for which we cannot hope to find a satisfactory general substitute in realistic terms.[2]

I shall return to this interesting example of Caesar and the atom bomb.

We could pursue textual interpretation without using contrary-to-fact conditionals. We could simply ignore the world of the past and respeak a text here and now for our present purposes. Logically, such an exclusive orientation to the present makes for a strong and consistent model of interpretation, and no metaphysical arguments about meaning or interpretation can succeed in undermining this hard-headed view. I find metaphysical arguments against legal realism unconvincing when they invoke conceptions like "the nature of language," or "the nature of texts." For there is nothing in the nature of language or texts that prevents legal realists (or postmodern literary critics) from proceeding in just the ways they actually proceed. A legal realist will hardly be impressed with being told he can't "really" do what he's really doing. And I don't see why Derrida should be impressed with being told that "the nature of language" requires him to be constrained by authorial intent. A strength of antihistorical positions like legal realism and poststructuralism is that they confine themselves to the world of the present, and thus avoid the uncertainties of the counterfactual conditional.

If we consider interpretation from the standpoint of interpretive norms—that is, from the standpoint of the question, What principle determines which inferences are acceptable and which are not?—the norms of interpretation reduce to two. And these exhaust the possibilities. I have argued this point elsewhere, and so I will not repeat the exposition at tedious length here.[3] Briefly, my argument is that the normative principles of interpretation all reduce to Humpty-Dumpty's question, "Who shall be master?" and that there are only two possible answers to that question: "the reader" or "the writer." Every other candidate is subsumed under one of these two categories. Such candidates as "codes," "institutions," or "interpretive communities" are always determined by one of these two fundamental norms, and so are all compromise positions that seem to be partly reader- and partly writer-oriented. For in all such in-between cases, the question can be asked, But who decides? and the answer will be either "the writer" or "the reader."

Some have objected that this choice is only apparent because there is really no writer norm at all. The reader of past texts does not defer to a real person, but only to his or her *idea* or *construct* of the writer. Hence all norms are reader norms. But this is a specious argument. Deference to the wishes or intentions of other persons is always deference to one's idea or construct of their wishes. And when their intentions are at odds with our own, the fact that we have constructed those intentions does not remove the conflict. A genuine choice does offer itself to interpreters as between the writer norm and the reader norm.

I have described the duality of interpretive norms in order to stress a further choice that is entailed by that duality, the choice between conceiving textual interpretation as communication or as exploitation. I do not want to suggest by these terms that exploitation is always the ethically inferior mode. On the contrary, exploitation of what comes down from the past is a way of making something valuable out of the past, and that approach is ethically superior to an antiquarian reverence which makes of the past nothing useful at all. Moreover, the exploitative mode can offer an intellectual simplicity that never has to submit to the uncertainties and complexities of historical speculation. My chief objection to the exploitative approach is that it suffers from practical and intellectual defects that make it unacceptable in a context of intellectual freedom. For, under the exploitative, reader norm, decisions about meaning are decisions about the best present uses of a text, and these decisions are based ultimately on nothing more stable or open to inquiry than the preferences of those readers who happen to be in power. The obvious arbitrariness of such a method reduces its persuasiveness and authority.

But, on the other hand, if we adopt the writer norm aren't we then condemned to antiquarianism? In past years my answer to that question has been as follows: I have said that we should distinguish between meaning and significance. Meaning is what the writer meant, what he or she intended to convey. Significance is what the modern reader makes out of that historical meaning after having construed the original sense. I said that the reader has an ethical obligation to base significance upon this historically defined, author-defined meaning.[4] That account was reasonable enough, but I now think it was not complex and subtle enough. It slid over some of the nuances between a significance that is constrained by the past and a significance that is not so constrained; it omitted details of the distinction between a significance that is communication and a significance that is exploitation.

The importance of the distinction between writing as communication and as exploitation comes into focus if we consider the origins of writing itself. Writing was invented to overcome the restriction of speech to a particular time and place, and chiefly the restriction to a particular time. The interpretive problem of yoking together two historical worlds was therefore implicit in the very origins of writing. Fixing speech in writing makes its meaning permanently available, and allows the present to build upon knowledge gained in the past. Writing has thereby been the chief agent of intellectual progress. But this momentous function of writing has required the concept of *communication* between the past and the present. Mankind advances in knowledge because what the writing says is communicated to another time. From the beginning, therefore, writing was regarded as analogous to normal speech where both speaker and audience inhabit the same moment and participate in a two-way exchange. But from the start this analogy with spoken communication was a metaphor, not a reality.

Does it make sense to continue to take this metaphor seriously? Is there any point in perpetuating the illusion that speechlike events are possible in the absence of a speaker, or that communication is possible in the absence of one of the parties to communication? Those who keep abreast of literary theory know that the communicative model of textual interpretation has come under disdainful attack by Derrida and other influential French writers, who have made the quasi-metaphysical objection that the author of a text, being absent, does not really exist for interpretation.[5] The author is just a construct. But this argument does not really amount to much. As I have just suggested, the speaker in an ordinary conversation is also, linguistically speaking, a construct in the mind of the other party to the conversation. Further, one can at times approach ordinary conversation in either an exploitative or a communicative spirit. In that respect the analogy between textual interpretation and ordinary speech is not a metaphor at all.

I shall not extend these introductory remarks any further. I have wanted to say enough in favor of the communicative model of textual interpretation to suggest that it is technically reasonable and harmonizes well with ordinary commonsense convictions about writing. In addition, I have wanted to avoid useless byways of polemics by conceding that interpretation-as-exploitation is also a tenable and tenanted position. I eschew metaphysical arguments which claim that the "nature" of language, or of anything else, requires us to take one position or the other. I set aside all such discussion and accept from the start the conclusion that a choice of one position or the other is inescapably ideological. Having acknowledged my ideological commitment to the communicative model (which I have by no means fully defended here), I can turn without distraction to the knotty problem of the counterfactual and other problems that arise when textual interpretation is regarded as communication.

I start with an example from literature, a poem by Blake. I have chosen it because W. K. Wimsatt has written a comment on it that brings out with great clarity some of the issues I wish to address. It is a short poem, and I shall quote it in full:

London

I wander thro' each charter'd street,
Near where the charter'd Thames does flow,
And mark in every face I meet
Marks of weakness, marks of woe.

In every cry of every Man,
In every Infant's cry of fear,
In every voice, in every ban,
The mind-forg'd manacles I hear.

How the Chimney-sweeper's cry
Every black'ning Church appalls;
And the hapless Soldier's sigh
Runs in blood down Palace walls.

But most thro' midnight streets I hear
How the youthful Harlot's curse
Blasts the new born Infant's tear,
And blights with plagues the Marriage hearse.

This poem is universally admired. It is firmly established in the canon of English literature, and will probably remain in the school and college curriculum for a long time. Is it not our duty to preserve its vitality and relevance through effective interpretation? Isn't it the responsibility of the literary professoriat to "save the texts"? That was the view of the late Professor W. K. Wimsatt. He used Blake's poem as an example of the need for *not* adopting a communicative model of textual interpretation. Thus Wimsatt:

> We are now seeking a maximum or crucial instance where a poet's private or personal and habitual meaning (as inferred from external documents) clearly clashed with what he managed to realize in . . . his poem. . . . But the following [instance] may serve . . . to define the issue. The materials are well known, but not the interpretive problem as I shall urge it. William Blake wrote in a sketchbook:

An Ancient Proverb

Remove away that blackning church
Remove away that marriage hearse
Remove away that man of blood
You'll quite remove that ancient curse.

These lines remained in the sketchbook, where they deserved to remain. They are a raw expression of certain soreheaded antinomian attitudes which are beyond doubt a part of Blake's biography at the period when he was writing . . . *London*.[6]

Then Wimsatt, after amiably calling me "one of the best informed and soberly reliable of recent Blake critics,"[7] quotes from my commentary on the poem, in which I had explained parts of it by taking into account Blake's other writings and beliefs at the time of composition. Wimsatt argues that I went wrong when I tried to explain "London" in terms of what Blake wanted to convey by the poem, and that I went egregiously wrong when I explained the phrase "marriage hearse" in light of Blake's hostile attitude to the institution of marriage.

> Mr. E. D. Hirsch, as I have said, is well informed about Blake and reliable, and I believe he gives us an accurate reading of a sort of intention which Blake probably did entertain . . . . "If there were no marriage, there would be no ungratified desires, and therefore no harlots." One thing, however, which perhaps he does not notice, or perhaps does not worry about, is that these ideas are silly. (Why wouldn't there be *many* ungratified desires, as many at least as there were losers in stag combats, or wooers rejected, or pursuers eluded, or matings frustrated? and *many* harlots? and *many* whoremasters?) An admirer of Blake the poet might well be content to leave these ideas, if he could, on a back shelf in the doctrinaire part of Blake's mind. What if we actually do find them or manage to put them in the poem? Won't this make the poem silly? And, since interpretation and evaluation are at the very least closely related, won't we be in danger of reading the poem as a pretty bad poem? And isn't this poem, in fact, supposed to be a masterpiece, "one of the best city poems ever written"?
>
> Isn't it, in fact, a masterpiece?[8]

I find these observations of Wimsatt's compelling. He has clearly laid out the puzzlements that arise when we are interpreting a canonical text whose original meanings do not fit the values and truths that current readers believe in. The Blake poem is a particularly useful example of the problem I want to examine because Wimsatt and I have agreed in this case about the premises of the problem. He accepts my view about what Blake originally meant, and I accept his view that some of Blake's ideas are wrong. Usually the dilemma produced by canonical works that contain false or outmoded meanings is hidden by disagreements about original meaning, but in this case, none of the usual confusions or evasions of the problem are available to the mind. And although Wimsatt thought the example rare, my own view is that it is paradigmatic for the interpretation of older texts.

Wimsatt's solution to the problem is to issue a reader-meaning rather than a writer-meaning. (I shall not go into the details of his interpretation of the poem.) By this procedure he protects the poem from silliness and justifies it as a good poem, a "masterpiece" that deserves to be kept in the canon and taught in the schools. Needless to say, Wimsatt here and elsewhere rejects a conception of literary interpretation as communication. Yet those who hold to that principle may have some tall explaining to do if they want to stay true both to Blake and to their own sense of the world. What can such interpreters say about outmoded medical theories in Shakespeare, or outmoded social theories in the law? How shall they practice their craft in a culture that differs from the culture of the past, yet lives by texts from the past? It is a question of some importance.

Responsible interpreters have generally taken an ad hoc approach to such problems of datedness, and in practice that is undoubtedly a good approach. But in areas of interpretation where a great deal is at stake—in religion and the law, for instance—an ad hoc approach should be buttressed by an explicit set of interpretive principles. Such principles are already followed implicitly by responsible interpreters. Here is a statement of them as I have come to perceive them. A responsible interpreter (a) tries to understand the original meaning; (b) tries to *accommodate* that meaning to present circumstances; (c) tries to distinguish between an accommodation that remains true to the spirit of the original and one that does not.

You will notice that these old-fashioned principles draw upon the language of biblical exegesis—"the spirit of the text" versus the "letter of the text"—and they draw also upon the religious principle of "accommodation." According to the theological doctrine of accommodation, when God revealed his truth to historical persons, he did so in a way they could understand in their own time and place. But with the passage of time, the spiritual progress of mankind has enabled us to comprehend God's truth more fully and accurately. When we interpret a text from the biblical canon we must grasp the spirit behind it, not just its original sense. We must reaccommodate its meaning to our own understandings in our own time and place. According to this principle, the canonical text has underneath its historical clothing an essential core meaning that is true in all times and places. It is the task of the interpreter to present this core meaning in the idiom of the present day.

I want to suggest that the three principles of responsible interpretation (listed above) constitute a secular version of the theological principle of accommodation. The key difference is this: the wordless divine meaning (the spiritual sense) behind Holy Scripture has been replaced in the secular account by a purely human meaning-intention whose core can be transported without change from one historical era to another. That texts in the secular as well as the sacred canon may exhibit this transhistorical core meaning is, I think, a root assumption of responsible interpretation. Before proceeding further with this theory of secular accommodation I want to return briefly to Blake's marriage hearse.

I concede that Blake was wrong in thinking that marriage is as dispensable a mind-forged manacle as religious superstition and political tyranny (the two other enslaving and perverting institutions presented in the poem). I can even agree with Wimsatt that Blake's idea is silly. Shall we therefore pretend that the poem doesn't really express the idea? I don't think that is the way responsible interpretation goes. What happens is more like this. We agree that Blake meant what he meant, and we agree that his meaning, following the letter of his text, is wrong. But we also think that the *spirit* of his text is neither silly nor wrong. There *are* mind-forged manacles, and there *are* enslaving institutions, which depress and debase people. Moreover, angry irony directed against avoidable human evils is a sentiment that transcends the circumstances of any particular historical era, and is applicable to all eras including, needless to say, our own.

If this is how responsible and sensitive interpreters understand texts from the past, another general principle of interpretation suggests itself: accommodation requires allegory. Here is the way Saint Thomas, with his customary clarity, defines it: "That first signification whereby words signify things belongs to the first sense, the historical and literal. That signification whereby things signified by words have themselves also a signification is called the spiritual sense, which is based on the literal and presupposes it. . . . Allegory alone stands for the spiritual senses" (*Summa* I, x). My discussion of the Blake poem suggests that the tradition of allegory is not just a medieval eccentricity, but is rather a necessary principle for the responsible interpretation of older texts. Indeed, that very necessity is the reason that medieval culture developed allegorical interpretation.

Yet allegory as a principle of interpretation exhibits the serious defect of permitting an interpreter to derive desired meanings at will. Allegory can easily be the handmaiden of what I have called the exploitative approach. That is why the principle of the counterfactual conditional is needed in responsible interpretation. It is a principle that can help to determine whether a given accommodation of a text to the present world is a valid accommodation. By "valid" I mean "governed by and consonant with original meaning." This conception of validity is implied in the original decision to regard textual interpretation as communication. In a successful communication of meaning a listener correctly grasps the meaning-intention of a speaker. In a successful textual communication between different temporal and cultural worlds, the reader correctly grasps the meaning-intention of the writer. But since in the latter case the cultural worlds are different, valid accommodation requires a transposition of the writer's intention from one world to another. (The structure of the task is similar to that of translation.) One way of testing whether an interpretation is a valid accommodation of the past to the present is to ask, "Would Blake intend that sort of meaning in the present world?"

Which is rather like asking, "If Caesar were in command would he use the atom bomb?"

Is there a valid answer to a question like that? Quine says no, but recently David Lewis and Saul Kripke have put new life and respectability into the counterfactual conditional. Such statements, they claim, can be true or false.[9] I lack the technical expertise to grasp all the details of Lewis's argument. (Kripke's discussion is en passant but easier for the layman because it avoids logical symbolism.) I shall deal here only with those aspects of the matter which are relevant to interpretation and can be grasped without using logical notation. At the intuitive level I am doubtful of Quine's claim that one counterfactual is about as good or bad as another, on the grounds that they are all hopelessly vague and are not expressible "in realistic terms." But since counterfactuals are staples of everyday talk and of science as well (natural laws can be viewed as counterfactual predictions: "If you dropped that pencil it would fall to the floor"), one feels skeptical of Quine's purism.

Certainly I am skeptical of Quine's example of Caesar and the atom bomb. If we use the counterfactual as an instrument for dealing with the real world, including the real historical world, then it is simply incorrect to say of the Korean War that if Caesar were in command he would use catapults. First of all, if Caesar would use catapults it is not possible that he would be in command. That particular counterfactual is almost certainly false. Even to entertain such an example is tantamount to what we would call in textual interpretation "the antiquarian fallacy." My second general observation about the example is that a valid use of such a counterfactual conditional requires us to identify an element that remains identical across time. In Quine's example, the identical element in both the ancient and the modern worlds would be something like: Caesar's character as a military tactician. To pretend that this aspect of his character is unknowable, or if it were knowable could not be validly applied to the present world, seems to me misplaced tough-mindedness. I don't imply that Caesar *would* use the atom bomb. I avoid taking a definite stand on that only because I don't know very much about Caesar. The validity of counterfactuals is like validity of historical propositions. One has to have a lot of relevant knowledge.

I mentioned just now that one also has to posit a transworld identity in order to make a translation of meaning from one world to another. The presence of an essential feature in both worlds enables us to conclude that the conterfactual inference is valid. For instance, "If pigs had wings they could fly." The proposition doesn't yet tell us enough about winged pigs for us to judge its validity. But assume we said, "If pigs had wings that were big and strong enough and if they could flutter them hard enough, and could get a fast enough start, they could fly." Of course the way that example is phrased, using "big enough," "strong enough," and so on, begs the question. But that is only because I have not taken the trouble to consult the universal laws and principles of aerodynamics to replace "strong enough," "fast enough," etc., with actual quantities. In order to produce a valid counterfactual you always need some kind of universal or essential feature, some element that is true for all worlds and is therefore true in the world at hand. Such a transworld structure is needed also in making analogies between worlds, and it remains for me an open question whether thinking by analogy is the basis of counterfactual thinking or vice versa.

In discussing the example of Blake's poem, I said that his original intention applied to our world because it embraced a human experience that is found in all periods. Such a broad intention is characteristic of literary texts. Their enduring value depends upon the existence of continuities throughout human experience. But I could not justifiably claim that I was being true to Blake's intentions just because I construed in his text some elements that are common to his world and our own. To be true to his poem, I would have to be able to justify the claim that I had been faithful to his *dominant* intentions.

The reason for this governance by dominant original intentions is that on a communicative conception of interpretation the text represents a speech act, a historical event that permanently determines the text's essence. In ordinary communication, speech acts are special kinds of historical events that are designed to be re-cognized in the mind of a listener or reader. What is normally re-cognized? First and foremost, the speaker's dominant intentions. For only by testing candidate meanings against an intention can a listener distinguish what was meant from what was not. Only an original structure of purposes can give a text an identity across possible worlds. The original intention "baptizes" the text, and gives it an essence that persists into the future. The act of composition is like the act of baptism. It is a historical event that determines an identity over future time. (If the same word sequence were respoken or rewritten with a new intention on another occasion that would be a different speech act and would baptize a different "text.") Baptism by original intention enables us to discriminate essence from accident in future appearances of a text in new cultural worlds.[10]

Would it be valid to say that Blake's poem applies to present-day New York City? "If Blake were in command, the Stock Exchange would be a mind-forged manacle." Yes, I think that's probably a valid counterfactual. Blake's dominant intentions, as far as we can judge them, included public institutions (the Church, the monarchy) which deprived the many and rewarded the few, so why not the Stock Exchange? A literary text, like a law or sacred scripture, is composed with future intentions. It is meant to be transported into new worlds. Its local meanings within its own immediate historical sphere are meant as allegories yielding further local meanings not only for contemporaries but also for those in other historical spheres. The criterion of applicability to other historical spheres is the same as the criterion in ordinary communication—faithfulness to the speaker's dominant intentions. Even in the original historical sphere a reader is in different circumstances from the writer, and needs to use imagination, counterfactual thinking. "If Blake were in my shoes, he would mean this and that aspect of my experience."

Kripke's reassurances about the validity of such modes of thinking are very much to the point: "in practice we cannot describe a complete counterfactual course of events and have no need to do so. A practical description of the extent to which the 'counterfactual situation' differs in the relevant way from the actual facts is sufficient; the 'counterfactual situation' could be thought of as a miniworld or a ministate, restricted to features of the world relevant to the problem at hand."[11]

I should like now to apply these observations about counterfactual thinking in interpretation to one of the key interpretive problems in literary culture and the law, the problem of datedness. Can the differences between the worlds of the writer and the reader become so great that counterfactual analogies can no longer be validly drawn? I think that situation can and does arise, and that it constitutes perhaps the chief practical justification for theorizing about interpretive counterfactuals.

One practical difference between the communicative and exploitative approaches to interpretation is that the communicative approach puts a limit on the principle of accommodation. Such a limit is important both intellectually and practically. Intellectually it is important that interpretation have principled constraints, because unconstrained accommodation can produce, ad libitum, quite contradictory interpretations. The freedom to make a text mean whatever one wishes brought allegorical interpretation into disrepute in the Middle Ages. (A famous example was "lucem a non lucendo," i.e., the text means "light" because no light is mentioned.) In the practical world, the importance of valid constraining principles in interpretation is owing to this intellectual consideration. For, in practice, an interpretation is unlikely to be accepted as valid by free people if it is arbitrary and in fact lacks intellectual validity.

The communicative approach, on the other side, carries the practical danger of a break with the past. Laws may be repealed, and literary works may be extruded from the canon when they can no longer be validly accommodated to the present world. Such extrusions from the canon should not be undertaken lightly. Edward Shils, in his profound book *Tradition*, has described the dangerous superficiality of attempts by society to regulate itself purely by truth and reason rather than by its inherited culture.[12] But in a literate society whose values and laws are recorded in texts, it is equally dangerous to preserve an inherited canon at all costs. For the canon itself may then fall into disrepute.

When tradition makes it an absolute principle to preserve at all costs the empty shell of a canonical text, the text is then allowed to take on whatever modern truth those in authority wish to pour into it. That kind of traditionalism will not effectively preserve a tradition in a literate society. Goody and Watt have argued that a chief historical effect of widespread literacy was that it enabled people to perceive a contrast between current experience and past texts; it thereby helped to create the critical, skeptical attitude to tradition that fostered modern science. Oral cultures, by contrast, can believe themselves traditional no matter how far they stray from the past, because they can gradually adjust their myths without knowing it, and no text will disabuse them.[13]

The theoretical principle that is needed for interpreting past texts in a literate society is therefore a compromise between two unacceptable extremes: between extreme literal-minded antiquarianism, and extreme laissez-faire exploitation. The need for a compromise is both intellectual and practical. This is where the counterfactual enters. My hunch is that counterfactual thinking has always been an implicit methodological principle behind good interpretive practice. A responsible interpreter will not want to subvert the main intentions behind a text. And an obvious way to avoid such misinterpretation is to ask, "If the author[s] were in this situation, would they, should they, accept this interpretation as being embraced by their meaning-intentions?" But this question can only recommend itself intellectually if it can be validly answered. It recommends itself practically only if it can exclude as well as accommodate meanings.

On the intellectual side, the validity of a counterfactual depends, as Kripke and Lewis have said, on there being a relevant something that is identical across the two worlds being contemplated. Kripke and Donnellan have argued that this something is not usually a literal picture or description, but is rather something referred to by an intention to refer.[14] Thus, I can refer to "Friday" even if I said "Thursday," and indeed even if I mistakenly thought that I *meant* "Thursday." If you point out to me that the day I was referring to was really Friday, I might very well say, "Oh yes, I *meant* 'Friday,' " and in some sense of *meant* I would be right. On the other hand, if I was very far off, if I had missed the date by three days, or by a decade, I might very well say, "Sorry, I got the date all wrong." In this example, the identical element demanded by the logicians might be "the latter part of the week," an element that would be lacking if I had said "Tuesday." Such everyday use of allegorical and counterfactual thinking exemplifies the difference between an accommodation to and a repudiation of a past text, between "Oh, that's what I meant," and "Oh, I was mistaken." In ordinary speech, the boundary line between these two results depends upon the degree of similarity between the literal sense and the figurative extension of meaning applied retrospectively to embrace the correct reference. Ordinary speech does not allow a big distance to develop between them. In this, ordinary speech displays deep methodological wisdom.

In the preceding example, I was willing to allow my intention to refer to "Friday" to embrace saying "Thursday," but not saying "Tuesday." The judgment we make in such cases connects with the old philosophical warhorse of identity. How much alteration of a thing is allowable before it becomes a different thing? How far can my literal sense be stretched figuratively before it can no longer represent the same meaning-intention? In science, a similar question arises. How many alterations can a theory accommodate before it becomes a different theory? Clearly the phlogiston theory of fire no longer represents, even figuratively, the current truths about fire. But Niels Bohr is rightly considered to be the author of the modern theory of large-scale atomic structure, even though a number of the literal details in his original theory have been abandoned.

If we go back to Blake's "London," we will discover that the poet himself presents us with an example of the boundary between accommodation and repudiation. At one point in his career, Blake himself removed "London" from his canon, because he no longer accepted the poem's dominant meanings. Blake's poem bases itself on the political principle that a lot of human misery is "mind-forg'd," and is caused by such despicable institutions as the monarchy and the Church. The poem dates from Blake's revolutionary phase, and implies the revolutionary doctrine that if we get rid of certain institutions a lot of the "marks of weakness, marks of woe" will disappear. Blake ceased to hold that belief in later years, and for a stretch of time he stopped offering the *Songs of Experience* (where "London" appears) to purchasers. The *Songs of Innocence*, on the other hand, imply that weakness and woe have deeper and more permanent causes than human institutions. Normally the two groups of *Songs* were issued together. But later in his life, Blake issued *The Songs of Innocence* as a separate work that excluded "London" and other poems like it.

There are obvious similarities between a poet's repudiating or radically altering a poem that he no longer believes in and a society's repealing or amending a law. The recent instance of *Brown* v. *Board of Education* is exemplary both as a removal from the canon and as an allegorical accommodation. The Court's decision rejected one text and created a replacement for it, thus acknowledging the principle of changing the canon. But the Court also claimed interpretive fidelity to the urtext, the Constitution, thus acknowledging adherence to and accommodation to deeper traditions. When it rejected *Plessy* v. *Ferguson*, the Court implied that we could not validly accommodate present truth to the past intentions of *Plessy*. On the other hand, it also said that the dominant intention of the Fourteenth Amendment to the Constitution (equal protection of the laws) was more truly interpreted by *Brown* than by *Plessy*. The Court's decision was not exploitative. An important consideration was that the *Plessy* conception of equal-but-separate facilities for different races was, according to modern sociologists, an impossibility, and hence failed to constitute equal protection of the laws. This allowed the inference that if the Framers were in command, they would reject *Plessy* and approve *Brown*.

So long as we interpret within a continuous legal or cultural tradition, the principle of accommodation justifies itself by the assumption that a text's original intention was to refer truly to the natural and cultural worlds, and we assume that our knowledge of those worlds is advancing. The meaning of the term *equal* in the Constitution can be accommodated to modern social science because we assume that the Framers truly intended the principle of equality, whatever it might turn out to entail. Such an assumption of intellectual progress in the continuous interpretive history of a text belongs also to the religious doctrine of accommodation. The New Testament is conceived to be an advance over the Old in the way *Brown* is conceived as an advance over *Plessy*. The later interpretations are literally truer. They have narrowed the distance between the literal and the figurative senses. The aim of the tradition of accommodation can be viewed as the gradual narrowing of the distance between the literal and the figurative senses. This can also be viewed as the aim of science.

What are the practical implications of these speculations? In the sphere of literary criticism, where I am most at home, one practical result of using the communicative model of interpretation more deliberately might be to encourage a more serious engagement with history, a greater concern with original historical intentions. At the same time, it would encourage a greater readiness to apply those historical intentions imaginatively to our world. On the communicative model, the imaginativeness of interpretation might take an even freer rein than on the exploitative model, because an understanding of the constraints on counterfactual thinking would go hand in hand with our having less anxiety about the genuine validity of counterfactual thinking. There would be more of it. So, paradoxically, a stonger commitment to history and the authorial norm might yield a greater commitment to the demands of present relevance. One might be more willing to banish a text from the canon because of its datedness, and less willing to preserve whatever is in the received canon at the price of interpretive arbitrariness and lack of validity. If these things happened, the consequence would be a more vigorous and credible literary culture.

The Misconceived Quest for the Original Understanding

Paul Brest

By *originalism* I mean the familiar approach to constitutional adjudication that accords binding authority to the text of the Constitution or the intentions of its adopters.[1] At least since *Marbury,* in which Chief Justice Marshall emphasized the significance of our Constitution's being a written document,[2] originalism in one form or another has been a major theme in the American constitutional tradition. The most widely accepted justification for originalism is simply that the Constitution is the supreme law of the land.[3] The Constitution manifests the will of the sovereign citizens of the United States—"we the people" assembled in the conventions and legislatures that ratified the Constitution and its amendments. The interpreter's task is to ascertain their will.[4] Originalism may be supported by more instrumental rationales as well: adherence to the text and original understanding arguably constrains the discretion of decision-makers and assures that the Constitution will be interpreted consistently over time.

The most extreme forms of originalism are "strict textualism" (or literalism) and "strict intentionalism." A strict textualist purports to construe words and phrases very narrowly and precisely. For the strict intentionalist, "the whole aim of construction, as applied to a provision of the Constitution, is . . . to ascertain and give effect to the intent of its framers and the people who adopted it."[5]

Much of American constitutional interpretation rejects strict originalism in favor of what I shall call "moderate originalism." The text of the Constitution is authoritative, but many of its provisions are treated as inherently open-textured. The original understanding is also important, but judges are more concerned with the adopters' general purposes than with their intentions in a very precise sense.

Some central doctrines of American constitutional law cannot be derived even by moderate originalist interpretation, but depend, instead, on what I shall call "nonoriginalism." The modes of nonoriginalist adjudication defended in this article accord the text and original history presumptive weight, but do not treat them as authoritative or binding. The presumption is defeasible over time in the light of changing experiences and perceptions.

This paper has two parts. The first takes originalism seriously as a theory of constitutional interpretation in order to understand its concepts, methodologies, and limitations. Part One concludes that neither strict textualism nor strict intentionalism is a tenable approach to constitutional decision-making, but that moderate originalism is coherent and workable. Part Two advances a normative thesis based on what I assert to be the ends of constitutional government. I argue that in resolving many constitutional disputes nonoriginalist adjudication better serves these ends than does moderate originalism.[6]

PART ONE: The Concepts and Methods of Originalism

Part One examines the three fundamental methods of originalism: interpretation of the text of the Constitution, interpretation of the intentions of its adopters, and inference from the structure and relationships of government institutions.

I. Textualism

Textualism takes the language of a legal provision as the primary or exclusive source of law (a) because of some definitional or supralegal principle that only a written text can impose constitutional obligations;[7] or (b) because the adopters intended that the Constitution be interpreted according to a textualist canon; or (c) because the text of a provision is the surest guide to the adopters' intentions. The last of these, probably the central rationale for an originalist-based textualism, is sometimes stated as a preamble to textualist canons. For example:

> It is a cardinal rule in the interpretation of constitutions that the instrument must be so construed as to give effect to the intention of the people, who adopted it. This intention is to be sought in the Constitution itself, and the apparent meaning of the words employed is to be taken as expressing it, except in cases where that assumption would lead to absurdity, ambiguity, or contradiction.[8]

Implicit in the preceding quotation is a canon of interpretation paradigmatic of textualism—the so-called plain meaning rule. Chief Justice Marshall invoked this canon in *Sturges* v. *Crowningshield*:

> [A]lthough the spirit of an instrument, especially of a constitution, is to be respected not less than its letter, yet the spirit is to be collected chiefly from its words. . . . [I]f, in any case, the plain meaning of a provision, not contradicted by any other provision in the same instrument, is to be disregarded, because we believe the framers of that instrument could not intend what they say, it must be one in which the absurdity and injustice of applying the provision to the case, would be so monstrous that all mankind would, without hesitation, unite in rejecting the application.[9]

The plain meaning of a text is the meaning that it would have for a "normal speaker of English" under the circumstances in which it is used.[10] Two kinds of circumstances seem relevant: the linguistic and the social contexts. The linguistic context refers to vocabulary and syntax. The social context refers to a shared understanding of the purposes the provision might plausibly serve.[11]

A tenable version of the plain-meaning rule must take account of both of these contexts. The alternative, of applying a provision according to the literal meanings of its component words, misconceives the conventions that govern the use of language.[12] Chief Justice Marshall argued this point eloquently and, I think, persuasively, in *McCulloch v. Maryland*,[13] decided the same year that he invoked the plain-meaning rule in *Sturges*. The state had argued that the necessary and proper clause authorized only legislation "indispensable" to executing the enumerated powers. Marshall responded with the observation that the word *necessary*, as used "in the common affairs of the world, or in approved authors, . . . frequently imports no more than that one thing is convenient, or useful, or essential to another."[14] He continued:

> Such is the character of human language, that no word conveys to the mind, in all situations, one single definite idea; and nothing is more common than to use words in a figurative sense. Almost all compositions contain words, which, taken in their rigorous sense, would convey a meaning different from that which is obviously intended. It is essential to just construction that many words which import something excessive, should be understood in a more mitigated sense—in that sense which common usage justifies. . . . This word, then, like others, is used in various senses; and, in its construction, the subject, the context, the intention of the person using them, are all to be taken into view.[15]

As Marshall implied, to attempt to read a provision without regard to its linguistic and social contexts will either yield unresolvable indeterminacies of language or just nonsense. Without taking account of the possible purposes of the provisions, an interpreter could not, for example, decide whether singing, flag-waving, flag-burning, picketing, and criminal conspiracy are within the protected ambit of the First Amendment's "freedom of speech,"[16] or whether the "writings" protected by the copyright clause include photographs, paintings, sculptures, perform-ances, and the contents of phonograph records.[17] She would not know whether the phrase, "No person except a natural born Citizen . . . shall be eligible to the Office of President,"[18] disqualified persons born abroad or those born by Caesarean section. We understand the range of plausi-ble meanings of provisions only because we know that some interpreta-tions respond to the kinds of concerns that the adopters' society might have while others do not.[19]

That an interpreter must read a text in the light of its social as well as linguistic context does not destroy the boundary between textualism and intentionalism. Just as the textualist is not concerned with the adopters' idiosyncratic use of language, she is not concerned with their subjective purposes. Rather, she seeks to discern the purposes that a member of the adopters' society would understand the provision to encompass.[20]

Suppose that phrases such as "commerce among the several states," or "freedom of speech," or "equal protection of the laws" have quite different meanings today than when they were adopted. An originalist would hold that, because interpretation is designed to capture the origi-nal understanding, the text must be understood in the contexts of the society that adopted it: "The meaning of the constitution is fixed when it is adopted, and it is not different at any subsequent time when a court has occasion to pass upon it."[21]

When a provision is interpreted roughly contemporaneously with its adoption, an interpreter unconsciously places the provision in its lin-guistic and social contexts, which she has internalized simply because she is of that society. But she cannot assume that a provision adopted one or two hundred years ago has the same meaning today as it had for the adopters' society. She must immerse herself in their society to under-stand the text as they understood it. Although many provisions of the Constitution may pose no serious interpretive problems in this respect, the textualist interpreter cannot be sure of this without first understand-ing the ordinary usage at the time of adoption. Did "commerce" include manufacture as well as trade?[22] Did the power to "regulate" commerce imply the power to prohibit it?[23] Did the power to "regulate commerce among the several states" include the power to regulate intrastate trans-actions which affected interstate commerce?[24] With what absoluteness did eighteenth-century Americans understand the prohibitions against "impairing" contractual obligations[25] and "abridging the freedom of speech"?[26] What did the words "privileges," "immunities," "due pro-cess," "equal protection of the laws," "citizen," and "person" mean to those who adopted the Fourteenth Amendment in 1868?[27]

Despite the differences between textualism and intentionalism, plac-ing a constitutional provision in its original contexts calls for a historical inquiry quite similar to the intentionalist interpreter's. I shall consider these together in section IV.

II. Intentionalism

By contrast to the textualist, the intentionalist interprets a provision by ascertaining the intentions of those who adopted it. The text of the provision is often a useful guide to the adopters' intentions, but the text does not enjoy a favored status over other sources.[28] Before turning to issues of intentionalism in constitutional interpretation, it is helpful to examine the underlying concepts through a simple example.

A. The Basic Concepts

1. The Adopters' Perspective

Suppose that you are the mayor of a small town and that you alone have the power to enact ordinances. The town maintains a park through which a dirt road runs. The road has traditionally been used as a shortcut by cars going to and from an adjacent residential neighborhood. It is also used by joggers. Last week, a blue 1973 Ford bumped into a jogger on this road. You immediately enacted an ordinance providing, "No vehicles shall be permitted in the park." When you came into your office this morning you were confronted by citizens asking whether you "intended" to prohibit various vehicles and activities from the park: Does the ordinance prohibit use of the park by a white 1975 Chevy sedan, a moped, a baby carriage? Does it forbid the local distributor of a crash-proof car from dropping it into the park from a helicopter as a publicity stunt?

These proposed uses have several features in common. First, each is prohibited by some literal interpretation of the ordinance. Second, each may annoy or endanger people using the park for recreational purposes. Third, you did not advert to any of these examples when you promulgated the regulation.[29] Nonetheless, you will almost surely conclude that your intentions were not the same with respect to all of the proposed uses. Just how you know what your intentions were is not crucial for our purposes. Yet it may be useful if, without any pretensions of rigor, I mention some aspects of the process of understanding or recollecting one's intentions.

You have three sources available. First, you can recall any instances of the rule's application which passed through your mind during the process of adopting it. I will call these your subjective exemplary applications of the rule. Second, you can look to the language of the rule you drafted, which implies conventional exemplary applications—those that your language would suggest to other members of your society. Third—though I am not certain how independent this is from the first two—you can recall the undesirable consequences that you hoped to avoid by enacting the rule. These may be conceptualized on different levels of generality. Moving from the abstract to the particular, you might have hoped to protect pedestrians using the park from harm, or from injury caused by vehicles, or from being run into by cars.

In reconstructing your intent, you will compare a proposed application with both conventional and subjective examples in the light of the consequences you hoped to avoid. The more a putative application differs from these applications, the less likely it falls within your intentions. "The more it differs"—but differs in what respect? Assuming that Fiat makes baby carriages as well as automobiles, is a Fiat sports car more like a Fiat baby carriage or more like a Chevrolet sedan? The concern, of course, is with salient differences, and salience is determined by the consequences you hoped to avoid, which in turn . . . .

However circular the process may seem, it often leads us somewhere. For example, you will surely conclude that you intended to prohibit the 1975 Chevy and that you intended not to prohibit the baby carriage. (Intent "to" and "not to" are mirror images, reflecting the same degree of determinacy.) What of the publicity stunt, dropping the vehicle into the park by helicopter? Of course, now that it comes to your attention, you would like to prohibit it. But it is too remote from either your subjective examples, or from society's conventional examples, to have been within your intentions when you enacted the ordinance. You did not intend the ordinance to prohibit this conduct.

And what of mopeds? Assume that you "intended not to" prohibit bicycles because you considered them among the legitimate uses of the park to be protected by the ordinance. Then mopeds probably lie on the periphery of the examples of both protected and prohibited uses: they both serve and disserve your purposes to some extent. Even if you had adverted to the issue you might not have reached a definite decision. Your intent with respect to mopeds was indeterminate.

2. The Interpreter's Perspective and the Application of Rules

Suppose that the mayor's intentions are as I have described them. The municipal court judge is an intentionalist interpreter and is therefore required to consult the mayor's intentions. How should she rule on the various constituents' requests for advisory opinions?

The decisions in the cases concerning the Chevy sedan and the baby carriage are clear-cut: the Chevy may not be driven through the park; the baby carriage may be perambulated. Assuming that the "no vehicles" regulation is the only colorably relevant law on the books, the car may be dropped from a helicopter. If this seems strange, suppose that a neighboring town has no ordinance whatever concerning vehicles in its park, and the car dealer wishes to perform the stunt there. That town's mayor would also have enacted a law prohibiting the stunt if only he had anticipated it, but of course he didn't. The only difference between that town and ours is that we have language on the books that conceivably applies. But from an intentionalist standpoint this is irrelevant, for our mayor never intended the words to deal with this situation. An intentionalist judge may no more prohibit the stunt based on what the lawmaker might have intended than a textualist may prohibit the stunt based on what a lawmaker might have written.

How should the judge decide the legality of mopeds in the park? By hypothesis the mayor's intent was indeterminate. Should the judge treat this as tantamount to a finding of no intent and therefore hold that mopeds are not prohibited by the regulation? Intentionalist theory alone does not warrant this conclusion any more than it does the opposite. Even if the judge also holds to an institutional theory that allocates "policy" decisions to nonjudicial agencies—in this case, the mayor—she would have no basis for preferring one or the other outcome, for a decision either way is equally one of policy. Thus, the judge's decision must be rooted elsewhere, perhaps in a libertarian disfavor of government regulation or an environmentalist disfavor of gas-powered vehicles. Even if these are values generally shared in the community, however, the judge's decision would not be determined by intentionalist interpretation.

3. The Interpretive Intent

Suppose that the mayor has the legal authority not only to adopt substantive regulations, but also to stipulate the canons by which the judge shall interpret them.[30] Suppose that when the judge inquires into the mayor's intentions about how his regulations should be interpreted—his interpretive intent—she discovers that he is a literalist, or perhaps a moderate intentionalist. That is, suppose that he intends his enactments to be interpreted either by the canon, "Adhere strictly to my language regardless of my intentions" or, "Take my language and what you understand to be my objectives as general guidelines, but don't try to figure out how I would have decided any particular case."[31]

If under these circumstances the judge continues to engage in strict intentionalist interpretation, she has subordinated fidelity to the adopter's intentions to some other value.

4. Individual and Institutional Intent

Imagine, finally, a less autocratic town in which ordinances are enacted by a five-member city council. Although the council unanimously enacts the "no vehicle" ordinance, its members have contradictory intentions concerning its application. What rules determine the intent of the city council—the institutional intent of a multimember body? If we make some simplifying assumptions, the same rules that determine whether a proposed enactment is binding law also determine what intentions are binding.

Consider how intentionalist lawmakers would respond to the disquieting prediction that their laws will be interpreted by purely textualist canons. They would try to specify their intentions in the text of the provision, and the text would, ideally, articulate all and only those intentions that gain a majority vote of the city council. Suppose, for example, that a five-member city council was deliberating the proposed "no vehicle" ordinance. Two council members oppose any regulation; two favor a regulation that prohibits mopeds. The fifth member favors the prohibition of motor vehicles in general but wishes to exempt mopeds. Under these circumstances, the two other proponents might accede to language explicitly exempting mopeds from the regulation in order to assure that at least some other motor vehicles are prohibited.

Of course, the intentionalist interpreter is concerned with the adopters' intentions whether or not these are embodied in the text. In effect, she accords each participant an intention-vote, and the counting of these votes determines the reach of the provision. If a version of the "no vehicles in the park" regulation that specified "this shall prohibit mopeds" would have failed by one vote, then, whatever its language, the regulation lacks the intention-votes necessary to prohibit mopeds and the intentionalist interpreter may not prohibit them.[32]

Let me conclude this section by defending it against the charge that I have created a straw intentionalist, for few if any intentionalist interpreters actually attempt to count the intention-votes of the adopters of statutory and constitutional provisions.[33] The preceding discussion does not purport to set out a methodology of intentionalist interpretation, but rather analyzes the concepts that underlie the practice. In the real world, of course, an interpreter must rely on quite different, and much cruder, ways of determining the adopters' intentions. Nonetheless, her methodology assumes the existence of an attainable ideal which is fairly described by the metaphor of intention-votes—the intentionalist analogue to actual votes. Much of the remainder of Part One inquires to what extent the intentionalist ideal can actually be achieved.

B. Intentions in Constitutional Interpretation

The artificially simple examples of the mayor and city council have allowed us to examine some of the basic concepts implicit in intentional-ism. I should like to explore these issues further in the context of constitutional interpretation.

1. Who Are the Adopters?

The adopters of the Constitution of 1787 were some portion of the delegates to the Philadelphia Convention and majorities or supermajorities of the participants in the ratifying conventions in nine states.[34] For all but one amendment to the Constitution,[35] the adopters were two-thirds or more of the members of each House of Congress and at least a majority of the legislators in two-thirds of the state legislatures.

For a textual provision to become part of the Constitution, the requisite number of persons in each of these bodies must have assented to it. Likewise, an intention can only become binding—only become an institutional intention—when it is shared by at least the same number and distribution of adopters. (Hereafter, I shall refer to this number and distribution as the "adopters.")

If the only way a judge could ascertain institutional intent were to count individual intention-votes, her task would be impossible even with respect to a single multimember lawmaking body, and a fortiori where the assent of several such bodies was required. Therefore, an intentionalist must necessarily use circumstantial evidence to educe a collective or general intent.

Interpreters often treat the writings or statements of the Framers of a provision as evidence of the adopters' intent. This is a justifiable strategy for the moderate originalist who is concerned with the Framers' intent on a relatively abstract level of generality—abstract enough to permit the inference that it reflects a broad social consensus rather than notions peculiar to a handful of the adopters. It is a problematic strategy for the strict originalist.

As the process of adoption moves from the actual Framers of a constitutional amendment, to the members of Congress who proposed it, to the state legislators who ratified it, the amount of thought given the provision surely diminishes—especially if it is relatively technical or uncontroversial, or one of several of disparate provisions (e.g., the Bill of Rights) adopted simultaneously. This suggests that there may be instances where a Framer had a determinate intent but other adopters had no intent or an indeterminate intent. For example, suppose that the Framers of the commerce clause considered the possibility that economic transactions taking place within the confines of a state might nonetheless affect interstate commerce in such a way as to come within the clause, and that they intended the clause to cover such transactions. But suppose that most of the delegates to the ratifying conventions did not conceive of this possibility and that either they "did not intend" that the clause encompass such transactions or else their intentions were indeterminate. Under these circumstances, what is the institutional intent, i.e., the intent of the provision?

If the intent of the Framers is to be attributed to the provision, it must be because the other adopters have in effect delegated their intention-votes to the Framers.[36] Leaving aside the question whether the adopters-at-large had any thoughts at all concerning this issue of delegation, consider what they might have desired if they had thought about it. Would they have wanted the Framers' intentions to govern without knowing what those intentions were? The answers might well differ depending on whether the adopters had "no intent" or "indeterminate intent."

A delegate to a ratifying convention might well want his absence of intention (i.e., "no intent") regarding wholly intrastate transactions to be treated as a vote against the clause's encompassing such transactions (i.e., "intent-not"): Since no intent is the intentionalist equivalent of no text, to accede to the Framers' unknown intentions would be tantamount to blindly delegating to them the authority to insert textual provisions in the Constitution.

Where the Framers intend that the activity be covered by the clause, and the adopters' intentions are merely indeterminate, the institutional intent is ambiguous. One adopter might wish his indeterminate intent to be treated as "no intent." Another adopter might wish to delegate his intention-vote to those whose intent is determinate. Yet another might wish to delegate authority to decision-makers charged with applying the provision in the future. Without knowing more about the mind-sets of the actual adopters of particular constitutional provisions, one would be hard-pressed to choose among these.

2. The Adopters' Interpretive Intent

The intentionalist interpreter's first task must be to determine the interpretive intentions of the adopters of the provisions before her—that is, the canons by which the adopters intended their provisions to be interpreted.[37] The practice of statutory interpretation from the eighteenth through at least the mid nineteenth century suggests that the adopters assumed—if they assumed anything at all—a mode of interpretation that was more textualist than intentionalist. The plain-meaning rule was frequently invoked: judicial recourse to legislative debates was virtually unknown and generally considered improper. Even after references to extrinsic sources became common,[38] courts and commentators frequently asserted that the plain meaning of the text was the surest guide to the intent of the adopters.[39]

This poses obvious difficulties for an intentionalist whose very enterprise is premised on fidelity to the original understanding.[40]

3. The Intended Specificity of a Provision

I now turn to an issue that lies at the intersection of what I have called interpretive and substantive intent: how much discretion did an adopter intend to delegate to those charged with applying a provision? Consider, for example, the possible intentions of the adopters of the cruel and unusual punishment clause of the Eighth Amendment. They might have intended that the language serve only as a shorthand for the Stuart tortures which were their exemplary applications of the clause. Somewhat more broadly, they might have intended the clause to be understood to incorporate the principle of *ejusdem generis*—to include their exemplary applications and other punishments that they found or would have found equally repugnant.[41]

What of instances where the adopters' substantive intent was indeterminate—where even if they had adverted to a proposed application they would not have been certain how the clause should apply? Here it is plausible that—if they *had* a determinate interpretive intent—they intended to delegate to future decision-makers the authority to apply the clause in light of the general principles underlying it. To use Ronald Dworkin's terms, the adopters would have intended future interpreters to develop their own "conceptions" of cruel and unusual punishment within the framework of the adopters' general "concept" of such punishments.[42]

What of a case where the adopters viewed a certain punishment as not cruel and unusual? This is not the same as saying that the adopters "intended not to prohibit the punishment." For even if they expected their laws to be interpreted by intentionalist canons, the adopters may have intended that their own views not always govern. Like parents who attempt to instill values in their child by both articulating and applying a moral principle, they may have accepted, or even invited, the eventuality that the principle would be applied in ways that diverge from their own views.[43] The adopters may have understood that, even as to instances to which they believe the clause ought or ought not to apply, further thought by themselves or others committed to its underlying principle might lead them to change their minds. Not believing in their own omniscience or infallibility, they delegated the decision to those charged with interpreting the provision. If such a motivation is plausible with respect to applications of the clause in the adopters' contemporary society, it is even more likely with respect to its application by future interpreters, whose understanding of the clause will be affected by changing knowledge, technology, and forms of society.

The extent to which a clause may be properly interpreted to reach outcomes different from those actually contemplated by the adopters depends on the relationship between a general principle and its exemplary applications. A principle does not exist wholly independently of its author's subjective, or his society's conventional exemplary applications,[44] and is always limited to some extent by the applications they found conceivable. Within these fairly broad limits, however, the adopters may have intended their examples to constrain more or less. To the intentionalist interpreter falls the unenviable task of ascertaining, for each provision, how much more or less.

III. Inference from Structure and Relationship

In an important lecture given in 1968, Professor Charles Black described a mode of constitutional interpretation based on "inference from the structures and relationships created by the constitution in all its parts or in some principal part."[45] Professor Black observed that in *McCulloch* v. *Maryland*,[46] "Marshall does not place principal reliance on the [necessary and proper] clause as a ground of decision . . . . [B]efore he reaches it he has already decided, on the basis of far more general implications, that Congress possesses the power, not expressly named, of establishing a bank and chartering corporations; . . . he addresses himself to the necessary and proper clause only in response to counsel's arguing its *restrictive* force."[47] Indeed, the second part of *McCulloch*, which held that the Constitution prohibited Maryland from levying a tax on the National Bank, rested exclusively on inferences from the structure of the federal system, and not at all on the text of the Constitution. Similarly, *Crandall* v. *Nevada*[48] was not premised on the privileges and immunities clause of either Article IV or the Fourteenth Amendment. Rather, the Court inferred a right of personal mobility among the states from the structure of the federal system:

> [The citizen] has the right to come to the seat of government to assert any claim he may have upon that government, or to transact any business he may have with it. To seek its protection, to share its offices, to engage in administering its functions. He has a right to free access to its sea-ports, through which all the operations of foreign trade and commerce are conducted, to the subtreasuries, the land offices, the revenue offices, and the courts of justice in the several States, and this right is in its nature independent of the will of any State over whose soil he must pass in the exercise of it.[49]

Citing examples like these, Professor Black argued that interpreters too often have engaged in "Humpty-Dumpty textual manipulation" rather than relying "on the sort of political inference which not only underlies the textual manipulation but is, in a well constructed opinion, usually invoked to support the interpretation of the cryptic text."[50]

Inference from structure and relationship is no less legitimate than other originalist modes of interpretation, nor less fraught with indeterminacy. Like the language of many constitutional provisions, the constitutional ordering of institutions permits alternative inferences. Contrary to Chief Justice Marshall's implication in *McCulloch*, for example, the nature of a federal constitution does not entail that the national legislative powers must be construed expansively[51] or that state taxation of the operations of a national bank is necessarily prohibited. Moreover, because an originalist interpreter is concerned only with the structure and relationships of institutions as of the time they were established or restructured, she confronts the same hermeneutical problems as the textualist and intentionalist. It is to these that I now turn.

IV. The Interpreter-Historian's Task

The interpreter's task as historian can be divided into three stages or categories. First, she must immerse herself in the world of the adopters to try to understand constitutional concepts and values from their perspective. Second, at least the intentionalist must ascertain the adopters' interpretive intent and the intended scope of the provision in question. Third, she must often "translate" the adopters' concepts and intentions into our time and apply them to situations that the adopters did not foresee.

The first stage is common to originalists of all persuasions. Although the textualist's aim is to understand and apply the language of a constitutional provision, she must locate the text in the linguistic and social contexts in which it was adopted. Similarly, the originalist "structuralist" interpreter must situate the institutions in their original contexts. The intentionalist would ideally count the intention-votes of the individual adopters. In practice, she can at best hope to discover a consensus of the adopters as manifested in the text of the provision itself, the history surrounding its adoption, and the ideologies and practices of the time.

The essential difficulty posed by the distance that separates the modern interpreter from the objects of her interpretation has been succinctly stated by Quentin Skinner in addressing the analogous problem facing historians of political theory:[52]

> [I]t will never in fact be possible simply to study what any given classic writer has *said* . . . without bringing to bear some of one's own expectations about what he must have been saying . . . . [T]hese models and preconceptions in terms of which we unavoidably organize and adjust our perceptions and thoughts will themselves tend to act as determinants of what we think or perceive. We must classify in order to

understand, and we can only classify the unfamiliar in terms of the familiar. The perpetual danger, in our attempts to enlarge our historical understanding, is thus that our expectations about what someone must be saying or doing will themselves determine that we understand the agent to be doing something which he would not—or even could not—himself have accepted as an account of what he *was* doing.[53]

To illustrate the problem of doing original history with even a single example would consume more space than I wish to here. Instead, I suggest that a reader who wants to get a sense of the elusiveness of the original understanding study some specific areas of constitutional history, reading both works that have been well received,[54] and also the controversy surrounding some of those that have not.[55]

The intentionalist interpreter must next ascertain the adopters' interpretive intent and the intended breadth of their provisions.[56] That is, she must determine what the adopters intended future interpreters to make of their substantive views. Even if she can learn how the adopters intended contemporary interpreters to construe the Constitution, she cannot assume they intended the same canons to apply one or two hundred years later. Perhaps they wanted to bind the future as closely as possible to their own notions. Perhaps they intended a particular provision to be interpreted with increasing breadth as time went on. Or—more likely than not—the adopters may have had no intentions at all concerning these matters.[57]

For purposes of analytic clarity I have distinguished between (a) the adopters' interpretive intent and the intended scope of a provision and (b) their substantive intent concerning the application of the provision. If interpretive intent and intended scope can be ascertained at all, they may instruct the interpreter to adopt different canons of interpretation than she would prefer. Under these circumstances, the intentionalist interpreter may wish to ignore these intentions and limit her inquiry to the adopters' substantive intentions. Leaving aside the normative difficulty of such selective infidelity,[58] this is a problematic strategy: to be a coherent theory of interpretation, intentionalism must distinguish between the adopters' personal *views* about an issue and their *intentions* concerning its constitutional resolution. And it is only by reference to their interpretive intent and the intended scope of a provision that this distinction can be drawn.

The interpreter's final task is to translate the adopters' intentions into the present in order to apply them to the question at issue. Consider, for example, whether the cruel and unusual punishment clause of the Eighth Amendment prohibits the imposition of the death penalty today. The adopters of the clause apparently never doubted that the death penalty was constitutional.[59] But was death the same event for inhabitants of the American colonies in the late eighteenth century as it is two centuries later? Death was not only a much more routine and public phenomenon then, but the fear of death was more effectively contained within a system of religious belief.[60] Twentieth-century Americans have a more secular cast of mind and seem less willing to accept this dreadful, forbidden, solitary, and shameful event.[61] The interpreter must therefore determine whether we view the death penalty with the same attitude—whether of disgust or ambivalence—with which the adopters viewed their core examples of cruel and unusual punishment.[62]

Intentionalist interpretation frequently requires translations of this sort. For example, to determine whether the commerce clause applies to transactions taking place wholly within the boundaries of one state, or whether the First Amendment protects the mass media, the interpreter must abstract the adopters' concepts of federalism and freedom of expression in order to find their analogue in our contemporary society with its different technology, economy, and systems of communication.[63] The alternative would be to limit the application of constitutional provisions to the particular events and transactions with which the adopters were familiar. Even if such an approach were coherent,[64] however, it would produce results that even a strict intentionalist would likely reject: Congress could not regulate any item of commerce or any mode of transportation that did not exist in 1789; the First Amendment would not protect any means of communication not then known.

However difficult the earlier stages of her work, the interpreter was only trying to understand the past. The act of translation required here is different in kind, for it involves the counterfactual and imaginary act of projecting the adopters' concepts and attitudes into a future they probably could not have envisioned. When the interpreter engages in this sort of projection, she is in a fantasy world more of her own than of the adopters' making.

* * *

Even when the interpreter performs the more conventional historian's role, one may wonder whether the task is possible. There is a hermeneutical tradition, of which Hans-Georg Gadamar is the leading modern proponent, which holds that we can never understand the past in its own terms, free from our prejudices or preconceptions.[65] We are hopelessly imprisoned in our own world views; we can shed some preconceptions only to adopt others, with no reason to believe that they are the conceptions of the different society that we are trying to understand. One need not embrace this essentially solipsistic view of historical knowledge to appreciate the indeterminate and contingent nature of the historical understanding that an originalist historian seeks to achieve.

None of this is to disparage doing history and other interpretive social science. It suggests, however, that the originalist constitutional historian may be questing after a chimera. The defense that "we're doing the best we can" is no less available to constitutional interpreters than to anyone else. But the best is not always good enough. The interpreter's understanding of the original understanding may be so indeterminate as to undermine the rationale for originalism. Although the origins of some constitutional doctrines are almost certainly established, the historical grounding of many others is quite controversial.[66] It seems peculiar, to say the least, that the legitimacy of a current doctrine should turn on the historian's judgment that it seems "more likely than not," or even "rather likely," that the adopters intended it some one or two centuries ago.

V. Two Types of Originalism

The originalist interpreter can approach her task with different attitudes about the precision with which the object of interpretation—the text, intentions, or structure—should be understood. In this section I describe the attitudes of "strict" and "moderate" originalism—two areas, not points, on a spectrum—and briefly survey the practices of American constitutional decision-making in terms of them.

I have devoted very little attention to the most extreme form of strict textualism—literalism. A thoroughgoing literalist understands a text to encompass all those and only those instances that come within its words read without regard to its social or perhaps even its linguistic context. Because literalism poorly matches the ways in which we speak and write, it is unable to handle the ambiguity, vagueness, and figurative usage that pervade natural languages, and produces embarrassingly silly results.

Strict intentionalism requires the interpreter to determine how the adopters would have applied a provision to a given situation, and to apply it accordingly. The enterprise rests on the questionable assumption that the adopters of constitutional provisions intended them to be applied in this manner. But even if this were true, the interpreter confronts historiographic difficulties of such magnitude as to make the aim practicably unattainable.

Strict textualism and intentionalism are not synergistic, but rather mutually antagonistic approaches to interpretation. The reader need only consider the strict textualist's and intentionalist's views of the First Amendment protection of pornographic literature.[67] By contrast, moderate textualism and intentionalism closely resemble each other in methodology and results.

A moderate textualist takes account of the open-textured quality of language and reads the language of provisions in their social and linguistic contexts. A moderate intentionalist applies a provision consistent with the adopters' intent at a relatively high level of generality, consistent with what is sometimes called the "purpose of the provision."[68] Where the strict intentionalist tries to determine the adopters' actual subjective purposes, the moderate intentionalist attempts to understand what the adopters' purposes might plausibly have been,[69] an aim far more readily achieved than a precise understanding of the adopters' intentions.

* * *

Strict originalism cannot accommodate most modern decisions under the Bill of Rights and the Fourteenth Amendment, or the virtually plenary scope of congressional power under the commerce clause. Although moderate originalism is far more expansive, some major constitutional doctrines lie beyond its pale as well.

A moderate textualist would treat almost all contemporary free speech and equal protection decisions as within the permissible ambit of these clauses, though not necessarily entailed by them. Because of our uncertainty about the original understanding, it is harder to assess the legitimacy of these doctrines from the viewpoint of a moderate intentionalist. For example, the proper scope of the First Amendment depends on whether its adopters were only pursuing "representation reinforcing" goals,[70] or were more broadly concerned to promote a free marketplace of ideas or individual autonomy.[71] The level of generality on which the adopters conceived of the equal protection clause presents a similar uncertainty, but whether or not a moderate intentionalist could accept all of the "new" or "newer" equal protection,[72] she could read the clause to protect "discrete and insular minorities" besides blacks.

On the other hand, a moderate originalist, whether of textualist or intentionalist persuasion, would have serious difficulties justifying (a) the incorporation of the principle of equal protection into the Fifth Amendment;[73] (b) the incorporation of provisions of the Bill of Rights into the Fourteenth Amendment;[74] (c) the more general notion of substantive due process, including the minimal rational relationship standard;[75] and (d) the practice of judicial review of congressional legislation established by *Marbury* v. *Madison*.[76] Although these doctrines strain or go beyond the text of the Constitution, for reasons made apparent in the preceding pages, one cannot say with certainty that they are not authorized by the original understanding. For purposes of Part Two it is enough that the legitimacy of their origins cannot be established with much certainty.[77]

PART TWO: The Authority of the Constitution

Throughout Part One we assumed that judges and other public officials were bound by the text or original understanding of the Constitution. Part

Two challenges this assumption. I begin by showing that the issue is not foreclosed by the written Constitution itself, and then offer some criteria for evaluating competing strategies of constitutional decision-making. I then describe a familiar alternative to originalism—(mere) adjudication. The remainder of Part Two compares the alternatives and concludes that adjudication which takes account of the text and original understanding without, however, treating them as authoritative generally serves the ends of constitutionalism better than originalist interpretation.

I. The Authority of the Constitution and the Purposes of Constitutional Decision-making

What authority does the written Constitution have in our system of constitutional government? This is not an empty question. The English experience demonstrates that a constitutional democracy—a government of limited powers ultimately responsible to its citizens—need not be premised on a written document.[78] And although Article VI declares that the Constitution is the "supreme law of the land," a document cannot achieve the status of law, let alone supreme law, merely by its own assertion.

According to the political theory most deeply rooted in the American tradition, the authority of the Constitution derives from the consent of its adopters.[79] Even if the adopters freely consented to the Constitution, however, this is not an adequate basis for continuing fidelity to the founding document, for their consent cannot bind succeeding generations.[80] We did not adopt the Constitution, and those who did are dead and gone.

Given the questionable authority of the American Constitution—indeed, of any (quasi) revolutionary constitution at the moment of its inception—it is only through a history of continuing assent or acquiescence that the document could become law.[81] Our constitutional tradition, however, has not focused on the document alone, but on the decisions and practices of courts and other institutions. And this tradition has included major elements of nonoriginalism. The doctrines described in the conclusion to Part One are as well-settled parts of the constitutional landscape as most originalist-based doctrines. They are among the principal subjects that occupy professionals who "do" constitutional law—lawyers, judges, law professors, and law students—and are considered part of constitutional law by the media and by the lay public. A description of the American legal system that omitted them or treated them as aberrational would be extraordinarily inaccurate. To make the point affirmatively, the practice of supplementing and derogating from the text and original understanding is itself part of our constitutional tradition.

The fact of this tradition undermines the exclusivity of the written document. It does not, however, establish the legitimacy of nonoriginalism. Acquiescence is not the same as "consent," which must be informed and knowingly and freely given. Those conditions have not in fact been met, and perhaps can never be met in a large industrial society.[82]

Actual consent is not, then, a practicable measure of the legitimacy of any system of government,[83] and a fortiori not of a particular practice or institution. Owen Fiss has suggested that it is not even an appropriate measure of institutional legitimacy:

> Consent goes to the system, not the particular institution; it operates on the whole rather than on each part. The legitimacy of particular institutions, such as courts, depends not on the consent—implied or otherwise—of the people, but rather on their *competence*, on the special contribution they make to the quality of our social life. Legitimacy depends on the capacity of the institution to perform a function within the political system and its willingness to respect the limitations on that function.[84]

Whether or not the practices of constitutional decision-making should ideally be validated by consent as well as competence, I think we must accept Professor Fiss's observation faute de mieux.

Having abandoned both consent and fidelity to the text and original understanding as the touchstones of constitutional decision-making, let me propose a designedly vague criterion: how well, compared to possible alternatives, does the practice contribute to the well-being of our society—or, more narrowly, to the ends of constitutional government? Among other things, the practice should (*a*) foster democratic government; (*b*) protect individuals against arbitrary, unfair, and intrusive official action; (*c*) conduce to a political order that is relatively stable but which also responds to changing conditions, values, and needs; (*d*) not readily lend itself to arbitrary decisions or abuses; and (*e*) be acceptable to the populace. The following paragraphs amplify the first two of these, and I shall discuss specific applications of all of them below.

Central to our constitutional order are the related though not always compatible concerns for individual rights and decision-making through democratic processes. For better or worse, the judiciary has assumed a major role in protecting both. In what has become a classic description of the special role of constitutional adjudication, Alexander Bickel wrote:

> [M]any actions of government have two aspects: their immediate, necessarily intended, practical effects, and their perhaps unintended or unappreciated bearing on values we hold to have more general and permanent interest. It is a premise we deduce not merely from the fact of a written constitution but from the history of the race, and ultimately as a moral judgment of the good society, that government should serve not

only what we conceive from time to time to be our immediate material needs but also certain enduring values. . . . But such values do not present themselves ready-made. They have a past always, to be sure, but they must be continually derived, enunciated, and seen in relevant application.[85]

In the same spirit, Owen Fiss argues that the judiciary should give "concrete meaning and application to our constitutional values"—the values which "give our society an identity and inner coherence [and] its distinctive public morality."[86]

Thus, the practice of constitutional adjudication should enforce those, but only those, values which are fundamental to our society. Adopting this vague norm does not automatically foreclose either strict or moderate originalism. It may still be contended that the ends of constitutionalism are best served by enforcing only values embodied in the text and original understanding of the Constitution.[87] However, originalism can no longer be defended a priori but must justify itself in the face of alternative approaches to constitutional decision-making.

One such alternative would safeguard two of our most fundamental values—the integrity of majoritarian processes and the rights of minorities. This special judicial role was suggested in footnote 4 of Justice Stone's opinion in the *Carolene Products* case.[88] It is the thesis of John Ely's recent book, *Democracy and Distrust: A Theory of Judicial Review*. Ely argues that the judiciary properly performs these "representation-reinforcing" functions, but that courts are not competent to ascertain and apply any other "fundamental values." A broader approach, implicit in Bickel's and Fiss's more general description of the judicial function, would protect all fundamental values against official intrusion, without inquiring whether the intrusion resulted from defects of democratic processes.

Independent of any of these views of the proper *domain* of judicial intervention are a variety of notions about the amount of *deference* that a court should accord a legislative or administrative decision under review. For example, although the substantive scope of Bickel's judicial function is broad, he, like many other scholars and judges in the "fundamental values" tradition, would accord legislation a very strong presumption of constitutionality.[89] Professor Ely, on the other hand, is less concerned with judicial deference within the more circumscribed sphere of intervention that he advocates.

The thesis of this article is not tied to Bickel's, Ely's, or any other particular nonoriginalist method. Rather, the thesis is that whether one views the appropriate realm of judicial inquiry as broad or narrow, and whether one approaches the enterprise with a deferential or interventionist bias, the aims of constitutionalism are best served by nonoriginalist adjudication which treats the text and original history as important but not necessarily authoritative.

II. Adjudication As an Alternative to Originalist Interpretation

Several features of adjudication[90] commend it as a plausible method for deriving and applying Bickel's "fundamental" values or Ely's "representation-reinforcing" values. Judges—especially federal judges—are relatively independent officials. Cases are presented through arguments based on precedent, policy, and principle, by parties who stand equally before the court. The court must justify its decisions by articulating reasons for them. The concreteness of the dispute, and the method of "testing" a result by articulating a governing principle and applying it to this and similar cases—real or hypothetical—induce the court to take responsibility for its decisions and to look beyond the circumstances of the particular dispute. And although the court gives strong presumptive weight to its precedents, the presumption is defeasible: precedents are modified and even overruled to reflect perceived changes in social needs and values. Therefore, a doctrine that survives over a period of time has the approval of a court composed, in effect, of all the judges who have ever had occasion to consider and apply it.[91]

This is, of course, an idealized[92] description of the Anglo-American "case" or "common-law" method, which derives legal principles from custom, social practices, conventional morality, and precedent. Most American constitutional doctrines have evolved through adjudication, for it is the method of moderate orginalism in the many cases where original sources alone cannot resolve the controversy before the court.[93]

The only difference between moderate originalism and nonoriginalist adjudication is one of attitude toward the text and original understanding. For the moderate originalist, these sources are conclusive when they speak clearly. For the nonoriginalist, they are important but not determinative. Like an established line of precedent at common law, they create a strong presumption, but one which is defeasible in the light of changing public values. The text and original understanding exert the strongest claims when they are contemporary and thus likely to reflect current values and beliefs, or simply the expressed will of a current majority;[94] or where they specify the procedures and numbers relating to elections, appointments to government offices, and the formal validity of laws, where certainty is an important objective or inherently arbitrary lines must be drawn.[95] The presumption is most likely to be overcome in adjudication under broad clauses involving issues of equality and liberty, where legal and moral principles are closely intertwined.

III. Originalism Evaluated

A. Strict Originalism

The discussion in Part One showed that strict textualism cannot produce sensible constitutional decisions. This section attempts to show why strict intentionalism is not well suited to eliciting fundamental or "representation-reinforcing" values.

Even if the adopters were extraordinarily wise and public-spirited, they were also self-interested: the Constitution reflects a pragmatic and not always principled compromise among a variety of regional, economic, and political interests. The strict intentionalist must winnow the adopters' underlying values from these interests.[96] Besides the methodological and historiographic difficulties of this enterprise, it is prey to a normative problem: the drafting, adopting, or amending of the Constitution may itself have suffered from defects of democratic process which detract from its moral claims. To take an obvious example, the interests of black Americans were not adequately represented in the adoption of the Constitution of 1787 or the Fourteenth Amendment. Whatever moral consensus the Civil War amendments embodied was among white male property-holders and not the population as a whole. Similarly, the assumption that the contract clause reflected widely held norms of eighteenth-century America is weakened to the extent that creditors were well represented and debtors underrepresented in the Philadelphia and state ratifying conventions.[97]

To characterize these as defects of democratic process may seem anachronistic or question-begging: even if we regard them as defects, they may not have been so regarded by many participants at the time. Moreover, the argument may prove too much, for the making of almost any law suffers from similar imperfections. But my point is not that an early nineteenth-century court should have tried to abolish slavery or guarantee full racial equality in the face of a contrary constitutional understanding. Rather, the fact that a provision was drafted by an unrepresentative and self-interested portion of the adopters' society weakens its moral claim on a different society one or two hundred years later.

Assume that the intentionalist interpreter can filter out the purely pragmatic factors and identify the moral consensus of an earlier era in American history. What is the likelihood that the same consensus exists today? Suppose, for example, that the prevalent public morality in 1868 did not extend beyond the limited formal racial equality mandated by a narrow reading of the Civil Rights Act of 1866.[98] Many intervening phenomena—including the achievements of blacks in the face of a century of discrimination, changes in the economy with attendant changes in migration and labor patterns, and direct evidence of attitude change—suggest that the nation's values had shifted significantly by 1954, and certainly by the mid 1960s.[99] The history of the preceding decades justifies Chief Justice Warren's comment in *Brown* that "[i]n approaching this problem, we cannot turn the clock back to 1868 when the Amendment was adopted, or even to 1896 when *Plessy v. Ferguson* was written."[100]

To return to the contract clause, assuming for the sake of argument that most eighteenth-century Americans believed that contractual obligations should be absolutely inviolate, how many of our contemporaries share that belief? Consider Chief Justice Hughes's response in the *Minnesota Mortgage Moratorium* case:

> It is manifest . . . that there has been a growing appreciation of public needs and of the necessity of finding ground for a rational compromise between individual rights and public welfare. The settlement and consequent contraction of the public domain, the pressure of a constantly increasing density of population, the interrelation of the activities of our people, and the complexity of our economic interests, have inevitably led to an increased use of the organization of society in order to protect the very bases of individual opportunity . . . . [T]he question is no longer merely that of one party to a contract as against another, but of the use of reasonable means to safeguard the economic structure upon which the good of all depends.[101]

Finally, strict intentionalism produces a highly unstable constitutional order. The claims of scholars like William Winslow Crosskey and Raoul Berger[102] demonstrate that a settled constitutional understanding is in perpetual jeopardy of being overturned by new light on the adopters' intent—shed by the discovery of historical documents, reexaminations of known documents, and reinterpretations of political and social history. Morever, constitutional interpretation is not a scientific process but a subjective undertaking which vests the historian with enormous discretion in ordering and analyzing her data. Novel interpretations are due as much to changes in the interpreter's perspective as to anything extrinsic. And we have witnessed enough dramatic revisions of social and political history to be sure that the past is not about to stand still.

B. Moderate Originalism

Moderate originalism is a perfectly sensible strategy of constitutional decision-making. But its constraints are illusory and counterproductive. Contrary to the moderate originalist's faith, the text and original understanding have contributed little to the development of many doctrines she accepts as legitimate. Consider the relationship between the original understanding of the Fourteenth Amendment and current doctrines prohibiting gender-based classifications[103] and discriminations in the political process.[104] For the moderate originalist these may be legitimately premised on the equal protection clause. But to what extent have originalist sources *guided* the evolution of these doctrines? The text is wholly open-ended; and if the adopters had any intentions at all about these issues, their resolution was probably contrary to the Court's. At most, the Court can claim guidance from the general notion of equal treatment reflected in the provision. I use the word "reflected" advisedly, however, for the equal protection clause does not establish a principle of equality; it only articulates and symbolizes a principle defined by our conventional public morality. Indeed, because of its indeterminacy, the clause does not offer much guidance even in resolving particular issues of discrimination based on race.[105]

To see this from a different perspective, suppose that the equal protection clause had provided: "No State shall deny any person the equal protection of the laws *on account of race.*"[106] If the Court had nonetheless expanded the requirement of equal treatment beyond racial classifications—under the aegis of, say, the due process clause—would the gender and voting decisions have been any less responsive to changing public values than they have in fact been under the actual clause? Or suppose that tomorrow it were demonstrated, as conclusively as such things ever can be, that the adopters intended to limit the clause to a narrow range of racially discriminatory practices:[107] would many decades of moderate originalist doctrine become retroactively misguided?[108]

We need not rely on counterfactual examples to examine the importance of the text and original understanding to sound constitutional decision-making. I have already noted that a moderate originalist cannot easily justify the incorporation of principles of equal treatment into the due process clause of the Fifth Amendment or the incorporation of most of the Bill of Rights into the Fourteenth Amendment. But these reciprocal incorporation doctrines are relatively easy to justify on nonoriginalist grounds. They did not require inventing any new rights as such, but only demanded that the federal government respect rights that were properly—from a moderate originalist standpoint—applied to the states, and vice versa. The main issue facing the Court was whether policies of federalism made it inapposite to impose on one government constraints that the Constitution placed on the other.

The Court incorporated the equal protection clause into the Fifth Amendment in a companion case to *Brown,* with the casual comment that "in view of our decision that the Constitution prohibits the states from maintaining racially segregated public schools, it would be unthinkable that the same Constitution would impose a lesser duty on the Federal Government."[109] I cannot think of a plausible argument against this result—other than the entirely correct originalist observation that it is not supported by even a generous reading of the Fifth Amendment.[110]

The selective incorporation of the Bill of Rights into the Fourteenth Amendment was not as easy, for it implicated venerable traditions of state diversity and autonomy. At first tentatively, then gradually with more authority, the Court proceeded to articulate a doctrine of incorporation[111] that reflected and contributed to a changing conception of federalism. I cannot prove the point, but the mature doctrine, though not necessarily every judicial gloss on particular clauses, seems responsive to current public norms.

Consider a final example. By the early 1970s it was well established that restrictions on access to the franchise violated the equal protection clause unless they served compelling state interests. In *Richardson* v. *Ramirez*[112] the Court refused to apply this doctrine to prohibit the disfranchisement of ex-felons. The Court noted that most nineteenth-century state constitutions denied the vote to ex-felons and that section 2 of the Fourteenth Amendment reduced a state's representation in Congress to the extent that it denied the vote to male citizens over twenty-one except those who had participated in rebellion "or other crime." With only two justices dissenting on the merits, the Court concluded that "those who framed and adopted the Fourteenth Amendment could not have intended to prohibit outright in section 1 of that Amendment that which was expressly exempted from the lesser sanction of reduced representation imposed by section 2 of the Amendment."[113]

This observation seems correct but beside the point. The adopters would probably have disapproved of all of the Court's modern voting-rights decisions, beginning with the *Reapportionment* and *Poll Tax* cases.[114] But the moral and political principles on which the modern decisions depend apply with equal force to convicted felons. To adhere to the general doctrine but not require the state to justify its discrimination is arbitrary and unprincipled.[115]

In sum, if you consider the evolution of doctrines in just about any extensively adjudicated area of constitutional law—whether "under" the commerce, free speech, due process, or equal protection clauses—explicit reliance on originalist sources has played a very small role compared to the elaboration of the Court's own precedents. It is rather like having a remote ancestor who came over on the Mayflower.

IV. The Ideology of Originalism and the Role of the Written Constitution

It has been said that the written Constitution lies at the core of the American "civil religion."[116] Not only judges and other public officials, but the citizenry at large habitually invoke the Constitution to justify and criticize judicial decisions and government conduct. Belief in the continuing authority of the document may contribute to a sense of national unity and to law-abiding behavior by officials and citizens. Thus, even though some of our most important constitutional practices are not originalist, the ideology of originalism may evoke concerns for a reader otherwise inclined to accept the practice of nonoriginalist constitutional decision-making.

One concern centers on informed consent and legitimacy. It is simply antidemocratic to conceal something as fundamental as the nature of constitutional decision-making—especially if concealment is motivated by the fear that the citizenry wouldn't stand for the practice if it knew the truth. If the Court can't admit what it is doing, then it shouldn't do it.

The premise that the government should be open about its practices seems right, as does the implication that the judiciary has not been fully candid about its decision-making processes: although the Supreme Court has often disavowed strict originalism and acknowledged its moderate originalist stance,[117] it has not usually admitted that some of its decisions go still further. Yet it is not plausible that the truth about constitutional adjudication has been successfully hidden in the face of almost two centuries of continual exposés of the Court's infidelities to the original meaning of the Constitution—criticisms levied by dissenting justices, lawyers, politicians, and newspaper editors, as well as scholars. The justices have not pulled the wool over the eyes of anyone who cared to see.

A second concern focuses on the decision-making process itself: even if judicial forays beyond the limits of moderate originalism are justified, perhaps they remain within proper bounds only because they occur within a pervasive originalist ethic. On this view, confining the Court to some form of originalism is rather like setting the speed limit at 55 miles an hour to keep cars from going faster than 65.[118]

The felt need to justify decisions by invoking the authority of the Constitution may indeed constrain decisions.[119] The question is whether it constrains them in ways conducive to the ends of constitutionalism. I have argued that the constraints imposed by adjudication which treats the text and original understanding as persuasive but not authoritative better serve these ends. Until and unless the Court abandons its moderate originalist pretensions we can only rely on our hunches.

A reader inclined to acknowledge the legitimacy of nonoriginalist decision-making may nonetheless intuit a distinction between supraconstitutional and contraconstitutional decisions, and find it easier to accept decisions that supplement the Constitution than those which ignore or derogate from the document. On this view, the Court's expansive readings of the Bill of Rights and the Fourteenth Amendment are legitimate, whereas the holding in the *Minnesota Mortgage Moratorium* case[120] may be unacceptable.

The distinction between supplementing and derogating from the Constitution does not readily fit most power-granting provisions. For example, a supraconstitutional expansion of Congress's powers under Article I would be contraconstitutional under the Tenth Amendment. The distinction probably has the most appeal when it is invoked to protect individual rights, where we hope to use the authority of the written document as a defense against the abuse of government power. But I think the hope is illusory. Many of what we have come to regard as the irreducible minima of rights are actually supraconstitutional; almost none of the others are entailed by the text or original understanding. To the extent that institutional safeguards—such as the independence of the judiciary—protect against the contraction of individual rights, they seem to do so whether the Court is engaged in originalist or nonoriginalist adjudication.

I come finally to the central problem posed for nonoriginalist adjudication by the fact of a written Constitution, adopted and amendable by supermajoritarian processes. Even if the adopters have no claim over citizens two centuries later, their Constitution remains the governing document of the United States. It establishes the national government, its branches and offices, its relationship to the states, and the states' relationship among themselves. And although the amending power has been used sparingly, it is a vital element in the constitutional scheme.

Even though nonoriginalist adjudication respects these features of the constitutional order by according presumptive weight to the text and original history,[121] the availability of the amending process specified by Article V poses two distinct challenges to my thesis. First, should not the absence of an amendment be taken as popular consent to the Constitution as written? A short but adequate answer is that if inaction can be read as tacit consent to anything—a problematic assumption in any case—it is to the Court's constitutional decisions, including its nonoriginalist doctrines.

Second, doesn't the possibility of constitutional amendment supplement originalist interpretation so that together they adequately serve the ends of constitutionalism? I think not. First, the formal process of amendment is too cumbersome to bear sole responsibility for constitutional change. The adoption of an amendment usually requires considerable mobilization and intense interest focused on a specific issue. But if constitutional adjudication is to perform the functions described earlier, its growth must proceed more incrementally. And it in fact has: if you consider the development of a line of doctrine, for example under the First Amendment or the equal protection clause, there have been few, if any, obvious focal points for an amendment—either because any particular point would lie such a short distance from antecedent judicial doctrine, or because the language already in the Constitution is capable of encompassing the change.[122]

At least equally important, the formal amendment process is poorly suited to protecting minorities against injuries currently sustained as a result of legislative action or neglect, for the initiation and adoption of an amendment depends on extraordinary action by these same institutions. Imagine, if you will, the fate of an amendment proposed in the mid fifties to protect Communists or to require school desegregation. Consider the history of the Equal Rights Amendment since it was most recently introduced in Congress in 1970.[123] Of course, if these examples imply that the amending process inadequately protects minority interests, they also highlight a difficulty with judicial intervention. If support cannot be gained for a constitutional amendment, what assurance is there that a judicial decision to the same effect embodies "fundamental values"? But to hold that a purpose of our Constitution is to protect individual rights, whether in Bickel's or Ely's sense, is to concede that there will be times when no majority, let alone a supermajority, will adequately protect those rights.

V. Conclusion

Because moderate originalism and nonoriginalism so often produce identical results, and their practices so often seem identical, it is useful to reiterate their attitudes toward original sources. The moderate originalist acknowledges that the text and original history are often indeterminate and that the elaboration of constitutional doctrine must often proceed by adjudication based on precedent, public values, and the like. But adjudication may not proceed in the absence of authorization from some original source, and when the text or original history speaks clearly it is binding. The nonoriginalist treats the text and original history as presumptively binding and limiting, but as neither a necessary nor sufficient condition for constitutional decision-making.[124]

The argument of Part Two is addressed chiefly to those who would have the judiciary serve the ends of constitutional government by enforcing "fundamental values" or by playing a "representation-reinforcing" role. In one form or another, these alternative views of the judicial function have dominated modern American constitutional theory and practice. The burden of my argument is that nonoriginalist adjudication serves these ends better than either strict or moderate originalism. To put it bluntly, one can better protect fundamental values and the integrity of democratic processes by protecting them than by guessing how other people meant to govern a different society a hundred or more years ago.

James Madison's Theory of Constitutional Interpretation

H. Jefferson Powell

Although the Virginia and Kentucky resolutions expressed an approach to constitutional construction that soon achieved canonical status in American politics, they did not themselves set forth a detailed interpretive methodology. That task remained for James Madison. As one of the prime movers in the Philadelphia Convention of 1787 and in the Virginia ratifying convention the following year, as one of the authors of *The Federalist*, and as the draftsman of both the Virginia Resolutions of 1798 and the Report of 1800, Madison played a critical role both in the process of framing and ratifying the Constitution and in the formulation of a consensus about its meaning. Although he would have been quick to distinguish his personal opinions from the public meaning of the Constitution, the coherent interpretive theory Madison expressed in speeches and letters over many years has special value for anyone seeking to discern the "interpretive intent" underlying the Constitution.

Madison's interpretive theory rested primarily on the distinction he drew between the public meaning or intent of a state paper, a law, or a constitution, and the personal opinions of the individuals who had written or adopted it. The distinction was implicit in the common law's treatment of the concept of "intent," but Madison made it explicit and thereby illuminated its implications and underlying rationale. Madison's reliance on this basic hermeneutical premise is evident in his correspondence with Secretary of State Martin Van Buren in 1830. Responding to President Andrew Jackson's citation of a veto message Madison had sent Congress in 1817, Madison wrote that Jackson's use of his message had misconceived his personal views. But Madison conceded that Jackson might have correctly interpreted the public meaning of the message: "On the subject of the discrepancy between the construction put by the Message of the President [Jackson] on the veto of 1817 and the intention of its author, the President will of course consult his own view of the case. For myself, I am aware that the document must speak for itself, and that that intention cannot be substituted for [the intention derived through] the established rules of interpretation."[1] Madison applied the same distinction between public meaning and private intent to statutes,[2] to the Report of 1800,[3] and to the Constitution. With respect to the Constitution, Madison described his knowledge of the views actually held by the delegates to the Philadelphia and Virginia conventions as a possible source of "bias" in his constitutional interpretations,[4] and cautioned a correspondent against an uncritical use of *The Federalist*, because "it is fair to keep in mind that the authors might be sometimes influenced by the zeal of advocates."[5] He explained that he had decided to delay publication of his notes of the Philadelphia Convention until after his death "or, at least, . . . till the Constitution should be well settled by practice, and till a knowledge of the controversial part of the proceedings of its framers could be turned to no improper account. . . . As a guide in expounding and applying the provisions of the Constitution, the debates and incidental decisions of the Convention can have no authoritative character."[6]

Madison employed the distinction between public meaning and private intent to differentiate the relative value of the various sources of information to which constitutional interpreters might turn for evidence on "the intention of the States."[7] The text itself, of course, was the primary source from which that intention was to be gathered, but Madison's awareness of the imperfect nature of human communication[8] led him to concede that the text's import would frequently be unclear.[9] Madison thought it proper to engage in structural inference in the classic contractual mode of the Virginia and Kentucky resolutions, and to consult the direct expressions of state intention available in the resolutions of the ratifying conventions.[10] He regarded the debates in those conventions to be of real yet limited value for the interpreter: evidentiary problems with the surviving records[11] and Madison's insistence on distinguishing the binding public intention of the state from the private opinions of any individual or group of individuals, including those gathered at a state convention, led him to conclude that the state debates could bear no more than indirect and corroborative witness to the meaning of the Constitution.[12] Madison allowed that contemporaneous expositions of the document by its supporters were of some value, but he cautioned that such statements were to be regarded strictly as private opinions, useful chiefly in shedding light upon the meaning of words and phrases that the fluidity of language might gradually change over time.[13] Last and least in value were the records of the Philadelphia Convention. Once again, there were significant evidentiary problems,[14] but Madison's objection to treating the Framers' views as authoritative was based chiefly on theoretical grounds.

Mr. [Madison] said, he did not believe a single instance could be cited in which the sense of the Convention had been required or admitted as material in any constitutional question. . . .

But, after all, whatever veneration might be entertained for the body of men who formed our Constitution, the sense of that body could never be regarded as the oracular guide in expounding the Constitution. As the instrument came from them, it was nothing more than the draft of a plan, nothing but a dead letter, until life and validity were breathed into it by the voice of the people, speaking through the several State Conventions.[15]

Madison was quite insistent that a distinction must be drawn between the "true meaning" of the Constitution and "whatever might have been the opinions entertained in forming the Constitution."[16] The distinction did not imply a refusal to recognize the purposive character of the instrument;[17] it simply denied that the Framers' subjective intent was the purpose that mattered.[18]

The dichotomy between public meaning and private intent also informed Madison's view of constitutional precedent. He consistently thought that "*usus*,"[19] the exposition of the Constitution provided by actual governmental practice and judicial precedents,[20] could "settle its meaning and the intention of its authors."[21] Here, too, he was building on a traditional foundation: the common law had regarded usage as valid evidence of the meaning of ancient instruments, and had regarded judicial determinations of that meaning even more highly.[22] Applying this view of interpretation to the Constitution, Madison felt himself compelled to change his position on the controversial issue of Congress's constitutional power to incorporate a national bank.[23] In the first Congress, Representative Madison opposed on constitutional grounds the bill establishing the First Bank of the United States;[24] as President, Madison twenty years later signed into law the act creating the Second Bank.[25] "But even here the inconsistency," Madison assured a correspondent, "is apparent only, not real." His own "abstract opinion of the text" remained unchanged: the words of the Constitution did not authorize Congress to establish the bank.[26] Nevertheless, he recognized that Congress, the president, the Supreme Court, and (most important, by failing to use their amending power) the American people had for two decades accepted the existence and made use of the services of the First Bank, and he viewed this widespread acceptance as "a construction put on the Constitution by the nation, which, having made it, had the supreme right to declare its meaning."[27] He had signed the Second Bank bill, Madison declared, in accordance with his "early and unchanged opinion" that such a construction by usage and precedent should override the intellectual scruples of the individual,[28] and he explained to his friend the Marquis de LaFayette, "I did not feel myself, as a public man, at liberty to sacrifice all these public considerations to my private opinion."[29] In Madison's eyes, precedents—at least those derived from "authoritative, deliberate, and continued decisions"—served to "fix the interpretation of a law."[30] Furthermore, Madison claimed, this view represented not just his opinion, but the general expectation—the "interpretive intention"[31]—that prevailed at the time of the Constitution's framing and ratification: "It could not but happen, and was foreseen at the birth of the Constitution, that difficulties and differences of opinion might occasionally arise in expounding terms and phrases necessarily used in such a charter . . . and that it might require a regular course of practice to liquidate and settle the meaning of some of them."[32]

The public character of long-settled precedent was for Madison the key to reconciling his acceptance of views inconsistent with his "abstract opinion" of the bare text and his commitment to the Republican version of the old anti-interpretive tradition. To the end of his life, Madison warned his fellow citizens against expansive innovations in constitutional interpretation, "new principles and new constructions, that may remove the landmarks of power."[33] But however strongly he might have fought constitutional error when it first appeared, for Madison there could be no return to the unadorned text from interpretations that had received the approbation of the people.[34] The Constitution is a public document, and its interpretation, for Madison, was in the end a public process.

Dead Letters: Wills and Poems

Michael Hancher

[W]ills and the construction of them do more perplex a man, than any other learning . . . .

Lord Coke (1614)

One writes with one's desire, and I am not through desiring.

Roland Barthes (1975)

I

A studied indifference to what the author meant has dominated English and American literary criticism in three successive eras: the era of critical impressionism, which lasted from the avowed impressionism of Walter Pater and Oscar Wilde through the twenties and beyond, sometimes in unavowed forms; the era of the New Criticism, which dignified impressionism by objectifying it, or by attempting to do so; and the recent poststructurist era inaugurated by Nouvelle Critique, which under the aegis of Roland Barthes restored to literary criticism the entertainment value that it had in the days of Pater and Wilde.

Common to each of these eras is the doctrine that the reader of a literary text should not bother himself with questions about what the author meant. Though its justifications have varied in subtle ways, the doctrine has been powerfully influential for a century.

Such an established order is bound to elicit the occasional protest. One loud protester early in this century was the late Elmer Edgar Stoll, for many years a professor of English at the University of Minnesota. In a characteristic essay on *The Tempest*,[1] after noting some critical aberrations that resulted from ignoring the question of what Shakespeare might have meant in writing the play, Stoll put a general question that is still worth consideration: "[I]s not a critic (*kritikos*) a judge, who does not explore his own consciousness, but determines the author's meaning or intention, as if the poem were a will, a contract, or the constitution? The poem is not the critic's own."[2] By recalling the etymology of *critic*, which derives from the Greek *kritikos* and *krites*, meaning "judge," Stoll suggested a radical similarity between the business of literary criticism and the interpretive responsibilities of a judge at law.[3]

Some fifteen years after Stoll put his question, W.K. Wimsatt and Monroe Beardsley published *The Intentional Fallacy*,[4] an essay that has long been famous as a theoretical manifesto for the New Criticism. They argued that "the design or intention of the author is neither available nor desirable as a standard for judging the success of a work of literary art,"[5] and they implied that the intention of the author was irrelevant also to any interpretation of the work's meaning. During the course of their argument they quoted Stoll's rhetorical question and so preserved it like a fly in amber.[6] They then chastised the intentionalism Stoll proposed as a form of "irresponsibility" just as deplorable as the form—unbridled impressionism—that he deplored.[7] They had no need to scrutinize Stoll's assumption that judges read wills and other legal documents with an eye toward what the author meant.

More recently the latent interest of that assumption has come to life thanks to Roland Barthes's celebration of "The Death of the Author." In the terse essay which bears that title, first published in 1968,[8] Barthes proclaimed that literary or noninstrumental writing—writing undertaken for what he called "intransitive ends"—necessarily involves the extinction of the writer. "[T]he voice loses its origin, the author enters his own death, writing begins."[9] Each particular author regularly dies in the act of writing; furthermore, the idea of the Author died a historical death in the recent past, a death that followed chronologically and logically from the death of God. "*Gott ist tot*," Nietzsche announced a century ago,[10] in the era of Pater and Wilde. The Author too is dead, Barthes announced in our own lifetime.[11] One demystification leads to another. He made the connection himself:

> We know that a text does not consist of a line of words, releasing a single "theological" meaning (the "message" of the Author-God), but is a space of many dimensions, in which are wedded and contested various kinds of writing, no one of which is *original*: the text is a tissue of citations, resulting from the thousand sources of culture.[12]

In this tissue no text has precedence over any other, and no interpretation of any text has special authority. Ultimately such demystification reaches even to the text of the law:

> Once the Author is gone, the claim to "decipher" a text becomes quite useless. To give an Author to a text is to impose upon the text a stop clause, to furnish it with a final signification, to *close* the writing. . . . [L]iterature (it would be better, henceforth, to say writing [*écriture*]), by refusing to assign to the text (and to the world as text) a

"secret," that is, an ultimate meaning, liberates an activity which we might call counter-theological, properly revolutionary, for to refuse to arrest meaning is finally to refuse God and his hypostases, reason, science, the law.[13]

As it draws to its end this argument takes on oedipal overtones. The Author, according to Barthes, conveniently erases himself in deference to the Reader, who is thereby freed to take his pleasure with the text. "[T]he birth of the reader," he says in conclusion, "must be ransomed by the death of the author."[14]

The trope of the author's death has an obvious and special relevance to the legal genre of wills and testaments. Professor Stoll was wrong to lump wills together with contracts and constitutions; it makes more sense to distinguish them, as the law usually does.[15] The authority of "the author" can be estimated most simply in the case of a text, such as a will, that has been written by or on behalf of one person. The trouble with the interpretation of statutes or of constitutions is the same as the trouble with the interpretation of folk songs: too many folks spoil (overcomplicate) the concept of "the author." It is easier to think about a single author, a single testator. And after the death of the author, if what he has written is a will that comes before a judge, how does the judge construe it? Does he read it like Stoll, trying to recover what the author meant? Or does he, like Barthes's liberated Reader, make it the occasion for a dance on the author's grave?

Apparently he does both—some judges mean to follow one procedure, while other judges manage to follow the other. It is true that, given a choice, most anti-intentionalist judges would prefer the more conservative rationalizations of Wimsatt and Beardsley to the more colorful declarations of Barthes and Wilde. (Wilde: serious criticism "does not confine itself . . . to discovering the real intention of the artist and accepting that as final."[16] The function of criticism is "to see the object as in itself it really is not."[17]) That is, jurists usually frame the dilemma of testamentary construction in terms of authorial intention versus verbal meaning (usually called "plain words" or "plain meaning"), rather than in terms of authorial intention versus judicial freedom.[18] Nonetheless, both an intentionalist and an anti-intentionalist position are firmly entrenched in the law of wills. In fact they have been distilled into antithetical maxims, both encoded, appropriately, in a dead language:

> *In testamentis plenius testatoris intentionem scrutamur.* In wills, we should search thoroughly for the intention of the testator.[19]

> *In testamentis ratio tacita non debet considerari, sed verba solum spectari debent; adeo per divinationem mentis a verbis recedere durum est.* In wills a secret intention ought not to be considered, but only the words ought to

be regarded; it is so difficult to recede from the words by guessing at the intention.[20]

Neither of these imperatives is futile; each serves an important legal end. In 1555 Chief Justice Robert Brook made a general justification of the anti-intentionalist imperative in terms of the social utility of enforcing a common linguistic code on the authors of legal documents:

> [T]he party ought to direct his meaning according to the law, and not the law according to his meaning, for if a man should bend the law to the intent of the party, rather than the intent of the party to the law, this would be the way to introduce barbarousness and ignorance, and to destroy all learning and diligence. For if a man was assured that whatever words he made use of his meaning only should be considered, he would be very careless about the choice of his words, and it would be the source of infinite confusion and incertainty to explain what was his meaning.[21]

But after summarizing this doctrine with the words, "the law rules the intent, and not the intent the law,"[22] Brook made an exception for the case of wills. His reasons were nominally practical ones, but they were implicitly responsive to considerations of fairness and equity:

> But in testaments the intent only shall be observed and considered, because it [is] presumed that the testator has not time to settle every thing according to the rules of law, and wills are most commonly made on a sudden, and in the testator's last moments; and so is the difference between them and acts executed in the party's life-time.[23]

Not long after Justice Brook framed this pragmatic justification for searching out the testator's intentions, the ecclesiastical lawyer Henry Swinburne offered a more sweeping theoretical justification. "It is written," he wrote, "that the will or meaning of the testator is the Queene or Empresse of the testament."[24]

> Because the *will* dooth rule and gouerne the testament, enlarge and restraine the testament, and in euerie respect moderate and direct the same, and is in deede the very efficient cause thereof. The will therefore and meaning of the testator, ought before all thinges to bee sought for diligently; and being found ought in any wise to be obserued faithfullye, it ought to bee sought for as earnestly as the hunter seeketh his game: And as to the sacred anker ought the iudge to cleaue vnto it: Pondering not the words, but the meaning of the testator. For although no man be presumed to thinke otherwise then hee speaketh, (for the tongue is the vtterer or interpreter of the heart[)], yet cannot euery man vtter al that he thinketh, and therefore are his wordes subiecte to his meaning. And as the mind is before the voyce, (for we conceiue before we speake) so is it of greater power; for the voyce is to the minde, as the seruant is to his Lord.[25]

Swinburne's basic linguistic assumption is that conception precedes expression: "we conceive before we speak." This assumption, most influentially articulated by John Locke a century later,[26] has not fared well in our own century. Our common wisdom is that ideas are formed not in the individual mind but in the system of language that determines the mind. There is no intuition without expression, no signification beyond the signifier. And Swinburne's ideological assumptions are now obsolete also; indeed a theological taint seems to color the emblematic relationship of "the seruant" to "his Lord," especially so soon after a mention of "the sacred anker." Barthes would find this a suspicious text.

Swinburne's leading metaphor of the testator's intent as the "Queene or Empresse" of the testament has had a lasting currency in the history of testamentary interpretation, but his other flourishes have not. Chief Justice Brook's more practical rationalization[27] speaks more directly to the basic dispute in English testamentary law down through the centuries. The conflict that he described, the conflict of institutional requirements versus individual needs, persisted well into the middle of the nineteenth century, with one important added complication—a seventeenth-century statute that outlawed merely oral wills.[28] This statute cast a shadow on all direct oral or written evidence of the testator's intention, the major class of evidence extrinsic to the will; for such "parol evidence" seemed to subvert the statutory requirement that the will be formal and in writing. Sir James Wigram, a Victorian authority on the law of evidence, was influenced by such considerations when he stated that "the question in expounding a will is not—What the testator meant? as distinguished from—What his words express? but simply—What is the meaning of his words?"[29]

In a speculative and sometimes subtle rejoinder to Wigram, the barrister F. Vaughan Hawkins objected to the notion that the testator's "words" alone meant anything determinate. For that notion must presuppose that language is "a perfect code of signals," whereas in fact "the convention on which usage of language rests, is not a single or fixed one, but is the aggregate of an innumerable number of lesser conventions, which intersect and conflict with each other, and are continually shifting and changing from year to year."[30]

In so varied and variable a linguistic world, even the most skillful writer must be at a disadvantage; and many ordinary writers of wills are not skillful at all. Ethical compassion for their plight moved Hawkins to proclaim interpretation to be "in truth a species of equity," with the judge acting as champion of the testator's subjective intention, rather than as the jealous guardian of legal niceties.[31]

The intentionalist principle that Hawkins advocated has been expressed in some catchy metaphors, of which Swinburne's "Queene or Empresse" metaphor is only the most imposing. Two of them are especially popular, the "armchair" metaphor and the "polestar" metaphor. In 1880 Lord Justice James advised judges construing a testator's will, "You may place yourself, so to speak, in his armchair, and consider the circumstances by which he was surrounded when he made his will to assist you in arriving at his intention."[32] This trope suggests a certain leisure and luxury on the part of the testator—probably the normal circumstance for the kind of case that made its way to Lord James's attention. In more than one way the metaphor suggests Descartes seated comfortably by the fireplace, emptying his mind of all distractions and preparing himself for philosophy. The polestar metaphor, a century older, has a more robust appeal, suggesting intrepid navigation. Mr. Justice Buller believed that "the question always must be, what was the intention of the testator? That is the polar star by which we must be guided."[33]

Despite such explicit allegiance to the author's intention, nineteenth-century English courts tended to ignore subjective and equitable concerns when construing wills. Dickens showed the Court of Chancery as indifferent to legatees;[34] there could also be a smooth indifference to the will of the testator. That is why the influential practical treatise that Hawkins eventually wrote turned out to be more rigid than his speculative paper. For he was bound to report and to publicize the restrictive rulings of various mid-nineteenth-century judges.[35]

The mood has changed somewhat since the nineteenth century; the authors of the current edition of one English treatise express a belief (or, perhaps, hope) that the English Court of Chancery is now beginning to show more sympathetic interest in the claims of individual justice as against those of institutional certainty.[36] Furthermore, the authors of the major American treatise on the subject report that, although American practice does vary considerably, sometimes preferring "certainty and uniformity" and sometimes "fairness and justice," on balance it has always been more liberal than the English tradition, more respectful of "the subjective intent of the testator."[37]

Nonetheless, it has never been sure (as Professor Stoll supposed) that a testator's will would be read with an eye toward what he meant, even supposing his intent could be plausibly surmised. A modern handbook on legal construction sports as its epigraph an excerpt from a crackling opinion by Lord Henley, Lord Chancellor, dated 1761, celebrating "the intent of the testator" as "another and stronger legal rule," one more powerful than any merely positive or conventional rule of the law.[38] But that same handbook also is obliged to recite the following melancholy history of a leading case:

> This was a case where a domiciled Scot left a legacy to the "National Society for the Prevention of Cruelty to Children." There is a Society with that exact name having headquarters in London and another

Society having the same name with the addition of the word "Scottish," the headquarters of which were in Edinburgh where the testator lived. There were a number of circumstances which rendered it highly probable that the testator would have preferred to extend his bounty to the Scottish Society, but the will contained no indication other than the name which accurately fitted the other Society and which accordingly was held to be the legatee intended.[39]

A more recent case, *In re Will of Rowland*,[40] points to the same moral. In his will Rowland gave all his estate to his wife, but in case of her death "preceding or coinciding with my own decease" he gave it to his brother and his nephew. His wife, who had considerably fewer assets, had made a similar will, naming relations of her own as secondary legatees. Eventually both husband and wife were lost at sea on a small ship that disappeared with dozens of persons on board, leaving hardly a trace. The question then was, Who was to inherit the husband's estate: the husband's relatives, or the wife's? That question turned on the question whether their deaths had "coincided" or not. It was plausibly argued on behalf of the husband's relations that for his purposes he had meant by the word "coincide" not absolute temporal simultaneity but rather a commonality of cause and occasion. (He had written the will in expectation of making a series of hazardous journeys together with his wife, journeys like the boat trip on which they both drowned.) Nonetheless, the court decided, with one outspoken dissent, to take the word "coincide" in a strict sense. Lacking evidence to prove that the deaths had indeed "coincided" *sensu stricto* or that one spouse predeceased the other, the court relied upon the statutory presumption that the wife, being younger, had survived her husband, and therefore had inherited from him. Therefore *her* family, not his, was awarded his estate. In his dissenting opinion in this case Lord Denning quoted a remark by Lord Atkin which drew attention to "the group of ghosts of dissatisfied testators who, according to a late Chancery judge, wait on the other bank of the Styx to receive the judicial personages who have misconstrued their wills."[41]

Cases like these show that Professor Stoll was unlucky in his choice of testamentary construction as a model of intentionalist understanding. As an English professor he might have taken instruction from the eighteenth-century English poet John Gay, who gave a more realistic account of the process in his verse fable of "The Dog and the Fox." Addressed to a lawyer, the fable includes the lines,

> Read o'er a will. Was't ever known,
> But you could make the will your own?
> For when you read, 'tis with intent
> To find out meanings never meant.[42]

II

Wills and testaments are the legal genre that most emphasizes the problem of the death of the author. The corresponding literary genre is elegy. The typical occasion for elegy is the death of someone, usually an author, who is too disturbingly like the poet-elegist himself. Besides the death of the departed, the elegist complains of his own impending death (at least by implication), and fears also the death of his poetry. *Debemur morti nos nostraque:* "death claims both us and our works." So Horace complained in an elegiac aside in the *Ars Poetica*, contemplating the mutability of language, which tends to make all texts obsolete and indecipherable:

> As forests suffer change of leaves with each declining year, so the earliest-invented words are the first to fall: an elder generation passes away and new-born words, like youth, flourish and grow. Death claims both us and our works.[43]

I don't know what Horace would have made of the actual fate of Latin, destined to become one of the most honored of dead languages. The death of Latin gave it a second life as the language of those who wanted to write immortal and unchanging texts—priests and lawyers especially, scientists also, and even poets who hoped to be read and understood long after their deaths. Petrification, supposedly, was preservation. So in the seventeenth century the poet Edmund Waller renewed Horace's complaint with a difference:

> Poets that lasting marble seek
> Must carve in Latin or in Greek;
> We write in sand . . . .[44]

What the elegist mainly desires is some sign that, despite the death of the body, the deceased has not really died. But he also wants to believe that the signs of language themselves survive as a medium for human communication; that the Muse will not finally prove "thankless" (as Milton feared in "Lycidas"), cheating the poet of his fame. In the greatest elegy of the last century, Tennyson's *In Memoriam*, the poet fulfills both of these desires at once. Reading over some of Arthur Hallam's letters after his death—"those fallen leaves which kept their green,/ The noble letters of the dead"[45]—Tennyson discovers in them the author's living voice:

> So word by word, and line by line,
>   The dead man touched me from the past,
>   And all at once it seemed at last
> His living soul was flashed on mine,
>
> And mine in his was wound . . . .[46]

Here the momentary contact made possible by language, even after death, leads "all at once" to something yet more mystical, a "trance" as Tennyson calls it; a vision of eternity, one that absorbs Tennyson's whole being until it is suddenly "cancelled"—like a text—"stricken through with doubt."[47] This transcendental vision, to which Tennyson devoted two awestruck stanzas,[48] is inevitably impermanent and dubious after the fact. But what of the hermeneutical moment that preceded it and prompted it, when "strangely on the silence broke" Hallam's "silent-speaking words"? However "strange" that experience was, it was not incredible; Tennyson does not call it into question. His lasting doubts are more theological than literary.

Which is not to say, of course, that a skeptical reader of the elegy cannot call Tennyson's scene of reading into question. Probably he was only projecting: the consciousness that he encountered in reading Hallam's letters was only his own. After all, Tennyson had long been subject to trances very like the one that followed his reading of Hallam's letters. On his own testimony he had experienced this kind of trance

> frequently . . . quite up from boyhood, when I have been all alone. This has come upon me through repeating my own name to myself silently, till all at once, as it were out of the intensity of the consciousness of individuality, individuality itself seemed to dissolve and fade away into boundless being, and this not a confused state but the clearest, the surest of the surest, utterly beyond words—where death was an almost laughable impossibility . . . .[49]

No doubt repeating one's name to oneself silently is the epitome of linguistic solipsism; and for it to have the same effect as reading Hallam's letters raises questions about the nature of that reading. But Tennyson felt no misgivings. His experience reading Hallam's letters stands as one of the strongest expressions in English literature of the power of writing and reading to annul the death of the author.

However uncritically, Tennyson believed in writing and reading as acts of literal communication: the bringing together of two consciousnesses, even after death. His belief contrasts sharply to the more "modern" and tough-minded attitude expressed by W.H. Auden in his wholly secular elegy, *In Memory of W.B. Yeats*. Auden wrote that the poet Yeats, in dying, "became his admirers."

> Now he is scattered among a hundred cities
> And wholly given over to unfamiliar affections;
> To find his happiness in another kind of wood
> And be punished under a foreign code of conscience.
> The words of a dead man
> Are modified in the guts of the living.[50]

This is a remarkable passage, finer than anything in *In Memoriam*.

Auden's matter-of-fact acceptance of punishment "under a foreign code of conscience" would recommend itself to any legal realist. The image of scattering is especially strong, incorporating as it does the ritual *sparagmos* celebrated by Greek myth (especially the myth of Orpheus), and the *dissémination* of the word celebrated in contemporary critical theory. There are connotations of the scattering of cremated ashes across an entire landscape, and of the repeated miraculous breaking of bread in the New Testament. The image of scattering mainly depends, however, upon the fact that copies of Yeats's poems were multiplied and widely distributed by being printed and published: many copies of a poem, many readers, many poems. Tennyson could have more confidence in his reading of Hallam's letters because he was the only reader of a unique text. (Furthermore, he had known the author, and recognized in his written words the sound of his speaking voice—a sound that readers do often recognize in the written words, even the printed words, of people they have known personally.) The general question is whether such confidence as Tennyson's can be extended to rationalize, as an act of communication, the reading of even published material; or whether, on the other hand, Auden's belief in the instability of reading published works has to be extended back to cover even unique readings of uniquely inscribed texts.

III

If the author of a will is dead, and the words of the decedent are "modified in the guts of the living," does that make a "dead letter" of the will that is being interpreted, in the sense that a statute is sometimes said to be made a "dead letter"—obsolete—through disuse? Not quite, since dead-letter statutes have been wholly neglected in recent times—not interpreted at all. But the phrase "dead letter" acquired this legal sense by extension from an older, originally theological meaning, which does apply to this situation. From the sixteenth century the phrase "dead letter" was used to denote "a writing, etc. taken in a bare literal sense without reference to its 'spirit,' and hence useless or ineffective";[51] and in this sense the phrase was supposed to allude to Paul's well-known distinction between the spirit and the letter. God "hath made us able ministers of the new testament," Paul wrote in 2 Corinthians, "not of the letter, but of the spirit: for the letter killeth, but the spirit giveth life."[52] Ironically this text has had its greatest influence as it has been misunderstood. First, the phrase "new testament" used in the King James translation is a misnomer, the result of an earlier mistake in translating from the Greek into Latin. Evidently Paul did not really have in mind a *testamentum*, or unilateral expression of "will," as a model for God's relation with man; rather, he compared that relation to a covenant (*diathēkē*) that required participation on both sides. More importantly, his distinction between the letter and the spirit is not, according to the chief biblical commentaries, a distinction between literal and liberal construction, but rather one between the old Hebraic law—deadly because insufficient—and the new gospel, fulfilled in Christ.[53]

Paul's words, however, have been so thoroughly "modified in the guts of the living" that they now commonly serve to distinguish two kinds of reading, one that responds to the spirit in which the author wrote the text, and another that mortifies the text by concentrating exclusively on its supposed "literal" sense. In the interpretation of wills some cases do seem to show the difference between the letter, which killeth, and the spirit, which giveth life. Of the Scottish charity case,[54] or *In re Will of Rowland*,[55] or many another, it would be fair to say that a "literal" reading kills the text. It makes the will a "dead letter" in the sixteenth-century sense—"useless or ineffective" because read "without reference to its 'spirit.' "[56] Or the testator's will in such a case becomes like a "dead letter" of another kind, one of the several kinds defined by the Post Office Department—the kind involving a letter "unclaimed or refused by the party addressed."[57] The death of Melville's Bartleby the scrivener, who labored in a dead-letter office before he languished in a law office,[58] suggests what follows from too strong a refusal of human discourse and desire.

IV: Envoi and Codicil

A few words may highlight connections between the argument made here and arguments that others have made. First, despite my epigraph from Lord Coke, the legal genre discussed here is simpler, more elemental, than the genres usually in question—statutes, constitutions, and other products of collaborative authorship. In recent essays both Sanford Levinson[59] and James White[60] question the possibility of recovering any univocal, specifiable intention from a multiply authored text. But holographic wills don't present quite such difficulties. An argument can of course be made at a high level of abstraction that *all* discourse, even individual discourse, is fundamentally collective, a text encoded not so much by the individual as by the shared conventions of discourse; but in practical terms the intention of the individual testator is a less obviously tricky concept than, say, the intention of the collective Framers of the Constitution.

White does advert to the simpler case presented by "one writer about whom you knew everything," but he goes on to worry:

> [H]ow would you define his relevant intention? Intention can after all be stated with generality or particularity, as a matter of motive or a matter of aim; we are always subject to conflicts in our intentions, many of which are to some degree unconscious and out of our control. To try to follow the intention of the writer seems an inherently unstable procedure, leading to a radical conceptual collapse.[61]

Certainly *intention* is a very broad term, which even as applied to discourse (ignoring broader uses of the term) can mean several things. One can "intend" *to write* the words "I leave my gold watch to my Uncle John" (what I have elsewhere called *programmatic intention*); and one can "intend" *to cause* Uncle Harry to be annoyed at being left out of the will (*final intention*). White implicitly notices both these kinds, minimizing the relevance of the latter and reducing the former to a matter of what-he-has-written-he-has-written.[62] But neither of these is the main kind of intention at issue, which I have called *active intention:* that is, the intention that one's words be understood as enacting one meaning rather than another; for example, the intention to bequeath one's watch to a particular uncle named John, rather than to another uncle who also happens to be named John. This is the "relevant intention" (in White's phrase); it is an intention worth seeking out, and in some cases it may be determinable with reasonable certainty.[63]

If one grants that the author's intention (in the relevant sense) may have a bearing on the interpretation of a will, it may not be obvious that the multiple intentions of a multiply authored text like a statute or constitution should be ignored, just because they are hard to discover and to reconcile. Collective intentions may be messy enough, and yet still suggest limits for interpretation; some readings may stand evidently within the pale of what the authors meant, and others beyond the pale.

But there is yet another respect in which reading statutes or constitutions is harder than reading a will: the passage of time can enlarge the hermeneutical gap that always exists between interpretation and application—the gap alluded to by Gerald Graff in an essay reprinted in this volume.[64] Furthermore, in time the same section of a statute or constitution may need to be applied again, and yet again, to novel circumstances extremely remote from the circumstances that framed the Framers' supposed intentions. The ordinary will does not invite such difficult rereading.[65]

Levinson, seconded by Gerald Graff, criticizes traditional reliance on "the allegedly plain words of the text";[66] and an article by Walter Michaels, reprinted here, backs them up: it forcefully discredits the "doctrine of plain meanings" in both the legal and literary enterprises.[67]

Stanley Fish, too, has skillfully combated such simple faith; but in some of his essays he verges upon another plainness, plain reading rather than plain meaning. According to Fish, arbitrarily fanciful readings never get a hearing, and therefore never even get proposed, because "[i]nterpreters are constrained by their tacit awareness of what is possible and not possible to do, what is and is not a reasonable thing to say, what will and will not be heard as evidence, in a given enterprise."[68] Such an awareness works to keep interpretation within culturally ratified bounds—even as the plain-meaning doctrine was once supposed to do.

In broad outline Fish's account makes sense: interpreters do respect conventional, generic expectations of what an interpretation has to be like to be heard as an interpretation. But often within an actual (not idealized) community there are conflicting sets of conventional expectations demanding to be satisfied.[69] The interesting disputes arise when it is not clear to all participants which "interpretive strategy" should be invoked.

The strategic question of the author's intention, for example, usually defies consensus: one interpretive strategy will sanction elaborate efforts to recover the author's subjective intention, but another will repudiate any interest in the matter. According to Fish, reading is conventionally and always a matter of constructing (projecting) the author's intention, as a kind of inevitable invention by the reader. *National Society for the Prevention of Cruelty to Children* v. *Scottish National Society for the Prevention of Cruelty to Children*[70] might at first seem to illustrate Fish's account; most of the prevailing opinions effectively subverted the intention of the testator (one Nasmyth), yet paid lip-service to that intention by professing doubt that Nasmyth "meant something different from what he said."[71] Lord Dunedin was more candid than his colleagues when he acknowledged that Nasmyth meant to benefit the Scottish charity, but he still did not let his beliefs about Nasmyth's meaning affect his interpretation of "the meaning of the words used."[72] For Dunedin at least, if not indeed for all the Lords who joined in deciding this case, the plain-words doctrine simply overcame the otherwise obvious intention of the testator.

What actually prevailed in this case was not any superior cogency of the plain-meaning doctrine (which does not bear philosophical examination), nor any consensus of plain reading, but rather the superior authority that was vested in the last court to hear the case—which happened to be the British House of Lords rather than the Scottish Second Division. The will was first read one way in Edinburgh, then another way in London. The "interpretive strategies" invoked for the different readings (intention versus plain meaning) were fundamentally irreconcilable; if any interpretive convention really decided the matter, it was merely the convention that the decision of the House of Lords is final.

Justice Jackson once described the similar situation of the United States Supreme Court: "We are not final because we are infallible, but we are infallible only because we are final."[73] In another article I have distinguished literary interpretation from legal interpretation in terms of just this matter of final authority.[74] Unlike literary critics, appellate judges can solve once and for all the Gordian knot of a disputed text.

Never being final, the interpretation of literature will always be fallible. There are many competing conventional standards for success or failure in literary criticism; fidelity to the author's intention is one only. But that standard has survived a century of neglect and rejection without ever quite disappearing; and I predict that literary critics as well as lawyers (who have debated this question much longer) will a hundred years from now still be pondering the importance of the author's intention.

Statutory Interpretation and Literary Theory: Some Common Concerns of an Unlikely Pair

Kenneth S. Abraham

I. Introduction

One of the most famous questions in all of English poetry still has no authoritative answer:

> Tyger Tyger, burning bright,
> In the forests of the night;
> What immortal hand or eye,
> Could frame thy fearful symmetry?[1]

Interpreters of William Blake's poem have suggested a number of answers to its central question, "Who made the tyger?" Some have characterized the tiger and his creator as evil,[2] a contrast to Blake's later reference in the same poem, "Did he who made the Lamb make thee?"[3] Others have thought the tiger to be good, the celebration of a divinity capable of such "fearful symmetry."[4] Concluding that the poetic question is rhetorical and therefore unanswerable, critics of both of these views have argued that it is wrong to suggest an answer at all, because Blake himself had none.[5]

The interpreters of "The Tyger" have differed not only in their answers to the question it poses, but also in the approaches they have chosen to reach an answer. One critic found the key in the poet's life and cited Blake's interest in gnosticism as a way of resolving the question.[6] A second saw the parallels between "The Tyger" and traditional biblical and Miltonic imagery as the most enlightening.[7] Others looked to the countenance of Blake's own engraving of the tiger for guidance, although, not surprisingly, the tiger each critic saw there hardly seems to be the same animal.[8] Proponents of still another point of view considered these interpretations to be attempts to understand Blake, not "The Tyger," and advised studying the poem instead of its author.[9]

Interpretation of a literary work such as "The Tyger" may appear to raise issues very different from those presented by statutory interpretation. The issues that trouble literary theory, however, are strikingly similar to those that have troubled thinking about statutory interpretation. Practitioners of both disciplines have debated at length about the nature of the texts with which they are concerned, the relation of the author's intention to the meaning of a text, and the character of the reader's knowledge of a text's meaning.[10] In this chapter I will explore some of the ways in which the debates in both disciplines have been about similar issues, and discuss how a common concern, the nature of texts and their interpretation, is a pivotal philosophical issue for both.

II. Interpretation: Objective or Subjective?

Every first-year law student is familiar with the central problem of statutory interpretation. Under the doctrine of the separation of powers the legislature has the sole power to enact law. The judiciary's role in interpreting the legislature's enactments is, therefore, a subordinate one. Conflicts between the legislative will and the judicial will must be resolved in favor of the legislature.[11] Subordination to the legislative will, however, requires that it be ascertained. Approaches to the problem of ascertaining the legislative will have varied. Those adopting a formal, mechanical view believe that some statutes need not be interpreted because their meaning is clear.[12] In contrast, the radical realist view is that subordination is a myth: "Whoever hath an *absolute authority* to *interpret* any written or spoken laws, it is *he* who is truly the Law-giver . . . and not the person who first wrote or spoke them."[13] In between are approaches that ground the judiciary's role in an interpretive method, by requiring a search for legislative intention[14] or statutory "purpose,"[15] or in a measured combination of the formalist and realist extremes.[16]

Analogous positions have emerged in literary theory. Reacting to what it saw as an overemphasis on the author's life history as an aid to literary interpretation, the "New Critical" school judges the author's intention neither "accessible nor desirable" as a consideration in interpreting a literary work.[17] Its adherents believe that the internal qualities of the work are the only proper subject of literary study, and that reliance on anything external to the text is not the study of literature, but of something else.

Recent writers, emphasizing the radically subjective potential of the interpreter[18] and the self-referential, indeterminate character of language itself,[19] have called into question the validity of the New Critical school's approach. Thus, as in law, there are two theoretical extremes. On one side is the belief in the determinacy of meaning in the literary text and in the validity of interpreting the text's linguistic elements; on the other is the contention that each reader determines his own meaning without objective linguistic or contextual limitations.

In literary theory as in legal theory, compromises lie between the extremes. One leading theorist in the intentional school would reinstate authorial intention as a principal criterion of meaning.[20] Still another theorist acknowledges the weaknesses of the New Critical school's formalism but nevertheless would limit interpretive "pluralism," the view that a text can have more than one meaning, to the area surrounding an indisputable core of linguistic meaning.[21] A third believes that the limits of "pluralism" will arise because of the practical need for some determinacy of meaning if the discipline of literary study is to survive.[22]

Those familiar with only literature or law may be struck by the similarity of the concerns of the disciplines. Both are concerned with the extent to which a text is "self-interpreting," with a meaning in the language of the text itself. Both are also troubled by claims that interpretation is a subjective and even arbitrary process by which individuals impose their prejudices onto texts in the guise of "interpreting" them. Moreover, even proponents of the polar positions are notably in agreement on a crucial point. At both extremes interpretation is seen as the operation of an independent, autonomous force that determines meaning. For the legal formalist and the New Critic, the text is a separate object with a meaning that inheres in its language. That meaning is simply discovered by the reader, whose views remain subordinate to the "plain meaning" of the text. In contrast, for the legal realist and the subjective or "deconstructive"[23] literary critic, the autonomous individual reader creates the text. For theoretical moderates, interpretation is, in the end, some combination of the two extremes; the text is determinate to a point, prescribing its own meaning, but is otherwise dependent on the creative powers of the interpreter.

Both H.L.A. Hart and Reed Dickerson have developed "moderate" theories of this sort. Professor Hart argues that although there are many "plain" cases where the meaning of the text is clear, there are others that have "open texture" and leave the reader "discretion" to interpret.[24] Professor Dickerson's theory of statutory interpretation turns on his distinction between the "cognitive" and the "creative" functions of the judge. The cognitive function involves the ascertainment of meaning; the creative function entails judicial lawmaking. Much of his book is devoted to elucidating and locating the proper scope of each function.[25]

The defining issue, then, is the same for both disciplines: to what extent does the text have a determinate meaning, and to what extent is the reader free to interpret it as he chooses? This tendency to account for meaning in the terminology of subject and object is part of a philosophical tradition that has existed for hundreds of years.[26] The pitfalls of accepting the distinction long have been recognized, yet the distinction has affected our understanding of the character of knowledge in a number of disciplines.[27]

In the following section I examine the way in which this distinction has affected thinking about a case that is an old favorite of the legal profession. I then attempt to show that a different conception of the interpretive process might better our understanding of both statutory interpretation and literary criticism.

III. The Significance of "Communities of Interpretation": *Riggs* v. *Palmer* and "The Tyger"

Legal theorists traditionally have paid less attention to statutory interpretation than to constitutional and common-law adjudication.[28] Perhaps this can be explained by the symbolic and political importance of decision-making in the Supreme Court and by the scholarly appeal of issues related to stare decisis that are posed in many common-law disputes. Because ours may be an "Age of Statutes,"[29] more attention to the problem of statutory interpretation may be warranted. In fact, many of the issues that trouble constitutional and common-law adjudication have counterparts in statutory interpretation. These issues emerged quite dramatically in the celebrated case of *Riggs* v. *Palmer*.[30] Several years before his death, Francis B. Palmer had executed a last will and testament in which he left most of his property to his grandson Elmer. Palmer later suggested that he might change the provisions of his will. To prevent Palmer from revoking the will and, as the court said, "to obtain the speedy enjoyment and immediate possession of his property,"[31] sixteen-year-old Elmer poisoned him. Palmer's daughters brought suit to prevent Elmer from taking Palmer's property under the will.

Elmer lost the case. For our purposes, the court's method of reaching its decision and the characterization of that method are more important than the result. The devolution of Mr. Palmer's property at death was governed by several statutes. One set of statutes authorized and regulated the execution and effectuation of wills,[32] another governed intestate succession.[33] The court's decision had to be, and in fact was, an exercise in statutory interpretation.[34] Yet not once did the court quote or paraphrase any of the applicable statutes.

The court began by acknowledging an argument advanced by Elmer's counsel that "statutes regulating the making, proof and effect of wills and the devolution of property, if literally construed, and if their force and effect can in no way and under no circumstances be controlled or modified, give this property to the murderer."[35] But this acknowledgment was not a concession that Elmer was entitled to the property. The court determined that the "literal" reading was incorrect, stating:

> The purpose of those statutes was to enable testators to dispose of their estates to the objects of their bounty at death . . . . It was the intention of the law-makers that the donees in a will should have the property given to them. But it could never have been their intention that a donee who murdered the testator to make the will operative should have any benefit under it . . . . It is a familiar canon of construction that a thing which is within the intention of the makers of the statute is as much within the statute as if it were within the letter; and a thing within the letter of the statute is not within the statute unless it be within the intention of the makers.[36]

The court did not consider itself restrained by the general language of the statute. Rather, it noted that the language could be narrowed, or broadened, by reference to the "intention" of the legislature. The court, however, did not discover the legislative intent directly. That intent was inferred by looking to the purpose of the statute.

The court continued by explaining its decision in a second way:

> Besides, all laws, as well as all contracts, may be controlled in their operation and effect by general, fundamental maxims of the common law. No one shall be permitted to profit by his own wrong, or to found any claim upon his own iniquity or to acquire property by his own crime. These maxims are dictated by public policy, have their foundation in universal law administered in all civilized countries, and have nowhere been superseded by statutes.[37]

Legal scholars in generations succeeding *Riggs* v. *Palmer* have had their say about the decision, each characterizing it within a theory of statutory interpretation. Dean Pound criticized *Riggs* as an example of spurious interpretation, a legislative, not a judicial, process designed "to meet deficiencies or excesses in rules imperfectly conceived or enacted."[38] This process, Pound stated, resulted in an attempt "to read into the statutes governing descent an exception."[39]

In accord with Pound, Dean Wade wrote that *Riggs* and other similar cases "engrafted an exception on the statutes."[40] The courts that have refused to follow *Riggs*, he indicated, did so "upon the expressed reason that they did not have power to change a statute."[41] Thus, both Pound and Wade believed that the statutory text was perverted by the court in *Riggs*. For them, the statute meant one thing until the court made it mean something else.

Those who approved of the *Riggs* court's decision characterized it differently. Cardozo noted that "in the end, the principle that was thought to be most fundamental, to represent the larger and deeper social interests, put its competitors to flight."[42] Professors Hart and Sacks suggested that "every statute is to be read as subject to established principles and policies of the general law save only as a decision to modify or depart from them is made unmistakedly plain."[43] Professor Dworkin placed *Riggs* within his general theory of adjudication.[44] He wrote, "[T]he Court cited the principle that no man may profit from his own wrong as a background standard against which to read the statute of wills and in this way justified a new interpretation of the statute."[45]

The contrast between the viewpoints of those who disapprove and those who favor the *Riggs* decision is as much a difference in the methods of reading the statute as it is between the actual readings. The approach of Pound and Wade, who might be called "textualists," emphasizes that the statutes contain no language specifically excepting claims such as Elmer's. For the textualist, the approach taken by the court can only be described as engrafting an exception onto the text. The textualist would assume that Elmer's claim must be allowed unless the statute had stated that "a murderer shall not inherit from his victim," or contained words to that effect. The proponents of this view would allow nothing less than a specific prohibition to defeat Elmer's claim.

How would a textualist support his approach? No doubt some textualists would explain their assumptions by simply repeating the language of the statute and insisting that it contains no words of limitation. The words of the statute, summarized roughly as "Every will conforming to the following requirements shall be enforced according to its terms," should, according to the textualist, be read according to their normal, everyday usage. For example, he might argue that the word *every* in normal speech is used to mean "without exception."

This argument, however, also contains a set of assumptions. First, it assumes that the word *every* has a discernible inherent meaning that always obtains regardless of the context in which it is used. Second, it assumes that the word *every*, whenever used, never admits of exceptions from the class to which it refers. And finally, the argument assumes that the statute as a whole is expressed in words which might well be uttered "every" day. Most statutes, however, are not drawn in "ordinary" language. Certainly nothing very similar to the New York Decedent's Estates Law is uttered in daily speech.[46]

The textualist might, however, adopt a different approach to support his method of interpretation. He could develop a theory that would link the meaning of the text to the legislature's intention. This theory, however, would also rest on assumptions or beliefs that we would have to share if we were to be persuaded. Thus, the textualist's argument would be based on a logic of persuasion, not a logic of demonstration. The textualist could argue, for example, that a legislature which did not include an express exception in the statute could not have intended the result in *Riggs*. This argument depends on the "fiction" of legislative intent. Legislatures, however, are corporate authors, and do not necessarily speak with a unified intention.[47] The majority voting in favor of the statute may not have agreed on its meaning. Moreover, individual legislators may not have been concerned with the potential for a problem like the one that arose in *Riggs* when they voted in favor of the statute.[48] Where this lack of awareness exists, the textualist will face a problem bringing him to the frontiers of the philosophy of language. May the legislature be deemed to have intended anything that was not consciously on the minds of a majority of legislators at the time of enactment?[49]

The textualist might buttress his assumptions about legislative intention with arguments from legislative history.[50] He could attempt to show that the problems which occasioned the consideration and passage of the statute do not suggest the existence of an intention to create any exceptions.[51] Reliance on legislative records, however, would present the same problem as reliance on the statutory text itself. Legislative records are also texts and do not come to the reader already interpreted. A reader's interpretation of these texts, therefore, must rest on a set of assumptions or beliefs about the setting in which he encounters them.

Finally, the textualist might offer an argument based on efficiency. To avoid the difficulty and uncertainty of interpreting statutory language and legislative history, the textualist might propose a "law" of interpretation.[52] For example, he might suggest a rule that general language should be read without exception.[53] If such a law existed, the legislature would be presumed to know that it will be deemed to have intended no exceptions in a statute unless they are "expressly" included. Even if we ignore the certainty that the rule would lead back into the interpretive thicket that it was designed to circumvent, the textualist's stance here is of a piece with his others. He has proposed the acceptance of a set of assumptions, how the legislature "shall" be taken to speak, that will render the meaning of legislation determinate. Only if this set of assumptions is accepted, and a "law" of interpretation is adopted, can his attempt succeed.[54]

It is important to see how far the textualist, while attempting to defend his original position, would have to depart from it. From the notion that the text carries a meaning on its face, he would necessarily move to find the source of meaning in "normal" usage, legislative intention, legislative history, or presumptions created for administrative convenience. In essence he would become a "contextualist," whose position, like that of Cardozo, Hart and Sacks, and Dworkin, presupposes the situation in which interpretation occurs.[55]

Once he has surrendered his pure literalism, the textualist in each instance will have asked his audience to share certain beliefs and assumptions. He will have asked, that is, that they join in what might be called a "community of interpretation."[56] I use the term "community of interpretation" as a way of speaking about the power of institutional settings, within which assumptions and beliefs count as facts. Membership in a community of interpretation means that one has accepted its beliefs. These beliefs determine readers' strategies of interpretation. Within a community of interpretation a text may be considered to be a self-interpreting and literal object, a reflection of legislative intention, or a product of the legislature's observance of a "law" of interpretation. Within a given community of interpretation the reader may believe that he is separate from the text, and can be considered a disinterested interpreter of it. But this separation of reader and text is only possible because membership in that community of interpretation often renders one's central beliefs transparent. These beliefs then become matters of common sense, and are so indisputable that their role in constituting the very objects of understanding goes unrecognized.

Thus, those who suggest that a text is an object entirely independent of its readers are ignoring the sense in which the bedrock beliefs of its readers actually constitute the text. Those, however, who suggest that reading is an individual, subjective activity equally ignore the idea that the reader is always within a community of interpretation, the acceptance of whose beliefs affects the meaning he attributes to a text. Our very selves, then, are the product of shared understandings. Under this view the notion of individual subjectivity in interpretation would become empty.

Since we are always operating within a community of interpretation, it is always possible, indeed necessary, to speak of texts as separate from their readers. Thus, the textualist's strongest asset is the human tendency to objectify—to put things "in" texts and then to find them there. The textualist's arguments may therefore appear to be derived *from* the nature of the text even though their function is to provide support *for* his particular conception of the nature of texts.

A different approach is taken by the contextualist, who does not begin with the text alone. His approach requires him to begin with the text together with its surroundings. He must build a theory of meaning that links text and context. When this linkage is examined, however, we find that the contextualist's arguments are not derived from the objective nature of the statutory text. Rather, they rest on beliefs which bring into being the text for whose existence they had argued. The dilemma of the contextualist, as we might call Cardozo, Dworkin, and Hart and Sacks, stems from his implicit acceptance of the textualist notion that principles of interpretation can be derived from the nature of the text being interpreted.

In discussing *Riggs* v. *Palmer,* for example, Professors Hart and Sacks suggest that the court could have made use of a presumption that the legislature would not contravene the fundamental principles and policies of the common law without so indicating in "unmistakably plain" language.[57] This proposal for a law of interpretation was designed to preserve the "precious inheritance" of "deeply-embedded principles and policies,"[58] the context surrounding the statute. Like the textualist's proposal for a law of interpretation, this recommendation rests on a set of beliefs and assumptions. Does the legislature necessarily speak in "unmistakably plain" language whenever it creates an exception to a "deeply embedded" principle? Is it appropriate for a court to dictate the form in which the legislature shall communicate its intentions? Answers to these questions depend on assumptions which make the statute what it is for the contextualist who follows Hart and Sacks's proposal—a text which never contradicts common-law principles without doing so in a prescribed fashion. If such assumptions were not in force, the statutory language might well have a different meaning.

Professor Dworkin also explains *Riggs* as a case in which a statute was read against a background standard of common-law principles.[59] For Dworkin, statutory interpretation calls for the application of a special political theory which provides a better justification for the statute than any alternative theory.[60] His examples suggest that a "special political theory" is a set of beliefs about the problems the statute was intended to deal with and about the factors the legislature might properly have considered when framing it.[61] Using the special political theory, the contextualist makes sense of the statute. Yet for Dworkin, language still plays a limiting role in interpretation. He emphasizes how great a role the canonical terms of the statute play in the process.[62] Thus his interpreter's special political theory is to be brought to bear only within the limits of the statutory language itself.

Dworkin's position raises problems similar to those which faced the textualist. How do the "canonical terms" of the statute set the limits of plausible interpretations? Like the textualist, he must ask his audience to adhere to a set of beliefs which, when accepted, will render the semantic limits of the statutory language determinate. For example, the court in *Riggs* understood the limits of the statutory language not by reading the words of the statute, but by isolating its purpose, "to enable testators to dispose of their estates to the objects of their bounty at death."[63] From that purpose the court derived the legislative intention. Purpose was logically prior to intention, and set the context within which the semantic limits of the statutory language came into being.

To defend against the textualist charge that such an interpretation ignores the language of the statute and creates a new meaning for it, contextualists such as Dworkin, or the *Riggs* court, must account for their understanding of the statute's purpose. They must, at least implicitly, call upon that "special political theory" which was thought to come into play only after language had set the bounds on interpretive possibilities. Of course that theory, which best justifies the statute within the legislature's general responsibilities, will be the product of a fundamental set of beliefs which the interpreter brings to his task.

In short, the contextualist no more ignores the language of the statute than the textualist really limits his reading to the words alone. They both do what all readers do: encounter the text in a situation which unavoidably includes the beliefs that the reader holds. When the interpreter has these beliefs in common with others, then they are, for that community, "facts." These facts are not immutable, as the objectivist would have it, nor individual or arbitrary in the sense that the subjectivist or radical realist might suggest. They do provide objectivity, however, within a community of interpretation where they need not be questioned.

The contextualist need be on the defensive, then, only if he accepts the textualist conception of the statutory text as an object whose nature determines its own method of interpretation. That conception cannot be maintained without acceptance of the beliefs about the legislative process that support it.[64] If, however, the contextualist recognizes that he is arguing *for* a particular conception of the institution of statutory interpretation, rather than *from* some fixed essence of the statutory text, he need not accept the idea of the textual object as his starting point. Instead, his arguments urge adopting an approach that actually brings the meaning of the text into being. Since he is attempting to persuade his audience to adopt his view of textuality, the contextualist's references to the nature of legal texts are really efforts to show the members of the audience that they already belong to the same community of interpretation.

It should come as no surprise that interpretations of literary works also depend on communities of interpretation for their persuasiveness. Answers to the question posed by "The Tyger," for example,[65] simply are not satisfactory until the reader accepts the premises of the critic proposing the interpretation. The premises vary. For example, Kathleen Raine, who inaugurated the modern debate about the tiger and his creator, has argued that the tiger is the product of an evil force. She seems to conclude that the two animals of the poem, the tiger and the lamb, are in sharp contrast. "The lamb is a symbol of the principle in nature that willingly dies in order that others may live . . . the tiger is the symbol of the opposite principle."[66] In fact, however, this "conclusion" was her starting point. From this assumed contrast between the tiger and the lamb Ms. Raine reasoned that an evil creative principle must be responsible for the tiger. She found the evil creator in the "demiurge," the third person of the gnostic and cabalistic trinity which Blake had studied.[67] Yet she felt compelled to indicate that "the grandeur of the poem does suggest some such emotion of admiration for the tyger."[68]

E.D. Hirsch, although using a similar approach to interpret the poem, was convinced that the tiger and the lamb had the same creator. "There can be no doubt," he wrote, "that 'The Tyger' is, among other things, a poem that celebrates the holiness of tigerness."[69] Doubt, of course, is exactly what there can be about such a proposition. Having decided that there is no doubt, however, Hirsch was able to "demonstrate in the poem itself" the presence of a holy tiger, the product of the biblical and Miltonic imagery which sees everything that God created as good.[70] So, however, had Ms. Raine been able to "demonstrate" the presence of an evil tiger in the same poem.

A number of critics have reacted strongly to the approaches of Raine and Hirsch. J. L. Swingle, for instance, has rejected their reliance on Blake's own preoccupations,[71] believing it to be misleading.[72] Swingle has argued that the critic must decide "whether he wants to understand Blake or 'The Tyger.' "[73] His view, it seems, is that interpretations such as those of Raine and Hirsch have led us astray, and that the proper solution is to focus on the poem alone.

As we saw, however, in examining the textualist position, it is impossible to get back to the text without adopting a set of beliefs that makes the text something in itself. Swingle does exactly this, but with the innocent sense that he has simply removed what was standing between the reader and the poem. "Understanding 'The Tyger,' " he asserted, "involves accepting the fact that the world of the poem prohibits understanding."[74] It is not, of course, a fact that the world of the poem prohibits understanding until we accept it as a fact. Once we have done so, "The Tyger" is a poem that only asks questions, just as for those who have accepted Raine's or Hirsch's facts, "The Tyger" is a poem that also answers them.

None of these critics was wrong in making assumptions which led them to find meaning in "The Tyger." On the contrary, interpretation of the poem could not have proceeded in any other way. If any meaning is to be discerned, there must be shared assumptions and beliefs which will allow the work of understanding to go forward. Like the statutory interpreter who claims that the proper approach to interpretation can be deduced from a text with an independent status, the interpreters of "The Tyger" each claim to be "discovering" a poem that is independent of their method of discovery. Such independence of reader and text, however, only seems to exist when shared assumptions produce an undisputed method of interpretation. In literary study, as in law, this ideal is likely never to be achieved, and the differences that are the product of multiple communities of interpretation will always be present.

IV. Interpretive Anarchy or Stability?

The differences between statutory and literary interpretation, then, are differences in communities of interpretation. Law and literature are structurally different disciplines, and interpreters within each discipline use different strategies to aid in understanding their texts. These differences, however, are not prescribed by intrinsic differences between statutory and literary language or texts. In an important sense, differences in structures and strategies actually constitute the differences between statutory and literary language. The court deciding *Riggs* v. *Palmer*, for example, was authorized to render a final adjudication of the meaning of a statute as it applied to the facts of the case. There is no analogous central authority in the literary world, although the imagination of a Huxley is no longer required to see that this is a possibility.

The *Riggs* court's conception of its proper relation to the legislature allowed, and in a sense required, that it speak the language of intention in interpreting the applicable statute. That statute was an "intentional object," the product of its authors' purposes, because the court's interpretive strategies made it so. These strategies are still so forceful that it would be astonishing to find a court today waxing eloquent about the alliterative qualities of the statute, the rich ambiguity of the word *person* in a phrase such as "[a]ny person may make a will," or the symbolism of the legislature's confrontation with the problems of mortality. It would be equally surprising for a literary critic to suggest that the meaning of the poem "The Tyger" depends on the effect of certain fundamental maxims, for example, that there is a God and that he is benevolent, which no poem may supersede.

Competent, professional interpreters of statutes know that there is no symbolism in statutes. Professional literary critics know that, today at least, poems are not interpreted against background standards of morality in the same way as are statutes. These professionals have been trained in disciplines guided by detailed codes of interpretive behavior. By virtue of conformity to these codes, their interpretations are both more competent than that of the initiate and more reckonable.[75] Indeed, part of their work may well be seen as "teaching" others how to read.

The theoretical controversies that now rage in both law and literary theory can be seen as concerned with characterizing the "knowledge" possessed by the competent reader. In jurisprudence, there has been an almost molecular examination of the propriety of judicial discretion in interpreting a statute or previous decision.[76] The issue recently has focused on Professor Ronald Dworkin's powerful formulation of the "rights thesis."[77] In elaborating his thesis, Dworkin has contended that in a developed legal system there is almost always one right answer to any legal question.[78] He argues that even when an answer is not demonstrable, the ground rules of any enterprise may characterize one answer as "right" because it best satisfies the enterprise's criteria of correctness. According to Dworkin, whether there is a right answer to a legal question will be a function of two factors: (1) "the density of the information supplied by the settled law" and (2) "the degree to which the question put by the case could be thought independent of whatever information is so supplied."[79]

Dworkin's citation of these two factors implies that he is arguing *from* a preconception of the character of legal texts rather than *for* his approach to interpretation. Where there are few precedents, the information an interpreter has at his disposal will be sparse. He suggests, however, that in a developed legal system there will be dense "intersections and interdependencies of different legal doctrine."[80] From this it would seem to follow that in a "developed" legal system there will almost always be one right answer to every legal question. Although it might be assumed that the "density of information" is somehow independent of the belief that the information contains a single right answer, this assumption is questionable; the two are closely connected. For the stronger the belief that the text, a body of settled law, contains a single right answer, the stronger would be the tendency for its readers to perceive the information it contains as sufficiently dense to supply one, at least if such "density" were thought necessary to the existence of a right answer. This would be as much the case in an "underdeveloped" legal system as it would be in a developed one.

Similarly, the notion that the question put by the case might be independent of whatever information is supplied by the settled law apparently assumes that the material in a text could be independent of its readers' interpretive strategies. Such independence, however, could not exist, since there is an intimate connection between the question put by the case and the information used to answer it. The more strongly the reader believes that there is one right answer to every legal question, the more likely he will be to find that answer in whatever information is supplied.

On the other hand, much of the extraordinary power of the rights thesis, and the concomitant notion that there is one right answer in legal disputes, lies in its normative rather than descriptive qualities. In this sense the thesis is not an argument about the independent character of a collection of texts, the law, but rather an argument for Dworkin's conception of the interpretive process.[81] From this normative point of view, the thesis has the value of what Professor H.L.A. Hart in another context has called a "regulative ideal."[82] This regulative ideal obligates the courts to justify their decisions on grounds acceptable to the legal community. For Dworkin, the only acceptable grounds are the principles embedded in the body of settled law.[83] As a result, there is no room left for judicial discretion.[84] Under this view, even decisions in "hard" cases can be subjected to critical scrutiny in a way that discretionary decisions cannot, since the reasons for a decision must be grounded in a common body of knowledge. Part of the appeal of the rights thesis thus lies in its elimination of judicial discretion from the interpretive process. It not only provides a rationale for the enormous adversity or benefit that judicial interpretation sometimes visits on individuals, but also carries the message that such consequences could not justifiably be otherwise.

Students of the law may at first glance find little here that is analogous to the study of literature. The results of a decision about the meaning or quality of a poem hardly seem comparable to the consequences of a lawsuit. Literary critics, however, still do a great deal of sorting and categorizing before lay readers come face-to-face with literature. Moreover, every discipline has a profound need to have right answers to the questions it studies. The members of a discipline or profession must be able to see themselves as possessing knowledge or expertise that is not available to those who are not members. Such knowledge provides the ability to discern right answers. Thus, the possession of such knowledge in fact may be what defines membership in the profession.

Certainly one of the main efforts of an individual's literary study is learning to be a sensitive reader, and for many this means the ability to reveal what beauty or truth is in the text. Other conceptions of the nature of interpretation are likely, therefore, to be very upsetting to those who pride themselves on possessing this ability. Those who suggest that interpretation is merely an exercise in individual subjectivity and that there are no proper limits to what can be said about a text's meaning imply that the professional's interpretation is no better than anyone else's. Those who hold that meaning is the product of beliefs shared within communities of interpretation suggest that the truth which the professional critic is so adept at discovering is grounded not in an unchanging text, but in the critic's own institutional allegiances. Both views threaten the discipline's self-image.

Thus, we find seemingly disparate theoretical approaches in service of the discipline's self-preservation. Wimsatt's classic anti-intentionalism rested not simply on his disrespect for interest in authorial intention, but on his conviction that the discipline of literary study should be primarily concerned with the semantics, syntax, and language of poetry.[85] E. D. Hirsch, a theorist violently opposed to Wimsatt's position, justified his intentionalism by indicating that searching for the author's meaning "might help correct some of the most serious faults of current criticism (its subjectivity and relativism) and might even make it plausible to think of literary study as a corporate enterprise and a progressive discipline."[86] Perhaps the most open expressions of this theme of disciplinary self-preservation come from Wayne C. Booth and

M. H. Abrams, both admitted interpretive "pluralists." Despite his recognition of the validity of many critical points of view, Abrams believes that the contention that literary meaning is indeterminate "goes beyond the limits of pluralism, by making impossible anything that we would account as literary and cultural history."[87] Booth accurately summarizes Abrams's argument as "Stop, you're killing me."[88] He then takes what seems to be the ultimate step in defense of the discipline. He does not reject any theory of meaning. Indeed, he seems to accept several, although they contradict each other. Rather, Booth embraces this pluralism and anchors its limits only in what is in his view necessary "to reconstruct a critical commonwealth"[89]—a willingness of the proponent of one interpretive approach to learn from that of another.

These defenses of interpretation suggest the threat felt by the discipline from arguments that call into question the reality of the objects, texts, and facts from which the central tenets of the discipline seem to be derived. Such arguments, however, are not threats to the discipline, since the forces which cement it are not those which the arguments attack. The objects, texts, and facts with which this and every other enterprise works are real in the only way that anything is real. And the knowledge that we all possess is therefore secure in the way that all knowledge is secure, by virtue of its acceptance within a community of interpretation whose existence is a prerequisite to the production of knowledge itself.

V. Conclusion

In describing the concerns which law and literature have in common, I have obviously ignored much of what distinguishes the two fields. My point, however, has been to demonstrate that the source of what distinguishes the two is the same as the source of their common concerns. The two fields of endeavor are closely related. Members of each must confront the problems of textuality, both as part of their everyday experience and, less directly, as a way of instilling in themselves a sense of the limits of their disciplines. A better understanding of the significance of these problems cannot help but further enrich both.

(B)
Formalism

An Essay on Constitutional Language

Frederick Schauer

Many contemporary constitutional scholars have explored the extent to which, if at all, judges should go "outside of" or "beyond" the constitutional text for decisional principles in constitutional cases.[1] Although the resulting discussions have been highly illuminating, I do not wish to deal directly with this controversy here. Rather, I propose to discuss what is logically a prior question. For before we can argue intelligently about whether to go outside of the text, we ought to explore the meaning of the words *inside* the text. Only then will we know what counts as going "outside," and until then, it is not clear that there even is an outside because *inside* and *outside* are relative terms.

We assume, perhaps too easily, that the language of the Constitution is neither the source of, nor the answer to, our problems, and we then head off into the forbidding jungles of history, political theory, moral philosophy, public policy, and what have you without any clear guide. An examination of the words in the Constitution has been merely the hors d'oeuvre, with high theory as the main course.

There is nothing unseemly about high theory in this sense. Nevertheless, we need to look at the words of the Constitution *as language*, and we need to examine closely some of our rarely questioned presuppositions about constitutional language. Although this examination logically is prior to any broader interpretation of the Constitution, it has received surprisingly little concentrated attention in the literature.[2]

Constitutional cognoscenti talk about "gaps," "great silences," "vague language," and "open texture" as if these were concepts of little controversy.[3] But what makes the requirement that the president be of "the Age of thirty five Years" specific and the requirement of "equal protection of the laws" vague? Why are there "loopholes" in the Internal Revenue Code, but not in the Constitution? In order to understand and to attempt to answer questions like these, we need a theory of constitutional language as much as we need theories of constitutional law.

The Constitution is, after all, a writing,[4] and at bottom we are interpreting the *words* of a written document. But how do we do this? What does it mean to "interpret" a constitutional provision? What do we mean when we say that a constitutional provision "means" something? How do we start such an analysis? These are hard and important questions, and we should not dismiss them as irrelevant philosophical speculation. Indeed, answers to these questions underlie any theory of constitutional adjudication, and this essay attempts to bring some of these answers to the surface for closer inspection.

My intention here is not to offer a completely mature theory of constitutional language. Rather, I wish to explore the way in which the conventions of language affect constitutional theory. At the end of this essay, I conclude that constitutional language acts as a significant restraint on constitutional decision, but I will not have developed a complete theory of constitutional language which directs any particular substantive outcomes. A complete theory will have to wait for another time.

I. On the Supposed Uniqueness of Constitutional Language

In his pioneering work on legal language, H.L.A. Hart argued that legal language is fundamentally different from ordinary language.[5] According to Hart, if one fails to recognize the unique context and the distinct presuppositions of legal discourse, then one commits the errors of formalism or conceptualism—giving to words in the abstract an aura of authority and of unique reference inconsistent with the view of language as an activity determined and governed by social rules.[6] If, as Hart and his philosophical contemporaries supposed, meaning is use,[7] then legal use ought to produce different meanings than a physicist's use, a sociologist's use, or the use of the man on the Clapham omnibus.[8] And, just as legal language is different in kind from ordinary language, constitutional language may be different from other legal language.[9] In fact, this hypothesis implicitly undergirds many different theories of constitutional interpretation.[10] The various theories of a "living" or "changeable" constitution each presuppose a view of the uniqueness of constitutional language, setting it off from the linguistic raw material with which lawyers normally deal.[11]

There *seem* to be readily apparent differences between constitutional language and other legal language. Grandiloquent phrases like "freedom of speech," "equal protection of the laws," "due process of law," and "privileges and immunities of citizens of the United States" have few counterparts in the Internal Revenue Code or the Public Utility Holding Company Act of 1935. Indeed, many constitutional provisions are more than merely indeterminate. They have a powerful emotive component. The Constitution is more an eloquently written manifesto[12] than it is a code, and in many ways we are much better for that. But the eloquence and emotive force of the document further reinforce the view that the Constitution's words are as different as they are special. To construe its language too literally or too much like the language in a conventional statute would be both unrealistic and inconsistent with its deeper purposes. In some ways, the Constitution is a metaphor.[13]

Not unrelated to the Constitution's metaphorical quality is its permanence. Statutes are frequently amended, and the common law is continually changing, but the Constitution has a special sort of durability. Not only is amending the Constitution extremely difficult, but we also seem remarkably averse to doing so.[14] Many have feared a constitutional convention because too much might be changed,[15] even though such changes would still require ratification by the states. On the other hand, we certainly do not suspend Congress or the state legislatures for fear that they might legislate too much—however appealing that suggestion may at times seem.

Despite these important differences, we would be mistaken to view constitutional language as a wholly unique creature. The seemingly intentional openness of many constitutional terms, upon which most of the supposition about the uniqueness of constitutional language is based,[16] has counterparts in other areas of law, especially in American law. The generality of "equal protection of the laws" or "the freedom of speech" differs little from the language in Rule 10b-5 of the Securities and Exchange Commission, which prohibits the employment of "any device, scheme, or artifice to defraud."[17] Likewise, the Fourth Amendment's prohibition of "unreasonable" searches and seizures provides no more guidance than the Sherman Act's ban on "[e]very contract, combination . . . or conspiracy, in restraint of trade or commerce."[18] As a result, the task of the courts in putting flesh on the skeleton of the Constitution is not wholly different from the task that courts have undertaken in developing the elaborate structure of tests, rules, and standards that surround and govern the application of the securities laws, the antitrust laws, and many other statutory schemes.[19]

If the openness of constitutional language does not provide its uniqueness, perhaps the notion of presupposition,[20] which undergirds Hart's argument in "Definition and Theory in Jurisprudence,"[21] can explain the uniqueness. Statements of law, or *in* law (as opposed to statements *about* law), presuppose the existence of a legal system, and particular statements of legal rules themselves contain presuppositions.[22] Thus, the statement "the corporation is liable in damages" presupposes a body of law creating and defining a "corporation." But presupposition is hardly unique to law. When we use *home run* or *small slam*, we presuppose the systems of baseball and bridge, respectively, and when we use *professor* or *hour examination*, we similarly presuppose the existence of a college or university, which is in turn defined by a (probably looser) set of constitutive rules.[23] Legal language is not special because it contains presuppositions, but rather because it alone contains presuppositions which relate to the existence of a legal system.

In this sense, then, constitutional language is unique because it, and no other language, presupposes the existence of a constitution, and incorporates those particular presuppositions which concern the role of a constitution in a given legal system. But this is not going to get us very far, because the presuppositions of constitutionalism are themselves both vague and contested. Unlike the specific terms of a general legal system, which, to some extent, relate to relatively uncontroversial presuppositions about the way the legal system operates, the terms of a constitution *themselves* determine the differences between the constitutional presuppositions and other legal presuppositions. Therefore, an initial search for constitutional uniqueness reduces itself to circularity because the presuppositions of a constitutional system are dependent on our view of the language of a constitution. Perhaps constitutional language *is* unique. But we cannot articulate the differences which make it unique simply by examining the presuppositions of constitutionalism. Rather, we must examine the *language* in order to discover the differences between the presuppositions embedded in that language and the presuppositions included in the language of statutes or the common law.

These observations on the presuppositional nature of constitutional language are neither interesting nor important enough to provide the touchstone for a theory of constitutional language. They show, however, that certain uses of language have distinct meanings because of the context in which they occur.[24] When an entomologist talks about "bugs," when a physicist describes something as "solid," and when a logician refers to "implication," each uses those terms in a more technical and precise sense than the ordinary person uses them. We know this because we know something about the special context in which entomologists, physicists, and logicians speak.[25] Similarly, the context in which lawyers talk determines their use of *real property* (which is not the opposite of *fake property*) or *wrongful* (which refers to conduct that may have no moral counterpart in ordinary language). Unlike strictly technical legal terms, such as *habeas corpus, demurrer,* and *curtesy,* which have no ordinary language meaning, the technical uses of *real property* and *wrongful* are parasitic on ordinary language.[26] If this phenomenon occurs in conventional (nonconstitutional) legal language, then the equally parasitic nature of certain consitutional terms, such as "equal protection of the laws," "free exercise of religion," and "search and seizure" should not surprise us. These are expressions derived from ordinary language, but their constitutional meaning in the context of constitutional adjudication diverges in important ways from the ordinary meaning that first generated each expression. The constitutional presuppositions of constitutional language may not establish the complete uniqueness of constitutional language, but they do emphasize the context from which the words take their meaning.

II. The Intentional Paradigm

Most discussion of constitutional language takes place within what I call the "intentional paradigm"—the assumption that any interpretation of the constitutional text must comport with the explicit, implicit, reconstructed, or fictionalized intentions of the drafters. In its crudest and least plausible version, the intentional paradigm focuses on the results that the drafters specifically had in mind.[27] Thus, because we can show that the drafters of the due process clauses of the Fifth and Fourteenth amendments intended to invalidate lengthy imprisonment without trial, we can be confident that we are correct in applying those provisions to that end.[28] Conversely, because we can fairly clearly infer that those same drafters did not intend to invalidate prejudgment real estate attachment for the purpose of securing a potential money judgment,[29] we can be equally confident that we are correct in refusing to apply the due process clause to invalidate prejudgment real estate attachment. Use of the same methodology would support the First Amendment's application to prior restraints and at the same time justify excluding its application to obscenity, defamation, commercial speech, and blasphemy.[30]

The specific-intention theories of constitutional interpretation, of which the writings of Raoul Berger represent the most extreme example,[31] are the least plausible of any of the theories discussed in this essay. They are implausible precisely because they ignore the distinction between the meaning of a rule (such as a constitutional provision) and the instances of its application.[32]

When we draft any rule, we envision certain particular applications of that rule, certain cases where the rule will produce a particular outcome. We do not merely list these outcomes in a series of specific commands because we do not see those particular outcomes as exhaustive. They are only instances of a more general problem, and we analyze the problem to discover some underlying unity in the instances that we wish to treat.[33] We then formulate the rule to deal with this general unitary problem. By formulating a rule in general terms, the rule extends, by the nature of language, further in time or space than those particular applications envisaged by the drafters of the rule.

This is a commonplace observation,[34] and we can easily imagine examples of the distinction between meaning and instances of application in constitutional interpretation. For example, punishment by electric shocks to the genitalia falls plainly within the Eighth Amendment's prohibition of cruel and unusual punishments even though the drafters could not have imagined this particular procedure in 1791.[35]

This much is relatively uncontroversial, but it does not take us very far because, at some point, the new applications are so different that the meaning has changed.[36] The "meaning" of a cruel and unusual punishment clause prohibiting only painful and humiliating punishment is different from one prohibiting capital punishment.[37] The "meaning" of an equal protection clause prohibiting only racial discrimination is different from the meaning of an equal protection clause prohibiting discrimination on the basis of, say, gender,[38] alienage,[39] illegitimacy,[40] or wealth.[41] And the meaning of "the freedom of speech" that includes only political argument[42] is different from the meaning of "the freedom of speech" that includes the right to advertise pharmaceutical prices[43] or the right to display a For Sale sign on a front lawn.[44]

I am not contending that such shifts in constitutional meaning are constitutionally impermissible. I am saying only that they *are* shifts in meaning, and thus are neither explained nor justified by the distinction between the meaning of a rule and the instances of its application. For such explanation or justification we must look elsewhere.

The defects of the specific-intention approach have been amply documented in the literature,[45] and there is little need for me to belabor these criticisms here. Intriguingly, however, even the most vehement critics of the specific-intention approach still feel obliged to tether their arguments to some form of original intent. According to Laurence Tribe[46] and Ronald Dworkin,[47] for example, the extremely general language in the Constitution conclusively proves the drafters' intent that subsequent generations should work out their own theories applying such phrases as "cruel and unusual punishment," "due process of law," "equal protection of the laws," and so on. John Hart Ely implicitly criticizes wide excursions from the text as a whole,[48] but his argument is as revealing as it is interesting. Ely bases his deference to the text on the idea that the text constitutes *the best evidence* of the drafters' intent.[49] The text, for Ely as for the others, is still a way of bringing forward the intentions of the Framers.

Those who argue within the framework of this "intentional paradigm" appear to operate on the model of the "convention" in the game of bridge. When bridge players reach a certain level of proficiency, they begin to use artificial conventions in bidding. These bids do not represent the intended contract, but rather aim at describing specific features of the bidder's hand or at asking questions about the partner's hand. The bids are in a *code* whose primary ordinary meaning (*clubs* means clubs) may be irrelevant to the specific contextual use. Most bridge players use simple conventions like Blackwood or Stayman, and more advanced players are likely to use complex systems containing a high percentage of so-called artificial bids. These systems and conventions are languages designed in part, like other languages, to convey information. But the important feature of a bridge convention (or indeed the notion of bidding at all) is that the use of conventions is derived from and directed toward one quite simple fact—in the game of bridge, you are not permitted to look at your partner's cards. If a player could look at his partner's hand before arriving at the final contract, he could dispense with every convention yet devised.

Many people understand constitutional language in much the same way as a bridge convention. Under the intentional paradigm, constitutional language exists only because we are unable to know the specific intentions (the cards) of the drafters. If we could ascertain that specific intention, or if we knew how the drafters would treat the constitutional problems of the present, we would have no need for constitutional language. To the extent that we know that intention, then the importance of the text is diminished *pro tanto*.[50]

This is not a useful model, for it fails to capture the sense in which a text is authoritative *as a text*. No amount of looking into the minds of the Framers, or constructing fictionalized intentions at various levels of abstraction, can render the text less authoritative.[51] The text is not only the starting point, but is also in some special way the finishing point as well. Constitutional language exists not only because the Constitutional Convention is not still sitting, nor because James Madison and his colleagues were not immortal. The text interposes itself between the intentions of the Framers and the problems of the present, cutting off the range of permissible access and references to original intent, thereby reducing the extent to which original intent persists after the text's adoption. A theory of constitutional language is incomplete if it does not recognize the way in which a text is authoritative—the way in which we treat the Constitution, but not, for example, the Declaration of Independence or the Mayflower Compact, *as law*.

The authoritativeness of a text is by no means a peculiar feature of a written constitution. Although constitutional law is exciting and popular at the moment, we should not forget our basic law school contracts principles. One such basic principle requires that the parties be held to the reasonable meaning of the terms they have used, regardless of their subjective intent at the time they used those words.[52] And the considerations that led to acceptance of this "objective" theory of contracts[53] are the same as those that generated other common-law rules, for example the "plain-meaning" rule in the common law of defamation.[54]

What the analogy with contract law shows us, however, is not something about contracts, or even about law. The analogy illuminates, rather, something about language in general, of which the language of a written constitution and the language of a contract are subsets. In order to make sense of language, we presume that it represents the intentional acts of human beings.[55] But there is a difference between the intention of a text and the human thoughts that accompanied the creation of that text. Although the authority of a text is derived in part from the intention that it be authoritative, a text can have purpose without reference to the psychological condition of its creator, as we see in the attempts of courts to derive purpose from statutes themselves.[56] As one philosopher has put it, "Communication is a public, social affair and [the communicator] is not exempted from responsibility for aspects of his performance he failed to notice."[57] Thus, "a speaker is not the sole arbiter over what import his utterances have,"[58] and our touchstone must be the rules of language rather than largely futile explorations into the mind of the communicator. So long as the distinction between "what he said" and "what he meant to say" is meaningful, then we must recognize that the conventions of language use are superior, in the hierarchy of interpretive tools, to the intentions of the speaker. This is even more true when the language used has an authoritative embodiment, as in a statute or in a written constitution.

The intentional paradigm implicitly confuses a language with a code (as in "Morse code" rather than in "Uniform Commercial Code"). Codes such as bridge conventions are only one form of language,[59] and it is wrong to assume that every language is a code. In theory, codes are dispensable, as the bridge example demonstrates, but language is not. Moreover, language operates only because *it* has meaning, quite apart from what the speaker may have *meant* to say.[60] Perhaps meaning is use,[61] but the intentions of the user do not exclusively, or even mainly, determine the use.

In arguing for greater attention to the Constitution as an authoritative text, I do not urge a literalist, conceptualist, or formalist approach to constitutional adjudication.[62] The view that the text can be interpreted as self-defining, or as ordinary language,[63] or without reference to purpose[64] does not follow from the proposition that the text is authoritative. In many instances, we can derive purpose from a text,[65] and we can apply canons of interpretation peculiar to the nature of the Constitution itself. Working out the details of such a program is difficult, but it is a task that cannot be avoided if we are to develop a theory of constitutional interpretation that captures both the authoritativeness of the text and the necessity of contextual interpretation.

III. Moral Theory and Constitutional Language

Many issues of constitutional interpretation concern the Constitution's incorporation or nonincorporation of moral values. We must, then, examine the way in which the text either mandates, prohibits, or permits the use of certain moral arguments. Thus, I will propose questions that are metaethical, but in a rather special way. For, unlike most of the others who have asked metaethical questions,[66] I will not ask how we reason about ethics, but rather *when* and *how much* we reason about ethics—at least in this constitutional law context.

At the conclusion of his essay "Constitutional Cases,"[67] Ronald Dworkin notes that the problem of rights against the state "argues for a fusion of constitutional law and moral theory, a connection that, incredibly, has yet to take place."[68] This statement is both revealing and ambiguous, for the key word *fusion* admits of a number of importantly different interpretations.[69] Two items may become fused in a strong sense when they are merged so that the two are no longer separately identifiable; or they may become fused in a weaker sense when, although they are tightly joined, we can continue to identify the originally separate components.

If we are to accept Dworkin's incredulity as justified, we must determine how much moral theory is to be merged into constitutional law, where and how that merger is to take place, and how much of the resultant product will be fused in the strong sense. I propose therefore to explore several "strategies of fusion," and their presuppositions about the Constitution and moral theory.

A. Moral Theory as Constitutional Command

In his essay "Cruel and Unusual Punishments,"[70] Jeffrie Murphy introduces his argument by saying that "if one can mount a good argument that to treat a person in a certain way is gravely unjust or would violate some basic human right of his, this is also and necessarily a good argument that it is unconstitutional to treat him in this way."[71]

The import of Murphy's characterization of constitutional argument is that if he is correct, then he has, in the same forty-six words, *just written the Constitution!* For if any good moral argument is *eo ipso* a good constitutional argument, the text becomes superfluous.[72] But surely the text must serve some purpose other than to offer a *carte blanche* for moral philosophizing. In fact, it defines the contours of permissible moral arguments. The authoritative nature of the text, and the existence of a substantive content beyond a mere formal authorization[73] for judges to philosophize, compels us to reject Murphy's notion of one-to-one fusion of constitutional law and moral theory. In addition, we can find counterexamples to

Murphy's theory; there are moral arguments that appear good yet irrelevant to the Constitution (for example, rights to safety in the workplace). Conversely, there are constitutional issues, even in the Bill of Rights, that are only dimly illuminated by moral argument (for example, the right to trial by jury in civil cases,[74] and the right to keep and bear arms).

Murphy's statement erroneously suggests a model of constitutional law and moral theory as congruent circles. The more apt geometric metaphor is that of intersecting circles, which leaves areas of both constitutionally irrelevant moral argument and morally sterile constitutional argument. Viewed in this way, a good moral argument is no longer "necessarily" a good constitutional argument. That one has a moral duty to support one's parents in their dotage is fairly clear, but the Constitution does not deal with this duty, nor does it require that it be enforced or supplemented by the state. Conversely, a good constitutional argument is not necessarily a good moral argument, as for example the argument one would deploy in challenging the constitutional qualifications of an able and mature thirty-three-year-old to hold office as President of the United States. A good moral argument is therefore a good constitutional argument only if it falls within that area of moral theory embraced by the Constitution as relevant. The crucial task remains, then, to define the contours of this area, and to determine the manner in which the constitutional text identifies constitutionally relevant moral theory.

B. The General/Particular Theory

A more plausible theory than an interpretation that takes the moral or political flavor of the Constitution as a mandate for rendering the text irrelevant is the "general/particular" theory of textual interpretation. This theory, which appears in various forms, takes the morally or politically oriented constitutional provisions—for example, freedom of speech, equal protection of the laws, and freedom of religion—not as discrete repositories of self-contained moral or political theories, but rather as instances, or more particularized expressions of the single moral or political theory embedded in the Constitution. The theory, as most commonly expressed, does not merely say that instantiated constitutional values are derived from higher and more general principles. It says that they are derived from *one* higher and more general principle. This theory is implicit in the work of theorists as diverse as David Richards[75] and John Hart Ely,[76] and is suggested in some parts of Ronald Dworkin's writings.[77] Its proponents view the text as the raw material from which to construct a general moral or political theory of the Constitution. Because the generated theory must encompass the more particularized values explicitly stated in the text, it is not totally unbounded, but can claim a mandate from the text itself.

The general/particular theory (or metatheory) is attractive because it evolves out of the text, while, at the same time, it is not constrained by the more uncomfortable moral or political gaps[78] in the Constitution. Thus, if we use the mentioned particulars as the building blocks for a theory, and then apply that general theory directly to future cases, we can easily find a particular right to privacy,[79] a particular right to travel,[80] and so on, as well as even more particular rights derived from these rights.[81] So long as these rights are part of the general theory constructed from the mentioned particulars and are not inconsistent with the text, the absence of these particular rights in the text does not undermine their existence and application. The text operates somewhat like a ladder.[82] We use it to build the theory, or perhaps to reconstruct the theory that was implicit all along. Having built the theory, we can kick away the ladder and then apply the theory directly.

This methodology appeals to us because it captures, at a rather high level of abstraction, the intuitive feeling that the Constitution is incomplete. It also reflects the sense in which not only particular applications but also more general principles must change to accommodate changing circumstances.[83] Moreover, it justifies a wide range of morally or politically attractive results without totally rejecting the importance of the text.[84] Indeed, this methodology would be ideal but for the fact that it rests on two mistakes and one controversial assumption.

First, any general/particular theory mistakenly assumes that one general principle (or theory) can be uniquely, or at least most correctly, derived from a set of particulars, or instances. This assumption, however, ignores the extent to which any theory—scientific, moral, or interpretive—is underdetermined by any number of specific instances or observations.[85] Theory is underdetermined in this sense because any number of empirical observations, or specific instances, can generate and be consistent with a large and perhaps infinite number of explanatory theories. Moreover, each such explanatory theory will yield different predictions or results for future cases.[86] For example, a given set of symptoms can be consistent with a number of different medical diagnoses, and to that extent the diagnosis is underdetermined by the observation of symptoms. Similarly, several different theories about the formation of the solar system might be equally consistent with our observations about the solar system. The principle of underdetermination of theory applies to a wide range of activities, and it has been frequently discussed in reference to the philosophy of science,[87] to literary criticism,[88] to historical explanation,[89] and so forth. In each of these disciplines, theory acquires a different role, but the point remains the same: specific examples, instances, observations, or events can produce more than one theory equally consistent with those examples, instances, observations, or events.

We see the same phenomenon in constitutional theorizing because a large number of different overarching theories would be consistent with the specific moral or political principles specified in the text. We may have good reasons to choose one theory rather than another, just as a doctor may have good reasons to choose one medical diagnosis over another that is equally consistent with the same symptoms. But the constitutional text does not determine the choice among theories equally consistent with it, and thus the argument that the theory is generated by the Constitution is seen to be a fake. Certainly we can require that the particular theory fit all of the textualized particulars as a necessary condition of its validity. But if this is taken to be a sufficient condition, then there is little limit on the extent to which quite different theories can find their source in the Constitution. If that is so, the text does not control the result in future cases and does not affect our decision of which competing coherent theory to accept. This does not mean that judges should be forbidden to construct moral or political theories,[90] but it does defeat the claim that the theory so constructed is either mandated by or derived from the text.

A general/particular theory makes its second mistake by presuming that the selection of particulars from which to construct or reconstruct the general theory is itself independent of theory. The process of selecting particulars is not and cannot be value-neutral.[91] Textually explicit particulars are analogous to observations from which we construct a theory, and we cannot lightly ignore the extent to which such observations are controlled by theory.[92] The instances are not just there waiting for us to build a theory around them. We have to select the particulars to use, and this selection process contains implicit judgments of value and importance.

Interestingly, in this connection, most people who seek to build unitary moral or political theories of constitutional rights select (i.e., observe) the same constitutional provisions—the First Amendment, the due process clause, the equal protection clause, the prohibition on cruel and unusual punishment, the amendments extending the franchise, and so on. They thus impose a theory on the Constitution more than they extract one from it.[93] If the process of selection concentrates on different provisions, a different theory results. For example, John Hart Ely,[94] who concentrates on the majoritarian provisions of the Constitution, derives a theory quite unlike the theories derived by Dworkin and Richards, who concentrate on individual rights and antimajoritarian aspects of the Constitution.[95] And imagine the theory we might derive if we concentrated on the property-protecting provisions of the Constitution,[96] perhaps including the Second Amendment as well. Our selection depends on what we think is most important, and what we think is most important is pretextual. Although some of these theories might be better than others, any theory based on something less than *all* of the constitutional text is selective,[97] and the process of selection is hardly value-neutral. We see what we want to see and ignore what we want to ignore, and theories that purport to "explain" the Constitution usually explain only those portions of the Constitution that the theorist finds, for non–textually based reasons, to be most significant.

The controversial assumption contained in any particular/general theory is that the morally or politically loaded clauses of the Constitution are particulars instead of more general irreducible principles, and also that they are particulars of the same general principle.[98] Some constitutional provisions, of course, are derived from higher principles. For example, the First Amendment's protection of freedom of speech might be plausibly derived from the political principle of popular sovereignty,[99] and the equal protection clause is plausibly derived from some sort of "golden rule" or universalization principle.[100] But in order to construct *a* theory of the Constitution, we must assume that all of the textual provisions are reducible to one overarching principle. Thus, the methodology of a particular/general theory presupposes a unitary moral or political theory (albeit perhaps a highly complex one[101]) that explains and unites all but the purely structural constitutional provisions.

In order to evaluate this presupposition, we must question whether such an overarching theory can conceivably exist. If we follow Rawls,[102] Richards,[103] Dworkin,[104] Gewirth,[105] and others in believing that such a theory exists or can be constructed, then the search for a unifying theory of constitutional morality is highly plausible. But if one accepts ethical pluralism[106] as a more accurate reflection of reality, then freedom of speech, fair procedure, equality, and so on may be ultimate and irreducible primary values with no necessarily coherent relationship.[107] If this is true, then we need not tie these values together nor fill the gaps between them. If there is a plurality of first principles, then that, of course, means that in some cases they will conflict.[108] The pluralist would not wish to deny this, but would deny the existence of any conflict-resolving higher theory.[109] This makes constitutional interpretation more difficult than it would be under a single unifying principle, but one cannot validly move from "it would be nice if it did" to "therefore it must," despite the prevalence of this move in many arguments for nonpluralist ethical theories.[110]

I do not wish here to join further the debate between the pluralists (Rawls's "intuitionists"[111]) and the coherence theorists.[112] But that dispute exists, and we must recognize that the argued mandate for constructing unitary moral theories around or through the Constitution derives from only one side of a highly contested deontological debate.

Moreover, this one-sided view presupposes not only that ethical pluralism is wrong, but it must presuppose as well that pluralism is totally implausible despite the structure of the constitutional text, which suggests plurality rather than unity. The arrangement of the text, with particular and discrete provisions and with no expressed unifying principle save a vacuous Preamble,[113] appears to be the embodiment of pluralistic ethics. Thus, the task of the constitutional coherence theorist is not only to show that ethical pluralism is wrong, but also to refute the appearance of ethical pluralism in the text of the Constitution.

IV. Language and Theory

In a much more promising start toward constructing a theory of constitutional language, Ronald Dworkin distinguishes "concepts" and "conceptions."[114] His theory is incomplete, but its gaps can direct us toward a more satisfactory formulation.

Despite its similarity to ordinary language associations, Dworkin's distinction between concepts and conceptions does not parallel the distinction between connotation and denotation, or between intension and extension. Rather, his distinction admits the existence of, and is derived from, differences in meaning rather than various applications of an agreed meaning.[115] A conception in Dworkin's scheme is a particular (but not necessarily particularized, in the sense of highly detailed) theory which is thought to explain the meaning of a concept.[116] A concept, therefore, allows competing theories of its meaning, and no one of these theories is necessarily more or less correct as a definition or explanation of the concept.[117] A concept is something[118] whose definition requires references to a theory, but no theory provides a uniquely correct definition. If only one plausible theory existed, then that theory would provide the definition of the concept, and there would be no need for the distinction between concept and conception. In order for the distinction to survive, then, there must be at least two competing conceptions (theories), neither of which is demonstrably better or more correct than the other as a definition of the concept.

This distinction seems to hold great potential for a theory of constitutional interpretation, because, as Dworkin maintains, it enables us to argue alternative conceptions within the framework of the existing concepts set forth in the constitutional text. But the utility of the distinction rests on the exact nature of a "concept." In order for any word, including a concept, to have a potential use, it must have some meaning which allows us to understand its use in the face of competing theoretical conceptions. One candidate for "some meaning" is the existence of a paradigm, or exemplar. W.B. Gallie contrasted "essentially contested concepts"[119] (the notion from which Dworkin derives his distinction[120]) with those words whose use was merely "radically confused."[121] For Gallie, the existence of an exemplar makes it possible to meaningfully use words whose essential characteristics are contested.[122]

Gallie offers the concept of a "champion" to demonstrate the operation of an exemplar.[123] Modifying this example, we might contend that the New York Yankees of 1927 were the exemplar of a "great" baseball team. If, in this context, "great baseball team" marks an essentially contested concept, we nonetheless understand the use of the concept because we recognize the authority and unattainable standards[124] of the exemplar. Thus, if one baseball team's hitting and depth were stronger than that of the 1927 Yankees, but its pitching was weaker, and if another team's pitching and depth were stronger but its hitting was weaker, we could contest whether either or both of these teams were entitled to the "great baseball team" designation. Although the concept is contested, it retains meaning through a core of settled meaning, the exemplar, which allows us to debate about the shape and extent of the fringe.

A more plausible candidate than the "exemplar," for "some meaning" that makes understanding of a contested concept possible, could be a "family resemblance."[125] Unlike the unattainable standards of the exemplar, the family resemblance has no set of necessary and sufficient defining characteristics,[126] but rather is an interlocking relationship among the appropriate uses of a term. Although the Wittgensteinian family resemblance does not admit of a core and fringe characterization,[127] it still contains exemplars. While we might debate whether some novel form of amusement is "really" a game, we have no doubt that Olympic games and party games are games, despite the absence of identifiable shared features. Without the existence of exemplars of some kind, we have not a contested concept, and perhaps not even Gallie's "radically confused" concept, but perhaps just loose talk, or, even worse, vacuous talk.

If this is so, then Dworkin's concepts have run into heavy weather. Almost certainly exemplars for freedom of speech, equal protection, and many other similar constitutional concepts have never existed. There are exemplars for some, and Dworkin properly points out that an exemplar exists for cruel and unusual punishment.[128] But surely no exemplar for "the freedom of speech" shares the common agreement implicit in Gallie's original formulation of the essentially contested concept. Is imprisonment of a newspaper editor for publishing criticism of the government the exemplar of a free speech violation? It is not if we understand an aversion to prior restraint to be the essential feature of the meaning of the "freedom of speech,"[129] or if we take individual self-expression through communication as the paradigm.[130] The identification of an exemplar in the absence of general agreement is dependent upon a particular theory.

In the absence of an exemplar, however, it is difficult to see how a particular theory or conception is or is not related to the concept at hand.

From this perspective, constitutional adjudication *builds* exemplars. But we encounter difficulty in locating the foundation on which to build the exemplar or theory. Though the words of the Constitution are the starting point, they give us very little guidance.

Perhaps we should forget about concepts and conceptions, and look instead at *words*, but words of a certain sort. Here we encounter a particular variety of words that cannot be understood without reference to a theory.[131] Not all words share this characteristic equally, but some words or terms, such as *anal-retentive personality* or *kinetic energy* or *wave function*,[132] can only be understood with reference to a theory. When we use terms such as these, we presuppose the existence of some theory, even though we do not explain the theory every time we use the terms. If theory-laden words can appear in nonlegal texts, then similar terms ought to be able to appear in legal texts, and it seems promising to look at terms such as "the freedom of speech" and "equal protection of the laws" as such theory-laden words, except that here the use of the term precedes the development of the theory, rather than following after it.

If the use of the terms precedes the development of the theory, the terms themselves may have no meaning other than some ordinary language associations and some syntactic meaning. Notwithstanding this fact, they are still in a text which we take to be authoritative. Their irremovable presence in the text must then be taken as a mandate for the development of a theory that will give content to the terms used. Significantly, the mandate does not derive from the personal intentions or states of the mind of the drafters of the document. It derives from the conventions that govern language use, conventions that operate without regard to the intentions of the user.[133] We argue unnecessarily and misleadingly when we argue that the use of such terms provides evidence of an original intent by the Framers that the underlying theories be developed and changed, an intent we can assume from the failure to use more specific terminology.[134] The constructed intent here is unnecessary, because the rules and conventions of language cut off the necessity and possibly even the permissibility of looking behind them into the mind of the speaker or writer.

Philosophers commonly argue that if a speaker says p, and p logically entails q, then the speaker is committed to q even if he had never thought of q and never would have intended to say q.[135] A similar convention of language use appears applicable to the use of theory-laden terms. When a speaker uses a theory-laden term, the speaker is committed to the theory that may at any time surround the use of the term, even if the speaker did not intend that result. If, for example, I accuse someone of having an anal-retentive personality, my use of that term commits me to accusing him of having whatever an anal-retentive personality entails as a matter of psychiatric theory. And if I use terms such as "equal protection of the laws," that too commits me to having authorized the incorporation (and, if necessary, the creation) of a theory without which the term's meaning is incomplete.

Given that theories change, we can legitimately commit the user of theory-laden terminology to the possibility of change implicit in any theory. Thus, the users of theory-laden language such as "the freedom of speech" and "privileges and immunities of citizens of the United States" are committed to the theory whose construction they have authorized by their choice of words. Whether or not the user of those terms intended to be so committed does not matter. It's just part of the rules of the game. Theory-laden terms are incomplete, and the use of an incomplete term commits the user to the fact that the completion is going to come from somewhere else. The interpreter of the Constitution is thus, in some sense, like a musician working with a score that is not complete until it is interpreted; and in some sense like a trial lawyer who is expected to make the best case possible with the available evidence. An interpretation becomes an explication rather than an explanation,[136] and we can hope for no more.

Additionally, we can argue that all of ordinary language is theory-laden,[137] and indeed this is the assumption of much of Western metaphysics, embodied, for example, in the categories of Aristotle[138] and Kant.[139] But even if not all of ordinary language is theory-laden, it is fairly uncontroversial that at least much of it is. In some sense, the word *lunch* is theory-laden, at least as compared to *eating* or *placing organic matter in one's mouth for the purpose of introducing it into the digestive system.* So, too, are terms like *time, space, hailing* a cab, *playing* a game, *sending* a letter, and *understanding* a book. We constantly use expressions which presuppose or incorporate theories that do more than identify a physical object or activity.

Thus, when we say that a term is theory-laden, we presuppose a particular point of view of the speaker with respect to which a term is theory-laden. I cannot explain to a person ignorant of baseball what a "home run" is without explaining a great deal of baseball, but it seems strange to describe *home run* as theory-laden when one baseball player is talking to another. Similarly, I cannot explain a "trick" to a non–bridge player without explaining at least the rudiments of the game of bridge, even though *trick* is not highly theory-laden in conversations between bridge players. But suppose that after a sequence of bidding I explain to my opponents at the bridge table that a particular bid was an "impossible negative." I must then explain a bidding system or theory known as "Precision," without which the term *impossible negative* cannot be understood.

We can clarify things by distinguishing between two forms of theory-ladenness. In the weaker sense, many of the terms of ordinary language are theory-laden. But in a stronger sense, terms are only theory-laden if they force us to go outside the domain of discourse in which they are used. Thus, *lunch* and *time* are theory-laden in the weaker sense but not in the stronger, because the theory that they presuppose is as much a part of ordinary language as is the language itself. But *straight flush* or *anal-retentive personality* or *habeas corpus*, if used in ordinary conversation, are theory-laden in the stronger sense because they presuppose theories outside the domain of ordinary discourse.[140]

Therefore, we can say that terms are theory-laden in a strong sense only when they require us to go outside the context in which we are speaking. And that is why *habeas corpus* may be theory-laden in ordinary language but not in law, as is even more true for terms like *pleading, statute of limitations,* or *appeal.*

This distinction applies directly to constitutional language. The requirement that the president shall have attained "the Age of thirty-five years" is theory-laden in the weak sense because it presupposes a theory of determining age. It also presupposes the deeper idea of determining growth with reference to chronology. But it is not theory-laden in the strong sense because it is uncontroversially known to all participants speaking *within* the domain. A reference in the Constitution to "habeas corpus," or "Congress," or "amendment" is similar. But a term in the Constitution is theory-laden in the strong sense when it sends us outside the legal domain. "Freedom of speech" and "equal protection of the laws" are different from "habeas corpus" or "Congress," because they send us outside of the legal domain and into the moral or the political. That is also why the use of terminology that lacks meaning within the domain in which it is used can be said to commit the user to whatever meaning may appear in or be provided by another domain.

V. Language as a Constraint

Characterizing constitutional terms as theory-laden is problematic because the language then provides little if any guidance in our search for theory. Perhaps, therefore, a theory-authorizing view of constitutional language gives no weight to the text of the Constitution. Yet this view would mistakenly ignore the important asymmetry between positive and negative responses.[141] Constitutional language can constrain the development of theory, or set the boundaries of theory-construction, without otherwise directing its development. Constitutional language can tell us when we have gone too far without telling us anything else.

The statement that "it doesn't mean that" need not necessarily occasion the response, "Then what does it mean?" I can know some of what a term does not mean without knowing what it does mean,[142] just as I can tell you quite confidently that *the theory of relativity* does not mean "shirt collar" even though I have only the dimmest perception of what *the theory of relativity* does mean.[143]

In this sense, we might do best to look at constitutional language as a frame without a picture,[144] or, better yet, a blank canvas. We know when we have gone off the edge of the canvas even though the canvas itself gives us no guidance as to what to put on it.

But if language constitutes the frame, then how does it do that? The ordinary language associations of theory-laden terms do not explain the framelike quality of the words, because we would not hesitate to extend freedom of speech to black armbands[145] or oil paintings, although neither is "speech" in ordinary language.[146] Furthermore, we would have little difficulty in holding universal tongue-boring to be a violation of the Eighth Amendment, although the universality would prevent a finding that the punishment was "unusual" in the ordinary language sense.[147] We do, however, incorporate some very rough, pretheoretical understandings into our sense of the limits of language. For example, it is probably largely pretheoretical that castration as a punishment for jaywalking does not violate the principles of freedom of speech and that a fine of $1.00 for criticizing the president does not violate the prohibition on cruel and unusual punishment.[148] But this helps very little in most real cases.

Perhaps, at best, we can only note the importance, as in all development of language, of moving in small steps. Highly theory-laden constitutional language is like the ship, imagined by the philosopher Neurath, which is to be rebuilt while afloat and therefore can only be rebuilt plank by plank.[149] So long as the ship stays afloat during the process, it is no objection that the finished product bears little or no resemblance to the original. With constitutional language, so long as the enterprise stays afloat it is no objection that the current conception bears no close relation to the ordinary language meaning of the text.[150] If we have moved in small steps from the original text, the enterprise stays afloat. The question, then, is not necessarily whether the putative move is justified by the text, but whether the move is justified by the last move.

In some ways, constitutional interpretation parallels some theories of literary criticism.[151] In literary criticism, or indeed in any artistic interpretation, we do not demand *the* uniquely correct interpretation, but only *an* interpretation justified by the text. The paint or text underdetermines an interpretation (a theory) of an oil painting or a literary work in the same way that the text of the Constitution underdetermines a constitutional theory.[152] The interpretation must be plausibly coherent with the painting or the text, but an interpretation cannot be uniquely derived from the text or painting alone. Therefore no one interpretation is uniquely acceptable, just as no constitutional theory is uniquely acceptable in terms of the text. Although nontextual sources may mandate a particular result, such a mandate is not the function of the language. The language limits, but does not command.

The analogy with literary criticism should not be pressed too far, because the literary critic has the freedom to select particularly important parts of his text for attention, a freedom not nearly as available in constitutional interpretation. But the analogy does effectively capture the relationship between flexibility and an authoritative text, a relationship that lies at the core of understanding the nature of constitutional adjudication.

Were this theory to be more fully developed, it might be said to be horizontally clause-bound, but not vertically clause-bound.[153] That is, it recognizes, as more free-wheeling theories do not, that the values specified in the text are more or less discrete, and that they have a textual preeminence over values not so specified. In this sense, it is horizontally clause-bound because each interpretation must derive originally from some particular portion of the text or from some justified interpretation of that portion of the text. It is vertically open because there is no limit on the source from which we can derive the full theory for the textually stated value, other than the intuitive, pretheoretical limits placed on that theory by the language.[154]

These discrete constitutional values are like a series of funnels, separate from each other, but open to receive anything of the right size that may be poured into them. Of course, if we extend the rims of funnels too far, the funnels bump into each other, and the important conceptual separation becomes difficult to maintain. But that is a caution against the extremes, and not necessarily a crippling failure of the notion of conceptual separation. Courts must supply content to those theory-laden terms that send us outside the domain of legal knowledge and legal discourse. That content need not come from philosophy (as argued by Dworkin[155] and Richards[156]) or from history (as argued by Berger[157]) or from somewhere else. As I have argued in this essay, the conventions of language demonstrate that Berger's extreme form of historical reference and even the more mild forms of historical interpretation[158] are mistaken as a matter of textual derivation. Historical reference is neither mandated nor implicit in a permanently authoritative constitutional text. But although the text does not require a reference to history, it does not necessarily prohibit such reference. The text requires that we supply the theory, but there may be extratextual, or extraconstitutional, reasons for constructing it from one source rather than from another. History is one possible source, but not the only possible source, and the same can be said for moral philosophy, or political policy, or any other source of values.

Conclusion

The Constitution has been written in a language, and a user of language must be taken to know and intend that the language is open to interpretation. Although a user of language has intentions that are relevant in determining what the user meant to say, the user has no power to veto the conventions of the language that have been used. Constitutional interpretations can change because the linguistic conventions and presuppositions change, even though the words remain the same.[159] Thus, a fixed reference to history or original intent seems curious. Even historians expect to interpret the past anew for each generation,[160] because perspective, and therefore meaning, is mutable. Of course, our craving for certainty[161] may cause us to search for the immutable. This is most apparent in law, where the myth of certainty has a persistent appeal.[162] But the law cannot be certain, in large part because language itself is not certain. What is unfortunate is that quixotic quests for certainty are likely to interfere with more fruitful quests for an intelligent understanding of the causes and management of our uncertainty.

Law as Literature

Sanford Levinson

I

[T]he process of reading is not a half-sleep, but, in highest sense, an exercise, a gymnast's struggle; . . . the reader is to do something for himself, must be on the alert, must himself or herself construct indeed the poem, argument, history, metaphysical essay—the text furnishing the hints, the clue, the start or frame-work. Not the book needs so much to be the complete thing, but the reader of the book does. That were to make a nation of supple and athletic minds, well-train'd, intuitive, used to depend on themselves, and not on a few coteries of writers.

Walt Whitman, *Democratic Vistas*

Ultimately, man finds in things nothing but what he himself has imported into them: the finding is called science. . . . Is meaning not necessarily relative mean-ing and perspective? All meaning is will to power (all relative meaning resolves itself into it).

Friedrich Nietzsche, *The Will to Power*

"Law," said Christopher Columbus Langdell, "considered as a sci-ence, consists of certain principles or doctrines. To have such a mastery of these as to be able to apply them with constant facility and certainty to the ever-tangled skein of human affairs is what constitutes a true law-yer."[1] Langdell's argument was twofold; his conceptualization of law as a science was only the first. The other was his assertion that "all of the available materials of that science are contained in printed books."[2] Both of these principles are crucial to his approach to law. For Langdell law was essentially a literary enterprise, a science of extracting meaning from words that would enable one to believe in law as a process of submission to the commands of authoritative texts (the rule of law) rather than as the creation of willful interpreters (with submission concomitantly produc-ing the rule of men).

To an extent never sufficiently acknowledged by his many detractors, Langdell was altogether correct in linking the legitimacy of the law to the mastery of texts, whether of cases, statutes, or the Constitution. How-ever much legal positivism justifiably emphasizes the origins of law in social facts,[3] the ordinary language of all developed legal systems in-cludes constant recourse to texts that authorize specific conduct. One does not have to accept the entire Langdellian system (indeed, I most certainly do not) in order to recognize the centrality of textuality to the lawyer's enterprise.

Perhaps the easiest way to confirm this point is simply to note that most controversial decisions of the past three decades, especially those of the United States Supreme Court, rest on purported interpretations of the United States Constitution. And the authority of the written Constitution is a prominent theme in American political thought. John Marshall, after noting the "reverence" with which Americans viewed written constitutions, went on to label such creations the "greatest improvement on political institutions" made by the citizenry of the new country.[4] And Marshall deftly asserted the power of the "obvious meaning" of the constitutional text to undergird his claim for the primacy of judicial review. "The powers of the legislature are defined, and limited; and *that those limits may not be mistaken*, or forgotten, the constitution is written."[5]

No sense can be made of even present-day American political discourse without recognizing the power of constitutional writtenness within our language. Thus Senator Dale Bumpers of Arkansas attacked a bill pending before the Senate, which would have stripped the federal courts of their power to order busing as a remedy for unconstitutional segregation, by calling it part of a "continuing, sinister, devious attack" on the Constitution. "We will today begin the erosion," announced Senator Bumpers, "of *the only document* that stands between the people and tyranny."[6] Anyone familiar with English political discourse, on the other hand, knows that it is almost impossible to imagine similar language there; debate in England centers on the right or wrong of a particular bill, not on its fidelity to a presumptively authoritative text that stands above parliamentary activity.[7]

Citizens of the United States, however, retain within their active political language the purported commands of an allegedly comprehensible Constitution.[8] Comprehensibility is nothing peculiar to constitutions, however, for its possibility arises from the presumed attributes of writtenness. "The physical presentation of a text," the literary theorist Jonathan Culler points out, "gives it a stability . . . . Writing has something of the character of an inscription, a mark offered to the world and promising, by its solidity and apparent autonomy, meaning which is momentarily deferred."[9] In a more ominous vein, the late French critic Roland Barthes described writing as "a hardened language." Writing, he went on to say, "manifests an essence and holds the threat of a secret."[10]

Constitutions, of the written variety especially, are usefully viewed as a means of freezing time by controlling the future through the "hardness" of language encoded in a monumental document, which is then left for later interpreters to decipher. The purpose of such control is to preserve the particular vision held by constitutional founders and to prevent its overthrow by future generations. The very existence of written constitutions with substantive limitations on future conduct is evidence of skepticism, if not outright pessimism, about the moral caliber of future citizens; else why not simply enjoin them to "be good" or "do what you think best"? Writers of constitutions must have a very high confidence in the ability of language both to "harden" and to control.

One form of "hardness" that any reader of written texts quickly becomes aware of, paradoxically, arises from the propensity of language to change, so that understanding past speech recorded in texts requires a "historical" dictionary. Consider, for example, the vicissitudes of the description of a person as "sentimental." The *Oxford English Dictionary* tells us: "Of persons, their dispositions and actions; characterized by sentiment. Originally in favourable sense: Characterized by or exhibiting refined and elevated feeling. In later use: Addicted to indulgence in superficial emotion; apt to be swayed by sentiment."[11] What has been a term of praise became one of mild reproach. What would be the task of a lawyer, then, if asked to construe a trust instrument written in 1720 establishing scholarships for "sentimental" youths?

Any writer, including a framer of constitutions, presumably imagines the following relationship between text and reader: "The reader sets himself to make out what the author has designed and signified through putting into play a linguistic and literary expertise that he shares with the author. By approximating what the author undertook to signify the reader understands what the language of the work means."[12] And, of course, in the case of those particular texts called legal, by understanding the meaning the conscientious adjudicator-reader becomes authorized to enforce it.

The remark just quoted comes from an essay vigorously attacking certain strains of contemporary literary criticism that Abrams finds insufficiently respectful to determinate meanings allegedly generated by disciplined study of texts. The disputes currently raging through literary criticism precisely mirror some of the central problems facing anyone who would take law seriously; the basis of this parallelism is the centrality to law of textual analysis.[13] If we consider law as literature, then we might better understand the malaise that afflicts all contemporary legal analysis, nowhere more severely than in constitutional theory.

II

The example given above regarding *sentimental* presents no shattering difficulty, for it rests on the notion that the word has a determinate meaning at a specific historical moment. But the emphasis of much contemporary theory is an attack on the stability of meaning (or, concomitantly, on the possibility of establishing techniques by which to retrieve meaning) at *any* given moment. Moreover, our increasing propensity to view all social activity as embedded within linguistic codes has universalized the scope of the inquiry regarding the difficulties of reading texts, whether formally written or not. Indeed, much contemporary writing and painting is explicitly self-referential in its demand that the reader-viewer confront the extent to which language and image are unavoidably ambiguous, and its assertion that any given ascription of narrative line or meaning is the product of an interchange between object and viewer rather than an attribute of the object itself.

There is less of a gap between contemporary legal theory and literature than we might suppose, for many practitioners of each are united by a pervasive anxiety generated by what has been well described as "the loss of the sense of doing and speaking in the name of someone or something recognizable and unquestionably valid."[14] This loss undercuts the confidence in one's ability to ground description or analysis in a purported reality beyond the descriptions or analyses themselves. For American lawyers the primary example, as already suggested, is constitutional law and its relationship to (something recognizable as) the Constitution. Paul Brest has recently noted that little contemporary constitutional doctrine explicitly relies on "originalist sources," i.e., on close analysis of the text or of the presumed intentions of the Framers. Instead what is increasingly important is "the elaboration of the Court's own precedents." So far as the documentary Constitution is concerned, "It is rather like having a remote ancestor who came over on the Mayflower."[15] Brest's image brilliantly conveys the sense of a distant Constitution which can be seen, if at all, only "through a glass darkly." To view it as a genuine source of guidance is naive, however heartbreaking this realization might be.

Two classic approaches to understanding a written constitution involve emphasizing either the allegedly plain words of the text or the certain meaning to be given those words through historical reconstruction. I think it fair to say that these particular approaches are increasingly without defenders, at least in the academic legal community.[16] Even so capable an analyst as Professor Monaghan, who is eager to return to the confines of a knowable "originalist" Constitution, admits that he has no way of handling the authority of judicial precedents that (he argues) violate initial understandings.[17]

There is not time in this essay to canvass the problems of originalism. Suffice it to say that the plain-meaning approach inevitably breaks down in the face of the reality of disagreement among equally competent speakers of the native language. Intentionality arguments, on the other hand, face not only the problem of explaining why intentions of long-dead people from a different social world should influence us,[18] but also, perhaps more importantly, the problem of extracting intentions from the collectivity of individuals and institutions necessary to give legal validity to the Constitution.[19] Even literary critics most committed to the existence of objective meaning through recovery of authorial intent, like E.D. Hirsch, admit that their approach applies only to individually authored works, and therefore cannot be used to analyze a document like the Constitution.[20]

As Richard Rorty has pointed out, however, there are at least two options open to critics who reject the two approaches outlined above but who, nonetheless, remain interested in interpreting the relevant texts. The first option involves the use of an allegedly more sophisticated method to extract the true meaning of the text. Thus Rorty refers to "the kind of textualist who claims to have gotten the secret of the text, to have broken its code," as a "weak" textualist,[21] where the term is seemingly a metaphor for the power of the individual critic. Whatever pyrotechnics might come from a critic who "prides himself on not being distracted by anything which the text might previously have been thought to be about or anything its author says about it,"[22] there remains the infatuation—110 years after Langdell—with the possibility of a science of criticism. A "weak" textualist "is just doing his best to imitate science—he wants a *method* of criticism and he wants everybody to agree that he has cracked the code. He wants all the comforts of consensus, even if only the consensus of readers of the literary quarterlies" (or law reviews).[23]

Perhaps the best current example of such a "weak" textualist is John Hart Ely, whose *Democracy and Distrust*,[24] however radical some of its criticisms of so-called interpretivism purport to be, is merely the latest effort to crack the code of the United States Constitution and discover its true essence. As James E. Fleming pointed out in a recent review, Ely is engaged in a "quest for the ultimate constitutional interpretivism" which would in effect foreclose further debate about the genuine meaning of the Constitution.[25]

Like Charles Black,[26] Ely is savagely critical of those who seek constitutional meaning in the isolated words of the clauses themselves. And, like Black, Ely looks instead to the overall structure of the Constitution for guidance. If the lines themselves are no longer a plausible source of meaning, there is still a Constitution to be discovered "between the lines," as it were, in the interplay of conceptual structures—states, nation, citizens, republican government—that are undoubtedly present in the constitutional text. Consequently, Ely's structuralism is no less addicted to a search for the "one-and-only truth" about the Constitution than are its discredited competitors. He continues to presuppose what Rorty calls a *"privileged vocabulary,* the vocabulary which gets to the essence of the object" and "expresses the properties which it has in itself as opposed to those we read into it."[27]

No one can read Ely and miss his anger at those who merely read their own views into the Constitution. Indeed, most of Ely's reviewers agree with him at least on this last point, even as they criticize him for reading *his* preferred views into the Constitution. What unites Ely and most of his critics, though, is the continued belief that there is something "in" the Constitution that can be extracted if only we can figure out the best method to mine its meaning.

Against such weak textualists—the decoders, whatever the fanciness of their methods of decoding—Rorty posits "strong" textualists, who reject the whole notion of questing for the essential meanings of a text. "Strong," it should be emphasized, refers to the power of the critic, not the power of the text (or of its author). According to Stanley Fish, one of the leading proponents of this approach, "Interpretation is not the art of construing but the art of constructing. Interpreters do not decode poems; they make them."[28] Fish has argued that "[t]he objectivity of the text is an illusion and, moreover, a dangerous illusion, because it is so physically convincing. The illusion is one of self-sufficiency and completeness. A line of print or a page is so obviously *there* . . . that it seems to be the sole repository of whatever value and meaning we associate with it."[29]

Instead Fish emphasizes the reader's active role and concomitant inability to measure any given interpretation against the "actual" text. He correctly insists that the debate about what it means to read a text is of more than academic interest:

> [D]ifferent notions of what it is to read . . . are finally different notions of what it is to be human. In [one] view, the world, or the world of the text, is already ordered and filled with significances and what the reader is required to do is get them out (hence the question, "What did you get out of that?"). In short, the reader's job is to extract the meanings that formal patterns possess prior to, and independently of, his activities. In my view [on the other hand], these same activities are constitutive of a structure of concerns which is necessarily prior to any examination of meaningful patterns because it is itself the occasion of their coming into being.[30]

As Fish notes, "The difference in the two views is enormous." The first one regards "human beings as passive and disinterested comprehenders of a knowledge external to them (that is, of an *objective* knowledge)."[31] It is worth noting, I believe, that Felix Frankfurter's favorite single word was "disinterested,"[32] and that the ideology of the Harvard Law School, from Langdell's time to the days of Hart and Sacks and afterward, can be regarded as centered around the search for a "disinterested," impersonal approach to legal analysis.

The view endorsed by Fish regards "human beings as at every moment creating the experiential spaces into which a personal knowledge flows."[33] Meaning is created rather than discovered, though the source of creative energy is the particular community within which one finds him- or herself. Critics more Emersonian in their inspiration, like Harold Bloom, are willing to credit individual acts of creativity, though Bloom's emphasis on the ubiquity of "misreadings," rather than "truthful" renderings of what is inside texts, links him to Rorty's "strong" textualists.[34] All such readers could well join the Whitmanian anthem, where all readings, whether of life or of texts, become songs of oneself.

The patron saint of all strong textualists is Nietzsche:

> [W]hatever exists, having somehow come into being, is again and again reinterpreted to new ends, taken over, transformed, and redirected by some power superior to it; all events in the organic world are a subduing, a *becoming master*, and all subduing and becoming master involves a fresh interpretation, an adaptation through which any previous "meaning" and "purpose" are necessarily obscured or even obliterated.[35]

And the argument of Fish, Bloom, and other strong textualists, whether American or Continental, is *not* that they prefer to do their thing as an alternative to the more banal work of "truth-seekers" like Abrams or Hirsch, but rather that the project of ultimate truth-seeking is based on philosophical error. At the very least it presumes a privileged foundation for measuring the attainment of truth, and it is precisely this foundation that Nietzsche and most of the more radical literary theorists deny. Like Rorty, they do not substitute a new candidate for a winning method of how to recognize literary truth when one sees it; rather, they reject the very search for finality of interpretation.

To be sure, none of the radical critics defend the position that any interpretation is just as good as any other. Stanley Fish, for example, notes that he genuinely believes in the validity of any given view that he happens to hold, and he can present reasons for rejecting the views of his opponents on the interpretation of a given text.[36] In this regard Fish seems similar to Ronald Dworkin, who views judging as including the phenomenological experience of feeling oneself to have achieved the uniquely correct solution even to a hard case.[37] But Fish, more candid than Dworkin on this point, admits that his own conviction of rightness will provide no answer at all to anyone who happens to disagree with him, and that there is no way to resolve the dispute. It is at this point that he retreats to his Kuhnian[38] emphasis on communities of understanding and shared conventions. It may be true that these communities will share, at any given moment, a sense of what distinguishes "on-the-wall" from "off-the-wall" arguments,[39] but Fish is acutely aware of the contingency of such judgments. They describe only our own temporal sense of what is currently acceptable, rather than anything genuinely mirroring the essential characteristics of the texts being discussed.[40]

III

Presumably only those professionally interested in literature are forced to wrestle with the issues presented by Abrams, Culler, and Fish regarding poetics or the interpretation of fiction. But if law is, in some meaningful sense, a branch of literature, then the problems discussed above take on new and bothersome implications. And nowhere is this more true within our own culture than in constitutional interpretation and its emphasis on writtenness.

The role of our Constitution is not only to enable us to pretend that past linguistic acts can control future action. It is also presumably to prevent the rise of Nietzschean "masters." Nietzsche seems to suggest, however, that a massive exercise in social deception is necessary if we are not to recognize the way that "interpretation" inevitably implies a struggle for mastery in the formation of political consciousness. For a Nietzschean reader of constitutions, there is no point in searching for a code that will produce "truthful" or "correct" interpretations; instead, the interpreter, in Rorty's words, "simply beats the text into a shape which will serve his own purpose."[41]

E.D. Hirsch, perhaps the most consistent opponent of the radical critics, notes that "[w]ith a numinous document like the Constitution or the Bible, the principles and methods of correct interpretation are as important as they are problematical."[42] If one takes seriously the views articulated by Nietzsche, Rorty, and Fish (among others), one must give up the search for principles and methods of constitutional interpretation. Instead, one assesses the results of an interpretive effort by something other than the criterion of adherence to an inner essence of the text being interpreted. Indeed, Robert Cover addresses this point directly in his remarkable review of Raoul Berger's *Government by Judiciary*, in which Berger vigorously attacks judges for allegedly straying from the original meaning (which is equated with the true meaning) of the Constitution. Cover himself quotes Nietzsche's comment that "[t]he knowledge of the past is desired only for the service of the future and the present"[43] and emphasizes that it is up to us, the living, to decide for our own reasons what we wish the Constitution to mean.

To put it mildly, there is something disconcerting about accepting the Nietzschean interpreter into the house of constitutional analysts, but I increasingly find it impossible to imagine any other way of making sense of our own constitutional universe. For some years I have organized my own courses in constitutional interpretation around the central question, But did the Court get it right? as if one could grade any given opinion by whether or not it measured up to the genuine command of the Constitution. Answering such a question, of course, requires the development of a full set of "principles and methods of correct interpretation," and my courses have involved a search for such principles and methods.

I still spend a great deal of time examining various approaches, ranging from the linguistic to the historical, from the structural to what my colleague Philip Bobbitt calls the "ethical,"[44] but I have less and less confidence that this is a sensible enterprise. At the very least there is no reason to believe that the community of persons interested in constitutional interpretation will coalesce around one or another of these approaches. Moreover, insofar as one accepts the plausibility of an analysis like Rorty's, there is no reason to regret this, for it is the result of a genuine plurality of ways of seeing the world, rather than of the obdurate recalcitrance of those who refuse to bend to superior argument.

Yet there are obvious difficulties in adopting Rorty's metaphor of the conversation (rather than the argument),[45] for the principal social reality of law is its coercive force vis-à-vis those who prefer to behave other than as the law "requires." As Chairman Mao pointed out, a revolution is not a tea party, and the massive disruption in lives that can be triggered by a legal case is not a conversation. The legal system presents a conversation from which there may be no exit, and there are certainly those who would define hell as the vision of their least favorite constitutional interpreter, whether the Court or a benighted law professor.

What does one do, then, when studying opinions, if one gives up the enterprise of determining whether or not they are "correct"? Are cases simply historical fragments which should be studied for insight into the ideology of the time?[46] One no longer would say, for example, that *Dred Scott*[47] or *Lochner* v. *New York*,[48] or any other case, was "wrongly" decided, for that use of language presupposes belief in the knowability of constitutional essence. One *can* obviously show that constitutional tastes and styles shift over time, but this retreat into historicism has nothing to do with the legal science so desperately sought by Langdell and his successors.

A study of shifts in legal styles, moreover, may force us to come to grips with the fact that there may be no guiding criteria to enable us to state with confidence that any given piece of writing is "legal" writing, as opposed to writing about a subject of interest to the legal system. Jonathan Culler has studied the ways in which readers use conventions to constitute something as a poem or a short story and to give it meaning.[49] It would be interesting to see what, besides identification of a particular piece of writing as emanating from a court, allows one with confidence to label it as peculiarly "legal."[50] Fish, as one might imagine, insists that poetry is anything we conventionally posit as such.[51] Is the same thing true of legal writing?[52]

These remarks have obvious implications for legal education. Here, too, there are parallels to literary education. Some of Culler's most convoluted paragraphs are spent defending the enterprise of specialized undergraduate and graduate education in literature in the face of the attack by radical critics on the very notion of a science of criticism.[53] It is tempting to paraphrase Dostoevski by saying that if there is no science, there is no truth, and if there is no truth, then anything is permitted. How does one describe education in such a climate of skepticism? As already indicated, Culler's major project is identifying the structured conventions by which readers supply meaning to texts; his own reference to only *"apparent* autonomy" in the remarks quoted earlier[54] indicates the limit of the extent to which he rejects reliance on the independent status of the language. It is we who establish what the monuments mean by ascribing content to them.

Insofar as Culler seeks the conventions that differentiate "competent" readers from incompetent ones, he faces the difficulty of establishing as well how one distinguishes "off-the-wall" readings that are the product of genuine incompetence from those that are simply brilliantly ahead of their time and in cadence with the next paradigm coming down the pike. Legal education too could devote itself more formally to studying the conventions of reading law and legal opinions, though such a move would face great hostility not only from students but from most present faculty members as well. I note the debate that raged in England over the appointment of Colin MacCabe to the English faculty at Cambridge.[55] MacCabe, with his interests in contemporary structuralism and post-structuralism, is fundamentally antagonistic to the view that the only task of students is to read set texts, without ever systematically reflecting on the notion of "reading" itself. Indeed, most constitutional law courses avoid discussing the assumptions not only that there are standard cases that must be read, but also that the act of reading itself is, when all is (un)said and done, unproblematic.[56]

Consider also the way we treat the innovative judges of our legal tradition, particularly as they appear in law school courses. Do we really wish to argue that John Marshall or Earl Warren (or the most recent dynamic innovator, William Rehnquist)[57] got the essence right in their interpretations of the Constitution, or do we recognize instead the extent to which we have been subdued by their political visions?

Perhaps the most significant example of this dilemma is John Marshall himself, or rather I should say our response to Marshall. I have little trouble stating that I consider his major opinions to run the gamut from the intellectually dishonest[58] to the majestically visionary,[59] and rarely to contain the only (or even the most) plausible rendering of the

Constitution. Yet there is also a profound irrelevance to such a criticism. Not only does it assume the existence of a privileged discourse that allows me to dismiss Marshall as "untruthful" rather than merely different, it also ignores the fundamental fact that John Marshall is as much a "founder" of the American legal system as those who wrote the Constitution he purported to interpret. He is, perhaps, the great Nietzschean judge of our tradition.

Indeed, Marshall is a worthy successor to the Founders of 1787, for they too were aware of the awesome role they played as visionary leaders. When it was pointed out to the Philadelphia Convention that it was without authority to "revise" the Articles of Confederation by obliterating them, the response was candid and to the point. "There are great seasons when persons with limited powers are justified in exceeding them, and a person would be contemptible not to risk it."[60] So spoke Edmund Randolph, later the attorney general in the Washington administration. Even James Madison, who gamely insisted that the convention was behaving properly, was reduced to arguing, in *The Federalist* Number 40, that the Philadelphia delegates "must have borne in mind, that as the plan to be framed and proposed, was to be submitted *to the people themselves* . . . its approbation [would] blot out all antecedent errors and irregularities."[61]

Madison's argument is significant, to be sure, and it serves to distinguish the Founders from twentieth-century authoritarians unconcerned with popular ratification of their acts. Nonetheless it establishes a powerful precedent for the general proposition that the people themselves can give their approval to what was arguably illegal conduct by visionary leaders, including judges who break the bonds of confining legal conventions and ultimately transform our vision of ourselves as a nation. Under this theory the difference between hero and villain is found not in fidelity to preexisting legal norms and adherence to their "correct" meaning, but in the ability of a hero-founder to impress the new understanding of the political order on the popular consciousness. And, in our particular culture we graft these new understandings, particularly if found in judicial opinions, onto something called "the Constitution" and pretend that the leader-judge has merely seen more deeply into its essence, rather than bent it to a new vision.

This description, of course, works only when a "strong" judge, like one of Harold Bloom's "strong" poets, successfully misreads the past to establish his or her own vision of reality as one for the writer's own time. But an age without such judges, or with contending candidates, can recognize only the existence of the competing visions themselves, with no recourse to the foundation document—the Constitution—being genuinely possible. It would obviously be nice to believe that *my* Constitution is the true one and, therefore, that my opponents' versions are fraudulent, but that is precisely the belief that becomes steadily harder to maintain. They are simply *different* Constitutions. There are as many plausible readings of the United States Constitution as there are versions of *Hamlet*,[62] even though each interpreter, like each director, might genuinely believe that he or she has stumbled onto the best answer to the conundrums of the text. That we cannot walk out of offending productions of our national epic poem, the Constitution, may often be anguishing, but that may be our true constitutional fate.

IV

Professor Owen Fiss has recently directed several arguments against the views expressed in an earlier version of the present essay.[63] Fiss forthrightly labels these views as "nihilism." He concludes his article by identifying what is at stake in the debate: "[T]his nihilism calls into question the very point of constitutional adjudication; it threatens our social existence and the nature of public life as we know it in America; and it demeans our lives." It is no surprise, then, that he goes on to state, "It must be combated and can be, but perhaps only by affirming the truth of that which is being denied—the idea that the Constitution embodies a public morality and that a public life founded on that morality can be rich and inspiring."[64]

In this section I shall first lay out what I perceive as the view of constitutional adjudication defended by Fiss. I shall then consider his response to those critics, like myself, who are unable to share it. I should emphasize at the outset that I share both Fiss's basic social and political values, even if not his theory of the Constitution, and his unhappiness about the implications of "nihilism." But a desire, however understandable, to combat it does not equal the ability to do so.

Professor Fiss first elaborated his views in a *Harvard Law Review* "Foreword."[65] For the purposes of this essay, the key paragraph is as follows:

> The right place of courts in our political system turns on the existence of public values and on the promise of those institutions—because they are independent and because they must engage in a special dialogue—to articulate and elaborate the true meaning of those values. The task [is] discovering the meaning of constitutional values such as equality, liberty, due process, or property . . . .[66]

A concomitant of "the meaning-giving enterprise implicit in constitutionalism itself"[67] is the judge's duty to be concerned with designing effective remedies. "The desire to be efficacious need not be seen as an assertion of will, but as a willingness of the judge to assume responsibility for practical reality and its consonance with the Constitution." Indeed, "[t]he judge might be seen as forever straddling two worlds, the world of the ideal and the world of the practical, the world of the public value and the world of subjective preference, the world of the Constitution and the world of politics." It is the judge among all officials of government who "is in the best position to discover the *true meaning* of our constitutional values."[68]

Fiss more recently has spoken of the judicial duty to interpret legal texts; in doing so the judge "gives meaning and expression to the values embodied in that text."[69] Like Ronald Dworkin,[70] Fiss seems to assert the existence of uniquely valid ("true") solutions to the conundrums about the implications of our "public values," assuming in the first place that such values exist and can be ascertained. Moreover, like Dworkin's, Fiss's Constitution turns out to contain only the good, the true, and the beautiful.

Fiss takes pains to distinguish himself from that "arid and artificial conception of interpretation" which some label " 'interpretivism,' but [is] more properly called 'textual determinism.' "[71] He links this conception with that form of legal positivism that emphasizes "the 'written constitution' and stresses factors like the use of particular words or the intent or beliefs of the framers, all of which have little or no moral relevance."[72] The problem with this mode of interpretation goes well beyond any theoretical difficulty in ascertaining the true meaning of the text or the intentions of its authors.[73] As Fiss notes, even if one assumes the theoretical coherence of positivism, there remains the problem that "[a] too rigid insistence on positivism will inevitably bring into question the ultimate moral authority of the legal text—the justness of the Constitution."[74] Thus he concedes that an all-too-comprehensible Constitution might well be read to have protected slavery, and this fact alone would justify raising the question as to why the Constitution is worthy of respect and obedience. Indeed, the mere presence of such a question indicates "[a] moment of crisis in the life of a constitution."[75]

A resolution to any such crisis is close at hand, however. A judge must be willing "[t]o read the moral as well as the legal text. The judge quickly learns to read in a way that avoids crises."[76] Indeed, Fiss accords the judiciary a "[s]pecial competence to interpret a text such as the Constitution, and to render specific and concrete the public morality embodied in that text."[77]

This assignment of authority to the judiciary is, allegedly, not a blank check, i.e., not an invitation to become a Nietzschean creator of meaning. Instead the judicial interpreter "is disciplined by a set of rules that specify the relevance and weight to be assigned to the material (e.g., words, history, intention, consequence), as well as by those that define basic concepts and that established the procedural circumstances under which the interpretation must occur."[78] There is, to be sure, no uniformity of rules of interpretation. Not only are the rules for interpreting poems different from those for interpreting legal texts, but, "even within the law, there may be different rules depending on the text—those for contractual interpretation vary from statutory interpretation, and both vary from those used in constitutional interpretation."[79] But in no case is an "interpreter . . . free to assign any meaning he wishes to the text," for the rules discipline the interpreter and thus succeed in "transforming the interpretive process from a subjective to an objective one, and they furnish the standards by which the correctness of the interpretation can be judged."[80] The disciplining rules derive from "an interpretive community consisting of those who recognize the rules as authoritative."[81]

Fiss's notion, of course, is very close to Fish's emphasis on the importance of interpretive communities,[82] and both have been influenced by the work of Thomas Kuhn.[83] It is easy enough to see why Fish and I find Kuhn's notions attractive, rooted as they are in the tradition of the sociology of knowledge and its rejection of the correspondence between ideas believed to be true and the external world itself.[84] It is harder to understand Fiss's embrace of Kuhn, given that the key element in Fiss's program is his defense of the objective truthfulness of claims about public and constitutional values.[85] The notions of "truth according to the conventions of my community" and "objective knowledge as determined by my reference group" differ substantially from notions of unmodified "truth" or "objective knowledge." The former exist within the language of skepticism, including that most virulent form castigated as nihilism. It was Nietzsche, after all, who emphasized the reduction of "truth" to the views of one's own perspective (and who thus went on to assert the possibility of changing our world by adopting different perspectives).

Fiss is aware, of course, that legal adepts argue vigorously among themselves over the meaning of the Constitution; he does not seriously suggest that legal academicians are significantly more in agreement with one another than are professors of literature debating the meaning of a poem or a novel. His most interesting (and dubious) move, however, is to differentiate the lawyer from the literary critic by asserting the significance of the membership of the former in an interpretive community presided over by authoritative courts and judges. The legal system offers procedures that can resolve disputes through, "for example, pronouncements by the highest court and perhaps even legislation and constitutional amendments. The presence of such procedures and a hierarchy of authority resolving disputes that could potentially divide or destroy an interpretive community is one of the distinctive features of legal interpretation."[86] Ultimately, then, the judge is "a combination of literary critic and moral philosopher. But that is only part of the picture. The judge also speaks with the authority of the Pope."[87]

This last assertion is directly relevant to an earlier essay of mine, in which I posited the existence of "protestant" and "catholic" approaches to the Constitution.[88] That Fiss embraces a "catholic" Constitution, in the senses of looking to unwritten norms and accepting the institutional authority of the judiciary, tells us a great deal about him but only a little about the interpretive community. Indeed, a recent article coauthored by Fiss, attacking Justice Rehnquist, manifests all too well the problems faced by those seeking to slay the nihilist dragon.[89]

V

The 10 March 1982 issue of *The New Republic* had as its cover story "The Rehnquist Court." The illustration of the cover is worth noting: a sphinx-like head of Justice Rehnquist perches atop the "body" of a Supreme Court building. Reaching out on each side of the steps are the menacing paws of Sphinx-Rehnquist. The head, incidentally, is gazing with an ominous serenity into the distance. The phrase "Equal Justice under Law" does not appear on the building. Finally, the magazine places the tag line ". . . and what it's doing to the Constitution" opposite the title. Fiss and his coauthor, Charles Krauthammer, claim to have decoded the riddle of this particular sphinx, however, and it is the purpose of their article to bring the alarming news to the public. Whether or not the reader is convinced by the argument that the intellectual leader of the current Court is Justice Rehnquist, the specific way Rehnquist is described and criticized in the article gives great insight into the operation of Fiss's overall approach to legal analysis.

According to the article, Rehnquist's "opinions fall radically short of the ideals of the profession. He repudiates precedents frequently and openly, and if that is impossible (because the precedent represents a tradition that neither the Court nor society is prepared to abandon), then he distorts them."[90] The "failings of craft," however, pale before the real problem, which "is substance. Rehnquist has a constitutional program for the nation: he wants to free the states from the restrictions of the national Constitution, particularly those emanating from the Civil War Amendments and The Bill of Rights."[91] Thus Rehnquist rejects the incorporation doctrine as it has been used by the Court in the past two decades to "nationalize" the Bill of Rights.[92] Moreover, Rehnquist has led the way in questioning the extent to which Congress may legislate the behavior of the states.[93] And, the authors point out, Rehnquist has scarcely shown himself a textualist in his theory of constitutional interpretation, for he has proved skillful in adopting structural arguments to defend his particular theory of federalism.[94] Rehnquist "is no conservative, as that term is ordinarily understood in the law, but rather a revisionist of a particular ideological bent. He repudiates precedents; he shows no deference to the legislative branch; and he is unable to ground state autonomy in any textual provision of the Constitution."[95]

Yet the authors point out that Rehnquist claims more than his personal views as authority for his opinions. Indeed, he disparages those who emphasize contemporary social needs or morality as authorizing a "living Constitution";[96] instead Rehnquist is an "originalist,"[99] who sees the Court's task as enforcement of the goals of the Framers themselves. Although Fiss and Krauthammer mention their doubts about the cogency of originalism,[98] they prefer to challenge Rehnquist on his own ground, for their argument is that he ignores the intent of the authors of the Civil War amendments to diminish the state autonomy that concededly might have been the vision of at least some of the Framers.[99] These amendments were not, they argue, "merely technical modifications to what Rehnquist claims to be the understanding at Philadelphia, corrections that assured all persons formal equality before the law. Rather, these amendments represent a second starting point, a basic change in the postulates of our constitutional system. Any appeal to history which ignores that is a sham."[100]

I have no trouble agreeing that Rehnquist's jurisprudence is questionable in theory and pernicious in practice. But the terms of this attack, derived as they are from the allegedly internal professional norms of the legal interpretive community, present the occasion for embarrassment, if not incoherence. For, as the authors recognize, "the Marshall Court (in its affirmation of nationalism) and the Warren Court (in its affirmation of equality) also repudiated strict constructionism and practiced judicial activism."[101] Indeed, for Fiss and Krauthammer, "[t]he most plausible interpretation of *Brown*[102] is that it simply repudiated *Plessy*,[103] in an attempt to reflect a truer understanding of the fourteenth amendment. For the Warren Court, as for Rehnquist, precedent had less force than the framers' original understanding of the text they wrote."[104] It is clear from Fiss's earlier comments, though, that he would defend *Brown* even if he were convinced beyond a reasonable doubt that the Framers of the Fourteenth Amendment did not understand that amendment to bar school segregation.[105]

If Rehnquist were simply a conservative law professor, like Robert Bork,[106] Ralph Winter,[107] or Richard Posner,[108] then it would be easy to dismiss his views by noting the extent to which they require the modification or abandonment of many of our "papal edicts" from the Warren Court. But the very point of the article, of course, is based on the proferred fact that Rehnquist is rapidly becoming the chief declarer of what the Constitution requires, and that the Court-directed interpretive community will increasingly revolve around him.

It is hardly likely, of course, that Professor Fiss (or I) will start teaching students the (normative) Constitution according to Rehnquist, even as we make our students aware of the existence of the appalling Rehnquist oeuvre. But will Professor Fiss argue that the interpretive community has been taken over by a false pope, a usurper, against whom the truly faithful must rally? Moreover, given the willingness of the voting public to elect a president and a majority of the Senate who share many of Rehnquist's values, how will Fiss (or anyone else) show that they contravene the public values embodied in the Constitution, especially given the undoubted interest of our Constitution-writers in protecting at least some measure of both state autonomy and the rights of private property owners?

Fiss's approach to the Constitution, like that of Professor Dworkin, ultimately rests on the premise that there is no genuine conflict among the values that animate the different parts of the public.[109] But, as Bray Hammond put it in his analysis of the early dispute in our history about the power of Congress to charter the Bank of the United States, "The controversy demonstrated at the very outset that the Constitution had not displaced rival principles or reconciled them but had become their dialectical arena."[110] This last term may bring to mind either the controversy of the seminar table or warfare in which each side claims adherence to the "true" meaning of the disputed document. It is the latter mode of dispute resolution that is suggested by Justice Black's comment that "the fundamental issues over the extent of federal supremacy had been resolved by war."[111] But surely there is something peculiar about the assertion that fundamental ideological issues are "resolved" by war, even if we concede that political power indeed often comes from the barrels of guns, and even if it is possible to identify clearly the doctrinal position that won or lost a particular battle. Indeed, Fiss and Krauthammer may even be correct that Rehnquist's views, taken to an extreme, reopen the dilemmas that ultimately led to the outbreak of war. But if that be so, it is only because of the continuing tension in American values and the inability of either armed victory or judicial articulation to settle the dispute firmly one way or another. Perhaps Rehnquist is attempting to resolve what he sees as a genuine legal crisis by reasserting certain traditional moral and legal values. That he cannot achieve resolution says more about the pervasiveness of the fundamental conflicts than it does about his mistake in reading our fundamental values.

The American wish is that one can avoid having to answer the political question posed by a Harlan County labor song, "Which side are you on?" by responding that one stands by the Constitution and that, in turn, the Constitution itself stands for the proper values. The transformation of political questions into legal questions, first emphasized by Tocqueville,[112] allows the "adjudication" of disputes. As Fiss notes, however, "The idea of adjudication requires that there exist constitutional values to interpret, just as much as it requires that there be constraints on the interpretive process. Lacking such a belief, adjudication is not possible, only power."[113]

As he portrays the bleakness of a world that rejects belief in the possibility of principled adjudication, Fiss speaks with much of the same eloquence and vigor as does Gerald Graff. It is worth noting that Richard Rorty, whose work has much influenced me, has indicated his own empathy with the attacks of Graff and others on the new literary criticism. What is at stake is a conception of the possibility of a shared moral life. Rorty refers to "the view that, in the end, when all the intellectuals have done all their tricks, morality remains widely shared and available to reflection—something capable of being discovered rather than created, because already implicit in the common consciousness of everyone."[114] Critics with this view "want criticism to bring an antecedent morality to light, enlarge upon it and enrich it," and they consequently "resist the suggestion that there is no common vocabulary in terms of which critics can argue with one another about how well this task has been performed."[115] No one with a democratic sensibility can easily reject the vision of a common discourse described by Rorty and evoked by Fiss.

Empathy, however, does not equal agreement. It would be contradictory to say that the historicist pragmatism celebrated by Rorty is "true," or that philosophy has "disproved" the possibility of true and certain knowledge about the natural world, including its moral component. But those who do not already share Fiss's faith are unlikely, I suspect, to be persuaded by his attack on positions like the one articulated in the present essay. The inability of Fiss and his coauthor to mount a persuasive attack on Justice Rehnquist in anything other than political terms reveals the parlous state of contemporary constitutional discourse. The united interpretive community that is necessary to Fiss's own argument simply does not exist.[116] What one does in the absence of such a community is, of course, a problem of more than merely theoretical import. The decreasing propensity of the body politic to accord the Supreme Court ultimate authority in constitutional interpretation may portend an ever deeper constitutional crisis, especially if any of the jurisdiction- and remedy-limiting bills now before Congress had passed and received presidential signature.[117]

VI

Even poets who emphasize the contingency of perception nevertheless continue to write their poems. "Even the linking of stars is a lie./ But for a while now let's be happy/ to believe the symbol. That's enough."[118] And so we who take the constitutional firmament seriously continue as well to write our articles and dispute with one another.[119] And, just as constellations are human attempts to link the separate stars, so are doctrinal analyses likely to serve as similar attempts to demonstrate that the cases themselves are meaningfully linked and intellectually patterned. All such writing (and reading) is a supreme act of faith. We can hope that some future conjunction of author and reader will provide a common language of constitutional discourse fit for "a nation of supple and athletic minds,"[120] but for now we can only await its coming and make do with the fractured and fragmented discourse available to us.[121]

Keep off the Grass, Drop Dead, and Other Indeterminacies: A Response to Sanford Levinson

Gerald Graff

> *In legal practice it is usually all right to treat laws as if they were solid things whose effects have definite spatial boundaries and material consequences. When a semiotician starts examining laws as a patterned system of meanings their insubstantiality becomes evident, and the inquiry presses on both jurisprudence and epistemology.*
>
> Mary Douglas, *The Future of Semiotics*

The anthropologist Mary Douglas's point here seems to me right, and insofar as Professor Levinson's paper echoes her point, it seems to me right too. Not only lawyers but most people harbor superstitions about the nature of language and meaning. These superstitions assume that meanings reside "in" language somewhat the way furniture resides in rooms—securely "there" where the interpreter can see, identify, and grasp them the way we can see, identify, and grasp tables and chairs. Holding this conception of language, one is naturally going to be disturbed when a semiotician or some other new-style theorist of language comes along and says it isn't so at all, and points out that meanings have nothing like the substantiality of tables and chairs. Even worse, this theorist says that the words by which we signify "tables" and "chairs" are only somewhat arbitrary sounds, that even the visible "furniture" of the world is insubstantial, for the language we use to describe that world segments it in culturally conditioned ways. The more vertiginous the theorist makes things appear, the more inclined we are to cling to what's left of the "commonsense" view of language, according to which words are essentially names of things and the meanings of words are securely fastened like barnacles onto the objects the words denote. Those professionally concerned with the law may feel an especially strong need to cling to such superstitions lest the stability of their occupation, not to mention the stability of the law itself, be threatened.

I suspect that the legitimate inspiration of Sanford Levinson's paper, "Law as Literature,"[1] was the fact that many lawyers, judges, and other professional students of the law hold these superstitions. Levinson observes—rightly, I would guess, though I haven't his inside knowledge—that much thinking about meaning and interpretation among legal professionals is badly outmoded, and that it remains intact only for fear of the Pandora's box that would be opened if more up-to-date theories were admitted into court.[2] He writes to unmask this outmoded thinking, and to that extent I find no fault with his project. The belief that meaning is a substance or spirit reposing *in* language can't be exploded too soon to suit me. But it makes some difference *how* one goes about exploding this belief and what one puts in its place. Here I find serious flaws in Levinson's argument.

That argument rests on a good many non sequiturs, most of which, however, can be reduced to a single major one: Levinson assumes throughout his paper that once the fallacy of semantic immanence which I've described above is discarded, our practical ability to make sense of texts and utterances is somehow endangered or impaired. He falsely assumes, in other words, that our ability to decipher a text—whether that text be a legal document or some other text need not concern us here—depends on our ability to grasp what he calls "some presumed inner essence" that reposes *in* the "text being interpreted."[3] Judging quite correctly that no such inner essence exists, Levinson leaps to several illogical conclusions: that legal and other texts are therefore marked by a radical indeterminacy,[4] that there is no real truth in interpretation and "anything is permitted,"[5] and that what eventually gets construed as the correct interpretation in any given instance is a function merely of the institutional fiat or "coerciveness" of the interpreter.[6]

Levinson actually makes the same mistake committed by those whom he is attacking. Like them, he believes that if meaning is not an inner essence in utterances, meaning is then indeterminate and disputes over meaning aren't susceptible to rational procedures of adjudication. The difference between Levinson and those he opposes is merely a tactical or political difference: whereas they would presumably keep the cat in the bag, Levinson would let it out. The mistake of both parties is in supposing that there is any radical consequence in letting the cat out, or indeed that there is any cat in the bag to begin with.

Instances of Levinson's faulty reasoning could be cited from many pages of his essay, but I'll content myself with one or two of the more glaring. Levinson asks whether meaning "is to be found *within* a case or do we as analysts participate in creating the meaning of a given case?"[7] If there's a right answer to this question (which I would not like to encounter in a true/false test), it would have to be "neither." The alternatives are misleadingly formulated. Any sophisticated theorist of language would point out that the meaning of an utterance isn't a function of the words themselves or even of sentences, but of the *use* to which the words and sentences are put by speakers and writers. The notion of meaning as something "to be found *within* a case," which is, again, Levinson's "inner essence," is wrong to begin with. Meaning is an affair of the use of words and sentences, not of words and sentences considered as things-in-themselves which somehow bear meanings within them. This use can be *inferred* from words and sentences, because words and sentences have recognizably conventional uses, which are the "meanings" listed in dictionaries. But strictly speaking, no word or sentence means anything determinate until it is used in a specific situation by somebody, until it is employed in a speech act.

To be sure, we can talk of what words or even sentences mean apart from their uses. Speech act theorists like John Searle and H.P. Grice distinguish between "sentence meaning" and "utterance meaning" to distinguish between the kind of understanding we can have of a context-free sentence like *keep off the grass* and of the same sentence when actually used by somebody to commit a speech act, say, of warning.[8] One might suppose that the expression *keep off the grass* is sufficiently familiar that we know what it means independent of any situation in which it may be used. In fact, the expression's familiarity depends on our imagining a standard situation with which we associate the words—a sign seen on a well-manicured lawn, say, or the cry of a gardener working on such a lawn while somebody is walking across it. *Keep off the grass* would *mean* something entirely different if we overheard the expression uttered by a narcotics counselor, in appropriate circumstances, to a person known to us as a marijuana user. Even sentences that lack the same potential for ambiguity as the example I've chosen (*keep off the tulips*) can be used to mean a great variety of things. Though we can say that certain utterances "normally" are used to mean one thing rather than others they might potentially be used to mean (and it's such normal expectations that enable us to make educated guesses of what is meant in particular cases), this fact itself demonstrates that interpretation is concerned not with what words or sentences mean "in themselves" but with how speakers actualize the semantic potential of words and utterances in particular speech acts.

In this sense, meaning is not a substance but an activity and has the determinacy of an activity rather than of a physical object. Guessing the meaning of a text or utterance is inferring what a writer or speaker was or is *doing* with language and not what some linguistic object essentially was or is. Now, what writers and speakers may be doing with words is as open to more or less reliable inference, according to the kind of evidence that guides such inference, as is any other kind of human action. The question of what any text means, then, is neither more nor less open to "determinate" inference than the question of whether a person did or didn't commit a particular act, or whether a historical event occurred or didn't occur. Just as we have reason to believe that we know a lot about some historical occurrences, less about others, and so little about still others that their very occurrence may be conjectural, so it is with texts: the degree to which we can be confident about our inferences depends on the amount of evidence available, evidence which itself is open to criticism and fallible.

Consider, for example, the problem of interpreting the words *drop dead*. We would interpret these words in one way if we heard them shouted by the driver whose car we had just cut in front of on the freeway, and quite a different way if we heard them spoken—even with the same intensity and tone of voice—by a friend whom we knew well, or one whom we knew to be a frequent kidder. Again, the example points up the fact that meaning doesn't reside *in* the expression *drop dead*, an expression which has acquired certain standard meanings only because of a history of use that has established those meanings as normal and conventional. And apart from some inferable situation in which *drop dead* is used to commit a speech act, whether it be to insult a passing motorist or to chide a friend gently, *drop dead* doesn't mean anything in particular. But Levinson, were he to remain faithful to the logic of his argument, would be obliged to conclude that since *drop dead* doesn't mean anything in particular in itself, it is therefore a radically indeterminate expression.

There are, to be sure, instances in which *drop dead* might very well be indeterminate. Suppose, for example, someone were to send me an unsigned note with those words on it. How would I be able to determine whether the note constituted a serious expression of ill will, a threat, or a put-on? The first thing most of us would do on receiving such a note would be to inventory our memories for circumstances that would explain its motivation. Might it have been that run-in one had a few days ago with an ill-tempered student? That colleague one does not know very well but who is suspected of instability? Could it have been a message intended for another recipient mistakenly delivered to oneself? If none of these explanations seems plausible, one would simply not know what to make of the note—its meaning in this case would be indeterminate.

Given the absence of sufficient evidence in such cases, evidence helping us identify the situations in terms of which speech acts are recognized, I am not going to be able to interpret that note. But this kind of frustration, stemming from relative lack of evidence, doesn't introduce any *radical* indeterminacy into the practice of interpretation, except insofar as it means we can never be *certain* we understand what any text or utterance means. The older a text is and the more alien the culture that produced it, the more difficult it is likely to be to reconstruct the conventional situations in terms of which interpreters fix the meanings of speech acts. What might count for us as a "normal" or "standard" contextual indicator of a threat, say, or of a warning, or of praise or blame, may not have so counted in the convention system of the culture that produced the text we are trying to decipher. A text produced by a culture in which masochism or sadism was the normal morality would be difficult for us to grasp, since we might mistake certain expressions of approval for disapproval.[9] There may in some instances be so little commonality between the convention system of the interpreter and that of another culture that it's not possible to crack the code of that culture's texts at all. There's no reason to suppose that all texts can be interpreted, that every hieroglyphic can be deciphered. Insofar as we take interpretation to be possible at all, however, we assume there is at least sufficient commonality (or commensurability) between different convention systems for areas of disparity and misunderstanding to be detected and defined.

What I think Levinson has failed to understand about interpretation is that it's essentially a messy business of guesswork predicated on practical knowledge of language, conventions, and the situations in which they operate. Levinson begins with an unrealistic expectation about interpretation and then adopts an unnecessary skepticism when the expectation isn't met. He supposes either that interpretations have the unchallenged authority of divine commandments, or else that they have no authority whatsoever except the coercive authority of institutional force. Again, to illustrate this charge fully would be tedious, so I'll content myself with a few flagrant examples. Levinson adverts to the "search for finality of interpretation"; he doubts the possibility of "final interpretive authority"; and he endorses "the proposition that there can be no ultimately provable right answer in legal discourse."[10] Just as Levinson had offered a false choice between understanding meaning as immanent in language and understanding it as indeterminate or determined only by whim or fiat, so here he offers another false choice between total absolutism and total uncertainty. In both cases, the choice is one of all or nothing.

The problem is that the practice of interpretation doesn't depend on interpreters' possessing godlike power to arrive at an "ultimately provable right answer" that closes the books on further argument about the meaning of a text. Therefore the lack of such godlike power doesn't entail indeterminacy in Levinson's sense of that word. (The statement that law and mathematics have "the same" indeterminacy "as literature" is question-begging, since it assumes that the indeterminacy of literature is already uncontroversial, which it isn't.) Levinson has merely inverted the gesture of the interpretive absolutist, who insists that there is One True Meaning and that he alone possesses it. Levinson turns this absolutism upside-down and comes out with an equally prescriptive No True Meaning. The alternatives he gives are simply unreal.

Legal texts do offer special problems of interpretation, especially when those interpretations are charged with an authority that interpretations of poems or casual remarks do not possess. Interpretive decisions may become difficult when, because of historical changes, the circumstances to which a constitution or statute is applied are ones the original framers could not have foreseen. In these and other situations, the intentions of the framers may be regarded as less important than the present consequences of the decision. Intentions can also be irrelevant in other situations, as in the case of a person who only jokingly shouts "Fire!" in a crowded theater or claims to be packing a weapon when passing through airport passenger inspection. In such cases, the practical concerns of the law occasion the imposition of a number of *artificial* or *stipulative* restrictions on interpretation.

Levinson is trapped in a muddle because his argument forbids him from distinguishing between interpretive truth and the forms of power and self-interest which, according to him, determine the truth. On the one hand, he wants to say that interpretation in general is radically "problematic," since it's determined not by considerations of truth or good reasons but merely by institutional power;[11] on the other hand, this argument proves inconvenient when he needs to give weight to his own interpretations. For example, Levinson says that the structuralist literary critic Colin MacCabe "is *correctly viewed* as fundamentally antagonistic to the view that the only task of students is to read set texts, without ever reflecting on the notion of 'reading' itself."[12] But according to what set of interpretive procedures is MacCabe "correctly viewed" the way Levinson says he's viewed? And why should the notion of correctness that's operating in such a judgment be taken seriously if, as Levinson has been arguing, such notions of correctness are the products of an institutional power that we ought to be trying to get out from under? What permits Levinson to appeal so selectively to an interpretive standard which, to this point, he has presented as an authoritarian fiction? One could cite other examples of Levinson's selective reliance on norms he appears to have discredited, but again I see no point in multiplying instances.

Does this mean that political power and bias, then, play no role in interpretation? Not at all, it merely means that to argue that an interpretation is distorted by political power or bias is itself to appeal to a normative position from which such a judgment can be made. No matter how self-critical they may claim to be, those who totalize the political motivation of interpretation apply a double standard which exempts their ideological demystifications from the blindness they attribute to others.

On the Use and Abuse of Nietzsche for Modern Constitutional Theory

Richard Weisberg

I

There is nothing less radical today than the position that textual mean-ings are indeterminate. As a Nietzschean, I say this not only because indeterminacy has become so popular; rather, I contend that the position itself is fundamentally conservative, if not reactionary. Conservative, lit-erally, because it conserves what Nietzsche perceived to be a two-thousand-year-old tradition of distorting texts to suit the given reader or community; conservative, figuratively, because removing the need "simply to understand what an author is saying" (Nietzsche's phrase) conserves the energies of the reader and is fundamentally lazy. Reaction-ary, finally, because any system, no matter how perverse, can be ratified if not authorized by deconstructive readings of central texts.[1] After all, this precisely occurred when, in Nietzsche's oft-cited sense, Paul twisted the Old Testament completely out of shape to provide a convenient pre-diction of his private messianic beliefs. Destabilizing text and tradition to implement subjectivist programs and desires has been, for two millen-nia, our prevalent hermeneutical mode.

Nietzsche always connected bad readings of texts with other faulty ele-ments of a disturbed will to power. To read well, for Nietzsche, was to live well. So only a postmodernist seeking to abuse Nietzsche would strive to deny or distort his notion of text and to see it as one more end-lessly interpretable, metaphorically fluid notion.

Indeed, Hendrik Birus has recently put forth a virtually definitive demonstration that Nietzsche's hermeneutics is text-oriented and sharp-ly critical of what today would be called "reader-response" reactions to written words.[2] Throughout his writings, Nietzsche chastises readers who run over a text attempting to make it their own. He sees false readings as both identifiable and closely related to the form of moral slavishness denominated "ressentiment."[3] Thus Nietzsche, in *Human, All-Too-Human*, tells us: "*The worst readers.* The worst readers are those who act like plundering soldiers. They take out some things that they might use, cover the rest with filth and confusion and defame the whole."[4]

This typically forceful statement matches hermeneutics to morals and does more than imply the independent existence of an entity outside the reader. And its message is repeated often in the late Nietzsche—who even believed in a truthful reading of his own *Genealogy of Morals,* but one that he presciently doubted would occur for a century[5]—and outweighs (as Birus shows) the occasional statement used by postmodernists to enlist Nietzsche into one self-serving hermeneutical camp or the other. One of these latter aphorisms will be identified and, so to speak, "deconstructed," in my next section.

A question left unanswered by Birus—namely *why* it was so important to Nietzsche to stress careful and relatively selfless readings of texts—I address more fully in another forum.[6] But for now it might be appropriate to identify a special use of Nietzsche's writing by lawyers over the past several years. This enterprise will inevitably move us toward the central issue of Nietzsche's hermeneutics and their relationship to his views on morality and justice.

II

The law school world has adopted Nietzsche to its purposes of late. The issue is fundamental and the stakes are high: how do we determine the meaning of our central political text, the United States Constitution? Here Professor Levinson has found grist for a postmodernist's mill in an aphorism found in the second essay of Nietzsche's *Genealogy of Morals,* which he has seized in order to justify the ostensible loss of textual autonomy and consequent complete control of reader over text: "Everything that exists, no matter what its origin, is periodically reinterpreted by those in power in terms of fresh intentions; . . . all processes in the organic world are processes of outstripping and overcoming. . . . In turn, all outstripping and overcoming means reinterpretation, rearrangement, in the course of which the earlier meaning and purpose are necessarily either obscured or lost."[7]

Like "the more radical literary theorists"—he cites Fish, Rorty, and Bloom—the Levinsonian Nietzsche asks us only to exercise our will to power over a text: "For a Nietzschean reader of constitutions, there is no point in searching for a code that will produce 'truthful' or 'correct' interpretations; instead the interpreter, in Rorty's words, 'simply beats the text into a shape which will serve his own purpose.' "[8] Levinson allows that "there is something disconcerting about accepting the Nietzschean interpreter into the house of constitutional analysis"[9] but eventually is able to call John Marshall himself "the great Nietzschean judge of our tradition"[10] and to conclude that power, not textual or communal restraint, alone defines the judge's methodology.

However one may stand on Levinson's concluding point, it is absolutely necessary to redeem Nietzsche from the strikingly inaccurate role cast for him in getting Levinson there. Ironically, the passage seized upon by Levinson (as it is also by Sarah Kofman in arguments that parallel Levinson's although they are unconcerned with American law[11]) lies in the midst of Nietzsche's most extensive excursion into legal theory, the Second Essay of the *Genealogy*. Nietzsche emerges as a firm believer in normative codes, but if and only if they have been produced by the performative speech acts of healthy and vitalistic wills to power. So, in the very aphorism chosen by Levinson, Nietzsche berates contemporary psychologists and criminologists for their resentful inversion of the notions of punishment and, more generally, justice. Not addressing written texts at all in that aphorism,[12] but rather concepts, Nietzsche suggests that a sound idea of justice does indeed exist, and that only the ressentiment-imbued nineteenth century has perverted it so as to forget completely its origin.

Thus, just prior to the passage chosen by Levinson to prove Nietzsche's textual nihilism, he calls for a return to an enduring, root notion of justice:[13]

> A word should be said here against certain recent attempts to trace the notion of justice to a different source, namely rancor [ressentiment]. . . . [W]e must not be surprised if we see these recent attempts hark back to certain shady efforts, discussed earlier, to dignify vengeance by the name of justice (as though justice were simply an outgrowth of the sense of injury) and to honor the whole gamut of reactive emotions. . . . Against Duhring's specific proposition that the native soil of justice is in the reactive emotions, it must be urged that the exact opposite is the case: the soil of the reactive emotions is the very last to be conquered by the spirit of justice. Should it actually come to pass that the just man remains just even toward his despoiler (and not simply cool, moderate, distant, indifferent; to be just is a positive attitude), and that even under the stress of hurt, contumely, denigration the noble, penetrating yet mild objectivity of the just (the judging) eye does not become clouded, then we have before us an instance of the rarest accomplishment, something that, if we are wise, we will neither expect nor be too easily convinced of. It is generally true of even the most decent people that a small dose of insult, malice, insinuation is enough to send the blood to their eyes and equity out the window. The active man,

the attacker and overreacher, is still a hundred steps closer to justice than the reactive one, and the reason is that he has no need to appraise his object falsely and prejudicially as the other must. It is an historical fact that the aggressive man, being stronger, bolder, and nobler, has at all times had the better view, the clearer conscience on his side. Conversely, one can readily guess who has the invention of "bad conscience" on his conscience: the vindictive man. Simply glance through history: in what sphere, thus far, has all legislation and, indeed, all true desire for laws, developed? In the sphere of "reactive" man? Not at all. Exclusively in the sphere of the active, strong, spontaneous, and aggressive. Historically speaking, all law. . . . is a battle waged against the reactive emotions by the active and aggressive, who have employed part of their strength to curb the excesses of reactive pathos and bring about a compromise. Wherever justice is practiced and maintained, we see a stronger power intent on finding means to regulate the senseless raging of rancor among its weaker subordinates. This is accomplished by wresting the object of rancor from vengeful hands, or by substituting for vengeance the struggle against the enemies of peace and order, or by devising, proposing, and if necessary enforcing compromises, or by setting up a normative scale of equivalents for damages to which all future complaints may be referred. But above all, by the establishment of *a code of laws* which the superior power imposes upon the forces of hostility and resentment whenever it is strong enough to do so; by a *categorical declaration of what it considers to be legitimate and right, or else forbidden and wrong. Once such a body of law has been established, all acts of highhandedness on the part of individuals or groups are seen as infractions of the law, as rebellion against the supreme power.* Thus the rulers deflect the attention of their subjects from the particular injury and, in the long run, achieve the opposite end from that sought by vengeance, which tries to make the viewpoint of the injured person prevail exclusively. *Henceforth the eye is trained to view the deed ever more impersonally*—even the eye of the offended person, though this, as we have said, is the last to be affected. It follows that only after a corpus of laws has been established can there be any talk of "right" and "wrong" (and not, as Duhring maintains, after the act of injury). (emphasis added)

In this marvelous aphorism, Nietzsche saves justice as an active, innate, almost biological need. What a magnificent concept! But he goes further. As though describing Moses in the wilderness, or at least the American constitutional generation, Nietzsche posits here the potential for *codification* of the basic notion of justice, an act performed by certain superior groupings of talented individuals. Once that "code of laws" arises, it may be, indeed should be, implemented "impersonally." In such happy generations, a set of speech acts follows hard upon a set of sound, vitalistic, and even aggressive physical acts; the result is a linguistic encoding of the preexisting vitalistic notion of justice.[14]

This is not to say that Nietzsche was a firm believer in legal systems, particularly those in nineteenth-century Europe.[15] But to confuse for a general relativism what were in fact his contemporary dissatisfactions would be a grave error. Levinson's chosen aphorism, in the context of the longer one preceding it, announces that justice has been misread for a long time but that it exists nonetheless, available for eventual rehabilitation in the tradition of its original purveyors and declarers.

It is not for nothing, then, that the Levinsonian act of "becoming master" over a text is clearly identified in the *Genealogy* as open to the harshest criticism if we find (as Nietzsche believes we can) that the proposed interpretation is *wrong.* For Nietzsche here and elsewhere advises us, particularly regarding the texts of just and vigorous wills to power, to seek "a strictly philological explanation, that is, the simple desire to comprehend what an author says."[16]

It is not gratuitous that, in the second essay of the *Genealogy*, Nietzsche links *textual accuracy* with the *urge to justice.* Clearly, for him, living well means reading well or, at a minimum, reading vitalistic, performative texts with an aspiration toward the dynamic growth and the necessary constraint[17] of the individual will to power.

III

Following Nietzsche, we must reconstruct the notion itself of a text. Stanley Fish tells us that the presentation of a text as a separate (usually bound) entity is deceptive.[18] Perhaps that formal hint of "otherness" is less deceptive than beneficial. It reminds us that almost everything we deal with everyday is, literally, outside of ourselves.

But once we reposit the objective existence of a physical text, can we be assured of finding anything within it besides ourselves? As Geoffrey Hartman says,

> to call a text literary is to *trust* that it will make sense eventually, even though its quality of reference may be complex, disturbed, unclear. . . . At some point the affective power of voice, as well as the relation of particular words to that resonating field we call the psyche, must be considered. Semiotic analysis of the word in the word, even when as penetrating as Derrida's . . . cannot reach that field of pathos or power. The interpreter at least, has also to understand the wound in the word.[19]

As when we deal with people, Hartman suggests that we open ourselves to the deepest otherness of the *textual* experience. Awareness of ourselves in this context is less to enhance than to *reduce* the chance that we will control the other. Surely this is what Heidegger would mean by "reader-response," and what his student Gadamer explicitly demands of the interpreter: to be wary of the inevitable imposition of oneself upon matter.[20]

Apparently unlike people, however, texts do not *seem* to evoke the nonverbal clues to meaning that we find in looks, attitudes, touches, tears. But, like a look, the structure of a text yields a sense; and like an attitude associated with a person over a long period of time, an ever-increasing knowledge of the author of the text assists us to understand specific words within a given structure.

If this be a return to structuralism,[21] or even to a modified version of intentionalism,[22] I will stand by that characterization, with one important caveat. These signposts should not deceive us into thinking we are truly deciphering *meanings*. The most we can hope for is that we have made ourselves alive to the *yearning for understanding* within the text, the reason it was probably set down to begin with. Clues are more likely to lead to an ideal *manner of interpretation* of the text than to an unmediated entry into its mysteries. The latter is something we may desire; the former is asked of us by the text.

Different texts, like different people, may call for different interpretive approaches. The key observation is that text leads to theory, and not the reverse.

So, as Nietzscheans, if we seek to grasp the text as text, we must start with its words, understood to be apart from us and embedded (usually) in a structure of other words assumed to have been generated by one or more authors. Often without enormous difficulty, or so I believe, these factors will yield (to a self-conscious but self-effacing reader) a broad hint as to the interpretive mode then to be followed in proposing the text's "meaning." I put *meaning* in quotation marks because I believe that few texts have a discernible meaning, and even then perhaps for only a few readers; but many texts display a discernible *desire to be understood a certain way*. Indeed, I will only search hard for "meaning" when I believe the text has asked its reader to do so. Therefore I would suggest a kind of spectrum of yearning, yielded by legal (performative) as well as literary (figurative) texts. On the right end of the spectrum are texts whose preliminary verbal and structural sense demands further close adherence to the objective or derivable text itself; in the middle are texts for which formal historical or generic elements alone will provide the best interpretive methodology; and on the left end are texts whose preliminary verbal and structural sense yields to the reader almost all further power to create textual meanings.

This preliminary, methodology-yielding step does not, ordinarily, require recourse to intentionalism. Structure, form, genre, and other elements usually suffice. But if the author or authors of a text have spoken generally about theories of interpretation or language, it strikes me as legitimate for the reader to integrate that knowledge into an understanding of the desired interpretive strategy. Thus, if Edgar Allen Poe and Henry James tell us what their stories *mean*, we should be relatively indifferent to their analyses; but if Dostoevski or Madison or Flaubert or Douglas tells us how he feels *about words* or about our *capacity to understand* texts, we should lend such statements great credence.

Examples at all ends of the spectrum are available in almost every historical period. The twentieth-century novel, at one extreme, offers texts such as Joyce's *Finnegan's Wake*, Ricardou's *La Prise de Constantinople*, or even Faulkner's *Sound and the Fury*, each of which breaks down the reader's traditional temporal expectations in such a way as to imply a maximum of subjective reader response. Ricardou's novel thus offers an opportunity to begin the act of reading anywhere along the physical text one might wish; and in Robbe-Grillet's *La Jalousie*, the reader is offered the choice of providing the subject itself of the novel.

But it would be a mistake to deduce from that list an assumption that all modern novels desire subjectivist readings, just as we shall learn in dealing with the Constitution that not all eighteenth-century neoclassical texts yearn for objectivist or even Aristotelian reader responses. Indeed, in other works by Faulkner, for example, particularly those dealing with legal themes, the reader is asked to be as careful as possible in absorbing the details and subjects generated by the author.

Text yields theory. But not all literary texts will yield a theoretical invitation to hew closely to the words themselves. Examples are not lacking in the domain of the novel, particularly (as we have suggested) the postwar novel. The readiness is all, our readiness to accept the text's desire to be approached a certain way.[23]

IV

I have suggested that one path to enlightenment about the correct interpretive strategy for a given text is provided by the author's statements about interpretation itself. The particular kind of intentionalism I am suggesting here can liberate a reader not so much to "find" meanings as to adopt appropriate interpretive strategies.[24]

Fortunately, some of the Framers of the 1787 document that still seeks our understanding today were quite overt about hermeneutics. If we take the *Federalist* papers as an important and authoritative statement of the Framers' linguistic beliefs, we find much food for thought. (It is worth answering right away a potential jibe at even this limited form of intentionalism, namely that it, too, is a form of interpretation requiring us to reopen all the theoretical questions about meaning that we pose about the text itself. Let us test that notion by reading through only once what the Founders had to say about interpretation.)

Perhaps the most cogent expression of the Founders' approach to words is found in *The Federalist* in its number 37, authored by Madison. Madison, a man richly trained in the various eighteenth-century schools of aesthetic theory (Hutchinson and Milord Shaftesbury among others[25]) was no Candide when it came to what today's social scientists cumbrously call the "communications arts." In number 37, Madison seizes a chance to express a hermeneutic theory; the context is his excoriation of those demanding perfection in the proposed Constitution, and his immediate example is the complex development of English law:[26]

> The use of words is to express ideas. Perspicuity, therefore, requires not only that the ideas should be distinctly formed, but that they should be expressed by words distinctly and exclusively appropriate to them. But no language is so copious as to supply words and phrases for every complex idea, or so correct as not to include many equivocally denoting different ideas. Hence it must happen that however accurately objects may be discriminated in themselves, and however accurately the discrimination may be considered, the definition of them may be rendered inaccurate by the inaccuracy of the terms in which it is delivered. And this unavoidable inaccuracy must be greater or less, according to the complexity and novelty of the objects defined. When the Almighty himself condescends to address mankind in their own language, his meaning, luminous as it must be, is rendered dim and doubtful by the cloudy medium through which it is communicated.

No clearer skepticism about plain meanings or textual objectivity could be extracted from the collected works of such ultramodernists as Derrida or Rorty. Yet this is a neoclassical passage, penned by a contemporary of Blackstone and Voltaire. The Constitutional fathers did not believe in words, which they called, quite simply, "the cloudy medium." If even the Bible as given to Moses—Madison's evocative textual example— yields "unavoidable inaccuracy," why should the readers of any constitution expect more?

For the Founders, words were a necessary impediment to the understanding of the vital constitutive concepts they were encoding. What they asked for, at the most, was the kind of structural sense discussed in my previous section. It was Hamilton, in fact, who shortly before (*The Federalist* number 32) set forth what he significantly calls *"a rule of interpretation out of the body of the act,"*[27] one which asks the Constitutional reader to find meanings in "the whole tenor of the instrument."[28] Text again yields theory, not the reverse.

I would like to follow the Founders' interpretive model and to suggest that the smallest detail in the text of the Constitution may illuminate a professedly murky whole. My final text is a two-word parenthetical in

Article I, section 7, relating to the veto power. Most will remember it, although it is seemingly not as provocative as those other dynamic verbal duos, "equal protection" or "due process." The parenthetical surrounds the cloudy words "Sundays excepted" and helps explain the rule that a law comes into existence (pocket vetos temporarily aside) "[i]f any bill shall not be returned by the President within ten days (Sundays excepted) after it shall have been presented to him. . . ."[29]

Woe unto the interpreter like Professor Monaghan,[30] who seeks the "plain meaning" of that innocuous parenthetical, for it could mean at least each of the following:

1. The president has only ten days unless the bill was presented to him on Thursday in which case he may take an extra day at the very end of the period (which is a Sunday);
2. The president has eleven days in any event, and sometimes twelve.

If, like Professor Michaels,[31] we believe that only intentions control meaning, we are equally as stymied. The debates, and sources like *The Federalist*, are virtually silent on the point.[32]

But suppose we utilize the parenthetical for a different kind of meaning-based constitutional theory? Removing ourselves one step from "plain meaning," suppose we seek, like Professor Perry, to find values "constitutionalized by the framers."[33] Although—surely to his credit—Perry does not so employ the parenthetical, might not a disciple seek to find there a ratification of his "religious understanding of ourselves as a people committed to struggle incessantly to see beyond, and there to live beyond, the imperfections of whatever happens at the moment to be the established moral conventions"?[34]

Or why might not a follower of Ely,[35] for example, "discover" in the parenthetical a value that might then permit an "interpretivist" judge to affirm the constitutionality of a state's Sunday blue laws?[36] Would it matter in such a view that the parenthetical also carries a totally secular alternative meaning?[37]

The fallacy of reasoning, in both these last cases, lies in the interpreter's conviction that certain meanings are embedded in the Constitution. In this sense Ely and Perry do not move us, as a theoretical matter, too far from Raoul Berger's "strict originalism"; they all seek meaning, albeit at different analytical stages, in the text or in the intentions of the Framers. But it suffices to seek, instead, an *interpretive* strategy in the text as a whole. Beyond this, as we have shown, the Framers did not want us to go, for they distrusted an overreliance on the medium of words.

Does this relegate an understanding of the parenthetical to a kind of nihilism or free-flowing subjectivism unbound to text, intention, or history? It is true that my approach looks, at first blush, like Paul Brest's practice—based on rejection of textual authority (and I do believe that

Brest's 1980 article[38] remains the best recent work on constitutional theory). There he identifies a position close to mine here, that of the "moderate originalist" (one interested in, but not fully constrained by, text or intention). Furthermore, Brest describes—without fully elaborating, however—the stance of a moderate originalist interested only in originalist interpretive theory, *not* originalist substantive meaning. But in his example, the application of the cruel and unusual punishment clause to twentieth-century death penalty cases, Brest seems to retreat from the implications of his dichotomy by having his moderate originalist "translate the adopters' intentions into the present in order to apply them to the question at issue."[39] This retreat does an injustice to the creative dichotomy Brest seemed to allow between the Founders' hermeneutics and their substantive positions. If we must constantly "update" the Framers' substantive vision, we are left with the kind of murky generalizations so intensely disliked by the Raoul Bergers of this debate:[40] "But was death," Brest asks, "the same event for inhabitants of the American colonies in the late 18th century as it is two centuries later? Death was not only a much more routine and public phenomenon then, but the fear of death was more effectively contained within a system of religious belief."[41] Although the author dutifully drops a footnote to substantiate this position, the idea that the human dread of death has changed at all through the millennia, or that it somehow was more "routine" or painless two centuries ago, is hardly credible.[42]

To put the argument this way is to impoverish the form of moderate originalism Brest had sketched for us earlier. Suppose our attention to originalist sources is solely to find out what interpretive methodology is asked of us and only then (if we are so asked) to help us detect substantive meanings? The approach I am suggesting tonight minimizes the importance of the adopters' substantive view of the death penalty but heightens our curiosity about their favored hermeneutical approach to the amendment. If there is no specific information on this approach (as there is, for example, about the trial-by-jury provisions),[43] we may fall back on the clear interpretive freedom otherwise allowed us by the Framers' word-skepticism, and not rely further on vague sociological generalizations totally outside of the lawyer's scope of competence.

Thus I am both to the right and the left of Professor Brest: to the right because I do not agree that we can junk the text altogether (his ultimate position, quite logical because of the dilemma he has unnecessarily imposed on the moderate originalist); to the left because I cannot accept the restraints he nonetheless finally imposes on the reader, who is meant to ask, "[H]ow well . . . does the practice contribute to the well-being of our society—or, more narrowly, to the ends of constitutional government?"[44] The first move wrongly unconstrains the reader from seeking the authors' interpretive strategy; the second wrongly moves the reader back into a theoretically contradictory reliance on "the ends of constitutional government," a far more circular move than either Perry's or Ely's.

But what of our "(Sundays excepted)"? To my mind this compelling constitutional detail is as significant as one of Melville's seeming digressions in *Billy Budd*, and we have been asked by Hamilton in fact to look at the document structurally, with a sense of the whole.

The text yields theory in that, by any account of meaning so far proposed, the parenthetical calls our attention to an extralegal, communal concept and assumes—without further explanation—that government should not contradict community. This is, however, not an assignment of "meaning" to the words of the parenthetical themselves, for we have yet to find or to credit any individual's or interpretive group's attempt to attach meaning to the words. All we have done is to recognize that at every point along the hermeneutical spectrum, the sign *Sunday* evokes a package of meanings completely dissociated from the stuff of the rest of the Constitution, and inclining the reader effortlessly toward community and away from prescriptive and normative law.[45] The text yields here an indication of the Federalist authors' belief that values are stronger than laws, that a phenomenon (here Sunday as a special day), so successfully proposed by the authors as to require only two words and no legalistic justification whatsoever, deserves to be constitutionalized. It is immaterial whether the parenthetical embodies religious values or merely the secular value of a day off from work; what it tells us is that law gives way to widely or universally held nonlegal beliefs. "Truths," as Hamilton puts it in *The Federalist* number 31—anticipating Nietzsche—are "antecedent to all reflection or combination."[46] The paucity through two centuries of case law on the parenthetical lends further credence to the simplicity and power of the concept.[47]

And it is precisely that extralegal power that the Framers intended to be part of a word-skeptical hermeneutical approach. I take their ultimate position on constitutional interpretive strategy to be that whoever fights for and wins authoritative status over constitutional meanings—whoever can articulate them in a way that to each generation of readers makes the same cogent sense as they did in framing the document (including the parenthetical)—deserves to win his or her way. Their position grants power over the text to the individual or group who successfully lays claim to it. But the power must be earned, with only partial assistance from the legalistic verbalizing they distrusted, through the call to communal good sense that was their special strength. This is what they expected and hoped to see repeated in each generation.

Faith in language was foreign to them. If it were not, they might have asked us to fix in granite the meanings they themselves brought to their new text. But they thought this both impossible and unwise. Meanings would follow hard upon the text, the result of struggle and compromise.

I do not think they particularly expected legislative majorities or any other egalitarian, function-oriented process to regulate meaning. Indeed, at least if we take *The Federalist* as authority for the point, they envisioned a two-pronged control on majorities, both from the courts and from the executive.[48] A kind of elitism pervades their thinking, hardly foreign, even to revolutionaries, in the neoclassical eighteenth century.[49] The "proper guardians of the public weal" were to control the "transient impulse," as Hamilton calls it in *The Federalist* number 71, the inevitable divergence from embedded political values that occasionally infects majorities. "An elective despotism," Jefferson reminds us, "was not the government we fought for."[50] Truths, at least constitutional truths, are neither majoritarian nor textual. Then where do we find them? Like Sundays, they are embedded as "ideas" in communities. Thus, if certain politicians today seek to correct not only the courts', but even the Congress's, view of the Constitution, the Framers would wish them well. That was exactly the function they prescribed for the executive branch.[51] Such politicians may be wrong (and on the view I've been expressing here, they are wrong) to insist that the Founders wanted the text's meaning to be fixed forever. But paradoxically, in saying so, they are only implementing the interpretive freedom desired by the Founders. Those of us who see the Constitution differently have the responsibility to find our own persuasive parentheticals. We will thus both accept the Nietzschean textual "constraint" and recognize that "there is emancipation in our very bonds."[52]

Following the Rules Laid Down: A Critique of Interpretivism and Neutral Principles

Mark V. Tushnet

The two leading modern constitutional theories are neutral principles and interpretivism. According to the former, "the main constituent of the judicial process is precisely that it must be genuinely principled, resting with respect to every step that is involved in reaching judgment on analysis and reasons quite transcending the immediate result that is achieved . . . [, resting] on grounds of adequate neutrality and generality, tested not only by the instant application but by others that the principles imply."[1] According to the latter, judges "should confine themselves to enforcing norms that are stated or clearly implicit in the written Constitution."[2] Such norms are found by interpreting the text, with recourse when necessary to the intent of the Framers. These formulations are of course only initial, but they state the theories in general terms. Roughly, they tell judges to do what the Constitution says and to do that in good faith, and in this way to commit themselves to the logical implications of what they decide.

Interpretivism and neutral principles are closely associated with the political philosophy of liberalism.[3] Liberalism's psychology posits a world of autonomous individuals, each guided by his or her own idiosyncratic values and goals, none of which can be adjudged more or less legitimate than those held by others. In such a world, people exist as isolated islands of individuality who choose to enter into relations that can metaphorically be characterized as foreign affairs.[4]

Constitutional theory is essentially a concomitant of liberalism. In a world of liberal individualism, the Hobbesian problem of order immediately arises. If one person's values impel that person, for example, to seize the property of another, the victim cannot appeal to some supervening principle to which the assailant must be committed. Individuals may try to protect themselves from assaults on their persons and property by arriving at mutual-assistance agreements with others. But if the parties to such agreements differ significantly in power, the weaker place themselves at the mercy of the stronger. Hobbes's solution was to transfer all authority to an all-powerful sovereign. Hobbes recognized that such a sovereign could itself threaten person and property, but regarded the gain in security against attack by all others to be worth the cost of insecurity against an attack by the sovereign. Those who understood the dangers of unconstrained private power but also feared the unconstrained power of the sovereign needed a different solution. The Glorious Revolution and John Locke seemed to have provided that solution by placing the sovereign itself under the rule of law. But law, of course, cannot rule on its own; it depends on human agents to give it force. In effect, sovereignty was diffused: instead of being concentrated in the person of a monarch, it was shared between the monarch and the legislature. The monarch in exercising his portion of sovereignty would act pursuant to and be constrained by the laws enacted by the legislature in exercising its portion of sovereignty.

The American Revolution eliminated the monarch from sovereignty and thereby sharply posed the problem of legislative tyranny. The Framers' solution, according to one view, was a revised version of Locke's diffused sovereignty, in which power was divided among the separate branches of government, each of which was expected to restrain the others. Yet the separation of powers merely reduced—without eliminating—the risk of oppression. Another view assigns a special role to the judiciary and to the constraints on power embodied in a written constitution. Because the division of power alone was insufficient to reduce the risk of tyranny to an acceptable level, the Framers called on the judiciary to serve a special function beyond its role in diffusing power: by commanding the judges to enforce constraints that the Constitution placed on the other branches, the Framers provided a check on even the few instances of tyranny that they thought might slip through the legislative and executive processes.

As long as the judges who enforced the constraints could themselves be seen to be somehow removed from self-aggrandizement and political contention, the Lockean solution was entirely satisfactory. Over time, however, it became clear—as a result, for example, of the first era of substantive due process and the legal realists' destructive rule skepticism—that judges no less than legislators were political actors, motivated primarily by their own interests and values. The Hobbesian problem was then seen to recur on a higher level. Its solution lay in the development of constitutional theory, which could serve as a constraint on judges by providing some standard, distinct from mere disapproval of results, by which their performance could be evaluated.

Interpretivism and neutral principles, as the two leading dogmas of modern constitutional theory, are thus designed to remedy a central problem of liberal theory by constraining the judiciary sufficiently to prevent judicial tyranny. But it turns out that the two theories are plausible only on the basis of assumptions that themselves challenge important aspects of the liberal world view. Interpretivism attempts to implement the rule of law by assuming that the meanings of words and rules are stable over extended periods; neutral principles does the same by assuming that we all know, because we all participate in the same culture, what the words and rules used by judges mean. In this way, interpretivism and neutral principles attempt to complete the world view of liberalism by explaining how individuals may form a society.

I argue below, however, that the only coherent basis for the requisite continuities of history and meaning is found in the communitarian assumptions of conservative social thought—that, in fact, only these communitarian assumptions can provide the foundations upon which both interpretivism and neutral principles ultimately depend. Conservative social thought places society prior to individuals by developing the implications of the idea that we can understand what we think and do only with reference to the social matrix within which we find ourselves. If I am correct, the liberal account of the social world is inevitably incomplete, for it proves unable to provide a constitutional theory of the sort that it demands without depending on communitarian assumptions that contradict its fundamental individualism.

Interpretivism and neutral principles are two powerful theories, but as we shall see, they cannot stand on liberalism's premises. And conservative social thought, because it rejects the individualist premises that make constitutional theory necessary, need not develop an alternative constitutional theory. The most it must do is elaborate the ways in which we are dependent on each other not merely for peace, as Hobbes would have it, or for material well-being, as Locke would have it, but also for the very conditions under which we can understand and communicate with each other and so form ourselves into a society. This chapter does not attempt this last task. I do note, though, that just as conservatism correctly emphasizes our mutual dependence, liberalism correctly emphasizes our individuality and the threats we pose to each other. It may be that we live in a world of tension, in which no unified social theory but only a dialogue between liberalism and conservatism is possible. In any case, it appears that the construction of a satisfactory constitutional theory will be either impossible or unnecessary.

Interpretivism and Historical Knowledge

It is commonplace to observe that interpretivism has its roots in *Marbury*

v. *Madison*, the Supreme Court's first assertion of the power of judicial review. In that case the Court thought it essential to decide whether a section of the statute organizing the federal court system was consistent with the distribution of judicial authority dictated by the Constitution. Chief Justice Marshall justified the exercise of the power of judicial review by a number of arguments, prominent among which was his appeal to the idea of a written constitution. According to the chief justice, the Constitution was law, albeit supreme law, and thus was to be treated just as other legal documents were. Therefore, when the Court was asked to determine the meaning of the Constitution, it was to do what it did when faced with other legal instruments. This enterprise is characteristically "interpretivist": judges must look both to the words of the document and, because such words as "equal protection" and "due process of law" are too opaque, to the intent of those who wrote the document.

A. The External Critique

For about thirty years, roughly from 1940 to 1970, interpretivism had a bad reputation, largely because, allied as it was to politically conservative positions, it seemed too vulnerable to external critique. That critique is captured by counterposing "the dead hand of the past"—interpretivism—to the need for "a living Constitution." That is, a strict adherence to interpretivism seems to require that we find legislation valid unless it violates values that are both old-fashioned and seriously outmoded. The interpretivist deflects this criticism by invoking the specter of judicial tyranny. Of course, the response goes, interpretivism does mean that we will be subject to the risk that the legislature will develop novel forms of tyranny. Empirically, however, novelty in tyranny is relatively rare, and because the Framers of the Constitution were rather smart, they managed to preclude most of the really troublesome forms of tyranny through the Constitution they wrote. Some risk of novel forms of tyranny remains, but that risk is significantly smaller than the risk of judicial tyranny that would arise were we to allow judges to cut free from interpreting the text. In this sense, according to the interpretivist, we are indeed better off being bound by the dead hand of the past than being subjected to the whims of willful judges trying to make the Constitution live.

This response is, I think, fairly powerful. But it rests in part on an empirical claim about novelty, a claim that is open to obvious external attacks. First, the possibilities of innovative legislative tyranny are in fact great because the social and material world in which we live has changed drastically since 1789. Wiretapping provides a standard example of innovation that interpretivism can accommodate only with great difficulty. The drafters of the Fourth Amendment obviously could not have contemplated wiretapping when they thought about searches. Yet if interpretivism means that we cannot respond to that kind of innovation, it fails to guard against legislative tyranny. Wiretapping is thus a prime illustration for the claim that, because of the broader scope of legislative action, the domain of innovation in legislative tyranny is more extensive than that in judicial tyranny.

Moreover, if we look to the historical record, we discover that, at least according to the interpretivist account, the Framers had a fairly limited conception of legislative tyranny. For example, Leonard Levy, the most careful recent student of the history of the First Amendment, concludes that the Framers did not intend it to prohibit sedition laws, that they meant it to prohibit only prior restraints on publication and not subsequent punishment, and that they did not intend the amendment to insulate speech from regulation simply because the speech was political.[5] Similarly, the Bill of Rights provided protection, such as it was, against encroachment only by the national government, not by the states. Because a genuine interpretivism would thus protect only against limited varieties of legislative tyranny, it fails to achieve its objective. When the real risks of legislative tyranny are recognized, they appear more serious than the prospects of judicial tyranny.

B. The Internal Critique

The internal critique cuts deeper; it undermines in several steps the plausibility of interpretivism as a constitutional theory. The first step is an argument that interpretivism must rest on an account of historical knowledge more subtle than the naive presumption that past attitudes and intentions are directly accessible to present understanding. The second step identifies the most plausible such account, the view—sometimes called hermeneutics—that historical understanding requires an imaginative transposition of former world views into the categories of our own. The third step is an argument that such an imaginative transposition implies an ambiguity that is inconsistent with the project of liberal constitutional theory (and interpretivism). The project of imaginative transposition can be carried through in a number of different ways, with a number of different results, none of which is more "correct" than the others. The existence of such an indeterminacy means that interpretivism, unless it falls back on nonliberal assumptions, cannot constrain judges sufficiently to carry out the liberal project of avoiding judicial tyranny.

I. Interpretivist History

We can approach the problems of historical knowledge by noting the standard criticism of "law office" history. Interpretivism calls for a historical inquiry into the intent of the Framers. That inquiry is conducted by lawyers imbued with the adversary ethic. The standard criticism is that lawyers are bad historians because they overemphasize fragmentary evidence and minimize significant bodies of conflicting or complicating evidence in the service of their partisan goals.

Though some lawyers surely deploy the kind of history thus criticized, interpretivism need not rest on that sort of bad history. But the difficulty goes deeper. Interpretivist history requires both definite answers (because it is part of a legal system in which judgment is awarded to one side or the other) and clear answers (because it seeks to constrain judges and thereby to avoid judicial tyranny). The universal experience of historians, however, belies the interpretivists' expectations. Where the interpretivist seeks clarity and definiteness, the historian finds ambiguity. I have already mentioned the interpretivist view of the history of the First Amendment. But if we were able to sit down for a talk with Thomas Jefferson about civil liberties, a good historian will tell us, we would hear an apparently confused blend of assertions: libertarian theory, opposition to the enactment of sedition laws, the use of sedition laws once in office, and so on. Jefferson's "intent" on the issue of free speech is nothing more than this complex set of responses.

2. Intentions and Liberal Thought

The interpretivist project requires the discovery and use of unambiguous historical facts; the only way that interpretivists can find such facts is to embrace what are fundamentally flawed historiographic methods. Underlying the interpretivists' reliance on these methods is the view that individuals are the primary units of human experience and history and that larger social wholes are best understood as aggregates of such individuals. From this view, it follows that an individual's beliefs, intentions, and desires have their character independent of, or prior to, the larger social and conceptual context in which they occur, a context that the liberal vision sees as a product of all antecedent individual perspectives. The project of the liberal historian thus is to study the historical record for evidence of what the intentions and beliefs of historical actors actually were.

On this account, intentions must be real, determinate entities; the interpretivist must be able to identify and understand specific intentions of the Framers with respect to one part of the Constitution or another. I can introduce the difficulties with this approach to historical knowledge by reference to two recent works on American history.

Leo Marx's *Machine in the Garden* discusses the ways in which

Americans thought about technological change. One of Marx's central items of evidence, used to great effect, is a painting of a pastoral scene through which a railroad train is peacefully passing.[6] Marx's point of view suggests that historians cannot reconstruct a world in which railroads did not exist but everything else remained the same. The existence of railroads affected how people thought about their relation to the natural world, and those conceptions in turn affected the desire to invest and the value placed on growth. As Marx shows, perspectives, beliefs, and intentions are thoroughly interwoven with the concrete social and economic realities of their day. Marx's insight is that the contents or meanings of beliefs and intentions are shaped by the entire societal context in which those beliefs and intentions arise and that they in turn alter. When interpretivists presume that they can detach the meanings that the Framers gave to the words they used from the entire complex of meanings that the Framers gave to their political vocabulary as a whole and from the larger political, economic, and intellectual world in which they lived, interpretivists slip into the error of thinking that they can grasp historical parts without embracing the historical whole.

3. The Hermeneutical Alternative

These examples raise doubts about easy acceptance of an interpretivism whose theory of historical knowledge presumes that past beliefs and intentions are determinate and identifiable. Those doubts can be deepened by comparing this theory of history to its main rival, the hermeneutical tradition.[7] In that tradition, historical knowledge is seen as "the interpretive understanding of [the] meanings" that actors give their actions.[8] The historian must enter the minds of his or her subjects, see the world as they saw it, and understand it in their own terms. Justice Brandeis's eloquent opinion in *Whitney* v. *California*,[9] which recreates one version of the world view of the Framers, is the best example in the case law of a hermeneutical effort to understand the past. Brandeis's reconstruction, though partial and largely unsupported by specific references to what any Framer actually said, does in the end bring us into the Framers' world:

> Those who won our independence believed that the final end of the State was to make men free to develop their faculties; and that in its government the deliberative forces should prevail over the arbitrary. They valued liberty both as an end and as a means. They believed liberty to be the secret of happiness and courage to be the secret of liberty. They believed that freedom to think as you will and to speak as you think are means indispensable to the discovery and spread of political truth; that without free speech and assembly discussion would be futile; that with them, discussion affords ordinarily adequate protection

against the dissemination of noxious doctrine; that the greatest menace to freedom is an inert people; that public discussion is a political duty; and that this should be a fundamental principle of the American government. They recognized the risks to which all human institutions are subject. But they knew that order cannot be secured merely through fear of punishment for its infraction; that it is hazardous to discourage thought, hope, and imagination; that fear breeds repression; that repression breeds hate; that hate menaces stable government; that the path of safety lies in the opportunity to discuss freely supposed grievances and proposed remedies; and that the fitting remedy for evil counsels is good ones. Believing in the power of reason as applied through public discussion, they eschewed silence coerced by law—the argument of force in its worst form. Recognizing the occasional tyrannies of governing majorities, they amended the Constitution so that free speech and assembly should be guaranteed.[10]

Here Brandeis recalls to us the Framers' belief in a republic dominated by civic virtue. It matters not very much that their views on specific aspects of governmental design may have differed in detail from Brandeis's reconstruction; what matters is that the Framers designed a government that comported with their sense of a world in which civic virtue reigned. The significance and the ramifications of this sense are what Brandeis strove to capture, and they are what interpretivism, too, must recognize to be central. The ways in which people understand the world give meaning to the words that they use, and only by recreating such global understandings can we interpret the document the Framers wrote.

The dilemma of interpretivism is that, if it is to rely on a real grasp of the Framers' intentions—and only this premise gives interpretivism its intuitive appeal—its method must be hermeneutical, but if it adopts a hermeneutical approach, it is foreclosed from achieving the determinacy about the Framers' meanings necessary to serve its underlying goals. The interpretivists' premise of determinate intentions is essential to their project of developing constraints on judges. But the hermeneutical approach to historical understanding requires that we abandon this premise. In imaginatively entering the world of the past, we not only reconstruct it, but—more importantly for present purposes—we also creatively construct it. For such creativity is the only way to bridge the gaps between that world and ours. The past, particularly the aspects that the interpretivists care about, is in its essence indeterminate; the interpretivist project cannot be carried to its conclusion.

Consider an example. In *Brown* v. *Board of Education* the Supreme Court said, "In approaching this problem, we cannot turn the clock back to 1868 when the [Fourteenth] Amendment was adopted. . . . We must consider public education in the light of its full development and its present place in American life throughout the Nation."[11] Chief Justice

Warren was not rejecting the use of historical inquiries in constitutional law; he was instead approaching the task of discovering the past in a hermeneutical way.

Suppose that we did turn back the clock so that we could talk to the Framers of the Fourteenth Amendment. If we asked them whether the amendment outlawed segregation in public schools, they would answer no. But we could pursue our conversation by asking them what they had in mind when they thought about public education. We would find out that they had in mind a relatively new and peripheral social institution designed (say) to civilize the lower classes. In contrast, they thought that freedom of contract was extremely important because it was the foundation of individual achievement, and they certainly wanted to outlaw racial discrimination with respect to this freedom. Returning to 1954 and the question for the Court in *Brown*, we might, in an antic moment, challenge the interpretivists with their own weapons. Our hermeneutical enterprise has shown us that public education as it exists today—a central institution for the achievement of individual goals—is in fact the functional equivalent not of public education in 1868, but of freedom of contract in 1868. Thus, *Brown* was correctly decided in light of a hermeneutical interpretivism.

The problem raised by this interpretation of *Brown* is that the need to identify functional equivalents over time necessarily imports significant indeterminacy—and therefore discretion—into the interpretivist account; alternative hermeneutical accounts of *Brown* are also possible. Consider, for example, the implications of Herbert Wechsler's argument that *Brown* was problematic because it failed to consider the effect of desegregation on the interest of white parents and students in associating only with those of whom they approved.[12] A hermeneutical defense of that criticism might argue that education today is an important part of American civil religion and that it is therefore the secular functional equivalent of true religion in 1868. The Framers would certainly have considered forced association in churches to be improper; thus, Wechsler's point is established. Interpretivists claim that their approach is at least able to limit judges, but, by allowing judges to look hermeneutically for functional equivalents, interpretivism reintroduces the discretion that it was intended to eliminate.

But the difficulty runs deeper than the indeterminacy of identifications of functional equivalents. The hermeneutical tradition tells us that we cannot understand the acts of those in the past without entering into their mental world. Because we live in our own world, the only way to begin the hermeneutical enterprise is by thinking about what in our world initially seems like what people in the past talked and thought about. Usually we begin with a few areas in which we and they use the same rather abstract words to talk about apparently similar things. Thus, we and the Framers share a concern for democracy, human rights, and limited government. But as we read what the Framers said about democracy and limited government, we notice discontinuities: they described their polity as a democratic one, for example, when we would think it obviously nondemocratic. As we examine this evidence, we adjust our understanding and attempt to take account of the "peculiarities." With a great deal of imaginative effort, we can indeed at the end of the process understand their world, because we have become immersed in it. But the understanding we achieve is not the unique, correct image of the Framers' world. On the contrary, our imaginative immersion is only one of a great many possible reconstructions of that segment of the past, a reconstruction shaped not only by the character of the past, but also by our own interests, concerns, and preconceptions. The imagination that we have used to adjust and readjust our understandings makes it impossible to claim that any one reconstruction is uniquely correct. The past shapes the materials on which we use our imaginations; our interests, concerns, and preconceptions shape our imaginations themselves.

Robert Gordon has offered a similar, but significantly different, account of the hermeneutical problem that faces us when we try to uncover the world of the Framers:

> The old text will be rendered almost wholly archaic if it can be shown to embody a set of conceptions—about human nature, property, virtue, freedom, representation, necessity, causation, and so forth—that was a unique configuration for its time and in some ways strikingly unlike what we believe to be our own. One naturally thinks in this connection of the remarkable recent work that has made the thought of this country's founders more intelligible by locating its terminology and major preoccupations in a Whig "republican" ideology with a foundation in Renaissance political thought. The lawyer who turns to the best available perspectives on the thinking behind the American Constitution may find herself in the position of the French humanist lawyers who hoped to uncover the universal basis for their own jurisprudence by freeing the Roman *Corpus Juris* from medieval corruptions, and then did such thorough scholarly work as to persuade many of them of Rome's irrelevance.[13]

The conclusion for the French lawyers was that Rome was irrelevant, and Gordon apparently would have us draw the same conclusion about the Framers. In fact, the conclusion for a hermeneutical interpretivism in consititutional law is weaker, but more interesting. The gap between the Framers and us is not nearly as wide as the gap between Rome and the French humanists. The intellectual world of the Framers is one that bears some resemblance, which is more than merely genetic, to ours. A hermeneutical interpretivism would force us to think about the social contexts of the resemblances and dissimilarities. It would lead us not to despair over the gulf that separates the Framers' world from ours, but rather to the crafting of creative links between their ideals and our own. But in recognizing the magnitude of the creative component, we inevitably lose faith in the ability of interpretivism to provide the constraints on judges that liberal constitutional theory demands.

Nonetheless, the hermeneutical tradition does identify something that constitutional theory should take seriously. The point is not, as some fanatic adherents of hermeneutical method might have it, that, because the world of the past is not the world in which we have developed our ways of understanding how others act, we can never understand that past world. That view would go too far. We can gain an interpretive understanding of the past by working from commonalities in the use of large abstractions to reach the unfamiliar particulars of what those abstractions really meant in the past. The commonalities are what make the past *our* past; they are the links between two segments of a single community that extends over time.[14] The commonalities are both immanent in our history and constructed by us as we reflect on what our history is. Interpretivism goes wrong in thinking that the commonalities are greater than they really are, but we would go equally wrong if we denied that they exist. The task is to think through the implications of our continued dedication to the large abstractions when the particulars of the world have changed so drastically. That project will lead us to face questions about the kind of community we have and want.

Neutral Principles and the Recognition of Rules

The hermeneutical tradition suggests that historical discontinuities are so substantial that interpretivism must make incoherent claims because it can achieve the necessary determinacy of past intentions only at the cost of an implausible claim about consistency of meaning across time. The theory of neutral principles fails for similar reasons. It requires that we develop an account of consistency of meaning—particularly of the meaning of rules or principles—within liberal society. Yet the atomistic premises of liberalism treat each of us as autonomous individuals whose choices and values are independent of those made and held by others. These premises make it exceedingly difficult to develop such an account of consistent meaning. The autonomous producer of choice and value is also an autonomous producer of meaning.

The rule of law, according to the liberal conception, is meant to protect us against the exercise of arbitrary power. The theory of neutral principles asserts that a requirement of consistency, the core of the ideal of the rule of law, places sufficient bounds on judges to reduce the risk of arbitrariness to an acceptable level. The question is whether the concepts of neutrality and consistency can be developed in ways that are adequate for the task. My discussion examines various candidates for a definition of neutrality, beginning with a crude definition and moving toward more sophisticated ones. Yet each candidate suffers from similar defects: each fails to provide the kinds of constraints on judges that liberalism requires. Some candidates seek to limit the results judges might reach, others the methods they may use. The supposed substantive bounds that consistency imposes on judges, however, are either empty or parasitic on other substantive theories of constitutional law, and the methodological bounds are either empty or dependent on a sociology of law that undermines liberalism's assumptions about society.

A. Neutral Method

If neutrality is to serve as a meaningful guide, it must be understood not as a standard for the content of principles, but rather as a constraint on the process by which principles are selected, justified, and applied. Thus, the remaining candidate explications of neutrality all focus on the judicial process and the need for "neutral *application*." This focus transfers our attention from the principles themselves to the judges who purport to use them.

I. Prospective Application

What then are methodologically neutral principles? To Wechsler, such principles are identified primarily by a forward-looking aspect: a judge who invokes a principle in a specific instance commits himself or herself to invoking it in future cases that are relevantly identical.[15] For example, a judge who justifies the holding in *Brown* v. *Board of Education* that segregated schools are unconsitutional by invoking the principle that the state may not take race into account in any significant policy decision is thereby also committed to holding state-developed affirmative action programs unconstitutional. The judge's interior · monologue involves specifying the principle about to be invoked, imagining future cases and their proper resolution, determining whether those cases are different from the present one in any ways that the proposed principle itself says are relevant, and asking whether the principle yields the proper results. But there is a conceptual problem that robs the very idea of prospective neutrality of any normative force.

Neutral application requires that we be able to identify *the* principle that justified the result in case 1 in order to be sure that it is neutrally applied in case 2. This requirement, however, cannot be fulfilled, because there are always a number of justificatory principles available to make sense of case 1 and a number of techniques to select the "true" basis of case 1. Of course, the opinion in case 1 will articulate a principle that purports to support the result. But the thrust of introductory law courses is to show that the principles offered in opinions are never good enough. And this indefiniteness bedevils—and liberates—not only the commentators and the lawyers and judges subsequently dealing with the decision; it equally affects the author of the opinion.

I draw my example from Michael Perry's discussion of the abortion funding cases.[16] Perry, in the best recent application of the theory of neutral principles, attempts to identify the operative principle in *Roe* v. *Wade*, a highly abstract principle concerning the relationship between governmental powers and constitutional protections, and to criticize the Court's later ruling in *Harris* v. *McRae* for inconsistency with that principle.

In 1973, the Supreme Court held in *Roe* v. *Wade* that state criminal statutes restricting the availability of abortions are unconstitutional.[17] Seven years later, it upheld legislation that denied public funds for abortions to those otherwise qualified for public assistance in paying for medical care.[18] Perry contends that the abortion funding decision is "plainly wrong" because it "is inconsistent with the narrowest possible coherent reading" of *Roe*.[19] Perry extracts that reading as follows: the Court struck down the statutes in *Roe* because the pregnant woman's interest in terminating her pregnancy was adjudged to be weightier than the government's interest in preventing the taking of the life of the fetus. According to Perry, this conclusion entails that "*no* governmental action can be predicated on the view that . . . abortion is per se morally objectionable."[20] Perry's premise is that government is permitted to use a factor as a predicate for restrictive legislation only if that factor is entitled to no constitutional protection.

Perry rejects as "deeply flawed" and "fundamentally confused" the position taken by the Court in the funding cases and repeated by Peter Westen.[21] That position is that *Roe* barred the government from criminalizing abortions only because criminal sanctions placed an *undue* burden on the woman's interest in termination of the pregnancy; refusing to fund abortions does not similarly burden that interest. Perry claims that *Roe* is coherent only if it precludes the government from taking *any* action predicated on the view that abortion is wrong. To allow the government to take such action would force us to the "rather strange" position that the Constitution simultaneously both permits the government "to establish a legal principle" and "protect[s] a person's interest in disregarding that principle once established."[22]

I confess that I have thought about this supposed paradox as hard as I can and that I do not see anything terribly strange about it; whether we think the position is strange in fact depends on how we define principles and interests. The governing general principle might be that the government can take all actions predicated on any given moral view except insofar as they unduly burden some individual interest. Perry presumably thinks that such a principle is inconsistent with other areas of constitutional law, for it recognizes a kind of acceptance of civil disobedience that is not recognized elsewhere in the Constitution.[23] But Westen gives the example of *Coker* v. *Georgia*, in which the Supreme Court held that, although Georgia could make unaggravated rape—if such there be—a crime because it is morally wrong, a state could not constitutionally make it a capital offense.[24] And even if Perry is right in thinking that we do not use the principle in other areas, it remains open to say that abortion is special because, for example, it imposes on us an agonizing dilemma between terminating (potential) life and eliminating unique demands on the pregnant woman. It may be that the two horns of this dilemma pose problems more difficult than those posed in other areas of constitutional law. Thus, if the entire area of abortion is relevantly different from other areas of constitutional law, it would not be nonneutral to adopt a special rule in abortion cases.

I have developed the argument this far by accepting Perry's identification of the "narrowest possible coherent principle" justifying *Roe*. But I could have directly attacked his specification of the narrowest principle. Here are two other candidates: (1) *Roe* rests on the principle that the state may take no action that would strongly influence a woman's decision to have an abortion. (2) *Roe* rests on the principle that the decision to have an abortion is entitled to special constitutional protection, the precise contours of which will vary depending on the circumstances. The funding cases are arguably consistent with both principles, and, strikingly, the first of these principles might make it unconstitutional for a state to subsidize abortions. Both principles would of course have to be fleshed out before they could be put to work.[25] But the point is that Perry in fact has identified neither the only nor the narrowest principle on which *Roe* could be justified.

The argument that I have just made can be generalized. At the moment a decision is announced, we cannot identify the principle that it embodies. Even when we take account of the language of the opinion, each decision can be traced to many different possible principles, and we often learn the justifying principle of case 1 only when a court in case 2 states it. Behind the court's statement of what case 1 meant lies all the creativity to which the hermeneutical theory of historical understanding directed our attention. When *Roe* was decided, we might have thought that it rested on Perry's principle, but the funding cases show us that we were "wrong" and that *Roe* "in fact" rested on one of the alternatives spelled out above. The theory of neutral principles thus loses almost all of its constraining force when neutrality has a prospective meaning.

What is left is something like a counsel to judges that they be sincere within the limits of their ability. But this formulation hardly provides a reassuring constraint on judicial willfulness.

2. Retrospective Application

Although Wechsler framed the neutral principles theory in prospective terms, it might be saved by recasting it in retrospective terms. The theory would then impose as a necessary condition for justification the requirement that a decision be consistent with the relevant precedents. This tack links the theory to general approaches to precedent-based judicial decision-making in nonconstitutional areas. It also captures the natural way in which we raise questions about neutrality. The prospective theory requires that we pose hypothetical future cases, apply the principle, and ask whether the judges really meant to resolve the hypothetical cases as the principle seems to require. Because the hypothetical cases have not arisen, we cannot know the answer; we can do little more than raise our eyebrows, as Wechsler surely did, and emphasize the "really" as we ask the question in a skeptical tone.

In contrast, the retrospective theory encourages concrete criticism of the sort that Perry produced. We need only compare case 2, which is now decided, with case 1 to see if a principle from case 1 has been neutrally applied in case 2. But if the retrospective demand is merely that the opinion in case 2 deploy some reading of the earlier case from which the holding in case 2 follows, the openness of the precedents means that the demand can always be satisfied. And if the demand is rather that the holding be derived from the principles actually articulated in the relevant precedents, differences between case 2 and the precedents will inevitably demand a degree of reinterpretation of the old principles. New cases always present issues different from those settled by prior cases. Thus, to decide a new case, a judge must take some liberties with the old principles, if they are to be applied at all. There is, however, no principled way to determine how many liberties can be taken; hence this second reading of the retrospective approach likewise provides no meaningful constraints.

The central problem here is that, given the difficulty of isolating a single principle for which a given precedent stands, we lack any criteria for distinguishing between cases that depart from and those that conform to the principles of their precedents. In fact, any case can compellingly be placed in either category. Although such a universal claim cannot be validated by example, examples can at least make the claim plausible. Therefore, the following paragraphs present a case that simultaneously departs from and conforms to its precedents.

The case is *Griswold* v. *Connecticut*, in which the Supreme Court held that a state could not constitutionally prohibit the dissemination of contraceptive information or devices to married people.[26] *Griswold* relied in part on *Pierce* v. *Society of Sisters*,[27] which held unconstitutional a requirement that children attend public rather than private schools, and *Meyer* v. *Nebraska*,[28] which held that a state could not prohibit the teaching of foreign languages to young children. In *Griswold*, the Court said that these cases relied on a constitutionally protected interest, conveniently labeled "privacy," that was identical to the interest implicated in the contraceptive case.

On one view, *Griswold* tortures these precedents. Both were old-fashioned due process cases, which emphasized interference "with the calling of modern language teachers . . . and with the power of parents to control the education of their own."[29] On this view, the most one can fairly find in *Meyer* and *Pierce* is a principle about freedom of inquiry that is rather narrower than a principle of privacy. Yet of course one can say with equal force that *Griswold* identifies for us the true privacy principle of *Meyer* and *Pierce*, in the same way that the abortion funding cases identify the true principle of *Roe* v. *Wade*. Just as hermeneutical interpretivism emphasizes the creativity that is involved when judges impute to the Framers a set of intentions, so the retrospective approach to neutral principles must recognize the extensive creativity exercised by a judge when he or she imputes to a precedent "the" principle that justifies both the precedent and the judge's present holding.

Once again the example illustrates a general point. In a legal system with a relatively extensive body of precedent and with well-developed techniques of legal reasoning, it will always be possible to show how today's decision is consistent with the relevant past decisions. Conversely, however, it will also always be possible to show how today's decision is inconsistent with the precedents. This symmetry, of course, drains "consistency" of any normative content. Just as we were forced to abandon prospective neutrality of application, we are now also forced to abandon retrospective neutrality of application as a source of meaningful constraints in a mature legal system like ours.

The difficulties with this variety of neutral principles theory are on a par with the problems in understanding interpretivism that were noted earlier. Understanding the intentions of the Framers required a special kind of creative re-creation of the past; the creativity involved in such a re-creation dashed any hopes that interpretivism could effectively constrain judicial decisions, because many alternative re-creations of the Framers' intentions on any given issue are always possible. In the same way, the result of the inquiry into retrospective neutral principles theory indicates that, though it is possible to discuss a given decision's consistency with previous precedents, requiring consistency of this kind similarly fails to constrain judges sufficiently and thereby fails to advance the underlying liberal project.

3. The Craft Interpretation

This critique of the retrospective-application interpretation points the way to a more refined version—what I will term the craft interpretation—of the calls of the neutral principles theorists for retrospective consistency. The failings of this final alternative bring out the underlying reasons that the demand for consistency cannot do the job expected of it.

The preceding discussion has reminded us that each decision reworks its precedents. A decision picks up some threads that received little emphasis before, and places great stress on them. It deprecates what seemed important before by emphasizing the factual setting of the precedents. The techniques are well known; indeed, learning them is at the core of a good legal education. But they are techniques. This recognition suggests that we attempt to define consistency as a matter of craft. When push comes to shove, in fact, adherents of neutral principles simply offer us lyrical descriptions of the sense of professionalism in lieu of sharper characterizations of the constraints on judges. Charles Black, for example, attempts to resolve the question whether law can rely on neutral principles by depicting "the art of law" living between the two poles of subjective preference and objective validation in much the same way that "the art of music has its life somewhere between traffic noise and a tuning fork—more disciplined by far than the one, with an unfathomably complex inner discipline of its own, far richer than the other, with inexhaustible variety of resource."[30] The difficulty then is to specify the limits to permissible craftiness. One limit may be that a judge cannot lie about the precedents—for example, by grossly mischaracterizing the facts. And Black adds that "decision [must] be taken in knowledge of and with consideration of certainly known facts of public life," such as the fact that segregation necessarily degrades blacks.[31] But these limits are clearly not terribly restrictive, and no one has suggested helpful others.

If the craft interpretation cannot specify limits to craftiness, another alternative is to identify some decisions that are within and some that are outside the limits in order to provide the basis for an inductive and intuitive generalization. As the following discussion indicates, however, it turns out that the limits of craft are so broad that in any interesting case any reasonably skilled lawyer can reach whatever result he or she wants. The craft interpretation thus fails to constrain the results that a reasonably skilled judge can reach, and leaves the judge free to enforce his or her personal values, as long as the opinions enforcing those values are well written. Such an outcome is inconsistent with the requirements of liberalism in that, once again, the demand for neutral principles fails in any appreciable way to limit the possibility of judicial tyranny.

The debate over the propriety of the result in *Roe* v. *Wade*[32] illustrates this problem. It seems to be generally agreed that, as a matter of simple craft, Justice Blackmun's opinion for the Court was dreadful. The central issue before the Court was whether a pregnant woman had a constitutionally protected interest in terminating her pregnancy. When his opinion reached that issue, Justice Blackmun simply listed a number of cases in which "a right of personal privacy, or a guarantee of certain areas or zones of privacy," had been recognized. Then he said, "This right of privacy, whether it be founded in the Fourteenth Amendment's concept of personal liberty . . . or . . . in the Ninth Amendment's reservation of rights to the people, is broad enough to encompass a woman's decision whether or not to terminate her pregnancy."[33] And that was it. I will provisionally concede that this "argument" does not satisfy the requirements of the craft.

But the conclusion that we are to draw faces two challenges: it is either uninteresting or irrelevant to constitutional theory. Insofar as *Roe* gives us evidence, we can conclude that Justice Blackmun is a terrible judge. The point of constitutional theory, though, would seem to be to keep judges in line. If the result in *Roe* can be defended by judges more skilled than Justice Blackmun, the requirements of the craft would mean only that good judges can do things that bad judges cannot without subjecting themselves to professional criticism. For example, John Ely argues that, although *Roe* is beyond acceptable limits, *Griswold* is within them, though perhaps near the edge.[34] Justice Douglas's opinion for the Court in *Griswold* identified a number of constitutional provisions that in his view explicitly protected one or another aspect of personal privacy. The opinion then noted that the Court had in the past protected other interests closely related to those expressly protected. By arguing that those "penumbral" interests overlapped in the area of marital use of contraceptives, Justice Douglas could hold the challenged statute unconstitutional.

If *Griswold* is acceptable, we need only repeat its method in *Roe*. Indeed, Justice Douglas followed just that course in a brilliant concurring opinion.[35] And even if *Griswold*'s logic is rejected, skilled lawyers could still rewrite *Roe* to defend Justice Blackmun's outcome. There is in fact a cottage industry of constitutional law scholars who concoct revised opinions for controversial decisions. Thus, the craft interpretation of neutrality in application is ultimately uninteresting for reasons that we have already seen. At most it provides a standard to measure the competence of judges, a standard that by itself is insufficient to constrain adequately the risk of tyranny.

The other difficulty with the craft interpretation runs deeper. Craft limitations make sense only if we can agree what the craft is. But consider the craft of "writing novels." Its practice includes Trollope writing *The Eustace Diamonds*, Joyce writing *Finnegan's Wake*, and Mailer writing *The Executioner's Song*.[36] We might think of Justice Blackmun's opinion in *Roe* as an innovation akin to Joyce's or Mailer's. It is the totally unreasoned judicial opinion. To say that it does not look like Justice Powell's decision in some other case is like saying that a cubist "portrait" does not look like its subject as a member of the Academy would paint it. The observation is true, but irrelevant both to the enterprise in which the artist or judge was engaged and to our ultimate assessment of his product.

B. Rules and Institutions

We can now survey our progress in the attempt to define "neutral principles." Each proposed definition left us with judges who could enforce their personal values unconstrained by the suggested version of the neutrality requirement. Some of the more sophisticated candidates, such as the craft interpretation, seemed plausible because they appealed to an intuitive sense that the institution of judging involves people who are guided by and committed to general rules applied consistently. But the very notions of generality and consistency can be specified only by reference to an established institutional setting. We can know what we mean by "acting consistently" only if we understand the institution of judging in our society. Thus, neutral principles theory proves unable to satisfy its demand for rule-guided judicial decision-making in a way that can constrain or define the judicial institution; in the final analysis, it is the institution—or our conception of it—that constrains the concept of rule-guidedness.

Consider the following multiple-choice question: "Which pair of numbers comes next in the series 1, 3, 5, 7? (*a*) 9, 11; (*b*) 11, 13; (*c*) 25, 18." It is easy to show that any of the answers is correct. The first is correct if the rule generating the series is "list the odd numbers"; the second is correct if the rule is "list the odd prime numbers"; and the third is correct if a more complex rule generates the series. Thus, if asked to follow the underlying rule—the "principle" of the series—we can justify a tremendous range of divergent answers by constructing the rule so that it generates the answer that we want. As the legal realists showed, this result obtains for legal as well as mathematical rules. The situation in law might be thought to differ, because judges try to articulate the rules they use. But even when an earlier case identifies the rule that it invokes, only a vision of the contours of the judicial role constrains judges' understanding of what counts as applying the rule. Without such a vision, there will always be a diversity of subsequent uses of the rule that could fairly be called consistent applications of it.

There is, however, something askew in this anarchic conclusion. After all, we know that no test-maker would accept (c) as an answer to the mathematical problem; and indeed we can be fairly confident that test-makers would not include both (a) and (b) as possible answers, because the underlying rules that generate them are so obvious that they make the question fatally ambiguous. Another example may sharpen the point. The examination for those seeking drivers' licenses in the District of Columbia includes this question: "What is responsible for most automobile accidents? (a) The car; (b) the driver; (c) road conditions." Anyone who does not know immediately that the answer is (b) does not understand what the testing enterprise is all about.

In these examples, we know something about the rule to follow only because we are familiar with the social practices of intelligence testing and drivers' education. That is, the answer does not follow from a rule that can be uniquely identified without specifying something about the substantive practices. Similarly, although we can, as I have argued elsewhere, use standard techniques of legal argument to draw from the decided cases the conclusion that the Constitution requires socialism,[37] we know that no judge will in the near future draw that conclusion. But the failure to reach that result is not ensured because the practice of "following rules" or neutral application of the principles inherent in the decided cases precludes a judge from doing so. Rather, it is ensured because judges in contemporary America are selected in a way that keeps them from thinking that such arguments make sense. This branch of the argument thus makes a sociological point about neutral principles. Neither the principles nor any reconstructed version of a theory that takes following rules as its focus can be neutral in the sense that liberalism requires, because taken by itself, an injunction to follow the rules tells us nothing of substance. If such a theory constrains judges, it does so only because judges, before they turn to the task of finding neutral principles for the case at hand, have implicitly accepted some image of what their role in shaping and applying rules in controverted cases ought to be.

Conclusion

The critiques of interpretivism and neutral principles have each led to the same point. To be coherent, each theory requires that our understandings of social institutions be stable. Interpretivism requires that judges today be able to trace historical continuities between the institutions the Framers knew and those that contemporary judges know. The theory of neutral principles requires that judges be able to rely on a shared conception of the proper role of judicial reasoning. The critiques have established that there are no determinate continuities derivable from history or legal principle. Rather, judges must choose which conceptions to rely on. Their choice is constrained, but explaining the constraints demands a sociological explanation of the ways in which the system within which they operate is deeply entrenched and resistant to change. If this sociological explanation is to have not merely descriptive validity, but normative force as well, we find ourselves drawn into the domain of conservative social theory, in which variable individual conceptions are seen to be derivative from—and subsidiary to—an underlying societal perspective.

The problem faced by both judge and constitutional theorist is how to find or construct the requisite shared conceptions. This problem is analogous to the interpretive difficulties that confront us in many aspects of our social experience. Consider an ordinary conversation between two people. Alice hears Arthur use the word *arbogast*. She thinks she knows what he means, but as the conversation continues Alice realizes that Arthur is using the word in a way that comes to seem a little strange. She interrupts, so that Arthur can explain what he means. But things get worse. His explanation shows that his entire vocabulary rests on the way that he has lived until that moment. Because Arthur's life is by definition different from Alice's, Alice finds herself left with only an illusory understanding of what Arthur says. Her task is then to identify the point at which she can, so to speak, think her way into Arthur's life, so that she can understand what he means through understanding how he has developed. In this story, "understanding what Arthur means when he says 'arbogast' " plays the role of "following the rule in *Roe* v. *Wade*" or "remaining faithful to the Framers' meaning of 'due process.' "

The question in each case is how to overcome the gaps that reflection has revealed. Of course, we go along each day with some taken-for-granted understandings of the world. But anyone can disrupt what is taken for granted simply by placing it in question. Courts are institutions in which challenges to the taken-for-granted may be made as a matter of course, and the individualist premises of the liberal vision both make such challenges inevitable and demand that they be heard. But if society is to be stable, those challenges must be rebuffed in ways that preserve the shared societal understandings.

Here the parable of the conversation is central. As experience has taught us, Alice and Arthur need not give up in despair; if they keep talking, they can build bridges between their two idiosyncratic dialects. Just as the historian can understand the past through hermeneutical efforts, so can we understand each other by creating a community of understanding. But the parable also reminds us that we cannot assume that people who talk to each other are part of such a community merely because they seem to be speaking the same language. Similarly, communities of understanding are not defined by geographical boundaries or by allegiance to a single constitution. They are painstakingly created by people who enter into certain kinds of relations and share certain kinds of experiences.

Some have argued that such relations demand complete equality of power and of access to material resources; others identify the requisite experiences as confrontations with scarcity or similar natural kinds of human experience. For my purposes, I need not identify exactly what the prerequisites for a community of understanding are. It is enough simply to recognize that we must develop a shared system of meanings to make either interpretivism or neutral principles coherent. But in developing such a system, we will destroy the need for constitutional theory, predicated as that need is on liberal individualism; the problem identified by Hobbes, Locke, and liberal thought in general disappears in a society in which such a shared understanding exists. In the end we may decide to retrieve individualism in order to reaffirm its insistence on the otherness of other people, but we can do so only after we have thought through the implications of our dependence on each other.

Against Formalism: Chickens and Rocks

Walter Benn Michaels

It may seem odd and even a little perverse to entitle an essay "Against Formalism" when we are supposed years ago to have gone beyond formalism at a time when what we were against was interpretation. But, as we may recall, Geoffrey Hartman's conclusions in that famous essay were skeptical: "[T]o go beyond formalism is as yet too hard for us," he wrote, "and may even be . . . against the nature of understanding."[1] And, of course, Susan Sontag was far from arguing against formalist criticism; her only complaint was that it wasn't formalist enough. What we needed, she thought, was criticism of the "sort that dissolves considerations of content into those of form."[2] It must have seemed to some readers even then that we had already had quite a lot of that — in any event, we have had a great deal of it since. But it is not really my purpose in this essay to take up lines of argument suggested by either Sontag or Hartman; that is, I don't mean to argue either for or against that kind of criticism we usually call formalist. What I want to question is not so much a kind of criticism as an account of meaning, an account of meaning which is held, I think, not only by avowedly formalist critics but by many critics who are far from thinking of themselves as formalists and indeed by many who are not critics at all but who are nevertheless concerned with the nature of language and of texts.

There is, however, a real connection between formalist criticism and what I am calling the formalist account of meaning. This connection has surfaced most obviously in the debate over intention that has for so long been prominent among the theoretical issues of modern American literary criticism. The central text in this debate, the text which began it and for some readers ended it, is, of course, Wimsatt and Beardsley's "The Intentional Fallacy." The central thesis of this essay was that "the intention of a literary artist qua intention is neither a valid ground for arguing the presence of a quality or meaning in a given instance of his literary work nor a valid criterion for judging the value of that work." And the debate which followed this assertion has usually (and quite naturally) taken the form of arguments for or against the proposition that knowledge of the author's intention is relevant to the determination of what his poem or novel means. And yet, this way of putting the question is somewhat misleading, for as constant as Wimsatt and Beardsley were in denying the relevance of authorial intention to interpretation, they were at least equally constant in denying one aspect of their denial. As "Mr. Beardsley and I were careful to point out . . .," Wimsatt wrote in 1968, "interpretation apparently based upon an author's 'intention' often in fact refers to an intention as it is found in, or inferred from, the work itself. Obviously the argument about intention . . . is not directed against such instances."[3]

Charges that Wimsatt wished to ignore the author's intention or that he misunderstood the "intentional" nature of the poetic object thus seem a little beside the point. The central thrust of his position was not completely to deny the relevance of authorial intention but rather to limit what would be allowed to count as evidence of that intention to the work itself. As such, the polemic against intention was part of the more broadly formalist polemic against discussion of the aesthetic object in what were perceived as fundamentally nonaesthetic terms (historical, biographical, psychological, etc.). The poem was to be regarded as an autonomous object and to be studied, in the famous phrase, "as a poem and not another thing." Seen in this light, it is, of course, very tempting to equate American formalism with a kind of (high-minded) aestheticism, but it is at the same time worth noting that the modern insistence on the determinate and autonomous status of the text itself has been by no means confined to aesthetics. In fact, some thirty years before the publication of "The Intentional Fallacy," Judge Learned Hand was writing, in language remarkably similar to Wimsatt's, as follows:

> A contract has, strictly speaking, nothing to do with the personal or individual intent of the parties. A contract is an obligation attached by the mere force of law to certain acts of the parties, usually words, which ordinarily accompany and represent a known intent. If, however, it were proved by twenty bishops that either party, when he used the words, intended something else than the usual meanings which the law imposes upon them, he would still be held, unless there were some mutual mistake, or something else of the sort.[4]

The point in law has, of course, nothing to do with the aesthetic status of contracts. It was rather an attempt to guarantee the objectivity of the contract by ensuring that both parties would be bound to what the words themselves said and not to anyone's "subjective" or "private" interpretation of what the words meant. Thus we find the primary tenet of literary formalism — that study be confined to the text *itself* — anticipated in a context utterly removed from any aesthetic concerns and associated not with a New Critical retreat to the ivory tower but with the interpretive demands of the marketplace.

In contract law, one of the primary ways in which the integrity of the text is protected is by something called the parol evidence rule, which in the *Restatement of Contracts* reads as follows: "the integration of an agreement makes inoperative to add to or to vary the agreement all contemporaneous oral agreements relating to the same subject matter; and also . . . all prior written or oral agreement relating thereto" (section 237). The force of this rule is clear enough; it is designed to ensure objectivity by providing a public standard of accountability. Since, in Justice Holmes's words, "the making of a contract depends . . . not on the parties having *meant* the same thing but on their having *said* the same thing,"[5] the parol evidence rule ensures that evidence of one party's subjective intent will not be introduced in order to alter the objective meaning of the contract itself, what the contract says. There are, however, exceptions to this rule. Extrinsic evidence is not admissible "if the written words are themselves plain and clear and unambiguous," but if the contract is itself vague or ambiguous, then extrinsic evidence will often be admitted to clear up the vagueness or resolve the ambiguity. The evidence serves not to vary the contract but to help the judge in interpreting it.

This interpretive scenario sounds reasonable enough, but, in fact, as the late Arthur L. Corbin argued, it is highly misleading, depending as it does on the implicit and in Corbin's view mistaken assumption that qualities like ambiguity and clarity are intrinsic properties of texts. A judge's decision as to whether or not a contract is ambiguous must inevitably be itself based on extrinsic evidence, Corbin argued, because "no man can determine the meaning of written words by merely gluing his eyes within the four corners of a square paper. . . . when a judge refuses to consider relevant extrinsic evidence on the ground that the meaning of the words is to him plain and clear, his decision is formed by and wholly based upon the completely extrinsic evidence of his own personal education and experience."[6] In support of this view, Corbin cited the example of *Frigaliment Importing Co.* v. *B.N.S. International Sales Corp.* (190 F. Supp. 116 [S.D.N.Y. 1960]).

The question in this case was the meaning of a contract in which a New York company called B.N.S. (the defendant) undertook to sell to a Swiss company called Frigaliment (the plaintiff), among other things, 75,000 lb. of U.S. fresh frozen chicken at a price of $33 per 100 lb. When the chickens arrived in Switzerland, the plaintiff was dismayed and outraged to discover that they were not the young "fryers" and "roasters" he had anticipated but were instead old "stewing chickens" or "fowl." According to the plaintiff and to witnesses on his behalf, the word *chicken* had a particular trade usage; it could mean a "broiler, a fryer, or a roaster" but not a stewing chicken. Hence, the plaintiff claimed, he had every right to expect, according to the terms of the contract, that he would be sent fryers and/or roasters, not stewing chickens. The defendant maintained, however, that being new to the chicken business he was not familiar with such usage and that, furthermore, such usage was by no means universal even in the trade. Among the witnesses called on behalf of the defendant was a Mr. Weininger, the operator of a chicken eviscerating plant in New Jersey, who testified, "Chicken is everything except a goose, a duck, and a turkey. Everything is a chicken but then you have to say, you have to specify which category you want or that you are talking about." The defendant thus maintained that it had every right to understand *chicken* to mean, among other things, stewing chicken, and so contended that it had complied with the terms of the contract.

The question was thus, as the judge put it, "What is chicken?" And, he wrote, "since the word 'chicken' standing alone is ambiguous," it was clearly relevant to admit extrinsic evidence as an aid to interpretation. From the theoretical standpoint, then, this case is a clear illustration of the parol evidence rule. The written word (*chicken*) is not "plain and clear and unambiguous," hence extrinsic evidence is appropriate. But what is it about the word *chicken* that is ambiguous? *Chicken* is not, after all, an example of lexical ambiguity; in fact, from the standpoint of the dictionary, *chicken* seems a more than usually precise word. If, to take a common example, someone tells you that he has spent the morning at the bank, you might reasonably (from a lexical standpoint) wonder whether he means the river or the First National. But if he tells you that he likes or doesn't like chicken you are likely to feel, and with reason, that you have some fairly concrete information about his dietary habits. If, then, the word *chicken* "standing alone" is ambiguous, it is not because *chicken* is a particularly ambiguous word.

In fact—and this is Corbin's central point—the judge's sense that *chicken* is ambiguous derives not from the word as it stands alone but from the extrinsic evidence of conflicting meanings. There is a problem with *chicken* not because it is itself ambiguous or, as some commentators have written, "vague," but because it is in dispute. The word *chicken*, standing alone, in itself, is neither ambiguous nor vague (nor clear nor precise) and the contract isn't either. To see this clearly, we have only to imagine some alternative sets of circumstances: suppose the defendant had been an old hand at the chicken business and had, like the plaintiff, regularly employed the trade usage in question. Or suppose the plaintiff had been a newcomer also and like the defendant ignorant of trade usage, understanding by *chicken* just a kind of fowl. In both cases, the meaning of the contract would have been plain and clear, with its clarity deriving not from less ambiguous or more explicit language (since the language in both cases is identical) but from shared understandings or what Corbin calls "undisputed contexts." And, of course, the meaning of the contract made by the neophytes would have been plainly and clearly different from the meaning of the contract made by the old chicken hands, although again the words would have been the same.

The moral Corbin draws from this story is essentially that the parol evidence rule must be liberally understood. "All rules of interpretation . . ." he writes, "are mere aids to the court . . . in ascertaining and enforcing the intention of the parties."[7] Evidence of these intentions can therefore never be irrelevant. But this does not mean that extrinsic evidence is always admissible. For "the courts are always correct when they say that they must not by interpretation alter or pervert the meaning and intention of the parties,"[8] hence, "[w]hen two parties have made a contract and have expressed it in a writing to which they have both assented as the complete and accurate integration of that contract, evidence, whether parol or otherwise, of antecedent understandings and negotiations will not be admitted for the purpose of varying or contradicting the writing."[9] Thus, where the *Restatement* admits extrinsic evidence only in the case of an ambiguity in the contract itself, Corbin would have required no such prima facie ambiguity. He insisted rather that ambiguity is itself a product of extrinsic evidence, and so would have allowed extrinsic evidence at all times so long as it was for the purpose of interpretation and not contradiction. "Contradiction, deletion, substitution: these are not interpretation."[10]

As a revision of the *Restatement*, this formulation seems once again reasonable enough but in fact it founders on almost exactly the same terms. For it is reasonable to insist that we allow extrinsic evidence for the purpose of interpreting but not for the purpose of contradicting or varying a contract only if we can make some neutral distinction between "interpreting" and "varying," some distinction which does not already involve a commitment to a particular interpretation. But this, as Corbin himself had shown, is what we can never do. We can only decide whether or not extrinsic evidence will *vary* the writing after we have decided what the writing means, and our decision about what the writing means is itself dependent on some form of extrinsic evidence, if only that of our own experience. We cannot therefore refuse to admit extrinsic evidence on the grounds that it will tend to vary the meaning of the contract without having already admitted extrinsic evidence in deciding what that meaning is. The distinction between interpretation and variation cannot be understood as the neutral and principled distinction Corbin wanted it to be. Interpreting and varying both involve extrinsic categories — the only difference between them is that evidence which according to the judge tends to serve "the purpose of varying or contradicting the writing" will be evidence for an interpretation the judge does not share — which is why it seems to him to vary or contradict the writing. Corbin's insistence that judges refuse to admit evidence that will vary the text then becomes an exhortation to interpret correctly instead of incorrectly and, as such, has no methodological significance whatsoever.

That Corbin could have been unaware of this contradiction may seem implausible, but actually this kind of blindness on this particular issue is by no means uncommon. In another celebrated case, *Pacific Gas and Electric Co.* v. *G.W. Thomas Drayage and Ry. Co.* (442 P.2d 641 [1968]), an opinion by Chief Justice Traynor of the California Supreme Court reversed a lower court decision on the grounds that it illegitimately excluded relevant extrinsic evidence. "Although," Traynor wrote, "extrinsic evidence is not admissible to add to, detract from, or vary the terms of a written contract, these terms must first be determined before it can be decided whether or not extrinsic evidence is being offered for a prohibited purpose." This sentence sits squarely on both sides of Corbin's fence. On the one hand, it asserts that the terms of a contract must not be altered by evidence which is extrinsic to the contract; on the other hand, it asserts that what the terms of a contract are can only be discovered by the use of evidence extrinsic to the contract. The implication is that while we must recognize the importance of extrinsic evidence (since to interpret a text is always to invoke some form of extrinsic evidence), we must still insist on a principled way of distinguishing between relevant extrinsic evidence (which will help us toward a correct interpretation) and irrelevant extrinsic evidence (which will serve to vary the contract). But, on Traynor's own terms, there can in principle be no such principle. Relevant evidence will be evidence that supports the interpretation we hold. Irrelevant evidence will be evidence that supports an interpretation with which we disagree.

Traynor's criticism of the trial court is thus double-edged. "Having determined that the contract had a plain meaning," he writes, "the court refused to admit any extrinsic evidence that would contradict its interpretation." As a criticism of the implicit claims made by the trial court for its own interpretation, this is perfectly valid, because the trial court maintained that the meaning of the contract was intrinsically clear, independent of any extrinsic evidence, and so refused to allow any extrinsic evidence. Traynor's criticism is thus directed against the trial court's account of what a "plain meaning" is. But if we replace the trial court's account of plain meaning with Corbin's and Traynor's, Traynor's criticism ceases to be a criticism at all and becomes instead an account of what every judge must always do. Whenever a court refuses to allow extrinsic evidence on the grounds sanctioned by Corbin and Traynor (that the evidence serves not to interpret but to vary the contract), the court will of necessity have already decided what the contract means. And having decided what the contract means, the evidence the court refuses to admit will of course be evidence that contradicts its interpretation. Corbin and Traynor both see that a text can have no meaning, plain or otherwise, independent of extrinsic evidence, but then they both imagine that a court can distinguish between evidence which will be a legitimate aid to interpretation and evidence which won't without having already reached an interpretation. But it can't and because it can't the parol evidence rule, no matter how liberally we construe it, is doomed to circularity. It can never provide a neutral procedure for deciding what extrinsic evidence should be admitted and what shouldn't; it can only provide an after-the-fact justification for excluding the evidence that seems to contradict the court's interpretation.

Literary criticism, needless to say, has no parol evidence rule to guarantee the text's autonomy, but the text has managed quite nicely on its own. The major thrust of "The Intentional Fallacy" was, as we have seen, to establish the priority of the text, insisting simultaneously on the intrinsic and objective character of meaning. The formal study of "the text itself," wrote Wimsatt and Beardsley, "is the true and objective way of criticism."[11] And, in fact, even some of the strongest arguments against Wimsatt and Beardsley have turned out to share some of their most important assumptions. A neat example of this phenomenon is E.D. Hirsch's seminal "Objective Interpretation," an argument against what Hirsch saw (in 1960) as the inevitable relativism of formalist criticism and in support of the proposition that meaning is "permanent" and "self-identical" and that "[t]his permanent meaning is, and can be, nothing other than the author's meaning."[12] One of Hirsch's more persuasive examples of the relevance of authorial intention and of the necessity to go outside the text in the effort to discover that intention is the critical controversy over Wordsworth's "A Slumber Did My Spirit Seal." The poem reads as follows:

> A slumber did my spirit seal;
> I had no human fears:
> She seemed a thing that could not feel
> The touch of earthly years.
>
> No motion has she now, no force;
> She neither hears nor sees;
> Rolled round in earth's diurnal course,
> With rocks, and stones, and trees.

Hirsch cites two conflicting interpretations. One emphasizes the poet's " 'agonized shock' " at Lucy's death, his horrified " 'sense of the girl's falling back into the clutter of things . . .chained like a tree to one particular spot, or . . .completely inanimate like rocks and stones.' " The other suggests that the poem climaxes not in horror but in two lines of " 'pantheistic magnificence.' " Lucy's fate is consoling not shocking because she " 'is actually more alive now that she is dead . . .she is now a part of the life of nature.' " These two critics, Cleanth Brooks and F.W.

Bateson, agree that Lucy is one with the rocks and stones but they disagree on what exactly is implied by oneness with rocks. The issue, as the judge in *Frigaliment* v. *B.N.S.* might have said, is "What is a rock?" To a pantheist, of course, rocks are living things, participants, as Bateson says, in "the sublime processes of nature," and if Lucy is rolling around with them she is fairly well off. To almost everyone else, however, rocks are, in Brooks's words, "completely inanimate," and Lucy's kinship with them is indeed unfortunate. The question "What is a rock?" can thus only be answered convincingly once we know whether or not Wordsworth was a pantheist. It cannot be answered by the text itself because the text, as Hirsch notes, permits both interpretations. The available historical evidence, however, seems to indicate that in 1799 (when the poem was written) Wordsworth probably regarded rocks not, according to Hirsch, as "inert objects," but as "deeply alive, as part of the immortal life of nature." Thus, he concludes, until and unless we uncover "some presently unknown data," we are entitled to conclude that Bateson's optimistic reading of the poem is more correct than Brooks's pessimistic one.[13]

This interpretive procedure is clearly similar to the legal procedure in cases which are understood to fall within the province of the parol evidence rule. The text itself is ambiguous (Hirsch prefers the term *indeterminate*, pointing out quite rightly that in literary criticism ambiguity tends to signify not the reader's inability to decide what the text means but the author's intention to have it mean more than one thing) — no matter how carefully we read, we cannot decide whether *chicken* means fryer or stewing chicken or both, whether rocks are alive or dead. Thus we turn to extrinsic evidence to make explicit which of the text's implicit meanings is correct. But to formulate the problem and its solution in these terms is also, I think, to point toward what is wrong with this account. For one thing, as we have already seen, the decision that a text is ambiguous cannot be made prior to the introduction of extrinsic evidence. And for another thing, while seeming to recognize and take into account the difficulty of interpreting a text on its own terms, Hirsch in fact demonstrates exactly the same kind of confidence with regard to intrinsically meaningful extrinsic evidence that the formalist has with regard to the text.

This sounds more paradoxical than it is. Imagine, for example, that rummaging through Dove Cottage, some diligent researcher were to come up with a letter dated February 1799 from Wordsworth to Coleridge, ending with the customary salutations, wish-you-were-here, etc., and then a P.S.: "I have definitely become a pantheist." Such a discovery of "new data" would seem on the face of it to end the matter. Bateson would be proven right; Brooks, if he were in a generous mood, might send him a congratulatory telegram. But it requires little more than a glancing familiarity with the academic (or any other) world to recognize the utopian character of this scenario. Rather we can imagine supporters of the "dead rocks" thesis maintaining that the postscript was not evidence of Wordsworth's pantheism but was in fact ironic, and hence was evidence of his skepticism in regard to the fundamental sentimentality of the pantheistic view of nature. The whole Lucy cycle, they might claim, insists on the inevitability of loss, on an "asceticism" which is the very denial of pantheistic "mysticism." How then could any critic take seriously such a disingenuously naive declaration of faith? In short, not only would the argument over the poem be simply reproduced in an argument over the postscript, but now the poem would be cited as extrinsic evidence to clear up the ambiguity of the text itself, the postscript.

The point of this example is not to suggest that, even in the face of incontrovertible evidence, people will stubbornly maintain their own positions but rather to call into question the notion of incontrovertible evidence. Or, in the terms we have been using, to suggest that explicitness is a function not of language but of agreement. The problem with *rock*, like the problem with *chicken*, is not that it is vague or ambiguous but that it is in dispute. Such a problem cannot be resolved by an appeal to words which are in themselves less vague or ambiguous (there are no such words); it can only be resolved by an appeal to words which are not in dispute. If we agree that "I am a pantheist" meant that Wordsworth was indeed a pantheist, then our dispute over the meaning he attached to the word *rock* will be at an end. If we don't, it won't. The process of adjudication thus depends not on words which have plain meaning and can be used as touchstones against which to measure words whose meanings are not so plain. It depends instead on what Corbin calls "undisputed contexts," agreement on the meaning of one piece of language which can then compel agreement on the meaning of another. No text by itself can enforce such an agreement, because a "text by itself" is no text at all.

To claim, then, as I do, that the phrase "the text itself" is oxymoronic is to argue not that formalism is undesirable and that we should stop being formalists but that formalism is impossible and that no one ever has been a formalist. To read is always already to have invoked the category of the extrinsic, an invocation that is denied, as I suggested earlier, not only by avowedly formalist critics but by all those who think of textual meaning as in any sense intrinsic. Many contemporary legal and literary theorists, for example, are accustomed to thinking of language as inherently "vague" or "ambiguous," a position that at least appears to be more responsive to the complexities of contracts and poems than any doctrine of plain meanings and that may also appear not incompatible with the account of interpretation I have sketched above. Thus, according to the legal scholar E. Allan Farnsworth, "all language is infected with ambiguity and vagueness,"[14] and, according to the literary critic Paul de Man, "literary . . . language is essentially ambivalent."[15] But does it really make sense to say that *chicken* is inherently ambiguous and *rock* inherently ambivalent? We can easily imagine contexts (in fact, we have already done so) in which the meanings of *chicken* and *rock* would be as clear and precise as anyone could wish—in an agreement between two experienced chicken merchants, for example, or in a conversation between pantheists. And of course we have also already imagined the contexts in which *chicken* and *rocks* become ambiguous again. The mistake is to conclude with Farnsworth and de Man that ambiguity is somehow more a property of language than clarity is. In fact, although some texts are ambiguous, no texts are inherently ambiguous, and although some texts are precise, no texts are inherently precise either. That is the point of chickens and rocks—no text is inherently anything. The properties we attribute to texts are functions, instead of situations, of the contexts in which texts are read.

But, it might be objected at this point, poems are not contracts. Isn't our response to poetic language quite different from our response to legal language, and doesn't this difference manifest itself very clearly in cases like the ones we have been talking about? In *Frigaliment* v. *B.N.S.*, after all, people stand to win or lose thousands of dollars, whereas the values of "A Slumber Did My Spirit Seal" must be calculated quite differently. Aren't chickens and rocks, like apples and oranges, incomparable? Isn't it a fundamental mistake to treat the two texts as if they were the same when they so clearly aren't?

The response to this objection is that, while there are indeed differences between poems and contracts, they are institutional not formal differences. We can, for example, easily imagine a certain brand of literary critic maintaining that the whole point of "A Slumber Did My Spirit Seal" was the ambiguity of "rocks and stones," emblemizing the poet's and the reader's uncertainty as to what exactly Lucy's absence means. To insist on either reading at the expense of the other, such a critic might maintain, would be to attribute to the poem a sense of resolution that the poet is precisely concerned to deny, etc. If, on the other hand, the judge in *Frigaliment* v. *B.N.S.* were to begin his decision by praising the art of the contract-makers, their subtle refusal to simplify experience by specifying fryers or stewing chickens, their recognition of the ultimately problematic character of the chicken itself, etc., we would know that something has gone radically wrong. Judges cannot decide that contracts are ambiguous in the same way and for the same reasons that literary critics can. But this is not because legal *language* is less tolerant of ambiguity than poetic language is; it is because the institution of the law is less tolerant of ambiguity than the institution of literary criticism is. Judges don't read the same way literary critics do.

These differences should not, however, be allowed to obscure some basic similarities. Legal and literary theorists both have been concerned with objectivity, they have attempted to guarantee that objectivity by a theoretical insistence on the primacy of the text, and their theoretical model has broken down when faced with what should, on their own terms, be easy questions: "What are chickens?" "What are rocks?" They should be easy because the formalist model assumes that texts have some intrinsic, plain, or literal meaning (even if that meaning is ambiguous), a lexical function of the language itself, not of the situations in which the language is being used. And we may have trouble defining *good* or *beautiful*, but we know what *chicken* means and we know what *rock* means. They are hard because our lexicon won't tell us if chickens are fryers or if rocks are dead—which doesn't mean that *chicken* and *rock* have no plain meanings but that plain meanings are functions not of texts but of the situations in which we read them. And which reminds us that the lexicon itself ("*chicken:* a common domestic fowl," "*rock:* a concreted mass of stony material") has meaning itself only against a background of assumptions and information which it too can never contain.

(C)
Objectivity

Objectivity and Interpretation

Owen M. Fiss

Adjudication is interpretation: adjudication is the process by which a judge comes to understand and express the meaning of an authoritative legal text and the values embodied in that text.

Interpretation, whether it be in the law or literary domains, is neither a wholly discretionary nor a wholly mechanical activity. It is a dynamic interaction between reader and text, and meaning the product of that interaction. It is an activity that affords a proper recognition of both the subjective and objective dimensions of human experience, and for that reason, has emerged in recent decades as an attractive method for studying all social activity.[1] The idea of a written text, the standard object of legal or literary interpretation, has been expanded to embrace social action and situations, which are sometimes called text-analogues. In one of the most significant works of this genre to date, Clifford Geertz's *Negara*, a nineteenth-century Balinese cremation ceremony is taken as "the text."[2]

Admittedly, to treat everything as a text might seem to trivialize the idea of a text, but the appeal of the interpretive analogy stems from the fact that interpretation accords a proper place for both the perspective of the scholar and the reality of the object being studied, and from the fact that interpretation sees the task of explicating meaning as the most important and most basic intellectual endeavor. This appeal is considerable and, as a consequence, liberties have been taken with the notion of a text, and interpretation is now accepted as central to disciplines that were once on the verge of surrendering to the so-called scientific ethos, such as politics and history (though interestingly, not economics—there the surrender to the pretense of science seems complete). The behaviorists or social scientists have hardly quit the field, but a new humanistic strand has emerged and, when pushed to define that strand, one would speak, above all, of interpretation.

To recover, then, an old and familiar idea, namely, that adjudication is a form of interpretation, would build bridges between law and the humanities and suggest a unity among man's many intellectual endeavors. A proper regard for the distinctive social function of adjudication, and for the conditions that limit the legitimate exercise of the judicial power, will require care in identifying the kinds of texts to be construed and the rules that govern the interpretive process; the judge is to read the legal text, not morality or public opinion, not, if you will, the moral or social texts. But the essential unity between law and the humanities would persist and the judge's vision would be enlarged.

A recognition of the interpretive dimensions of adjudication and the dynamic character of all interpretive activity and its capacity to relate constructively the subjective and objective will also deepen our understanding of law and in fact might even suggest how law is possible. It might enable us to come to terms with a new nihilism, one that doubts the legitimacy of adjudication—a nihilism that appears to me to be unwarranted and unsound, but that is gaining respectability and claiming an increasing number of important and respected legal scholars, particularly in constitutional law. They have turned their backs on adjudication and have begun a romance with politics.[3]

This new nihilism might acknowledge the characterization of adjudication as interpretation, but then would insist that the characterization is a sham. The nihilist would argue that for any text—particularly such a comprehensive text as the Constitution—there are any number of possible meanings, that interpretation consists of choosing one of those meanings, and that in this selection process the judge will inevitably express his own values. All law is masked power. In this regard the new nihilism is reminiscent of the legal realism of the early twentieth century. It too sought to unmask what was claimed to be the true nature of legal doctrine, particularly the doctrine that insulated laissez-faire capitalism from the growth of the activist state and the reforms pressed by Progressives and the supporters of the New Deal. It saw law as a projection of the judge's values.

In the decades following the Second World War, particularly in the sixties, at the height of the Warren Court era, a new judicial doctrine arose to replace the doctrine that was associated with laissez-faire capitalism and that was ultimately repudiated by the "Glorious Revolution" of 1937 and the constitutional victory of the New Deal. It embraced the role of the activist state and saw equality rather than liberty as the central constitutional value. Scholars turned to defending this new doctrine and in so doing sought to rehabilitate the idea of law in the face of the realist legacy.[4] They sought to show that *Brown* v. *Board of Education*[5] was law, not just politics. So were *Reynolds* v. *Sims*,[6] *New York Times* v. *Sullivan*,[7] and *Gideon* v. *Wainwright*.[8]

The nihilism of today is largely a reaction to this reconstructive effort of the sixties. It harks back to the realist movement of an earlier era, and coincides with a number of contemporary phenomena—the transfer of the judicial power from the Warren Court to another institution altogether; a social and political culture dominated by the privatization of all ends; and a new movement in literary criticism and maybe even in philosophy called deconstructionism, which expands the idea of text to embrace all the world and at the same time proclaims the freedom of the interpreter.[9]

I

The nihilism of which I speak fastens on the objective aspiration of the law and sees this as a distinguishing feature of legal interpretation. The judge, the nihilist reminds us, seeks not just a plausible interpretation, but an objectively true one. Judges may not project their preferences or their views of what is right or wrong, or adopt those of the parties, or of the body politic, but rather must say what the Constitution requires. The issue is not whether school desegregation is good or bad, desirable or undesirable, to the judge, the parties, or the public, but whether it is mandated by the Constitution. The law aspires to objectivity, so the nihilist observes, but he concludes that the nature of the constitutional text makes this impossible. The text is capable of any number of possible meanings, and thus it is impossible to speak of one interpretation as true and the other false. It is impossible to speak of law with the objectivity required by the idea of justice.

The nihilist stresses two features of the legal text in explaining why objectivity is impossible. One is the use of general language. The Constitution does not, for example, contain a specific directive about the criteria for assigning students among the public schools, but provides that no state shall "deny to any person within its jurisdiction the equal protection of the laws." There is no further specification of what is meant by *state, person, jurisdiction, protection, laws,* or most importantly, *equal.* The potential of *equal* is staggering, and the nihilist is confounded by it. A second feature of the text is its comprehensiveness. The Constitution is a rich and varied text. It contains a multitude of values, some of which potentially conflict with others. It promises equality *and* liberty. In fact, at times it seems to contain almost every conceivable value, especially when one refers to such provisions as the privileges and immunities clause of Article IV or the Fourteenth Amendment, or the provision of the Ninth Amendment that reserves to the people rights not otherwise enumerated in the Constitution.

In coming to terms with this nihilism, one must begin by acknowledging the generality and comprehensiveness of the constitutional text and also by insisting that in this regard the Constitution is no different from a poem or any legal instrument. Generality and comprehensiveness are features of any text. Though the Constitution may be more general and comprehend more than a sonnet or a contract, it is comparable in this regard to an epic poem or some national statutes. Few, if any, statutes touch as many activities as the Constitution itself (which, after all, establishes the machinery of government) but many, if not most, embody conflicting values and are in that sense comprehensive. It should also be understood that generality and comprehensiveness do not discourage interpretation but are the very qualities that usually provoke it. Interpretation is a process of generating meaning, and one important (and very common) way of both understanding and expressing the meaning of a text is to render it specific and concrete.

There are some legal theorists who would limit legal interpretation to highly specific constitutional clauses. This school, misleadingly called "interpretivism" but more properly called "textual determinism," operates with a most arid and artificial conception of interpretation.[10] For an interpretivist only a specific text can be interpreted. Interpretation is thus confused with execution—the application of a determinate meaning to a situation—and is unproblematic only with regard to clauses like that requiring the president to be at least thirty-five years old. Most interpretivists, including Justice Black, would recognize the narrowness of such a perspective and want to acknowledge a role for less specific clauses, like freedom of speech; but in truth such provisions are hardly obvious in their meaning and require substantial judicial interpretation to be given their proper effect. Does *speech* embrace movies, flags, picketing, and campaign expenditures? What is meant by *freedom*? Does it, as Isaiah Berlin wondered, pertain exclusively to the absence of restraint, or does it also embrace an affirmative capacity for self-realization?[11]

To endorse active judicial interpretation of specific clauses and to caution against judicial interpretation of the more general and potentially more far-reaching clauses, such as due process and equal protection, represents an attempt at line-drawing that cannot itself be textually justified. It is instead motivated by a desire—resting on the most questionable of premises—to limit the role of constitutional values in American government and the role of the judiciary in expressing those values. And the line itself would be illogical. It would require that small effect be given to the comprehensive constitutional protections while full effect is given to the narrow ones. I reject this attempt at line-drawing because I reject the premises and the result, but it must be emphasized that, for purposes of this essay, the critical question is not whether judicial interpretation of specific clauses, understood in any realistic sense, is legitimate and that of general clauses is not, since, as we saw in the case of the First Amendment, both require substantial interpretation. Rather, the question is whether *any* judicial interpretation can achieve the measure of objectivity required by the idea of law.

Objectivity in the law connotes standards. It implies that an interpretation can be measured against a set of norms that transcend the particular vantage point of the person offering the interpretation. Objectivity implies that the interpretation can be judged by something other than one's own notions of correctness. It imparts a notion of impersonality. The idea of an objective interpretation does not require that the interpretation be wholly determined by some source external to the judge, but only that it be constrained. To explain the source of constraint in the law, it is necessary to introduce two further concepts: one is the idea of disciplining rules, which constrain the interpreter and constitute the standards by which the correctness of the interpretation is to be judged; the other is the idea of an interpretive community which recognizes these rules as authoritative.

The idea of objective interpretation accommodates the creative role of the reader. It recognizes that the meaning of a text does not reside in the text, as an object might reside in physical space or as an element might be said to be present in a chemical compound, ready to be extracted if only one knows the correct process; it recognizes a role for the subjective. Indeed, interpretation is defined as the process by which the meaning of a text is understood and expressed, and the acts of understanding and expression necessarily entail strong personal elements. At the same time, the freedom of the interpreter is not absolute. The interpreter is not free to assign any meaning he wishes to the text. He is disciplined by a set of rules that specify the relevance and weight to be assigned to the material (e.g., words, history, intention, consequence), as well as by those that define basic concepts and that established the procedural circumstances under which the interpretation must occur.

The disciplining rules may vary from text to text. The rules for the interpretation of a poem differ from those governing the interpretation of legal material; and even within the law, there may be different rules depending on the text—those for contractual interpretation vary from statutory interpretation, and both vary from those used in constitutional interpretation. Though the particular content of disciplining rules varies, their function is the same. They constrain the interpreter, thus transforming the interpretive process from a subjective to an objective one, and they furnish the standards by which the correctness of the interpretation can be judged. These rules are not simply standards or principles held by individual judges, but instead constitute the institution (the profession) in which judges find themselves and through which they act. The disciplining rules operate similarly to the rules of language, which constrain the users of the language, furnish the standards for judging the uses of language, and constitute the language. The disciplining rules of the law may be understood, as my colleague Bruce Ackerman has suggested, as a professional grammar.

Rules are not rules unless they are authoritative, and that authority can only be conferred by a community. Accordingly, the disciplining rules that govern an interpretive activity must be seen as defining or demarcating an interpretive community consisting of those who recognize the rules as authoritative. This means, above all else, that the objective quality of interpretation is bounded, limited, or relative.[12] It is bounded by the existence of a community that recognizes and adheres to the disciplining rules used by the interpreter and that is defined by its recognition of those rules. The objectivity of the physical world may be more transcendent, less relativistic, though the Kuhnian tradition in the philosophy of science throws considerable doubt on that commonsense understanding;[13] but as revealed by the reference to language, and the analogy I have drawn between the rules of language and the disciplining rules of interpretation, the physical does not exhaust the claim of objectivity, nor does it make this bounded objectivity of interpretation a secondary or parasitic kind of objectivity. Bounded objectivity is the only kind of objectivity to which the law—or any interpretive activity—ever aspires and the only one about which we care.[14] To insist on more, to search for the brooding omnipresence in the sky,[15] is to create a false issue.

Nihilism is also fashionable in literary criticism today and is represented there by what I referred to as the deconstruction movement.[16] Deconstructionists exalt the creative and subjective dimension of interpretation. For them, interpretive freedom is absolute. Deconstructionists reject the idea of objectivity in interpretation, presumably even the bounded objectivity of which I speak, because they would deny that an interpretive community possesses the necessary authority to confer on the rules that might constrain the interpreter and constitute the standards of evaluation. Competing interpretive communities, and the freedom of the literary critics to leave one community and to join or establish another, are considered by the deconstructionists as inconsistent with the authoritativeness that rules need in order to constrain. Authority that depends completely on members' agreement is not authority at all.

I will not here attempt to dispute the notion that literary critics are so unconstrained that no claim of objectivity can be made for any of their interpretations, though my instinct is to be wary of this form of nihilism too.[17] For my purposes, it is sufficient to recognize the distinctive feature of legal interpretation: in law the interpretive community is a reality. It has authority to confer because membership does not depend on agreement. Judges do not belong to an interpretive community as a result of shared views about particular issues or interpretations, but belong by virtue of a commitment to uphold and advance the rule of law itself. They belong by virtue of their office. There can be many schools of literary interpretation, but, as Jordan Flyer put it, in legal interpretation there is only one school and attendance is mandatory. All judges define themselves as members of this school and must do so in order to exercise the prerogatives of their office. Even if their personal commitment to the rule of law wavers, the rule continues to act on judges; even if the rule of law fails to persuade, it can coerce. Judges know that if they relinquish their membership in the interpretive community, or deny its authority, they lose their right to speak with the authority of the law.

Nothing I have said denies the possibility of disagreement in legal interpretation. Some disputes may be centered on the correct application of a rule of discipline. For example, a dispute may arise over a rule that requires the interpreter to look to history. Some may claim that the judge has misunderstood the history of the Fourteenth Amendment or that he is using a level of generality that is inappropriate for constitutional interpretation.[18] They may claim, for example, that the focus should not be on the existence of segregated schools in 1868 or on the willingness of those who drafted and adopted the Fourteenth Amendment to tolerate segregated schools, but on the Framers' desire to eradicate the caste system and the implication of that desire for segregated education today. Disputes of this kind are commonplace, but they pose little threat to the legitimacy of the disciplining rules; they pose only issues of application.

Other disputes may arise, however, and they may involve a challenge to the very authority or existence of a rule. Some judges or lawyers may, for example, deny the relevance of history altogether in constitutional interpretation.[19] Disputes of this type pose a more serious challenge to the idea of objectivity than those over the application of a rule, for such disputes threaten the source of constraint itself. It should be remembered, however, that in the law there are procedures for resolving these disputes—for example, pronouncements by the highest court and perhaps even legislation and constitutional amendments. The presence of such procedures and a hierarchy of authority for resolving disputes that could potentially divide or destroy an interpretive community is one of the distinctive features of legal interpretation. One should also be careful not to exaggerate the impact of such disputes. The authority of a particular rule can be maintained even when it is disputed, provided the disagreement is not too pervasive; the integrity of an interpretive community can be preserved even in the face of a dispute or disagreement as to the authority of some particular disciplining rule. The legal community transcends cliques; some cliques may dissolve over time, others may come to dominate the community.

Just as objectivity is compatible with a measure of disagreement, it should also be stressed that objectivity is compatible with error: an objective interpretation is not necessarily a correct one. *Brown* v. *Board of Education* and *Plessy* v. *Ferguson*,[20] one condemning segregation, the other approving it, may both be objective and thus legitimate exercises of the judicial power, though only one is correct. To understand how this is possible, we must first recognize that legal interpretations can be evaluated from two perspectives, one internal, the other external.

From the internal perspective, the standards of evaluation are the disciplining rules themselves, and the authority of the interpretive community is fully acknowledged. The criticism, say, of *Plessy* v. *Ferguson* might be that the judges did not correctly understand the authoritative rules, or may have misapplied them; the judges may have failed to grasp the constitutional ideal of equality imported into the Constitution by the Fourteenth Amendment, or incorrectly assumed that the affront to blacks entailed in the Jim Crow system was self-imposed. Though such a criticism argues that the interpretation is mistaken, it might well acknowledge the objective character of the interpretation on the theory, borrowed from Wittgenstein,[21] that misunderstanding is a form of understanding, that a judge could misunderstand or misapply a rule and still be constrained by it. An objective but (legally) incorrect interpretation partakes of the impersonality or sense of constraint implied by the idea of law. Not every mistake in adjudication is an example of lawlessness.

The internal perspective permits another type of criticism in which both the objectivity and the correctness of the decision may be challenged. The charge may be that the judge utterly disregarded well-recognized disciplining rules, such as those requiring the judge to take account of the intention of the Framers of the Fourteenth Amendment or those rules prohibiting the judge from being influenced by personal animosities or bias. If these are the bases of criticism of the judicial decision, and arguably they may have some relevance to *Plessy*, then the claim is that the interpretation is both wrong and nonobjective. I imagine that it is also possible for an interpretation to be both nonobjective and correct, as when a judge pretty much decides to do what he wishes, that is, once again utterly disregards the disciplining rules, and yet in this instance gives the text the same meaning—in a substantive sense—as would a fair and conscientious judge constrained by all the appropriate rules. Such a situation does not seem to be of great practical importance, but it once again illustrates the analytic distinction between objectivity and correctness, even from the wholly internal perspective. Both qualities arise from the very same rules: objectivity speaks to the constraining force of the rules and whether the act of judging is constrained; correctness speaks to the content of the rules and whether the process of adjudication and the meaning produced by that process are fully in accord with that content. From the internal perspective, legitimacy largely turns on objectivity rather than correctness; judges are allowed to make some mistakes.

The internal perspective does not exhaust all evaluation of legal interpretation. Someone who stands outside of the interpretive community and thus disputes the authority of that community and its rules may provide another viewpoint. A criticism from this so-called external perspective might protest *Plessy* on the basis of some religious or ethical principle (e.g., denying the relevance of any racial distinction) or on the grounds of some theory of politics (e.g., condemning the decision because it will cause social unrest). In that instance, the evaluation is not in terms of the law; it matters not at all whether the decision is objective. It may be law, even good law, but it is wrong, whether morally, politically, or from a religious point of view.

The external critic may accept the pluralism implied by the adjectives *legal, moral, political,* and *religious,* each denoting different standards of judgment or different spheres of human activity. The external critic may be able to order his life in a way that acknowledges the validity of the legal judgment and that at the same time preserves the integrity of his view, based on nonlegal standards, about the correctness of the decision. He may render unto the law that which is the law's. Conflict is not a necessity, but it does occur, as it did over the extension of slavery in the 1850s and over the legalization of abortion in the 1970s. The external critic will then have to establish priorities. He may move to amend the Constitution or engage in any number of lesser and more problematic strategies designed to alter the legal standards, such as packing the court or enacting statutes that curtail jurisdiction. Failing that, he remains free to insist that the moral, religious, or political principle take precedence over the legal. He can disobey.

One of the remarkable features of the American legal system is that it permits such a broad range of responses to the external critic, and that over time—maybe in some instances over too much time—the legal system responds to this criticism. The law evolves. There is progress in the law. An equally remarkable feature of the American system is that the freedom of the external critic to deny the law, and to insist that his moral, religious, or political views take precedence over the legal interpretation, is a freedom that is not easily exercised. Endogenous change is always preferred, even in the realm of the wholly intellectual. The external critic struggles to work within the law, say, through amendments, appointments, or inducing the Supreme Court to recognize that it had made a mistake. An exercise of the freedom to deny the law, and to insist that his moral, religious, or political views take precedence, requires the critic to dispute the authority of the Constitution and the community that it defines, and that is a task not lightly engaged. The authority of the law is bounded, true, but as Tocqueville recognized more than a century ago, in America those bounds are almost without limits.[22] The commitment to the rule of law is nearly universal.

II

Viewing adjudication as interpretation helps to stop the slide toward nihilism. It makes law possible. We can find in this conceptualization a recognition of both the subjective and the objective—the important personal role played by the interpreter in the meaning-giving process, and yet the possibility of an intersubjective meaning rooted in the idea of disciplining rules and of an interpretive community that both legitimates those rules and is defined by them. I have explained how objective interpretation becomes possible in the law, even if it is not possible in literature. But a number of other distinguishing features of adjudication remain to be considered: the prescriptive nature of the text, the claim of authoritativeness for the interpretation, and the desire for efficacy. These differences seem to deny the essential unity between the ways of the law and those of the humanities and may well cast doubt on my claim about the existence of constraint in the law. The question is whether we can insist that adjudication is an interpretive activity and still find that it possesses an objective character in the face of these differences. I think we can.

A. The Prescriptive Nature of the Text

Legal texts are prescriptive. Though they presuppose a state of the world, and employ terms and concepts that are descriptive or representational, their purpose is not to describe, but to prescribe. For example, the statement in the Fourteenth Amendment that "[n]o State shall . . . deny to any person within its jurisdiction the equal protection of the laws" is not meant to depict what is happening, much less what has happened, but to prescribe what should happen. It embodies a value—equality—and I see adjudication as the process by which that value, among others, is given concrete meaning and expression.

Adjudication and morality both aspire to prescribe norms of proper conduct. Both state the ideal. The ultimate authority for morality is some conception of the good. The ultimate authority for a judicial decree is the Constitution, for that text embodies public values and establishes the institutions through which those values are to be understood and expressed. When asked to justify why the schools of a community must be desegregated, reference will first be made to some lower-court decision, then to a Supreme Court decision, and finally to the Constitution itself, for it is the source of both the value of equality and the authority of the judiciary to interpret that value.

The prescriptive element in adjudication and legal texts does not preclude objective interpretation. Prescriptive texts are as amenable to interpretation as descriptive ones. Those who might think otherwise would point to the profound and pervasive disagreement that often characteriz-es moral life—that people disagree about what is right and good, as, for example, whether the separate-but-equal doctrine is consistent with equality or whether the state should be allowed to interfere with the free-dom of a woman to decide to have an abortion. The existence of this disagreement cannot be denied, but I fail to see why it precludes inter-pretation or is inconsistent with objectivity.

Interpretation does not require agreement or consensus, nor does the objective character of legal interpretation arise from agreement. What is being interpreted is a text, and the morality embodied in that text, not what individual people believe to be the good or right. An individual is, as I have already noted, morally free to dispute the claim of the public morality embodied in the Constitution and its interpretation—he can be-come a renegade—but that possibility does not deny the existence or va-lidity of either that morality or its interpretation. Neither the objectivity nor the correctness of *Brown* v. *Board of Education* depends on the una-nimity of the justices, and much less on the willingness of the people—all the people, or most of the people—then or even now—to agree with that decision. The test is whether that decision is in accord with the au-thoritative disciplining rules. Short of a disagreement that denies the au-thority of the interpretive community and the force of the disciplining rules, agreement is irrelevant in determining whether a judge's decision is a proper interpretation of the law.

Moreover, though the celebration of disagreement in the realm of mo-rality has become commonplace, it is far from clear that disagreement is more pervasive in the interpretation of prescriptive texts than descriptive or representational ones: consensus as to the meaning of a play by Shakespeare, a novel by Joyce, or a historical text by Thucydides seems no more likely than it does in the interpretation of the Constitution. Con-sensus becomes possible in the interpretation of descriptive or represen-tational texts only if we trivialize those texts (e.g., reduce them to statements like "there is a tree in my back yard"). That move is equally available in the treatment of prescriptive texts (e.g., "equality is good"), though I see no value in insisting upon it.

The prescriptive nature of the text therefore should not be seen as a bar to objective interpretation, but it does have an important impact on the content of the disciplining rules, that is, the rules through which the law is defined. Legal interpreters are under constant pressure to abide by the constraints that govern moral judgments, for both law and morals seek to establish norms of proper behavior and attempt to describe the ideal by similar concepts, such as liberty and equality. Law borrows from morals (and, of course, morals from law). The borrowing is sometimes substantive; more often it is procedural.

Different schools of interpretation contemplate different degrees of borrowing. The natural law tradition, for example, demands that the judge give morality the decisive role in the interpretation of the legal text, or, to put the same point somewhat differently, that the judge read the legal text in light of the moral text, the so-called unwritten constitution.[23] In this instance the substantive borrowing would be most pronounced, but in fact the natural law tradition has never dominated American jurisprudence. That school has remained a clique. It has been largely overshadowed by legal positivism, which emphasizes the analytical distinction between law and morals, between what is legal and what is good. Legal positivism celebrates the "written constitution" and stresses factors like the use of particular words or the intent or beliefs of the Framers, all of which have little or no moral relevance.

Positivism tries to separate law from morals, and keeps the substantive borrowing to a minimum, but as I suggested in my account of the so-called external criticism, and my depiction of the pressures forcing the external critic to work within the law, the separation will, in fact, never be complete. Two forces modulate the commitment to positivism and thus minimize the separation. The first derives from the facts that the judge is trying to give meaning and expression to public values (those that are embodied in a legal text) and that his understanding of such values—equality, liberty, property, due process, cruel and unusual punishment—is necessarily shaped by the prevailing morality. The moral text is a prism through which he understands the legal text. The second force relates to an intellectual dilemma of positivism: a too-rigid insistence on positivism will inevitably bring into question the ultimate moral authority of the legal text—the justness of the Constitution.

Judges ardently committed to legal positivism will ultimately be asked—as they were in the debates over the constitutionality of slavery before the Civil War[24] and in response to the judicial efforts to protect industrial capitalism in the early part of the twentieth century[25]—to justify the public morality embodied in that text and the processes by which those values are expressed. Slavery may be protected by the Constitution; so may industrial capitalism and the inequality of wealth and privilege it invariably produces; but why must we respect the Constitution? The answer to such a question is not obvious or easily discovered, for one must transcend the text and the rules of interpretation to justify the authority of the text; to justify the Constitution itself or explain why the Constitution should be obeyed, one must move beyond law to political theory, if not religion. Such questioning can itself become a moment of crisis in the life of a constitution, and since it is occasioned by a rigid insistence on the principles of positivism and the separation of law and morals, judges have an incentive to temper their commitment to that legal theory and thus to read the moral as well as the legal text. A judge quickly learns to read in a way that avoids crises.

An even more pronounced measure of borrowing occurs in formulating the disciplining rules that govern the procedures of legal interpretation. Above all, it is the procedures of morals that the law borrows.[26] One vision of the procedures of morals is conveyed by the vivid and powerful image created by John Rawls of the original position—of a group of people deliberating behind a veil of ignorance and reaching agreement on the principles of justice in a situation that entails divorcement from interests, a willingness to engage in rational dialogue, and a willingness to universalize the principles agreed upon.[27] Rawls was speaking of morals, but we can see in the law an insistence on an analogous set of procedural norms to discipline the interpreter: the judge must stand independent of the interests of the parties or even those of the body politic (the requirement of judicial independence); the judge must listen to grievances he might otherwise prefer not to hear (the concept of a nondiscretionary jurisdiction) and must listen to all who will be directly affected by his decision (the rules respecting parties); the judge must respond and assume personal responsibility for that decision (the tradition of the signed opinion); and the judge must justify his decision in terms that are universalizable (the neutral principles requirement). These rules reflect the inherently prescriptive character of the legal text and the identity of concepts used by law and morals to describe the ideal.

These procedural constraints are not, mind you, mere techniques of administration, to be dispensed with whenever the need or desire to do so arises. They are an essential component of the body of disciplining rules that govern the interpretive process known as adjudication and that constitute the standards for evaluating a legal interpretation. The correctness of any interpretation is relative to a set of standards, and in law those standards are composed of procedural as well as substantive norms. This is partly due to the prescriptive nature of the text and the fact that the judge is trying to state the ideal, which has the effect of blending the idea of "correctness" into "justness": a just interpretation speaks to process as well as outcome. The role of procedure is also attributable, though perhaps in a secondary way, to certain institutional facts. The judiciary is a coordinate agency of government, always competing, at least intellectually, with other agencies for the right to establish the governing norms of the polity. The judiciary's claim is largely founded on its special competence to interpret a text such as the Constitution, and to render specific and concrete the public morality embodied in that text; that competence stems not from the personal qualities of those who are judges—judges are not assumed to have the wisdom of philosopher-kings—but rather from the procedures that limit the exercise of their power. It is as though they operate under the procedural constraints of the original position and from that fact obtain a measure of authority over the other branches.

B. The Claim of Authoritativeness

I have pictured the judge as an individual essentially engaged in interpretive activity. I have also suggested a moral dimension to legal interpretation—the judge interprets a prescriptive text and in so doing gives meaning and expression to the values embodied in that text. The judge seems to be a combination of literary critic and moral philosopher. But that is only part of the picture. The judge also speaks with the authority of the Pope.

Some literary critics aspire to a kind of authority: they search not just for a plausible interpretation, but for the correct interpretation of a text. The same is true for moral philosophers: they do not simply express what they believe to be good, but try to identify principles of morality that are objective and true. Both the literary critic and the moral philosopher aspire to a kind of authority we might term intellectual, an authority that comes from being right in their intellectual endeavor. Judges also attempt to achieve intellectual authority, yet this is only to supplement a powerful base of authority that they otherwise possess. Judicial interpretations are binding, whether or not they are correct. The decision of *Brown* v. *Board of Education* was not only right but had the force of law; *Plessy* v. *Ferguson* may have been wrong, from either the internal or external perspective, in 1896 as well as now, but it was nonetheless binding.

In what ways is the interpretation of the judge uniquely authoritative? There are two answers to this question. The first, emphasized in the work of John Austin,[28] is based on power: by virtue of the rules that govern their behavior, the officers of the state are entitled to use the power at their disposal to bring about compliance with judicial interpretations. Sometimes the power is brought to bear on the individual through contempt proceedings; sometimes through criminal prosecutions and police action; sometimes through supplemental civil proceedings. Sometimes, as with the desegregation of the public schools at Little Rock or the admission of James Meredith at Ole Miss, the power is expressed through brute force—bayonets, rifles, clubs, and tear gas.[29] A judicial interpretation is authoritative in the sense that it legitimates the use of force against those who refuse to accept or otherwise give effect to the meaning embodied in that interpretation.

The second sense of authoritativeness, suggested by the works of other positivists, namely Herbert Hart[30] and Hans Kelsen,[31] stresses not the use of state power, but an ethical claim to obedience—a claim that an individual has a moral duty to obey a judicial interpretation, not because of its particular intellectual authority (i.e., because it is a correct interpretation), but because the judge is part of an authority structure that is good to preserve. This version of the claim of authoritativeness speaks to the individual's conscience and derives from institutional virtue, rather than institutional power. It is the most important version of the claim of authoritativeness, because no society can heavily depend on force to secure compliance; it is also the most tenuous one. It vitally depends on a recognition of the value of judicial interpretation. Denying the worth of the Constitution, the place of constitutional values in the American system, or the judiciary's capacity to interpret the Constitution dissolves this particular claim to authoritativeness.

Belief in the institutional virtue of judicial interpretation may proceed from a variety of theories. One theory stresses the importance of having questions of public values settled with some finality through procedures unique to the judiciary. Another centers on the desirability of maintaining continuity with our traditional values and sees adjudication as the process best designed to promote that end. A third theory emphasizes the need to maintain the stability of the larger political system and the role of the judiciary in maintaining that stability. Taken together, or maybe even separately, these theories have sufficient force, at least to my mind, to create a presumption in favor of the authoritativeness of judicial decisions. Any interpretation of a court, certainly that of the highest court, is prima facie authoritative. On the other hand, none of these theories, taken individually or collectively, can assure that this presumption will withstand a decision that many, operating from either the internal or external perspective, perceive to be fundamentally mistaken, an egregious error. In such a situation, the judge may be unable to ground his claim to obedience on a theory of virtue, but may have to assert the authoritativeness that proceeds from institutional power alone.

It is important to note that the claim of authoritativeness, whether it be predicated on virtue or power, is extrinsic to the process of interpretation. It does not arise from the act of interpretation itself and is sufficient to distinguish the judge from the literary critic or moral philosopher who must rely on intellectual authority alone. Moreover, though the claim of institutional authoritativeness is not logically inconsistent with objective interpretation, but rather presupposes it, the authoritative quality of legal interpretation introduces certain tensions into the interpretive process. It creates a strong critical environment; it provides unusually strong incentives to criticize and defend the correctness of the interpretation. Something practical and important turns on judicial interpretations. They are binding. Institutional authoritativeness also produces psychological strains in the interpreter. It at once oppresses and liberates the interpreter.

From one perspective, the claim of authoritativeness acts as a weight: it creates additional responsibility. The search for meaning is always arduous, but even more so when one realizes that the interpretation will become authoritative. *Brown* must have been agonizing. The justices had to determine what the ideal of racial equality meant and structure its relation to liberty. This task was hard enough, especially given the legacy of

Plessy v. *Ferguson*, but the difficulty was compounded because the justices knew they were also establishing the course of the nation. They were authoritatively deciding whether more than one-third of the states could adhere to their long-established and passionately defended social order. Authoritativeness confers a responsibility that is awesome, probably at times disabling. It appears that in at least one instance, when Justice Whittaker had to decide the reapportionment issue in *Baker* v. *Carr*,[32] this responsibility produced a nervous breakdown.[33]

The contrasting perspective is best captured by the work of Justice Douglas and a judicial quip that became popular in the mid 1960s, at the height of the Warren Court era: "With five votes we can do anything." From this perspective, the claim of authoritativeness liberates the judge, dangerously so; he works with the knowledge that his words will bind whether or not he has correctly interpreted the text. This sense of security is not completely well founded, for, as we saw, insofar as the judge claims authoritativeness based on the virtue of the institution, the claim can be overcome or defeated by what others perceive to be a particularly serious mistake. Even from the perspective of power, the judge must recognize that a serious abuse of the judicial office may also incline the executive against using the force at its disposal to compel obedience. (Eisenhower's hesitation in deploying the federal troops in Little Rock is ample warning on that score.) But these limitations on the claim of authoritativeness depend on a complicated chain of reasoning and presuppose the most egregious of errors, and as such, only circumscribe the judge's sense of freedom. The larger fact is the freedom itself: an interpretation is binding even if mistaken. The judge enjoys a protection that is not shared by the literary critic or the moral philosopher, and that might allow a casual indifference to the integrity of the interpretive enterprise. The impact of the disciplining rules may be dulled. The search for meaning may be less than complete.

The mention of Justice Whittaker and Justice Douglas is not meant to suggest that each dimension of this conflicting dynamic finds expression in a different person. I assume that the psychological conflict resulting from the claim of authoritativeness is present in all judges, perhaps all the time. The existence of this conflict does not deny the interpretive character of judging, or make that task impossible to perform. The great judge—I have Earl Warren very much in mind—is someone who can modulate these tensions, someone whom the specter of authority both disciplines and liberates, someone who can transcend the conflict.

C. Efficacy and the Element of Instrumentalism

The claim of authoritativeness, like the prescriptive nature of the text, complicates and defines the distinctive nature of legal interpretation. There is a third dimension that informs the task of the judge and that probably plays an even greater role in giving legal interpretation its distinctive cast: the judge tries to be efficacious. The judge seeks to interpret the legal text and then to transform social reality so that it comports with that interpretation.

The literary critic, no doubt, often finds himself anxious whether his audience will accept his interpretation as the true one, and he will polish his rhetorical skills and participate in institutional politics to that end. But the personal anxieties of the literary critic are raised to a duty in the law. The judge must give a remedy; it is part of the definition of his office. The duty of the Supreme Court in *Brown* was to interpret the ideal of racial equality in terms of concrete reality and to initiate a process that would transform that reality so that it comports with the ideal—to transform, as the slogan reads, the dual school systems into unitary, nonracial ones.

The authoritativeness of a legal interpretation is an essential ingredient of this transformational process. Faced with the Little Rock crisis, the Supreme Court felt compelled to reaffirm *Brown* and to put its authority on the line. But the reassertion of the authority of its interpretation, the achievement of *Cooper* v. *Aaron*,[34] did not itself desegregate the schools. Authoritativeness is a necessary, not a sufficient, condition of efficacy. Efficacy also requires measures that will transform social reality.

Part of that transformational process entails further specification of the meaning of the text, an explication of the ideal of racial equality in the context of a particular social setting: does the commitment to racial equality allow freedom of choice as the method of student assignment in this particular city? Does it allow a neighborhood school plan? The answers to these questions depend in part on a specification of the imperatives of the ideal of racial equality and its relation to other constitutional ideals, such as liberty. In this regard, the transformational process also entails interpretation, with, so to speak, one eye on the Constitution and the other on the world—the world that was and the one that should be. But there is another dimension of the transformational process that is not properly considered interpretive: instrumentalism. The judge must know how to achieve specific objectives in the real world.

The meaning the court gives the constitutional value, in the general and in the specific, defines and structures the end to be achieved by this transformational process. The objective established in *Brown* is to desegregate the schools. The question then becomes one of deciding how to achieve this objective, and in resolving that question the judge will have to make certain technical judgments: choosing the schools to be paired, designing bus routes, deciding which teachers are to be reassigned, adjusting the curriculum and sports schedule, etc. He may rely on the initiative of the parties and their so-called experts to help in these matters, but in the end, he will have to assume responsibility for the technical judgments—the judge must be an architect and engineer, redesigning and rebuilding social structures.

This is, however, only one facet of the instrumentalism. We also know, especially from the history of *Brown*, that a deeper and more intractable set of obstacles may confront the judge in his effort to give the value of racial equality a practical meaning: resistance by those who must cooperate in order for the meaning to become a reality—parents, children, teachers, administrators, citizens, and politicians. Collectively, and sometimes even individually, these people have the power to frustrate the remedial process. In ways that are both subtle and crude, they may refuse to recognize the authoritativeness of the judge's interpretation. They can boycott the schools, attack the minority students, withdraw from the public school system and flee to the suburbs or private schools, or refuse to appropriate money needed for buses.

In the face of this resistance, the judge can reassert his authority either by proclaiming the virtues of his office and the place of the judiciary in the political system, or by employing the power at his disposal. When the resistance is deep and sufficiently widespread, however, such an action is likely to be hollow and unavailing. Then the judge must be able to manage his opposition: he must transform resistance into cooperation. He must win the support of those he needs. He must bargain and negotiate. To succeed in achieving his remedial objectives, the judge must be as much a political strategist as he is a social architect and engineer.

This journey into instrumentalism, perhaps most vividly symbolized by the "all deliberate speed" formula of the second *Brown* decision,[35] may cause important departures from the interpretive paradigm, for the legal text cannot inform, in any important sense, the technical and strategic judgments that are an integral part of the remedial process. The Constitution establishes the values and establishes the institutions for expressing those values, but is not a significant source for understanding how those values might be effectively implemented. It is not a manual of the type Machiavelli might write. The judge can, of course, read another text, such as the one read by legislators—public opinion—but it is not an authoritative text for the judge. Moreover, there is no reason to assume that instrumental judgments should be or even could be constrained by the disciplining rules that characteristically govern judicial interpretation—for example, the rules assigning weight to precedent or requiring dialogue or independence of the judiciary from the political process. Indeed, it is not at all clear why the instrumental judgments are entrusted to the same officials who are charged with interpreting the constitutional text. At best, one can employ an argument of necessity—the instrumental judgments must be entrusted to the judge as a way of preserving the integrity of the meaning-giving enterprise, because the meaning of a value derives from its practical realization as well as its intellectual articulation.

The concern with efficacy may have even greater consequences. Instrumentalism may not only call for a departure from the interpretive paradigm, it may actually interfere with the interpretive process. It may make the judge settle for something less than what he perceives to be the correct interpretation. The technical and strategic obstacles to efficacy may humble the judge and remind him that even with five votes he cannot do everything, for they reveal the practical limits of his authority; but there is always the risk that the humility will be excessive. It may be crippling. Fearing he lacks the ability—the technical expertise or political power—to implement the right answer, and determined to avoid failure, even if it means doing nothing, the judge may tailor both the remedy and the right to what he perceives to be possible, and that may be considerably less than what he believes the text—the appropriate text—requires. That fear may drive the judge to read a lesser text—public opinion—or even worse, it might lead the judge to embrace what might be regarded as Frankfurter's axiom—it is better to succeed in doing nothing than to fail in doing something. Doubting that he has the ability to change social mores[36] or to implement desegregation plans that involve the suburbs as well as the city,[37] the judge may so modify his reading of the equal protection clause as to produce an interpretation of equality that tolerates separation.

The desire for efficacy may, as a result of this dynamic, corrupt, but it need not. The need to address complex social situations with creative and often complicated remedies and then to manipulate power so as to make them reality is undeniable, but these needs do not necessarily cause the judge to compromise the integrity of his interpretation. A secure concept of the judicial role, and the priorities within that role, and a proper recognition of the source of legitimacy, may enable the judge to order and perhaps even reconcile tasks that may otherwise tend to conflict. The core of adjudication, objective interpretation, can be protected from the pressures of instrumentalism, as it can be protected from the tensions produced by the claim of authoritativeness. The multiple demands of adjudication often make law an elusive, partly realized ideal, for they mean the judge must manage and synthesize a number of disparate and conflicting roles—literary critic, moral philosopher, religious authority, structural engineer, political strategist; but it would be wrong to abandon the ideal in the face of this challenge. The proper response is increased effort, clarity of vision, and determination, not surrender.

III

The nihilism that I have addressed is based on the premise that for any text there are any number of possible meanings and the interpreter creates a meaning by choosing one. I have accepted this premise, but have tried to deny the nihilism by showing why the freedom is not absolute. I have argued that legal interpretations are constrained by rules that derive their authority from an interpretive community that is itself held together by the commitment to the rule of law. There may, however, be a deeper nihilism that I have not yet addressed, and that also seems part of the present moment in American intellectual life.

For the deconstructionist, it makes little difference whether a text is viewed as holding all meanings or no meaning: either brand of nihilism liberates the critic as meaning-creator. My defense of adjudication as objective interpretation, however, assumes that the Constitution has some meaning—more specifically, that the text embodies the fundamental public values of our society. I have confronted the nihilism that claims the Constitution means everything; but my defense does not work if the alternative version of the literary nihilism is embraced and applied to the law. My defense does not work if it is said that the Constitution has no meaning, for there is no theory of legitimacy that would allow judges to interpret texts that themselves mean nothing. The idea of adjudication requires that there exist constitutional values to interpret, just as much as it requires that there be constraints on the interpretive process. Lacking such a belief, adjudication is not possible, only power.

The roots of this alternative version of nihilism are not clear to me, but its significance is unmistakable. The great public text of modern America, the Constitution, would be drained of meaning. It would be debased. It would no longer be seen as embodying a public morality to be understood and expressed through rational processes like adjudication; it would be reduced to a mere instrument of political organization—distributing political power and establishing the modes by which that power will be exercised. Public values would be defined only as those held by the current winners in the processes prescribed by the Constitution; beyond that, there would be only individual morality, or even worse, only individual interests.

Against the nihilism that scoffs at the idea that the Constitution has any meaning, it is difficult to reason. The issue seems to be one of faith, intuition, or maybe just insight. This form of nihilism seems so thoroughly at odds with the most elemental reading of the text itself and with almost two hundred years of constitutional history as to lead me to wonder whether anything can be said in response. On the other hand, I believe it imperative to respond, in word and in deed, for this nihilism calls into question the very point of constitutional adjudication; it threatens our social existence and the nature of public life as we know it in America; and it demeans our lives. It is the deepest and darkest of all nihilisms. It must be combated and can be, though perhaps only by affirming the truth of that which is being denied—the idea that the Constitution embodies a public morality and that a public life founded on that morality can be rich and inspiring.

Fish v. Fiss

Stanley Fish

I. The Rules of the Game

On the first page of his essay "Objectivity and Interpretation," Owen Fiss characterizes interpretation as "neither a wholly discretionary nor a wholly mechanical activity," but a "dynamic interaction between reader and text" of which meaning is the "product."[1] This middle way, he asserts, "affords a proper recognition of both the subjective and objective dimensions of human experience."[2] The alternatives Fiss rejects will be familiar to all students of both literary and legal interpretation. The "wholly mechanical" alternative is the view, often termed positivist, that meaning is a property of—is embedded in—texts and can therefore be read without interpretive effort or intervention by a judge or a literary critic. The "wholly discretionary" alternative is the opposite view, often termed subjectivist, that texts have either many meanings or no meanings, and the reader or judge is free to impose—create, legislate, make up, invent—whatever meanings he or she pleases, according to his or her own whims, desires, partisan purposes, etc. On the one view, the text places constraints on its own interpretation; on the other, the reader interprets independently of constraints. Fiss proposes to recognize the contributions of both text and reader to the determination of meaning by placing between the two a set of "disciplining rules" derived from the specific institutional setting of the interpretive activity. These rules "specify the relevance and weight to be assigned to the material" and define the "basic concepts and . . . procedural circumstances under which the interpretation must occur."[3] They thus act as constraints on the interpreter's freedom and direct him to those meanings in the text that are appropriate to a particular institutional context.

On its face, this proposal seems reasonable enough, but ultimately it will not do, and it will not do because the hinge on which Fiss's account turns is not sufficiently fixed to provide the stability he needs. That hinge is the notion of "disciplining rules" that will constrain readers or interpreters and mitigate (if not neutralize) the inherent ambiguity of texts.[4] The claim is that, given a particular situation, the rules tell you what to do and prevent you from simply doing whatever you like.

The trouble is that they don't. If the rules are to function as Fiss would have them function—to "constrain the interpreter"—they themselves must be available or "readable" independently of interpretation; that is, they must directly declare their own significance to any observer, no matter what his perspective. Otherwise they would "constrain" individual interpreters differently, and you would be right back in the original dilemma of a variously interpretable text and an interpretively free reader. To put the matter another way, if the rules tell you what to do with texts, they cannot themselves be texts, but must be—in the strong sense assumed by an older historiography—documents.[5] Unfortunately, rules *are* texts. They are in need of interpretation and cannot themselves serve as constraints on interpretation.

That at least is my argument, and we can test it by trying to think of some rules. Fiss does not spend much time telling us what the disciplining rules are like, but the general form they would take is clear from what he does say. They would be of at least two kinds, particular and general. A particular rule would be one that "specif[ied] the relevance and weight to be assigned to the material,"[6] and would presumably take a form like: "If someone takes the property of another without his consent, count that as larceny." A general rule would be one that defined the "basic concepts and . . . procedural circumstances under which the interpretation must occur,"[7] and its form would be something like: "Always consult history" (one of Fiss's examples, in fact).[8] The problem with the particular rule is that there will always be disputes about whether the act is indeed a "taking" or even about what a "taking" is. And even where the fact of taking has been established to everyone's satisfaction, one can still argue that the result should be embezzlement or fraud rather than larceny. The same analysis holds for the more general rules. To say that one must always consult history does not prevent—but provokes—disagreements about exactly what history is, or about whether or not this piece of information counts as history, or (if it does count) about what its factual configurations are.

Fiss himself acknowledges the possibility of such disputes, but says that they "pose only issues of application";[9] that is to say, they do not affect the "legitimacy of the disciplining rules," which are still doing their disciplining. "The authority of a particular rule can be maintained even when it is disputed . . . ."[10] But how can "it" be maintained *as a constraint* when the dispute is about what "it" is or about what "it" means? Fiss assumes that one first "has" a rule and then interprets it. But if the shape of the rule could be had without interpretation, then the interpretation would be superfluous.[11] And if interpretation is not superfluous to the "reading" of rules (Fiss would agree that it is not), then one only has rules in an interpreted shape. Thus we are back once again to my assertion that a so-called disciplining rule cannot be said to act as a constraint on interpretation because it is (in whatever form has been specified for it) the product of an interpretation.

This is true even in those cases where there are no disputes, where there is perfect agreement about what the rule is and what it means. There is a temptation (often irresistible to those on Fiss's side of the street) to assume that such cases of perfect agreement are normative and that interpretation and its troubles enter in only in special circumstances. But agreement is not a function of particularly clear and perspicuous rules; it is a function of the fact that interpretive assumptions and procedures are so widely shared in a community that the rule appears to all in the same (interpreted) shape. And if Fiss were to reply that I am not denying the existence—and authority—of disciplining rules, but merely suggesting a new candidate for them in the "persons" of interpretive assumptions and procedures, I would simply rehearse the argument of the previous paragraphs all over again, pointing out this time that interpretive assumptions and procedures can no more be grasped independently of interpretation than disciplining rules can; thus they cannot be thought of as constraints upon interpretation either.[12]

The difficulty, in short, cannot be merely patched over; it pervades the entire situation in which someone (a judge, a literary critic) faced with the necessity of acting (rendering a judgment, turning out a reading) looks to some rule or set of rules that will tell him what to do. The difficulty becomes clear when the sequence—here I am, I must act, I shall consult the rule—becomes problematic in a way that cannot be remedied. Let us imagine that the president of the United States or some other appropriate official appoints to the bench someone with no previous judicial or legal experience. This person is, however, intelligent, mature, and well informed. As she arrives to take up her new position she is handed a booklet and told, "Here are the rules—go to it!" What would happen? The new judge would soon find that she was unable to read the rules without already having a working knowledge of the practices they were supposed to order, or, to put it somewhat more paradoxically, she would find that she could read the rules that are supposed to tell her what to do only when she already knew what to do. This is so because rules, in law or anywhere else, do not stand in an independent relationship to a field of action on which they can simply be imposed; rather, rules have a circular or mutually interdependent relationship to the field of action in that they make sense only in reference to the very regularities they are thought to bring about. The very ability to read the rules in an informed way presupposes an understanding of the questions that are likely to arise (Should liability be shared or strictly assigned?), the kinds of decisions that will have to be made, the possible alternative courses of action (to dismiss, to render a summary judgment), the consequences (for future cases) of deciding one way or another, and the "deep" issues that underlie the issue of record (Are we interested in retribution or prevention?). Someone who was without this understanding would immediately begin to ask questions about what a rule *meant*, and in answer would be told about this or that piece of practice in a way that would alert her to what was "going on" in some corner of the institutional field. She would then be able to read the rule because she would be seeing it as already embedded in the context of assumptions and practices that make it intelligible, a context that at once gives rise to it (in the sense that it is a response to needs that can be felt) and is governed by it.

Even that would not be the end of the matter. Practices are not fixed and finite—one could no more get out a list of them than one could get out a list of *the* rules. Sooner or later the new judge would find herself "misapplying" the rules she thought she had learned. In response to further questions she would discover that a situation previously mastered also intersected with a piece of the field of practice of which she had been ignorant; and in the light of this new knowledge she would see that the rule must be differently applied because in a sense it would be a different, though not wholly different, rule.

Let me clarify this somewhat abstract discussion by juxtaposing to it another example. Suppose you were a basketball coach and had taught someone how to shoot baskets and how to dribble the ball, but had imparted these skills without reference to the playing of an actual basketball game. Now you decide to insert your student into a game, and you equip him with some rules. You say to him, for instance, "Take only good shots." "What," he asks reasonably enough, "is a good shot?" "Well," you reply, "a good shot is an 'open shot', a shot taken when you are close to the basket (so that the chances of success are good) and when your view is not obstructed by the harassing efforts of opposing players." Everything goes well until the last few seconds of the game; your team is behind by a single point; the novice player gets the ball in heavy traffic and holds it as the final buzzer rings. You run up to him and ask, "Why didn't you shoot?" and he answers, "It wasn't a good shot." Clearly, the rule must be amended, and accordingly you tell him that if time is running out, and your team is behind, and you have the ball, you should take the shot even if it isn't a good one, because it will then *be* a good one in the sense of being the best shot in the circumstances. (Notice how both the meaning of the rule and the entities it covers are changing shape as this "education" proceeds.) Now suppose there is another game, and the same situation develops. This time the player takes the shot, which under the circumstances is a very difficult one; he misses, and once again the final buzzer rings. You run up to him and ask, "Didn't you see that John (a teammate) had gone 'back door' and was perfectly positioned under the basket for an easy shot?" and he answers "But you said . . . ." Now obviously it would be possible once again to amend the rule, and just as obviously there would be no real end to the sequence and number of emendations that would be necessary. Of course, there will eventually come a time when the novice player (like the novice judge) will no longer have to ask questions; but it will not be because the rules have finally been made sufficiently explicit to cover all cases, but because explicitness will have been rendered unnecessary by a kind of knowledge that informs rules rather than follows from them.

Indeed, explicitness is a good notion to focus on in order to see why Fiss's disciplining rules won't do what he wants them to do (namely, provide directions for behavior). On the one hand, no set of rules could be made explicit enough to cover all the possible situations that might emerge within a field of practice; no matter how much was added to the instruction "Take only good shots," it could never be descriptive of all the actions it was supposed to direct, since every time the situation changes, what is or is not a "good" shot will change too. On the other hand, for someone already embedded in a field of practice, the briefest of instructions will be sufficient and perhaps even superfluous, since it will be taken as referring to courses of action that are already apparent to the agent; upon hearing or remembering the rule "Take only good shots," a player will glance around a field already organized in terms of relevant pieces of possible behavior. A rule can never be made explicit in the sense of demarcating the field of reference independently of interpretation, but a rule can always be received as explicit by someone who hears it within an interpretive preunderstanding of what the field of reference could possibly be. [13]

The moral of the story, then, is not that you could never learn enough to know what to do in every circumstance, but that what you learn cannot finally be reduced to a set of rules. Or, to put the case another way (it amounts to the same thing), insofar as the requisite knowledge *can* be reduced to a set of rules ("Take only good shots," "Consult history"), it will be to rules whose very intelligibility depends on the practices they supposedly govern. Fiss believes that the rules must exist prior to practice, or else practice will be unprincipled; but as the examples of the judge and the basketball player have shown, practice is already principled, since at every moment it is ordered by an understanding of what it is practice *of* (the law, basketball), an understanding that can always be put into the form of rules—rules that will be opaque to the outsider—but is not produced by them.

The point has been well made by Thomas Kuhn when he wrote that "scientists . . . never learn concepts, laws, and theories in the abstract and by themselves." "Instead," he adds, "these intellectual tools are from the start encountered in a historically and pedagogically prior unit that displays them with and through their application." [14] As an illustration Kuhn offers an example that is on all fours with the ones we have already considered. His text is an eighteenth-century law of rational mechanics: "Actual descent equals potential ascent."

> Taken by itself, the verbal statement of the law . . . is virtually impotent. Present it to a contemporary student of physics, who knows the words and can do all these problems but now employs different means. Then imagine what the words, though all well known, can have said to a man who did not know even the problems. For him the generalization could begin to function only when he learned to recognize "actual descents" and "potential ascents" as ingredients of nature, and that is to learn something, prior to the law, about the situations that nature does and does not present. That sort of learning is not acquired by exclusively verbal means. Rather it comes as one is given words together with concrete examples of how they function in use . . . . To borrow . . . Michael Polanyi's useful phrase, what results from this process is "tacit knowledge" which is learned by doing science rather than by acquiring rules for doing it.[15]

In another place Kuhn characterizes this process as one "of learning by finger exercise" and identifies it with "the process of professional initiation."[16] The generality of this assertion can be seen immediately when one considers what happens in the first year of law school (or, for that matter, in the first year of graduate study in English). The student studies not rules but cases, pieces of practice, and what he or she acquires are not abstractions but something like "know-how" or "the ropes," the ability to identify (not upon reflection, but immediately) a crucial issue, to ask a relevant question, to propose an appropriate answer from a range of appropriate answers, etc. Somewhere along the way the student will also begin to formulate rules or, more properly, general principles, but will be able to produce and understand them only because he or she is deeply inside—indeed, is a part of—the context in which they become intelligible.

II. Independence and Constraint

To have said as much is already to have taken the next step in my argument. In the course of explaining why rules cannot serve as constraints on interpretation, I have explained why rules (in that strong sense) are not necessary; and in the course of explaining why rules are unnecessary, I also have explained why the fear of unbridled interpretation—of interpreters whose determinations of meaning are unconstrained—is baseless.[17] It is this fear that animates Fiss's entire enterprise, but it is a fear that assumes an interpreter who is at least theoretically free to determine meaning in any way he or she likes, and who therefore must be constrained by something *external*, by rules or laws. But on the analysis offered in the preceding paragraphs there can be no such interpreter. To be, as I have put it, "deeply inside" a context is to be already and always thinking (and perceiving) with and within the norms, standards, definitions, routines, and understood goals that both define and are defined by that context.

The point is an important one because it clarifies the relationship between my argument and Fiss's (which is not simply one of opposition, as it is, for example, in the dispute between Fiss and Sanford Levinson[18]). The notion of disciplining rules is crucial to Fiss's account because it represents for him the chief constraint on the process of adjudication; and by taking away the firmness and independence of those rules I may seem to have undermined the process altogether by leaving an undisciplined interpreter confronting a polysemous text, with nothing between them to assure that the assignment of meaning will proceed in one direction rather than another. But these consequences follow only if readers and texts are in need of the constraints that disciplining rules would provide, and the implication of what I have already said is that they are not.

To see why they are not, one must remember that Fiss's account takes the form it does because he begins by assuming two kinds of independence, one good and one bad. The bad kind of independence attaches to readers and texts: readers are free to choose any meanings they like, and texts contain too many meanings to guarantee a principled choice. The good kind of independence attaches to rules: because they stand outside of or are prior to a field of interpretive practice, they can guide and control it in appropriate ways. The good kind of independence controls and disciplines the bad. My contention is that by showing why the good kind of independence can never be achieved, I have shown at the same time why the bad kind is never a possibility. Just as rules can be read only in the context of the practice they supposedly order, so are those who have learned to read them constrained by the assumptions and categories of understanding embodied in the same practice. It is these assumptions and categories that have been internalized in the course of training, a process at the end of which the trainee is not only possessed *of* but possessed *by* a knowledge of the ropes, by a tacit knowledge that tells him not so much what to do, but already has him doing it as a condition of perception and even of thought. The person who looks about and sees, without reflection, a field already organized by problems, impending decisions, possible courses of action, goals, consequences, desiderata, etc., is not free to choose or originate his own meanings, because a set of meanings has, in a sense, already chosen him and is working itself out in the actions of perception, interpretation, judgment, etc., he is even now performing. He is, in short, already filled with and constituted by the very meanings that on Fiss's account he is dangerously free to ignore.

This amounts finally to no more, or less, than saying that the agent is always and already situated, and that to be situated is not to be looking about for constraints, or happily evading them (in the mode, supposedly, of nihilism), but to be constrained already. To be a judge or a basketball player is not to be able to consult the rules (or, alternatively, to be able to disregard them) but to have become an extension of the "know-how" that gives the rules (if there happen to be any) the meaning they will immediately and obviously have.[19]

Of course, what holds for the rules holds too for every other "text" encountered in a field of practice, including the text with which Fiss is most concerned, the Constitution. Fiss believes that texts present the same liabilities (the liabilities of independence) as interpreters. Interpreters have too many choices; texts have too many meanings. "[F]or any text," he says, "there are any number of possible meanings and the interpreter creates a meaning by choosing one."[20] I have tried to show why this is the wrong account of the position occupied by interpreters, and I shall now show why it is also (and for the same reasons) the wrong account of texts. Although Fiss says that any text has any number of possible meanings, we have already seen that for his system to work there must be at least some texts—i.e., disciplining rules—that have only one meaning, and we have seen too that (a) there are no such texts, and (b) the fact that there are no such texts is not fatal to the goal of principled interpretive behavior. The reason that this fact is not fatal is that there are also no texts that have a plurality of meanings, so that there is never a necessity of having to choose between them.

Now I know that this will seem immediately paradoxical. How can there be at once no texts that have a single meaning and no texts that have many meanings, and how can this impossible state of affairs (even if it could exist) be seen as a *solution* to the problem of interpretation? The answer to this question will emerge once we are no longer in the grip of the assumption that gives rise to the paradox, the assumption that texts "have" properties before they are encountered in situations, which is also the assumption that it is possible to encounter texts in anything but an already situated—that is, interpreted—condition. It is this assumption that impels the project of formal linguistics, the project of specifying the properties of sentences as they exist in an acontextual state, so that one could finally distinguish in a principled way between sentences that were straightforward, ambiguous, multiply ambiguous, etc. But as I have argued elsewhere,[21] sentences never appear in any but an already contextualized form, and a sentence one hears as ambiguous (for example, "I like her cooking"[22]) is simply a sentence for which one is imagining, at the moment of hearing, more than one set of contextual circumstances. Any sentence can be heard in that way, but there are conditions under which such imaginings are not being encouraged (although they are still possible), and under these conditions any sentence can be heard as having only a single obvious meaning. The point is that these conditions (of ambiguity and straightforwardness) are not linguistic, but contextual or institutional. That is to say, a sentence does not ask to be read in a particular way because it is a particular kind of sentence; rather, it is only in particular sets of circumstances that sentences are encountered at all, and the properties that sentences display are always a function of those circumstances. Since those circumstances (the conditions within which hearing and reading occur) can change, the properties that sentences display can also change; and it follows that when there is a disagreement about the shape or meaning of a sentence, it is a disagreement between persons who are reading or hearing (and therefore constituting) it according to the assumptions of different circumstances.

Everything that I have said about sentences applies equally, mutatis mutandis, to texts. If there are debates about what the Constitution means, it is not because the Constitution "provokes" debate, not because it is a certain *kind* of text, but because for persons reading (constituting) it within the assumption of different circumstances, different meanings will seem obvious and inescapable. By "circumstances" I mean, among other things, the very sense one has of what the Constitution is *for*. Is it an instrument for enforcing the intentions of the Framers?[23] Is it a device for assuring the openness of the political process?[24] Is it a blueprint for the exfoliation of a continually evolving set of fundamental values?[25] Depending on the interpreter's view of what the Constitution is for, he will be inclined to ask different questions, to consider different bodies of information as sources of evidence, to regard different lines of inquiry as relevant or irrelevant, and finally, to reach different determinations of what the Constitution "plainly" means. Notice, however, that these differences are not infinite; at any one time there are only so many views as to what the Constitution is for;[26] and therefore even those who are proceeding within different views and arguing for different meanings are constrained in their proceedings by the shared (if tacit) knowledge that (a) the number of such views is limited, and (b) they are all views of the *Constitution*, a document whose centrality is assumed by all parties to the debate. (Here is a way in which it does make a kind of sense to say that the Constitution "provokes" debate—not because of any properties it "has," but because the position it occupies in the enterprise is such that specification of its meaning is the business everyone is necessarily in.) Even when the central text of the enterprise is in dispute, all parties to the dispute are already situated within the enterprise, and the ways of disputing and the versions of the Constitution produced by those ways are "enterprise-specific." What this means is that the Constitution is never in the condition that occasions the urgency of Fiss's essay—it is never an object waiting around for interpretation; rather, it is always an already-interpreted object, even though the interpretations it has received and the forms it has taken are in conflict with one another.

How are these conflicts to be settled? The answer to this question is that they are always in the process of being settled, and that no transcendent or algorithmic method of interpretation is required to settle them. The means of settling them are political, social, and institutional, in a mix that is itself subject to modification and change. This means, of course, that the *arena* of settling is never purely internal; and indeed the distinction between the internal and the external is in general less firm and stable than Fiss assumes. He makes the point that judgments concerning the law are sometimes made from an "external perspective" by someone who is operating "on the basis of some religious or ethical principle (such as denying the relevance of any racial distinction) or on the grounds of some theory of politics (such as condemning the decision because it will cause social unrest)."[27] In such instances, he concludes, "the evaluation is not in terms of the law."[28] Well, yes and no. If Fiss means by this that the evaluation originates from a source that is not part of the "judicial system," narrowly conceived, then his statement is both true and trivial; but if he means that an evaluation emanating from some social, political, religious, or moral concern is not a legal one, then he is propounding a notion of the law that is as positivistic as it is impossible. Instead, one might say (to take up just one of Fiss's examples) that the desire to avoid social unrest is one of the enabling conditions of law; it is one of the tacitly assumed "goods" that dictate the shape of the law even when particular laws nowhere refer to them. For the most part the stated purpose of a statute is the regulation of some precisely defined set of activities in industry or public life (for instance, traffic laws); but it is some unstated general purpose on the order of "avoiding social unrest" that impels the very attempt at regulation and determines the details of the statute as it is finally written. The content of the law, even when its manifestation is a statute that seems to be concerned with only the most technical and mechanical of matters (taxes, for example), is always some social, moral, political, or religious vision; and when someone objects to a decision "on the basis of some ethical or religious principle," his objection is not "external" to the law (except in the narrow procedural sense acknowledged above), but represents an effort to alter the law, so that one's understanding of what was internal to it would be different. If that alteration were effected, it would not be because a structure of the law had been made to bend to the pressure of some moral or political perspective, but because a structure *already* moral and political had been given another moral and political shape.

How might that happen? Just as Fiss says it would, when he enumerates the courses of action available to the "external critic": "He may move to amend the Constitution or engage in any number of lesser and more problematic strategies designed to alter the legal standards, such as packing the court or enacting statutes that curtail jurisdiction."[29] However, in calling these latter strategies "lesser" and "more problematic," Fiss once again assumes a distinction that cannot be maintained. Presumably they are "lesser" and "more problematic" because they are more obviously political; but in fact the entire system is political, and the question at any moment is, From which point in the system is pressure being applied, and to what other points? It is no more illegitimate to enact statutes or to make appointments than it is to engage in the slower and less theatrical activity of amending the Constitution. The processes for executing any of these courses of action are already in place, and they have been put in place by political acts. The fact that one rather than another course is taken reflects the conditions obtaining in the entire system, not a bypassing of the system or an unwarranted intrusion on proper legal procedure.

Consider, for example, the course of "packing the Court." That phrase, now laden with pejorative connotations, refers to an attempt by Franklin Delano Roosevelt to assure that the ethical and social philosophy informing the Court's decisions was similar to his own. Roosevelt made that attempt not as an anarchist or an outlaw but as a political agent whose actions were subject to the approval or disapproval of other political agents, all of whom were operating within a system of constraints that make it possible for him to do something but not everything. In other words, "packing the Court" is a possible legal strategy, but it can be successful only if other parts of the legal system assist it or fail to block it. The fact that Roosevelt was in fact blocked is not to be explained by saying that a "lesser" strategy was foiled by a legitimate one, but by saying that the political forces always as work in the system exist in ever-changing relationships of strength and influence. (It is not the case that because Roosevelt was unable to do it it can never be done; but it is true that doing it has been made harder by the fact that he tried and failed.)

At times the disposition of the entire system will be such that the judiciary can settle constitutional questions by routine procedures and in accordance with principles that have been long articulated and accepted; at other times the legislature or the executive will feel called upon to intervene strongly in an attempt to alter those principles and institute new procedures. The mistake is to think that one state of affairs is normative and "legal" while the other is extraordinary and "external." Both are perfectly legal and normative; they simply represent different proportions of the mix of agencies that participate in the ongoing project of determining what the Constitution is. The same analysis holds for the oft-opposed policies of judicial restraint and judicial activism. It is often assumed that the one indicates a respect for the Constitution while the other is an unwarranted exercise of interpretive power, as influenced by social and political views; but in fact, so-called judicial restraint is exercised by those judges who, for a variety of reasons, decide to leave in place the socially and politically based interpretations of the activists of an earlier generation.

III. Interpretive Authority and Power

It is time, I think, to take stock and look back at the argument as it has unfolded so far. The first thing to recall is that Fiss's account of adjudication is inspired by the fear that interpretation will be unprincipled, either because (*a*) the "interaction" between the reader and the text is not sufficiently constrained by rules that put limits on the freedom of the one and the polysemy of the other, or because (*b*) interpretive authority is simply a function of the power wielded by those who happen to occupy dominant positions in certain political or bureaucratic structures. I have argued against the first version of this fear by pointing out that readers and texts are never in a state of independence such that they would need to be "disciplined" by some external rule. Since readers are already and always thinking within the norms, standards, criteria of evidence, purposes, and goals of a shared enterprise, the meanings available to them have been preselected by their professional training; they are thus never in the position of confronting a text that has not already been "given" a meaning by the *interested* perceptions they have developed. More generally, whereas Fiss thinks that readers and texts are in need of constraints, I would say that they *are* structures of constraint, at once components of and agents in the larger structure of a field of practices, practices that are the content of whatever "rules" one might identify as belonging to the enterprise. At every point, then, I am denying the independence (of both the "good" and "bad" kinds) that leads Fiss first to see a problem and then to propose its solution.

The second version of Fiss's fear—that the law may be nothing but "masked power"[30]—is merely a "bogeyman" reformulation of the first, and it can be disposed of in the same way. By "masked power," Fiss means authority that is not related to any true principle, but that instead represents a "mere" exercise of some official will. The opposition surfaces most revealingly when Fiss contrasts two claims that a judge might make in his efforts to secure obedience to a decision. In the best of circumstances the judge may base his claim "on a theory of virtue," but in some situations he "may have to assert the authoritativeness that proceeds from institutional power alone."[31] Once again the mistake is to imagine two pure entities—"institutional virtue" and "institutional power"[32]—which can then be further conceived of as alternative and mutually exclusive bases for action in a community. And, once again, the way to see past the mistake is to challenge the independence of *either* entity.

To begin with "institutional virtue": what exactly would that be? The answer is that it would be precisely *institutional*, virtue defined not in some abstract or asitutional way, but in terms of the priorities, agreed-upon needs, long- and short-term goals, etc., of an ongoing social and political project. It would, in short, be virtue in relation to the perspective of an enterprise, and an appeal to it would be compelling only to someone with a commitment to that enterprise. To that same someone the threat of a contempt proceeding or some other punitive action would be no less compelling, *and for the same reason.* That is to say, the person who on one occasion complies with a decision because he agrees with it and on another occasion because of a judicial threat is in each instance signifying his commitment to the legal institution and its principles. Adherence to the rule of law does not mean agreement with its decisions but a respect for its procedures and its power, including the power to fine, to cite, and to imprison. Such power is not, as Fiss believes, a matter of "brute force," even when its instruments are "rifles, clubs, and tear gas,"[33] but is instead an extension of the standards and norms—indeed, of the "theory of virtue"—that inform the decision in the first place. "Institutional power" is just another (and unflattering) name for an obligation, inherent in an office, to decide this or enforce that, and therefore it is not something extrinsic to a principled enterprise but is itself principled.

This is not to say that there are no differences between immediate compliance and compliance under threat, or compliance in the form of undergoing incarceration. The differences are real, but they cannot simply be characterized as the difference between obedience to a principle and obedience to brute force. Neither the principle, which is authoritative (i.e., *forceful*) only because of the political enactment (sometimes following upon revolution) of some vision or agenda, nor the force, which is an etiolated version of the authority vested in the principle, can be sufficiently distinguished in a way that would make the one a threat to the integrity of the other. Of course, force can be abused—I am not proposing anything as crude as "might makes right"—but the decision that it had been abused is itself an institutional one, and such a decision implicitly entails the recognition that under certain well-defined institutional circumstances force is legitimate and—in terms of the institution's assumed goals and purposes—even virtuous.

The opposition between legitimate (virtue-based) and illegitimate (power-based) authority is for Fiss part of a broader opposition between authority of any kind and interpretation: "It is important to note that the claim of authoritativeness, whether it be predicated on virtue or power, is extrinsic to the process of interpretation. It does not arise from the act of interpretation itself and is sufficient to distinguish the judge from the literary critic or moral philosopher who must rely on intellectual authority alone."[34]

Obviously there is a harmless (and trivial) sense in which what Fiss says is true: arriving at a judicial decision and subsequently enforcing it are distinct processes, in the sense that the one precedes the other; but to say that one is *extrinsic* to the other is to attribute to both of them an independence and purity that neither could have. That is to say, neither "arises" from the other, since they both "arise" from the same set of institutional imperatives. Interpretation is not an abstract or contextless process, but one that elaborates itself in the service of a specific enterprise, in this case the enterprise of the law; the interpretive "moves" that occur to a judge, for example, occur to him in a shape already informed by a general sense of what the law is *for*, of what its operations are intended to promote and protect. Even when the particulars are the subject of debate, it is that general sense that legitimizes interpretation, because it is the content of interpretation. As we have seen, it is that same general sense that legitimizes (because it is the content of) authority, whether of the virtue-based or power-based variety. To put the matter starkly, interpretation is a form of authority, since it is an extension of the prestige and power of an institution; and authority is a form of interpretation, since it is in its operations an application or "reading" of the principles embodied in that same institution. So while it is possible to distinguish between these two activities on a narrow procedural level (on the level, for example, of temporal precedence), it is not possible to distinguish between them as activities essentially different in kind.

Nor is it possible to distinguish between the law and literary criticism or philosophy by saying that practitioners of the latter "must rely on intellectual authority alone."[35] Again there is a fairly low-level sense in which this is true: the decisions or interpretations of literary critics and philosophers are not backed up by the machinery of a court. But Fiss means more by "intellectual authority"; he means the authority exerted by arguments that make their way simply by virtue of a superior rationality and do not depend for their impact on the lines of power and influence operating in an institution.[36] That kind of authority, I submit, does not exist. In literary studies, for example, one possible reason for hearkening to an interpretation is the institutional position occupied by the man or woman who proposes it, the fact that he or she has a record of successfully made (that is, influential) arguments, or is known as the editor of a standard text, or is identified with an important "approach," or is highly placed in a professional organization (a department, a professional society), or all of the above. These and other institutional facts are not external to the issue of intellectual authority, because the very shape of intellectual authority—in the form of "powerful" arguments and "decisive" evidence and "compelling" reasons—has been established (not for all time, but for a season) by the same processes that have established these facts—by publications, public appearances, pedagogical influence, etc. When a Northrop Frye or a Jacques Derrida speaks, it is with all the considerable weight of past achievements, battles fought and won, constituencies created, agendas proposed and enacted; and that weight is inseparable from the "intellectual" decision to "comply" with what they have said. (They are the E.F. Huttons of our profession.) Of course, Frye and Derrida cannot call in the judiciary or the Congress or the president of the United States to implement their interpretations, but there are other means of implementation at their disposal and at the disposal of their adherents. They can influence decisions about tenure, promotion, publications, grants, leaves, appointments, prizes, teaching assignments, etc. Although the "compliance" secured by these and other means is more diffuse and less direct than the compliance secured by a judge, it is rooted in authority nevertheless, and this authority, like that wielded in the law, is *at once* intellectual and institutional. This is not to deny that literary and legal practice are importantly different, but their differences cannot be captured by drawing the kind of line Fiss draws.

It may seem that by collapsing so many distinctions—between the intellectual and the institutional, between authority and power, between virtue and authority—I am undermining the possibility of rational adjudication; but in fact, everything I have said points to the conclusion that adjudication does not need these distinctions (any more than it needs "disciplining rules") to be rational. All it needs is an understanding, largely tacit, of the enterprise's general purpose; with that in place (and it could not help but be) everything else follows. Fiss knows this too, but not in a way that figures strongly in his analysis. He knows, for example, that a "judge quickly learns to read in a way that avoids crises,"[37] and that "[t]he judge must give a remedy";[38] but he does not recognize such facts for what they are: the very motor of adjudication and a guarantee of its orderliness. The judge who has learned to read in a way that avoids crises is a judge who has learned what it means to be a judge, and has learned that the maintenance of continuity is a prime judicial obligation because without continuity the rule of law cannot claim to be stable and rooted in durable principles. It is not simply that crisis would be disruptive of the process, but that crisis and disruption are precisely what the process is supposed to forestall. That is why the judge must give a remedy: not only because the state, defendant, and plaintiff have a right to one, but also because every time a remedy is given the message is repeated that there is always a remedy to be found, and that the law thereby underwrites and assures the ongoing and orderly operations of society.

The situation is exactly the reverse in literary studies, at least in the context of a modernist aesthetic where the rule is that a critic must learn to read in a way that *multiplies* crises, and must never give a remedy in the sense of a single and unequivocal answer to the question, What does the poem or novel or play mean? This rule is nowhere written down, and the ways of following it are nowhere enumerated. But it is a rule inherent in the discipline's deepest beliefs about the objects of its attention, in its deepest understanding of what literary works are for—for contemplation, for the reflective exploration of complexity, for the entertainment of many perspectives, for the *suspension of judgment*. Critics who hold these beliefs (and, for many, to hold them or be held by them is what it means to be a critic) interrogate texts assumed to be literary in such a way as to "reveal" the properties—ambiguity, irony, multivalence—a literary text is supposed to have. That is to say, the procedures of literary criticism— its methods of inquiry, notions of evidence, mechanisms for evaluation—flow naturally from a sense, already in place, of what literature is and should be; and it follows that these same procedures are not in need of any external or independent constraints to assure their orderliness. A literary critic faced with an interpretive task always knows in general what to do (find interpretive crises), although the ways of doing it will vary with the circumstances, with his commitment to this or that methodology, with the currently received wisdom about a text or a period, with the scope of the project (a teaching of a single poem, of an entire oeuvre, of a genre, of a period). And, by the same reasoning, a judge always knows in general what to do (avoid crises, give a remedy), although his ways of doing it will vary with the nature of the case, with the forces (political, social, legislative) pressing for this or that decision, with the (interpreted) history of previous decisions.[39]

In neither discipline, then, does rationality depend on the presence of "disciplining rules"; nor is the shape of rationality a function of different kinds of texts. Legal texts might be written in verse or take the form of narratives or parables (as they have in some cultures); but so long as the underlying rationales of the enterprise were in place, so long as it was understood (at a level too deep to require articulation) that judges give remedies and avoid crises, those texts would be explicated so as to yield the determinate or settled result the law requires. In both law and literature it is ways of reading, inseparable from the fact of the institution itself, and not rules or special kinds of texts that validate and justify the process of rational interpretation, whether it leads to the rendering of a clear-cut legal decision or to the demonstration that what is valuable about a poem is its resolute refusal to decide.

All of which is to say that, while I stand with Fiss in his desire to defend adjudication in the face of "nihilist" and "subjectivist" arguments, I do not believe that this defense need take the form of asserting a set of external constraints, because the necessary constraints are always already in place. Indeed, I would put the case even more strongly: it is not just that the dangers Fiss would guard against—the dangers of excessive interpretive freedom, of "masked power," of random or irresponsible activity—have been neutralized, but that they are *unrealizable*, because the conditions that would make them the basis of a reasonable fear—the condition of free subjectivity, of "naturally" indeterminate texts, of unprincipled authority—could never obtain; the worst-case scenario that Fiss calls up in his penultimate paragraph could never unfold:

> The great public text of modern America, the Constitution, would be drained of meaning. It would be debased. It would no longer be seen as embodying a public morality to be understood and expressed through rational processes like adjudication; it would be reduced to a mere instrument of political organization—distributing political power and establishing the modes by which that power will be exercised. Public values would be defined only as those held by the current winners in the processes prescribed by the Constitution; beyond that, there would be only individual morality, or even worse, only individual interests.[40]

Were I to attempt a full-fledged analysis of this paragraph, I would find myself repeating everything I have said thus far, for it has been the business of this essay to redefine and recharacterize every one of the concepts and entities Fiss here invokes. On my analysis, the Constitution cannot be drained of meaning, because it is not a repository of meaning; rather, meaning is always being conferred on it by the very political and institutional forces Fiss sees as threats. Nor can these forces be described as "mere," because their shape and exercise are constrained by the very principles they supposedly endanger. And, since the operation of these forces is indeed principled, the fact that they determine (for a time) what will be thought of as "public values" is not something to be lamented, but simply a reflection of the even more basic fact that values derive from the political and social visions that are always competing with one another for control of the state's machinery. Moreover, such values are never "individual," since they always have their source in some conventional system of purposes, goals, and standards; therefore, the very notion of "merely individual" interests is empty.[41] In short, if *these* are the fears that animate Fiss's efforts, then there is nothing for him to worry about.

Paradoxically, he need not even be worried by the possibility that his account of adjudication might be wrong. Fiss believes that it is important to get things right because, if we don't, nihilism might triumph. Nihilism must therefore be "combated" in "word and in deed" because it "calls into question the very point of constitutional adjudication."[42] But if I am right, nihilism is impossible; one simply cannot "exalt the . . . subjective dimension of the interpretation"[43] or drain texts of meanings, and it is unnecessary to combat something that is not possible. Of course, there may be people who regard themselves as nihilists or subjectivists (whether these are the people who promote "deconstruction" is the subject of another essay), and who try to instruct others in nihilist ways, but the fact that they intend the impossible does not make them capable of doing it; they would simply be conferring meanings and urging courses of action on the basis of principles they had not fully comprehended. One could of course combat those principles and dispute those meanings; but in doing so one would simply be urging alternative courses of action, not combating nihilism.

Another way of putting this is to say that nothing turns on Fiss's account or, for that matter, on my account either. To be sure, one would rather be right than wrong, but in this case being right or wrong has no consequences for the process we are both trying to describe.[44] Fiss thinks otherwise; he thinks that there are consequences and that they are grave ones: "Viewing adjudication as interpretation helps to stop the slide toward nihilism. It makes law possible."[45] But if the slide toward nihilism is not a realizable danger, the urging of nihilist views cannot accelerate it, and, conversely, the refutation of nihilist views cannot retard it. From either direction, the account one has of adjudication is logically independent of one's ability to engage in it. Your account may be nihilist or (as it is for Fiss) objectivist or (as it is for me) conventionalist, and when all is said and done, adjudication is still either possible or it is not. The empirical evidence is very strong that it is; and it has been my argument that its possibility is a consequence of being situated in a field of practice, of having passed through a professional initiation or course of training and become what the sociologists term a "competent member." Owen Fiss has undergone that training, but I have not; and, therefore, even though I believe that his account of adjudication is wrong and mine is right, anyone who is entering the legal process would be well advised to consult Fiss rather than Fish.

The Poetics of Legal Interpretation

Jessica Lane

The editors had initially planned to include at this point an essay by Professor Ronald Dworkin, "How Law is Like Literature," which can be found in his A Matter of Principle *(Cambridge, Mass.: Harvard University Press, 1985), pp. 146–66. Professor Dworkin informed the editors, however, that he wished not to have the essay reprinted, as it does not represent his most mature thinking about interpretation. The editors, of course, respected his wishes in this matter.*

Professor Dworkin's earlier views have, though, taken on a certain life of their own; they have been the subject of much scholarly writing. The editors have therefore chosen to include the following review of A Matter of Principle *by Jessica Lane, in which she summarizes and discusses some of his arguments. Students interested in Professor Dworkin's most recent statement of his position should consult* Law's Empire *(Cambridge, Mass.: Harvard University Press, 1986), pp. 45–87, 228–38.*

Homer's *Odyssey* principally chronicles the difficulties encountered by Odysseus on his return from the Trojan War. But Homer speaks also of Menelaus, stranded on the island of Pharos. There Menelaus sought out the sea-god Proteus, whose counsel he wished to obtain. This god had the power to change shape when apprehended. Thus he eluded any seeker. Menelaus, however, unwilling to be shaken off, grasped Proteus relentlessly through each appalling change, until at last the god took on his own form and submitted to questioning.

This myth illustrates the reading of texts generally, but is especially pertinent to Ronald Dworkin's work. Dworkin is unusually susceptible to misreading, perhaps because he never adverts to any first principles but his own. Thus, more than with many texts, dismaying—even chimerical—shapes appear to readers who come without knowing, or without sharing, its assumptions or aims. Moreover, after an exchange with his critics, Dworkin has sometimes revised his own estimate of the shape he meant his work to take. Interpretation, then, is like the task of holding Proteus: readers must keep a grip while the object of attention assumes provisional, often unappealing shapes. But they must also recognize when the text has assumed its true shape and can give an answer.

In *A Matter of Principle*, Dworkin collects a series of essays written in the seven years since publication of *Taking Rights Seriously*. Several pieces tackle the hoary Dworkinian issue of the distinction between policy and principle, showing the practical effect of the distinction on our view of different forms of civil disobedience, or of censorship.[1] Other chapters take up questions such as the philosophical status of judicial decisions framed according to an economic analysis, the legitimacy of affirmative action, and the appropriate basis for freedom of the press. The material with the greatest long-term significance for Dworkin's work, however, appears in the essay "How Law Is Like Literature" (hereafter HLL).[2]

Dworkin argues that law is an arena where principles of political morality necessarily inform judicial decision-making. At the same time, he wants to show that such decisions, though "deeply and thoroughly political," are not contaminated by the vagaries of judicial whim, or even by personal politics (p. 146). Yet it is the difficulty of distinguishing between personal politics and political morality that has given force to the legal realists' critique. Dworkin has explained the distinction, in principle, in various ways. Recently, he has found his answer in the talismanic phrase, "interpretation." Indeed, his most recent book, *Law's Empire*, is an attempt to construct a theory of law from the theory of interpretation sketched in HLL. Although Dworkin has succeeded in shedding light on how law and literature approach texts, he fails to persuade that a unitary conception of interpretation can be specified for all disciplines. Interpretation, as in the case of Menelaus, answers questions regulated by purposes that a reader brings to a text. It is precisely because the disciplines aim at quite different ends, and wish to work out quite distinct social and psychological imperatives, that even literary critics who substantially agree with Dworkin have engaged him in bitter debate.[3]

I. Interpretation within the Chain

Dworkin's theory of interpretation involves two essential components, both of which are couched in literary terms. First, Dworkin describes the imperative he believes all literary interpretation seeks to fulfill: "the aesthetic hypothesis" (pp. 149–54). Second, he proposes a model for interpretation as a social practice: "the chain novel" (pp. 158–62). The essay begins with a definition of this "aesthetic hypothesis," which, for legal interpretation, might be called "the political morality hypothesis." Dworkin's aesthetic hypothesis states: "Interpretation of a text attempts to show *it* as the best work of art *it* can be, and the pronoun insists on the difference between explaining a work of art and changing it into a different one" (p. 150).

Briefly, Dworkin proposes that differences in the interpretation of a text are theory-dependent[4] insofar as they can be ascribed to different beliefs on the part of interpreters about what is valuable in literature (or political morality) (pp. 150–51). On this view, each interpreter inevitably reads the text as the best example it can be of the complex of aesthetic values (or values of political morality) that dominate the interpreter's thought (pp. 151–52).

Dworkin depicts the social practice of interpretation as a "chain novel." In this literary form, used in parlor games or perhaps the rare avant-garde novel, chapters are written sequentially by different authors (p. 150). For Dworkin, this is a game with strict procedural rules. Each author must "interpret" rather than "invent" the meaning of the novel previously created. Moreover, each must *continue* the novel rather than starting anew, or striking out in a new direction. Even when a new start would improve the novel, the interpreter is bound by the task of continuing. Put another way, each author must write the next chapter of "a single unified novel," not one of a series of discrete episodes (p. 159).

Within the chain, however, participants may engage in very distinct practices. Of what these practices are, Dworkin says very little, beyond the proviso that they be understood by the person using them as practices of "interpretation" (p. 161). Yet for interpreters with different aesthetic values (or political morality values, in the case of law), the legitimacy of any practice can become a matter of dispute. For example, one interpreter's idea of a plot device that continues the novel may seem an abrupt change in course, even a violation of the novel's meaning, to another. Disagreements will persist so long as interpreters have differing values, whether about aesthetics or about any of the other substantive issues involved in novel-writing. Nonetheless, in a chain novel, such diverse efforts properly constitute a common enterprise.

Dworkin links literary and legal interpretation by drawing a parallel between the writing of a chain novel and judicial decision-making.

> Each judge must regard himself, in deciding the new case before him, as a partner in a complex chain enterprise of which these innumerable decisions, structures, conventions, and practices [of "arguably similar cases decided over decades or even centuries past"] are the history; it is his job to continue that history into the future through what he does on the day. He *must* interpret what has gone before because he has a responsibility to advance the enterprise in hand rather than strike out in some new direction of his own. So he must determine, according to his own judgment, what the earlier decisions come to, what the point or theme of the practice so far, taken as a whole, really is. [P. 159]

Joining the political morality hypothesis to the chain novel model, Dworkin posits a theory by which even the great controversies of legal interpretation can be seen as part of a unified, if heterogeneous, enterprise of lawmaking. What will be shared among interpreters will be not a list of results, but a set of practices. In this way, the theory tries to increase the resiliency of a communal undertaking that is structurally a battleground for the resolution of bitter disputes.

The controversial nature of judgments has always threatened the legitimacy of law. Law's pressure point comes when conflicting interpretations of the way things "are" collide in litigation. Acting through official interpreters, the law legitimates one answer and rejects the other. Since law is inextricably involved in reconciling "irreconcilable" differences, any theory of law must account for the persistent presence of incompatible interpretations. Each argument's claim to truth is advocated by one party to the dispute; indeed, if the opposing arguments were not at least colorable, the dispute would not become a "legal" one.

When Dworkin wrote "Model of Rules I,"[5] the positivist analysis of law saw judicial discretion as the chief threat to legitimacy. In that essay, Dworkin denied the possibility of "strong" discretion. Ultimately he grounded judicial authority not in rules, but in the "articulate consistency" of opinions as written instances of a judge's comprehensive theory of rights.[6] Public scrutiny and rational debate assured judicial competence. Moreover, Dworkin implied that the need to offer consistent arguments capable of withstanding scrutiny would do the work of constraining arguments to be sincere in the absence of transparent truth. It would itself, in other words, militate against self-interest.

A different threat to legitimacy attends a theory of law as interpretation. Dworkin is plagued by the charge that theory dependence is skeptical, because it must admit that there is no right answer (pp. 168–69).[7] Each value-laden theory, say the skeptics, will produce its own right answer, but none will have a paramount claim to that right necessary to ground the legitimacy of law, as more than a display of power. Nor will there be any way to adjudicate among right answers since any adjudicator will also have adopted a set of personal values.

Dworkin has essayed the Gordian knot of the right answer before. Indeed, after each contest, he emerges the embattled victor—yet the tangle seems always to persist.[8] He never addresses this problem squarely in HLL, although in the essay that is an earlier version of his chapter "On Interpretation and Objectivity," Dworkin links the concept of "the right answer" to an interpreter's belief that he can distinguish his inventions from his interpretations:

> [N]o interpreter can accept a right/wrong picture unless he can distinguish (or in any case thinks he can distinguish) between his own interpretive beliefs and his own inventions, unless the activities of interpreting and inventing seem different to him. And his way of making these distinctions, for himself, must correspond to the way others make the same distinctions for themselves. . . . So we must ask: "How *do* we distinguish between interpreting and inventing?

How *do* we decide that one interpretation or one argument for an interpretation is better than another?"[9]

Dworkin takes for granted that most interpreters accept the "right/wrong picture." Moreover, he recasts this distinction as one between interpreting and inventing, as if these were two separate activities. Yet, as I will suggest, is seems more likely that in the process of interpreting, "inventions"—ranging from stray thoughts and irrational associations to cliches—form the groundwork for what will later be called the interpretation. Dworkin also seems to assume that interpreters will come to believe in the validity of their own distinctions if and only if the distinctions correspond to those made by others in the interpretive community.[10]

Nevertheless, Dworkin never gives an answer to the questions that close the quoted paragraph. The distinction between interpreting and inventing is at the core of an argument that Dworkin has yet to explore fully—despite a dramatic initial claim that any theory of law that so fails must remain suspect. He begins, "law is not a matter of personal or partisan politics, and a critique of law that does not understand this difference will provide poor understanding and even poorer guidance" (p. 146).

Dworkin's model of legal interpretation, the chain novel, erodes the wall between interpreting and creating, blurring the distinctions between the impersonal and the personal, the right and the wrong, the interpreted and the invented. Indeed, the author of each chapter will inevitably invent new elements of plot and may even introduce new characters into the narrative. The problem of serial invention goes beyond the addition of new material, however. It invades the interpretation of what has come before as well.

The process of interpretation is a complex introspective discipline, a movement from conflicting hypothetical thoughts toward a rationalized structure of beliefs. This movement involves an unobservable and often disorganized attempt to adapt various possible readings to one another and to discard those readings that are, on the whole, not as satisfying as the readings kept in play. Moreover, an interpreter must simultaneously distinguish not only which crucial passages in the text will stand for the text as a whole, but which reading of each passage is most susceptible to the exigencies of system formation. The question that Dworkin must answer is, What is there in this inchoate process that protects the interpreter from the impermissible forms of interest that color the inventor's product? Dworkin's one glancing reference to this problem comes in his assertion that interpretations state beliefs about the formal properties and normative qualities of the interpreted object rather than being mere inventions. "These beliefs may be inarticulate (or 'tacit'). They are still genuine beliefs (and not merely 'reactions') because their force for any critic or reader can be seen at work not just on one isolated occasion but in any number of other occasions, and because they figure in and are amenable to argument" (p. 152).

But can these beliefs really be seen so readily on any number of occasions? Moreover, since inevitably there will be occasions where particular beliefs will seem to be put aside in favor of other, apparently supervening beliefs, what number of occasions is necessary to validate belief? The critic Paul de Man, in an influential book, *Blindness and Insight*, has argued that it is precisely in their conflicting impulses, their oversights, and subtle reversals that texts bear their most powerful messages.[11] Such problems of consistency and uncertainty—and for the law they clearly are problems—inevitably cast doubt on the validity of *any* interpretation. That they cannot be finally resolved, except in closing down debate, gives force to the critique of the legal realists and their descendants.

Dworkin's view to the contrary, it seems that the raw material of interpretation is reaction and therefore invention. We work toward and retrospectively attribute consistency and coherence to the system that evolves, always bringing forward arguments for its rationality ad hoc. But each inspection of the interpretive system is limited by our inability to perceive the system from the outside. Indeed, all we can do is attempt to articulate its coherence from somewhere within the system, our judgment necessarily skewed by the distinct pressure point of that part which is our immediate concern.

What connects Dworkin's new theory with his prior work is the aura of romance with which he surrounds the idea of rationality. Dworkin worked strenuously to invent Hercules, the ideal interpreter and embodiment of rationality in human affairs. His concession to human imperfection was the corrective mechanism of rational debate. Together, these have provided the infrastructure of Dworkin's belief in the legitimacy of the law. They allowed mistakes to be defeated by argument, not power, and to be reversed in a communal and progressive approximation of the global rationality of a Hercules.

The image of the chain novel lends to interpretation a very different character from the global rationality of the Hercules model. Hercules represents a completely coherent and consistent system of thought. Yet Hercules, as Dworkin imagines him, is fundamentally a static concept. Hercules' system, although it might be elaborated over time, would presumably develop solely by virtue of the further unfolding of distinctions that are already perfectly rationalized. The model does not work if Hercules suddenly discovers that a concept he had never before imagined cuts across many of his subtly balanced and weighted principles, or casts them in an entirely different light. However, even the history of an individual interpreter's thought shows that judgments taken at one point will be overthrown later, perhaps because the context itself forces the questions being asked to take on new dimensions. In keeping with this, the chain novel evokes a positional rationality, one that is continually reintegrating the meaning of the moves previously made. Thus as a model for law as a communal enterprise, the chain responds to the observation that the history of the judicial system is riddled with twists and turns embarrassing to the Hercules model.

Thus, even in terms of its explanatory power, the chain is a more adequate conception of law. On the surface, the Hercules model may have seemed a more secure foundation for the legitimacy of state power. Yet this surface perception is an illusion. Perfect rationality may be the perfect instrument of a monumental tyranny. No argument is adduced for the justice of the system, only for the probity of its internal logic. The chain novel is rationality on a more human scale. But even here, Dworkin's work implies a faith in a convergence, a natural sympathy between the world interpreters have created and what should be. This is the romance of the rational. However, Dworkin himself would surely concede that an internal logic, no matter how self-adapted, cannot by itself satisfy the requirement of legitimacy. Rationality alone, then, cannot do the work that he requires of it.

II. The Problem of Intentionalism

A. Is Intentionalism Really Necessary?

One great virtue of his theory, Dworkin asserts, lies in its power to shed new light on the question whether the Constitution—or indeed any legal document—should be interpreted according to the authors' intention. Dworkin's attack on intentionalist interpretation[12] has obvious implications for recent debate on constitutional interpretation. On one side, "originalists" (or "interpretivists") propose that the proper aim of constitutional interpretation is to understand and deploy the intention of the Framers;[13] on the other side, "nonoriginalists" (or "noninterpretivists") argue that in order to adapt the Constitution to changing conditions, the courts must go beyond the Framers' intentions.[14] However, both sides of the originalist debate misconceive the role of the author's intention in textual interpretation by improperly conflating originalism with intentionalism. Any reading requires the use of a conception of the author's intention. However, this is not to privilege in advance any particular conception of that intention; each reading will stipulate (or will simply assign) intentions in its own way.

Dworkin seems to act on what are to him two insurmountable

objections to intentionalism. First, he appears to believe that adopting the intentionalist view would require him to accept the originalist conception of author's intention.[15] Second, he insists that intentionalists inevitably and impermissibly substitute their own beliefs for the author's intentions (p. 158).[16]

What Dworkin, and indeed even the so-called originalists themselves, fail to see is that all interpretation involves the explication of the intention of the text's author, whose "intention to mean" x or y is embodied in the text. The very thing that makes a text a text, rather than a clump of squiggles or a knot of empty vocables, is the fact that an author or authors, meaning something by the words, wrote them down. However difficult this makes interpretation of a document like the Constitution, which has many putative authors, it is the unavoidable fact.

The originalists' claim is simply one, by no means necessary, conception of how intention should be stipulated for reading the Constitution. However—and this is a large however—any such particular conception will become *the* way of interpreting, indeed of reading, for those who hold it. Of course, those who do not share this conception of intention will be considered by its proponents to be making incorrect interpretations, or even not to be interpreting at all. Ironically, it is the entrenchment of the originalist conception of author's intention that poses an obstacle to the understanding of intentionalism's larger point.[17]

Nonoriginalists like Dworkin, then, also have too rigid an idea of what counts as intention. In essence, the nonoriginalists have needlessly conceded the field of "intention" to originalists, rather than making arguments for their own ways of stipulating and deriving intention. Dworkin persists in this mistake in part because he argues that any consideration of author's intention must necessarily reflect what he characterizes accurately as "doctrinaire author's intention theories," involving "what the author in some narrow and constrained sense intended to put there" (p. 154).[18] In a sense, Dworkin's characterization of the interpretivist position as a "narrow and constrained" conception of author's intention is exactly right; the puzzle is why he then proceeds to ban intentionalism altogether.

During his debate with the literary critic Stanley Fish, however, Dworkin conceded, if backhandedly, that intention is somehow important.[19] Fearing that this requires every concrete intention attributable to the Framers be enforced in perpetuity, Dworkin thinks that he must contrive an escape from intentionalism. He proposes that the intention specified by the interpreter be taken not as the intention of the real author, but of an imagined author whose intention, if it had existed, would have required the reading that the interpreter has made. But he insists that the chimerical intentions of this imagined author not be identified with the "intentions of the particular historical person whom we identify as its actual author."[20] This proposal is designed to cut interpreters loose from the framers' "real" intentions, while acknowledging the role that the idea of intentionality plays in interpretation. Yet this is nonsensical, particularly from someone who begins with the belief that continuing the chain rather than starting anew is the signal trait of interpretation. It is precisely the attempt to distinguish what the original author meant that constrains the interpretive enterprise. The chain is, in fact, a chain of intentions held together by the shared interpretive project of reconstituting, under changing conditions, the force of the intentions that animated, and animate, a central document.

Dworkin has forgotten that, according to his political morality hypothesis, the interpreter's values will necessarily provide the terms for ascribing intention to the author.[21] But to provide such terms is not to substitute interpretation for intention, but rather to interpret in the only way one can, viz., in one's own terms. Dworkin's suggestion, moreover, leads to some peculiar results. According to Dworkin, in conversation with a friend, an intentionalist interpreter would be substituting her interpretation for her friend's intentions, while they spoke.[22] Far from understanding what her real friend intended to say, she would be constructing an imagined friend whose intentions corresponded to the ones that she was interpretively inclined to hear.[23] Such conversational interpretations would be carried out, as Dworkin says, according to a friendly-conversation hypothesis, including values for how friends should (and do) act and whatever the subject of the conversation was. But then we would all walk in a world of phantasmic acquaintances, despite the fact that all our hypotheses about meaning are intended to produce "reality," not imaginary worlds.

B. Can "Formal Values" Displace the Author?

Constraining interpretation is all the more urgent for Dworkin's theory of law, for it acknowledges the pervasive instability of the interpretive enterprise. This instability, finally clarified by theory-dependent explanations of meaning, arises from the fact that different interpreters will frequently have different values. Moreover, as is generally accepted, language is indeterminate and its meanings contextually derived. Dworkin here is cutting himself loose from those experiential constructs—the author and the intention—whose inscription within our imagination acts as an unconscious constraint on the meanings we ascribe.

Yet Dworkin thinks he can escape from intentionalism because he has translated the constraining structure of the idea of author's intention into what he calls the "formal dimension" of interpretation. His general strategy is to say that interpreters apply not only substantive values—

values, say, for "law and order" or "equal rights"—but also formal values, when they interpret. However, it is naive to think that the elements of the formal dimension are being applied *except* through the deep structures that give shape to what we think. An analysis of Dworkin's interpretive "dimensions" reveals that Dworkin's success in describing the formal dimension misleads him into thinking that he can eliminate the author, and thus the intentionalist argument.

Dworkin suggests that in interpreting a text, readers read it according to both substantive and formal values. Substantive values have to do with "the function or point of art more broadly conceived" (p. 151). For example, nineteenth-century interpreters of Jane Austen's *Persuasion* were often concerned with the heroine's obedience to her misguided elders and the possible weakening effect this could have on the moral constitutions of women readers.[24] Twentieth-century interpretations have either centered on Austen's irony, often as a means of shedding light on her own psychology,[25] or on questions of class conflict and change,[26] and in feminist criticism, with Austen's critique of patriarchy.[27]

Substantive values define the kinds of content an interpreter will think a text (or author) has "in mind." The objection may be raised that Austen had no thoughts such as those feminists now read in (or, in this objection, "read into") her novels. But, of course, feminists answer that Austen need not have been aware of her indictment of her own society; she need not have put it in terms of our polemics. Nevertheless, she surely did intend *this* portrait, even if she believed, as feminists do not, that this is how things must and even, in part, should be. Indeed, if Austen makes readers uneasy or raises doubts about a society that allows women such as her protagonist to waste their lives in submissive remorse, it may be that she had such doubts as well. This last suggestion hints at how difficult it may be to disentangle the author's and reader's values on sensitive matters.

Dworkin's formal dimension, however, which includes such textual properties as "identity" and "integrity," is far more difficult to grasp (pp. 150–52). This dimension concerns more inchoate decisions about how an interpretation establishes its accuracy and completeness. Substantive values usually can be formulated independent of a reading.[28] Formal values, on the contrary, which organize the text as an exemplar of the governing substantive values, are realized in a reading, but cannot be abstracted from it, even if in any particular instance readers can explain specific formal decisions. The impossibility of prescribing, and thus regularizing, formal values is made clear by Dworkin's own attempt to do so.

> An interpretive style will also be sensitive to the interpreter's opinions about coherence and integrity in art. An interpretation cannot make a

work of art more distinguished if it makes a large part of the text irrelevant, or much of the incident accidental, or a great part of the trope or
style unintegrated and answering only to independent standards of fine
writing. [P. 150]

Dworkin's explanation is seriously misleading. Every interpretation
necessarily makes much of a text irrelevant. In the process of interpreting, key phrases come to stand paradigmatically for the text as a whole.
Additionally, interpreters of necessity privilege passages that suggest
their own substantive values. It is equally possible to regard certain parts
of the text as flawed and undeserving of attention. Certainly, literary critics feel free to concentrate on selected portions of a work, an approach at
odds with Dworkin's holistic view. For example, books 11 and 12 of *Paradise Lost* were long considered inferior to the rest and consequently were
neglected in scholarship. Moreover, parts of Webster's *The Duchess of
Malfi* are currently thought to be bizarre and assignable to no intention
we wish to recognize. Yet the play is taught in Renaissance Drama
courses and is considered one of the most important non-Shakespearean
tragedies. In law, too, part of a judge's opinion is not infrequently given
great importance in determining future results while another part is entirely ignored.[29] This is especially true since law is a discipline that deals
with discrete issues.

Dworkin's idea of identity, a primary component of his formal dimension, is intimately connected to his idea of textuality.

Contemporary theories of interpretation all seem to use, as part of their
response to [the] requirement [of identity], the idea of a canonical text
(or score, in the case of music, or unique physical object, in the case of
most art). The text provides one severe constraint in the name of identity: all the words must be taken account of and none may be changed to
make "it" a putatively better work of art. (This constraint, however familiar, is not inevitable. A joke, for example, may be the same joke told
in a variety of forms, none of them canonical . . .). [P. 150]

Even on its face, Dworkin's point about canonicity is open to attack.
With the advent of variorum editions, the idea of a single text that represents an author's "final" intentions—as canonical texts have been
thought to do—has become more difficult to sustain.[30] My point is not
that canonicity is unimportant, but that Dworkin's counterexample, the
joke, may be the paradigm of canonicity in the sense that any number of
texts may legitimately claim to be "the" canonical text, none of them to
the exclusion of the others. One might then consider all texts that included certain features as versions of the "same poem" (as opposed to "different poems"), as one would with a joke. In law, where the need is for
integration of efforts, rather than for a proliferation of subtly innovative
readings, having one, absolutely uniform text may be of paramount

importance. If that is so, law is on an extreme end of an interpretive spectrum.[31]

Dworkin's requirement that "none [of the words] may be changed to make 'it' a putatively better work" is logical only if interpreters are trying to preserve an author's intention. Why *not* make the work better? The necessity of one, universally consulted text is one answer. But we could agree to change the words if this substantially improved the text. Indeed, textual scholars do change the words of a text intermittently over the span of its history. Notably, such changes are always made in the name of recovering the author's true intention.[32]

Moreover, Dworkin's analogy to a unique physical object masks the complexity of textual identity. If disputes over identity had to do only with defining the canonical text, they would be, as Dworkin says, of minor significance. However, canonicity does not exhaust, but only makes possible, the struggle over the identity of a text. The problem of identity is how a reader can determine which word any word "is"—precisely what it refers to.[33] It is how words reach out into the system of language, so far and no farther, that defines the invisible identity of that text alone. Reading is the process of delineating the reach of the associative net that words cast out into the language. But only the belief that marks on a page stand for the intention of their author to use words in precisely the way that *that* author would use them—to refer to *that* context in precisely *that* way—tells an interpreter how to cast the net.[34] Hence, contextuality is constructed around, and then insinuates meaning back into, texts.[35]

Indeed, Dworkin's notion of identity cannot give a manageable account of intertextuality. In following the associative thread, other texts—whether poems, letters, diaries, or critical writings—often affect our understanding of the text we are interpreting. Only the idea of the author can explain how we sort out these pressures—why texts by the same person are thought to bear more strongly on the text at hand than texts by any other person, even one writing in the same historical context.[36]

In deciphering the author's intention, "who" the author is, is pivotal. Yet even *that* identity is subject to the vicissitudes of interpretation. To know, for example, that Milton wrote *Paradise Lost* is only a first step. What an interpreter thinks Milton meant by a line of poetry will depend on the interpreter's view of what kinds of things "Milton" is likely to mean, based on an understanding of Milton in psychological, religious, political, or poetical terms. The author, then, embodies the idea of the integrated identity that informs the text. Integrity and identity are the concepts that an interpreter intuitively puts into practice by thinking concretely and carefully about an author's intention.[37]

Dworkin argues that intentionalism "does not challenge the political hypothesis but contests for its authority" (p. 163). In other words, intentionalism is a conception of interpretation; however, it is only one among many such conceptions which vie, as Dworkin seems to imagine it, for the nod of the political morality hypothesis. Intentionalism is inextricably involved with notions of language as communication and as context-bound. What follows from Dworkin's demotion of intentionalism is that interpretation is cut loose from both communication and context in a way that implies that meaning can be constructed in their absence. Moreover, his essays show that he believes that interpretation is "structured" in such a way as to divorce the level of author's (or speaker's) meaning from the level of the meaning of the work as a whole.[38] In contemporary debate, these positions have been staked out by the French philosopher Jacques Derrida in favor of such values as free play and indeterminacy.[39] It is true that the value of communication may compete against values such as indeterminacy and free play for the "crown" that the political morality hypothesis has in mind. These values hardly seem to be what Dworkin has in mind. Although his theory never directly confronts the problem of indeterminacy, free play seems distinctly inimical to it.

Two of Dworkin's premises may explain his drastic underestimation of the problems that afflict any theory of interpretation cut loose from intentionalism. First, Dworkin's notion of the chain novel suggests that, over time, rationality will prevail, so that debates which were open to extremes of opinion at the beginning of the chain will be resolved by the "novel's" end.[40] What deceives him is the analogy between law as a historical process and the novel as an aesthetic event. The novel has, as part of its formal structure, a thrust toward closure, a property any parlor-game novel writer will take into account. There is nothing analogous to these structures of closure in law; nor could techniques be developed to achieve closure, in view of law's inscription in history, where succeeding contexts motivate the substitutions and displacements of "free" play.

A second factor is Dworkin's idea that most disagreements in law take place on the substantive level (p. 151). Interpreters can debate substantive issues directly; and although the debates may not in practice be susceptible of resolution, they seem theoretically limitable because subject to the scrutiny of rational analysis. This, however, is one of the myths of rationality that Dworkin purveys. He overlooks that substantive meaning is filtered through the interpreter's formal values. These values make the text what it is; and interpreters with different substantive values are essentially disputing the identity of the text. In this sense, interpreters with different values are reading "different" texts. The difference here is felt to be a metaphoric one because it is the identity of the text that holds together the interpretive community; but the difference is real nevertheless. Thus interpreters who hold the substantive values of law and order will give priority to phrases that embody those values; indeed, they will read all passages in terms of how they fulfill the imperatives of law and order. On the other hand, interpreters who value "human dignity" will emphasize other passages, and will read each phrase with the imperatives of "human dignity" in mind. Thus when Dworkin claims that most debates are about substantive value, he ignores the fact that substantive debate inescapably uses arguments derived from and realized through formal values—arguments resolvable, if at all, only on that plane. Intentionalism, as a way to understand what is otherwise dissolved in the subliminal play of formal values, thus gives back to interpreters a means of arguing substantively about the formal dimension.

C. The Consequences of Intentionalism

Dworkin's second objection to intentionalism is a practical one. He worries about the effect that intentionalist interpretation might have on how, for example, one would read the equal protection clause (p. 163). The question is whether, in holding that the clause does not permit segregation, interpreters are not substituting their values for the intentions of the "real, historical" authors—or creating imagined authors whose intentions conform to their antisegregationist beliefs. Intentionality here becomes a multidimensional problem. Different literary, psychological, and legal interpretations will be directed toward, and will excavate, different, sometimes mutually exclusive, intentions. But, more important, any single interpretation will necessarily find many conflicting intentions in the text. A theory that understands intention as monolithic, and not composed of many impulses, some more consistent than others, is a reductive theory of intention.

The antisegregationist interpretation is not a "substitution" because the essential axiom of legal interpretation—the belief holding together the chain—is that the real authors (and thus their text) share the values of the interpreter to some important degree. Suppose a reader believes the authors of the Fourteenth Amendment intended to create a government in which citizens were afforded the equal protection of the laws. Suppose the reader also believes that they did not want to associate with black people and that this reservation may have confused them in applying their own good purpose, or that they did not believe that education was a central public good. This conflict would be resolved somewhat along the following lines. First, in light of the increased importance of public education or because of the understanding that the desire for nonassociation comes from illegitimate feelings that black people are not quite equal, does the principle of equal protection now require an antisegregationist result? Second, do abstract principles have greater weight in determining constitutional meanings or the concrete practices by which the principles were thought to be captured? The problem would be to look back, in such terms, to the authors, both of the Constitution and the relevant judicial opinions, and to tell the best story of what the point or value of the equal protection enterprise is.[41]

If the result of this interpretive process is a conclusion that the Constitution sanctions segregation in public schools, then citizens must reevaluate its political morality. In some cases, they must amend it, or, if the document is riddled with injustice, write an entirely new document. Indeed, the Thirteenth, Fourteenth, and Fifteenth amendments comprise a partial rewriting of the original Constitution.

What binds individuals into interpretive communities is the drive toward "commensurability"—toward enough agreement on terms of discourse, and thus a conviction of many shared interpretive beliefs. Without this conviction, the chain will be broken. This drive is present in the debate over constraints. For example, interpreters need canonical texts because the words on the page are what all interpreters share. However, different social practices require different degrees of commensurability. Thus, while Dworkin's obsession with the right answer, for example, would be baffling in a literary critic, among lawyers he might be called a principled legal realist.

Finally, one questions the appropriateness of Dworkin's foray into literary theory. As social practices, law and literature speak to vastly different human impulses and needs. Theory dependence, as a system, directs us to examine the purposes any theory means to fulfill in order to understand the force of its interpretations. If this is so, then interpretation must be a different thing when understood by literary critics from what it is when understood by lawyers. Each discipline will conceive of interpretation as a method for serving its particular aims. Even at the most abstract level, ideas are shaped by the agendas out of which they arise and by the ideas in whose company they appear.

The differences between the aims of literary and legal studies can be seen in the different practices and communities each has spawned. It has been pointed out that there is no Pope of literary criticism (although the poet delighted in the pun)—and certainly no Supreme Court. Nor is there any one great text that all literary critics pore over. The literary critical fascination with upheaval and novelty would, as a rule, be disquieting among lawyers. Dworkin's idea of the chain, and particularly of the absolute requirement of continuing, has less power in the context of literary studies. In this respect, the imperative of precedent, while it may be privately respected, is not as compelling a motive of legitimacy as it is in law. Literary criticism is the most highly developed arena we have for the study of the discourse in all its manifestations. Language, the symbolic order, through its construction of the subject, is what constitutes the world, its most perfect products being the texts of reality and art. Consequently, literary criticism responds more deeply to the need for individuation, for elaboration of the intricate possibilities hidden in the dialectic of writing and reading. Law comes into play in regularizing social structures. It works most actively when incommensurable disputes arise, when competing interpretations face one another, and only one must remain at the end. Social integration demands one right answer, even if it strives to meet the condition of individual rights.

Dworkin begins HLL with a strikingly apt question: What is the point of *Hamlet*, as a whole? Fittingly enough, given Dworkin's own struggles, one response is that *Hamlet* is a play about the extreme difficulty of finding the right answer—the answer that action must put into play—and the maddening uncertainty of all evidence. Is the ghost Hamlet's own father, calling him to revenge, or is it a demon, come to lead him to hell? Even though the play lets us (but not Hamlet) know Claudius's own guilty thoughts, it never answers that critical question. Hamlet becomes convinced of Claudius's guilt, yet never arrives at "ocular proof"[42]— proof making the right answer absolute and undeniable. Instead, he depends on an interpretation of an interpretation: it is Claudius's reaction to the play-within-the-play that confirms his belief.[43] Nor does Hamlet act on his answer; he delays until, knowing his own death to be imminent, he lashes out in hopeless brutality.

On one hand, Hamlet. On the other, Hercules. It's a wonder lawyers get any sleep at all.

An Essay in the Deconstruction of Contract Doctrine

Clare Dalton

> [A]pparently the realization of deepgoing antinomies in the structure of our sys-
> tem of contracts is too painful an experience to be permitted to rise to the full level
> of our consciousness.
>
> Friedrich Kessler,
> "Contracts of Adhesion—Some Thoughts about Freedom of Contract"

Introduction

Law, like every other cultural institution, is a place where we tell one another stories about our relationships with ourselves, one another, and authority.[1] In this, law is no different from the *Boston Globe*, the CBS evening news, *Mother Jones*, or a law school faculty meeting. When we tell one another stories, we use languages and themes that different pieces of the culture make available to us, and that limit the stories we can tell. Since our stories influence how we imagine, as well as how we describe, our relationships, our stories also limit who we can be.

In this chapter, by examining the rules of contract law as applied by judges and elaborated by commentators, I ask whether we can begin to understand the particular limits law stories impose on the twin projects of self-definition and self-understanding.[2] Can we, in other words, expose the way law shapes all stories into particular patterns of telling, favors certain stories and disfavors others, or even makes it impossible to tell certain kinds of stories?[3]

The stories told by contract doctrine[4] are preoccupied with what must be central issues in any human endeavor of our time and place. One set of questions concerns power: What separates me from others and connects me to them? What is the threat and the promise to me of other individuals? Can I enjoy the promise without succumbing to the threat? Am I able to create protective barriers that will not at the same time prevent me from sharing the pleasures of community? What is the role of the state in regulating my relations with others? The other set of questions concerns knowledge: How can I know what others see, what they intend? On what basis can I share my understanding of the world with others? Is there a reality separate from my grasp of it? Is communication possible? These central questions of power and knowledge devolve from the split between self and other, subject and object, which structures our experience of the world. This chapter examines precisely how this split structures our contract doctrine—how doctrine devotes its energies to describing, policing, and disguising the divide.

A. The Project Described

In this chapter, I give an account of selected portions of contract doctrine and the themes and problems that permeate them. I demonstrate how our preoccupation with questions on power and knowledge is mirrored in doctrinal structures that depend on the dualities of public and private, objective and subjective, form and substance.[5] I suggest that it is these problems of power and knowledge, these doctrinal structures, which contribute to the inconsistency and substantial indeterminacy of contract doctrine.

In elaborating doctrinal dichotomies, I suggest that contract doctrine consistently favors one pole of each duality: contract law describes itself as more private than public, interpretation as more about objective than subjective understanding, consideration as more about form than about substance. And I suggest further that while the method of hierarchy in duality allows our doctrinal rhetoric to avoid the underlying problems of power and knowledge, it is an avoidance that is also a confession: the problems are only displaced, not overcome. This displacement is both diachronic and synchronic: the problems are frequently presented as having been then and not now, and equally frequently presented as being there and not here. To answer the strategy of displacement, my account necessarily deals with historical moments in the development of doctrine, as well as with doctrine in its current state. My claim is that the problems are now as well as then, here as well as there.

I begin the chapter with a discussion of the public-private distinction in contract law, as reflected in the law's treatment of the implied contract. The implied-in-law contract or quasi contract is traditionally considered an exceptional supplement to the body of contract doctrine; its reliance on social norms to create a public obligation is traditionally viewed as a deviation from contract doctrine's focus on the facilitation of private intent. But I demonstrate that the same factors that lead judges to impose quasi-contractual obligations influence both the "finding" of obligations implied-in-fact and the interpretation of express contracts. In this sense all contracts are public. The courts' creation of categories of contract of varying degrees of privateness is therefore only a strategy of displacing and containing, not resolving, the public threat to the private world of contract.

In part II, I discuss the objective-subjective dichotomy in the context of those areas of contract doctrine—contract formation, the parol evidence rule, and mistake—that directly address questions of communication between parties, and questions of interpretation. I focus on the way doctrine favors objective interpretations of contracts over subjective ones by using devices that deflect attention from the threat objectivity poses to the claim that contract law is more private than public. These devices disguise the law's inability to maintain an objective sphere uncontaminated by subjectivity.

B. Method

To demonstrate my thesis that contract doctrine is organized around the problems of power and knowledge, and that certain areas of doctrine contain particular manifestations of these difficulties, I rely on very close analyses of comparatively few texts. In part because the thinking that has gone into this piece began and continues in the classroom, my selected texts are familiar classroom materials: an assortment of older, well-known cases and recent, less-well-known ones, some seminal articles, and the recently published *Restatement (Second) of Contracts*.[6] My claim is that the patterns of conflict I uncover in the texts I examine, and the mediating devices I identify, are characteristic.

I support this claim in various ways throughout the chapter. First, I draw on cases from different historical periods to show that the central problems of any area of doctrine, and the elements through which the problems are sought to be resolved, remain the same over time, although particular approaches to the resolution of these problems may come and go. Similarly, I draw on some very recent cases to demonstrate that these core problems cannot be consigned to history, but continue to plague the application of contract doctrine in our own time.[7]

My major source of older cases is Kessler and Gilmore's *Contracts: Cases and Materials*.[8] Its disdain for the general rule, its methodical collection of contradictory decisions, and its insistence on contextualization make it perhaps the most skeptical of the traditional teaching materials. I find it particularly useful because of the editors' respectful refusal to edit the heart out of the texts they include, and their preference for opinions in which judges pay close attention to doctrine and wrestle with its limitations. In addition, the editors' many scholarly notes provide a good foil against which to test the possibility of a postrealist reconstruction of the world of doctrine.[9]

I have also chosen to supplement case material with the more general account provided by the *Restatement*. It is often suggested that the *Restatement* sits uneasily between description and prescription, offering both a general account of the statement of doctrine as practiced in the courts, and a preferred vision of what that doctrine should be. For my purposes, either view of the enterprise of the *Restatement* is valuable. Viewed as description, the fact that, as I will show, the *Restatement* shares the patterns I have found to operate in the cases confirms my thesis. Viewed as prescription, it serves as further evidence of our culture's inability to progress beyond the problems I suggest plague the cases. Some might argue, "Yes, but everyone knows that the *Restatement* is an internally conflicted committee product." To this my reply would be, "Isn't it interesting that those same internal conflicts exactly characterize the work of any individual judge?" Still others might charge, "Doesn't your reliance on idiosyncratic judicial products undermine your conclusions?" To this I would answer, "Isn't it interesting that the flaws in the judicial product are exactly those present in the *Restatement?*"

Where I have used particular articles to support my arguments, I have chosen them either because the article itself is recognized as a particularly valuable addition to the literature, or because the author, at least in his own time, was held in high regard. I draw on articles because they, too confirm that the problems inherent in judicial opinions are not the result of judicial inability or inattention, but are instead faithful reflections of the same difficulties that inhere in academic treatments of the same issues. In addition, the article writer often is forced into more complex and more thorough efforts at mediation because of the broader scope of his inquiry. The judge can often write an opinion that appears more coherent because of what he is able to leave out.

It is always possible to cast doubt on an argument by suggesting that it has been insufficiently proven, or proven only by judicious selection of evidence. I would simply have readers ask themselves whether the analyses I suggest are ones that shed light on the material to which they apply those analyses. That a reader is intrigued enough to attempt such further applications, and in trying finds his perceptions altered by the framework I have offered, would make the project, for me, a successful one.

C. The Project Located

My approach to contract doctrines owes much to traditions of scholarship outside of law, and shares much with other attempts to bring these traditions to bear on legal materials and issues. At one level I incorporate a critique of liberal political theory and legal liberalism that has provided a consistently fruitful perspective on structures of legal argumentation.[10] The liberal conception criticized is that individuals can remain free to experience positive interactions with one another without interference by the state, while relying on the state to protect them from negative interactions. Under this liberal conception, clear guidelines as to what are positive and what negative interactions, guidelines formulated as legal rules, prevent the state from overstepping its proper boundaries.[11]

The critique seeks to demonstrate how the various guidelines proposed by liberal legalism lack the clarity on which the liberal order presents itself as depending.[12] The critique further reveals that this lack of clarity represents our inability to decide how we should conceive relationships between people, how we should understand and police the boundary between self and other.[13] Liberalism's obsession with, and inability to resolve, the tension between self and other suggests that our stories about politics, policy, and law will be organized along dualities reflecting this basic tension.[14]

The critique of liberalism connects this central tension within legal thought to the possibility for systematic (although not necessarily conscious) oppression by the "haves" of the "have-nots" through the manipulation of inconsistent but equally legitimate strands of legal argument. This is not a crude determinism, but an explanation of how a legal order that proclaims itself to be based on democratic principles, individual rights, due process, and equal protection can still operate to exclude important constituencies from the benefits available within the society.[15]

If this critique of liberal legal argument has weight, as I believe it does, we need first to understand more concretely how doctrinal inconsistency necessarily undermines the force of any conventional legal argument, and how opposing arguments can be made with equal force. We need also to understand how legal argumentation disguises its own inherent indeterminacy and continues to appear a viable way of talking and persuading. We need, finally, to understand how legal argumentation is used, knowingly or unknowingly, to perpetuate a world view that imposes itself upon constituencies that it simultaneously leaves essentially without power or resources.

In addressing the way legal doctrine is unable to provide determinate answers to particular disputes while continuing to claim an authority based on its capacity to do so, I have drawn on another critical tradition, described loosely as poststructuralism.[16] In particular, I have benefited from the "deconstructive" textual strategies developed by Jacques Derrida,[17] and from the input of colleagues who are incorporating various of these techniques into their own work.[18]

Derrida affirms the role of conceptual duality in the discourse of philosophers since the eighteenth century, and observes that all discourse tends to favor one pole of any duality over the other, creating a hierarchical relationship between the poles.[19] The disfavored pole he calls the dangerous supplement, "dangerous" because of its undermining potential, its role in revealing to us that things are not, after all, what they seem.[20]

Taking as his starting point that philosophy as a discipline depends on a capacity for objective reason and transparent communication, Derrida is concerned to expose the sleight of hand by which philosophers convince their readership that language can represent an objective reality, and serve as a transparent medium of thought. He would restore us to a world in which we would be not only without a false confidence in either the power of objective reason or the possibility of transparent communication, but also without a sense of false constraint.[21] I believe Derrida's strategies are singularly apt for the analysis of a legal order that has, like the philosophy he critiques, founded its authority on objectivity, and that presumes access to individual intentions and understandings.

In aspiring to a perspective external to the dominant discourse—an aspiration necessary for the type of analysis I develop in this piece—I have also drawn strength from feminist theory and from attempts to bring feminism to bear on legal theory.[22] In understanding the central problem of our legal discourse to be a corrosive preoccupation with self and other, I see correspondences among the "liberal" world depicted by legal scholars, the "rational" world depicted by Derrida, and the "male" world depicted by feminists.[23]

D. Implications

It is distressingly common to interpret the kind of analysis I undertake in this chapter as an attack on doctrine, as a claim that doctrinal talk is somehow "meaningless." I hope to show that such interpretations are misperceptions. At the most practical level, my analysis suggests that the advocate's task is precisely as traditionally imagined, a job requiring a most sophisticated sense both of the array of available argument and of the limits of legal discourse. At the level of theory, my account suggests that doctrine is redolent with meaning, that it incorporates debates about commitments and concerns central to our society. However, the usefulness of those debates is unfortunately limited by their stylized distance from the core issues they represent. Debate on these core issues is further limited by doctrine's pretense that it can resolve these issues rather than simply articulate them in a fashion that would allow a decision-maker to make a considered choice in the case before her.

To expose the limitations of doctrine—to reveal the poverty of legal discourse, its dependence on only a few types of feint and parry, eminently graspable—is one of the major goals of this piece. That done, it becomes possible systematically to surface the core issues underlying contractual disputes, by decoding the doctrinal formulations.

My analysis, which supports the idea that judicial decision-making is indeterminate, is rendered vulnerable by our experience of being able to speculate successfully about how at least some cases will come out. One response is that our ability to speculate has less to do with the determinacy of doctrine than with our sensitivity to cultural values and understandings as they impinge on and are created by our decision-makers. This implies that while "doctrine-as-rule-system" is indeterminate, "doctrine-in-application" is after all determinate, needing just that infusion of (determinate) cultural value and understanding to make it so. But if doctrinal indeterminacy is produced, as I have suggested, by the *same* dualities that structure the rest of our life and thought, that affect the very development of our cultural values and understandings, then indeterminacy must exist at *all* these levels. Our seeming ability nonetheless to understand and to predict (in a historically contingent fashion) the particular links that decision-makers create between particular arguments, and the particular fact situations decision-makers construct from the testimony submitted to them, requires us to search for other explanations.[24] The devaluing of doctrine clears the ground for this further work.[25]

I. Public and Private

The opposing ideas of public and private have traditionally dominated discourse about contract doctrine. The underlying notion has been that to the extent contract doctrine is "private," or controlled by the parties, it guarantees individual autonomy or freedom; to the extent it is "public," or controlled by the state, it infringes individual autonomy.

Since at least the mid nineteenth century, the discourse of contract doctrine has tried to portray contract as essentially private and free.[26] At all times, nonetheless, traditional doctrine has uneasily recognized a public aspect of contract, viewing certain state interests as legitimate limitations on individual freedom. But this public aspect has traditionally been assigned a strictly supplemental role; indeed, a major concern of contract doctrine has been to suppress "publicness" by a series of doctrinal moves.

The public aspect of contract doctrine is suppressed differently in each area of that doctrine, and in each historical period. The method of suppression is generally either an artifical *conflation* of public and private, in which the public is represented as private, or an artifical *separation* of public from private, which distracts attention from the public element of the protected "private" arena by focusing attention on the demarcated (and limited) "public" arena.

The current mainstream treatment of quasi contracts and implied contracts illustrates doctrine's techniques of separation and conflation. The prevailing position, represented by the *Second Restatement*, but also by cases and commentary from the 1850s to the present, is that quasi contracts are not contracts at all, but constitute instead an exceptional imposition of obligation by the state in order to prevent unjust enrichment. An artificially sharp line of demarcation is therefore presented as separating quasi contracts from implied-in-fact contracts, and public from private. But this position obscures the fact that the finding of contractual implication is guided in the so-called private sphere by the same considerations that dictate the imposition of quasi contract. Any inquiry into a party's intent must confront the problem of knowledge—our ultimate inability to gain access to the subjective intent underlying any particular agreement. The indicia or manifestations of intent, discussed in detail in part II, serve as substitutes for subjective intent. But in relying on this objective evidence, we move from the realm of the private to that of the public. Calling implied contracts based on party intention "private," and thereby ignoring the extent to which their consent is shaped by external norms, conflates public with private.

My analysis of public and private starts with a brief historical overview of the way these themes have been treated in contract doctrine since the nineteenth century. I then examine in greater detail the suppression of the public aspect of contract in doctrine's treatment of quasi contract.

A. A Brief History

In the earlier part of the nineteenth century, a will theory of contract dominated the commentary and influenced judicial discussion.[27] Contractual obligation was seen to arise from the will of the individual. This conception of contract was compatible with (and early cases appear sympathetic to) an emphasis on subjective intent: judges were to examine the circumstances of a case to determine whether individuals had voluntarily willed themselves into positions of obligation.[28] In the absence of a "meeting of the minds," there was no contract.[29] This theory paid no particular attention to the potential conflict between a subjective intention and an objective expression of that intention.

The idea that contractual obligation has its *source* in the individual will persisted into the latter part of the nineteenth century, consistent with the pervasive individualism of that time and the general incorporation into law of notions of liberal political theory.[30] Late nineteenth-century theorists like Holmes and Williston, however, began to make clear that the proper *measure* of contractual obligation was the formal expression of the will, the will objectified. Obligation should attach, they reasoned, not according to the subjective intention of the parties, but according to a reasonable interpretation of the parties' language and conduct. Enforcement of obligation could still be viewed as a neutral facilitation of intent, despite this shift, if the parties are imagined as selecting their language and conduct as accurate and appropriate signals of their intent.[31] Thus, even in this objectified form, the will theory of contract was equated with the absence of state regulation: the parties governed themselves; better yet, each party governed himself.[32]

The realists made it impossible to believe any longer that contract is private in the sense suggested by this caricature. By insisting that the starting point of contract doctrine is the state's decision to intervene in a dispute, the realists exposed the fiction of state neutrality. As Morris Cohen argued, "[I]n enforcing contracts, the government does not merely allow two individuals to do what they have found pleasant in their eyes. Enforcement, in fact, puts the machinery of the law in the service of one party against the other. When that is worthwhile and how that should be done are important questions of public policy."[33] From this vantage point, the objectivist reliance on intent as the source of contractual obligation was blatant abdication of responsibility, a failure to address and debate the substantive public policy issues involved in decisions about when and how courts should intervene in disputes between contracting parties.

This basic challenge to the "privateness" of contract, however, was accompanied by a continuing faith in the ability of courts to understand the agreements made by contracting parties. For example, the contract was felt to restrain the terms on which the court, if it chose to intervene, would favor one party over the other. In the hands of the realists, then, a sensitivity to the problem of power was coupled, by and large, with an apparent lack of sensitivity to the problem of knowledge, and to the way in which power could be subtly exercised through the interpretation and construction of intention.[34]

In the decades since, the realist challenge to the "privateness" of contract has been assimilated and defused, a process aided by the incomplete nature of the realist assault. Thus our principal vision of contract law is still one of a neutral facilitator of private volition. We understand that contract law is concerned at the periphery with the imposition of social duties, that quasi contract governs situations where obligation attaches even in the absence of agreement, that doctrines of duress and fraud deprive the contracting reprobate of benefits unfairly extorted. But we conceive the central arena to be an unproblematic enforcement of obligations voluntarily undertaken. We excise regulated and compulsory contracts from the corpus of contract doctrine altogether and create special niches for them, as in labor law and utility regulation. Although we concede that the law of contract is the result of public decisions about what agreements to enforce, we insist that the overarching public decision is to respect and enforce private intention.

Thus, for better than a hundred years, contract doctrine and the commentary it has generated have been characterized by a concern with public imposition and private volition. In the remainder of this section, I explore in much more detail how the public-private dichotomy has influenced doctrine in the area of the implied contract. I begin with some history, and end by suggesting that our modern formulations do nothing more than give a new disguise to age-old problems.

B. The Implied Contract Story: Wrestling with the Problem of Knowledge

The implied-in-law or quasi contract plays a crucial role in sustaining the notion that contract law is essentially private. The implied-in-law contract is portrayed as essentially noncontractual and public, in contrast to the implied-in-fact contract in which the private is dominant. In this account, the implied-in-fact contract is presented as kin to the express contract, the only difference being that the former is constituted by conduct and circumstance rather than words.[35] An examination of how and when courts choose to impose quasi contractual obligations, however, reveals the essential similarity between this decision and the supposedly dissimilar decision that a given situation evidences implied-in-fact contractual obligations. Thus, although the distinction between the two types of implied contracts accords with our experience—we intuitively know that being bound by one's word is different from being bound by an externally imposed obligation—the methods of legal argument used for over one hundred years to distinguish the two situations do not and cannot hold.

1. Hertzog—The Constructive Contract

Hertzog v. Hertzog,[36] decided by the Pennsylvania Supreme Court in 1857, is reputedly the first American case to distinguish the quasi contract from the implied-in-fact contract. The themes and method of analysis present in *Hertzog* still reverberate in the treatment of implied contract found in the *Second Restatement* and in modern case law.

In *Hertzog*, an adult son lived and worked with his father until his father's death, at which point the son sued the estate for compensation for services rendered.[37] The trial judge instructed the jury that John Hertzog could recover only if an employment contract existed between father and son. Two witnesses gave testimony that could be interpreted as evidence of such an agreement: one Stamm testified that he "heard the old man say he would pay John for the labour he had done,"[38] while one Roderick swore that the father "said he intended to make John safe."[39] The jury found for John, and the defendant appealed, successfully.

Pennsylvania Supreme Court Justice Lowrie begins the opinion by distinguishing express, implied-in-fact, and implied-in-law contracts.[40] In advancing this categorization, Lowrie particularly criticized Blackstone for failing to distinguish the implied-in-fact from the implied-in-law contract.[41]

Blackstone had suggested that "[i]mplied [contracts] are such as reason and justice dictate; and which, therefore, the law presumes that every man undertakes to perform."[42] Lowrie, true to his advanced understanding of the implications of the will theory of contract, observes, "There is some looseness of thought in supposing that reason and justice ever dictate any contracts between parties, or impose such upon them. All true contracts grow out of the intentions of parties to transactions, and are dictated only by their mutual and accordant wills."[43] The only "contracts" that reason and justice dictate, according to Lowrie, are "*constructive* contracts" in which the contract is "mere fiction," a form adopted solely to enforce a duty independent of intention.[44] "In one," says Lowrie, "the duty defines the contract; in the other, the contract defines the duty."[45]

Lowrie offers this definition of quasi contract: "[W]henever, not our variant notions of reason and justice, but the common sense and common justice of the country, and therefore the common law or statute law, impose upon any one a duty, irrespective of contract, and allow it to be enforced by a contract remedy, [this is] a case of [quasi] contract."[46] For Justice Lowrie, quasi contract, unlike contract proper, reflects public norms. Public norms, however, require legitimation, and Lowrie offers two types—one positivist, the other dependent on natural law. The norms are "positively" binding because they are part of the body of common law or statute recognized as authoritative. They are "naturally" binding because they reflect "common sense and common justice."[47] While Lowrie distinguishes these public obligations from obligations based on consent, he invokes consent to legitimize public norms: consent underlies his distinction between "*variant* notions of reason and justice" and "*common* sense and *common* justice."[48]

Lowrie avoids the need to devote more time and attention in *Hertzog* to quasi contract by stating that "[i]n the present case there is no pretence of a constructive contract, but only of a proper one, either express or implied."[49] The focus on the opinion, then, is on whether John Hertzog can demonstrate the existence of a contract by words spoken or by an account of the relationship and circumstances.

As to express contract, Lowrie explicitly uses the parties' relationship and their circumstances to "frame" the words spoken in such a way that they become words of "noncontract" instead of contract: "The court told the jury that a contract of hiring might be inferred from the evidence of Stamm and Roderick. Yet these witnesses add nothing to the facts already recited, except that the father told them, shortly before his death, that he intended to pay his son for his work. This is no making of a contract or admission of one; but rather the contrary. It admits that the son deserved some reward from his father, but not that he had a contract for any."[50] The father-son relationship clearly influences Lowrie's conclusion. *Hertzog* thus illustrates that words of intention are inconclusive until they are shaped by a judicial reading of the context in which they are uttered. Even the paradigmatically self-sufficient "express" contract, in which "the terms of the agreement are openly uttered and avowed at the time of the making,"[51] is invaded by "publicness" in its interpretation and enforcement.

In regard to the implied-in-fact contract, Lowrie says that "[t]he law ordinarily presumes or implies a contract whenever this is necessary to account for other relations found to have existed between the parties."[52] In *Hertzog*, Lowrie's willingness to find an employment contract will therefore turn on whether the parties are related: he assumes that strangers assist one another only on the expectation of reward,[53] whereas precisely the opposite is true of employment between intimates.[54]

Lowrie thus bases his conclusion that no implied contract exists almost entirely upon "the customs of society"[55] and commonly accepted notions about human nature in general and family relationships in particular.[56] But his reliance on such customs and commonalities hopelessly undermines his distinction between contracts implied-in-fact and quasi contracts. Lowrie's treatment of the absence of a contract proper could just as easily be read as an account of the absence of a quasi contract. Plainly he has decided that common sense and common justice demand a finding that no contract exists here. The advantage of his contractual analysis is that it permits public considerations to be introduced as if they were private, without the elaborate scrutiny of their source and justification that a quasi-contractual analysis would require.

Lowrie's concluding ruminations about the jury's finding for the son ironically illustrate his obliviousness to the "publicness" of his analysis:

> The difficulty in trying causes of this kind often arises from juries supposing that, because they have the decision of the cause, therefore they may decide according to general principles of honesty and fairness,

without reference to the law of the case. But this is a despotic power, and is lodged with no portion of this government.

Their verdict may, in fact, declare what is honest between the parties, and yet it may be a mere usurpation of power, and thus be an effort to correct one evil by a greater one. Citizens have a right to form connexions on their own terms and to be judged accordingly. When parties claim by contract, the contract proved must be the rule by which their rights are to be decided. To judge them by any other rule is to interfere with the liberty of the citizen.[57]

The moralizing might be more convincing if the judge had not just exercised, in the guise of fact-finding, the type of state power he now labels "despotic."[58]

In resolving the dispute, then, Lowrie proves incapable of sustaining the distinction between public and private on which he places so much emphasis. He asserts that the intrusion of the state into the relationships of private individuals is generally undesirable. He suggests that in extreme circumstances such intrusion can be justified, provided we impose only those obligations grounded both in community standards and in positive promulgation. In normal circumstances, however, contract law is purely about the intentions of the parties. Disciplined and rational judges, aware of the limitations of their authority, are better equipped to discern these intentions than undisciplined and irrational juries who confuse their sense of what is fair and honest with what the parties had in mind. But when it comes to deciding the case, Lowrie uses standards that were neither explicitly adopted by the parties nor promulgated by the state. In determining that the relationship between the parties was not contractual, he invokes common understandings about the context of the agreement to transform words of agreement into evidence of noncontract. In so doing he avoids the problem of power by appearing to endorse the parties' own choice that their relationship be without legal consequence, and avoids the problem of knowledge by presenting his own normative interpretation of the situation as nothing more than a transparent reading of the parties' intentions.

2. Since *Hertzog*—*Plus Ça Change* . . .

By the first decades of this century, theorists had begun cautiously to explore the extent to which an objectified will theory required public intrusion on private volition. In 1920, for example, Costigan[59] suggested that the quasi-contractual obligations could not be successfully separated from implied-in-fact obligations without recognizing that there were, in addition to "meeting-of-the-minds implied-in-fact contract[s],"[60] those implied-in-fact contracts that were *not* based on meetings of minds. Costigan's prime example was the implied warranty, which he described in terms that would also apply to Lowrie's analysis of the absence of contract in *Hertzog*: "Implied warranties are founded upon the implied facts of general . . . experience and understanding—implied because people in general, and not necessarily the particular parties concerned, when acting understandingly and fairly, normally agree upon such an assumed factual basis . . . ."[61] As the quotation suggests, Costigan explicitly recognizes that the actual intent of the parties is not the basis of the obligation in these cases. At the same time, rather than asserting explicitly the "public" interest in the imposition of such terms, he "privatizes" the imposition of obligation by reference to what other fair-minded people *would* intend under similar circumstances.

Costigan is left having to explain why his category of "no-meeting-of-the-minds" contracts are still contracts rather than quasi contracts. To this end, he focuses initially on the remedy attached: where the court awards a restitutionary measure, the action is quasi-contractual; where an expectation measure is awarded, the action is contractual.[62] Costigan himself, however, later recognizes that his position is indefensible: he acknowledges that "[t]he contractual right justifies the measure of damages, not the measure the right."[63] Ultimately, then, he fails to demonstrate how these cases can be viewed as contractual without the parties' minds having met.[64]

As I have already sketched,[65] the realist approach to contract involves a radical shift of emphasis from the private to the public aspects of enforcement. Predictably, then, when the realist Cohen addresses the question of interpretation, he sees and describes its public face. He pinpoints the way in which judges, in the guise of interpretation, "decide the 'equities,' the rights and obligations of the parties . . . . [T]hese legal relations are determined by the courts and the jural system and not by the agreed will of the contesting parties."[66] Cohen also identifies how rules of interpretation serve as state regulation: "When courts follow the same rules of interpretation in diverse cases, they are in effect enforcing uniformities of conduct. We may thus view the law of contract not only as a branch of public law but also as having a function somewhat parallel to that of the criminal law. Both serve to standardize conduct by penalizing departures from the legal norm."[67]

Cohen laments that while the fictional nature of the will theory is at one level a commonplace, it is at the same time ignored, forgotten, or otherwise resisted—in part, because of the force of the traditional language.[68] And indeed, the realists did generally fail to explore the implications of the will theory's fictional basis. They tended to be much more concerned with problems of coercion and of relief from the bad bargain. The realist focus was the public-private split as it implicates the problem of power, not the public-private split as it implicates the problem of knowledge. Since the line of inquiry initiated by those such as Costigan has been given only scant attention in the following decades, Cohen's criticism could be leveled with equal force today.

The position taken by the *Second Restatement* is essentially that of Justice Lowrie. The *Second Restatement* divides the universe of contracts along the private-public axis into express contracts, contracts implied-in-fact, and contracts implied-in-law or quasi contracts. It defines the express contract as an agreement made up of words, either oral or written, and the implied-in-fact contract as one that a court infers wholly or partly from conduct or circumstances.[69] Quasi contracts, in contrast, are "public." And because they are not concerned with the intentions of the parties, they are not really contracts at all.[70] That quasi contracts even share the appellation "contract" is a matter of historical accident.[71] Like torts, quasi contracts are "obligations created by law for reasons of justice."[72] Their noncontractual nature is so essential that they are separated out for treatment in the *Restatement of Restitution*.[73] Only that fact even alerts us that the "reasons of justice"[74] that dictate the imposition of the quasi-contractual obligations have to do with the idea of unjust enrichment.

At the same time, the *Second Restatement of Contracts* confesses that this analytically clear distinction between contract and quasi contract does not always work in practice, that "in some cases the line between the two is indistinct."[75] The *Restatement* attributes the potential for confusion to the difficulties of "Conduct as Manifestation of Assent."[76] Except where formal requirements give words special significance as evidence of agreement, "there is no distinction in the effect of the promise whether it is expressed in writing, orally, or in acts, or partly in one of these ways and partly in others."[77] But conduct "is more uncertain and more dependent on its setting than are words."[78] The uncertainty of conduct as evidence of agreement can make it unclear whether a particular relationship should be considered contractual or quasi-contractual.

This explanation allows the *Restatement* to save the express contract from involvement in potential confusion between public and private. Words that directly express the parties' intentions make state intrusion unnecessary. Only conduct, inherently more ambiguous and open-textured, threatens the public-private distinction by requiring the interpreter of fact to add his sense of the context to the acts of the parties in order to understand them.[79]

As *Hertzog* demonstrates, however, the division between public and private cannot be so neatly made. Divining intention in order to find an implied-in-fact contract depends on understanding the societal background against which a relationship is formed: a knowledge of private thus requires a knowledge of public. Deciding that a social relationship requires the imposition of a quasi contract depends on knowing which relationship the parties have entered: a knowledge of public thus requires a knowledge of private.

In failing to account successfully for the kinship of the implied-in-fact and quasi contract, the *Restatement* is not an aberration in modern treatments. The note in Kessler and Gilmore's casebook[80] introducing the topic of the implied contract also fails in this regard. The note begins by repeating the standard distinction between "genuine" contracts and the fictional quasi contract, but warns that the "famous, plausible and innocent-looking" distinction raises "a host of troublesome questions."[81] The next passage of the note is a spectacular account of how what is commonly conceived of as private in the realm of contract formation and interpretation is in fact public. In a short compass, Kessler and Gilmore suggest that in one sense all contracts, even express ones, are implied: that express contracts are possible only through "a regulation which is originally social";[82] that "environment" is crucial;[83] that "official control becomes an integral part of the contract itself";[84] and that the courts' habit of presenting their enforcement task as one of "interpretation" obscures the "degree of control over private volition thus exercised."[85]

Then, abruptly, the note introduces the concept of quasi contract. Early in its treatment we are warned: "If it [quasi contract] is unduly extended, private autonomy . . . will suffer erosion."[86] The degree of erosion demonstrated in the interpretation of contracts proper was never explicitly presented as this kind of a threat, however, and it is not clear why the threat inheres in quasi contract and not in contract.

At this point the very distinction about which the authors expressed doubt in their opening paragraphs is reintroduced as essential: although the "borderline" may be "wavering and blurred,"[87] the boundary is "necessary," and "not to be ignored."[88] The separation of quasi contract and contract is vital, not just for the sake of private autonomy, but because of the different remedies attaching, even though in many situations the measure of recovery is the same.[89] We are also warned that judges are not as good at recognizing the essentially different natures of these kinds of contracts as we will presumably be once we have digested the elaborate "guidance" the note provides.[90]

There are manifold messages here. Kessler and Gilmore understand the world of contract to be more complicated and difficult than the standard division into implied-in-fact and implied-in-law would indicate. They fully and sympathetically present the problem of knowledge as it affects issues of interpretation. But this insight is not permitted to influence their treatment of the quasi contract, which is still presented as the place where the real threat to privateness exists. In shoring up the distinction between real and quasi contracts by referring to the remedies attached, Kessler and Gilmore repeat Costigan's mistake—unless their point is instead that we *should* draw this distinction in order to know what remedy is appropriate. This is different from Costigan's claim that the remedy given lets us know what kind of action we are dealing with, but it leaves us asking why we should base a choice of remedy on so weak a foundation. Kessler and Gilmore's final move of pinning the blame on judges deflects attention from the inadequacies of the conceptual scheme itself.

The inadequacies of Kessler and Gilmore's treatment echo those evident in the *Second Restatement* and in *Hertzog*. None of the accounts fully acknowledges the interrelationship of public and private. None adequately recognizes that public concerns and conceptions necessarily inform the judicial decision about whether to impose contractual obligations. None suggests that quasi-contractual obligation depends on prior understandings of the private relationship of the parties. Once these interrelationships are understood, as the (failed) attempt to distinguish contract from quasi contract allows us to understand them, the public-private dichotomy threatens to dissolve.

[Omitted here is a discussion of Duress and Unconscionability.]

C. Summary

In the implied contract story, we saw how public and private were confounded, how our understanding of implied-in-fact and express contracts requires us to draw on a fund of public information and values that influences our judgment of what we see. Similarly, our imposition of a public quasi-contractual obligation requires us to look for private signals from the parties about their conception of their relationship. Rather than banishing quasi contract as a dangerous public exception to a private law of contract, therefore, we embraced its lesson that all contract is as public as it is private. This theme is elaborated in the discussion of manifestation and intent in part II.

II. Manifestation and Intent: Communication in the Law of Contract

Underlying the realms of contract doctrine concerning how agreements are formed, how they should be interpreted, and how contractual risks are allocated are models of how the parties communicate with one another and construct the meaning that is their contract, as well as models of how courts gain access to that meaning. In the previous section I suggested that it is not in practice possible to separate out a court's understanding of the parties' meaning from a meaning made for and imposed on the parties by the court. Here I elaborate on the theme, through an analysis of doctrinal categories including offer and acceptance, the parol evidence rule, disclosure, misunderstanding, and mistake.

My goal in this section is to articulate precisely how, according to contract doctrine, meaning is made and communicated. I suggest that close examination reveals the doctrinal model to be at once unconvincing and incomplete. To the extent judges attempt to describe communication in doctrinal terms, they are forced into accounts that tend to distort what we imagine the actual process of communication between the contracting parties to have been. To the extent the doctrinal model leaves judges without guidance, they are left ascribing meaning according to unarticulated criteria. Both these problems emphasize the gap between the contract as the parties may have understood it and the contract as ultimately described by the court.

At the root of these difficulties lies the problem of knowledge—the gulf between self and other, subject and object. Translated into doctrinal discourse, this becomes the distinction between subjectivity, substance, and intent on one hand, and objectivity, form, and manifestation on the other. Our legal culture appreciates the difference between what someone subjectively intends, and the form in which he makes that intention available to others (the objective representation of his thought or wish). That we concede the possibility of "mis-understanding" demonstrates our awareness of this dichotomy and our recognition that the signs can be read to manifest something other than the "actual" or "real" intent of their author. Appreciating the difference, our legal culture has explicitly opted to favor objective over subjective, form over substance, and manifestation over intent, in the areas of doctrine with which this part deals. Yet the suppressed subjective constantly erupts to threaten the priority accorded the objective, is subdued, and erupts again. The details of this dynamic occupy the following pages.

Doctrinal obsession with the competing claims of objective and subjective, manifestation and intent, dates perhaps from the time at which a "will theory" of contract, initially conceived as emphasizing the subjective "meeting of the minds,"[91] was "objectivized" by the likes of Holmes and Williston.[92] In this second incarnation, while the subjective intentions of the parties were still felt to provide the legitimating basis of contractual obligation, the measure of intention became overwhelmingly objective. The tension between these two aspects of doctrine and the need to reconcile them did not become urgent until a couple of decades into the twentieth century.[93]

The *Second Restatement* provides an up-to-the-minute account of how that tension is managed today. We see that objectivity is still accorded an initial priority. Take, for example, the *Restatement's* formulation of "promise" as "a manifestation of intention to act or refrain from acting in a specified way, so made as to justify a promisee in understanding that a commitment has been made."[94] Here the *Second Restatement* directs us to focus, not on all intentions, but only on manifested ones. The commentary elaborates on the significance of this distinction: "The phrase 'manifestation of intention' adopts an external or objective standard for interpreting conduct; it means the external expression of intention as distinguished from the undisclosed intention."[95] At first glance, this constrained notion of intent seems pragmatic. To base contract interpretation on undisclosed intention is surely to invite chaos, perjury, a whole catalog of evils. At a more theoretical level, we might also imagine a concern with undisclosed intention to be senseless. At some point the undisclosed must be disclosed or we can have no concrete knowledge of it. Intent, in this view, is wholly dependent on manifestation—the only questions left are, What count as manifestations? To whom must they be made? In what form? At what time?

But even while objectivity retains its priority, subjectivity is accorded a vital and subversive supplementary role. According to the *Restatement* scheme, recognizing a manifestation requires a knowledge of intent. The *Restatement* demands that we categorize manifestations: only manifestations *of intent* qualify as promises,[96] only manifestations *of assent* qualify as assent.[97] Doctrinally we cannot, it turns out, sort or interpret manifestations without reference to an intent we have already acknowledged to be beyond our grasp save through the graspable reality of manifestations that we cannot comprehend without recourse to an unknowable intent . . . and so on.

In the various doctrinal areas rendered problematic by this basic conundrum, the *Restatement* attempts three different, although related, solutions. One proposed escape route treats "intent," in the formulation "manifestation of intent," as mere verbiage, not as an indication that the decision-maker in fact needs to take account of intent. A second route suggests that in concrete disputes the problem of recognizing manifestations is reduced to the problem of choosing between two competing sets of manifestations, so that the adoption of a formal hierarchy that privileges certain classes of manifestations will provide criteria of choice not dependent on intent. It is clear how these two devices can work together: having dismissed the idea of "actual" intent from the rule formulation, the formal hierarchy purports to provide the substitute criteria. The third proposed escape route attempts to resolve the set of "communication" problems by reference to a standard of "responsibility," as a substitute for reliance on "manifestations of intent."

Just as the basic conundrum is unresolvable, so the proposed escape routes turn out to be dead ends. All three routes lead to endless struggle with the unknowability of intent on the one hand, and the legitimation problems involved in the use of nonconsensual or non-intent-based criteria on the other. Each leads to a choice between basing liability on an unreliable assertion of private intention, or admitting and justifying the imposition of public law on the parties. I shall demonstrate how this dynamic operates to ensure that (*a*) any standard that begins by emphasizing intention winds up depending on equally unsatisfying models of formal hierarchy or responsibility; (*b*) any standard that begins by emphasizing formal hierarchy winds up depending on equally unsatisfying models of intention or responsibility; and (*c*) any standard that begins by emphasizing responsibility winds up depending on equally unsatisfying models of formal hierarchy or intention.

A. Intention Ousted: The Objective Theory of Contract

A standard history of contract doctrine represents that, from the sixteenth to the early nineteenth century, contract formation depended upon a subjective "meeting of the minds."[98] Despite the accordance of this subjective theory with the nineteenth-century "will theory" of contract, by the middle of the nineteenth century "the tide had turned in favor of an objective theory of contract."[99] To see the sequence as one in which objectivism replaced subjectivism is to discount the crucial, although supplementary, role that subjective will as a *source* of obligation continued to play. But the story accurately portrays the increased insistence on objectivity as an interpretive standard.

Holmes's article "The Theory of Legal Interpretation" illustrates the fundamental challenge of objectivism to the subjective theory it came to overshadow.[100] According to Holmes, the "intent" of the parties was never the issue in any case of contract interpretation. To determine the meaning of a word used in a contractual situation, Holmes believed the first step should be to consider its meaning in the context of surrounding words. But this was an exercise in applying the "general usages of speech" and did not reflect any concern with the "idiosyncrasies of the writer."[101] Admitting evidence of circumstances, and reading a contractual document in light of them, was also not about divining the intent of the parties. We were to ask instead, Holmes suggested, what the words used by the speaker would mean "in the mouth of a normal speaker of English, using them in the circumstances in which they were used."[102] In the case where the speaker uses a proper name that could refer to more than one person or thing (because there are, for example, two Blackacres or ships Peerless),[103] Holmes saw the inquiry into circumstance revealing which of two different *words* the speaker used, rather than revealing the speaker's intention.[104]

Mainstream twentieth-century thinkers came to accept the most extreme manifestations of the Holmesian doctrine. "It is even conceivable," Williston observes, "that a contract may be formed which is in accordance with the intention of neither party."[105] Learned Hand puts it more vividly when he suggests, "A contract is an obligation attached by the mere force of law to certain acts of the parties, usually words, which ordinarily accompany and represent a known intent. If, however, it were proved by twenty bishops that either party, when he used the words, intended something else than the usual meaning which the law imposes upon them, he would still be held [to the usual meaning] . . . ."[106]

This analysis forces us to ask what justifies the departure from intent. The central argument advanced is that replacing the unknowable and possibly idiosyncratic intentions of the contracting party with "that stubborn anti-subjectivist, the 'reasonable man,' "[107] is an advance. It seems insufficient to suggest that this substitution merely satisfies an aesthetic impulse.[108] At one level the substitution can be seen as a shift to a "responsibility" model: you are responsible for what you would appear to the reasonable man to be saying, rather than for what you actually meant to say. In this sense the standard seems tortious rather than contractual, even as "reliance" strikes us as a tortious notion. But at another level it can be reconciled with intention and the contractual model. If the reasonable man is a businessman assessing the words and conduct of businessmen, then in most instances appearance and reality will converge. Alternatively, if the ranking of manifestations is seen as a tool available to businessmen in their contract planning, they will be sure to shape in the proper legal form the deal they intended to make.[109]

It seems fair to say that the credibility of these arguments depends on two things: First, on the extent to which we can believe in the "reasonable man," as represented by his interpreters, the jurors and trial judges. As Frank puts it, "we must recognize, unless we wish to fool ourselves, that although one area of subjectivity has been conquered, another remains unsubdued. . . . We ask judges or juries to discover that 'objective viewpoint'—through their own subjective processes. Being but human, their beliefs cannot be objectified, in the sense of being standardized."[110] Second, the credibility of these arguments depends on our valuing objectivity and stability (to the extent we think the rule does or can promote them) more than we value the effort at divining "real" intention, in situations where the intention appears from the evidence to have been understood by both parties, but is different from the intention objectively constructed. It is this latter concern, more than anything else, that appears to have evoked the conviction that the objectivists went "too far."[111]

Hayden v. *Hoadley*,[112] decided in 1920, is an example of an objectivist position that seems extreme by today's standards. The parties exchanged property through a written agreement that bound Hoadley and his coseller to make certain repairs on the property conveyed to the Haydens.[113] Nothing in the agreement spoke to the timing of the repairs, the amount to be expended, or the quality of materials to be used. The trial court excluded evidence of oral agreements as to these matters in a decision upheld by the Supreme Court of Vermont.[114]

Justice Powers, for the court, began his analysis with an unexceptional statement of the parol evidence rule: "A written contract which contains no latent ambiguity cannot be qualified, controlled, contradicted, enlarged, or diminished by any contemporaneous or antecedent understanding or agreement . . . ."[115]

In Powers's view, however, the rule governs not merely the express terms of the contract, but also its "legal intendment."[116] This view severely erodes the role of the parties' intentions. In the absence of any express provision as to the timing of the repairs, for example, the law would imply a requirement that they be completed within a reasonable time.[117] Because any oral supplementary term as to timing would contradict the "reasonable time" provision, it may not be included: "To admit the testimony offered by the defendants to the effect that the parties agreed upon October 1 as the limit of the time given for the repairs would be to allow the plain legal effect of the written contract to be controlled by oral evidence. That is not permissible."[118]

While Justice Powers is firm in asserting the "unquestioned soundness" of the rule that "an incomplete writing may be supplemented by parol,"[119] his conclusion that this contract is "unequivocal and complete"[120] makes clear that the exception is to be narrowly construed.[121] Powers, like Holmes and Williston, disregards the particular parties and their intentions in the name of a "legal intendment," the justification for which is apparently so obvious to the author that it goes virtually unarticulated.[122]

B. Formal Hierarchy: Manifestations Multiplied

In the cut and thrust of contract disputes, we imagine the abstract, open-ended problem of finding manifested intent reduced to the concrete restricted choice between the different versions that the two contracting parties urged upon the decision-maker. This gives credibility to a formal model of determining contractual content: some manifestations simply take precedence over other manifestations, so that conflicts of interpretation can be resolved by favoring the hierarchically superior manifestation. Thus, as I explore below, speech is superior to silence, while final writings are superior to earlier writings or speech.

Current contract doctrine, as reflected by the *Second Restatement*, reacts to the perceived excesses of objectivism by consistently invoking intent as the ultimate justifier of hierarchy. In general terms, the justification is that hierarchy reflects intention because intention corresponds to hierarchy. This general statement, however, hides the existence of two quite separate themes: intention may correspond to hierarchy because the rules carefully mirror what people ignorant of the rules intend, or because people take account of the legal rules in expressing their intentions. While these two accounts contain dramatically different visions of the relationship between law and life, judges cheerfully adopt one or the other as it suits their purpose. They may even adopt both at once, which leads to entirely circular reasoning.[123]

The reconnection of formal hierarchy with intention, in whatever form, serves to subdue the argument that rules that arbitrarily accord priority to some manifestations of intention take contract doctrine too far from party intention and voluntary obligation. But modern doctrine must still wrestle with the problem created by convincing evidence that the interpretation yielded by the formal hierarchy is not the "real" interpretation. If the hierarchy triumphs, then the question reemerges of what—if not intent—legitimates it; if the hierarchy does not triumph, then its value as a constraint on decision-making is undercut.

I examine how this dynamic plays itself out in three examples. An analysis of *Restatement* section 203, "Standards of Preference of Interpretation," yields a crude understanding of the difficult relationship between formal hierarchy and intention. My second example is the parol evidence rule, where final writings take precedence over other evidence, most commonly earlier speech. The *Restatement* treatment of the rule provides an elaborated statement and attempted resolution of the same problem, introducing the way in which a second level of doctrinal play between form and substance can mediate the primary tension between hierarchy and intention. My final example is the group of rules about silence as assent, where speech or writing takes precedence over silence.

1. Standards of Preference in Interpretation

Restatement section 203 is an elaborate, painstaking, and thorough attempt to create a formal hierarchy of manifestations. It is a miracle of orderly privileging: whole interpretations win over partial, and specific terms over general; relevant categories of interpretive context are identified and ranked.[124] Unfortunately, however, the commentary undermines whatever sense of order and security the text conveys.

According to comment *a*, "The rules of this Section are applicable to all manifestations of intention and all transactions. They apply only in choosing among reasonable interpretations. *They do not override evidence of the meaning of the parties, but aid in determining meaning or prescribe legal effect when meaning is in doubt.*"[125] The first two sentences of the comment confirm our sense of what the section is about: it allows us to choose between and among possible meanings. It provides the way to sort conflicting evidence of the content of the parties' agreement. Then the comment proceeds to contradict itself, and negate the text of the section: the formal hierarchy may not be employed to "override evidence of the meaning of the parties."[126] But the hierarchy was supposed to *produce* the meaning of the parties. The rules of the hierarchy were applicable to "all manifestations of intention,"[127] which are our only sources of intention. If the meaning they produce is now open to challenge, how are we to derive the alternative meanings that might challenge it, and by what criteria are we to assess the success of the challenge?

At one level we appreciate the realistic "flexibility" in ascertaining meaning that the section and comment combine to give us: it accords with our sense that the formal hierarchy is not sufficient to explain how judges derive meaning when they decide cases. The structure of section 203 deceives us, however: the text of the section stands as an affirmation of formal hierarchy, while the comment does not spell out the full extent of its undermining function. We are not told what the real story of section 203 demands we be told: "The formal hierarchy is a reliable guide to what manifestations should count, except when it isn't. It can be trumped by other evidence of the parties' meaning." What other evidence? When? No answers are forthcoming.[128]

Underlying the undermining language of the comment is the concern that manifestations, after all, are empty unless they signify intent, and that without some such qualifications the "real" intent will lurk in the wings to delegitimate the device of formal hierarchy. At one level the fear is a groundless one: all intent requires manifestation to be known, while all manifestations are threatened by irrelevance without reference to the intent they signify. If the text of section 203 were truly to limit the scope of our inquiry, it would inhibit us from *finding* other evidence of the "meaning of the parties."[129] It would not, of course, protect us from doubts and fears that we had looked at empty vessels and missed the boat. These same doubts and fears are what have guided the interpretation and application of the parol evidence rule in its development from the classical period to the present.

2. The Parol Evidence Rule

The thrust of the parol evidence rule is that an "integrated" writing,[130] or one that contains the "final expression"[131] of the parties with respect to any terms of their agreement, cannot be contradicted or even supplemented with respect to those terms by other writings, speech, or conduct of the parties.[132] While the most frequent issue in application of the rule is perhaps the priority of later writing over earlier speech, the priority is more accurately that of final writing over other types of evidence. The very use of the adjective *final* suggests that the hierarchy is at the same time based on intention, that it applies where the parties see the writing as their "last word" on the subject.

The standard story about the parol evidence rule is that, while designed to prevent fraud and introduce stability by permitting businessmen to record their transactions, it has a disturbing tendency to promote fraud by allowing one party to limit a liability which attention to all evidence of agreement would indicate is more substantial than the integrated writing alone reflects. The standard story, told in a tone of exasperation, is that efforts to prevent fraud both by exaltation of the final writing and by subversion of the final writing necessarily make the rule one riddled with exceptions, virtually incapable of being applied.[133]

We should begin our examination of the rule with a quick survey of the principal ways in which evidence external to the writing is admissible. Since the writing does not announce its finality or its scope, external evidence is needed on the question of whether and to what extent the writing is integrated.[134] In addition to these qualifications, the final writing does not interpret itself, so reference to evidence external to the writing is required for interpretation.[135] Finally, the writing cannot be conclusive as to its legitimacy, so evidence can be admitted to show mistake, fraud, duress, lack of consideration, or the existence of a condition precedent.[136]

This tedious taxonomy demonstrates how a rule that purports to be about the privileging of "final writings" turns out to be surrounded by rules that reverse the privilege, so that prior evidence of a condition can supersede the written testament of the agreement, or so that prior evidence of trade usage can supersede the dictionary meaning of the written terms.[137] It is important to realize, however, that the precise formulation of the rule with its exceptions represents a second-level effort to sustain the very hierarchy that has, at the first level, proved unsatisfactory.

The first sustaining device, exactly analogous to the relationship between the text and the comment of section 203,[138] is a reversion to the idea of intent. When the formal hierarchy seems insupportable, intent is reintroduced in an attempt to legitimate it. This occurs, for example, when the *Restatement* talks about proving an integration,[139] proving a complete integration,[140] and distinguishing an integrated from a completely integrated agreement.[141]

It is easy to state the anxiety that underlies the reintroduction of intent in this subversion of formal hierarchy. To call an agreement integrated purely because of its length, complexity, or apparent completeness seems an arbitrary statement of judicial or legal preference. To call it integrated because most people who write such agreements intend them to be final statements allows the unscrupulous to exploit some particular people with a definition drawn from the abstract "most people." Interpreting such contracts according to their dictionary meaning is a similarly arbitrary exercise of authority with similar potential for exploitation. Yet, inexorably, the reintroduction of intent undercuts the hierarchy of form without yielding firm guidelines for deciding cases.

Having created this subjective threat to the rule's objective hierarchy, the *Restatement* then shores up the rule by recreating formal hierarchy at a second, "softer" level. Where the first level of formal hierarchy directly ranked the expressions of the parties—privileging writings over words or conduct—this second level works more indirectly through three devices we could loosely call procedural: (1) using *presumptions* that favor certain manifestations over others, while avoiding any absolute privileging; (2) ordering the different tasks that constitute application of the parol evidence rule, so that evidence may be included in one stage of the proceedings but legitimately excluded in another; and (3) dividing issues of proof between law and fact, judge and jury, in a fashion that diverts attention from the evidence-to-be-considered to the identity of the decision-maker.[142]

Let me first illustrate the use of presumptions. While the apparently integrated agreement does not necessarily qualify as an integrated agreement, it is presumed to be integrated.[143] In interpreting an integrated agreement, the written words, while not the only admissible evidence of the parties' meaning, are given a similar procedural priority.[144] Any apparent reassurance provided by the "weighting" technique evaporates once you ask what *other* evidence would establish that a writing was not integrated, or what *other* evidence of the transaction could override the apparent meaning of the written words of the agreement.

The next device is that of sequencing. In the context of the parol evidence rule, the *Restatement* suggests that the first decisions must be whether the writing is an integration,[145] and if so, whether it is a complete or only a partial integration.[146] The next decisions are whether the agreement reflected by the writing is affected by an invalidating cause and, provided it is not, how it should be interpreted.[147] Only a written agreement duly identified, validated, and interpreted "renders inoperative prior written agreements as well as prior oral agreements."[148]

The message of this task management scheme appears to be that the decision-maker need not be swamped by the boundless context of the agreement. Although the privileged position of the final writing in the hierarchy of interpretive sources has not completely isolated the writing from the context of the agreement, the specificity and temporal spacing of the questions posed can limit the impact of that context on interpretation. No matter that each preliminary question requires the decision-maker to consider "all relevant evidence, including the circumstances in which the writing was made or adopted."[149] We have still "managed" the context and, most critically, have prevented it from completely undermining the sanctity of the integrated agreement.

The final re-creation of hierarchy is achieved by the division of issues between judge and jury. Unlike other areas of law, there is no clear link, in this context, between judge and law, jury and fact; the *Restatement* is quite clear that some of the issues reserved for the judge are nonetheless issues of fact. For example, the question of whether there is an integrated agreement "is to be determined by the court,"[150] even though it is "a question of fact to be determined in accordance with all relevant evidence."[151] Interpretive questions with respect to an integrated agreement are to be decided as questions of law, unless they depend on the credibility of extrinsic evidence or on a choice among reasonable inferences to be drawn from extrinsic evidence, in which case they go to the "trier of fact."[152]

There are at least two messages of reassurance here. The first is that, while in some cases application of the parol evidence rule requires an expanded and complex inquiry into circumstance, there are still easy cases. For example, the claim of section 212(2) that some writings can be interpreted without reference to any evidence extrinsic to the document comes close to being a reincarnation of the "plain meaning" rule so explicitly abandoned by the *Restatement* elsewhere. Section 212(2) perpetuates the idea of the writing being independent, in at least some instances: it avoids the recognition that the writing is truly never self-limiting.[153]

The second message of reassurance is that the task of implementing the rule as a rule about party intention need not devolve into idiosyncratic instability. In this story the jury becomes the scapegoat. While unruly fact-finders, constantly tempted "to exercise a dispensing power in the guise of a finding of fact,"[154] need the constraining influence of the hierarchy, we can trust our judges reliably and objectively to weigh all the evidence of party intention. We are asked to transfer our faith from the objectivity of the written document to the objectivity of the decision-maker. Facts are made lawlike, stable, not manipulable; indeed, facts recover the characteristics the objectivists imbued them with when they held the final writing to be the only source of evidence.

But this story diverts us from the real lesson of these provisions. The unruliness of the inquiry does not arise from the level of objectivity, discipline, or good faith exercised by the decision-maker. Rather, it is the result of our inability to identify intention in any reliable way, and our equal incapacity to live with a rule structure that resolutely disregards intention. Instead of openly acknowledging this difficulty, the *Restatement* presents us with a system that turns irresolutely between the poles as it pretends to provide a determinate guide to decision-making.

3. Silence as Assent

Just as the parol evidence rule sought to privilege the "final writing" as evidence of agreement, so the rules about when silence can function as assent create a hierarchy that delegitimates silence. As with the parol evidence rule, however, the attempt to invoke this formal hierarchy fails, forcing doctrine either back into the rhetoric of intent or into another mediating rhetoric—in this case, that of responsibility. Since the hierarchy was initially invoked to rescue decision-makers from the problems of intent, the reversion to intent is plainly unsatisfactory. The particular force of this analysis, therefore, is the way in which it shows the rhetorics of intent and responsibility working together to shore up a frail appeal to formal hierarchy.

Restatement section 69 provides that a manifestation of assent may take the form of written or spoken words, or of acts or failures to act.[155] Failing to act, however, is an underprivileged form of conduct, since silence and inaction are *generally* disqualified as manifestations of assent.[156] If absolute, the rule would appear to solve a (perhaps limited) set of assent puzzles in a purely "formal" way, but without any pretense that intent was the crucial criterion; some other "public" justification would have to be invoked for such a rule.[157] The disqualifying presumption is a qualified effort in the same direction.

The question now is how we apply the rule, how we recognize the "exceptional"[158] case where silence may be assent. According to the *Restatement*, there are in fact two classes of exceptional cases: "those where the offeree silently takes offered benefits, and those where one party relies on the other party's manifestation of intention that silence may operate as acceptance."[159] The first type of case shifts us from "contract proper" into "restitution," and introduces the theme of unjust enrichment.[160] But, as it turns out, the enrichment is defined as unjust according to models of intent and responsibility: the offeree must have a *"reasonable opportunity"* to reject the services, and *"reason to know"* that they were offered with the *"expectation of compensation."*[161] The "expectation" idea is a reversion to an intent standard, the intent of the offeror to receive compensation. The "reason to know" and "opportunity to reject" formulas reflect responsibility notions: they incorporate a standard based on what the reasonable person might be expected to know, and how that reasonable person might be expected to act.

The second type of exceptional case exactly replicates the moves of the first. Silence may operate as assent "[w]here the offeror has stated or given the offeree *reason to understand* that assent may be manifested by silence or inaction, and the offeree in remaining silent and inactive *intends* to accept the offer, [or w]here because of previous dealings or otherwise, it is *reasonable* that the offeree *should notify* the offeror if he does not intend to accept."[162] Thus one situation depends on making the offeror responsible, by his manifestation of intent, for the offeree who by his silence actually intends to accept. The other depends on making the offeree responsible for communicating his nonacceptance.

To summarize, one way of explaining this doctrinal corner is to say that section 69 creates a (by now familiar) refuge from the conundrum of intent—formal hierarchy: in disputes over assent, words of action trump silence or inaction. But the internal structure of section 69 subverts the formal hierarchy with exceptions: words or actions trump silence or inaction except when the reverse is true. The reverse is true, in part, when dictated by standards of intent; the exorcised ghost reappears in the heart of the mansion. Alternatively, the reverse may be true when dictated by standards of responsibility.

[Omitted here is a discussion of the Responsibility Model.]

D. Summary

I have been describing the dynamic that operates in areas of doctrine caught between the commitment to objectivity expressed as reliance on "manifestation," and the commitment to subjectivity expressed as reliance on "intent." I have suggested that while contract doctrine on occasion relies squarely on divining intent, and ignores the gulf between subjective intent and the communication of that intent to others, by and large those acknowledged difficulties of communication drive doctrine to use other interpretive or liability-fixing devices. Formal hierarchy and standards of responsibility are two such devices.

The central problem in this area is that of knowledge—of access to intent, or understanding. But if contract doctrine is no longer to rely on intent and understanding as the basis of liability, then contract becomes something other than a system of voluntary obligation. And as a body of public rather than private obligation, it then must articulate the public norms on which it rests. In relying on formal hierarchy, doctrine occasionally makes a weak appeal to the public values of certainty and stability. More often, doctrine completes a circle by justifying hierarchy as the expression of intention. In relying on responsibility, doctrine attempts to evade the problem of knowledge by straying into territory made equally treacherous by the problem of power. As suggested by our earlier look at the doctrines of duress and unconscionability, and affirmed here, we have no reliable, and therefore no legitimate, basis for allocating responsibility between contracting parties. Finally, then, it is the interaction of the problems of power and knowledge that leaves these areas of doctrine without a determinate basis for resolving contractual disputes.

[Omitted here is Part III: Form and Substance: Consideration and the Question of Value.]

IV. Conclusion: Doctrine, the Cohabitation Contract, and Beyond

Doctrinal arguments cast in terms of public and private, manifestation and intent, and form and substance, continue to exert a stranglehold on our thinking about concrete contractual issues. By ordering the ways in which we perceive disputes, these arguments blind us to some aspects of what the disputes are actually about. By helping us categorize, they encourage us to simplify in a way that denies the complexity, and ambiguity, of human relationships. By offering us the false hope of definitive resolution, they allow us to escape the pain, and promise, of continual reassessment and accommodation.

In this final section, I will illustrate the poverty of traditional doctrinal arguments by examining the use of contract doctrine in recent cases involving the agreements of nonmarital cohabitants. These opinions deploy many of the doctrinal maneuvers exposed in this chapter. Distinctions between private and public realms, between contracts implied-in-fact and contracts implied-in-law, play an important part in the decisions. Interpretive questions and questions about the basis for enforcement—about consideration—also loom large, reiterating the concern with private and public, but couching that concern in the competing terms of subjective and objective, form and substance.

Significantly, the opinions largely ignore the aspect of the public-private debate that appears in contract doctrine as the set of rules governing duress and unconscionability. The concerns of those doctrines—preventing oppression of each party by the other, while preventing oppression of both by the state—are nonetheless highly relevant. For at the heart of these cases lies the problem of power. It is only because the exercise of power in this context is not seen as fitting the traditional rubrics of duress and unconscionability that courts are able to ignore and avoid it.

Once the convoluted play of doctrine in this area has been exposed, we can see that traditional formulations are not the only means for understanding how and why decision-makers reach their decisions. At this point, other inquiries become both possible and legitimate. In suggesting what some of those other inquiries might be, my conclusion points toward possible ways of expanding our thinking about the issues of contract law.

[The detailed doctrinal discussion of the cohabitation contracts is omitted.]

There are several ways to begin a richer examination of the cohabitation cases. First, we can learn from the truth underlying contract doctrine while rejecting the idea that the doctrine alone can lead us to correct answers. The dichotomies of public and private, manifestation and intent, form and substance, do touch on troubling questions that are central to our understanding of intimate relationships and the role of the state in undermining or supporting them. The problem with doctrinal rhetoric is twofold. First, it recasts our concerns in a way that distances us from our lived experience of them. Second, the resolution of the cases that the application of doctrine purports to secure offers us a false assurance that our concerns can be met—that public can be reconciled with private, manifestation with intent, form with substance.

Once we realize that doctrinal "resolutions" are achieved only by sleight of hand, consideration of the identified dichotomies helps us to explore more fully the cohabitation agreement. What is the nature of this relationship, or what range of cohabitation arrangements precludes us from making general statements about the nature of the relationship? To what extent do these relationships need protection from authority, and to what extent do they require nurturing by authority? To what extent do they reflect the shared expectations of their participants, and to what extent the imposition of terms by one party on another? How can we harbor intimacy within institutions that offer the flexibility to accommodate individual need, while at the same time providing a measure of predictability and stability? What stake does the society have in limiting the forms of association it will recognize? Given our dependence on our social and cultural context, what freedom does any of us have to reimagine the terms of human association?

Study of the play between public and private, objective and subjective, shows us that these same dichotomies organize not only the strictly doctrinal territory of contract interpretation or consideration, but also the broader "policy" issues that are folded into the cases. Questions of judicial competence, for example, turn out to involve precisely the question of whether a private sphere can be marked off from the public sphere.[163] Similarly, whether enforcement of cohabitation agreements is a pro-marriage or an antimarriage position turns out to depend on questions of intention and power.[164] Even as this analysis illuminates the policy dimension of the cases, it refutes the claim that the addition of policy considerations can cure doctrinal indeterminacy.

If neither doctrine nor the addition of policy can determine how decision-makers choose outcomes in particular cases, the next question is whether the opinions contain other material that illuminates the decision-making process. The dimension of these cohabitation cases that cries out for investigation is the images they contain of women, and of relationship. And since images of women and of relationship are the central concern of feminist theory, I have used that theory as the basis for my enquiry. This does not, of course, foreclose the possibility that other enquiries, in this or other settings, might prove equally possible and promising once doctrine is opened up to make room for them.

I am not claiming that judges decide cohabitation cases on the basis of deeply held notions about women and relationship in the sense that these notions provide a determinate basis for decision. For this to be true, attitudes toward women and relationship would have to be free from contradiction in a way that doctrine and policy are not. I believe instead that these notions involve the same perceived divide between self and other that characterizes doctrine, and are as internally contradictory as any doctrine studied in this chapter. My claim, therefore, is only that notions of women and relationship are another source of influence, and are therefore as deserving of attention as any other dimension of the opinions. These notions influence how judges frame rule-talk and policy-talk; in a world of indeterminacy they provide one more set of variables that may persuade a judge to decide a case one way or another, albeit in ways we cannot predict with any certainty.

One introductory caveat is in order. To say that "the opinions" convey images of woman and relationship is to miss the distinction between images that appear to inhere in the doctrine as it has developed, and images woven into the texture of opinions seemingly at the initiative of a particular judge. I think this distinction is worth noting, even though in practice it cannot always be made. It becomes clearest, perhaps, when a judge struggles *against* images he sees embedded in the doctrine, and offers new images that in turn provide him with new doctrinal choices.[165]

One powerful pair of contradictory images of woman paints the female cohabitant as either an angel or a whore. As angel, she ministers to her male partner out of noble emotions of love and self-sacrifice, with no thought of personal gain.[166] It would demean both her services and the spirit in which they were offered to imagine that she expected a return— it would make her a servant.[167] As a whore, she lures the man into extravagant promises with the bait of her sexuality—and is appropriately punished for *her* immorality when the court declines to hold her partner to his agreement.[168]

Although the image of the whore is of a woman who at one level is seeking to satiate her own lust, sex—in these cases—is traditionally presented as something women give to men. This is consistent both with the view of woman as angel, and with the different image of the whore as someone who trades sex for money. In either event, the woman is a provider, not a partner in enjoyment. When a judge invokes this image, he supports the view that sex contaminates the entire agreement, and that the desire for sex is the only reason for the male partner's promises of economic support. If sex were viewed as a mutually satisfying element of the arrangement, it could be readily separated out from the rest of the agreement. In most cases, the woman's career sacrifices and childbearing and homemaking responsibilities would then provide the consideration for the economic support proffered by the man.

Marriage is often presented in the cases as the only way in which men and women can express a continuing commitment to one another.[169] This suggests that when men do not marry women, they intend to avoid all responsibility for them.[170] Women therefore bear the burden of protecting themselves by declining the irregular relationship.[171] At the same time, the institution of marriage as an expression of caring is portrayed as so fragile that only the most unwavering support by the state will guarantee its survival.[172] This could mean that other expressions of caring would entirely supplant marriage without vigilant enforcement of the socially endorsed forms of relationship, although that would be inconsistent with the portrayal of marriage as the only expression of commitment. Alternatively, it could mean that men and women would not choose to enter relationships of caring without pressure from the state.

These nightmarish images have much in common with what other disciplines tell us men think about women and relationship. The conception of women as either angels or whores is identified by Freud,[173] and supported by feminist accounts.[174] The evil power of female sexuality is a recurrent subject of myth and history.[175] The contrast of men fearing relationship as entrapping, and women fearing isolation, is the subject of Carol Gilligan's work in the psychology of moral development;[176] others have explored the origins of that difference in the context of psychoanalytic theory.[177] Raising these images to the level of consciousness and inquiry therefore seems to me an important aspect of understanding this particular set of cases. It is also a way of stepping beyond the confines of current doctrine and beginning to think about other ways of handling the reciprocal claims cohabitants may make of one another.[178]

Epilogue

The stories told by contract doctrine are human stories of power and knowledge. The telling of those stories—like the telling of any story—is, in one sense, an impoverishing exercise: the infinitely rich potential that we call reality is stripped of detail, of all but a few of its aspects. But it is only through this restriction of content that any story has a meaning. In uncovering the way doctrine orders, and thereby creates, represents, and misrepresents reality, I have suggested and criticized the particular meaning created by doctrinal stories, the particular limitations entailed in the telling of those stories.

My critique is in turn a story, which itself creates order and meaning. My story, too, is subject to the charge that it has reduced the richness of contract law and the multiplicity of its concerns to a few basic elements, that it misrepresents as much as it reveals. And, in fact, I do not believe that my story is the only one that can be told about contract doctrine. I insist only that it is *an* important story to tell.

My story reveals the world of contract doctrine to be one in which a comparatively few mediating devices are constantly deployed to displace and defer the otherwise inevitable revelation that public cannot be separated from private, or form from substance, or objective manifestation from subjective intent. The pain of that revelation, and its value, lies in its message that we can neither know nor control the boundary between self and other. Thus, although my story has reduced contract law to these few basic elements, they are elements that merit close scrutiny: they represent our most fundamental concerns. And the type of analysis I suggest can help us to understand and address those concerns.

By telling my story, I also hope to open the way for other stories—new accounts of how the problems of power and knowledge concretely hamper our ability to live with one another in society. My story both asks why those problems are not currently addressed by doctrine and traditional doctrinal analysis, and suggests how they might be. By presenting doctrine as a human effort at world-making, my story focuses fresh attention on those to whom we give the power to shape our world. My story requires that we develop new understandings of our world-makers as we create them, and are in turn created by them. This kind of inquiry, exemplified for me by feminist theory, can help us see that the world portrayed by traditional doctrinal analysis is already not the world we live in, and is certainly not the only possible world for us to live in. And in coming to that realization, we increase our chances of building our world anew.

Interpreting the Law: Hermeneutical and Poststructuralist Perspectives

David Couzens Hoy

I. Critical Theory and Poststructuralism

Since 1960, when Gadamer published *Truth and Method*, hermeneutics has been criticized and taken in different directions. These developments have implications for legal interpretation, and the current task is to spell them out. I will discuss two ways of going beyond the hermeneutic theory I have sketched so far. The first development is Jürgen Habermas's attempt to avoid the threat of relativism by giving hermeneutics a "transcendental" turn. The second development is French poststructuralism, which is critical of both Gadamer's and Habermas's theories. Some poststructuralists who offer a radically different account of textual interpretation are Derrida, Foucault, Deleuze, Blanchot, and Barthes, but for present purposes I will refer mainly to Derrida since his work has been so influential for American literary theorists of deconstruction. I think there are important parallels in Anglo-American jurisprudence between the poststructuralists and the Critical Legal Studies movement, but first I will discuss the disagreement between Habermas and Gadamer.

A. The Habermas-Gadamer Debate

1. Gadamer on Tradition

Despite Gadamer's disclaimers, his theory is generally conceived as conservative. Although his view is that a text is always understood differently by different people, and thus that there will always be a need to criticize and revise previous interpretations, his critics find his account lacking in two important respects. First, given Gadamer's stress on the historical change of understanding, there seems to be no ground on which to base criticism. The interpreter cannot simply say that the *text* disconfirms prior interpretations and confirms the present one, since there is no text independent of some interpretation, and what counts as relevant in the text is dependent on the interpretation. (That is to say, there is no reading that is not already theory-laden.) Second, Gadamer's notion of the constitutive force of the *Wirkungsgeschichte*[1] leads him to suggest that the *tradition* supplies the most important standard for criticism. Any reading is said to be conditioned by the prior history of related readings, and thus to stand in a tradition of interpretation. Gadamer is frequently misread as saying that an interpretation must stay in contact with that tradition and that "nontraditional" readings are therefore wrong. This interpretation of Gadamer mistakes a descriptive claim about the nature of understanding for a normative one about what an understanding ought to do. What Gadamer in fact maintains is that often an interpretation will correct the traditional way of reading a text. He can say this because what comes to be taken as traditional may be only a partial feature of what the tradition really involves when it is not obscured by overemphasizing a derivative part and thus distorting the whole. In other words, what counts as the tradition is itself a matter of interpretation, and one that any interpretation ought to address.

To illustrate Gadamer's point, consider the force of precedent in legal reasoning. The appeal to precedent is an excellent example of what Gadamer means by *Wirkungsgeschichte* and *wirkungsgeschichtliches Bewusstsein*. Legal interpretation is a clearer case than literary interpretation of the constitutive force that the history of a text's reception has for the formation of further interpretations. But the fact that precedents are sometimes declared mistaken and overruled also sharpens the question about the basis on which an intervening interpretation can be disconfirmed.

A passage from Raoul Berger cited by Michael Perry illustrates how an interpretation of the tradition established in a precedent can be challenged by claiming that interpretation to be a false perception of what the genuine tradition is. As the same time, this passage attests to the ocurrence of the objectivist and intentionalist theory of interpretation to which hermeneutic theory is opposed.

> Why should "adherence to precedent" rise above effectuation of the framers' clearly expressed intention, which expresses the value choices of the sovereign people, not merely of judicial predecessors? . . .
>
> I assert the right to look at the Constitution itself, stripped of judicial encrustations, as the index of the constitutional law and to affirm that the Supreme Court has no authority to substitute an "unwritten Constitution" for the written Constitution the Founders gave us and the people ratified.[2]

Perry cites a similar passage from Garry Wills's book *Inventing America*, arguing that to recreate the original world of the text "we must forget what we learned, or what occurred, in the interval between our time and the text's."[3]

According to hermeneutical theory, this forgetting would be neither possible nor desirable. Naturally we should avoid anachronism, but why should we posit the impossible methodological ideal of forgetting all we have learned? More problematically, although these passages deny the force of tradition in one sense (namely, the history of precedents and "judicial encrustations"), they nevertheless appeal to tradition in another (the original tradition or context in which the document was adopted). So the force of tradition (whatever is taken as the real tradition) is not denied but instead confirmed by this objectivist theory which diverges from Gadamer's hermeneutical theory in every other respect. Hermeneutics wins out over objectivism here, since objectivism undermines its own argument against the constitutive force of the intervening history of interpretations (or *Wirkungsgeschichte*) by tacitly relying on a commitment to tradition. Or at least it can be said that the disagreement does not take place at the most basic philosophical level of the theory of understanding and interpretation (where Gadamer's theory is to be placed), but at a different level, closer to the details of particular practical interpretations and concerns about which aspects of tradition to emphasize and which to play down.

Even criticism of the intervening conceptions of the tradition can involve, then, an underlying normative commitment to continuity with the tradition. Criticism of what is commonly but superficially taken as "traditional" may be advanced for the sake of recovering lost aspects of the real tradition. There is another problem with the appeal to tradition, though, and that is the apparent emptiness of the notion of tradition as a standard for criticism. Two conflicting interpretations could both be based on an appeal to the tradition, but also on divergent understandings of the tradition. The appeal to continuity with tradition is not decisive. Professor Ely gives a concrete illustration of this problem[4] in terms of the *Regents of the University of California* v. *Bakke* case.[5] He maintains that there is more than one American tradition on the question whether racial majorities can aid minorities, and at best the traditions are ambiguous enough to lend support to both sides of the case. He also thinks that in addition to these practical difficulties there are theoretical ones. As a source of constitutional values, tradition's "overtly backward-looking character highlights its undemocratic nature: it is hard to square with the theory of our government the proposition that yesterday's majority, assuming it was a majority, should control today's."[6] Ely thinks that the appeal to tradition is not a primary criterion, but is derivative from what he calls "the most common reference-in-chief, the genuine consensus of contemporary American thought."[7]

I will turn to the notion of consensus shortly, for that is precisely the notion Habermas substituted for Gadamer's concept of tradition. The practical problem about tradition that Ely raises is a variant of the more general criticism by Habermas and the poststructuralists of Gadamer's notion of the tradition-laden character of understanding. The question is why tradition should be valued so highly. Even if our understanding is conditioned by a tradition of interpretation, and even if the ideal of a complete break with past traditions is merely utopian (or dystopian), there may be more point to changing than to restoring tradition.

Gadamer's reply depends precisely on recognizing that to talk about change is to presuppose an understanding of the history that has led up to the need for change. This understanding must be assumed to be correct, and thus an element of the call for change will be the willingness to discuss the importance of this history for the present. Furthermore, to call for change is at the same time to have a view about how change is possible. In order for change to be practicable, and to avoid empty utopianism, it must be to some extent consistent with the tradition and the antecedent history out of which it grows.

Admittedly, Gadamer's theory is abstract and general, but its consequences are not such as to discourage or retard practical efforts at formulating new interpretations, whether these interpretations rely on precedent or whether they significantly revise precedent. The charge of emptiness is not directly relevant to Gadamer's theory, then, since by *tradition* he does not mean established conventions, privileges, or values. He simply tries to describe how the process of understanding and interpretation works, even when the interpretation radically alters previous understandings of the tradition. Of course, the attempt to revise precedent can be overturned. However, insofar as the arguments for doing so are based not on a denial of tradition, but on the hope of becoming part of tradition, Gadamer's model stands.[8] Gadamer's conception of the methodological role of the tradition in understanding is thus more descriptive than normative. The normative component becomes more explicit, however, when the interpretation tries to become conscious of how it is both enabled and limited by antecedent history, including traditional preconceptions not only about doctrine but also about method. That is, the interpretation may need to make explicit the intervening history (or *Wirkungsgeschichte*) that inevitably plays a role in the formation of the interpretation. Hermeneutical philosophy does not tell interpreters what to do, but it does imply that an understanding that tries to understand itself (including both its doctrinal and methodological commitments) is better than one that does not. For the issue of judicial review, this point suggests that in the making or appraising of judicial decisions, the theory of judicial review behind those decisions also ought to be made clear. Then if the theory can be challenged (for instance, by arguing for a hermeneutical conception of interpretation over the intentionalist, objectivist one stated by Berger and Wills), that result will be a factor in appraising the substantive decision.

2. Habermas on Consensus

Professor Ely maintains that the appeal to tradition never stands alone, but always smuggles in the ideal of consensus. That is to say, the appeal to tradition will not by itself settle a dispute unless there is general agreement in the present that the traditional features in question ought to be preserved. Habermas makes much the same point against Gadamer's conception of the tradition-bound character of understanding, except that Habermas maintains further that all discursive understanding presupposes the ideal of consensus. Habermas thinks that the hermeneutical insistence on the context-bound character of understanding must be supplemented by some contextless (or quasi-"transcendental") conception of "reason"—that is, some universal standard for the rational discussion of conflicts of interpretation and for the adjudication of principles. Ely's analysis of the appeal to consensus in determining what the contemporary values are runs directly counter to Habermas's theory, however, since Ely thinks consensus does not in fact give any content to the "inherently contentless notions of 'reason' and 'principle.'"[9] Gadamer makes a similar charge against Habermas's attempt to take hermeneutics in a transcendental direction.

I will summarize the disagreements between Habermas and Gadamer before returning to the ramifications for the issue of judicial review. I see Habermas's position as leading toward noninterpretivism and Gadamer's objections as holding back. But the issue is now a broader one than what judges can do within the confines of current legal practices. Habermas raises the larger question about how current practices could themselves become the object of criticism, or how they could be legitimated. He does not call into question the whole idea of the "rule of law" as dramatically as the French poststructuralists do, but he sets up a framework in which the question of the legitimacy of the rule of law could be asked. He constructs, in Thomas McCarthy's words, "a theoretically grounded form of advocacy in situations of social conflict."[10] In doing so, he appears to go beyond Gadamer's theory, which seems to presuppose the rule of law, or at least does not specify how it could be genuinely challenged.

Habermas's basic worry about Gadamer's historicist hermeneutics is that not enough is said about how the interpreter can transcend and criticize the present context. Habermas thinks that there must be some ideal of truth which transcends the particular interpretation if the interpretation is believed to be not merely plausible, or the best we can do, but also right, and therefore binding on everybody. In a conflict of interpretations there could be no rational attempt to adjudicate the dispute unless the interpretations shared some standards for resolving disagreement. Any interpretation claiming to be correct would have to presuppose a notion of truth common to any other interpretation. In Habermas's terms, all rational discourse presupposes, at least counterfactually, the ideal of a speech situation in which the participants are not constrained by any interfering factors and can consider all the relevant information until the best argument wins unanimous consent. Such consensus is for Habermas presupposed by any claim to know what is true, and by appeals to the morally right as well.

Habermas thinks this notion of truth as consensus in an ideal speech situation is required to avoid the relativism he fears in Gadamer's theory.[11] Gadamer's objectivist critics accuse him of diminishing the status of the text by denying that the text has any standing independent of an interpretation. In contrast, Habermas argues that Gadamer overemphasizes the text. In *Theorie des kommunikativen Handelns*,[12] Habermas maintains that Gadamer is overly influenced by the paradigm of the classical philologist and incorporates into the relation of the text and the interpreter an asymmetry in favor of the text.

The difficulty arose in Gadamer's earlier reply to Betti, where Gadamer had defended himself from the charge of relativism (and of underemphasizing the role of the text) by arguing that his objectivist critics failed to appreciate his insistence on what he called the *Vorgriff der Vollkommenheit* (the anticipation of the completeness or perfection of the text). For Gadamer interpretation does not involve simply understanding the text, but also the text's subject matter. That is, the interpreter should have an understanding of the issues or ideas gained independently from reading the text, or perhaps as the result of being motivated by the text to think independently about the subject matter. The interpreter who has no understanding of the issues and questions that the text addresses obviously does not understand what the text is about. Habermas thinks Gadamer is right to maintain that questions about what a text means cannot be completely separated from those about how to determine its validity or value. However, he believes Gadamer privileges the text too much. At times Gadamer, who is himself a scholar of Plato and Aristotle, implies that the best way to approach eminent texts is to assume that they are unlikely to be wrong, however difficult or alien they seem initially. The dialogue between text and interpreter would thus be asymmetrical, and weighted in favor of the text.

To show that Gadamer has not correctly analyzed the structure of all understanding, Habermas points to a different case of understanding where the superiority of the interpreted object over the interpreter is not assumed. Anthropologists, Habermas maintains, cannot always presuppose the superiority of their object; instead, they must reconstruct the learning processes that separate their beliefs from those of the tribe being studied, and that distinguish modern from mythical thinking. Because Gadamer's hermeneutics is based on the paradigm of the interpretation of eminent texts (for example, legal, sacred, and artistic ones), Habermas thinks that the account of understanding is too one-sided and does not account for the need of the interpreter to criticize the object of interpretation. The backward-looking humanist is less likely than the present-oriented social scientist or the forward-looking social critic to recognize the need for a conception of progress. Some account is required of why we can believe we know more than the past did, or why our society is better than it was, or why society's critics can believe it could be improved. Habermas does not find this critical dimension in Gadamer's theory. He thinks Gadamer's position abets the mistaken tendency of confusing *Verständnis* and *Einverständnis*, comprehension and consent. To understand something is not necessarily to believe it.

Gadamer's position does not entail, however, that understanding is believing. In response to Betti he had pointed out that his stress is as much on the *Vorgriff*, the anticipation, as on the *Vollkommenheit*, or perfection of the text. That is, the notion is not intended as a metaphysical claim about the sacrosanctity of the classics (or, I presume, the infallibility of the law). Instead, it is a heuristic recommendation to the interpreter, suggesting that it will be more useful to go along with the text as far as possible than to dismiss the text's truth claims as outdated or its arguments as primitive. Of course, Habermas is forcing the issue to make clearer why the interpreter must be able not only to understand that which is being interpreted (whether a text or a tribe), but also to *criticize* it. He sees Gadamer's argument that all thinking is conditioned by *Vorurteile* (prejudgments or prejudices) as presupposing a deeply conservative belief in the legitimate and inevitable authority of the tradition. Like Heidegger, Gadamer thinks that any of these prejudgments could be brought to thought—they are not ineffable or inarticulable—but he denies that they could *all* be articulated at once. We could not end with a completely self-transparent thinking, with what Hegel called "absolute knowledge." Gadamer thinks that authority is inevitably involved in understanding insofar as it is always constrained in some respects by tradition and precedent, that is, by preunderstanding. Gadamer sees vestiges of this ideal of reason lurking in Habermas's conception of rationality, which appears utopian in its model of discourse unconstrained by authority or by unexamined assumptions.

Habermas's view is roughly that no authority is legitimate unless an enlightened discussion would result in consenting to it. Since agreements in the everyday world may not include all the relevant parties affected, or since constraints may force an agreement contrary to the participants' real interests, Habermas says the ideal speech situation may be only a counterfactual assumption. That is, discourse in the real world may generally fall short of the ideal, but nevertheless the discussants could not engage in anything that could be called rational discussion unless they presupposed the possibility of attaining an uncoerced consensus based on the best arguments. So, although this ideal may be counterfactual, it is nevertheless a necessary presupposition of all real discourse (i.e., all language activity aiming at cognitive results). To believe their discourse rational, the participants must assume that in the ideal speech situation, reason (i.e., the best arguments) would prevail and the authority to be legitimated would no longer be functioning as *authority*.

Habermas's theory applies to normative as well as cognitive matters. In fact, there is a more natural tendency to think of ethical norms as being validated by consensus, however cognitive claims are validated. The rightness of a normative principle is certainly connected with its being acceptable to all who are affected by it. To extend his theory to ethics, Habermas first denies that the foundation of the binding character of norms is a monological reflection about whether any other agent ought to do what a particular agent is considering. Whereas in Kant's theory reflection on the universalizability of moral maxims is conducted monologically, Habermas thinks that the proper basis for a universalistic ethics is interpersonal dialogue aiming at unanimous agreement. He thus calls his theory "communicative ethics." This ethics is a cognitivist one, because norms are not simply noncognitive, subjective preferences, but the results of objective, public, and legitimate procedures. Ethics is as cognitive as science since the process for validating norms is the same as the process of determining truths. Both science and ethics presuppose the possibility of consensus as the source of the legitimacy of belief. Unlike Kant's moral philosophy, which separates morality and legality because only the former involves internal autonomy whereas the latter presupposes external authority, Habermas thinks that agreement is also the basis for both moral and legal norms:

> Only *communicative ethics* guarantees the generality of admissible norms and the autonomy of acting subjects solely through the discursive redeemability of the validity claims with which norms appear. That is, generality is guaranteed in that the only norms that may claim generality are those on which everyone affected agrees (or would agree) without constraint if they enter (or were to enter) a process of discursive will-formation. The question of which sectors should, if necessary, be regulated through compromise or formal norms of action can also be made

the subject of discussion. Only communicative ethics is universal (and not, as is formalistic ethics, restricted to a domain of private morality separate from legal norms). . . .[13]

Again, however, the ideal and counterfactual status of such agreement makes the theory seem more applicable to a utopian world than to our own. Habermas admits that in an unjust world there will be conflicts between private morality and public mores. His argument is that merely to *conceive* of resolving these conflicts requires us to hypothesize an ideal speech situation in which norms would be discursively determined through consent. But he realizes that

> [t]his does not exclude the necessity for compelling norms, since no one can know (today) the degree to which aggressiveness can be curtailed and the voluntary recognition of discursive principles attained. Only at that stage, at present a mere construct, would morality become strictly universal. It would also cease to be "merely" moral in terms of the distinction made between law and morality. Internalization too would only be complete when the principle of the justification of possible principles (that is, the readiness to engage in discursive clarification of practical questions) was alone internalized, but in other respects the continuous interpretation of needs was given over to communication processes.[14]

To critics of this thesis of the "withering away" of morality who accuse him of utopianism, Habermas admits the utopian component of his theory, but stresses that it is only a formal one of procedure. His model does not specify anything about the actual makeup of the ideal society: "Ethical universalism does indeed have a utopian content, but it does not *sketch out* a utopia."[15] Habermas thinks this minimal utopian component is necessary if social theory is to be *critical* theory, and if we are to be able to transcend our historical conditions in the attempt to criticize our own or other societies.

The challenge I think both Gadamer and such French poststructuralists as Michel Foucault would raise here is why we need this utopian projection to criticize the present. Does this eternal, unhistorical, and supposedly impartial and impersonal ideal really have enough content to show that we have progressed over the past, and to help us decide what would constitute moral and social progress in the future? Habermas, however, clearly thinks his counterfactual, regulative ideal does have real critical bite. Although there is no appeal to a speculative philosophy of history in the notion of the ideal speech situation, Habermas says this notion is both (1) a necessary condition of all real communication, and (2) a political ideal we must try to achieve, and that can be more or less achieved in real societies. We will criticize ourselves and others according to the degree the procedural ideal is approached.

The critical theorist attempts a counterfactually projected reconstruction of social institutions guided by the question,

> How would the members of a social system, at a given stage in the development of productive forces, have collectively and bindingly interpreted their needs (and which norms would they have accepted as justified) if they could and would have decided on the organization of social intercourse through discursive will-formation, with adequate knowledge of the limiting conditions and functional imperatives of their society?[16]

Gadamer's response to Habermas's notion of the ideal speech situation is to say that this idealization is too formal and empty to have any bearing on practice. He could supplement his argument by pointing to the practical problems Ely sees, namely, that there is not likely to be a consensus on the questions that come up for adjudication in a forum like the courts, or that consensus could not be reliably discoverable, at least by responsible social agencies like the courts.

These practical objections to consensus as a legitimation of interpretations will not apply to a minimal (but then uncontroversial and trivial) version of Habermas's transcendental claim. If Gadamer is right that the ideal is a purely formal one, then he could equally well accept as reject it. Gadamer could agree without undermining his own theory that when particular prejudices do become conscious, we can test them with counterfactual reasoning procedures of the sort Habermas (and Rawls) describes. The intuitions at stake here are not mutually exclusive. Habermas thinks correctly that any rational participant in a dialogue would ideally want to articulate a consistent set of beliefs. Those who are on Gadamer's side are equally right to insist that whatever holds under ideal circumstances, we ordinary agents need not believe that all our beliefs are consistent. We could believe they are not, though we do not yet know in what respects, and still believe in our rationality and the rationality of our practices. To think we are irrational so long as all our beliefs are not explicitly examined and consciously formed into an error-free, coherent set condemns us to irrationality permanently.

However, this argument that rationality is better modeled on everyday rather than ideal circumstances does not invalidate Habermas's account of how we could go about deciding whether particular beliefs are rational and coherent with our other beliefs. Habermas can be understood as making a *procedural* point that is legitimate and potentially useful, as hermeneutic theorists could acknowledge. They may think too much is claimed for this procedure and that there are other, equally legitimate procedures, such as appeal to continuity with tradition. The case for each such procedure can be made independently of the others, though, and the only real disagreement will be about whether the ideal of "rationality" requires that there be only one supreme procedure. Hermeneutic theorists who do not think interpretation requires a transcendental foundation can resist the ideal of such a supreme procedure because it will be too thin to be of use in practical criticism, which can legitimately take many forms and which is not helped by the philosophical construction of a transcendental theory of truth. This point could be made another way by arguing that the procedure of agreement, as one procedure among others, will have independent appeal and does not have to be grounded in something more basic, such as the nature of discursive communication.[17] Habermas may think that his ethical theory has more force if it is transcendentally grounded in a necessary presupposition of the use of language. But if the concept of agreement has more intuitive connection with moral rightness than with truth, the case for the ethical theory should be kept separate from that for the theory of truth.

B. Deconstruction and the Critical Legal Studies Movement

1. "New Nihilism"?

With the discussion of Habermas, the question of interpreting the law has moved from the limited problem of how to interpret the law without at the same time challenging its legitimacy, to the larger issue of the legitimacy of both particular laws and the legal organization of society. This larger question is no longer one about interpreting the law in the sense of reading particular statutes and applying them to hard cases. Instead, it is about interpreting "the law" as such; that is, it is about justifying or rectifying the political and social organization that the code of laws and the judiciary serve and perpetuate. Since the object of interpretation is different at this level, the discussion might seem to be safely beyond the questions involved in the dispute about interpretivism versus noninterpretivism in judicial review. The larger questions seem more like ones for political theorists than for judges or constitutional theorists. However that may be, in the theory of interpretation there is now a tendency to push beyond the hermeneutical position I have sketched so far, in a way that would undermine even legal interpretation's minimal claim to rationality (let alone to objectivity or correctness).

Professor Fiss has labeled this tendency "a new nihilism, one that doubts the legitimacy of adjudication" and that has begun "a romance with politics."[18] I do not know for certain whom he would include among the new nihilists. Both Ronald Dworkin and Roberto Unger, for instance, argue that interpretivism is closely bound up with politics, but as I will show, they have different conceptions of politics as well as of the interconnection between law and politics. Whether all noninterpretivists would be nihilists is also not clear, but I assume that many representatives of the Critical Legal Studies movement would be. Fiss mentions deconstruction under this rubric,[19] so I assume a French poststructuralist like Derrida is to be included, as well as some American critics. Fiss identifies a basic premise of this trend toward nihilism in the theory of interpretation as follows: "[F]or any text there are any number of possible meanings and the interpreter creates a meaning by choosing one."[20] He says that he accepts this premise, but thinks that the interpreter's freedom is "constrained by rules that derive their authority from an interpretive community that is itself held together by the commitment to the rule of law."[21]

Given Fiss's intention, I think there are several reasons why he should not grant the premise at all. First, the theoretical model that says an interpreter creates a meaning by choosing one misdescribes what interpreters must believe about their interpretations. Second, when textual meaning is distinguished from utterance meaning, it does not follow that the textual meaning can be interpreted arbitrarily. Context will still constrain the possible alternatives, and variations or shifts between possible contexts will be constrained by factors such as suitability, purpose, and plausibility. Third, I think a hermeneutic theory should be cautious about making the consensus of an existent interpretive community the sole source of interpretive authority. Whether Habermas is right about the necessity of presupposing an ideal speech situation, he is right that real speech situations are imperfect and frequently distorted by the inadequate self-understanding of the discussants. Before deciding whether a hermeneutical line of defense against the new nihilism is needed, however, I should first state how I understand this tendency that Fiss deplores.

Pushed to its limits, this new nihilism would show that all interpretation, even the "interpretivist" attempt to stick to the statutes, is "noninterpretive" in the sense of imposing the interests of the interpreter and deliberately distorting the language of the law. What this position holds in common with noninterpretivism is the view that (a) the language of the law (the textual meaning) is not identical to the psychological intentions of the authors of the law, and (b) the interpreter may candidly manipulate the language to serve other purposes. Procedurally, then, this new tendency and noninterpretivism seem equivalent. Where they diverge is in political doctrine. But noninterpretivism is vulnerable in that its theory of interpretation is a slippery slope that may not be able to stop the slide toward a political outcome that it would find undesirable. Although noninterpretivists discount the author's or framers' intentions, they continue to assume that the language of the law has a coherence and unity, and is in principle capable of being in harmony with the moral and social order, which is also assumed to be coherent and unified. The new nihilists' conception of meaning and interpretation sees the language as either incoherent or else a disguised attempt to impose the interests of the dominant social group. The interpreters (for instance, the judges), who invariably belong to the dominant social group, overlook the contradictions either within the law or between their legal-moral ideals and the existent social structure. Whereas the interpreters may think of themselves as finding the inner harmony between the rationale of the law and the social order, in actuality they are reinforcing their own social power by imposing their illusory social and moral vision on everybody else.

The difficulty here is a general one for "institutional" theorists of interpretation. Any theory suggesting that the standards for adjudicating conflicts of interpretations are simply internal to different (actual, not counterfactual) social groups or institutions seems to have no satisfactory answer to the charge that interpretation is nothing more than an institutionalized way of reinforcing unequal social power relations. Most literary critics fail to take this problem seriously, for two reasons. First, they do not perceive themselves as exercising social power directly the way a judge does (or theologians used to do). Second, literature and art (unlike the law now, and formerly, Scripture) do not seem to be powerful social institutions. Literary theorists can therefore espouse and practice interpretive techniques more or less harmlessly, while interpreters in spheres such as law and theology cannot. The sacrosanctity of religious texts, for instance, would not survive deconstructive readings, and an interpreter holding a text sacred could hardly attempt its deconstruction.

Like Hegel's owl of Minerva, deconstruction would seem to emerge only when a text no longer had an unquestionable authority, or in a culture in which no text was in principle sacrosanct. As used by Derrida on philosophical texts, deconstruction does not take apart a text that is working, but instead it shows why something (for instance, either a central philosophical metaphor or an entire metaphysics) that seemed to work, never really did work. The deconstructive textual analysis then shows how the illusion is perpetrated by syntactical and rhetorical devices in the text.

Does deconstructionist theory really threaten legal interpretation and adjudication? One might think so, given that one of its central tenets is that the referents and truth values of discursive language are "undecidable."[22] This notion of undecidability has some kinship with hermeneutics, particularly with the insistence that interpretation is not a voluntaristic, fully conscious act, and should not be represented as an algorithmic decision procedure. Derrida means much more than this, however, since he holds up the undecidability of specific texts in the history of philosophy and literature as a sign of the inevitable failure of the hermeneutical attempt to find an interpretation that will integrate the elements of a text into a maximally coherent account. The hermeneutical search for the meaning of the literary, philosophical, or historical text, or the judge's attempt to interpret the legal text and to decide the case, would always be self-deceptive if all texts were in principle shot through with undecidability.

As a theory of poetry and literature this idea of undecidability may have a certain applicability since fictional and figurative discourse can reasonably be said to block attempts at decipherment.

As a theory of philosophical discourse, at least in the history of philosophy, it could also apply since no one will deny that metaphysical constructions often rely on literary devices. Thus, questions about whether there really are forms, monads, sense data, and other such posits no longer seem genuine. In other words, there is no longer a viable vocabulary or research program in which anyone would try to decide whether assertions using these notions were genuinely referential. However, what it would be like for our own vocabulary to be similarly a dead language is impossible for us to say, and it still seems reasonable and important to us to decide what we mean by crucial terms such as rationality, rights, obligation, justice, and fairness. In principle, we cannot accept the thought that these terms are undecidable, or that they do not have a genuine use, however difficult it is in practice to work out exactly how the terms are best used.

On my hermeneutical view, deconstruction exaggerates the theory of interpretation in two respects. First, from its destruction of the ideal of determining from the author's intention the one and only appropriate reading of the text, it tends to conclude too quickly that the text could mean anything to any number of different readers. This inference is mistaken, however, since from the fact that any particular context for making sense of a text can be called into question it does not follow that no context is reasonable or justifiable. Deconstruction infers from the collapse of the ideal of absolute justification that no justification is possible. Alternatively one may say that justification is misdescribed in the first place if it is thought that some belief or theory is justified only if all the possible evidence and arguments have been examined and accounted for.

The second exaggeration is to take what is only one moment of the process of interpretation as the inevitable outcome of all interpretation. This one-sidedness distorts interpretation, and would make it an incoherent and unrecognizable practice. Any interpretation should try to avoid reading into the text only what is already familiar. Deconstruction is a reasonable procedure as the practical attempt first to find the rhetorical devices that function to give the text the appearance of coherence, and then to show that since they are *rhetorical* devices there are other elements that disrupt this coherence. But to disrupt the apparent unity or sense of a text there must be another, hermeneutical moment of finding unity in the textual complexity, of making sense of difficult figurative devices. Deconstruction (or "dissemination," as Derrida calls it) goes as far as it can with the thought that the text might be infinitely complex, and allow infinitely many readings. This thought may be well-intended in its desire to insure that the potential complexity of the text is not underestimated, but projecting it as a fundamental principle of understanding and interpretation is philosophical overkill.

The hermeneutical moment is also required since we cannot really contemplate an infinity of meanings and still claim to be understanding the text. Understanding necessarily involves the hermeneutical moment of making sense of the text, of eliminating some possible readings, and therefore of not overestimating the textual possibilities. Hermeneutics denies that the interpreter can read anything and everything into the text and still claim to be understanding the text. I prefer to think of understanding as a matter of balancing two factors that are rarely in equipoise, namely, complexity and sense.[23] A reading is precisely an attempt to gain a reflective equilibrium in which the two appear as balanced as possible. The equilibrium is a reflective one since intuition alone will not settle all the questions. However, reflection is not the same as consciously choosing or creating a meaning

The thought that the interpreter is completely free to vary the context and thus the meaning of the language to be interpreted is wrong for at least two reasons. First, only some of the logical or syntactical possibilities are real ones, and the interpreter does not understand at all if this difference does not make a difference. Second, the lack of equipoise must be found by the interpreter to be a problem in itself. The interpreter does not simply choose arbitrarily and disinterestedly between possibilities, but finds interpretation difficult because it puts prior commitments up for reassessment. As John Rawls describes reflective equilibrium in moral interpretation, it is a matter of confronting our intuitions with our principles, such that we may have to revise either in terms of the other.[24] This description is not simply a better phenomenological characterization of moral reasoning, but also a corrective to a rigid philosophical picture of rationality. Similarly, the notion of reflective equilibrium I have sketched generates a different philosophical picture of interpretation and justification than the absolutist one the deconstructionist successfully attacks. On this hermeneutical model there is no privileged starting point for the interpretation, and no self-evident data. Furthermore, there is no ideal final resting place in the search for equilibrium, no point at which we would have examined *all* the relevant observations and arguments. The ideal is not implicated even counterfactually, for what sense we could make of such an ideal is not apparent. New cases will always call on us to reconsider our assumptions and weightings, so that the ideal of a final consensus determining a correct and unchangeable outcome is inappropriate.

The theory behind deconstruction thus starts from the implausibility of a rigid and absolutist model of what understanding and interpretation are, as well as what is involved in the justification of interpretations or the adjudication of conflicts of interpretation. Although it is correct in this regard, it mistakenly infers from the failure of the absolutist model that no understanding is justified and that no attempt at adjudication of conflicts can claim to be correct or rational. What should instead be inferred is that a more plausible account of understanding and rational justification is required. The account should not make it seem impossible to decide how a text applies in different circumstances, but should show that a reasonable interpreter can legitimately claim to be understanding the text and not simply to be articulating extratextual values. A theory of interpretation concluding that undecidability is inevitable is by *reductio* shown to be wrong. Since it could not decide the truth values of its own claims, it could not exclude contradictory principles, and thus refutes itself.

2. Unger and Dworkin on Politics

Professor Unger's manifesto for the Critical Legal Studies movement is not paradoxical in the same way, but it too argues from the collapse of an overly demanding theory of interpretation to one that risks a "paradoxical voluntarism."[25] Unger begins by distinguishing the procedural belief in value-neutral methods of legal interpretation from the substantive belief in the morality and justice of the laws, however ad hoc the process of legislation seems. He calls the former belief "formalism" and defines it as "a commitment to . . . a method of legal justification that can be clearly contrasted to open-ended disputes about the basic terms of social life, disputes that people call ideological, philosophical, or visionary."[26] The latter is called "objectivism" and is defined as the belief that the "authoritative legal materials" ("the system of statutes, cases, and accepted legal ideas") are "not merely the outcome of contingent power struggles or of practical pressures lacking in rightful authority"; instead, the laws are thought to "embody and sustain a defensible scheme of human association" and to "display, though always imperfectly, an intelligible moral order."[27] Formalism is said to presuppose a qualified objectivism since either the moral order would be completely extrinsic to the laws or it could coincide with the laws by "a sheer miracle."[28]

The rhetorical stage is already set with these definitions, however, since if the internal rationale of the legal system, "the intelligible moral order," cannot be specified in detail, then the only alternative appears to be that the legal system is not a system at all, that the laws have only an instrumental rationality and are simply the result of ad hoc power plays. On Unger's initial presentation of the situation of legal interpretation, there now seem to be only two possible accounts of interpretation. Either the legal interpreter has a "single cohesive theory" explaining how "the many conflicts of interest and vision that law-making involves, fought out by countless minds and wills working at cross-purposes, would have to be the vehicle of an immanent moral rationality," or legal reasoning becomes "a game of easy analogies" in which every thoughtful lawyer can argue "too well or too easily for too many conflicting solutions."[29]

Even Hegel would have balked at this characterization of the alternatives. Hegel did write a philosophy of right trying to show the rationale for the existent social order,[30] but he did not try to show that it fit the contemporary laws precisely. Presumably one purpose of a general philosophy of right would be to criticize some of the existent statutes and practices as inconsistent with other, more important ones. The interpreter has alternatives other than to assume either that there is a miraculous "preestablished harmony" between the laws and a complete theory of right, or the laws are merely ad hoc. If we give up the idea that justification is possible only through a complete and consistent set of verified beliefs, it does not follow that we are condemned to believe our interpretations are unjustifiable and arbitrary. A conception of rationality which humans could not live up to absent a miracle should be rejected as irrational.

If we think of interpretation not in this ultrarationalistic fashion, but as the hermeneutical process of balancing the principles implied in the legal language with the exigencies of particular cases, then we need not think of the laws as either miraculously rational or merely ad hoc. They are not ad hoc if some reasoning about principles and policies is involved at their inception, and they can be rationally and justifiably understood and applied if similar reasoning is used. Exactly the same reasoning both at the inception and at the later interpretation is not required, though, since the circumstances will be different; it will be sufficient if the later interpretation is a continuation and development of the earlier instances, given that how we understand principles and policies depends on what we learn from our attempts to act on them.

What I have said should not be taken as a defense of formalism and objectivism, as Unger defines them, but simply as a reaction to starting from what seems like a false dilemma. Unger is correct in objecting to the claim that lawmaking and law application "differ fundamentally" in "both how they work and how their results may properly be justified."[31] I have also not mentioned anything about the substantive theses of the Critical Legal Studies movement. A claim to the effect that the law and society are in an antagonistic relationship is not one that could be challenged a priori. It can be considered only in terms of a detailed, empirical interpretation. Furthermore, an ideal such as the "cumulative loosening of the fixed order of society"[32] is not objectionable, even if one thinks, as Hegel did, that any society will have some fixed order. A cumulative loosening is still a form of *Wirkungsgeschichte* and still involves some connection or continuity with tradition.

Calling his position a "superliberalism,"[33] Unger insists he is best understood as pushing liberal premises about freedom to their limits and trying "to remake social life in the image of liberal politics" (although doing so requires changing the liberal conception and practice of politics). A hermeneutical theory of interpretation cannot object to the thought that legal interpretation always involves, whether implicitly or explicitly, political commitments arising from continuity with a tradition. This thought is itself one way of illustrating the notion of the *wirkungsgeschichtliches Bewusstsein*, or hermeneutical awareness of the interpretive context.

The claim that legal interpretation always involves, and ought to involve, *politics*, however, can mean different things. While Professors Unger and Dworkin both make this claim, I question whether either could agree with the other's meaning. Roughly, the difference between what they mean by *politics* is the difference between political action and political theory. Dworkin thinks, for instance, that how the equal protection clause is interpreted necessarily presupposes "some theory about what political equality is and how far equality is required by justice."[34] Theory is not simply political theory either, for he thinks it would be possible to trace different political theories back to distinctive epistemological theories, and perhaps also to work out from these toward matching aesthetic theories: "politics, art, and law are united, somehow, in philosophy."[35]

In contrast, Unger thinks of politics more in terms of instrumental calculation and strategies of domination—in short, power relations. He accuses the "rights and principles school" of legal interpretation of being a "watered-down version" of nineteenth-century legal science, itself merely a "diluted version" of the conservative social doctrines that served to justify and perpetuate a stratified society before the emergence of the rights orientation of modern social theory.[36] He thinks that both liberal and conservative political theory rest on a prior political choice that results from the perceived dilemma: "either resign yourself to some established version of social order, or face the war of all against all."[37]

Thus, Dworkin argues against conservative lawyers who appeal to an author's-intention style of interpretation, that this style itself represents a political theory, and that therefore these lawyers undermine themselves in believing political theory to be a corruption of interpretation. Political theory for him is "part of what interpretation means."[38] But whereas Dworkin sees the practice of interpretation as grounded in political theory, Unger sees political theory as grounded in a self-deceptive attempt to preserve the political status quo through the practice of legal interpretation. For Dworkin, the theory can be masked by an interpretive practice that refuses to think itself through, and thus that lacks hermeneutical awareness. The better interpretations would be aware of the interconnection of political theory and interpretive practice, although this awareness is clearly not the same thing as simply imposing one's own values on the text. For Unger, in contrast, what is masked by both the theory and the interpretive practice is the political struggle for power, the interpretation being an ad hoc element of the power play. Better interpretation for him is that which does not try to avoid seeing the social conflicts that produce the interpretive conflicts. Instead of trying to discover an inherent harmony, the better interpretation recognizes the lack of congruence between the available social ideals and their flawed institutional actualizations. Unger thus calls for a self-reflective rationality or "internal development" model that will try either to revise the ideals or to transform the actualization. For this more modest conception of rationality I should think the reflective equilibrium model would be equally appropriate.

There should be a sharp contrast in style between the ways a rights-and-principles theorist and a Critical Legal Studies theorist read the legal material. The former searches for the unity and coherence in the law by specifying the systematic interconnection of politics, morality, and legality, holding out the possibility of finding the right interpretations of hard cases and apparent conflicts. The latter tries instead "to recognize and develop the disharmonies of the law: the conflicts between principles and counterprinciples that can be found in any body of law."[39] These disharmonies within the legal materials suggest that there is not a single vision of human association operant in them, but several alternatives in addition to the dominant one. For this reason, I think it is appropriate to consider the style of interpretation used by the Critical Legal Studies movement as deconstructive, as opposed to Dworkin's reconstructive style.

It would be facile to conclude, however, that both can legitimately claim to be equally correct understandings of different aspects of the texts. There is clearly a conflict here, and much will depend on how strong a case each can make for its own readings. Of course, neither side thinks there is a neutral way to adjudicate the conflicting readings, so how good the case appears to be will depend on the political commitments of the observer. What I wish to stress, however, is that as radical a conflict of interpretations as this is, it is better described by the hermeneutical model of interpretation than by either the objectivist picture I discussed earlier or the noninterpretivist model. Both parties deny a nonpartisan way of adjudicating their conflicting interpretations. Yet if I understand them correctly, both claim to be articulating what is really going on in the text, or what is the best explanation of how the text applies to a given situation. To recognize that in all candor each would have to believe its understanding of the text was not simply invented, one would have to recognize that interpreting is not the same as inventing. However, there are inventive interpretations, that is to say, original interpretations that make us find in the text or the situation points and possibilities we would otherwise not have seen. I do not believe a philosophical theory of interpretation could say in advance how to distinguish novel strategies of reading from arbitrary impositions on the text. In this chapter I have argued against the conception of philosophical theory expecting philosophical theories to be capable of drawing this line. I conclude with the hope that the arena of interpretation is encompassing enough for adjudication and criticism not only of conflicting interpretations, but also of conflicting philosophies of interpretation.

Rhetorical Politics

Introduction

The essays in this final section take up, implicitly or explicitly, the anti-foundationalist arguments that have appeared earlier in this collection. Several of the previous selections, especially those by Abraham, Dalton, Fish, Levinson, Michaels, and Tushnet, call into question foundationalist claims that interpretive theory can provide hermeneutic methods—Lieber's "safe rules"—that will guarantee correct (or at least uncontroversial) interpretations of legal and literary texts. All of these authors reject essentialist proposals to ground interpretation in textual givens unmediated by interpretation; and they also object to other foundationalist attempts to constrain readings through self-interpreting rules. All provide powerful critiques of formalist and objectivist theories and present strong arguments for abandoning the goal of a general hermeneutics.

The essays in this final section build on these negative, therapeutic critiques by proposing positive, rhetorical projects. They argue, by assertion or example, for a shift away from debates about objective texts, "safe rules," and the other issues troubling foundationalist hermeneutics. Instead, they put forth a new set of topics and narratives, focusing on rhetorical strategies displayed within the ongoing practices of legal and literary interpretation.

Chaim Perelman helped open up the space in which these essays now work, and a brief introduction to his "New Rhetoric" will set the stage for the readings to follow. Perelman began by wrestling with problems in "the analysis of informal reasoning," examining "the actual process of deliberation that leads to decision making in practical fields" such as politics, law, and ethics.[1] He rejected the dismissal of rhetoric by traditional philosophy going back to Plato; and he attempted to redirect philosophical inquiry toward the investigation of informal reasoning and rhetorical justification. The fine detail of Perelman's theory can be found in *The New Rhetoric: A Treatise on Argumentation*, coauthored with L. Olbrechts-Tyteca.[2]

The New Rhetoric is first of all a "theory of argumentation" which provides an account of how an author or orator "aims at obtaining or reinforcing the adherence of an audience" through nonformal argument.[3] For Perelman, this project entails a repudiation of philosophical orthodoxy, which he summarizes as the view that "Truth, reality and objectivity mark out the straight road of knowledge and put us on our guard against all deviations" by providing "the norm to which it is proper to submit opinions, appearances and impressions whose status is equivocal and whose basis uncertain, since they are the source at once of knowledge and of error." In place of this absolutist view with its privileging of self-evident truths, Perelman proposes an alternative in which the difference between truth (the province of philosophy) and opinion (the realm of rhetoric) is "no longer one of kind but of degree. All opinions become more or less plausible, and judgments that form the basis of that plausibility are not themselves clear of all controversy."[4] Thus, Perelman reconceives philosophy rhetorically, defining it not "as the search for self-evident, necessary, universally and eternally valid principles but, rather, as the structuring of common principles, values, and loci, accepted by what the philosopher sees as the universal audience."[5]

For Perelman's New Rhetoric, the concept of the universal audience is crucial. At one point he defines it as "the whole of mankind" and more exactly as "all reasonable and competent men."[6] Though there are disquieting suggestions of transcendental (yet gendered) universality in such definitions, Perelman usually takes care to historicize this notion of audience and thus practically limit its domain of universality. For example, he argues that the "way the philosopher sees this universal audience, which is the incarnation of his idea of reason, depends on his situation in his cultural environment. . . . Therefore, each philosophy reflects its own time and the social and cultural conditions in which it is developed." Elsewhere he asserts, "Each individual, each culture, has thus its own conception of the universal audience."[7] The "universal audience" is best understood, therefore, not as a transcendental criterion for judging the validity of all arguments but rather as a rhetorical feature of the historical contexts in which particular arguments take place.

This rhetoricizing of philosophy leads Perelman toward an anti-foundationalist pragmatism.[8] He rejects the "classical idea of justification" based on an "absolutist vision," which "looks for an absolute, irrefutable, and universally valid foundation." Instead, he argues the rhetorical line that precedents, models, convictions, and values "are relative to a specific discipline and a specific environment and can vary in time and in space." Thus, criticism and justification are never "non-temporal or universally valid"; they "are always found in a historically determined context." Although there are, in "all societies and for all intellects," certain acts, beliefs, and values "that are approved without reservation and accepted without argument," this historical fact has no transcendental implications.[9] Such cultural exemplars are simply contingent acts, values, and beliefs in part defined through a community's inability to recognize or accept their contingency.

It is in law that Perelman finds his best example of a practical discipline constituted throughout by historically situated rhetorical practices. In his analysis of the juridical process, Perelman emphasizes "the paramount importance of practical reason—that is, of finding 'good reasons' [i.e., arguments acceptable to the relevant audience] to justify" interpretations, decisions, or actions. For Perelman, legal reasoning is rhetorical through and through. "Criticism and justification are two forms of argumentation that call for the giving of reasons for or against, and it is these reasons that ultimately enable us to call the action or decision reasonable or unreasonable," the interpretation correct or incorrect, and the application acceptable or unacceptable. Furthermore, because of the rhetorical nature of legal reasoning, justification "always occurs within a social context; it is always 'situated.' "[10]

Thus, juridical practices, including legal interpretation, provide excellent examples of rhetorical practices embedded in specific sociohistorical contexts. For Perelman, the question of legal hermeneutics is not about the relation between judges and texts but between interpreters and their audiences. Rather than individually derived or transcendentally ascertainable "safe rules," there is only what pragmatists call "warranted assertibility" within specific communities.[11] In such a rhetorical theory, one analyzes legal reasoning, not by measuring interpretations against texts or a set of formal rules, but by examining how interpreters justify meaning through nonformal argumentation within a given cultural setting. As Perelman puts it more generally:

> Reason, the heritage and glory of every human being, is not that eternally invariable and fully developed faculty whose products are alleged to be self-evident and universally accepted. The rationality of our opinions cannot be guaranteed once and for all. It is in the ever-renewed effort to get them accepted by what in each field we regard as the universality of reasonable [people] that truths are worked out, made specific and refined—and these truths constitute no more than the surest and best tested of our opinions.[12]

Rhetorical Hermeneutics

Steven Mailloux

The Space Act of 1958 begins, "The Congress hereby declares that it is the policy of the United States that activities in space should be devoted to peaceful purposes for the benefit of all mankind." In March 1982, a Defense Department official commented on the statute: "We interpret the right to use space for peaceful purposes to include military uses of space to promote peace in the world."[1] The absurdity of this willful misinterpretation amazed me on first reading, and months later it readily came to mind when I was looking for an effective way to illustrate the politics of interpretation. With just the right touch of moral indignation, I offered my literary criticism class this example of militaristic ideology blatantly misreading an antimilitaristic text.

"But . . . the Defense Department is right!" objected the first student to speak. Somewhat amused, I spent the next ten minutes trying, with decreasing amusement, to show this student that the Reagan administration's reading was clearly, obviously, painfully wrong. I pointed to the text. I cited the traditional interpretation. I noted the class consensus, which supported me. All to no avail. It was at this point that I felt the "theoretical urge": the overwhelming desire for a hermeneutic account to which I could appeal to prove my student wrong. What I wanted was a general theory of interpretation that could supply rules outlawing my student's misreading.

This little hermeneutical fable introduces the three topics of my essay. One topic is the *theoretical moment* that concludes the narrative; another is the simple plot, a brief *rhetorical exchange;* and finally there's the *institutional setting* (a university classroom) in which the exchange takes place. These three topics preoccupy the sections that follow. Section 1 analyzes the problems resulting from the theoretical urge, an impasse in contemporary critical theory. Section 2 proposes my solution to this impasse, a solution I call rhetorical hermeneutics, which leads in section 3 to a rhetorical version of institutional history.

I

The theoretical urge is a recurrent phenomenon within the present organization of American literary studies. For within that discipline, the task of explicating individual texts remains the privileged activity; and, historically, this primary task has always brought in its wake a secondary one: critical practice inevitably leads to its self-conscious justification in critical theory. Every time a new challenger to the critical orthodoxy comes along, the discipline's theoretical discourse renews itself in an attempt to provide a rationale for interpretation. In simplified form, the institutional catechism during the last forty years has gone something like this: What is the purpose of literary studies as an institutionalized discipline? To produce knowledge about literature. How can this best be accomplished? By doing explications of texts. What should be the goal of explication? To discover the correct interpretation, *the* meaning of the text.[2] Once the theoretical dialogue gets this far, the agreement among theorists begins breaking down. How can we guarantee that critics produce correct interpretations? Formalists respond, "By focusing on the text"; intentionalists, "By discovering the author's meaning"; reader-response critics, "By describing the ideal reader's experience"; and so on.

As dissimilar as these theoretical answers appear, they all share a common assumption: validity in interpretation is guaranteed by establishing norms or principles for explicating texts, and such rules are best derived from an account of how interpretation works in general. In other words, most traditional theorists assume that an accurate theoretical description of interpreting will give us binding prescriptions for our critical practice, prescriptions that can assure (or at least encourage) correct readings. The classic statement of this assumption is E. D. Hirsch's in "Objective Interpretation": "When the critic clearly conceives what a correct interpretation is in principle, he possesses a guiding idea against which he can measure his construction. Without such a guiding idea, self-critical or objective interpretation is hardly possible."[3]

In this way, contemporary literary theory comes to focus on a question it takes as basic: how does interpretation—the accomplishment of meaning—take place? Two hermeneutic positions have developed in response to this central question: textual realism and readerly idealism. Hermeneutic realism argues that meaning-full texts exist independent of interpretation. From this perspective, meanings are discovered, not created. The facts of the text exist objectively, prior to any hermeneutical work by readers or critics, and therefore correct interpretations are those corresponding to the autonomous facts of the text. Realism often views the interpreter's mind as passive, simply acted upon by the words on the page. Though the text must be read, in correct interpretation it speaks itself. If the reader needs to do anything, it is only the mechanical activity of combining word meanings into larger thematic units and formal relationships. This is a "build-up" model of interpretation. For hermeneutic realism, texts are the primary source and test of readings; they constrain and ultimately determine interpretations.

In contrast, hermeneutic idealism argues that interpretation always creates the signifying text, that meaning is made, not found. In this view, textual facts are never prior to or independent of the hermeneutical activity of readers and critics. Idealism claims not only that the interpreter's mind is active but that it is completely dominant over the text. There are no semantic or formal givens; all such textual givens are products of interpretive categories. This is a "build-down" model of interpretation. From this perspective, what counts as a correct reading depends entirely on shared assumptions and strategies, not autonomous texts. In hermeneutic idealism, a text doesn't constrain its interpretation; rather, communal interpretation creates the text.

As theories of interpretation, textual realism and readerly idealism share a common institutional concern: to establish a foundation for validating knowledge. I call this an *institutional* concern because traditional theorists claim that, without principles of correct interpretation, an institutionalized discipline has no way of grounding its production of new knowledge. Once again Hirsch is the paradigmatic theorist: he claims that, without a proper theory of correct interpretation, we cannot avoid "subjectivism and relativism" and cannot think of "literary study as a corporate enterprise and a progressive discipline."[4] It follows from this view that theory serves the corporate enterprise by making explicit the norms and principles of valid readings. Any such theory attempts to derive these norms and principles from its general account of how interpretation works. Whether the account is realist, idealist, or some combination of the two, it must provide an *intersubjective* ground for correct interpretation, and it is traditionally thought that only by establishing such a ground can the dangers of relativism and subjectivism be avoided.

With such a high value placed on intersubjective foundations for interpreting, it should come as no surprise that the concept of conventions plays an important—even central—role in hermeneutic accounts, whether realist or idealist.[5] Thus, with some justification, the following discussion takes the conventionalist version of the realist/idealist debate as a synecdoche for all "foundationalist" arguments in recent critical theory.

Theorists of the realist persuasion have long turned to textual conventions to explain literary interpretation. Formalists, intentionalists, structuralists, and even some reader-response critics locate conventions in a text in order to guarantee intersubjective foundations in their hermeneutic accounts. An especially interesting case of realist conventionalism can be found in the work of Monroe Beardsley, who with W. K. Wimsatt codified the prescriptions of New Critical formalism. In essays on the affective and intentional fallacies, Wimsatt and Beardsley proposed an "objective criticism" that would avoid the dangers of "impressionism," "skepticism," and "relativism."[6] In his *Aesthetics*, Beardsley later developed this formalism into a foundationalist theory, asking, "What are we doing when we interpret literature, and how do we know that we are doing it correctly?" and answering, "There are *principles of explication* for poetry in terms of which disagreements about the correctness of proposed explications can be settled."[7] These principles can be summed up in the realist's slogan "Back to the text."[8]

Beardsley explains his realist hermeneutics further in *The Possibility of Criticism*, where he argues that the "literary text, in the final analysis, is the determiner of its meaning."[9] At this point conventions enter into Beardsley's account. In his chapter "The Testability of an Interpretation," he attempts to defend his formalist theory by arguing that "there really is something in the poem that we are trying to dig out, though it is elusive" (*PC*, p. 47). This "something"—the meaning in the text—is the object of interpretation, and Beardsley proposes to define it more rigorously by appropriating the conventionalism of speech-act theory. In another place, Beardsley succinctly describes J. L. Austin's account of language use: "To know what illocutionary action [requesting, promising, asserting, and so on] was performed is to know what action the production of such a text generated by the appropriate conventions."[10]

Austin's conventionalism can be pushed in two very different directions: toward readerly idealism, with conventions placed in hearers, or toward textual realism, with conventions posited in texts. Predictably, Beardsley's adaptation of speect-act theory takes the realist route. Rather than having speakers or hearers "take responsibility" for performing certain illocutionary acts and for committing themselves to certain conventional conditions (for example, in promising that the speaker can do a certain act in the future), Beardsley prefers to say that literary texts imitate illocutionary acts and "represent" that certain conditions are in fact the case (*PC*, p. 115, n. 38). This is a shrewd maneuver: instead of readers taking responsibility for conventions of language use, texts represent those conventions; conventions move from outside to inside the text. This realist placement of conventions gives Beardsley just what his formalist theory requires—an autonomous text against which all interpretations can be tested. "I am arguing that there are some features of the poem's meaning that are antecedent to, and independent of, the entertaining of an interpretive hypothesis; and this makes it possible to check such hypotheses against reality" (*PC*, pp. 57–58). And these semantic features that test interpretations include conventions embedded in the text.

Realist theories like Beardsley's emphasize that conventions display shared practices for writing literature and that readers and critics must recognize these textual conventions in order to achieve valid interpretations. But such theories inevitably suffer from incomplete coverage and lack of specificity as exhaustive accounts of interpreting. No matter how comprehensive it tries to be, the realist conventionalism of genre critics, formalists, and semioticians remains unsatisfying as a complete description of even a single text's literary meaning. The common notion of an artwork's irreducible uniqueness refuses to go away, even when a significant portion of the text's sense is attributable to an author following, modifying, or rejecting traditional conventions. But perhaps the literary text's uniqueness is simply an illusion fostered by the humanistic tradition, on the one hand, and supported by the needs of a critical profession, on the other. Even if this were the case and a text's meaning really could be explained as completely conventional, realist accounts would continue to be embarrassed by their contradictory descriptions of the uninterpreted givens in the text and by their many unconvincing explanations of how such textual givens cause interpretations. Realist conventionalism only restates these essentialist and causal problems: How exactly are conventions manifested in the text? How do such textually embedded conventions determine interpretation? The latter question usually leads realists toward some kind of correspondence model: interpreters recognize conventions in a text because they have literary competence, an internalized set of interpretive conventions.[11] Realists who take this route move toward idealist solutions and in so doing also move toward idealist incoherencies.

In contrast to realism, idealist theories emphasize conventions as shared practices for interpreting literature, conventions present in readers and critics, not in texts. Important idealist theories include those of Stanley Fish in "Interpreting the *Variorum*" and Jonathan Culler in *Structuralist Poetics*. Fish argues that communal interpretive strategies are the only constraints on the production of meaning. Texts are products of interpretive communities, which "are made up of those who share interpretive strategies not for reading . . . but for writing texts, for constituting their properties."[12] In *Structuralist Poetics*, Culler more fully elaborates an idealist-oriented account of using conventions in interpretation. Though at times he refers to "potential" properties "latent" in the text itself, he more often emphasizes interpreters' reading conventions, which determine the sense they make of the literary work.[13] He talks of the poem offering a structure for the reader to fill up, but he stresses the interpretive conventions competent readers use to invent something to fill up that structure. He suggests that it is not the text but the reading conventions that "make possible invention and impose limits on it."[14]

While realist accounts posit textual conventions that are recognized by readers, idealist accounts place interpretive conventions in readers who then apply them to create meaningful texts. Idealists fare no better than realists, however, in using conventions to avoid epistemological embarrassment. True, they do avoid the realist problems connected with essentialism and causation by arguing that the content of the text is produced by the interpretive conventions employed and that texts do not cause interpretations at all. But entirely new problems arise out of these supposed solutions. The two most important involve the infinite regress of conventions and the unformalizable nature of context. In a particular case of interpretation, what determines the interpretive conventions to be used? Idealists cannot answer by proposing metaconventions, because this would lead to an infinite regress within their theories: each set of conventions at a lower level requires metaconventions at a higher level to determine the appropriate lower-level conventions. Then these metaconventions themselves need metaconventions, and so on. One way to avoid this pitfall is to argue that context always determines the interpretive conventions to employ. But such a claim only leads to a more difficult question for the idealist: what constrains the use of interpretive conventions in a specific context?

Both Fish and Culler, among others, have recently suggested the impossibility of adequately answering this question. As they fully realize, such a suggestion entails a critique of their past conventionalist accounts of interpretation. I will limit my discussion here to Culler's recent observation that the interpretive conventions on which he focused in *Structuralist Poetics* should be seen as part of a "boundless context."[15] Culler states his new position in this way: "Meaning is context-bound, but context is boundless" (*OD*, p. 123). Culler seems to be claiming two rather different things, only the first of which helps explain why the contextual nature of interpretation makes idealist conventionalism inadequate.

Culler first seems to be arguing that any full account of meaning must include a notion of boundless context. By characterizing context as boundless, Culler means that any hermeneutic theory trying to specify a particular context exhaustively is doomed to failure: "Any given context is always open to further description. There is no limit in principle to what might be included in a given context, to what might be shown to be relevant to the interpretation of a particular speech act" ("CM," p. 24). Every specification is open to questions asking for further specifications.[16] In such an account, conventions are, at best, only first approximations of boundless context. Conventions begin the specification of relevant contextual features, designating the relation of the words, persons, and circumstances required for a speech act to have the specific meaning it has in a given context (compare *OD*, p. 121).

But conventions alone are inadequate as explanatory concepts. *Either* the description of the conventions must reductively and arbitrarily leave out relevant contextual features, *or* the specification of the relevant conventions would have to be so open-ended that conventions would become indistinguishable from context and lose their identity. A hermeneutic theory using conventions in conjunction with other contextual features will fare no better as an exhaustive account of meaning since there is no limit in principle to the features relevant to the interpretation of specific speech acts. Another way of putting this is to say that context is unformalizable. Any account that uses "context" to constrain interpretation thus has only two options: either it must simply name "context," "situation," or "circumstances" as a constraint and not elaborate any further, or it must carry out an infinite listing of all aspects of context and their interrelations, that is, bring everything in.[17] In other words, interpretive theories of context must either never begin the process of specification or never end it.

Culler's first claim about boundless context agrees with what I have been saying so far: boundless context determines meaning, and context is boundless because it is ultimately not formalizable. Unfortunately, Culler confuses things with a second, entirely different argument about meaning and context, in which he asserts the "impossibility of ever saturating or limiting context so as to control or rigorously determine the 'true' meaning" ("CM," p. 28). In this deconstructionist claim, context is boundless not in the first sense—that it is unformalizable—but in a second sense: new contexts can always be imagined for a particular speech act, and thus meaning is in principle radically indeterminate (see *OD*, pp. 124, 128). Culler ends up using context here as an interpretive device for making meaning undecidable rather than as an explanatory concept in accounting for meaning's determinate shape.

Culler's two uses of context are not necessarily irreconcilable; but to make them strictly consistent, he needs to give up his assertion about the absolute indeterminacy of meaning. As it happens, doing this would not be difficult given his initial explanatory use of context. Indeed, though he claims to be doing otherwise in his deconstructive maneuvers, Culler actually demonstrates not that meaning is always indeterminate but that meaning has one determinate shape in one situation and another in a different situation. Though a speech act's meaning can change from context to context, this meaning is always determinate *within a given context.* In the cases Culler suggests—situations in which the proposal of an imagined context shows how a meaning could change—one of two things happens: the meaning remains the same because, in the present situation, the proposed context is perceived as imaginary; or the meaning changes because, in the present situation, the proposed context is incorporated into the present circumstances. In this second possibility, meaning changes because the context changes. In neither situation is meaning indeterminate; it is determinate (even if ambiguous) because of the context it is in.[18]

But whichever way Culler uses context—whether as explanatory concept or interpretive device—he goes far beyond simply showing that "if language always evades its conventions, it also depends on them" ("CM," p. 29). What he demonstrates instead is something he admits in a footnote: that the distinction between convention and context breaks down (see "CM," p. 30, n. 12). Indeed, all idealist theories of interpretive conventions tend to self-destruct when they adopt the notion of context to solve their conventionalist problems. Do either realist or idealist uses of conventions, then, provide a full account of literary interpretation? The answer must be no, for both theoretical positions fail to avoid radical embarrassments in their accounts.

Nor do theories combining realism and idealism avoid the hermeneutic problems. Typically, such theories argue that realism and idealism are each only partially right, that neither the text alone nor the reader alone determines meaning, that meaning is contributed by both text and reader. This comfortable compromise is understandably popular in contemporary theory, but it solves none of the realist/idealist problems.[19] What it does do, however, is cagily cover up those problems by continually postponing their discovery. In conventionalist theories, for instance, we noted how some realists move from conventions in a text to conventions matched in a competent critic's mind. Such theories, by moving toward idealism, avoid the realist problem of explaining textual causation. But when those same theories run up against the idealist problem of determining appropriate interpretive conventions in a given situation, they turn back to the text for a solution. Thus, we end up with a cunningly circular argument: stay a realist until you have problems, then move toward idealism until you get embarrassed, then return to realism, and so forth, ad infinitum. No amount of tinkering or conflating can save realist and idealist conventionalism from similar dead ends and vicious circles.

It would be a mistake, however, to think that any other account—objective or subjective, conventionalist or nonconventionalist, or some admixture of these—could provide a general theory of interpretation, something we can call Theory with a capital T, something which could solve the hermeneutic problems we have discussed in this section. As Steven Knapp and Walter Benn Michaels have recently shown, Theory is impossible if it is defined as "the attempt to govern interpretations of particular texts by appealing to an account of interpretation in general."[20] My critique of realist and idealist conventionalism is another version of the attack on Theory so defined. The solution to the realist/idealist debate in hermeneutics is not, then, the proposal of still another Theory. The way to answer the realist/idealist question "Is meaning created by the text or by the reader or by both?" is simply not to ask it, to stop doing Theory.

II

The anti-Theory argument opens up two possibilities: a Theorist can be convinced by the argument and stop doing Theory, or he can remain unpersuaded and continue business as usual. Let's take up the second and more likely scenario first. If Theory simply continues, what will happen? According to Knapp and Michaels, Theory depends on logical mistakes like Hirsch's separation of meaning from intention in *Validity in Interpretation*.[21] Since to see a text as meaningful *is* to posit an author's intention and vice versa, a Theory built on the separation of meaning and intention includes prescriptions—"Discover meaning by first searching for intention"—that are impossible to follow. Thus, according to Knapp and Michaels, Theory in its general descriptions is illogical and in its specific prescriptions is inconsequential.

But Knapp and Michaels's thesis needs to be qualified in an important way. Certainly they are right in claiming that Theory cannot have the consequences it wants to have, that it cannot be a general account that guarantees correct interpretations. It can, however, have other kinds of consequences. For example, in advocating a search for the historical author's meaning, intentionalists promote the critic's use of history and biography, what formalists call external evidence. Thus, if a critic is convinced by intentionalist Theory, her interpretive method would employ historical and biographical as well as textual facts and thus could establish a meaning for a text that was different from one where extratextual evidence was scrupulously ignored.[22]

But such methodological consequences might not be exactly what Knapp and Michaels mean by consequences. Fish has recently made a related argument for Theory's inconsequentiality, an argument which suggests that my objection is entirely beside Knapp and Michaels's point:

> Interpretation is a function of the way human beings know, of what it is possible and not possible for the mind to do, of epistemology; and epistemology—the conditions of human knowing—is logically independent of any account one might give of it. I could be wrong about the way interpretation works, or I could be right; but the fact of my being either right or wrong would have no bearing whatsoever on the interpretive act I (or anyone persuaded by me) might perform.[23]

In this sense, Fish would argue, accurate or inaccurate Theory has no consequences.

I agree that having a correct or incorrect account of interpretation neither enables nor disables the critic in doing interpretation. She interprets in any case. But having *this* rather than *that* hermeneutic account does affect the *kind* of interpretation done. One account, for example, might restrict the critic to the published text; another might encourage her to examine manuscript material and biographical evidence. Fish, Knapp, and Michaels would not, I suppose, call these effects theoretical because, over and above such methodological prescriptions, the Theorist claims that the correctness of his account determines the effects it has. The anti-Theorists argue that since this Theoretical claim can't be true, the hermeneutic account has no methodological consequences. But delimiting "methodological consequences" in this way is certainly misleading. True, Theories do not have the kind of consequences a Theorist thinks they have in the way he thinks they have them. Still, the *attempt* to do the impossible (to have a correct Theory that guarantees valid interpretations because it is correct) does have consequences for practice that directly follow from the Theoretical attempt, consequences such as critics talking about the author's mind or becoming preoccupied with biography.

This, then, is my answer to the first question, "If a Theorist continues doing Theory, what is he doing?" If it persuades other critics, his Theory continues to have consequences, but they are not exactly what he thinks they are. He has not provided an idealist or realist account of interpretation that can be appealed to in order to adjudicate readings. He has, however, affected critical practice by encouraging one type of interpretive method rather than another. But now I turn to the second question, "What will happen to theory if the anti-Theory argument *is* accepted?" Of course, Theory would end, but what can take its place? What happens when the Theorist stops searching for that general account that guarantees correct readings? Where does he go once he quits asking realist or idealist questions about interpretation?

One route to follow takes a turn toward rhetoric. I take this path in the rest of my essay, where I propose a *rhetorical hermeneutics,* an anti-Theory theory. Such a hermeneutics does not view shared interpretive strategies as the creative origin of texts (in what George Orwell calls an act of "collective solipsism") but, rather, as historical sets of topics, arguments, tropes, ideologies, and so forth, that determine how texts are established as meaningful through rhetorical exchanges. In this view, communities of interpreters neither discover nor create meaningful texts. Such communities are actually synonymous with the conditions in which acts of persuasion about texts take place. Concepts such as "interpretive strategies" and "argument fields" are, we might say, simply tools for referring to the unformalizable context of interpretive work, work that always involves rhetorical action, attempts to convince others of the truth of explications and explanations.[24]

A rhetorical hermeneutics must, by necessity, be more therapeutic than constructive.[25] To be otherwise, to construct a new account of interpretation in general, would simply reinvoke the same old problems of realism and idealism. Rather than proposing still another interpretive system on all fours with realist and idealist theories, rhetorical hermeneutics tries to cure theoretical discourse of its Theoretical tendencies. It might, then, restate the critique I made in section I: various hermeneutic accounts make the Theoretical mistake of trying to establish the foundations of meaning outside the setting of rhetorical exchanges. All Theories believe that some pure vantage point can be established beyond and ruling over the messy realm of interpretive practices and persuasive acts. Only in this way, it is thought, can correct interpretation, privileged meaning, be accounted for. Hermeneutic realism, for example, assumes a stability of meaning before any rhetorical acts take place. Meaning is determinate, objective, and eternally fixed because of constraints in the text itself that are independent of historically situated critical debates. In a strangely similar way, hermeneutic idealism also assumes stability of meaning outside situated practices. Meaning is determinate, intersubjective, and temporarily fixed because of constraints provided by the communal conventions in readers' and critics' minds. When hermeneutic idealists attempt to describe the system of interpretive conventions that determine meaning, either they describe this system as independent of rhetorical situations or they do not realize that the conventions themselves are the topic of critical debate at specific historical moments. In either case, idealists make a mistake similar to that of realists by presupposing the possibility of meaning outside specific historical contexts of rhetorical practices.

Rhetorical hermeneutics tries to correct this mistake, but simply showing the problems with hermeneutic realism and idealism is not enough. It must also explain why realism and idealism are such attractive theories of interpretation in the first place. We can best do this by redefining realist and idealist claims in terms of a rhetorical hermeneutics. What exactly do these past theories teach us about rhetorical exchanges in interpretation? The realists' claims about constraints in the text testify to the common assumption in critical debates that interpretive statements are about texts. References to the text are therefore privileged moves in justifying interpretations. The idealists' claims about the constitutive power of critical presuppositions exemplify the common pluralist belief that if you change the questions being asked about texts, you change the answers you get, and if you can convince someone else to ask *your* questions, you are that much closer to convincing her to accept your interpretation of a specific text. A rhetorical hermeneutics does not reject any of these assumptions. In fact, it uses their widespread acceptability to explain the rhetorical dynamics of academic interpretation in late twentieth-century America. But to acknowledge the power of these assumptions in rhetorical exchanges today does *not* entail making any claims about whether they are epistemologically true. Such epistemological questions are simply beside the point for a rhetorical hermeneutics. Asking them always leads back to the dead ends of realism and idealism.

Rhetorical hermeneutics, then, gives up the goals of Theory and continues theorizing about interpretation only therapeutically, exposing the problems with foundationalism and explaining the attraction of realist and idealist positions. But a rhetorical hermeneutics has more to do: it should also provide histories of how particular theoretical and critical discourses have evolved. Why? Because acts of persuasion always take place against an ever-changing background of shared and disputed assumptions, questions, assertions, and so forth. Any full rhetorical analysis of interpretation must therefore describe this tradition of discursive practices in which acts of interpretive persuasion are embedded.[26] Thus rhetorical hermeneutics leads inevitably to rhetorical histories, and it is to one of these histories I now turn.

III

Recently more and more attention has been paid to the institutional politics of interpretation, and this attention has proven salutary for histories of literary criticism.[27] Traditional histories tended to minimize the importance of social, political, and economic factors in the development of American literary study; the focus was almost exclusively on abstract intellectual history. In the introduction to one paradigmatic text, *Literary Criticism: A Short History*, Wimsatt and Cleanth Brooks claimed to "have written a history of ideas about verbal art and about its elucidation and criticism," stressing "that in a history of this sort the critical *idea* has priority over all other kinds of material."[28] Such histories of critical ideas not only downplayed the political and economic context in which those ideas developed; they also ignored the effects of literary study's institutionalization within the American university of the late nineteenth century. In a moment I will try to show how this historical event transformed the critical tradition by adding specific institutional requirements to the more general cultural and political determinations that affected the rhetorical shape of American literary study.

More comprehensive than descriptions of critical ideas is a newer kind of critical history: explanations of literary study in terms of social, political, and economic forces. In *English in America*, for example, Richard Ohmann shows how "industrial society organizes the labor of people who work with their minds"; in *The Critical Twilight*, John Fekete situates modern critical theory within the American network of social ideologies manipulated by corporate capitalism.[29] Such studies take account of literary criticism as part of a discipline which is situated within an institution, the modern university. Indeed, Ohmann, Fekete, and others have done valuable work in revealing the institutional mechanisms that constrain the development of academic literary study. But though these historical analyses do acknowledge the importance of institutional constraints, such determinations are secondary to their primary interest in economic and political formations in society at large. The result is that (at least in Fekete's case) such accounts sometimes overlook or distort the institutional role of literary studies in the development of critical ideology. Whereas Fekete argues that, in the modern critical tradition, "cultural methodology reveals its politics directly,"[30] I would say that social and political formations reveal themselves only indirectly, through the mediation of criticism's place within institutions for producing knowledge— universities generally and literature departments specifically. That is, the establishment, maintenance, and development of literary study in universities can only be partially explained through analysis of factors outside these institutions. A more intrainstitutional explanation must also be attempted because, once the institutional space has been established for literary study, the specific interpretive work and rhetorical practices within this space seem only crudely affected by extrainstitutional factors.

Let me use the institutional history of New Critical formalism to illustrate what I mean. Traditional accounts of critical ideas and more recent sociopolitical analyses of criticism give a prominent place to the hegemony of New Criticism in American literary study during the 1940s and 1950s. Traditional histories of criticism usually recount the genealogy of New Critical ideas but fail to explain adequately why those ideas came to dominate literary study. Sociopolitical analyses like those of Ohmann and Fekete have much more explanatory power. For instance, Fekete skillfully shows how agrarian social ideology, which attacked modern industrial civilization, was easily accommodated to corporate capitalism through the institutionalization of New Criticism within English departments. Fekete's otherwise insightful analysis, however, does not grant the institutional setting of literary study its full share in determining the shape and hegemony of New Criticism. In fact, Fekete distorts the nature of the institutionalized discipline when he suggests that New Criticism filled a vacuum created in the 1930s by the failure of socialist criticism within the discipline.[31] Actually, there was no vacuum: literary study within the academy was dominated by historical scholarship, which provided the discipline with a professional training program, shared research goals, and interpretive conventions for viewing literature. The rhetorical shape of New Criticism—its theory and practice— was influenced significantly by its institutional attempt to displace this scholarship as the dominant approach to literary texts. To understand exactly what was required of New Criticism, we need to trace the institutional history of literary study. In what follows I will briefly present a rhetorical version of this history, emphasizing only those forces and events that contribute to an intrainstitutional analysis of why New Criticism achieved its persuasive authority in the American study of literature. Such a rhetorical history follows directly from the rhetorical hermeneutics I have proposed because, to understand the discursive practices of interpretive rhetoric, we must also understand their past and present relations to the nondiscursive practices of institutions.

In the 1870s and 1880s the American university expanded its collegiate curriculum to include scientific and humanistic disciplines previously ignored, and it utilized the model of German scientific research for its conception of knowledge production.[32] The influence of this scientific ideology can be seen in the particular way literary study was institutionalized. Various critical approaches were available to those in the university who wanted literature to be made part of the curriculum—for example, moral or didactic criticism, impressionism, and liberal social criticism. But the approach that made possible the institutionalization was German philology, the scientific study of modern languages and a linguistic and historical approach to literature.[33] Philology provided the scientific rhetoric needed to justify literary and linguistic study to the rest of the academic community. This scholarship allowed the discipline to take advantage of all the mechanisms for the production and dissemination of knowledge that other institutionalized disciplines were developing. Philological study provided a methodology that could be used for the classroom practices derived from the German scientific model: the seminar, the specialized lecture, and the research paper. It also made use of the agencies that the emphasis on research had created for the diffusion of knowledge: scholarly journals, university presses, and the annual conventions of learned societies.

But philology did not simply plug into an institutional compartment set aside for literary studies; it also effectively designed the interior of that compartment. In the early twentieth century, philology allowed the discipline to develop historical scholarship in all its forms (source and influence studies, examinations of historical backgrounds, and so forth). Indeed, philological research provided much of the agenda for the future of the discipline. The narrower view of philology gave literary study such basic projects as textual editing, variorum commentaries, bibliographical descriptions, and linguistic analyses. The broader view of philology gave historical scholarship its most ambitious rationale: philology as "the cultural history of a nation."[34] As philology modulated into a less linguistically oriented historicism in America, it maintained the ideal of this study of a national spirit. Thus philology did its part for Americanism in the academy's cultural politics as the

United States emerged a world power during the first decades of the century.

In the first quarter of the twentieth century, then, philological research and historical scholarship filled the institutional space provided for literary studies. These communal practices shaped and were shaped by the institutional nature of the discipline, and the functions they served became an important part of the institutional demands that the rhetoric of any new approach needed to address. I would now like to outline some of the ways in which New Criticism effectively served and, in turn, revised institutional functions when it came to dominate the discipline by displacing historical scholarship.[35]

First of all, New Criticism provided an ingenious rhetorical accommodation of scientific ideology. As I've noted, scientific research provided the model of knowledge production through which literary study and several other disciplines were institutionalized. The prestige of science continued to grow within the academy during the early twentieth century, but at the same time some members of the humanistic disciplines grew increasingly discontented with scientific ideology and its positivistic assumptions. In literary study, these two conflicting trends came together in the way the New Critics theorized about literature and criticism in the second quarter of the century. On the one hand, New Critics defended literature against the onslaught of positivist values by claiming that literary discourse presented a kind of knowledge unavailable in scientific discourse. On the other hand, New Criticism itself was promoted as a "scientific" method of getting at this nonscientific, literary knowledge. This strategic manipulation of scientific ideology can be seen in the rhetoric of John Crowe Ransom. In the early 1940s, Ransom distinguished science from poetry, arguing that poetry recovers "the denser and more refractory original world which we know loosely through our perceptions and memories." Poetry treats "an order of existence . . . which cannot be treated in scientific discourse."[36] Though he distanced literature from science, Ransom advocated a closer relationship between literary *criticism* and science: "Criticism must become more scientific, or precise and systematic, and this means that it must be developed by the collective and sustained effort of learned persons—which means that its proper seat is in the universities."[37] Here Ransom recognized the importance of proposing a "scientific" method of criticism to replace the "scientific" method of philological scholarship dominating the discipline. In this way, New Criticism accommodated itself to the institutionally entrenched model of knowledge production and simultaneously provided a defense of its subject matter as autonomous and uniquely worthy of study. It is beside the point that New Criticism actually laid claim to only a few characteristics of scientific method (technical precision, objectivity, neutrality) or that sciences such as physics were calling these scientific ideas into question. What is important institutionally is that New Criticism rhetorically adapted to the scientific ideology in such a way that it provided continuity as well as revitalization for the discipline.

This revitalization included a humanistic critique of carefully chosen aspects of scientific ideology. Some New Critics extended a humanistic attack on scientific relativism to the scientism of historical scholarship. In "Criticism, History, and Critical Relativism," Brooks took exception to Frederick Pottle's historical study, *The Idiom of Poetry*, and was particularly upset with the book's historicist premises. Critical evaluation is always relative, Pottle argued, because "poetry always expresses the basis of feeling (or sensibility) of the age in which it was written" and therefore earlier poetry can never be judged by twentieth-century standards. *"The poetry of an age* [in a collective sense] *never goes wrong."*[38] Brooks opposed these historicist assumptions with his own formalist claims about poetic structures that are transhistorical: "functional imagery, irony, and complexity of attitude" can be used to evaluate poems in all ages ("CHCR," p. 209). Brooks argued further that a debilitating relativism would certainly result if historical study continued to ignore the universal criteria of formalist evaluation. "I am convinced," he wrote, "that, once we are committed to critical relativism, there can be no stopping short of a *complete* relativism in which critical judgments will disappear altogether" ("CHCR," p. 212). Attributing this growing danger to the fact that "teachers of the Humanities have tended to comply with the [scientific] spirit of the age rather than to resist it," Brooks argued that in literary studies we have tried "to be more objective, more 'scientific'—and in practice we usually content ourselves with relating the work in question to the cultural matrix out of which it came" and thus irresponsibly avoid normative judgments ("CHCR," pp. 213, 198). The New Critical accommodation to scientific ideology, then, simultaneously approved one form of objectivity and criticized another: Ransom advocated a "good" kind of formalist objectivity in interpreting literature, and Brooks condemned a "bad" kind of historicist objectivity in not evaluating it. In this strategic way, New Criticism incorporated into its rhetorical appeal the strengths of both scientific and humanistic programs within the institutionalized discipline.

New Criticism satisfied a second institutional requirement when it became an effective means for increased specialization. The New Critical assumption that literature was an ordered object independent of social and historical context entailed a formalist methodology that could reveal the unified complexity of that literary object. Since literary meaning was also assumed to be independent of authorial intention and reader response, New Critics stressed the details of the text in-and-of-itself. They therefore developed their methodology by focusing on the literary text in a vacuum, or, as they preferred to say, on literature as literature. New

Critics thus tried to elaborate a technical criticism that derived its interpretive categories exclusively from literature and not psychology, sociology, or history. This rejection of "extrinsic" approaches conveniently included a rejection of the historical assumptions of philological scholarship. The rhetoric of this new "intrinsic" criticism served the institutional function of reinforcing the independence of literary study within the academy, an accomplishment that was part of a general institutional tendency in American universities between 1910 and 1960. As Stephen Toulmin points out, "During those years . . . the academic and artistic professions moved into a new phase of specialization. Each 'discipline' or 'profession' was characterized by, and organized as the custodian of, its own corpus of formal techniques, into which newcomers had to be initiated and accredited, as apprentices. So, there was a general tendency for each of the professions to pull away from its boundaries with others, and to concentrate on its own central, essential concerns."[39] In literary study, it was New Criticism that fulfilled this institutional need for increasing differentiation and specialization.

A third function of New Criticism was its usefulness as a means of further professionalization. Since institutional specialization also requires professionalism, the discipline of literary studies also needed an approach that fulfilled what Ohmann calls "the professional mission of developing the central body of knowledge and the professional service performed for clients."[40] New Criticism easily satisfied both of these professional requirements. It redefined the nature of the knowledge produced by the discipline, moving it from the historical and linguistic knowledge of philology to formalist knowledge about the literary text in-and-of-itself. It also changed the priority of the discipline's practices as it moved away from scholarship to criticism, giving ultimate value to explication of individual texts. The formalist assumptions and textual explications presented the discipline with a new pedagogy, one that Brooks and Robert Penn Warren's *Understanding Poetry* (1938) rapidly taught to members of the profession. More slowly, these same New Critical assumptions and practices also displaced philological scholarship as a methodology for training and accrediting the growing number of new recruits to the profession.

The close readings of New Critical formalism represent the fulfillment of the final institutional function I will point out. New Criticism constituted a discursive practice for the discipline, one that could be easily reproduced and disseminated within a growing profession. It gave the members new things to do with old texts, using an interpretive machine that was easy to operate without the traditional and lengthy training of philology. Literary critics exploited this machine to fill the increasing number of monographs and journals the expanding institution demanded.

In the 1940s and 1950s, New Critical formalism showed that it could fulfill all the institutional demands I have outlined. It did this more persuasively than any other available critical approach, even as it simultaneously modified these demands. Again, as with philology, the dominant critical practice and the institutional space were mutually defining. Today, debates in critical theory take place in terms set by New Critical formalism: Is authorial intention relevant to correct interpretation? Is textual meaning separate from reader response? Is the literary work independent of historical context? But even more important than setting the current agenda for theoretical debate is the hegemonic discourse contributed by New Critical close readings, the detailed explications of individual texts. It is no accident that the most popular forms of poststructuralist criticism are those that most closely resemble the interpretive rhetoric of New Criticism, a rhetoric emphasizing the complexity of the unique literary work. Thus, despite being constantly attacked and supposedly outmoded, formalist rhetoric still remains a dominant presence in literary thought and critical practice within the discipline of American literary studies.[41]

By presenting this schematic history, I am not arguing that intrainstitutional accounts are the only relevant narratives for understanding the rhetorical evolution of the academic study of literature. In fact, I believe that such histories must be supplemented by more comprehensive analyses relating the institutionalized discipline to the sociopolitical forces originating outside the university. By including this brief history in my presentation, however, I do mean to illustrate how a rhetorical hermeneutics is composed of therapeutic theory *and* rhetorical histories. More exactly, such narratives are not simply added onto theory; rather, interpretive theory must become rhetorical history. Thus, rhetorical hermeneutics joins other recent attempts to incorporate rhetoric at the level of literary theory and its analysis of critical practice.[42] Such attempts share a suspicion of Theory and a preoccupation with history, a skepticism toward foundational accounts of interpretation in general, and an attraction to narratives surrounding specific rhetorical acts and their particular political contexts. Such attempts place literary theory and criticism within a cultural conversation, the dramatic, unending conversation of history that is the "primal scene of rhetoric."[43] A rhetorical hermeneutics, then, is not so much theory leading to history but theory as history.

From *Constitutional Fate: Theory of the Constitution*

Philip Bobbitt

A Typology of Constitutional Arguments

The central issue in the constitutional debate of the past twenty-five years has been the legitimacy of judicial review of constitutional questions by the United States Supreme Court. This issue is thought to have been given heightened attention owing to the Court's historic decision in *Brown* v. *Board of Education of Topeka, Kansas*[1] and thereafter to have achieved status as the question of the hour in the legal academy with Judge Learned Hand's Holmes Lectures at the Harvard Law School in 1958.[2] Throughout the sixties the activism of the Warren Court kept the issue of this legitimacy alive, and interest was intensified by the controversial decision in *Roe* v. *Wade*[3] in the seventies. I think it is fair to say that the question of the legitimacy of judicial review has claimed more discussion and more analysis than any other issue in constitutional law. This chapter is an examination of the question of such legitimacy. It may strike some, however, as going about an answer in a rather odd and roundabout way.

For it is customary among essayists in constitutional law to address such questions in one of two ways. Judges and academic lawyers tend to examine the events surrounding the adoption of the Constitution, its homely but interesting text, the political relationships the Framers were trying to establish and those they sought to make impossible,[4] even sometimes what the Court itself has said about its own role.[5] And from a competition among the arguments arising from such examinations, critics purport to determine the proper scope for the Court's role. On the basis of such arguments it has been artfully argued that to legitimate the acts of Congress the Court must have the power of review, since the power to affirm necessarily predicates the power to strike down.[6] Elsewhere it has been noted that parts of the text, for example the supremacy clause, authorize the Court's review of acts of the state legislatures.[7]

Others following a different reasoning have said that the legitimacy of review is confirmed by a study of discussions at the Constitutional Convention addressed to whether or not to include the justices of the Supreme Court in a Council of Revision whose duty it would have been to review all laws before they became effective—since all the arguments for and against this proposal appear to share the assumption that the courts were empowered to determine the constitutionality of those laws they encountered in the process of deciding cases.[8] Correspondence among the Framers regarding a Bill of Rights also appears to reflect this assumption.

Still others have argued that institutional features of the Court arising from precisely that insulation from political reaction that is often thought to make the Court ill-suited for final review actually fit the Court to be the conservator of constitutional principles, the development and preservation of which take place by means of judicial review.

These various arguments all constitute one sort of analysis and come mainly from academic lawyers who are the priestly critics and opening-night reviewers of the legal profession.

The second kind of examination begins a little farther back. Judicial review of legislative acts, it is said, is proper because it is likeliest to assure just accommodations. This is so, on one view of the matter, because the terms of the original social contract would inevitably be varied by political majorities with the power to do so, so that these majorities, and their agents the legislatures, must be restrained in the same way that courts must often prevent the coercive renegotiation of contracts between private parties of unequal bargaining power.[9] But since only a long-dead majority can be said to have originally agreed to such a contract, the full force of this argument can perhaps be avoided.[10] It may instead be offered, however, that courts are the best final arbiters of the sort of hypothetical contract that would be agreed to by all citizens at any time (in ignorance of any particular personal advantage), since legislatures must respond to the powerful and to shifting majorities within their constituencies[11] and do not have to justify their decisions by appeals to the principles of such an "original contract."[12] This argument depends on the acceptance of the idea that those rules one would have agreed to without reference to one's own position in life do, in fact, reflect and will yield a condition of disinterested justice. Philosophical argument of this kind for judicial review will depend on an assumption that the Constitution is, or can be interpreted to be, this sort of original contract. This throws us back on legal argument. Thus the usual philosophical bases for judicial review take us only to the doorstep of legitimacy, since it must still be shown that a particular use of the Constitution actualizes the role for which review is justified.

And yet legal argument—the analysis of the Constitution to which so many able minds have devoted themselves this last quarter century—cannot establish independent legitimacy for judicial review, for its debates and its analyses are conducted by means of arguments that themselves reflect a commitment to such legitimacy. So although a general theory of constitutional law may appear to establish the legitimacy of certain kinds of arguments—as when a social contract theorist might wish to confine courts to a textual analysis of the Constitution[13]—it is in fact the other way round. It is because we are already committed to the force of an appeal to text that such an argument can be used in support of a court's role. When one argues that a court's experience with parsing documents, or its time for reflection, or its relative insulation from political pressure, and so forth, fit it as an institution for the task of assessing the constitutionality of legislation, one is already committed to the view that enforcing rules derived from the constitutional text is the legitimate task at hand.

In the ensuing pages therefore I will not take the conventional tack of raising arguments that appear to define the scope of legitimate review. Instead, I will present a typology of the kinds of arguments one finds in judicial opinions, in hearings, and in briefs. Each kind of argument must be one with which each of my readers could agree, though each may of course differ as to its force.

In this task it is not necessary to appeal to rules. You cannot *decide* to be convinced by any of these arguments; nor, of course, need you decide whether they are convincing. There is a legal grammar that we all share and that we have all mastered prior to our being able to ask what the reasons are for a court having power to review legislation.

If you doubt this, imagine for a moment some of the arguments that will not appear in this constitutional typology. One does not see counsel argue, nor a judge purport to base his decision, on arguments of kinship; as for example, that a treaty should be held to be supreme with respect to a state's statute because the judge's brother has a land title that would be validated thereby. Nor does one hear overt religious arguments or appeals to let the matter be decided by chance or by reading entrails. These arguments and a great many others are not part of our legal grammar, although there have been societies and doubtless are still societies within whose legal cultures such arguments make sense.

This suggests that arguments are conventions, that they could be different, but that then we would be different. This is evident in Orwell's description of the revolutionary whose house is searched without a warrant. "They can't do this to me," he says. "I've got my rights."

This point is not always appreciated. Indeed some commentators are inclined to ignore the significance of constitutional argument altogether, as when a political scientist boasts that he can predict the vote divisions in Supreme Court cases and coolly concludes that political bias decides most cases. It is not relevant for the time being whether constitutional arguments decide cases or *are* the decision itself, by which I mean that they form the structure of meaning the case ultimately achieves as precedent. What is now important is that the Court hears arguments, reads arguments, and ultimately must write arguments, all within certain conventions.

I will explore the various types of constitutional argument. I shall begin by saying that there are five types. As will become clear, these five are really archetypes, since many arguments take on aspects of more than one type. Eventually I hope to persuade the reader that these five types are not all there are.

Historical argument is argument that marshals the intent of the draftsmen of the Constitution and the people who adopted the Constitution.[14] Such arguments begin with assertions about the controversies, the attitudes, and decisions of the period during which the particular constitutional provision to be construed was proposed and ratified.

The second archetype is *textual argument*, argument that is drawn from a consideration of the present sense of the words of the provision. At times textual argument is confused with historical argument,[15] which requires the consideration of evidence extrinsic to the text.

The third type of constitutional argument is *structural argument*. Structural arguments are claims that a particular principle or practical result is implicit in the structures of government and the relationships that are created by the Constitution among citizens and governments.

The fourth type of constitutional argument is *prudential argument*. Prudential argument is self-conscious to the reviewing institution and need not treat the merits of the particular controversy (which itself may or may not be constitutional), instead advancing particular doctrines according to the practical wisdom of using the courts in a particular way.

Finally, there is *doctrinal argument*, argument that asserts principles derived from precedent or from judicial or academic commentary on precedent. One will not find in the text of the Constitution the phrases "two-tier review" or "original package" or any of the other necessary and ephemeral modes of analysis by which the Constitution is adapted to the common-law case method, yet these doctrines are every bit as potent as those phrases originally printed in Philadelphia.

To an exploration of these five types of argument—historical, textual, structural, prudential, and doctrinal—I shall devote the remainder of Book I. It will become apparent that what is usually called the *style* of a particular judge, as well as the very different notions of style in particular eras, can be explained as a preference for one type of argument over others.

My typology of constitutional arguments is not a complete list, nor a list of wholly discrete items, nor the only plausible division of constitutional arguments. The various arguments illustrated often work in combinations. Some examples fit under one heading as well as another. For example, the constitutional argument that a particular sort of question is best suited to be decided by one institution of government and ill-suited to another may in some cases be thought of equally plausibly as a prudential argument or a structural one. For that matter, structural argument itself contains a prudential component just as arguments of any kind may be said to be "doctrinal," since the various approaches and kinds of constitutional arguments are embodied in constitutional doctrines. A different typology might surely be devised through some sort of recombination of these basic approaches, and there can be no ultimate list because new approaches will be developed through time.

Ethical Argument

I have attempted to construct a typology of constitutional arguments whose existence I should think few would deny.[16] I now turn to one particular sort of argument whose very status as a coherent convention would be perhaps controversial. For reasons I will discuss later, I have called this approach "ethical" argument. For the moment I will only try to show that an ethical approach exists, that it is reflected in the U.S. Reports, and that it is often the animating argumentative factor in constitutional decision-making.

Thus far I have discussed the following types of constitutional arguments: historical, textual, structural, prudential, and doctrinal. If you were to take a set of colored pencils, assign a separate color to each of the kinds of arguments, and mark through passages in an opinion of the Supreme Court deciding a constitutional matter, you would probably have a multicolored picture when you finished. Judges are the artists of our field, just as law professors are its critics, and we expect the creative judge to employ all the tools that are appropriate, often in combination, to achieve a satisfying result. Furthermore, in a multimembered panel whose members may prefer different constitutional approaches, the negotiated document that wins a majority may, naturally, reflect many hues rather than the single bright splash one observes in dissents.

If you ever take up my suggestion and try this sport you will sometimes find (leaving aside the statement of facts and sometimes the jurisdictional statement) that there is nevertheless a patch of uncolored text. And you may also find that this patch contains expressions of considerable passion and conviction, not simply the idling of the judicial machinery that one sometimes finds in dictum. It is with those patches that I am concerned here.

By ethical argument I mean constitutional argument whose force relies on a characterization of American institutions and the role within them of the American people. It is the character, or ethos, of the American polity that is advanced in ethical arguments as the source from which particular decisions derive.

Let me say at once that I am aware of some of the difficulties created by my choice of this particular name. As I shall use the term, ethical arguments are not *moral* arguments. Ethical constitutional arguments do not claim that a particular solution is right or wrong in any sense larger than that the solution comports with the sort of people we are and the means we have chosen to solve political and customary constitutional problems.

I might have chosen the word *ethological* to describe such argument, but the cultural anthropologists have taken over that word; or I might have invented a word like *ethetic* which bears a relationship to *ethos* much like that borne by the word *pathetic* to the word *pathos*. I might have especially done this since *pathetic* has to do with the idiosyncratic, personal traits and thus reflects one feature of illegitimate judicial opinions which is often confounded with the class of arguments I am interested in illuminating. In the end I decided on the term *ethical* largely because of its etymological basis. Our word *ethical* comes from the Greek *ethikos*, which meant "expressive of character" when used by the tragedians. It derives from the term *ethos*, which once meant the "habits" and character of the individual, and is suggestive of the constitutional derivation of ethical arguments.

There is an almost utter absence of the discussion of ethical arguments *as arguments* in the teaching of constitutional law. Either they are instead regarded as disreputable reflections of the moral and political positions of the judge who lacks sufficient willpower to keep them properly cabined, or they are indulged by both the cynical and the sentimental for being what "real" judging is all about, having little to do with the competition of arguments per se. I think that even the mere recognition of ethical arguments may have some salutary effect. To that task of observation—though of course no observation of this kind is not theory-laden—I shall devote the remainder of this chapter.

Let us begin with some recent examples of ethical argument. In *Moore v. City of East Cleveland*,[17] the Supreme Court confronted an Ohio zoning ordinance that limited occupancy of a dwelling unit to members of a single family. Inez Moore, who was sixty-three years of age, lived in her own home with her son and two grandsons. One grandson was the child of the son living at home. The other grandson was the son's nephew. She was convicted for the crime of having failed to remove the nephew as an "illegal occupant" as defined by the Ohio ordinance which did not permit collateral relations to share a home within a certain area prescribed by the zoning code.

Precedent in the form of previous cases sympathetic to the integrity of the family had focused on the childbearing and child-rearing functions of the *nuclear* family, as Justices Stewart and Rehnquist pointed out. At the same time, the recent case of *Village of Belle Terre* v. *Boraas*[18] had upheld a zoning ordinance that, in restricting land uses, had excluded groups of students, friends living together, and unmarried groups like the Moores that were not couples.

Nevertheless, a plurality of the Supreme Court struck down the Ohio statute. Justice Powell read the earlier decisions not in terms of their doctrinal consistency, that is in terms of the arguments and rationales they shared, but in terms of the ethical approach to constitutional questions that they embodied. Thus he wrote,

> Our decisions establish that the Constitution protects the sanctity of the family precisely because the institution of the family is deeply rooted in this Nation's history and tradition.[19]

Justice Powell placed the decision on an ethical ground—one based on the American ethos and not shared by all cultures—that values and utilizes extended kinship.

> Ours is by no means a tradition limited to respect for the bonds uniting the members of the nuclear family. The tradition of uncles, aunts, cousins, and especially grandparents sharing a household along with parents and children has roots equally venerable and equally deserving of constitutional recognition. Over the years millions of our citizens have grown up in just such an environment, and most, surely, have profited from it. Even if conditions of modern society have brought about a decline in extended family households, they have not erased the accumulated wisdom of civilization, gained over the centuries and honored throughout our history, that supports a larger conception of the family.[20]

This is a clear and, to my mind, persuasive exposition of an ethical argument. As a distinct approach it not only enables us to deal with precedent in a way quite distinct from that taken by the dissenters, but it also establishes the opinion as a different precedent when understood in light of the approach. The value of this characterization may be appreciated when contrasted with more conventional analyses. Professor Tribe, for example, in his interesting and useful treatise, is forced to resort to extraordinary doctrinal pyrotechnics to rationalize *Moore* with *Belle Terre*. He notes that *Belle Terre* involved students who did not claim "an enduring relationship" with one another. Consequently, *Moore* should stand for the proposition that "governmental interference with *any* [enduring] relationship should be invalidated unless compellingly justified."[21] We are then told that *Belle Terre*, "the earlier case," cannot be said to foreclose this position.[22]

I fear that counsel who rely on this view are apt to be disillusioned. There is nothing clearly discernible in the American ethos that relies on the value of enduring relationships generally, except possibly magazine subscriptions and appeals from one's old college. I suggest that it is because he has elected a different constitutional approach than that taken by the Court that so able a reader as Professor Tribe is led to so profound a misconstruction.

Good and Bad/Good and Evil

I hope the examples given in the previous sections reaffirm the very existence of ethical arguments in constitutional law. Their absence from discussions in law school classrooms has, I believe, yielded the cynical conclusion that mere expediency governs constitutional decision-making. Ignoring the existence of ethical arguments has had other costs as well: not only candor, but simplicity too is sacrificed. Most importantly, the exile of ethical argument from the domain of legitimate constitutional discussion has denied an important resource to the creative judge who exploits all the various approaches from time to time and case to case.

Ethical argument has been neglected because it is feared. We are unwilling to use constitutional institutions as a supreme moral arbiter, and therefore many would like to remove moral argument from constitutional law altogether.

Why are we unwilling to view ethical argument as appropriate to constitutional decision-making? There have obviously been many societies (indeed, we may soon see the emergence of one in Iran) which have wholly integrated ethical and constitutional functions. There are two reasons, I think; one is widely accepted in various forms, and the other is correct.

The first view is roughly analogous to the empiricist's hostility to moral observations generally. One reason we are disinclined to admit moral statements into a calculus of truth functions about the world, and are not opposed to admitting scientific hypotheses, is that the latter are verifiable by observation evidence. If I observe a vapor trail in an electron chamber, I am inclined to count this as evidence of an electron. If, on the other hand, I feel moral indignation at the government's decision to suspend food stamps, this scarcely establishes the wrongness of the government's act. It only counts as evidence of my feelings.[23] Conventional constitutional arguments appear to have the same epistemological basis as statements of scientific observation. There are independent phenomena—the text, or historical events, or the political structure, or the calculus of costs and benefits, or previous case law—that stand for a state of affairs independent of our feelings. True, you and I may put different interpretations on a piece of historical evidence, but this is no different than our trying out different scientific hypotheses for fit. There is an objective fact. But when I say that a statute is unconstitutional because it violates the ethic to which our government ought to cleave, am I not simply saying something about my perception, a conclusion perhaps, but not anything about the Constitution per se?

This view of things is, I think, quite probably wrong about science and the role of observation evidence,[24] but I am certain it is wrong about the process of constitutional law. In both cases this view treats an object—the constitutional rule or the electron—as severable both from our apprehension of it and from our use of it with other concepts. This is an error with respect to the Constitution since the choice of a particular mode of approach and argument is not the product of an "objective" fact. There is not only nothing in the Constitution which dictates, for example, the use of historical argument, but even if there were, our application of such a provision would be made in light of how we apply textual provisions generally. I am not saying that there were an infinite number of kinds of constitutional argument available, "logically" as it were, to the authors of The Federalist or to the first litigants before the Supreme Court. Of course, the Constitution was written by men with certain kinds of institutions and arguments integrated into their very debates. In those debates one finds the full range of arguments I have discussed, and I derive from them the principle of constitutional construction that none of these modes can be shown to be necessarily illegitimate.

The second objection to ethical argument is more telling. It admits that we see our Constitution through various legal conventions, that the Constitution is inseparable from the organizing framework of these conventions, and that the Constitution we are to apply will appear differently depending on which convention is chosen. But it is observed that competing moral conventions generally do not themselves provide the methods for resolution which are provided by competing legal approaches. Thus, for example, a change in a statute may cause some things to cease being illegal, while they may well still be immoral. Since ours is a society of considerable moral pluralism, to admit ethical arguments in the constitutional arena is to sacrifice the ameliorative, assimilative power of constitutional law, to take advantage of which, political questions, as Tocqueville observed, are in America so often transmuted into legal questions.[25] One fears the result would be the kind of intractable ideological conflict so notable on the European scene. The conventions of a legal language are then exchanged for ideologies, in the face of which no event, much less an argument grounded in a differing approach, can but confirm to each side the rightness of their principles and their desires.

This is a substantial and highly important shortcoming of ethical argument in constitutional law. When the authoritative decider is the Supreme Court, this shortcoming is greatly worsened, since the finality of a constitutional decision by that Court often freezes the situation, limiting action by other constitutional institutions. Indeed, given the federal structure of law in our society, a good argument might be made that moral arguments should generally be excluded from the constitutional discourse.

I believe that this argument justifies, for example, the phenomenon of federal habeas corpus, for which it is otherwise difficult to give good grounds. Habeas corpus severs the constitutional decision from the moral question of guilt or innocence, so that the former can be dispassionately weighed as one suspects it seldom can be in the context of a trial. At the same time federal habeas corpus gives the matter to a group of deciders whose customary business is, by comparison to state courts, largely amoral. It is the state courts that must confront questions of moral blame, broken promises, negligent or intentional harm, marital collapse, and virtually all crime. The federal courts, on the other hand, except for their diversity jurisdiction, are largely given over to matters of government regulation, intergovernmental conflict, and national commerce. Federal habeas corpus enables the constitutional questions to be given the priority they can seldom achieve when held in the balance with a moral conviction widely enough shared to have found its way into a state's criminal code.

But doesn't such a distinction between moral argument and moral deciders on the one hand, and constitutional argument and federal judges on the other, actually reflect a way of compensating for the principal shortcoming of ethical argument, that is, its lack of a nonethical referent? Aren't the values of the Fourth and Fifth amendments, which habeas corpus has protected to the extent of turning many guilty men free, also "ethical"? If so, then we may be able to identify a class of ethical arguments that originate in a specifically *constitutional* ethos and hence avoid the difficulties of ethical and moral arguments generally.

Change and the Constitution

> Dying for the "Truth": *We should not let ourselves be burnt for our opinions: we are not that sure of them. But perhaps for this: that we may have and change our opinions.*
>
> Nietzsche, *The Wanderer and His Shadow*

Change comes to the Constitution through many different channels and is mediated by different agencies. The most frequent processes are the incremental corrections in course that courts make as they confront unanticipated fact-situations and must apply old rules reconsidered in the light of new cases. Beyond this, sometimes courts use the earlier language in a new way to bring about the re-cognition of issues, the same clouds making a different face.

As both the interstitial and the reviewed methods of change operate from the past, they also operate on the past. It has been remarked that every artist creates his own precursors.[26] I must read Keats differently having read Yeats and perhaps read both differently having read Auden. So I must read *Pierce* and *Meyer* differently having read *Griswold* and must read them all differently having read *Roe*.

Yet re-cognition differs from the incremental working out of doctrine because it acts to make available different arguments. The work of Calabresi may truly be called seminal because it brought to the academy a different analysis, which, in the pattern of ideas circulating between the three branches of our profession, will find its way into acceptable arguments in accepted opinions.[27] These arguments will come to be proffered by counsel who would otherwise lose or risk loss in the competition of previously accepted arguments. The accepted arguments will become opinions. The opinions will be accepted, first as fragments for higher courts mending their own internal conflicts, and later by lower courts seeking to explain the rules that are the products of such conflict, and later still in that temporary finality that occurs when a particular case is over. That acceptance will make such arguments part of lawyers' functioning perception of problems, "for reality in a world, like realism in a picture, is largely a matter of habit."[28]

There is also the rare, utterly transforming change which shatters the existing symmetry. In constitutional law, the Civil War was such a change. One of the principal analytical changes it brought about underscores the point that constitutional approaches often evolve in response to theoretical rather than practical needs. This was the development of substantive due process and the creative response this development called forth from the constitutional conventions of argument—the mistaken superimposition onto the states of the federal model of enumerated powers. The transforming constitutional event then becomes less important than the change by which we know it (as it has been said that Thucydides' *Peloponnesian Wars*[29] has replaced the war itself since the event can't stay in print).

Such constitutional transformations do not give us new conventions, new approaches. They change the context in which these conventions are applied and therefore the sense of "fit" which each will provide in a particular setting. This sense has been elsewhere discussed,[30] in the context of allocating scarce resources, creating great cultural drama. There exists a parallel phenomenon here. Our constitutional processes having created these conventions, there is no one truth outside of them. This allows our constitutional institutions to take advantage of the insight captured by Niels Bohr's remark that "the opposite of a correct statement is a false statement. But the opposite of a profound truth may well be another profound truth."[31]

Within the conventions we may have correct or incorrect statements. For example, the position has been maintained that, as a matter of textual argument, the term "during such time" in the emoluments clause implies, as a matter of contemporary usage, "inclusive of the end of such period." Therefore a senator nominated for a cabinet post, the salary of which had been raised during the senator's tenure, could nevertheless hold that office if, while still a senator, he saw to it that the salary was lowered again. By this method, the nomination would avoid violating the provision of Article I, section 6, that "No Senator shall, during the time for which he was elected, be appointed to any civil office under the Authority of the United States . . . the Emoluments whereof shall have been increased during such time."[32]

I think this is incorrect. But I cannot say that the further view that the text shouldn't govern at any rate is incorrect. We must test this solution against our larger sensibility to see if it comports comfortably with the other sorts of conventions for decision we have in this society, in law generally, and in constitutional law. We must see if it is meet and right for us, as the people we are. Fortunately, this test is done by the case method,[33] and we may test one judgment in varying contexts, no one of which commits us irrevocably to a single approach. Indeed, I am inclined to paraphrase Constable's famous remark about painting and say that "law is a Science, of which cases are the experiments." By the case method, doctrine tends to correctability within a stable convention and competing conventions gain ascendancy or decline with respect to particular sorts of problems.

This process of constitutional change is sometimes misunderstood by those unfamiliar with judicial review. For example, an article by the president of the Southwestern Political Science Association concludes that

> [o]ur Constitutional system has become self-destructing. The source of this Constitutional destruction lies in the Constitution and its inappropriateness to modern society. Essentially, the Constitution provides no structure or function to Congress that would nurture internal power centralization and institutional cohesion. It merely assumes that these will be maintained by the natural operation of political life in an uncomplicated, agrarian society.[34]

The author would resolve this crisis by a "Constitutional change." I have omitted his arguments since I do not intend to answer them. They are by and large not really arguments at all but highly questionable assertions about the cycles of power between the president and Congress, quite devoid of historical evidence and flimsily buttressed by warnings that current appearances to the contrary are but illusion. What I am concerned with is the general view of constitutional change. Not only does the article's author wish to reorient the relationship between two branches of the federal government, something no amendment has ever done, but he evidently believes that such an external, imposed change will set measures right.

This attitude is nothing new in political science. In 1934, Roger Pinto of the University of Paris, in a monograph on the dissenting opinions of the Supreme Court, is said to have contended that judicial review of legislation of the American type may have been useful and appropriate for a young and immature nation when the people were unwilling to trust themselves or their elected representatives.[35] He then raised "the query whether the American people have not grown up and whether they are not at the present time able to stand upon their own feet instead of continuing to depend in their economic and political conduct so largely upon the judgments of a few legal conservators."[36]

Such a view of the Constitution and of the institution of judicial review would be impossible for someone holding the positions I have described concerning arguments and functions and the reflexive quality of each within the legal and more general culture. Such a view is, instead, the position of those who think the Constitution and its institutions are models, blueprints as it were, and that blueprints are simplifications of structures. One sees this view in the current (and to my mind misguided) call for a constitutional convention. This view is as naive and inattentive to the way in which the Constitution actually works as is its cynical counterpart, the view that the Constitution is irrelevant to the wholly "subjective" directions of judges and politicians. Both views begin with the notion that constitutional law is the appeal to declared rules.

The more carefully we examine the actual uses of the Constitution in constitutional decision, the sharper becomes the conflict between those uses and our requirement that they follow inexorably from a constitutional command. So if the investigator were looking for evidence of this, it is quite natural that he would be disillusioned. Sir George Thomas observed, "What it comes to when you say you repeat an experiment is that you repeat all the features of an experiment which a theory determines are relevant. In other words, you repeat the experiment as an example of the theory."[37] Thus the investigation of constitutional law by the leading legal realist disclosed that

> [t]here is, in a word, one reason and one only, for turning in this day to the Text. A "written constitution" is a system of unwritten practices in which the Document in question, by virtue of men's attitudes, has *a little influence. Where it makes no important difference which way the decision*

goes, the Text—in the absence of countervailing practice—is an excellent traffic-light. Aside from such cases, any Text of fifty years of age is an Old Man of the Sea.[38]

Llewellyn said he determined this by simple observation. All he was recounting, he wrote, was the

> *tacit* doing of the Court, [drawing] from that doing conclusions not to be avoided by a candid child. The whole expansion of the due process clause has been an enforcement of the majority's ideal of government-as-it-should-be, running free of the language of the Document. Whatever the Court has *said*, it has departed from its own precedents whenever it saw fit to do so.[39]

This "observation" has given unjustifiable confidence to those who think constitutional judgment to be wholly without meaningful standards. Llewellyn certainly didn't believe this; and yet he didn't see the operation of the conventions there were, because he was captivated by the old pictures to whose discrediting he was devoted. Today this view is as true and yet as period-bound as a Braque or a cubist Picasso. Of course, that doesn't mean one is any less likely to encounter vulgarized copies tacked up in the interiors of everyday life.

Someone must have noticed that the number of Supreme Court justices is the same as the number of the Muses. I have not seen this commented upon; perhaps it is thought that if judges are the artists of constitutional opinions, it would be unlikely that they could be inspirers and inspired at the same time. I have tried to show how this is possible. The Constitution is the principal medium by which the relationship between our society and our government is displayed in meaningful patterns. As there is nothing more revolting than a cynical lawyer deriding the constitutional process he scarcely comprehends, so there are few things more noble than the Constitution's work on all of us—and our work on it. Of this, too, one might say, "it is here before necessity that old morality is unmade and then remade into a new thing."[40] In the final sections of this chapter, I shall explore the implication of this view for the question of the legitimacy and scope of the judicial review of constitutional questions.

Legitimacy and Review

In this chapter I have been engaged in a study of the legitimacy of judicial review. I have, however, gone about it in an odd way, beginning with the rejection of the usual justifications for this review and taking up instead a consideration of the kinds of argument that are customarily used in proving one justification or the other. I hope this approach has not reminded you, as it has sometimes reminded me, of Steinberg's first cartoon in the *New Yorker* magazine in 1941. In it a female art student faces a stern instructor and defends her painting of a centaur—equine head, human hindquarters—by saying, "But it *is* half man, half horse."[41]

I have gone about my investigation in a topsy-turvy, upside-down way because it really was an investigation. I did not impose on the cases, briefs, and oral arguments the requirement that they share some characteristics which would qualify them as being properly legitimate constitutional decisions. More importantly, I could not have begun with such a requirement since it would have derived from one of the various justifications for judicial review, which justification itself, I felt, was arrived at only by using a particular kind of argument as a vehicle. Each justification, it seemed, was the culmination of a proof in a competition of arguments played by rules which reflected a commitment to a particular form of argument. So I began instead with an examination of constitutional arguments—no, *examination* is misleading, is too strong; I began moving among different constitutional arguments. Now, we are almost finished with our tour. From our experience we ought to be able to give answers to some of the questions with which we began, questions which bear on the legitimacy of constitutional review by courts.

1. Do judges and commentators decide to adopt a particular approach or does the Constitution require one approach rather than another?

To the extent that one is attracted to natural law, it will perhaps seem that choosing a particular approach is a matter of finding that approach, latent in the Constitution, most suitable for a particular problem. To the extent that one is attracted to positivist or existentialist perspectives, it will often seem that choosing one of these approaches is a creative decision which, over time, yields an artifact that is the body of law expressing this approach. Some judicial activity appears to support both these views. I have discussed in the preceding section how particular factual features of a problem suit it to treatment by a particular approach. In the sections preceding that, however, I discussed the relationship between a particular approach and the function served by a single decision displaying this approach. I concluded that the use of a particular function is made actual by the conventions.

To the layman, without these conventions, all legal opinions will appear to be creative acts, choices. To a judge or commentator working within a particular convention, its application will appear to be determined for us. This accounts for the genuine sincerity of judges who claim they only apply the law. Thus it is quite understandable but quite unfortunate that constitutional law will often appear to have a bewildering formlessness to, say, the trusts and estates lawyer who is nevertheless confident of particular rules and their operation within his or her own area of expertise.

Each is wrong. Legal truths do exist within a convention. But the conventions themselves are only possible because of the relationship between the constitutional object—the document, its history, the decisions construing it—and the larger culture with whom the various constitutional functions serve to assure a fluid, two-way effect on the ongoing process of constitutional meaning. We have, therefore, a participatory Constitution.

2. Is the Constitution a realist's or a formalist's institution?

Neither. Realism and formalism are two different reactions which depend on a shared expectation. That expectation is that the statement of a legal rule is either true or false depending on whether it stands for a legal fact. For the formalist as for the realist, a law statement is a proposition, the assertion of a state of affairs. If a law statement is a true proposition, then it is true of something. The formalist looks at the body of constitutional law and, trimming away inconsistent decisions as wrongly decided (as they must be if there is to be a set of true legal propositions), is confirmed in his view. If there were no legal truths, he asks, how would we know when a decision was wrongly decided? The formalist is smug, reactionary, and suspicious of the motives of those who have forsaken his faith.

The realist looks at law as what judges in fact do and, finding a mass of contradictory statements, concludes that legal truth can only have an arbitrary correctness. Since there are no legal objects in the world—there is not "sovereignty" unless a court chooses to use that term as a way of resolving a case or, for that matter, "negligence" or "consideration"—the realist concludes that legal rules are false statements about the world; they are illusions. The realist is tough, battered, making a style out of despair. Some realists are nihilists, refusing to claim a special validity for any set of rules. Others are constructivists trying to create a structure, admittedly imposed, within which a statement is either correct or incorrect. Perhaps Llewellyn's work on the Uniform Commercial Code was a response of this kind. By the same token, some formalists are positivists, taking the law statement to be true insofar as it corresponds with authoritatively declared law. Other formalists are attracted by natural law, and they may take the Constitution to be its crystallization.

All this depends on treating legal rules as if they derived their validity from the truths they express about a world. This is a mistake. When we understand the notion of a participatory Constitution, we will reject both formalism and realism. The expression of law will be seen to be the formulation of rules and not propositions. These rules allow us to do constitutional law. They direct operations within the various conventions. Law consists of resolving questions in the context of the conventions that provide the methods for answering them.

In the opinion for the Court in *McCulloch* v. *Maryland*, Chief Justice Marshall proves, by means of structural arguments, that a national institution—a federal bank—is immune from state taxation. This holding may be roughly phrased as the proposition, "No state may tax a federal instrumentality per se."

If we are interested in the legitimacy of judicial review, we will want to be able to establish the validity of its holdings by determining the source of this validity. So, it is thought, we must ask whether the constitutional proposition of law is true and, if it is true, how we know it is true.

One classic position is that judicial review is legitimate only if the holding is logically true, that is, if it follows necessarily from the Constitution. This is Thayer's rule, announced in his famous article, "The Origin and Scope of the American Doctrine of Constitutional Law,"[42] first published in 1893 and excerpted countless times since. Thayer's rule does not, I think, justify the holding in *McCulloch* v. *Maryland*.

Another view is that the holding in a constitutional case is true because the Court said so, and no other authoritative decision-maker contradicted it. But courts have often disobeyed the Supreme Court with impunity, indeed without rebuke. In any event, this is scarcely a guide to a judge making a new decision: it tells him that whatever he decided will be correct while at the same time whatever was decided before, which he may now ignore or even overrule, was also correct.

Yet another reply is to say that the holding will become true as it becomes legitimate in the eyes of the public. A particular holding is therefore a kind of guess, and only time will say whether it is, or was, true. One more view is that a holding is true insofar as courts and others have agreed to call it true when it is arrived at within a certain system. The holding is true so long as the system is agreed upon and it is consistent with other holdings within that system. Thus a holding might be true only conventionally, i.e., true in the Commonwealth of Ames, or "true" for first-rate lawyers. Each of these views depends upon the holding being a proposition. I would like to say that a holding is not an assertion of a state of affairs, not a proposition at all (except for the single case in which it is stated). A holding is simply a rule for our future guidance. It may appear to us to be a proposition, an assertion about the Constitution or what courts will do or even what the people will accept. But it is not. Even when a holding seems to point to a reality outside itself, still it is only the expression of acceptance of a new measure of reality.[43]

This view of constitutional law is not mere conventionalism (which is the source of the positivism of the formalist and the constructivism of the realist), because, as we shall see, a participatory Constitution is not an invention of judges. At the same time it is not a matter of finding law in the world, either (a task to which formalists respond by "putting the Constitution next to a statute and seeing if it squares with it" and to which realists respond by choking), because the resulting statements are not statements about the world and hence cannot be deduced from it.

The concepts which occur in constitutional law must also occur and have a meaning in everyday life. We must argue in everyday life. We must arrive at decisions by way of arguments. It is the use of these concepts outside law (and this use is of course influenced by the reports of legal decisions, opinions, and so forth) that makes their use within constitutional law meaningful. "If there is a mystery to constitutional law," T. R. Powell once wrote, "it is the mystery of the commonplace and the obvious, the mystery of the other moral contrivances that have to take some chances, that have to be worked by mortal men."[44] The rules of constitutional law are not *derived* from these everyday uses, however, but result from the operations of the various conventions.

3. What is the fundamental principle that legitimizes judicial review?

There is none. It follows from what I have said thus far that constitutional law needs no "foundation." Its legitimacy does not derive from a set of axioms which, in conjunction with rules of construction, will yield correct constitutional propositions.

Indeed, I would go further and say that the attempt to provide such a formulation for constitutional law will likely lead to the superimposition of a single convention on the Constitution, because only within this do we achieve the appearance of axiomatic derivation that the foundation-seeker is looking for. See, for example, John Ely's remarkable *Democracy and Distrust*. We do not have a fundamental set of axioms that legitimize judicial review. We have a Constitution, a participatory Constitution, that accomplishes this legitimation.

The physicist John Wheeler has told this story about the game of Twenty Questions.

> You recall how it goes—one of the after-dinner party [is] sent out of the living room, the others agreeing on a word, the one fated to be questioner returning and starting his questions. "Is it a living object?" "No." "Is it here on earth?" "Yes." So the questions go from respondent around the room until at length the word emerges: victory if in twenty tries or less; otherwise, defeat.
> Then comes the moment when I am . . . sent from the room. [I am] locked out unbelievably long. On finally being readmitted, [I] find a smile on everyone's face, sign of a joke or a plot. [I] innocently start [my] questions. At first the answers come quickly. Then each question begins to take longer in the answering—strange, when the answer itself is only a simple "yes" or "no." At length, feeling hot on the trail, [I] ask, "Is the word 'cloud'?" "Yes," comes the reply, and everyone bursts out laughing. When [I was] out of the room, they explain, they had agreed not to

agree in advance on any word at all. Each one around the circle would respond "yes" or "no" as he pleased to whatever question [I] put to him. But however he replied he had to have a word in mind compatible with his own reply—and with all the replies that went before.[45]

This story is an illuminating metaphor of the process of constitutional decision. Note that if Wheeler had chosen to ask a different question, he would have ended up with a different word. But, by the same token, whatever power he had in bringing a particular word—*cloud*—into being was only partial. The very questions he chose arose from and were limited by the answers given previously.

The Fate of the Constitution

Walter Benn Michaels

In a recent issue of the *Texas Law Review* devoted to the question of interpretation,[1] G. Edward White finds himself provoked to ask an odd but interesting question. The provocation for the question consists of arguments by Stanley Fish and Sanford Levinson proposing what White calls "a political determinism that leads very rapidly to nihilism,"[2] and White's inquiry is meant to serve as a reminder of something "elementary" that Fish and Levinson have overlooked.[3] Why is it, White asks, that when we are doing interpretation we begin with a text?[4] "Why not teach a class on constitutional law without the Constitution, or a course on the *Iliad* . . . without the *Iliad*?"[5] The question seems odd for obvious reasons—how could we imagine a class in constitutional interpretation without a constitution to interpret? But this is precisely what White thinks theorists like Fish and Levinson do imagine. According to White, they have forgotten that "[o]ne need only believe that it is relevant and necessary, in order to clarify the meaning of a designated source, to use the source itself as a basis for extracting the meaning."[6] White criticizes Fish and Levinson for "epistemological overkill": "in order to prevent texts from being a source of *objective* meaning . . . [they] are attempting to prevent texts from being a source of *any* meaning."[7] Hence their nihilism, their belief that *"no answers that do not flow from one's prejudices are ever possible."*[8]

On this account, then, Fish and Levinson have not so much forgotten the text as they have deposed it, and, given this scenario, we can begin to see the interest as well as the oddness of White's question. The question seems odd because it seems self-contradictory—if we had a class in interpreting the Constitution without the Constitution, why would it be a class in interpreting the Constitution? But White's point is not that if we want to interpret texts we need texts to interpret. The reason we need texts, according to him, is to serve as the "source" of our interpretations, since if our interpretations do not come from the text, they will "flow from" our "prejudices." What makes his question interesting, then, is that it concerns not the objects of interpretation but the sources. Both the threat of nihilism and the promise of at least a limited objectivity, for White, depend on an account of where our interpretations come from: if they derive from the text, we are in relatively good shape; if they derive from our prejudices, we are in trouble.

White's interest in a causal account of interpretation is, of course, shared by his opponents in this debate. Levinson approvingly quotes Fish: "Interpretation is not the art of construing, but the art of constructing. Interpreters do not decode poems; they make them."[9] Levinson then speaks of meaning as being "created rather than discovered."[10] Both sides thus fall into (actually, leap into) what Richard Rorty has called "the basic confusion contained in the idea of a 'theory of knowledge,'" the "confusion between justification and causal explanation."[11] White, Levinson, and their allies proceed as if a narrative of the origins of interpretations will necessarily provide the best test of their truth or falsehood. But if, as Rorty points out, there is no logical relation between justification and causal explanation, then the best tests of truth and falsehood are just the usual ones—not where the interpretation comes from, but whether it explains what seem to be crucial aspects of the text; whether it accounts for evidence outside the text that we may have about the text; and whether it coheres with other things we believe about the world. None of these tests bears any relation to the genetic concerns of White and Levinson; none bears any relation to what Philip Bobbitt attacks as the desire "to get behind arguments to causes."[12]

This desire, Bobbitt writes in his important new book, *Constitutional Fate*, has produced an "entire enterprise . . . based on a confusion between the justification for judicial review . . . and a hypothesized causal explanation for judicial review derived from sociopolitical theories."[13] *Constitutional Fate* is written in a spirit of opposition to the genetic enterprise. Instead of "measuring our arguments against the social and political realities that are thought to account for them in the first place,"[14] Bobbitt wants us to think of constitutional arguments as "legal conventions," or, better, as "moves" in the "game" of interpreting the Constitution and justifying one's interpretation.[15]

As Bobbitt remarks, *Constitutional Fate* might even have been entitled " 'The Rules of the Game' since it attempts a showing of how justification is brought forth from conventional practices."[16] The point of the analogy is to direct attention away from "causal explanation . . . derived from socio-political theories"[17] and toward the "theoretical moves" themselves. The best way to understand how a game is played, Bobbitt seems to be saying, is to learn the rules and explore the strategies those rules make possible, not to hypothesize about what economic interests created the game and about what social interests are served by the various ways of playing it. Of course, this is not to deny that historical accounts of the interests motivating certain interpretations of the Constitution are possible and even, in certain contexts, essential. It is only to deny that such accounts have any special relevance to what Bobbitt calls the "legitimation" of those interpretations, that is, the determination of their truth. Because Bobbitt thinks that certain conventions of constitutional argument legitimate interpretations, his book begins with a typology of these arguments.

According to Bobbitt, there are basically six kinds of constitutional argument: historical, textual, doctrinal, prudential, structural,[18] and (his own contribution) ethical.[19] His account of these arguments is fascinating; mixing formal definition with historical example, Bobbitt is wonderfully adept at giving the reader a clear view of what each argument claims and a concrete sense of how each one works. At the same time, however, he is concerned not so much with producing a definitive typology as with providing an outline of the central issues in constitutional interpretation, one that will grant all these arguments a place while honoring their differences, and that will demonstrate the importance of their "interplay" in "Constitutional decision making."[20]

Having sketched his outline and having, in particular, unpacked the category of ethical argument, Bobbitt links ethical argument to what he calls the "expressive function" of constitutional interpretation, the rule of the Supreme Court in giving "concrete expression to the unarticulated values of a diverse nation."[21] Ultimately, ending his "tour" of the "conventions" of constitutional argument and of the "values" expressed in constitutional interpretation, Bobbitt is led to consider (and attempt to answer) such fundamental interpretive questions as "whether Constitutional law is found or made, whether Realism or Formalism most appropriately fits the Constitution, and . . . how the legitimacy of judicial review is established and maintained."[22] Of these questions, the first—whether constitutional law is found or made—is clearly the most fundamental, and Bobbitt's answer to it—his doctrine of the "participatory Constitution"—constitutes his most ambitious theoretical claim. But to understand and assess this claim, we must begin by taking a look at some of the arguments that make up his original typology.

Historical argument, for example, "marshals the intent of the draftsmen of the Constitution and the people who adopted the Constitution."[23] Committed to the notion that "construction of the Constitution must rely on 'the meaning and intention of the convention which framed and proposed it,' "[24] historical arguments customarily invoke records of the convention's debates and the writings, published and unpublished, of the Framers. The goal here is "the authoritative reading in a particular context,"[25] a goal that Bobbitt finds implausible and that other forms of argument utterly reject. Prudential argument, for instance, far from concerning itself with the historical circumstances in which the Constitution was written, "is accentuated by the political and economic circumstances surrounding the decision."[26] For the prudentialist, such as Brandeis, even the decision to decide depends on arguments drawn not "from the Constitution itself but from the institutional consequences of deciding."[27] And ethical argument, as Bobbitt uses the term,[28] concerns itself neither with the particular intentions of the Framers nor with the political and economic interests immediately at hand, but with a "characterization of American institutions and the role within them of the American people."[29] Ethical arguments will thus appeal to an almost anthropological sense of values "based on the American ethos and not shared by all cultures."[30]

Bobbitt's understanding of these arguments as conventional moves made possible by the rules of the game leads him to think of them essentially as different ways of doing the same thing—you can develop and argue an interpretation historically or prudentially just as, say, you can try to score six points either running the ball or passing it. By the same token, the moves you make will be dictated largely by strategic concerns—if the Constitution and the records of constitutional debate do not say much in support of your thesis, then prudential argument will be the way to go; if you have the ball on your own ten-yard line and you're down by four with a minute to play, then the pass makes a lot more sense than the run. But this way of thinking about constitutional arguments does not, in fact, survive Bobbitt's own account of his typology, and the way in which it breaks down seems to me instructive for the whole debate about interpretation in which *Constitutional Fate* means to have its say.

If, for example, we compare historical argument to Bobbitt's own contribution, ethical argument, it becomes clear that two quite different things are going on. The essence of historical argument is its claim that because the Constitution should be understood to mean what its authors intended it to mean, the best evidence of its meaning is the historical record surrounding its production. Ethical argument, however, appeals not to historical records but to what Bobbitt sometimes calls the "American ethos" and more often calls the "constitutional ethos." So far, so good; we have what look like parallel appeals to two different aids in interpreting the Constitution. But if we look a little more closely, the parallel breaks down, for where historical argument consists of instructions about where to look to find out what the Constitution really means, ethical argument turns out already to have articulated the meaning for which one was searching. Ethical argument, Bobbitt says, "is bottomed on the notion that to some extent in every matter, and wholly in some matters, the government is just not 'sovereign' as to its people."[31] And elsewhere, the "complementary features of ethical argument . . . are that while it confines government in few respects it provides an absolute bar as to the rights it does protect."[32]

Ethical argument depends on, or rather consists of, some fairly substantive claims about the kind of government provided for in the Constitution, above all the claim that it is meant to be a "limited government" in precisely the ways Bobbitt describes. And whether the account of the Constitution proposed in these descriptions is true or false, Bobbitt clearly uses ethical argument to do a very different job from historical argument. If you want to know what kind of government the Framers meant us to have, historical argument tells you what evidence to look at; ethical argument tells you what the evidence says. Thus, where historical argument has no necessary connection to any particular meaning, ethical argument is already an account of the meaning historical argument is supposed to help you locate. In other words, you cannot turn to the constitutional ethos for help in producing an interpretation of the Constitution—not because it won't enable you to come up with an interpretation, but because if you know what the constitutional ethos is you already have the interpretation you were supposed to be looking for.

Bobbitt's alternative formulation, the "American ethos," offers, at first sight anyway, an escape from this dilemma; an American ethos, unlike a constitutional ethos, need not at its outset amount to an interpretation of the Constitution. But there are at least two problems with invoking this American ethos as an aid in interpreting the Constitution. The first difficulty is empirical—one doesn't exactly know what the American ethos is. At one point, Bobbitt associates the ethical approach with Chief Justice Warren's tendency to confound lawyers by neglecting their technical legal arguments in favor of questions like "Is that fair?" or "Is that what America stands for?"[33] At another point, Bobbitt associates the ethical approach with President Carter's remark at a press conference in the wake of two Supreme Court decisions limiting the rights to abortion that "Life is unfair."[34] The notion that life in America is both fair and unfair has a certain intuitive plausibility, but it is hard to see how that intuition can usefully be converted into a principle helpful in interpreting the Constitution.

The empirical perplexities posed by the American ethos are, however, only symptomatic of a second, deeper problem. For even if we could get a good picture of what the American ethos is, why would it be any help to us in interpreting the Constitution? Why, that is, should an account of what we as Americans believe today be any help to us in interpreting a document not written by any of us and written instead by people whose beliefs may have been, in crucial respects, quite different from our own? Or, to put the theoretical point more precisely, why should an account of what a reader believes have any relevance to what a writer means?

Bobbitt answers the first of these questions by denying, in effect, any difference between the Constitution and its interpreters. The Constitution, he writes, "is in great measure what we are" and "we are . . . in part, what the Constitution is."[35] Hence the great interpretive problem—whether constitutional law is made or found—turns out to be, for Bobbit, a false problem. Why? Because the problem assumes a distance between the Constitution and its interpreters, a distance so great that interpretation can rarely if ever extract a past meaning from the text and so must customarily impose upon it a present meaning. According to Bobbitt, however, there is no great distance between the Constitution and its interpreters. Hence the interpreters are never simply makers or finders, they are "participant-spectators."[36] And the Constitution is neither simply made nor found; it is the product of a "fluid, two-way effect," it is "a participatory Constitution."[37]

But to put the interpretive problem and its solution in this way is to do precisely what Bobbitt seems to have been determined not to do—substitute "causal explanation" for "justification." In place of arguments for our interpretations, we are once again given a narrative of where they come from. Is the "source" of our interpretations our "prejudices" or the "text itself"? Instead of asserting the logical irrelevance of this question, Bobbitt answers it. Both, he says—we are the text, the subject is the object. In a paroxysm of geneticism, he goes beyond establishing an epistemologically uncontaminated relation between knower and known and simply makes them identical. Interpreting the Constitution becomes an act of Cartesian introspection, and the desire to establish knowledge on a genetically secure base is not repudiated but embraced.

This solution to the problem of constitutional interpretation raises some difficult questions; for example, what exactly does it mean to claim that persons are identical to a text? But there is at least one important sense in which such a claim seems plausible; we must, in many respects, think we believe what the Framers believed, otherwise why would we retain the Constitution they wrote? This, however, is a political point, not an interpretive one; from the standpoint of interpretation, even if we really are the Constitution, what difference does it make? We can be as mistaken about ourselves as we can about anything else; we can misinterpret our own utterances as easily as we can anyone else's.

Even if we agree that greater proximity to the object of interpretation may make it easier to get true interpretations, such proximity need not itself constitute an argument for the truth of those interpretations. In other words, nothing about the conditions in which we interpret has any necessary relation to the correctness or incorrectness of our interpretations. To say this, of course, is only to restate Bobbitt's own complaint against those whose "enterprise . . . seems to be based on a confusion between the justification for judicial review . . . and a hypothesized causal explanation for judicial review."[38] Ultimately inscribing a version of this geneticism at the heart of his own enterprise, Bobbitt turns out to have demonstrated its persistence while powerfully asserting its irrelevance.

The example of so intelligent and determined a thinker going astray may be enough to give any putative successor pause, but perhaps, with Bobbitt's help, it is still worth imagining for a minute what an account of constitutional interpretation indifferent to genetic concerns might look like. Suppose, for example, we simply say that the job of the Supreme Court is to interpret the Constitution and that by interpreting the Constitution we mean giving an account of what its authors intended. What does this commit us to? To begin with, we can say what it does *not* commit us to, and it certainly does not commit us to the historical method. It does not follow from the fact that interpreting the Constitution involves giving an account of the Framers' intentions that the best evidence for determining those intentions will always, often, or ever be the records of debate among the Framers, or their correspondence, or their journalism. Two hundred years of experience indicates that sometimes these documents will seem useful and sometimes they won't.

To indicate the inadequacies of historical argument is not in any way to weaken the claim that in interpreting the Constitution we are giving an account of what its authors intended. Bobbitt shows this when, contrasting two other kinds of argument in his typology (doctrinal with textual), he remarks, "Doctrinal argument does not depend so much on how the drafters actually intended a specific passage to be applied as on the application of doctrines which serve or can be assumed to serve a general purpose sought by the drafters."[39] The point here is that the invocation of the authors' intentions is central—although, of course, one might have a different sense of what that intent is if one tries to account for the text as a whole rather than focusing on its individual parts. The claim that the Constitution means what its authors intended it to mean is thus neutral with respect to the relative merits of doctrinal and textual arguments or, for that matter, with respect to the merits of historical and structural arguments. It simply suggests that all these approaches attempt to find out what the drafters intended.

Bobbitt's category of "prudential" argument seems more difficult to explain, since if prudential arguments are "actuated by the political and economic circumstances surrounding the decision,"[40] and if "prudentialists generally hold that in times of national emergency even the plainest of constitutional limitations can be ignored,"[41] then it seems highly implausible to claim that prudentialists are somehow interpreting the authors' intentions. Nevertheless, they are, and, again, Bobbitt's own formulation brings this out. Consider the situation of the prudentialist who decides in a national emergency that "the plainest of constitutional limitations" should be ignored. Such a prudentialist isn't arguing that the Constitution means something other than what its authors intended it to mean; he is arguing that given (what is in this case) its plain meaning, the Constitution should be ignored.

Even in situations where neither the meaning nor the emergency is so plain that the Constitution must be ignored, prudentialists customarily argue not for rereading but for what amounts to a rewriting of the Constitution. A rewriting is called for by the text's irrelevance to the matter at hand; called for, that is, by the reading the prudentialist has already obtained. "Our problems," writes Alexander Bickel, "have grown radically different from those known to the Framers, and we have had to make value choices that are effectively new. . . . Anything that might still be called 'construction' of the written Constitution has come to suffice less and less."[42] Whether the Constitution should be judicially rewritten and whether the intentions of the Framers are relevant to American life today are real questions but not interpretive ones. Indeed, they presuppose an interpretive answer—the Constitution means what the Framers intended it to mean—an answer acknowledged in practice, if not in theory, by every interpreter of the Constitution.

At a time when, as Sanford Levinson has remarked, "intentionality arguments" are "increasingly without defenders . . . in the academic legal community,"[43] it may seem perverse not only to defend intention but to claim that every interpreter is always and only looking for authorial intention. Such perversity seems to me justified, however, by the ultimate implausibility of the alternative, which is a formalism that requires us to believe that sounds in the air and marks on paper are intrinsically meaningful. My contention is not only that no one *should* believe this but that no one *does* believe it; no one treats sounds or marks as words unless he or she thinks of them as speech acts expressing the intentions of some agent.[44] No one would even try to interpret the Constitution if everyone thought it had been put together by a tribe of monkeys with quills. And to grant the existence of human Framers but insist that their intentions should not be binding on subsequent generations is only to introduce the monkeys at a later date.

Of course theorists who think that texts can be separated from intention do not really imagine the Constitution to have been originally produced or subsequently altered in some bizarre way. Instead, they imagine that the passage of time and the problems of multiple authorship have eventually separated the text from its original authors and given it a life of its own. Although one can readily acknowledge that old texts written by many people may prove difficult to interpret correctly, it is hard to see how (absent some theory of spontaneous generation) difficulty can produce autonomy. Perhaps theorists opposed to interpreting the Constitution as the expression of its authors' intentions could more plausibly claim that although reading a text may well involve reading it as the expression of *someone's* intention, we needn't read the Constitution as the expression of the *Framers'* intentions. We can read it instead as expressing the intentions of people closer to us in time and spirit. But this clearly doesn't help. For, if the Framers wrote the Constitution and the text we are reading does not express their intentions but expresses instead the intentions of someone else, why is it the Constitution? And if it is not the Constitution, what does our interpretation of it have to do with constitutional interpretation?

At this point, it may seem that we have painted ourselves into a politically uncomfortable corner. Having determined that the Constitution can only mean what its authors intended it to mean, we are left with "the problem of explaining," in Levinson's words, "why intentions of long-dead people from a different social world should influence us."[45] But this is an objection to constitutional government, not to intentionalist interpretation. Intentionalists are as free to think that the Constitution should be jettisoned as they are free to think of it as a sacred text. Furthermore, intentionalists, when they do engage in constitutional interpretation, need not be committed to the sorts of interpretations that accompany what is sometimes called "strict construction." Indeed, one of the many merits of Bobbitt's *Constitutional Fate* is that it shows us how ways of reading that have little to do with strict construction can still be understood as attempts to account for the Framers' intentions. Bobbitt's own "ethical" argument, for example, with its claim that the Constitution articulates an "ethos of limited government"[46] with respect to individual rights, is a perfectly plausible reading of the Framers' intentions. What makes it plausible is not, however, some mysterious identity of subject and object, people and text, but its explanatory power with regard to a wide range of evidence: the text itself, documents relating to the composition of the text, early traditions of interpretation, and other indicia.

Of course, explanatory power alone does not guarantee the truth of the interpretation. Nothing does and nothing could. Perhaps the Constitution is much less committed to individual rights than many of us think. As interpreters, we must be concerned with such questions, and, as citizens, we may well believe that a good deal rides on the answer to them. We may even be dismayed by the political consequences of our inability to decide with certainty just what the Constitution does mean. But, whatever the Constitution means, whatever rides on our beliefs about what it means, whatever may be the consequences of our inability to know with any certainty what it means, there is one certain thing we *can* know—it means what its authors intended it to mean.

Judicial Criticism

James Boyd White

Today I shall talk about the criticism of judicial opinions, especially of constitutional opinions. This may at first seem to have rather little to do with our larger topic, "The Constitution and Human Values," but I hope that by the end I will be seen to be talking about that subject too. In fact I hope to show that in what I call our "criticism," our "values" are defined and made actual in most important ways.

I will begin with a double quotation. I recently heard my friend and colleague Alton Becker, who writes about language and culture, begin a lecture by saying that one universal aspect of cultural life is the keeping alive of old texts, a reiteration of what was said before in a new context where it can have a life that is at once old and new. (The Javanese even have a name for it.) The text that Becker chose to keep alive in his lecture was a remark made by John Dewey when, toward the end of his long life, he was asked what he had learned from it all. He said, "I have learned that democracy begins in conversation." In this lecture I will try, by locating it in a new context, to give that same sentence a continued life.

The process of giving life to old texts by placing them in new ways and in new relations is of course familiar to us as lawyers. It is how the law lives and grows and transforms itself, for the law is nothing if it is not a way of paying attention and respect to what is outside of ourselves: to texts made by others in the past, which we regard as authoritative, and to texts made in the present by our fellow citizens, to which we listen. We try to place texts of both sorts in patterns, of what has been and what will be, and these patterns are themselves compositions. The law is at its heart an interpretive and compositional, and in this sense a radically literary, activity.

Such at least is my view: for others the law is policy, nothing but policy, and the only question what results we prefer; or power, nothing but power, and the only question who has it; or perhaps it is morality, and the only question what is "right" or "wrong." So in these remarks I will be making a claim for the character of law itself, as a way of reading, composing, and criticizing authoritative texts, and in so doing, as a way of constituting, through conversation, a community and a culture of a certain kind. In doing this I will try to give two other texts renewed life too, namely the opinions of Chief Justice Taft and Justice Brandeis in the famous case of *Olmstead* v. *United States*.[1]

I

Much of my previous work has been devoted to trying to work out a method of criticism, or what I call a way of reading, that can afford the grounds upon which we can engage with legal and literary texts alike. This is the object especially of my book *When Words Lose Their Meaning*,[2] in which I elaborate a way of reading that focuses attention (*a*) upon the state of the language and culture that a particular writer inherits and must use; (*b*) upon the ways in which that language is reconstituted, for good or ill, in his or her use of it; and (*c*) upon the social, ethical, and political relations that the text establishes both with its reader and with others. The first stage of the criticism is cultural; the second is literary; and the third ethical and political. A full essay in judicial criticism would address all of these questions, but today I shall direct your attention especially to this last aspect, that is, to the way a judge constitutes a social and political world in his writing: to the way his opinion constitutes him as a mind and as a judge, his colleagues as a court, and his readers as lawyers, citizens, or other kinds of legal and nonlegal actors.

In every opinion a court not only resolves a particular dispute one way or another, but validates or authorizes one kind of reasoning, one kind of response to argument, one way of looking at the world and at its own authority, or another. Whether the process is conscious or not, the judge seeks to persuade the reader not only of the rightness of the result reached and the propriety of the analysis used, but of his or her understanding of what the judge, the law, the lawyer, and the citizen are and should be—in short, of his or her conception of the kind of conversation that does and should constitute us. In rhetorical terms, the court gives itself an ethos, or character, and does the same both for the parties to a case and for the larger audience it addresses—the lawyers, the public, and the other agencies in government. It creates by performance its own character and role and establishes a community with others. This is, I believe, the most important part of the meaning of what a court does: what it actually becomes, independently and in relation to others. It is here that we can find its values most fully defined and realized.

The life of the law is in large part a life of response to these judicial texts. They invite some kinds of response and preclude others; as we deal with these invitations, both as individuals and as a community, we define our own characters, our minds and values, not by abstract elaboration but in performance and action. The life and meaning of an opinion, or a set of opinions, lie in the activities it invites or makes possible for judges, for lawyers, and for citizens; in the way it seeks to constitute the citizen, the lawyer, and the judge, and the relations among them; and in the kind of discoursing or conversational community it helps to create.

When we turn to judicial opinion, then, we can ask not only how we evaluate its "result" but, more importantly, how and what it makes that result mean, not only for the parties in that case, and for the contemporary public, but for the future: for each case is an invitation to lawyers and judges to talk one way rather than another, to constitute themselves in language one way rather than another, to give one kind of meaning rather than another to what they do, and this invitation can itself be analyzed and judged. Is this an invitation to a conversation in which democracy begins (or flourishes)? Or to one in which it ends?

II

I turn now to the famous case of *Olmstead* v. *United States*, to ask of each of the two primary opinions how it constitutes the conversation that defines us. How does it define the Constitution it is interpreting; the process of constitutional interpretation in which it is engaged; the meaning of the Fourth Amendment; the place and character of the individual citizen in our country, and that of the judge, the law, and the lawyer? What conversation does it establish, with what relation to "democracy"? What community does it call into being, constituted by what practices and enacting what values?

To start with the facts of the case: federal officials, with some state police assistance, systematically tapped the telephone wires of persons they suspected to be involved in a large-scale bootlegging operation. They did so without probable cause or a warrant, and in violation of state laws that made wiretapping a crime. Upon the basis of evidence obtained as a result of this activity, the defendant was convicted of a federal offense and appealed. The question is whether the wiretapping violated the defendant's Fourth Amendment rights, for if it did, the government concedes that the exclusionary rule applies to prohibit the admission of that evidence.[3]

It is important to emphasize that the question is not whether the intrusion was justified—by reason of the degree of probable cause, by the presence of a judicial warrant, or on some other ground—but whether or not what the officers did counts as an intrusion to which the Constitution speaks at all. If it does not, then the police may tap the wires not only of suspected criminal but of everyone, without constitutional consequence. In this respect *Olmstead* is one of a series of cases that mark out what we are now likely to call the "privacy interests" protected by the Fourth Amendment, the invasion of which requires prior or after-the-fact judicial approval.[4] Subsequent cases have involved such things as affixing a beeper to a car in order to trace its movements;[5] scraping paint from a car in order to make a chemical analysis;[6] taking fingerprints, blood samples, or hair clippings; stopping and frisking people;[7] examining bank records or employment files;[8] and using marijuana-sniffing dogs and undercover agents.[9] The Court's view on these questions does much to define what it means to be a citizen in our country, for these cases tell us what actions by officials count as intrusions to which the Constitution speaks.

The text of the Fourth Amendment is as follows: "The right of the people to be secure in their persons, houses, papers, and effects, against unreasonable searches and seizures shall not be violated; and no warrant shall issue but upon probable cause, supported by oath or affirmation and particularly describing the place to be searched and the persons or things to be seized."[10]

A.

In his opinion for the majority, Chief Justice Taft makes short work of the defendant's claim:

> The Amendment itself shows that the search is to be of material things—the person, the house, his papers or his effects. The description of the warrant necessary to make the proceeding lawful, is that it must specify the place to be searched and the person or *things* to be seized. . . .
> . . .The Amendment does not forbid what was done here. There was no searching. There was no seizure. The evidence was secured by the sense of hearing and that only. There was no entry of the houses or offices of the defendants.[11]

The Fourth Amendment does not apply, he says, because there was no "search" and there was no "seizure," defining these words in terms of trespass and materiality. This definition is itself arguable—in his dissent, for example, Justice Brandeis will argue that the Fourth Amendment should be conceived of as protecting privacy rather than property.[12] But let us suppose for the moment that we are not to go so far as that, but actually accept Taft's view that the Fourth Amendment requires a trespassory invasion of an individual's right. Let us also put aside the argument that the illegality of the conduct itself should require exclusion. Accepting Taft's property-trespass theory, then, is the result in *Olmstead* as self-evidently clear and correct as the opinion makes it seem?

I think not. Even on Taft's view of the law the defendant has much to say. After all, the officials undoubtedly trespassed against the telephone company in inserting tapping wires into its lines, and the defendant might well be given standing to protect that interest, especially since in this case the telephone company entered an appearance to argue on his behalf. Or, if a "property" or "possessory" interest on the part of the defendant himself is required, one might argue that he had a leasehold or easement in the wires, created by contract with the telephone company, or an interest created by the operation of trust law—the telephone company holding the wires beneficially for the defendant—or even by the penal law of Washington that made the tapping of the wires a crime. Or the company could be seen as the custodian of the defendant's interests by contract, just as the bank that holds papers in a safe deposit box, the lawyer who holds papers in a file, the United Parcel Service which contracts to deliver a package, can be said to be custodians of someone else's interest. There was, in brief, a trespass, notwithstanding Chief Justice Taft's claim; and there are at least colorable arguments either that the trespass was upon an interest of the defendant, or that, owing to his relation to the holder of the primary right, the defendant ought to have standing to raise the question. But in the Taft opinion no response whatever is made to these lines of argument.

Taft makes another conclusory claim that is also based on what appears to him the plain language of the Fourth Amendment. The amendment speaks of the seizure of "persons or things," and requires a warrant "particularly describing" the "persons or things to be seized." Taft reads this language as saying that intangibles are not protected by it. This is of course one possible reading, but even if it is accepted, it does not necessarily follow that the officer's testimony as to the overheard words should not be excluded. Even if the words themselves are not seizable objects under the Fourth Amendment, their exclusion could be required, for example, because the proffered testimony is the fruit of the admittedly unlawful trespassory invasion.[13]

Moreover, a different reading of the language of the amendment is itself also possible, namely that the seizure of words, oral words, is not covered by the amendment in another sense: not that they are unprotected by the amendment, but that under its provisions they are immune from seizure, at least whenever there is an ancillary trespass. This immunity, it would be argued, arises from the fact that no warrant could properly issue for them (since it would never be possible to meet the particularity requirements of the warrant clause). Finally, and most significantly, it is simply conclusory to say that words cannot be seized—in fact, what took place in this case could fairly be described without any violence to the term as the "seizure" of words. Analogies from property law can be employed to support this result, for under federal law today, and under state and federal law then, words can be made the object of property under copyright laws. The right to say or to write them can be bought and sold. And if the state may create a property right directly, through its copyright laws, why can it not do so indirectly, through its penal law, prohibiting the seizure of some words in some circumstances?

The point of these remarks is not to argue that words are seizable objects, or that a trespass against the defendant occurred, or any of the other matters suggested above, but merely to make plain that colorable arguments along these lines can be developed, none of which was addressed by Taft. If Taft did not meet such obvious arguments in his opinion, upon what do you suppose he relied to make the conclusory language quoted above persuasive to his readers? You will read his opinion in vain for an explicit justification of those characterizations. He discusses cases, but only in the most conclusory way, summarizing their facts and sometimes their holdings, but never attempting to draw in an analytic way a connection between those cases and the case before him. (He says, for example, of *Gouled* v. *United States*,[14] which dealt with a surreptitious filching of papers, that it "carried the inhibition against unreasonable searches and seizures to the extreme limit."[15] But he says nothing to explain or validate that characterization.)

I think that the answer to the question of what Taft relies upon to make his conclusions persuasive to his reader is that he depends more than anything else upon the very power of characterization that he has exemplified throughout his opinion, upon the voice of authority with which he has been speaking. For he repeatedly characterizes both the facts and the other judicial opinions with a kind of blunt and unquestioning finality, as if everything were obviously and unarguably as he sees them, and in doing this he prepares us for the conclusory and unreasoned characterizations upon which the case ultimately turns. He makes a character for himself in his writing and then relies upon that created self as the ground upon which his opinion rests. This character, as I will suggest more fully below, is that of a simple, even simple-minded, authoritarian.

There is a kind of self-evident circularity about this, of course, but here as elsewhere arguments from self-evidence have a remarkable power, at least to those disposed to share the basic premises. And if we accept his lesser characterizations of fact and law, for whatever reason we do so, we find ourselves increasingly ready to submit to the final and conclusive characterization.

What is the view of the Constitution, the law, the citizen, the reader, that is enacted in this writing? For Taft the Constitution is a document that is in its own terms authoritative, telling the rest of us what to do. It has, so far as can be gleaned from this opinion, no higher purposes, no discernible values, no aims or context; it is simply an authoritative document, the ultimate boss telling the rest of us what to do. The task of the judge is to be an intermediate boss, producing a text that has a similar structure: not reasoned, not explained, not creating in the reader the power that reason and explanation do—for if you are unpersuaded by an opinion that purports to rest upon reason you may reject the authority of the opinion itself—but an act of power resting upon power, pure and simple. The Constitution is a document written in plain English making plain commands: if you think they are not plain, wait till I have spoken and I will make them plain.

If one were to read this text as a literary text, and ask what it is that Taft really values and thinks is important, the first answer would be his own voice and his own power; the second, rather surprisingly, would be the criminal enterprise itself. He describes this at great length and in glowing terms:

> The evidence in the records discloses a conspiracy of amazing magnitude to import, possess and sell liquor unlawfully. It involved the employment of not less than fifty persons, of two seagoing vessels for the transportation of liquor to British Columbia, of smaller vessels for coastwise transportation to the State of Washington, the purchase and use of a ranch beyond the suburban limit of Seattle, with a large underground cache for storage and a number of smaller caches in that city, the maintenance of a central office manned with operators, the employment of executives, salesmen, deliverymen, dispatchers, scouts, bookkeepers, collectors and an attorney. In a bad month sales amounted to $176,000; the aggregate for a year must have exceeded two millions of dollars.[16]

Taft then describes with similar, but perhaps somewhat less intense, feeling the attempts of law enforcement agencies to bring this conspiracy to its knees: "The gathering of evidence continued for many months. Conversations of the conspirators of which refreshing stenographic notes were concurrently made, were testified to by government witnesses. They revealed the large business transactions of the partners and their subordinates."[17] That is what this voice admires: organization, scale, enterprise, and success. It would be possible to imagine someone saying, "The Constitution of the United States is an achievement of amazing magnitude." But Taft's enthusiasms and admiration, as expressed in this text at least, lie elsewhere.

Not that he makes no reference to the Constitution: at the end of this long statement of the facts Taft abruptly interposes the language of the Fourth Amendment, flopped before us like a pancake. The reader cannot help wondering what this language can possibly have to do with the detective story we have just read, with this thrilling world of organized scale and competition, for Taft—in this sense a "realist"—the real world.

This is of course exactly the feeling that Taft's opinion is designed to elicit in us, the sense that the Fourth Amendment has nothing to do with what is really at stake in the case. And this narrative implicitly supports the constitutional ideology he has been obeying, for it invites us to see power and force as real, language as simple, and government as about the struggle between the forces of good and the forces of evil. Nothing more than that and nothing less. And law is simply the will of good authority.[18]

To sum up: Taft has, and exemplifies in this opinion, a view of the process in which he is engaged that goes something like this: "My job is to decide this case in light of the Constitution. Here are the facts. They are as plain as can be. Here is the text. It is as plain as can be. It speaks of searches and seizures and here there is neither." This is a commitment by Taft to a particular text and to a particular way of reading it: for him it is simply authoritative, composed in plain English—therefore plainly readable and simple—and to be read "literally." Since there is no such thing as "literal" reading of words, that repudiation of ambiguity and complexity itself works as an unexposed, unexplained, and unjustified claim to authority, including the authority to reduce difficulty to simplicity—a claim to an authority that is in fact implicit in every claim to read language "literally."

The function of the court as Taft enacts it is thus not to reason, not to argue, not to explain, but to declare the meaning of an authoritative text. The judge is qualified for this function primarily by his position as judge; but also self-qualified, in the opinion itself, by the skill and force with which the facts and law are stated, and by the very force of his voice: in this instance a no-nonsense voice, business-like, a bit that of a crusty old boss from a 1930s movie. And the congruence or harmony between Taft's view of the Constitution and his view of his own role under it, between his voice and his sense of the Constitution's voice, gives his performance the great rhetorical force that arises when different dimensions of meaning coincide.

What kind of argument does this opinion invite in future cases, what kind of conversation does it establish? The answer is, "Make any argument you want and I'll tell you what the result is." The opinion invites a conversation of countering characterizations, conclusory in form, between which the judge will choose, or which he will resolve by making characterizations of his own.

What kind of education is required to perform the function Taft defines, or to argue to him, or to be a lawyer or judge in our system as he sees it? The answer is very little. You must know the legal categories in which the conclusions will be stated, and be able to relate them to each other. But the only question contemplated in this opinion is whether the person speaking has the authority to make his characterizations, not whether something is right or wrong. Legal training, if it were guided by this opinion, would be training in making one's voice authoritative, unquestioning and unquestionable.[19]

To judge from this opinion, what is the Constitution in general, the Fourth Amendment in particular, really about? What values do these texts establish, what values do we serve in our reading of them? For Taft, as he writes here, neither the Constitution nor the Fourth Amendment is about anything very important or valuable; it is simply a set of words that tells us what to do. Real value is to be found in the fact of authority, in the reduction to simplicity, in the "no-nonsense" voice, in the very control, acquiesced in by his reader, over the facts and the language of the case.

Why does this kind of performance work as well as it does? I think because it appeals to our desires for simplicity, for authority of a certain kind, and for a boss who will tell us what things mean and how they are. These desires show up again, with quite a different quality, in the work of Justice Black, who struggled valiantly to see in the Bill of Rights a certain and clear body of law by which "due process of law" could be defined.[20] We often see a similarly authoritarian claim, acquiesced in for similar reasons, in the interpretation of sacred texts: a person, or a group, claims the authority to declare the meaning of the sacred language, with which it is in fact the individual's responsibility to engage as an autonomous and present person, and we yield to the claimed authority. We do so because it relieves us of the task and responsibility of facing what is difficult, complex, and uncertain, of making judgments of our own, of responding as ourselves. To yield in either context is to destroy the life the text makes possible; yet we do it. When we do so we participate in a conversation that is not the beginning but the end of democracy.

B.

The opinion of Mr. Justice Brandeis, justly famous, is different in almost every respect. To begin with the statement of the facts, Justice Brandeis (not surprisingly) describes not the "conspiracy of amazing magnitude"[21] of the defendants but the behavior of the federal officials who arranged to tap the defendant's telephone wires: "To this end, a lineman of long experience in wire-tapping was employed, on behalf of the Government and at its expense . . . . Their operations extended over a period of nearly 5 months. The typewritten record of the notes of conversations overheard occupy 775 typewritten pages."[22] This is to focus the reader's attention not on the criminal enterprise engaged in by the defendant but upon the government's conduct. Brandeis concludes by saying that the government concedes that its conduct was unreasonable and thus, if there is a search or seizure, that the evidence must be excluded. It "makes no attempt to defend the methods employed by its officers," but instead "relies on the language of the Amendment; and it claims that the protection given thereby cannot properly be held to include a telephone conversation."[23]

This is to put directly in issue the question how that language should be read. Instead of simply asserting a conclusion, or implying as Taft did when he quoted the language, that one answer was obviously right, Brandeis focuses our attention on the general question of interpretation and puts the burden of advancing its interpretation on the government. He thus poses a question, never explicitly addressed by Taft: how are we to think about our reading of this text?[24]

His first step in responding to that question is to begin his next paragraph with the famous remark of Chief Justice Marshall: "We must never forget that it is *a constitution* that we are expounding."[25] This is to assert, against Taft, that the question how the Constitution ought to be read, or expounded, deserves explicit thought of a special kind. Brandeis next defines what *expounding* has meant in the past by summarizing cases in which the Court sustained the exercise of powers by Congress over "objects of which the Fathers could not have dreamed."[26] This is a way of showing that the kind of "nonliteralist" reading he favors, which he calls "expounding," has been part of our tradition not only on behalf of the individual in his struggles with the government, but on behalf of Congress itself. The next series of examples shows that the Court has expressed a similar view of the Constitution in its approval of state regulations which, quoting *Euclid v. Ambler Realty Co.*, "a century ago, or even half a century ago, probably would have been rejected as arbitrary and oppressive."[27] Only then does Brandeis move to clauses protecting the individual and claim that they must be read in the way he has now established as traditional and neutral, to allow for adaptation to a changing world.

But exactly what is this way of reading? If a "literalist" reading of the Constitution will not do, what will? Brandeis has given examples of flexibility but no general principle, and the principle of "adaptation" alone will not do, for it is a principle of change for its own sake. To meet the need he has created, he now quotes from *Weems v. United States*:[28]

> Legislation, both statutory and constitutional, is enacted, it is true, from an experience of evils, but its general language should not, therefore, be necessarily confined to the form that evil had theretofore taken. Time works changes, brings into existence new conditions and purposes. Therefore a principle to be vital must be capable of wider application than the mischief which gave it birth. This is particularly true of constitutions . . . . [O]ur contemplation cannot be only of what has been but

of what may be. Under any other rule a constitution would indeed be as easy of application as it would be deficient in efficacy and power.[29]

Brandeis uses this language to define his own fundamental attitude: that the interpretation of the general language of the Constitution, though naturally to be informed by the nature of the evils or mischiefs which gave rise to the language in the first place, must not be limited by those configurations, but should be guided by an understanding of the general evils, or goods, of which these are local examples. This view of what the Constitution is and how it is made is altogether different from Taft's, and it is ultimately based on a different vision of human life: that we have limited intelligence, limited imagination, limited grasp of facts; that our thinking is naturally shaped by our immediate experience; that we live in time, through which our experience and every aspect of our culture changes; that a central object of collective life is at once to maintain a central identity while undergoing this process of change and to learn from that process; and that all this was as true of the Framers of the Constitution as it is of us today.

In Brandeis's view the Constitution in fact addresses these very limitations, for it provides us with collective experience and with institutions by which we can to some degree transcend our circumstances. The point of the Constitution is to enable us to bring into our minds at once both our own experience and that of our predecessors, and to think about that experience as a whole in a disciplined way: it is in principle a mode of education and self-creation over time.

The Framers, that is, sought at once to establish and to limit their government, basing their effort on views of the individual, of democracy, and of republican government that made sense to them, and that were partly—but like all views, only partly—susceptible to definition and expression in their own language. They spoke that language directly and with confidence. But they also wished this text to be authoritative in other contexts, in other configurations of social reality, in conjunction with other languages. They therefore must have meant it to be read in a way that would permit it to be relocated in a new, and in principle to them unknowable, context, that is, "nonliterally." What is required in interpreting the Constitution, therefore, is something like translation, a bringing into the present a text of the past. But we all know that perfect translation is impossible—no one thinks that Chapman's Homer is Homer, or Lattimore's either—and this in turn requires us to recognize that our own formulations of the meaning of the text to which our primary fidelity extends must be made in the knowledge that they are in part our own creation.

This view of constitutional interpretation requires of the reader not merely the explication of plain English, as Taft's method does, but the capacity to penetrate the surface of language, and of social and cultural reality as well, in order to reach an understanding of the deepest questions that arise in social life, forever changing their particular forms. It requires, as all translation does, an attempt to be perfectly at home in two worlds, an attempt that must always fail. Our compositions should therefore reflect an awareness of the silence, the ignorance, that surrounds them. What Brandeis asks of the judge, and therefore of the lawyer, is not merely the ability to characterize facts and language as meaning one thing or another, but the capacity to find out what has been, what is, and what shall be, and to conceive of the Constitution as trying to provide, through its language, and through the general principles that it expresses, a way of constituting ourselves in relation to our self-transforming world.

But how is all this to be done? Brandeis has implicitly committed himself to exemplifying the process that he recommends, and he proceeds to do that. He says, "When the fourth and fifth amendments were adopted, 'the form that evil had theretofore taken,' had been necessarily simple. Force and violence were then the only means known to man by which a government could directly effect self-incrimination."[30] But circumstances have since changed—"time works changes"—and the government has already discovered other means for achieving its primary objective, "to obtain disclosure in court of what is whispered in the closet."[31] And since we are to think about "what may be," it also becomes important for Brandeis to say that "the progress of science in furnishing the Government with means of espionage is not likely to stop with wiretapping."[32] One can scarcely imagine what may be possible in the future. He concludes by asking, "Can it be that the Constitution affords no protection against such invasions of individual security?"[33]

Or, to put his question slightly differently, are we unable to think about this question in any terms other than those actually used by the Framers, not only in the Constitution but in the rest of life? If so, the Constitution in the nature of things cannot endure, for its continued life requires its constant translation into new circumstances, new terms, a translation to which the Constitution itself offers guides, through what Brandeis calls its "principles." The text must be removed from the web of associations that once gave particular meaning to its terms and relocated in a new set of such associations. The text remains the same, but its translation—its being carried over—to our own time locates it in a new context of particularities which will, and should, give it a transformed meaning.

How is this to be done in practical terms? Here Brandeis shows what is peculiar to the lawyer's way of facing these questions, by turning to precedent. He begins with *Boyd* v. *United States*,[34] defined now not merely as an invoice-discovery case, but as establishing the right to personal security, personal liberty, and private property. For Brandeis *Boyd* is about the relation between the individual and the government on the most fundamental level, establishing zones into which the government may not enter. *Ex parte Jackson*,[35] which held that a sealed letter in the mails was entitled to Fourth and Fifth amendment protection, is for him not distinguishable, as it is for Taft, but squarely on point. Taft had wanted to say that *Jackson* was different from *Olmstead* because the government had created the monopoly involved in that case. Brandeis denies the distinction: "The mail is a public service furnished by the government. The telephone is a public service furnished by its authority. There is, in essence, no difference between the sealed letter and the private telephone message."[36] It is true that one is tangible and the other not, but the evil—the invasion of privacy—of wiretapping is actually far greater than that involved in tampering with the mails. That is, when you look at judicial precedent the way that Brandeis's conception of the Constitution and of law more generally requires us to do, with an eye to the general principles and aims of the texts in question, the distinctions upon which Taft relies disappear. Conceived of as a case about privacy, as Brandeis says it should be, *Jackson* actually establishes the principle for which the defendants argue.

Brandeis then turns again to the general question of constitutional construction, arguing that "an unduly literal" method of construction ought to be rejected in this case as it has been in others. The nature of the Constitution requires an examination not merely of its words but of its "underlying purposes." In this spirit he summarizes the holdings of the cases since *Boyd*, which have, he says, settled the following things:

> Unjustified search and seizure violates the Fourth Amendment, whatever the character of the paper; whether the paper when taken by the federal officers was in the home, in an office, or elsewhere; whether the taking was effected by force, by fraud, or in the orderly process of a court's procedure. From these decisions, it follows necessarily that the Amendment is violated by the officer's reading the paper without a physical seizure, without his even touching it; and that use, in any criminal proceeding, of the contents of the paper so examined—as where they are testified to by a federal officer who thus saw the document or where, through knowledge so obtained, a copy has been procured elsewhere—any such use constitutes a violation of the Fifth Amendment.[37]

This is an argument from a series of holdings to a general conclusion (which he will shortly state in terms of "privacy") that determines the result in the particular case. Brandeis here exemplifies the process by which the Constitution, according to him, should be read—the method of "expounding" that is required by the temporal and shifting nature of our experience, and by the central aim of the Constitution, which is to provide a matrix of relations between the individual and the government that can endure throughout the changes of social and intellectual forms. In making the translation from one context to another, in pushing the old text into current life, Brandeis shows that the lawyer and judge are not at sea but have the assistance of precedent, the set of prior translations, that themselves form a kind of bridge from one world to the other.

In his most famous passage Justice Brandeis states as fully as he can the general principle which he perceives lying behind the constitutional language.

> The makers of our Constitution undertook to secure conditions favorable to the pursuit of happiness. They recognized the significance of man's spiritual nature, of his feelings and of his intellect. They knew that only a part of the pain, pleasure and satisfactions of life are to be found in material things. They sought to protect Americans in their beliefs, their thoughts, their emotions and their sensations. They conferred as against the Government, a right to be let alone—the most comprehensive of rights and the right most valued by civilized men.[38]

This is a translation not only into contemporary legal language but beyond it, into contemporary ordinary language, into the vernacular. It thus invites a conversation not only among lawyers but among citizens, a conversation in that sense democratic. But this language does not supplant the law—the last thing Brandeis argues for is the elimination of our cultural past in favor of the uninformed view of the moment. It is in fact his work with the legal language preceding this passage that has both made possible and justified this return of the Constitution to the people.[39]

As a second ground of reversal, Brandeis says that the crime committed by the federal officers renders the evidence seized inadmissible. "Here, the evidence obtained by crime was obtained at the Government's expense, by its officers, while acting on its behalf."[40] For Brandeis the admission of the evidence constitutes a ratification of the lawbreaking. "When these unlawful acts were committed, they were crimes only of the officers individually. The Government was innocent, in legal contemplation; for no federal official is authorized to commit a crime on its behalf."[41] But the admission of evidence constitutes a deliberate ratification of the illegal conduct, and this is violation of the deepest principles of self-government. He also invokes the settled principle that a court will "not redress a wrong when he who invokes its aid has unclean hands," and applies it to the present case.[42] What is significant here, especially after his earlier invocation of the vernacular, is his confidence in traditional legal language and categories—"ratification," "clean hands"—as his language of judgment. This embeds his opinion in the legal context as his earlier paragraph embedded it in the vernacular.

In his final paragraph he establishes himself, and his voice, in the following terms:

> Decency, security and liberty alike demand that government officials shall be subjected to the same rules of conduct that are commands to the citizen. In a government of laws, existence of the government will be imperiled if it fails to observe the law scrupulously. Our Government is the potent, the omnipresent teacher. For good or for ill, it teaches the whole people by its example. Crime is contagious. If the Government becomes a lawbreaker, it breeds contempt for law; it invites every man to become a law unto himself; it invites anarchy. To declare that in the administration of the criminal law the end justifies the means—to declare that the Government may commit crimes in order to secure the conviction of a private criminal—would bring terrible retribution. Against that pernicious doctrine this Court should resolutely set its face.[43]

It is not only the government that is the teacher: Brandeis establishes his own voice as that of a teacher, a teacher who must first learn, and who by having learned may teach. This is in turn to define the law, legal education, the Constitution, and all that is involved in thinking about a case such as this, as challenging every intellectual and moral capacity.

So what for Brandeis is a constitution? What is the judge's role? How is one to be qualified for the role that he defines? What is the meaning and importance of the enterprise in which he is engaged?

As for the Constitution, his view is, as I said above, that the Framers, located in one cultural and social context, sought to create a document that would establish a government, limit that government, and protect individuals, all in the service of a larger understanding of the individual and his relation to his polity. The formulations employed by the Framers were necessarily rooted in their experience, and have a necessarily incomplete reach because the power of the human imagination to grasp the future is limited. For the most part they employed not archetypal examples or strict rules, but generalizations as their way of establishing a set of relations, a set of institutions, and a set of ways of thinking and talking that could structure our common life in the future. Certain language was broken out of its original context, set aside, and given special authority, so that it could be given a new range of significances, in new and in principle unknowable contexts, for it was meant to reach not only what was but what might be.

Since everything shifts constantly, as time goes on, how can the Constitution possibly reach what might be? The answer is only through the process by which we read it correctly and well. The Constitution is made, then, according to Brandeis, not merely by the Framers, but by those who read the language of the Framers well, who translate—"carry over"—its terms to the contemporary world, aided as they are by the earlier efforts at translation.

What is involved in this enterprise as Brandeis defines it? The answer is everything: the intellect, the capacity to read and express, the ability to penetrate surface forms to underlying truths, the sensitivity to shifts in social and intellectual forms, all in the service of the wise and just definition of the individual and his government. The reading of the Constitution is a stage in the making of the Constitution, and everything that is present in that activity is present in this one: the definition of a civilized polity operating under the rule of law and protecting the deepest values of the culture. Accordingly, to become a good judge requires the greatest education imaginable: education that will train us to see what the Framers saw; to hear their language and to penetrate it; to see by analogy what fits and what does not; to see through the surface to the underlying truth, almost as Plato says one sees through the surfaces to permanent ideas and ideals; to translate an old text into the current world.

But more even than this is required, for the opinion, on Brandeis's view, is constitutive in another way: it becomes part of the Constitution itself, and this means that the judge must be able to create a constitution, with his readers, of a kind that fits with, and carries forward into the future, the earlier constitution out of which he speaks. This requires Brandeis to become a maker and remaker of language. He makes a formulation, "the right to be let alone," that connects our own vernacular with the language of the Constitution and our past. A proper legal education, for lawyer as well as for judge, will be an education into the past as well as the present, an education of the vision and the imagination, and will ultimately require all of us to be, as Brandeis demonstrates himself to be, a teacher. For as judges, as well as in our other capacities, we teach our values by what we do, whether we know it or not. In the world defined by Brandeis, who would not be a lawyer?

The heart of Brandeis's opinion lies in a vision of human culture working over time, in a sense that we have something to learn from the past as well as something to give to the future. Nothing could be farther from our contemporary idea of the individual as sovereign consumer, implementing his tastes in competition with others. Brandeis had a vision of the individual and the community alike engaged in a continual process of education, of intellectual and moral self-improvement, and of the law in general, and the Constitution in particular, as providing a central and essential means to this process. The community makes and remakes itself in a conversation over time—a translation and retranslation—that is deeply democratic not in the sense that it reflects, as a market or referendum might, the momentary concatenation of individual wills, but in the sense that in it we can build, over time, a community and a culture that will enable us to acquire knowledge and to hold values of a sort that would otherwise be impossible. The conversation is democratic in its ultimate subjection to popular determination, in its openness to all who learn its terms, in its continuity with ordinary speech, but most of all in its recognition that the essential conditions of human life that it takes as its premises are shared by all of us.

C.

One final point remains. The reader will have noticed that in this case it is the law-and-order man who is authoritarian in his voice and style, and the defender of individual rights who speaks as an individual himself and to us as individuals. Could this pattern be reversed?

I certainly think it would be possible to write an opinion that was as authoritarian as Taft's but came out the other way, say by simply declaring that this is a search or that the amendment protects privacy and stop. (Some of Justice Douglas's opinions have that flavor,[44] as indeed does Justice Stewart's opinion in *Katz* v. *United States*,[45] the case that finally overruled *Olmstead:* "The Fourth Amendment protects people, not places."[46] It is also true that I would not subscribe to every aspect of Brandeis's opinion; his prose is sometimes too heavy-handed for me, and I would have preferred to expand the meaning of "search" and "seizure" rather than leaping to "the right to be let alone," language that in fact has authoritarian elements of its own.

But how about an opinion "coming out" the way Taft's opinion does: can one imagine a good opinion doing that? It is certainly possible to imagine a better opinion doing so: one, for example, that spoke of the dangers that a new technology presented in the hands of lawbreakers, of the national crisis of law enforcement presented by bootlegging, of the respect to be accorded the judgment made by the executive (which is, after all, democratically accountable), of the reasons why the states should not be able to interfere with a national solution to a national problem, of the need for adaptation in constitutional interpretation, and so on, or perhaps one explaining by reference to history why a strictly material conception of "search" or "seizure" is appropriate. As you can tell from this summary, I think it would be hard to do this very persuasively, but we cannot know that until someone has earnestly tried it.

To return now to my earlier claim that the distinction between opinion and result, form and content, ultimately disappears: for me all this means that the standards of excellence by which I have suggested that we measure the literary work of the judge—his definition of himself, of us, and the conversation that constitutes us—are not merely technical, or verbal, but deeply value-laden and substantive. If we can arrive at shared standards of excellence in the domain that has been my main concern today, that of the nature and quality of judicial thought, of the ethics and politics of the judicial text, I think this will limit the range of substantively permissible, or reachable, decisions, including in "hard" cases. You cannot write a great novel in support of anti-Semitism, says Sartre, and I think you cannot write a great opinion that denies that sense of the ultimate value of the individual person that is necessarily enacted in any sincerely other-recognizing expression.

Will the range of permissible or good decisions ever narrow to "one correct result" in every case? Not while we are human beings, living in the world Brandeis defines—full of ignorance, with disturbed and feeble imaginations, caught by motives of which we are incompletely aware. We will always have much to disagree about. But if we focus real attention on the aspects of meaning I have tried to identify above, and ask ourselves and each other what excellences we demand there, we shall be engaging in a conversation that will move us in the direction of enlightenment and justice in our votes, as well as our expressions.

III

I have offered you one reading of these opinions. There is much more to say about them, for example that it is in some sense "unfair" to abstract Taft's opinion from the larger context of his work as a whole, or, more accurately, to draw sweeping conclusions about his work as a whole from this one text; that a part of the meaning of both opinions, untraced here, lies in their interactions with each other, with the other opinions in the same case—especially the striking opinion by Holmes—and with those from earlier cases as well; and that the soundness of Brandeis's claims about "privacy" and the intentions of the Framers is open to question. It is certainly true that Brandeis's image of the Framers is romantic and itself unargued; that his talk about "principles" is a bit simple-minded and his application of them more than a bit authoritarian; and that he may be thought inadequately respectful of the language actually used in the constitutional text.

I also want to make explicit what the reader has no doubt felt, that I myself give, by construction, Brandeis's opinion some of the meaning I claim for it, just as he gives the Fourth Amendment some of the meaning he claims for it. This, I think, is inevitable. The reader of this paper will in turn give it much of whatever meaning he claims for it. The text at once creates and constrains a liberty (or a power) in its reader, and in doing so defines for the reader a particular kind of responsibility. It is in that combination—liberty, constraint, and responsibility, for the reader and maker of texts—that the ethical and intellectual heart of the law can be found.

Contributors

Kenneth S. Abraham is Associate Professor of Law at the University of Maryland.

Philip Bobbitt is Professor of Law at the University of Texas.

William J. Brennan, Jr., is an Associate Justice of the Supreme Court of the United States.

Paul Brest is Dean of the Stanford Law School.

Clare Dalton is Assistant Professor of Law at Harvard Law School.

Stanley Fish is Arts and Sciences Professor of English and Law at Duke.

Owen M. Fiss is Professor of Law at Yale University.

Charles Fried, on leave from the Harvard Law School, is the Solicitor General of the United States.

Gerald Graff is the John C. Shaffer Professor of Humanities and English at Northwestern University.

Michael Hancher is Professor of English at the University of Minnesota.

E. D. Hirsch, Jr., is the Kenan Professor of English at the University of Virginia.

David Couzens Hoy is Professor of Philosophy at the University of California, Santa Cruz.

Jessica Lane is a doctoral candidate in the English department at Johns Hopkins University.

Sanford Levinson is Charles T. McCormick Professor of Law at the University of Texas.

Steven Mailloux is Professor of English at Syracuse University.

Philip Martin is Senior Lecturer in English at Monash University, Melbourne.

Edwin Meese III is the former Attorney General of the United States.

Walter Benn Michaels is Professor of English at the Johns Hopkins University.

H. Jefferson Powell is Associate Professor of Law at the University of Iowa.

Frederick Schauer is Professor of Law at the University of Michigan Law School.

Mark V. Tushnet is Professor of Law at Georgetown University Law Center.

Richard Weisberg is Professor of Law at Cardozo School of Law, Yeshiva University.

James Boyd White is the L. Hart Wright Professor of Law, Professor of English Language, and Adjunct Professor of Classical Studies at the University of Michigan.

Notes

Preface

1. Hans-Georg Gadamer, *Reason in the Age of Science* 88 (Cambridge: M.I.T. Press, 1981). Gadamer is one of the principal figures in the contemporary revival of interest in hermeneutics. His major work is *Truth and Method* (New York: Seabury Press, 1975). See also Joel Weinsheimer, *Gadamer's Hermeneutics* (New Haven: Yale University Press, 1985).

2. A good historical overview is contained in Peter Goodrich, "Historical Aspects of Legal Interpretation," 61 *Ind. L.J.* 331 (1986).

3. E. D. Hirsch, Jr., *The Aims of Interpretation* 19–20 (Chicago: University of Chicago Press, 1972).

4. The book was reprinted as late as 1880. All quotations are taken from the third edition (St. Louis: F. H. Thomas, 1880).

5. P. 52.

6. P. 53.

7. Roy J. Howard, *Three Faces of Hermeneutics: An Introduction to Current Theories of Understanding* 1–2 (Berkeley: University of California Press, 1982). See also Richard E. Palmer, *Hermeneutics: Interpretation Theory in Schliermacher, Dilthey, Heidegger, and Gadamer* (Evanston: Northwestern University Press, 1969).

8. Jacques Derrida, *Of Grammatology* 158 (Gayatri Spivak, trans. Baltimore: Johns Hopkins University Press, 1976).

9. Jacques Derrida, in "Deconstruction: A Trialogue in Jerusalem," *Mishkenot Sha'ananim Newsletter*, no. 7 (December 1986), p. 2.

10. Interview in *Criticism in Society* 164 (Imre Salusinszky, ed. New York: Methuen, 1987).

11. Brook Thomas, *Cross-Examinations of Law and Literature* 15 (Cambridge: Cambridge University Press, 1987). See also Robert Ferguson, *Law and Letters in American Culture* (Cambridge, Mass.: Harvard University Press, 1985).

12. The next two paragraphs are taken substantially from Levinson, "On Dworkin, Kennedy, and Ely: Decoding the Legal Past," 51 *Partisan Review* no. 2, p. 257 (1984).

13. Gerald Graff, "Textual Leftism," 49 *Partisan Review* 566 (1982).

Section I Introduction

1. Michael Kammen, *A Machine That Would Go of Itself: The Constitution in American Culture* 396 (New York: Alfred Knopf, 1986).

2. See "The Justice and the Radical," *New York Times*, 16 September 1986, p. 30.

3. William Rehnquist, "The Living Constitution," 54 *Tex. L. Rev.* 693, 695, 706 (1976).

4. Robert H. Bork, "Tradition and Morality in Constitutional Law," *Views from the Bench: The Judiciary and Constitutional Politics* 71 (Mark Cannon and David O'Brien, ed. Chatham, N.J.: Chatham House, 1985). See also Judge Bork's "The Constitution, Original Intent, and Economic Rights," 23 *San Diego L. Rev.* 823 (1986).

5. Edwin Meese, "Toward a Jurisprudence of Original Intention," 2 *Benchmark* 5 (Janu-

ary–February 1986). It has also been reprinted in *The Great Debate: Interpreting Our Written Constitution* 1–10 (Occasion Paper no. 2, The Federalist Society, 1986). This pamphlet reprints, in addition, the speech of Justice Stevens that is discussed in this introduction, as well as the speeches by the attorney general and Justice Brennan that are included below and the speech of Judge Bork cited in footnote 4.

6. Ibid., pp. 7–8.

7. One is tempted to say "found in the Bill of Rights," though that formulation would beg the central question posed by the materials in this book: Are texts repositories of inherent meaning that allow diligent readers to "find" or "discover" what is "in" them or, instead, do readers "construct" or otherwise "create" the texts that they ostensibly interpret? Thus the use of "associated with the Bill of Rights" allows for the possibilities that (*a*) the association is the result of a "correct" interpretation accurately finding that the protections are "in" the Bill of Rights; (*b*) it is the result of an inventive construction of such protections, subsequently assigned to the language of the Bill of Rights, but not otherwise "caused" by that language; or (*c*) as our last section suggests, the "discovery" versus "invention" opposition is not the most helpful way to frame the question.

8. 83 U.S. (16 Wall.) 36 (1873). The case involved New Orleans butchers who claimed that a slaughterhouse monopoly established by the local government violated their rights as independent businessmen.

9. The case is Adamson v. California, 332 U.S. 46 (1947). See also Fairman, "Does the Fourteenth Amendment Incorporate the Bill of Rights? The Original Understanding," 2 *Stan. L. Rev.* 5 (1949); and Michael Kent Curtis, *No State Shall Abridge: The Fourteenth Amendment and the Bill of Rights* (1986), for a taste of the scholarly debate on the issue.

10. *Los Angeles Times,* 21 July 1985, pt. IV, p. 3. See also Commager, "Meese Ignores History in Debate with Court," *New York Times,* 20 November 1985, p. A-31, responding to Meese's speech reprinted in this book.

11. Lincoln Caplan, *Baltimore Sun,* 16 August 1985, p. 15-A. See also Brian Dickerson, "Meese's Backward Vision," *Miami Herald,* 22 October 1985, p. 15A.

12. Justice Stevens's remarks, presented to the Federal Bar Association on 23 October 1985, were reprinted in 19 *U.C. Davis L. Rev.* 15–21 (1986), as part of a symposium on "Construing the Constitution." The quoted passages come from pp. 19–20.

13. It was also reprinted in the *Davis* symposium, as was the Meese speech mentioned at the close of this paragraph.

14. *Wall Street Journal,* 18 October 1985, p. 28. See also Walter Berns's analysis of "The Words According to Brennan" in the *Wall Street Journal,* 23 October 1985, p. 32.

15. Hugo Black, "The Bill of Rights," in Cannon and O'Brien, *Views from the Bench,* p. 222.

Section II Introduction

1. W. K. Wimsatt, Jr. and M. C. Beardsley, "The Intentional Fallacy," 54 *Sewanee Review* (July–September 1946), rpt. in W. K. Wimsatt, *The Verbal Icon: Studies in the Meaning of Poetry* 21 (1954; rpt. New York: Farrar, Straus, 1964); hereafter *VI.*

2. W. K. Wimsatt, "Genesis: A Fallacy Revisited," in *The Disciplines of Criticism: Essays in Literary Theory, Interpretation, and History* 193–225 (Peter Demetz, Thomas Greene, and Lowry Nelson, Jr., ed. 1968); further citations will be given in the main text.

3. Max Radin, "Statutory Interpretation," 43 *Harv. L. Rev.* 884, 885 (1930); hereafter "SI."

4. E. E. Stoll, "The Tempest," 44 *PMLA* 703 (1932); quoted in *VI,* p. 5.

5. E. D. Hirsch, Jr., *Validity in Interpretation* 31 (1967); further citations will be given in the main text. For further refinements of his intentionalist theory, see E. D. Hirsch, Jr., *The*

Aims of Interpretation (1976) and his "Meaning and Significance Reinterpreted," 11 *Critical Inquiry* 202 (1984).

Sonnet LXV and the "Black Ink" of the Framers' Intention

1. For the most comprehensive call for this approach, see Kennedy, "Form and Substance in Private Law Adjudication," 89 *Harv. L. Rev.* 1685 (1976).

2. See, e.g., Williams v. Walker-Thomas Furniture Co., 350 F.2d 445 (D.C. Cir. 1965) (Wright, J.). See generally Kennedy, "Distributive and Paternalist Motives in Contract and Tort Law, with Special Reference to Compulsory Terms and Unequal Bargaining Power," 41 *Md. L. Rev.* 563 (1982).

3. See, e.g., Lochner v. New York, 198 U.S. 45 (1905).

4. See, e.g., Stanley v. United States, 786 F.2d 1490 (11th Cir. 1986), *cert. granted*, 55 *U.S.L.W.* 3405 (U.S. 9 December 1986) (no. 86–393); Hector v. INS, 782 F.2d 1028 (3d Cir.), *rev'd per curiam*, 55 *U.S.L.W.* 3351 (1986); authorities cited inf. notes 15–17.

5. See Shapiro, "In Defense of Judicial Candor," 100 *Harv. L. Rev.* 739–42 (1987).

6. 246 N.Y. 369, 159 N.E. 173 (1927).

7. See idem at 371–79, 159 N.E. at 174–77.

8. See C. Fried, *Contract as Promise* 54–56 (1981); *Restatement (Second) of Contracts* § 87(2) (1981).

9. 64 F.2d 344 (2d Cir. 1933).

10. Idem at 346. Interestingly, empirical research appears to vindicate the terse hard-headedness of Learned Hand as against the more prolix — and I now think sometimes sentimental — ruminations of Roger Traynor. For a discussion of bid practices and of how contractors use Justice Traynor's rule in Drennan v. Star Paving Co., 51 Cal. 2d 409, 333 P.2d 757 (1958), to "shop" bids, thus unfairly squeezing subcontractors, see J. Dawson, W. Harvey and S. Henderson, *Cases and Comment on Contracts* 352–53 (4th ed., 1982).

11. 17 Cal. 3d 425, 551 P.2d 334, 131 Cal. Rptr. 14 (1976). See generally Stone, "The *Tarasoff* Decisions: Suing Psychotherapists to Safeguard Society," 90 *Harv. L. Rev.* 358 (1976).

12. 17 Cal. 3d at 433–47, 551 P.2d at 339–51, 131 Cal. Rptr. at 21–31.

13. 784 F.2d 942 (9th Cir. 1986).

14. See idem at 943–46.

15. Here one might cite as examples a string of cases in which lower courts, responding to what seemed to be sympathetic claims for avoiding deportation, found reasons to overturn the discretionary authority of the immigration authorities. Several of these have been reversed summarily by the Supreme Court. See, e.g., Miranda v. INS, 673 F.2d 1105, 1105–06 (9th Cir.) (*per curiam*) (holding that immigration authorities were estopped from denying an alien permanent resident status by their eighteen-month delay in acting on his visa petition), *rev'd*, 459 U.S. 14 (1982) (*per curiam*); Wang v. INS, 622 F.2d 1341, 1347–48 (9th Cir. 1980) (holding that immigration authorities erred in not considering the hardship that would be suffered by citizen children if their parents were deported), *rev'd*, 450 U.S. 139 (1981) (*per curiam*).

16. For a recent dramatic example of a court ignoring a statute of limitation in favor of "substantive justice," see Hohri v. United States, 782 F.2d 227 (D.C. Cir. 1986), *cert. granted*, (U.S. 17 November 1986) (no. 86–510). The circuit court held that the six-year statute of limitations for claims brought under the taking clause would not bar a suit brought by Japanese-American citizens imprisoned in internment camps during World War II. The statute did not begin to run, the court held, if plaintiffs could prove that the government had concealed information contradicting the "military necessity" for mass imprisonment. The court held that the statute only began to run by virtue of an act of Congress conceding the injustice but not by an earlier presidential proclamation to the same effect, and that the

flood of books and articles analyzing every aspect of the historical record also had been insufficient to cause the statute to begin to run (see idem at 246–53).

17. Such failures to exhaust administrative remedies occur quite frequently in Social Security and disability cases. See, e.g., Ringer v. Schweiker, 697 F.2d 1291, 1295–96 (9th Cir. 1982) (holding that the claimants could maintain their action under the Medicare Act although they had not exhausted administrative channels, when such exhaustion would have been futile and an appeal would have failed to vindicate all the interests pressed by claimants), rev'd sub nom. Heckler v. Ringer, 466 U.S. 602 (1984); Salfi v. Weinberger, 373 F. Supp. 961, 964 (N.D. Cal. 1974) (holding that the plaintiffs need not exhaust their administrative remedies in a Social Security action when such exhaustion would be futile), rev'd, 422 U.S. 749 (1975); cf. City of New York v. Heckler, 742 F.2d 729, 736–37 (2d Cir. 1984) (upholding the district court's waiver of the exhaustion requirement in a Social Security action in which exhaustion would have been futile, the harm suffered pending exhaustion might have been irreparable, and the plaintiffs' legal claims were substantially collateral to the demand for benefits), aff'd sub nom. Bowen v. City of New York, 106 S.Ct. 2022 (1986).

18. See S. 2440 & H.R. 4770, 99th Cong., 2d Sess. (Federal Tort Claims Reform Act of 1986); S. 2441 & H.R. 4765, 99th Cong., 2d Sess. (Government Contractor Liability Reform Act of 1986); H.R. 4766, 99th Cong., 2d Sess. & S. 100, 99th Cong., 2d Sess. amend. 1814, Cong. Rec. S5106–107 (daily ed. 30 April 1986) (Product Liability Reform Act of 1986); Atty. Gen.'s Tort Policy Working Group, Report of the Tort Policy Working Group on the Causes, Extent and Policy Implications of the Current Crisis in Insurance Availability and Affordability (1986).

19. See Memoranda from Edwin Meese III to Assistant Attorneys General and United States Attorneys (13 March 1986) (regarding department policy on consent decrees and settlement agreements and on special masters).

20. See Brief for a Writ of Certiorari to the United States Court of Appeals for the Eleventh Circuit, United States v. Stanley, Slip Op. 8 December 1986 (no. 86–393); Brief for the United States and the Equal Employment Opportunity Commission as Amici Curiae Supporting Affirmance, Ansonia Bd. of Education v. Philbrook, 55 U.S.L.W. 4019 (1986) (no. 85–495); Brief for the United States as Amicus Curiae Supporting Petitioners, School Bd. v. Arline, 106 S.Ct. 1633 (1986) (no. 85–1277); Brief for the United States as Amicus Curiae in Support of Appellants, Thornburgh v. American College of Obstetricians and Gynecologists, 106 S.Ct. 2169 (1986) (nos. 84–495 & 84–1379); Brief for the United States as Amicus Curiae Supporting Reversal, Evans v. Jeff D., 106 S.Ct. 1531 (1986) (no. 84–1288); Brief for the United States as Amicus Curiae Supporting Affirmance, Board of Governors of the Fed. Reserve Sys. v. Dimension Financial Corp., 106 S.Ct. 681 (1986) (no. 84–1274); Brief for the United States as Amicus Curiae Supporting Respondents, Davidson v. Cannon, 106 S.Ct. 668 (1986) (no. 84–6470).

21. Goldberg, "Ed Meese vs. John Marshall," Christian Sci. Monitor, 10 February 1986, 20, col. 1.

22. See, e.g., R. Dworkin, Taking Rights Seriously 137 (1977) (stating that "[t]he program of judicial activism holds that courts . . . should work out principles of legality, equality and the rest, revise those principles from time to time in the light of what seems to the Court fresh moral insight, and judge the acts of Congress, the states, and the President accordingly"); L. Tribe, American Constitutional Law 892 (1978). Tribe states that "the Constitution is an intentionally incomplete, often deliberately indeterminate structure for the participatory evolution of political ideals and governmental practices. . . . The best we can hope for is to encourage wise reflection — through strict scrutiny of any government action or deliberate omission that appears to transgress what it means to be human at a given time and place" (p. 892). For an interesting criticism of this view, see Posner, "The Constitution as Mirror: Tribe's Constitutional Choices," 84 Mich. L. Rev. 560–64 (1986). Those who agree with Tribe argue that their perspective is required because original intent is unknowable and, therefore, irrelevant. See C. Ducat, Modes of Constitutional Interpretation 103 (1978) (observing that "the framers, after all, are dead, and in the contemporary world, their views are neither relevant nor morally binding").

23. W. Shakespeare, Shakespeare's Sonnets 149 (T. Brooke, ed. 1936).

24. Lawyers should appreciate the legal metaphor here: beauty holds a plea, but its

"action" — that is, its cause of action — "is no stronger than a flower." Shakespeare's Sonnet XXX contains another such hidden legal metaphor:

> When to the *sessions* of sweet, silent thought
> I *summon up* remembrance of things past
> [P. 116; emphasis added].

25. I am reminded of the end of a poem by Philip Larkin:

> Only one ship is seeking us, a black-
> Sailed unfamiliar, towing at her back
> A huge and birdless silence. In her wake
> No waters breed or break.
> ["Next, Please," in *The Less Deceived*, p. 20].

26. See note 22 sup. and accompanying text.

27. See S. Kripke, *Wittgenstein on Rules and Private Language* 7–54 (1982).

28. R. Dworkin, *Law's Empire* (1986).

29. Ibid., pp. 54, 57.

30. Ibid., pp. 55–56 (discussing art in general).

31. Ibid., pp. 359–65.

Counterfactuals in Interpretation

1. The modal logicians I chiefly refer to are David Lewis and Saul Kripke, and to the following two works in particular: David Lewis, *Counterfactuals* (Cambridge, Mass.: Harvard University Press, 1973) and Saul Kripke, *Naming and Necessity* (Cambridge, Mass.: Harvard University Press, 1980).

2. W.V.O. Quine, *Word and Object* 222 (Cambridge, Mass.: M.I.T. Press, 1960).

3. "The Politics of Theories of Interpretation" *The Politics of Interpretation* (W.T.J. Mitchell, ed. 1983).

4. *Validity in Interpretation* (New Haven: Yale University Press, 1967).

5. See for example, R. Barthes, "The Death of the Author," *Critical Essays* (R. Howard, trans. 1972) and M. Foucault, "What is an Author?" *Textual Strategies* (J.V. Harari, ed. 1979).

6. W.K. Wimsatt, *Day of the Leopards: Essays in Defence of Poems* 30-31 (New Haven and London: Yale University Press, 1976).

7. Ibid., p. 32.

8. Ibid., pp. 32–33.

9. D. Lewis, *Counterfactuals*, and S. Kripke, *Naming*.

10. This idea derives from Kripke's analysis of the initial act of naming.

11. S. Kripke, *Naming*, p. 18.

12. Edward Shils, *Tradition* (Chicago: University of Chicago Press, 1981).

13. Jack Goody and Ian Watt, "The Consequences of Literacy," *Literacy in Traditional Societies* 27–68 (J. Goody, ed. 1968).

14. Keith Donnellan, "Speaker Reference, Description, and Anaphora," *Contemporary Perspectives in the Philosophy of Language* 28–44 (P. French, T. Uehling, and H. Wettstein, eds. 1981)

The Misconceived Quest for the Original Understanding

1. John Ely uses the term *interpretivism* to describe essentially the same concept. J. H. Ely, *Democracy and Distrust: A Theory of Judicial Review*, chaps. 1–2 (1980). At the cost of

proliferating neologisms I have decided to stick with *originalism*. Virtually all modes of constitutional decision-making, including those endorsed by Professor Ely, require interpretation. The differences lie in what is being interpreted, and I use the term *originalism* to describe the interpretation of text and original history as distinguished, for example, from the interpretation of precedents and social values.

2. Marbury v. Madison, 5 U.S. (1 Cranch) 137 (1803).

3. Idem at 175–80.

4. In a somewhat modified form of the theory, the sovereign people are our contemporaries, and it is their will that officials be bound by the text and original understanding. See p. 85 inf.

5. Home Bldg. & Loan Ass'n v. Blaisdell, 290 U.S. 398, 453 (1934) (Sutherland, J., dissenting).

6. Throughout the chapter I refer to actual constitutional doctrines to illustrate points and test arguments. This should not obscure my underlying purpose, which is not to describe, explain, or justify the Supreme Court's practices, but rather to argue what the practice should be.

7. For example, on the ground that the law must be available to all citizens. Cf. L. Fuller, *The Morality of Law* 34–35, 43–44 (1964) (exploring through allegory the importance of "a published code declaring rules to be applied in future disputes" and suggesting moral and legal foundations for "formalization of the desideratum of publicity").

8. H. Black, *Handbook on the Construction and Interpretation of the Laws* 20 (1911).

9. 17 U.S. (4 Wheat.) 202–3 (1819).

10. Holmes, "The Theory of Interpretation," 12 *Harv. L. Rev.* 419 (1899). Holmes also noted that "the normal speaker of English is merely a special variety, a literary form, so to speak, of our old friend the prudent man. He is external to the particular writer, and a reference to him as the criterion is simply another instance of the externality of the law" (ibid., p. 418).

11. A third circumstance—the occasion for the utterance—may also be relevant. For example, words formally promulgated by a legislature may sometimes have a different meaning than in casual conversation. This may be true of phrases that are used as legal terms of art but also have looser ordinary usages. For example, while "ex post facto law" is often used by laypersons to mean any sort of retroactive decision, a legislature might use it as a legal term of art limited to criminal retroactivity. See, e.g., Calder v. Bull, 3 U.S. (3 Dall.) 386 (1798). But see W. W. Crosskey, *Politics and the Constitution in the History of the United States*, chap. 11 (1953).
The mere fact that a phrase appears in a formal legal utterance, however, does not entail that it was used as a term of art. This is especially true of constitutional provisions. Although the ratifying conventions that adopted the Constitution and the legislatures that adopted the amendments included many lawyers, the vast majority of participants were laypersons, and it cannot simply be assumed that they used the phrase in its technical sense.

12. See H. L. A. Hart, *The Concept of Law* 125–26 (1961); Curtis, "A Better Theory of Legal Interpretation," 3 *Vand. L. Rev.* 407 (1950); Schulman, "Reason, Contract, and Law in Labor Relations," 68 *Harv. L. Rev.* 1003–5 (1955).

13. 17 U.S. (4 Wheat.) 316 (1819).

14. Idem at 413.

15. Idem at 414–15.

16. See, e.g., G. Gunther, *Constitutional Law* 1234–59 (9th ed. 1975) (collecting cases); Nimmer, "The Meaning of Symbolic Speech under the First Amendment," 21 *UCLA L. Rev.* 29 (1973).

17. See generally 1 M. Nimmer, *Copyright* § 8 (1973).

18. U.S. Const. art. II, § 1, cl. 5.

19. One can imagine a society having our vocabulary and syntax, but in which these provisions would properly be understood to encompass instances which seem absurd to us. For example, the eligibility clause would have quite a different meaning in a culture which supposed that people born by Caesarean were evil, stupid, or dangerous. See P. Brest, *Processes of Constitutional Decisionmaking* 31–32 (1975) [hereafter cited as *Processes*]. See generally Fuller, "Positivism and Fidelity to Law—A Reply to Professor Hart," 71 *Harv. L. Rev.* 662–64 (1958).

20. See pp. 77–79, 81–82 inf.

21. T. M. Cooley, *A Treatise on the Constitutional Limitations Which Rest upon the Legislative Power of the States of the American Union* 124 (Carrington's 8th ed. 1927) (n.p. 1868). See also South Carolina v. United States, 199 U.S. 448 (1895) (Brewer, J.). ("The Constitution is a written instrument. As such, its meaning does not alter. That which it meant when adopted it means now.")

One could imagine a version of textualism that incorporates at least *evolutionary* changes in the meaning of a provision. This approach would typically produce applications consistent with the adopters' intentions on a relatively broad or abstract, rather than a particularistic, level. See pp. 79–80 inf. But unless an interpreter were a priori committed to incorporating all such changes, she would need to know both the original meaning of the provision and the history of its evolution, to assure that the present meaning has a "legitimate" genealogy. Without elaborating on the criteria for legitimacy, it might matter who bears primary responsibility for the evolution. For example, assume that "freedom of speech" had a much narrower meaning in the late eighteenth century than it does today, and that "due process" originally dealt solely with the fairness of adjudicatory procedures but now also evokes the notion of so-called substantive due process. Perhaps a better case can be made for incorporating the former change, which likely reflects a more general change in social and political attitudes, than the change of meaning in a term of art that has been largely (albeit not exclusively) in the control of an elite professional group. Having said this, however, I think that an *originalist* interpreter would reject evolutionary changes of any sort.

22. See Carter v. Carter Coal Co., 298 U.S. 238 (1936); United States v. E.C. Knight Co., 156 U.S. 1 (1895); Kidd v. Pearson, 128 U.S. 1 (1888).

23. See Champion v. Ames, 188 U.S. 321 (1903). Cf. Ratner, "Congressional Power over the Appellate Jurisdiction of the Supreme Court," 109 *U. Pa. L. Rev.* 168–71 (1960) (discussing the eighteenth-century meanings of "exception" and "regulation").

24. See Stern, "That Commerce Which Concerns More States than One," 47 *Harv. L. Rev.* 1335 (1934).

25. See B. Wright, *The Contract Clause of the Constitution* 3–27 (1938).

26. See Note, "The Speech and Press Clause of the First Amendment As Ordinary Language," 87 *Harv. L. Rev.* 374 (1973).

27. See Murray v. Hoboken Land & Improvement Co., 59 U.S. (18 How.) 272 (1855); H. Graham, *Everyman's Constitution* 152, 295 (1968); Shattuck, "The True Meaning of the Term 'Liberty' in Those Clauses in the Federal and State Constitutions Which Protect 'Life, Liberty, and Property,' " 4 *Harv. L. Rev.* 365 (1890); Warren, "The New 'Liberty' under the Fourteenth Amendment," 39 *Harv. L. Rev.* 431 (1926).

28. Indeed, for an intentionalist, the main function of a written provision is that its adoption provides a moment in time for locating the adopters' intentions: the formalities that enact a particular text into law simultaneously enact the adopters' intentions.

29. The last point may seem incorrect at least with respect to the white 1975 Chevy, which is about as standard as cars can get. But put yourself in the mayor's position and ask just what vehicles you adverted to in the course of adopting the regulation. Did the images of *any* particular cars pass through your mind? If so, did they include a white '75 Chevy? (After all, it was a blue '73 Ford that you saw at the scene of the accident.) If by chance you imagined a 1975 Chevy, was it the particular car belonging to this citizen? If none of these, then in what sense did you advert to his car?

30. Legal codes commonly stipulate canons for their interpretation. See, e.g., Pa.

Cons. Stat. Ann. tit. 46, §§ 503–601 (Purdon 1969); *National Conference of Commissioners on Uniform State Law, Uniform Statutory Construction Act* (1965).

31. There is nothing paradoxical in these instructions so long as the adopter distinguishes between his interpretive and substantive intentions and intends the interpretive instructions to apply only to the latter.

32. It is possible for a provision to be enacted without a majority of intention-votes either for or against a controverted application. For example, two members of the city council may intend to prohibit mopeds; two may intend not to prohibit them; and the fifth may be utterly indifferent. An intentionalist interpreter should probably treat this as an instance of "intent-not-to": the textual analogue is a proposed text that fails to be adopted for want of a majority.

The institutional intention of a multimember body is fraught with other complexities. For example:

(1) Except for evidentiary purposes, it does not matter whether the fifth council-member explicitly withholds his vote in exchange for the other proponents' agreement to his limitations or harbors his limitations in private: there simply are not enough intention-votes for the more far-reaching measure. However, the fact that an intention was not expressed might sometimes cast doubt on the meaning of the other votes, for in some sense nobody knew precisely what issue was being voted on.

(2) Suppose a textualist legal system, in which the city council is divided over the moped issue. When the fifth member threatens to withhold his vote, the two proponents follow either of two strategies: (*a*) Believing that the fifth member desires some regulation more than he opposes a regulation that prohibits mopeds, they refuse to compromise on a less inclusive regulation. (*b*) Alternatively, they remind the fifth member that he needs their support on an unrelated measure that means a lot to him. He accedes, and the regulation as adopted prohibits mopeds from using the park. This is a common occurrence in multimember lawmaking bodies. A textualist judge should—and judges usually do—apply the law as it is written.

Suppose that the identical political dealings occur within an intentionalist legal system, where the issue is not the language of the regulation—in either case it will simply say "no vehicles"—but rather what intentions it will incorporate. By analogy, the intentionalist interpreter must apply the regulation to prohibit mopeds. Although the fifth council-member desired to permit mopeds in the park, he alienated his intention-vote in the same way that the lawmaker in a textualist system alienated his actual vote. That is, moved by whatever considerations, he agreed to intend, and hence for these purposes intended, that mopeds be prohibited from the park.

33. But see C. Beard, *An Economic Interpretation of the Constitution of the United States* 73–151 (2d ed. 1935).

34. See S. Padover, *The Living U.S. Constitution* 37–43 (1953).

35. The Twenty-first Amendment was ratified by state conventions.

36. See MacCallum, "Legislative Intent," 75 *Yale L.J.* 780–84 (1966).

37. The municipal court judge in our earlier example does not confront the same task. For the mayor probably lacks the authority to determine how his enactments will be interpreted, and is bound by established conventions of interpretations. Not so the adopters of the Constitution. Whether or not they assumed that certain conventions would govern the interpretation of their document, they were not bound by them. A contrary view at least poses serious difficulties for originalist political theory and interpretation.

38. See generally tenBroek, "Use by the United States Supreme Court of Extrinsic Aids in Constitutional Construction," 26 *Calif. L. Rev.* 441–43, 448 (1933).

39. G. Endlich, *A Commentary on the Interpretation of Statutes*, § 27 (1888); T. Sedgwick, *A Treatise on the Rules Which Govern the Interpretation and Construction of Statutory and Constitutional Law* 194 (1874). See pp. 70–71 sup.

40. But see note 87 inf.

41. On a rather restrictive view, "would have found" means that, although the adopters did not advert to a punishment, they nonetheless intended that it be prohibited.

42. R. Dworkin, *Taking Rights Seriously* 135 (1977).

43. Ibid., p. 134.

44. If you and I purport to agree that "punishment must not be excessive and degrading" but we cannot agree on any applications of this principle, then our agreement probably is illusory.

45. C. Black, *Structure and Relationship in Constitutional Law* 7 (1969).

46. 17 U.S. (4 Wheat.) 316 (1819).

47. C. Black, *Structure and Relationship* 14.

48. 73 U.S. (6 Wall.) 35 (1868).

49. Idem at 44.

50. C. Black, *Structure and Relationship* 29.

51. See generally G. Gunther, *John Marshall's Defense of* McCulloch v. Maryland (1969).

52. Skinner, "Meaning and Understanding in the History of Ideas," 8 *Hist. & Theory* 3 (1969). Skinner is one of several scholars whose work has focused on historiographical problems in political theory. See also J. G. A. Pocock, *Politics, Language, and Time* (1973); "Political Thought and Political Action—A Symposium on Quentin Skinner," 2 *Pol. Theory* 251 (1974). Although these historians are concerned with the intentions of individual theorists rather than with the meaning of a text having thousands of adopters, the originalist constitutional interpreter confronts many of the same difficulties.

53. Skinner, "Meaning and Understanding" 6. J. G. A. Pocock has similarly written, "It is part of normal experience to find our thought conditioned by assumptions and paradigms so deep-seated that we did not know they were there until something brought them to the surface: we suspect, if we are historians, that there are others present and operative of which we shall never be aware because they will only be visible from the vantage-points provided by historical moments in the future" [*Politics*, p. 32].

54. See, e.g., C. Fairman, *Reconstruction and Reunion, 1864–88*, Pt. 1 (1971); L. Levy, *Origins of the Fifth Amendment* (1968); L. Levy, *Legacy of Suppression* (1960). See also I. Brandt, *The Life of James Madison* (1941–61); G. Wood, *The Creation of the American Republic, 1776–87* (1969).

55. A recent example is Raoul Berger's *Government by Judiciary: The Transformation of the Fourteenth Amendment* (1977), which argues that almost all of the Supreme Court's decisions under the Fourteenth Amendment are incorrect. See, e.g., Kutler, "Raoul Berger's Fourteenth Amendment: A History or Ahistorical," 6 *Hastings Const. L.Q.* 511 (1979); Murphy, Book Review, 87 *Yale L.J.* 1752 (1978); Soifer, Review Essay, 54 *N.Y.U. L. Rev.* 651 (1979). But see Perry, Book Review, 78 *Colum. L. Rev.* 685 (1978).

A somewhat older example is William Winslow Crosskey's two-volume *Politics and the Constitution in the History of the United States* (1953). Based on massive research in eighteenth-century lexicography and politics, Crosskey argued that the received interpretations of various constitutional provisions were incorrect. He urged, for example, that Article I granted Congress plenary power to regulate commerce without regard to whether it was inter- or intrastate; that the Supreme Court was to have general common lawmaking authority binding on state courts, but that the Court lacked any general authority to review the constitutionality of congressional legislation; and that the "ex post facto" clause included retroactive civil as well as criminal legislation. Although *Politics and the Constitution* received some favorable reviews [see, e.g., Corbin, Book Review, 62 *Yale L.J.* 137 (1953): Sharp, Book Review, 54 *Colum. L. Rev.* 439 (1954); Sholley, Book Review, 49 *Nw. U.L. Rev.* 114 (1954)], the dominant reaction was highly critical of Crosskey's historiographic assumptions and methods [see, e.g., Brown, Book Review, 67 *Harv. L. Rev.* 1439 (1954); Goebel, "Ex Parte Clio," 54 *Colum. L. Rev.* 450 (1954); Hart, Book Review, 67 *Harv. L. Rev.* 1456 (1954)].

56. See 78–80 sup.

57. In any case, the adopters' sense of time and change—of the relationship between present and future—was almost certainly not the same as ours, which has been affected by

such phenomena as the industrial revolution, theories of evolution, relativity and quantum mechanics, and the possibility of annihilation.

58. See note 87 inf.

59. Or so one might assume from the practice of the time and from the casual references to the practice in the Fifth Amendment. See McGautha v. California, 402 U.S. 183, 226 (1971) (separate opinion of Black, J.).

60. See P. Aries, *Western Attitudes toward Death* 11–13 (1974): D. Stannard, *The Puritan Way of Death* 93 (1977).

61. See *Death in American Experience* 102 (A. Mack, ed. 1973); P. Aries, *Western Attitudes* 85–86.

62. See Granucci, " 'Nor Cruel and Unusual Punishment Inflicted': The Original Meaning," 57 *Calif. L. Rev.* 839 (1969).

63. The First Amendment issue would not be resolved by the (unlikely) conclusion that the adopters intended the free speech clause to apply "absolutely"—unless (equally unlikely) they intended it to apply absolutely to circumstances they could not have envisioned.

64. The problems with coherence lie in the indeterminacy of the level of abstraction on which one characterizes the "event" or "transactions" arguably familiar to the adopters. See pp. 73–74 sup.

65. See Hans-Georg Gadamer, *Truth and Method* (Eng. trans. 1975). See also P. Winch, *The Idea of a Social Science and Its Relation to Philosophy* (1958); Taylor, "Interpretation and the Sciences of Man," 25 *Rev. of Metaphysics* 3 (1971). For a sharply critical review of Gadamer's work, see E. D. Hirsch, *Validity in Interpretation* 245 (1967).

66. See p. 85 inf.

67. Compare Roth v. United States, 354 U.S. 476, 508 (Douglas J. dissenting) with Bork, "Neutral Principles and Some First Amendment Problems," 47 *Ind. L.J.* 1 (1971).

68. See, e.g., L. Fuller, *Morality of Law* 86–87; Frankfurter, "Some Reflections on the Reading of Statutes," 47 *Colum. L. Rev.* 538–39 (1947); Fuller, "Positivism and Fidelity" 661–66. See also *Processes* 41–43.

69. See Moore, "The Semantics of Judging" 54 *S. Cal. L. Rev.* 151 (1981).

70. See J. H. Ely, *Democracy and Distrust*, chaps. 4–6. See also Mills v. Alabama, 384 U.S. 214, 218–20 (1966); Bork, *Neutral Principles* 20–35.

71. See, e.g., J. S. Mill, *On Liberty* (1859); Richards, "Free Speech and Obscenity Law: Toward a Moral Theory of the First Amendment," 123 *U. Pa. L. Rev.* 45 (1974); Scanlon, "A Theory of Free Expression." 1 *Phil. & Pub. Affairs* 204 (1972).

72. See generally, *Processes* 809–93; Gunther, "In Search of Evolving Doctrine on a Changing Court: A Model for a Newer Equal Protection," 86 *Harv. L. Rev.* 1 (1972).

73. See, e.g., Frontiero v. Richardson, 411 U.S. 677 (1973); Bolling v. Sharpe, 347 U.S. 497 (1954); Linde, "Judges, Critics, and the Realist Tradition," 82 *Yale L.J.* 233–34 (1972).

74. Compare Justice Black's and Justice Frankfurter's views in Adamson v. California, 332 U.S. 46 (1947). See also L. Levy, "The Fourteenth Amendment and the Bill of Rights" in *Judgements: Essay on American Constitutional History* 64 (1972); Fairman, "Does the Fourteenth Amendment Incorporate the Bill of Rights? The Original Understanding," 2 *Stan. L. Rev.* 5 (1949); Morrison, "Does the Fourteenth Amendment Incorporate the Bill of Rights? The Judicial Interpretation," 2 *Stan. L. Rev.* 140 (1949).

75. See, e.g., R. Berger, *Government by Judiciary*; C. Fairman, *Reconstruction* 1207; H. Graham, *Everyman's Constitution*; Corwin, "The Doctrine of Due Process of Law before the Civil War," 24 *Harv. L. Rev.* 460 (1911); Shattuck, "The True Meaning of the Term 'Liberty' " 365 (1891); Warren, "The New 'Liberty'."

76. See L. Boudin, *Government by Judiciary* (1932); A. Westin, Introduction and Historical Bibliography to C. Beard, *The Supreme Court and the Constitution* (1912); *Judicial Review and the Supreme Court* 1–12 (Levy, ed. 1967). But see R. Burger, *Congress v. The Supreme Court*

(1969); E. Corwin, *Court over Constitution* (1938); Corwin, "Marbury v. Madison and the Doctrine of Judicial Review," 12 *Mich. L. Rev.* 538 (1914); Hart, Book Review 1456. See generally Van Alstyne, "A Critical Guide to Marbury v. Madison," 1969 *Duke L.J.* 1.

77. See pp. 91–93 inf.

78. See generally Friedrich, "Constitutions and Constitutionalism," in 3 *Ency. Soc. Sci.* 318 (1966); Grey, "Constitutionalism: An Analytic Framework," in *Constitutionalism: Nomos* XX 189 (J.R. Pennock & J. W. Chapman, eds. 1979).

79. J. Locke's "Second Treatise" (1690) was the classic theoretical formulation and the Declaration of Independence the major political statement.

80. See D. Hume, "Of the Original Contract," in *Philosophical Works* 443 (T. Green & T. Gross, eds. 1964). It might be thought that judges and other officials have expressly consented to be bound by the Constitution by virtue of their oath of office "to support this Constitution" (U.S. Const. art VI, § 3). But the oath must be understood in the context of two centuries of constitutional decision-making. Cf. also Eakin v. Raub, 12 S. & R. 330, 353 (Pa. 1825) (the oath "is designed rather as a test of the political principles of the man, than to bind the officer in the discharge of his duty").

81. Compare H.L.A. Hart, *Concept of Law,* chap. 6 with Stampp, "The Concept of a Perpetual Union," 65 *J. Am. Hist.* 5 (1978).

82. See J. Tussman, *Obligation and the Body Politic* (1960); D. Hume, "Original Contract."

83. See generally R. Flathman, *Political Obligation* (1972); C. Pateman, *The Problem of Political Obligation* (1979); Pitkin, "Obligation and Consent," 59 *American Political Science Review* 990 (1965), 60 *American Political Science Review* 39 (1966).

84. Fiss, "The Supreme Court, 1979 Term—Foreword: The Forms of Justice," 93 *Harv. L. Rev.* 38 (1979).

85. A. Bickel, *The Least Dangerous Branch* 24 (1962).

86. Fiss, *The Supreme Court* 9, 11.

87. This approach may, indeed, partially extricate the originalist from a bind that a naive theory of political obligation puts her in. We saw earlier that a thoroughgoing originalist must adhere to the adopters' interpretive intent and their intended scope of provisions, even if this requires her to be less strictly originalist than she wishes. However, if she chooses to adhere to the adopters' "substantive" intentions, not because they are binding as such, but rather because this practice conduces to the ends of constitutionalism, she is not necessarily bound to adhere to their interpretive intentions.

There is a catch, however. Even—or perhaps especially—the intentionalist interpreter must recognize a difference between the adopter's views on an issue and their intentions for its constitutional resolution. See p. 82 sup.

88. United States v. Carolene Prod. Co., 304 U.S. 144 (1938).

89. See A. Bickel. *Least Dangerous Branch,* passim.

90. I shall refer to nonoriginalist strategies of constitutional decision-making collectively as adjudication.

91. See generally *Processes,* chap. 12; L. Fuller, *Anatomy of a Law* 84–112 (1968); Simpson, "The Common Law and Legal Theory," in *Oxford Essays in Jurisprudence* (2d ed. 1973); Wellington, "Common Law Rules and Constitutional Double Standards: Some Notes on Adjudication," 83 *Yale L.J.* 221 (1973). See also Shapiro, "Stability and Change in Judicial Decision-Making: Incrementalism or Stare Decisis?" 2 *Law in Transition Quarterly* 134 (1968).

92. In real life, adjudication is subject to the vicissitudes of stupidity, prejudice, carelessness, and self-interest. A skeptic might in any case question the judges' ability to discern fundamental public or social values. See, e.g., J. H. Ely, *Democracy and Distrust,* chap. 3. I am not defending adjudication as an intrinsically desirable mode of constitutional decision-making, however, but only arguing that it is better than originalism. Judges who avowedly pursue an originalist strategy are, after all, also susceptible to idiocy, corruption, and bias.

93. It is also the method of much statutory interpretation. See generally G. Calabresi, *A Common Law for the Age of Statutes* (Cambridge, Mass.: Harvard University Press, 1982).

94. Because of the centrality of the democratic ideal and the importance of external checks on judicial decision-making, it is almost inconceivable that the Court could ignore the mandate of a contemporary constitutional amendment. But see Murphy, "An Ordering of Constitutional Values," 52 *S. Cal. L. Rev.* (1980).

95. See Williams v. Florida, 399 U.S. 78, 122–29 (1970) (Harlan, J., dissenting); National Mut. Ins. Co. v. Tidewater Transfer Co., 337 U.S. 582, 646–55 (1949) (Frankfurter, J., dissenting); Corwin, "Judicial Review in Action," 74 *U. Pa. L. Rev.* 659–60 (1926).

96. To be sure, no society's moral principles exist in a vacuum, and courts as well as the drafters of a constitution respond to pragmatic concerns. In the area of individual rights, however, the moral dimension is paramount. Moreover, even if the constitutional protection of individual rights must be tempered by pragmatic constraints, there is no justification for binding the present to the compromises of another age.

97. See C. Beard, *Economic Interpretation* 73–151. For a useful survey of the controversy over Beard's thesis, see *The Reinterpretation of the American Revolution, 1763–1789*, 59–67 (J. P. Greene, ed. 1968).

98. See R. Berger, *Government by Judiciary* 222–29. The Act only prohibited discrimination with respect to the imposition of punishments and the rights to own property, enter into contracts, sue and be sued, and testify in court.

99. See generally G. Myrdal, *An American Dilemma* (1944); C. V. Woodward, *The Strange Career of Jim Crow* (1957); Kelly, "The School Desegregation Case," in *Quarrels That Have Shaped the Constitution* 247–49 (J. Garraty, ed. 1964).

100. Brown v. Board of Educ., 347 U.S. 483, 492 (1954).

101. Home Bldg. & Loan Ass'n v. Blaisdell, 290 U.S. 398, 442 (1934).

102. See note 55 sup.

103. E.g., Craig v. Boren, 429 U.S. 190 (1976).

104. E.g., Harper v. Virginia Board of Elections, 383 U.S. 663 (1966).

105. See Brown v. Board of Educ., 347 U.S. 483, 489–91 (1954); Bickel, "The Original Understanding and the Segregation Decision," 69 *Harv. L. Rev.* 1 (1955); Kelly, "The Fourteenth Amendment Reconsidered: The Segregation Question," 54 *Mich. L. Rev.* 1049 (1956).

106. Cf. U.S. Const. amend. XV ("The right of citizens of the United States to vote shall not be denied or abridged . . . on account of race . . . .").

107. See R. Berger, *Government by Judiciary.*

108. An originalist may wish to insulate a long-standing constitutional doctrine, untenable under originalist canons, by invoking a sort of statute of limitations. For example, Raoul Berger, after arguing that almost every twentieth-century equal protection clause decision is inconsistent with the original understanding of the Fourteenth Amendment, writes: "It would . . . be utterly unrealistic and probably impossible to undo the past in the face of the expectations that the segregation decisions, for example, have aroused in our black citizenry . . . . That is more than the courts should undertake and more, I believe, than the American people would desire" (R. Berger, *Government by Judiciary* 412–13). This qualified version of originalism is quite different from nonoriginalism. The nonoriginalist purposely departs from the text and original understanding; the very endurance of deviant doctrine is evidence that it reflects contemporary norms and hence becomes an independent basis for its legitimacy. By contrast, the originalist regrets that the erroneous doctrine ever came into existence and treats it as a burden that must be borne because of the mistakes or willful infidelities of her predecessors. Even if she acknowledges the doctrine, she must not encourage its growth or even strive officiously to sustain it. The originalist program of dealing with an illegitimate doctrine is one of minimum maintenance and, if possible, gradual death. Thus Berger continues: "But to accept thus far accomplished ends is not to condone the continued employment of the unlawful means. . . . [T]he difficulty of a

rollback cannot excuse the continuation of such unconstitutional practices. This is not the place to essay the massive task of furnishing a blueprint for a rollback. But the judges might begin by . . ." (ibid., p. 413).

109. Bolling v. Sharpe, 347 U.S. 497, 500 (1954) (footnotes omitted).

110. See Linde, *Judges* 233–34.

111. For a brief review of the history of incorporation, see Duncan v. Louisiana, 391 U.S. 145, 147–58 (1968).

112. 418 U.S. 24 (1974).

113. Idem at 43.

114. See Harper v. Virginia Board of Elections, 383 U.S. 663 (1966); Reynolds v. Sims, 377 U.S. 533 (1964).

115. Arguably, a moderate originalist would not have had to reach this result. As Justice Marshall wrote in dissent. "[s]ection 2 provides a special remedy . . . to cure a particular form of electoral abuse—the disenfranchisement of the Negro. There is no indication that the framers of the provisions intended that special penalty to be the exclusive remedy for all forms of electoral discrimination. This Court has repeatedly rejected that rationale"(418 U.S. at 74). True, but this presents the greater embarrassment that the adopters of the equal protection clause probably intended it not to encompass voting discrimination at all. See Reynolds v. Sims, 377 U.S. 533, 589–625 (1964) (Harlan, J., dissenting). But see Van Alstyne, "The Fourteenth Amendment, the 'Right' to Vote, and the Understanding of the Thirty-ninth Congress," 1965 *Sup. Ct. Rev.* 33.

116. Levinson, " 'The Constitution' in American Civil Religion," 1979 *Sup. Ct. Rev.* 123. See also Lerner, "Constitution and Court as Symbols," 46 *Yale L.J.* 1290 (1937).

117. See, e.g., Harper v. Virginia Board of Elections, 383 U.S. 663 (1966); Brown v. Board of Educ., 347 U.S. 483 (1954); Home Bldg. & Loan Ass'n v. Blaisdell, 290 U.S. 398 (1934); Weems v. United States, 217 U.S. 349 (1910).

118. Cf. M. Kadish & S. Kadish, *Discretion to Disobey* 45–66, 138–40 (1973) (arguing that in order to keep the jury's power to nullify laws within its proper scope, the jury must not be instructed that it has the power).

This position is not inconsistent with the radical hermeneutic notion that an interpreter can never grasp the original meaning but can only interpret the intervening tradition of changing meanings—the tradition of interpretations of prior interpretations—and that her own interpretation is inextricably bound up with her preconceptions. See pp. 83–84 sup. One might accept this and yet conclude that the best constitutional decisions will emerge from a process in which the interpreter self-consciously focuses on the original sources.

119. See, e.g., R. Wasserstrom, *The Judicial Decision* 25–30 (1961). See generally *Processes* 1086–98.

120. Home Bldg. & Loan Ass'n v. Blaisdell, 290 U.S. 398 (1934).

121. Factors besides perceived changes in social values—such as stability, continuity, and respect for democratic decisions—bear on the circumstances in which the presumption may be overcome. See G. Calabresi, *A Common Law for the Age of Statutes.*

122. Of course, the broader one's view of what is fairly encompassed by the text and original understanding, the more change moderate originalism can accommodate and the less persuasive this point becomes as an argument for nonoriginalist adjudication.

123. Proposals for an equal rights amendment were unsuccessfully introduced as early as 1923. See Brown et al., "The Equal Rights Amendment: A Constitutional Basis for Equal Rights for Women," 80 *Yale L.J.* 871, 886–87 (1971).

124. I have focused on constitutional adjudication designed to protect individual rights and the integrity of majoritarian processes. These are not the only ends of constitutionalism, however, and adjudication is not the only method of constitutional decision-making. The bulk of the written Constitution, as its names implies, is constitutive—establishing and marking the boundaries of government entities and determining how the branches of the federal government shall be staffed. And if the judiciary has borne primary responsibility

for the development of constitutional liberties, their protection—as well as the implementation of other constitutional norms—is no less the business of other agencies. How, then, does the thesis of this chapter bear on these different sorts of constitutional decision-making?

As a descriptive matter, constitutional decision-making concerning the allocation of powers within the national government and between nation and states has not been particularly faithful to the text and original understanding of the Constitution. Changes in the relations between the federal Executive and Congress, and between national and state governments, have occurred primarily through the assertion of power followed by counterassertion or acquiescence, with political factors serving a function somewhat akin to the constraints of adjudication. Analytically and normatively, I see no essential differences among the various areas of constitutional concern that would automatically insulate any of them from the possibility of nonoriginalist decision-making. This is not to say that interests such as certainty and stability do not make some deviations from the text almost unthinkable: it is hard to imagine Congress or the Court changing the number of Senators allocated to each state other than by constitutional amendment. But even this cannot be determined a priori by any timeless principle. It seems both simpler and more accurate to say that there are some instances in which the nonoriginalist presumption of fidelity to the text and original understanding is very unlikely to be rebutted.

James Madison's Theory of Constitutional Interpretation

1. Letter from James Madison to Martin Van Buren (5 July 1830), reprinted in *Letters and Other Writings of James Madison* 89 (Philadelphia, 1865) [hereafter *Madison Letters*]. In an earlier letter to Van Buren, on 3 June 1830, Madison had written that he believed his own present understanding of the 1817 veto message "was the general understanding" in 1817, but conceded that "[w]hether the language employed duly conveyed the meaning of which J.M. retains the consciousness, is a question on which he does not presume to judge for others." Letter from James Madison to Martin Van Buren (3 June 1830), reprinted in 4 *Madison Letters* 88; see also letter from James Madison to N.P. Trist (3 June 1830), reprinted in 4 *Madison Letters* 87 (Madison again speaks of the meaning of the 1817 veto "[t]o my consciousness," while admitting that "the entire text" of the message may have conveyed that meaning faultily).

2. See letter from James Madison to Edward Livingston (10 July 1822), reprinted in *Mind of the Founder: Sources of the Political Thought of James Madison* 338–39 (M. Meyers's rev. ed. 1981).

3. See letter from James Madison to N.P. Trist (15 February 1830), reprinted in 4 *Madison Letters* 61 (acknowledging distinction between "the object of the member who prepared the documents in question" and their "fair import," while asserting in that particular case the identity of the two).

4. Letter from James Madison to Henry St. George Tucker (23 December 1817), reprinted in 3 *Madison Letters* 54.

5. Letter from James Madison to Edward Livingston (17 April 1824), reprinted in 3 *Madison Letters* 436.

6. Letter from James Madison to Thomas Ritchie (15 September 1821), reprinted in 3 *Madison Letters* 228.

7. Letter (not posted) from James Madison to John Davis (ca. 1832), reprinted in 4 *Madison Letters* 243–44. This letter illustrates well the variety of uses Madison could make of the rhetoric of "intention" without indicating any change or uncertainty in his basic interpretive stance: within a few paragraphs, Madison refers to "the intention of those who framed, or, rather, who adopted the Constitution"; he immediately states that the interpreter "must decide that intention by the meaning attached to the terms by the 'usus' [governmental and judicial precedent]"; he remarks that it "need scarcely to be observed that" the intention so determined "could not be overruled by any latter meaning put on the phrase, however warranted by the grammatical rules of construction"; and he finally men-

tions the "intention of the parties to the Constitution" and the "intention of the States" (pp. 242–43; emphasis omitted). The apparent inconsistency of Madison's use of the term to the modern reader is due to the fact that for Madison the word still retained its traditional common-law meaning.

8. See *The Federalist* no. 37 (J. Madison); letter from James Madison to N.P. Trist (2 March 1827), reprinted in 3 *Madison Letters* 565.

9. See letter from James Madison to N.P. Trist (2 March 1827), reprinted in 3 *Madison Letters* 565; letter from James Madison to Judge Spencer Roane (2 September 1819), reprinted in 3 *Madison Letters* 145; cf. letter from James Madison to Thomas Grimké (15 January 1828), reprinted in 3 *Madison Letters* 611 (laws are "always liable, more or less, till made technical by practice, to discordant interpretations").

10. See letter from James Madison to Judge Spencer Roane (6 May 1821), reprinted in 3 *Madison Letters* 220 (advocating structural inference about the intentions of the states); letter from James Madison to Joseph Cabell (22 March 1827), reprinted in 3 *Madison Letters* 571–72 (same); letter from James Madison to Andrew Stevenson (27 November 1830), reprinted in 4 *Madison Letters* 129–30 (amendments proposed by state ratifying conventions are evidence of states' intentions); Madison also made reference at times to the weaknesses in the previous federal system that the Constitution was intended by the states to correct—a combination of the intentionalism of the Resolutions and the traditional common-law approach to statutory interpretation. See letter from James Madison to Joseph Cabell (30 October 1828), reprinted in 3 *Madison Letters* 655.

11. See letter from James Madison to Jonathan Elliot (14 February 1827), reprinted in 3 *Madison Letters* 552.

12. See letter from James Madison to Andrew Stevenson (27 November 1830), reprinted in 4 *Madison Letters* 128 (interpreter must look for the meaning given the text "by the Conventions, or, rather, by the people, who, through their Conventions, accepted and ratified" the text).

13. See letter from James Madison to H. Lee (25 June 1824), reprinted in 3 *Madison Letters* 442–43 (arguing that literal meaning of text varies as language changes); letter from James Madison to Andrew Stevenson (25 March 1826), reprinted in 3 *Madison Letters* 521–22 (noting value of "contemporary expositions"); letter from James Madison to N.P. Trist (2 March 1827), reprinted in 3 *Madison Letters* 565 (Constitution affected by the imprecision and mutability of language).

14. See letter from James Madison to Robert Garnett (11 February 1824), reprinted in 3 *Madison Letters* 367; letter (not posted) from James Madison to John Davis (ca. 1832), reprinted in 4 *Madison Letters* 253–54 (noting difficulties in interpreting convention's proceedings); letter (not posted) from James Madison to John Tyler (1833), reprinted in 4 *Madison Letters* 288–89 (criticizing as biased and inaccurate Robert Yates's and Luther Martin's accounts of the convention. The problem of accuracy could of course have been cured, at least to Madison's satisfaction, by publication of his journal, which he regarded as "a pretty ample view of what passed in that Assembly." Letter from James Madison to Thomas Ritchie (15 September 1821), reprinted in 3 *Madison Letters* 228.

15. 5 *Annals of Cong.* 776 (1796) (remarks of Rep. James Madison).

16. Letter from James Madison to John Jackson (27 December 1821), reprinted in 3 *Madison Letters* 245.

17. See *The Federalist* no. 37, p. 179 (J. Madison) (G. Wills, ed. 1982) ("The use of words is to express ideas.").

18. "But whatever respect may be thought due to the intention of the Convention which prepared and proposed the Constitution, as presumptive evidence of the general understanding at the time of the language used, it must be kept in mind that the only authoritative intentions were those of the people of the States, as expressed through the Conventions which ratified the Constitution" [letter from James Madison to M.L. Hurlbert (May 1830), reprinted in 4 *Madison Letters* 74].

In 1791, in the heat of the congressional debate over Hamilton's bank bill, Madison, like other opponents of the bill, occasionally referred to the Philadelphia Convention's failure to adopt a proposal giving Congress the power to charter corporations. See 2 *Annals of Cong.* 1937–60 (1791) (remarks of Rep. James Madison). Thereafter, Madison's understanding of the task of constitutional interpretation remained remarkably consistent over a period stretching from 1796 (when he was a leader of the embattled Republican opposition that was resting its hopes on the states as a counterweight to the federal government) until the early 1830s (when, as an elder statesman, he was contributing his prestige to the support of federal authority against a states' rights challenge by self-proclaimed followers of the "doctrines of '98").

19. Letter (not posted) from James Madison to John Davis (ca. 1832), reprinted in 4 *Madison Letters* 242.

20. See letter from James Madison to Judge Spencer Roane (2 September 1819), reprinted in 3 *Madison Letters* 143 (a constitution's meaning, "so far as it depends on judicial interpretation," is established by "a course of particular decisions"); letter from James Madison to Joseph Cabell (7 September 1829), reprinted in 4 *Madison Letters* 47 ("definitive power" to settle constitutional questions on the allocation of power between federal and state governments is lodged in federal Supreme Court).

21. Letter (not posted) from James Madison to John Davis (ca. 1832), reprinted in 4 *Madison Letters* 249.

22. Madison also referred to this legal background in *The Federalist* Papers. See *The Federalist* no. 37, 179 (J. Madison) (G. Wills, ed. 1982).

23. In later life Madison was accused by states' rights advocates of inconsistency in his constitutional opinions—a charge that he denied. See letter from James Madison to W.C. Rives (21 October 1833), reprinted in 4 *Madison Letters* 309–10. He would admit to even the appearance of inconsistency only in the National Bank case. See letter from James Madison to N.P. Trist (December 1831), reprinted in 4 *Madison Letters* 211.

24. See A. Koch, *Jefferson and Madison: The Great Collaboration* 108–10 (1950).

25. Ibid., p. 254.

26. Letter from James Madison to C.E. Haynes (25 February 1831), reprinted in 4 *Madison Letters* 165.

27. Letter from James Madison to Marquis de LaFayette (November 1826), reprinted in 3 *Madison Letters* 542; see also letter from James Madison to Thomas Jefferson (17 February 1825), reprinted in 3 *Madison Letters* 483 (stating that Congress, in legislating in accordance with the Constitution, will inevitably reflect the will of the people).

For Madison, the most unequivocal exercise by the people of their power "to declare [the Constitution's] meaning" was the formal procedure of amendment or constitutional convention. See, e.g., Madison, Veto Message (3 March 1817), 30 *Annals of Cong.* 1061 (1817) (in vetoing on constitutional grounds an internal improvements bill, Madison expressed his approval of the bill's object, "cherishing the hope" that an amendment rendering the bill constitutional would be secured). But Madison feared the unsettling effects of resorting too frequently to formal constitutional revision. See letter from James Madison to Thomas Jefferson (4 February 1790), reprinted in 1 *Madison Letters* 504. In Madison's view, the ordinary and indeed preferable mode for popular declaration of the Constitution's meaning was the deliberate construction put on it by the people's organs of government and confirmed by the acquiescence of officials and voters. See letter from James Madison to C. J. Ingersoll (25 June 1831), reprinted in 4 *Madison Letters* 183–87.

28. Letter from James Madison to C.E. Haynes (25 February 1831), reprinted in 4 *Madison Letters* 165; letter from James Madison to N.P. Trist (December 1831), reprinted in 4 *Madison Letters* 211.

29. Letter from James Madison to Marquis de LaFayette (November 1826), reprinted in 3 *Madison Letters* 542.

30. Letter from James Madison to N.P. Trist (December 1831), reprinted in 4 *Madison Letters* 211. The obligation of legislator or judge henceforth was to follow the meaning as construed, and not his "solitary opinions." Letter from James Madison to C.J. Ingersoll (25 June 1831), reprinted in 4 *Madison Letters* 184–86.

31. On the concept of "interpretive intention," see Brest, "The Misconceived Quest for the Original Understanding," 60 *B.U.L. Rev.* 215–16 (1980).

32. Letter from James Madison to Judge Spencer Roane (2 September 1819), reprinted in 3 *Madison Letters* 145.

33. Letters of Helvidius No. 4 (1793), reprinted in *Mind of the Founder* 210; see also letter from James Madison to James Monroe (27 December 1817), reprinted in 3 *Madison Letters* 56 ("Serious danger seems to be threatened to the genuine sense of the Constitution . . . by an unwarrantable latitude of construction"); letter from James Madison to Joseph Cabell (18 September 1828) (published with Madison's approval in the *Washington National Intelligencer* in December 1828), reprinted in *Mind of the Founder* 375 (contrasting congressional power to enact a protective tariff, sanctioned by 40 years' exercise, with a "novel construction however ingeniously devised"). Madison's reluctance to categorize a constitutional development as sufficiently erroneous to warrant resistance was based in part on his belief that interpretation is only partially "objective." See, e.g., 5 *Annals of Cong.* 494 (1796) (remarks of Rep. James Madison acknowledging that "[n]o construction" can be "perfectly free from difficulties," but recommending his own as "subject to the least").

34. Madison's view of interpretation is exemplified in his warning to one correspondent that "some care in discussing the question of a distinction between literal and constructive meanings may be necessary in order to avoid the danger of verbal character to the discussion." Letter from James Madison to N.P. Trist (1 March 1829), reprinted in 4 *Madison Letters* 17. For Madison, the (legitimate) "constructive" meaning of the Constitution is no less that instrument's "intention" than is the "literal"; and indeed the former may be the legally appropriate "intention" in the event of a conflict. Madison did not deny that some constructions of the Constitution would so transform the nature of the federal compact that nothing less than a formal exercise of the amending power could justify them, but in his view such a case would be "of a character [so] exorbitant and ruinous" as to justify revolution. See letter from James Madison to Joseph Cabell (30 October 1828), reprinted in *Mind of the Founder* 387; J. Madison, "Notes on Nullification (1835–1836)," reprinted in *Mind of the Founder* 418. Madison himself was confident that "the barrier" against any such usurpation was now "happily too strong in the text of the Instrument, in the uniformity of official construction, and in the maturity of public opinion, to be successfully assailed." Letter from James Madison to C. J. Ingersoll (17 November 1927) reprinted in 3 *Madison Letters* 601.

Dead Letters: Wills and Poems

1. W. Shakespeare, *The Tempest.*

2. Stoll, "The Tempest," 47 *PMLA* 703 (1932).

3. Despite Stoll's implication, *kritikos* seems not to have had a narrowly legal denotation in classical Greek. Cf. P. Chantraine, 2 *Dictionnaire Etymologique de la Langue Grecque* 584–85 (1970).

4. Wimsatt and Beardsley, "The Intentional Fallacy," 54 *Sewanee Rev.* 468 (1946), reprinted in W. Wimsatt, Jr., *The Verbal Icon* 3 (1954).

5. Ibid. (Wimsatt and Beardsley), p. 468 or Wimsatt, p. 3.

6. Ibid. (Wimsatt and Beardsley), p. 470 or Wimsatt, p. 5. They drop "kritikos" from the quotation.

7. Ibid. Wimsatt later made explicit the implication that their argument applied to interpretation as well as evaluation: "The statement in our essay of 1945 should certainly have read: 'The design or intention of the author is neither available nor desirable as a standard for judging either the meaning or the value of a work of literary art.' " Wimsatt, "Genesis: A Fallacy Revisited," in *The Disciplines of Criticism: Essays in Literary Theory, Interpretation, and History* 222 (1968).

The phrase "neither available nor desirable" discredits intention twice over: not only in terms of epistemological doubt, but also as a matter of policy—here, aesthetic policy. In all disputes about intention the radical concern is the epistemological one; but the argument can also be conducted almost purely in terms of policy. As will be seen below, in the law of wills relatively mild epistemological misgivings tended to harden into an anti-intentionalist policy that could prevail even when the testator's intentions were not seriously in doubt.

8. Barthes, "The Death of the Author" (R. Howard, trans. 1968), in *The Discontinuous Universe* 7 (S. Sears and G. Lord, eds. 1972).

9. Ibid., p. 8.

10. Nietzsche, *Die Fröhliche Wissenschaft* 5 in 2 *Werke* 255 (1973).

11. Barthes, "Death of the Author," p. 8.

12. Ibid., p. 10.

13. Ibid., p. 11 (emphasis in original).

14. Ibid., p. 12.

15. For wills as sui generis with respect to the question of intention, see Throckmerton v. Tracy, 1 Plowden 145, 162, 75 Eng. Rep. 222, 250 (1555) (Brook, C.J.); see also 4 W. Bowe and D. Parker, *Page on the Law of Wills* 2-3, 8 (1960); R. Burrows, *Interpretation of Documents* 96 (2d ed. 1946).

16. Wilde, "The True Function and Value of Criticism," 28 *XIX Century* 144 (1890), reprinted as "The Critic as Artist: Part I," in O. Wilde, *Intentions* 142 (1905).

17. *Intentions*, p. 144.

18. In statutory and constitutional law the claims of judicial freedom are less muted, however. For a colorful example, see J. Frank, *Courts on Trial* 292–315 (1949) ("a comparison between (1) the interpretation of statutes by judges and (2) the interpretation of musical compositions by musical performers" (p. 295)).

19. *Ballentine's Law Dictionary* 657 (1969).

20. Ibid.

21. Throckmerton v. Tracy, 1 Plowden 145, 162, 75 Eng. Rep. 222, 251 (1555) (Brook, C.J.).

22. Idem.

23. Idem at 162a, 75 Eng. Rep. at 251.

24. H. Swinburne, *A Briefe Treatise of Testaments and Last Willes* 9 (London 1590 and photo. reprint 1978) (citations omitted). This was the first English treatise on wills. Swinburne glosses the "Queene or Empresse" metaphor by referring to "Sichard. in Rub. de testa C.n.2 in fin"—presumably the now scarce commentary on Justinian by Johannes Sichardus (1586), cf. 221 *British Museum General Catalogue of Printed Books* 896 (1964).

25. H. Swinburne, *Briefe Treatise*, p. 9 (emphasis in original).

26. J. Locke, *An Essay Concerning Human Understanding* 404–5 (P. Nidditch, ed. 1975).

27. See text accompanying notes 21–25 sup.

28. Statute of Frauds, 29 Car. 2, ch. 3, § 5 (1677), renewed by Wills Act, 1837, 7 Will. 4 & 1 Vict., ch. 26, § 9. For discussion see note 30 inf.

29. J. Wigram, *An Examination of the Rules of Law Respecting the Admission of Extrinsic Evidence in Aid of the Interpretation of Wills* 9 (3d ed. London 1840) (1st ed. London 1831) (footnote omitted). Wigram's statement is modeled on the opinion of Justice Parke in Doe d. Gwillim v. Gwillim, 5 B. & Adol. 129 (1833). ("In expounding a will, the Court is to ascertain, not what the testator actually intended, as contradistinguished from what his words express, but what is the meaning of the words he has used"), quoted in J. Wigram, p. 9 n. 1.

30. Hawkins, "On the Principles of Legal Interpretation, with Reference Especially to the Interpretation of Wills," in 2 *Papers Read before the Juridical Society* 305, 307 (1858–63).

The relative autonomy that attached to written wills is indicated by an influential remark of Lord Wensleydale in Abbot v. Middleton, 7 H.L.C. 68, 114, 21 Eng. Rep. 28, 46

(1858) quoted in F. Hawkins, *A Concise Treatise on the Construction of Wills* 2 (C. Sanger's 2d ed. 1912) (emphasis added by Hawkins): "The use of the expression that the intention of the testator is to be the guide, unaccompanied with the constant explanation, that it is to be sought in his words, and a rigorous attention to them, is apt to lead the mind insensibly to speculate upon what the testator may be supposed to have intended to do, instead of strictly attending to the true question, which is, *what that which he has written means*. The will must be expressed in writing, and that writing only is to be considered."

There was one well-established exception to the conservative bias against extrinsic evidence of the testator's intention. Such evidence was regularly admitted to resolve a specific reference in the will—one not *patently* vague, which nonetheless fit more than one referent—that is, what F. Bacon, "Maxims of the Law" (ca. 1597) Regula XXIII, in 7 *Works of Francis Bacon* 385 (J. Speading, R. Ellis, and D. Heath, eds. 1879), characterized as a "latent ambiguity." This topic gets amply discussed in the standard treatises. See Warren, "Interpretation of Wills—Recent Developments," 49 *Harv. L. Rev.* 706–7 (1936). Warren, incidentally, praises Hawkins's paper on legal interpretation (ibid., p. 714).

A well-known paper by Oliver Wendell Holmes, "The Theory of Legal Interpretation," 12 *Harv. L. Rev.* 417 (1899), was conceived as a refutation of Hawkins: Holmes would replace the concept of the author's actual intention with the fictional construct of what "the normal speaker of English would have meant . . . by the same words" in the same circumstances (p. 419).

31. Hawkins, "Principles," p. 310. This vision of testamentary interpretation as "a species of equity" has much in common with E.D. Hirsch's general account of interpretation as subject to a Kantian "ethical imperative of speech." See E. Hirsch, *The Aims of Interpretation* 90 (1976).

32. Boyes v. Cook, 14 Ch. D. 53, 56 (1880), quoted in E. Ryder, *Hawkins and Ryder on the Construction of Wills* 12 (1965). The metaphor is still alive; witness Lord Denning's statement in In Re Jebb, [1966] Ch. 666, 672: "In construing this will, we have to look at it as the testator did, sitting in his armchair, with all the circumstances known to him at the time. Then we have to ask ourselves: 'What did he intend?' We ought not to answer this question by reference to any technical rules of law. Those technical rules have only too often led the courts astray in the construction of wills. Eschewing technical rules, we look to see simply what the testator intended."

33. Smith v. Coffin, 2 Henry Blackstone's English Common Plea Reports 444, 450, 126 Eng. Rep. 641, 644 (1795). The currency of the metaphor is reported on and maintained in H. Broom, *A Selection of Legal Maxims Classified and Illustrated* 372 (10th ed. 1939); see W. Bowe and D. Parker, *Page on the Law of Wills* 32–33 (citing many American instances).

34. See, e.g., C. Dickens, *Bleak House* (London 1853).

35. See, e.g., F. Hawkins, "Concise Treatise" 2 (quoting Lord Wensleydale in Abbot v. Middleton, 7 H.L.C. 68, 114, 21 Eng. Rep. 28, 46 (1858)); see also Shore v. Wilson, 9 Clark & Finnelly 355, 8 Eng. Rep. 450 (1842), which cast a negative spell over much nineteenth-century practice. The judges in this influential case, which was argued before the House of Lords, were firm in repudiating any evidence of the testator's intention outside the will if the will taken by itself seemed to expound a plain sense. They drew a sharp and prejudicial distinction between what the testator actually wrote and what he had "intended only to have written." Idem at 526, 8 Eng. Rep. at 518. I have argued elsewhere that such "intentions to write" are not really the point at issue, and that to conceive of verbal intention as being merely intention-to-write is to trivialize it. See Hancher, "Three Kinds of Intention," 87 *Mod. Language Notes* 827–51 (1972).

It is worth noting that after inscribing upon the law of wills their opinions about the ordinary inadmissibility of external evidence, the judges went on to make exception for external evidence showing the conventional historical (but not personal) meaning of a disputed phrase in the will, and to decide the case upon the basis of that evidence. This is much like the surprising bow to the "history of words" that Wimsatt and Beardsley make. See Wimsatt and Beardsley, "Intentional Fallacy" 478. They go even further, and class the evidence of philology as part of the "internal evidence" (p. 477).

36. S. Cretney and G. Dworkin, *Theobold on Wills* 9–10 (13th ed. 1971).

37. See 4 W. Bowe and D. Parker, *Page on the Law of Wills,* pp. 7–9.

38. R. Burrows, *Interpretation.*

39. National Soc'y for the Prevention of Cruelty to Children v. Scottish Nat'l Soc'y for the Prevention of Cruelty to Children, 111 L.T.R. 869 (1915), summarized in R. Burrows, *Interpretation* 22. For an otherwise parallel case that was decided differently, in favor of what the testator meant rather than what she said, see *In re* Gibbs' Estate, 14 Wis. 2d 490, 111 N.W.2d 413 (1961).

40. [1963] 1 Ch.

41. Lord Denning objected to the nineteenth-century doctrine of the-meaning-of-the-words:

> [T]he argument . . . which urges that in this case the deaths of Dr. Rowland and his wife did not coincide . . . proceeds on the assumption that, in construing a will, "It is not what the testator meant, but what is the meaning of his words." That may have been the nineteenth-century view; but I believe it to be wrong and to have been the cause of many mistakes. . . . For in point of principle the whole object of construing a will is to find out the testator's intentions, so as to see that his property is disposed of in the way he wished. True it is that you must discover his intention from the words he used: but you must put on his words the meaning which they bore to him. . . . What you should do is to place yourself as far as possible in his position, taking note of the facts and circumstances known to him at the time: and then say what he meant by his words. [Pp. 9–10; footnote omitted]

For a discussion of this and related cases, see G. Dworkin, *Odger's Construction of Deeds and Statutes* 40–43 (5th ed. 1967).

42. J. Gay, 2 *Fables* 2 (V. Dearing, ed. 1967).

43. *Horace on the Art of Poetry* 43 (E. Blakeney, ed. and trans. 1928).

44. E. Waller, "Of English Verse," quoted in 1 W. Wimsatt and C. Brooks, *Literary Criticism: A Short History* 215 (1978).

45. Tennyson, "In Memoriam A.H.H.," XCV, ll. 23–24, in *The Poems of Tennyson* 946 (C. Ricks, ed. 1969).

46. Ibid., XCV, ll. 33–37. The reading followed here is that of the original edition (1850). Later (1872), Tennyson depersonalized the mystical vision by changing "His living soul" in line 36 to "The living soul"; similarly, "his" in line 37 became "this."

47. Ibid., ll. 43–44.

48. Ibid., ll. 37–44.

49. From a letter of Tennyson's quoted in W. James, *The Varieties of Religious Experience* 384 (1902). For a discussion of the letter, see Grant, "The Mystical Implications of *In Memoriam,*" in 2 *Stud. in Eng. Literature* 482–84 (1962).

50. W. Auden, *The English Auden* 242 (E. Mendelson, ed. 1977).

51. *Oxford English Dictionary,* s.v. "dead letter."

52. 2 Cor. 3:6 (King James).

53. See J.-F. Collange, *Enigmes de la Deuxième Epître de Paul aux Corinthiens 64* (1972); 10 *The Interpreter's Bible* 305–7 (1953); R. Strachan, *The Second Epistle of Paul to the Corinthians* 80–85 (1935); Schneider, "The Meaning of St. Paul's Antithesis 'The letter and the Spirit,' " 15 *Cath. Biblical Q.* 163 (1953).

54. National Soc'y for the Prevention of Cruelty to Children v. Scottish Nat'l Soc'y for the Prevention of Cruelty to Children, 111 L.T.R. 869 (1915).

55. [1963] 1 Ch. See text accompanying notes 40–41 sup.

56. *Oxford English Dictionary,* s.v. "dead letter."

57. *Bouvier's Law Dictionary* 271 (W. Baldwin, ed. 1948).

58. H. Melville, "Bartleby," in *The Portable Melville* 465 (J. Leyda, ed. 1952).

59. Levinson, "Law as Literature," 60 *Texas L. Rev.* 378–79 (1982).

60. White, "Law as Language: Reading Law and Reading Literature," 60 *Texas L. Rev.* 418 (1982).

61. Ibid., p. 419.

62. Ibid., pp. 438–41.

63. See Hancher, "Three Kinds of Intention"; Skinner, "Motives, Intentions, and the Interpretation of Texts," 3 *New Literary History* 393 (1972). The two-uncles-named-John example happens to involve "latent ambiguity" (see sup. note 30), but active intention is a broader category.

64. Graff, "*Keep off the Grass, Drop Dead,* and Other Indeterminacies: A Response to Sanford Levinson,' " cf. pp. 175–80.

65. However, wills establishing trusts may require such labor, as in the case Levinson cites of an old trust established in a will to benefit "sentimental" youths. "Law as Literature" 376.

66. Ibid., p. 379.

67. Michaels, "Against Formalism: The Autonomous Text in Legal and Literary Interpretation," 1 *Poetics Today* 32 (1979); See also Searle, "Literal Meaning," in *Expression and Meaning: Studies in the Theory of Speech Acts* 117–36 (1979).

68. Fish, "Working on the Chain Gang: Interpretation in Law and Literature," 60 *Texas L. Rev.* 562 (1982).

69. Fish does acknowledge that an "interpretive community" need not be "monolithic." S. Fish, *Is There a Text in This Class?* 343 (1980). "Within the literary community," for example, "there are subcommunities" which prefer different "interpretive strategies" (pp. 343–44).

70. 111 L.T.R. 869 (1915).

71. 1915 A.C. 207, 213 (1914).

72. Idem at 214.

73. Brown v. Allen, 344 U.S. 443, 540 (1953) (Jackson, J., concurring).

74. See Hancher, "What Kind of Speech Act Is Interpretation?" 10 *Poetics* 263 (1981).

Statutory Interpretation and Literary Theory

1. W. Blake, "The Tyger," in *The Poetry and Prose of William Blake* 24 (D.V. Erdman, ed. 1965).

2. Raine, "Who Made The Tyger?" *Encounter* (June 1954), 43–44.

3. See W. Blake, "The Tyger," p. 24.
> When the stars threw down their spears
> And water'd heaven with their tears:
> Did he smile his work to see?
> Did he who made the Lamb make thee? [P. 25]

4. See, e.g., E.D. Hirsch, *Innocence and Experience: An Introduction to Blake* 244–52 (1964).

5. See, e.g., Hobsbaum, "A Rhetorical Question Answered: Blake's Tyger and Its Critics," 48 *Neophilogus* 151 (1964); Swingle, "Answers to Blake's 'Tyger': A Matter of Reason or of Choice?" 2 *Concerning Poetry* no. 1, p. 61 (1970).

6. Raine, "Who Made the Tyger?" 44–48.

7. E. D. Hirsch, *Innocence and Experience* 250.

8. Compare Baine and Baine, "Blake's Other Tigers, and 'The Tyger,' " 15 *Studies in Eng. Lit. 1500–1900* 563–64 (1975) (fearful, ugly and stupid tiger), with D. Erdman, *Blake: Prophet against Empire* 179–80 (1954) (tame-looking cat).

9. See, e.g., Swingle, "Answers" 61.

10. For modern treatises on statutory interpretation see F.R. Dickerson, *The Interpretation and Application of Statutes* (1975); Maxwell, *The Interpretation of Statutes* (12th ed.; P. Langan, ed. 1969); and Sutherland, *Statutes and Statutory Construction* (4th ed.; C. Sands, ed. 1972–1975). Leading articles include Curtis, "A Better Theory of Legal Interpretation," 3 *Vand. L. Rev.* 407 (1950); Frank, "Words and Music: Some Remarks on Statutory Interpretation," 47 *Colum. L. Rev.* 1259 (1947); Frankfurter, "Some Reflections on the Reading of Statutes," 47 *Colum. L. Rev.* 527 (1947); Landis, "A Note on 'Statutory Interpretation,' " 43 *Harv. L. Rev.* 886 (1930); Llewellyn, "Remarks on the Theory of Appellate Decision and the Rules or Canons about How Statutes Are to Be Construed," 3 *Vand. L. Rev.* 395 (1950); Miller, "Statutory Language and Purposive Use of Ambiguity," 42 *Va. L. Rev.* 23 (1956); and Radin, "Statutory Interpretation," 43 *Harv. L. Rev.* 863 (1930).

For discussions of analogous problems in literary theory, see J. Culler, *Structuralist Poetics: Structuralism, Linguistics, and the Study of Literature* (1975); E.D. Hirsch, "Objective Interpretation," in *Validity in Interpretation* 209 app. (1967); Wimsatt and Beardsley, "The Intentional Fallacy," in *The Verbal Icon* 3 (1967); P. De Man, "Form and Intent in the American New Criticism," in *Blindness & Insight: Essays in the Rhetoric of Contemporary Criticism* 20 (1971).

11. F.R. Dickerson, *Interpretation and Application* 8.

12. See Caminetti v. United States, 242 U.S. 470, 485 (1917); Jones, "The Plain Meaning Rule and Extrinsic Aids in the Interpretation of Federal Statutes," 25 *Wash. U. L.Q.* 2 (1939).

13. Quoted in J. Gray, *The Nature and Sources of the Law* 172 (2d ed. 1921).

14. See Landis, "Note" 886.

15. See H. Hart and A. Sacks, *The Legal Process: Basic Problems in the Making and Application of Law* 1153–57 (Tent. ed. 1958) [hereafter Hart and Sacks].

16. "Then, after measuring the legislative contribution, the court, where necessary, may add its own contribution." See F.R. Dickerson, *Interpretation and Application* 15.

17. See Wimsatt and Beardsley, *Verbal Icon* 3.

18. See, e.g., D. Bleich, *Subjective Interpretation* (1978).

19. See, e.g., J. Derrida, *Of Grammatology* (1976).

20. See, e.g., E.D. Hirsch, *Innocence and Experience* 209. For a contrast of the text-focused terminology of the New Critical school—integrity, unity, subtlety—with the concerns of the "intentional school," whose passwords are author-focused—sincerity, fidelity, authenticity—see Wimsatt and Beardsley, *Verbal Icon* 9.

21. See Abrams, "Rationality and Imagination in Cultural History: A Reply to Wayne Booth," 2 *Critical Inquiry* 447 (Spring 1976); Abrams, "The Deconstructive Angel," 3 *Critical Inquiry* 425 (Spring 1977). Abrams writes, "All I claim—all that any traditional historian needs to claim—is that, whatever else the author also meant, he meant, at a sufficient approximation, at least *this* . . ." (p. 427). Cf. Hart, "Positivism and the Separation of Law and Morals," 71 *Harv. L. Rev.* 593, 607 (1958) ("There must be a core of settled meaning, but there will be, as well, a penumbra of debatable cases in which words are neither obviously applicable nor obviously ruled out.")

22. See Booth, " 'Preserving the Exemplar': or, How Not to Dig Our Own Graves," 3 *Critical Inquiry* 407 (Spring 1977).

23. Deconstruction is an interpretive technique that follows from the view that language itself contains infinite possibilities of meaning. The deconstructive critic unravels the text in order to demonstrate that it has no correct interpretation. See, e.g., Miller, "The Critic as Host," 3 *Critical Inquiry* 439 (Spring 1977).

24. H.L.A. Hart, *The Concept of Law* 124 (1978).

25. See F.R. Dickerson, *Interpretation and Application* 13–33.

26. The tradition is usually traced to Descartes's *Meditations on First Philosophy*. See Michaels, "The Interpreter's Self: Pierce on the Cartesian 'Subject' ", *The Georgia Rev.* 383 (Summer 1977).

27. See generally H.G. Gadamer, *Philosophical Hermeneutics* (1976) (philosophy); L. Wittgenstein, *Philosophical Investigations* (3d ed. 1958) (philosophy); M. Polanyi, *Personal Knowledge: Towards a Post-critical Philosophy* (1974) (philosophy); E. Carr, *What Is History* (1969) (history); W. Gallie, *Philosophy and the Historical Understanding* (2d ed. 1968) (history); R. Bernstein, *The Restructuring of Social and Political Theory* (1978) (social science); P. Feyerabend, *Against Method* (1978) (natural science); T. Kuhn, *The Structure of Scientific Revolutions* (2d ed. 1970) (natural science); Fish, "Interpreting the *Variorum*," 2 *Critical Inquiry* 465 (Spring 1976) (literary theory); Michaels, "The Interpreter's Self" (literary theory).

28. For a discussion of interpretive issues in constitutional law see A. Bickel, *The Least Dangerous Branch* (1962); A. Bickel, *The Supreme Court and the Idea of Progress* (1970); H. Wechsler, *Principles, Politics and Fundamental Law* (1961); Deutsch, "Neutrality, Legitimacy and the Supreme Court: Some Intersections between Law and Political Science," 20 *Stan. L. Rev.* 169 (1968); Ely, "The Wages of Crying Wolf: A Comment on *Roe* v. *Wade*," 82 *Yale L.J.* 920 (1973); Grey, "Do We Have an Unwritten Constitution?" 27 *Stan. L. Rev.* 703 (1975); Monaghan, "Foreword: Constitutional Common Law," 89 *Harv. L. Rev.* 1 (1975). For a discussion of the manner in which such issues arise in common law adjudication see K. Llewellyn, *The Common Law Tradition: Deciding Appeals* (1960); R. Wasserstrom, *The Judicial Decision* (1961); Dworkin, "Hard Cases," 88 *Harv. L. Rev.* 1057 (1975); Greenawalt, "Discretion and Judicial Decision: The Elusive Quest for the Fetters That Bind," 75 *Colum. L. Rev.* 359 (1975); Kennedy, "Form and Substance in Private Law Adjudication," 89 *Harv. L. Rev.* 1689 (1976); Wellington, "Common Law Rules and Constitutional Double Standards: Some Notes on Adjudication," 83 *Yale L.J.* 221 (1973).

29. G. Calabresi, "The Common Law Function in the Age of Statutes" (March 1977) (Oliver Wendell Holmes, Jr. Lectures, Harvard Law School).

30. 115 N.Y. 506, 22 N.E. 188 (1889).

31. Idem at 509, 22 N.E. at 189.

32. Separate provisions governed real and personal property. See N.Y. Dec. Est. Law art. 2, § 10 (McKinney 1949) (derived from Rev. Stats., pt. 2, ch. 6, tit. 1, § 1, as amended by L. 1867, ch. 782, § 3) (superseded by N.Y. Est., Powers & Trusts Law § 3-1.1 (McKinney 1967)) which provided, "All persons, except idiots, persons of unsound mind and infants, may devise their real estate, by a last will and testament, duly executed, according to the provisions of this article"; N.Y. Dec. Est. Law art. 2, § 15 (McKinney 1949) (derived from Rev. Stats., pt. 2, ch. 6, tit. 1, art. 2, § 21, as amended by L. 1867, ch. 782, § 4) superseded by N.Y. Est., Powers & Trusts Law § 3-1.1 (McKinney 1967)) which provided, "Every person of the age of eighteen years or upwards, of sound mind and memory, and no others, may give and bequeath his or her personal estate, by will in writing."

33. See N.Y. Dec. Est. Law art. 3, § 83 (McKinney 1949) (derived from N.Y. Real Prop. Law, ch. 547, § 281 (1896)) (current version at N.Y. Est., Powers & Trusts Law § 4-1.1 (McKinney 1967).

34. It has been argued that the court might also have interpreted Palmer's will so as to defeat Elmer's claim. See F.R. Dickerson, *Interpretation and Application* 200. This approach would have raised somewhat similar interpretive issues. The problem also arises when the beneficiary of a life insurance policy slays the insured and the insurer attempts to interpret the policy so as to defeat payment. See, e.g., Filmore v. Metropolitan Life Insur. Co., 82 Ohio St. 208, 92 N.E. 26 (1910).

35. 115 N.Y. at 509, 22 N.E. at 189.

36. Idem.

37. Idem at 511, 22 N.E. at 190.

38. Pound, "Spurious Interpretation," 7 *Colum. L. Rev.* 381 (1907).

39. Ibid., p. 382.

40. Wade, "Acquisition of Property by Willfully Killing Another—A Statutory Solution," 49 *Harv. L. Rev.* 716 (1936).

41. Ibid.

42. B. Cardozo, *The Nature of the Judicial Process* 42 (1921).

43. Hart and Sacks 101.

44. Dworkin argues that judges are bound to decide cases in accordance with "principles" concerning individual or group rights, and that these principles are derived from the political morality presupposed by the laws and institutions of the community. See R. Dworkin, *Taking Rights Seriously* 126 (1977).

45. Dworkin, "The Model of Rules," 35 *U. Chi. L. Rev.* 29 (1967), reprinted as "The Model of Rules I," in R. Dworkin, *Taking Rights Seriously* 28–29 (1977).

46. For excerpts from the New York Decedent's Estate Law, see note 32.

47. See MacCallum, "Legislative Intent," 75 *Yale L.J.* 755–56 (1966).

48. See Hart and Sacks 98.

49. See L. Wittgenstein, *Investigations* ("The intention with which one acts does not 'accompany' the action any more than the thought 'accompanies' speech. Thought and intention are neither 'articulated' nor 'non-articulated'; to be compared neither with a single note which sounds during the acting or speaking, nor with a tune").

Commentators also disagree about whether the court may take into account its estimate of what the legislature would have done had it considered the question. Compare Burnet v. Gugenheim, 288 U.S. 280, 285 (1933) (Cardozo, J.) ("which choice is it more likely that Congress would have made?") with Frankfurter, "Reflections" 539 ("thus to frame the question too often tempts inquiry into the subjective"). See also Curtis, "A Better Theory of Legal Interpretation," 3 *Vand. L. Rev.* 415 (1950) ("better deal with the future than the past, better pay a decent respect for a future legislature than stand in awe of one that has folded up its papers and joined its friends in the country club or in the cemetery"); MacCallum, "Legislative Intent" 773 ("But what he [the legislator] did not think of does not make a difference unless he would have excepted it had he thought of it").

50. Records of committee hearings or floor debates may provide a basis for drawing such inferences.

51. This approach has been designated the "mischief" rule, and seems to be derived from Heydon's Case, 30 Co. Rep. 7a, 76 Eng. Rep. 637 (Ex. 1584). See Hart and Sacks 1144.

52. For a proposal that such "laws" be created, see Silving, "A Plea for a Law of Interpretation," 98 *U. Pa. L. Rev.* 499 (1950).

53. See Hart and Sacks 98.

54. In addition to these doubts about such a "law," it is an open question whether the courts have the constitutional authority to impose rules on the legislature concerning the manner in which the latter shall conduct its affairs. See ibid., p. 101.

55. See text surrounding notes 57–66 inf.

56. This term was first used by Josiah Royce. See 2 J. Royce, *The Problem of Christianity* 211–75 (1967). See also Fish, "Interpreting the *Variorum*" 483–84; Michaels, "Interpreter's Self" 395.

57. Hart and Sacks 101.

58. Ibid.

59. See text at note 45 sup.

60. Dworkin, "Hard Cases" 1086; reprinted in R. Dworkin, *Taking Rights Seriously* 108 (1977).

61. See Dworkin, "Hard Cases" 1086–87.

62. Ibid., pp. 1087–1089.

63. 115 N.Y. at 509, 22 N.E. at 189.

64. For a discussion of these assumptions, see text accompanying notes 47–54 sup.

65. See text accompanying note 1 sup.

66. Raine, "Who Made the Tyger?" 43.

67. Idem at 48.

68. Idem at 43.

69. E. D. Hirsch, *Innocence and Experience* 248.

70. Ibid., p. 250.

71. See text at note 67 sup.

72. Swingle, "Answers to Blake's 'Tyger' " 66.

73. Ibid., p. 65.

74. Ibid., p. 67.

75. See K. Llewellyn, *Common Law Tradition* 17–18.

76. See, e.g., H.L.A. Hart, *The Concept of Law* 121–50. But see Hart, "Problems of Philosophy of Law," 6 *Encyclopedia of Philosophy* 264, 271 (1967), in which he states, "It may well be that terms like 'choice,' 'discretion,' and 'judicial legislation' fail to do justice to the phenomenology of considered decision: its felt involuntary or even inevitable character which often marks the termination of deliberation on conflicting considerations. P. 271, quoted in Greenawalt, "Policy, Rights and Judicial Decision," 11 *Georgia L. Rev.* 991 n.2 (1977).

77. See R. Dworkin, *Taking Rights Seriously* 82–90.

78. See Dworkin, "No Right Answer?" in *Law, Morality and Society* 58 (P. Hacker and J. Raz, eds. 1977).

79. Ibid., pp. 83–84.

80. Ibid., pp. 84.

81. Professor Dworkin seems to adopt this view when, in discussing the analogy between the judge and the referee in a chess game, he indicates, "The proposition that there is some 'right' answer . . . does not mean that the rules of chess are exhaustive and unambiguous; rather it is a complex statement about the responsibilities of its officials and participants." R. Dworkin, *Taking Rights Seriously* 104.

82. Hart, "American Jurisprudence through English Eyes: The Nightmare and the Noble Dream," 11 *Georgia L. Rev.* 981 (1977).

83. See Dworkin, *Taking Rights Seriously*.

84. Ibid., p. 125.

85. See Wimsatt and Beardsley, "Intentional Fallacy" 10.

86. See E. D. Hirsch, "Objective Interpretation" 209.

87. Abrams, "Rationality and Imagination" 425.

88. Booth, "Preserving the Exemplar" 418.

89. Ibid., p. 423.

An Essay on Constitutional Language

1. The contemporary jargon draws a distinction between "interpretivism" and "noninterpretivism," but this is merely one characterization of an issue that predates the current labels. See generally J.H. Ely, *Democracy and Distrust* 1–14 (1980); Brest, "The Misconceived Quest for the Original Understanding," 60 *B.U.L. Rev.* 204 (1980); Grey, "Do We Have an Unwritten Constitution?" 27 *Stan L. Rev.* 703 (1975) [hereafter "Unwritten Constitution"]; Grey, "Origins of the Unwritten Constitution: Fundamental Law in American Revolutionary Thought," 30 *Stan. L. Rev.* 843 (1978) [hereafter "Origins"]; Linde, "Judges, Critics and the Realist Tradition," 82 *Yale L.J.* 227 (1972); Monaghan, "Of 'Liberty' and 'Property,' " 62 *Cornell L. Rev.* 405 (1977); Monaghan, "The Constitution Goes to Harvard," 13 *Harv. C.R.-C.L. L. Rev.* 117 (1978) [hereafter Monaghan, "The Constitution"]; Perry, "Substantive Due Process Revisited: Reflections on (and beyond) Recent Cases," 71 *Nw. U.L. Rev.* 417 (1976); Richards, "Human Rights as the Unwritten Constitution: The Problem

of Change and Stability in Constitutional Interpretation," 4 *U. Dayton L. Rev.* 295 (1979); "Constitutional Adjudication and Democratic Theory," 56 *N.Y.U. L. Rev.* 259 (1981); "Judicial Review versus Democracy," 42 *Ohio St. L.J.* 1 (1981).

2. One notable exception is Munzer and Nickel, "Does the Constitution Mean What It Always Meant?" 77 *Colum. L. Rev.* 1029 (1977). See also Alexander, "Modern Equal Protection Theories: A Metatheoretical Taxonomy and Critique," 42 *Ohio St. L.J.* 4–16 (1981); Smith, "Rights, Right Answers, and the Constructive Model of Morality," 5 *Soc. Theory and Prac.* 421–25 (1980). Philosophy is at the moment having a good run in the constitutional arena, but, with few exceptions, it is moral philosophy rather than the philosophy of language that is taken to be the most useful for constitutional inquiries. Given that we have a written constitution, this lack of attention from the perspective of the philosophy of language seems a bit surprising. Although not directed specifically toward constitutional interpretation, there has been some recent attention to legal language from a philosophical perspective. Moore, "The Semantics of Judging," 54 *S. Cal. L. Rev.* 151 (1981); Stone, "From a Language Perspective," 90 *Yale L.J.* 1149 (1981).

3. In addition to the works cited sup. note 1, see L. Tribe, *American Constitutional Law* iii (1978) ("[T]he Constitution is an intentionally incomplete, often deliberately indeterminate structure for the participatory evolution of political ideals and governmental practices"); L. Tribe, *American Constitutional Law* 1979 Supp. 2 ("open-textured" provisions such as "equal protection" and "due process"; use of "broad terminology" in the Constitution). See also Baker v. Carr, 369 U.S. 186, 242 (1962) (Douglas, J., concurring) ("large gaps in the Constitution"); H.P. Hood & Sons, Inc. v. Du Mond, 336 U.S. 525, 535 (1949) (Jackson, J.) ("great silences of the Constitution"); Prudential Ins. Co. v. Benjamin, 328 U.S. 408, 413 (1946) ("great constitutional gaps").

4. Although it illustrates the focus both of this inquiry and of my conclusions, the phrase in the text is, at this stage, question-begging. For even if we note that the Constitution is written, what does this say about the constitution? This question can be expressed in terms of how much of the constitution is contained or captured in the (written) Constitution. It is this question that this essay is intended to address. Positing the question in this way suggests the Continental distinction between a material constitution and a formal constitution. See H. Kelsen, *The Pure Theory of Law* 222–24 (M. Knight, trans.; 2d ed. 1967).

5. Hart's original foray into the field was "The Ascription of Responsibility and Rights," in *Logic and Language* (first ser.) 145–66 (A. Flew, ed. 1955). Hart's later repudiation of this strictly performative view of legal language (H.L.A. Hart, *Punishment and Responsibility* v (1968)) was the result of the more complex, presupposition-oriented theory first put forth in Hart, "Definition and Theory in Jurisprudence," 70 *Law Q. Rev.* 37 (1954) [hereafter "Definition and Theory"], and embellished in H.L.A. Hart, *The Concept of Law* 13–17 (1961). See also Cohen, "Theory and Definition in Jurisprudence," 29 *Proc. Aristotelian Soc. (Supp.)* 213 (1955); Hart, "Theory and Definition in Jurisprudence," 29 *Proc. Aristotelian Soc. (Supp.)* 239 (1955). See generally N. MacCormick, *H.L.A. Hart* (1981); Hacker, "Hart's Philosophy of Law," and Baker, "Defeasibility and Meaning," in *Law, Morality, and Society: Essays in Honour of H.L.A. Hart* 26 (P. Hacker and J. Raz, eds. 1977).

6. See H.L.A. Hart, *The Concept of Law* 126–27; Sartorius, "Hart's Concept of Law," in *More Essays in Legal Philosophy* 131–61 (R. Summers, ed. 1971). See also G. Gottlieb, *The Logic of Choice* 48 (1968); Hart, "Problems of Philosophy of Law," in 6 *Encyclopedia Phil.* 266, 270 (P. Edwards, ed. 1967); Stone, "Ratiocination Not Rationalisation," 74 *Mind* 463 (1965).

7. See L. Wittgenstein, *Philosophical Investigations* §§ 30, 43, 120, 138, 340, 532 (G. Anscombe, trans. 1958). Although Wittgenstein was the guiding light of the "meaning is use" approach, that approach was in fact the standard under which most of Anglo-American philosophy operated in the 1950s and 1960s. See, e.g., J. Austin, *How to Do Things with Words* (J.O. Urmson and M. Sbisa's 2d ed. 1975) [hereafter *Words*]; J. Austin, *Philosophical Studies* (3d ed. 1979); Grice, "Meaning," 66 *Phil. Rev.* 377 (1957); Strawson, "Propositions, Concepts, and Logical Truth," 7 *Phil. Q.* 15 (1957).

8. The man on the Clapham omnibus is most frequently taken to be the prototypical reasonable man for purposes of tort law (see, e.g., Bolam v. Friern Hospital Management Committee, 1 W.L.R. 582, 586–87 (Q.B. 1957)), but he is also the ordinary speaker of ordina-

ry English. See, e.g., Woodhouse A.C. Israel Cocoa Ltd. S.A. v. Nigerian Produce Marketing Co., 2 Q.B. 23, 63 (C.A. 1971). Although we need not recount Hart's arguments, those arguments do suggest that constitutional language may possess a uniqueness of its own. For summary and critique, see N. MacCormick, *H.L.A. Hart;* Baker, "Defeasibility and Meaning"; Hacker, "Hart's Philosophy of Law". See also Shuman, "Jurisprudence and the Analysis of Fundamental Legal Terms," 8 *J. Legal Educ.* 437 (1956).

9. "[I]t was by no means self-evident in 1789 that judges should use the same techniques in the construction of constitutional provisions as in the interpretation of ordinary statutory and decisional sources." H. Jones, "The Common Law in the United States: English Themes and American Variations," in *Political Separation and Legal Continuity* 134 (1976). See also Bridwell, Book Review, 1978 *Duke L.J.* 914–15 (reviewing R. Berger, *Government by Judiciary: The Transformation of the Fourteenth Amendment* (1977)).

10. Thus, when John Marshall observed that "we must never forget that it is a constitution we are expounding," McCulloch v. Maryland, 17 U.S. (4 Wheat.) 316, 407 (1819), he was adopting the thesis discussed in the text, although McCulloch is significantly obscure in that Marshall did not explain in what way constitutional interpretation was unique. See Frankfurter, "John Marshall and the Judicial Function," 69 *Harv. L. Rev.* 217 (1955). For a sampling of the various theories that embody this view in one way or other, see C. Black, *Structure and Relationship in Constitutional Law* (1969); C. Miller, *The Supreme Court and the Uses of History* (1969); Llewellyn, "The Constitution as an Institution," 34 *Colum. L. Rev.* 1 (1934); Murphy, "The Art of Constitutional Interpretation: A Preliminary Showing," in *Essays on the Constitution of the United States* 130 (M. Harmon, ed. 1978).

11. See, e.g., R. Dworkin, *Taking Rights Seriously* 131–49 (1980); H. McBain, *The Living Constitution* (1927); Brest, "The Misconceived Quest"; Grey, "Unwritten Constitution"; Munzer and Nickel, "Does the Constitution Mean What It Always Meant?"; Perry, "Substantive Due Process"; Miller, "Notes on the Concept of the 'Living' Constitution," 31 *Geo. Wash. L. Rev.* 881 (1963); Reich, "The Living Constitution and the Court's Role," in *Hugo Black and the Supreme Court* 133 (S. Strickland, ed. 1967); Richards, "Human Rights." Contra Rehnquist, "The Notion of a Living Constitution," 54 *Tex. L. Rev.* 693 (1976). In terms of a theory of meaning, some of the foregoing theses could be said to assume that the meaning of constitutional provisions changes over time, while others would hold that the meaning remains the same while the applications change. Exploring that distinction at this point would serve little purpose, because it and related issues are the focus of the balance of this essay.

12. In this sense, the Constitution combines both argument and aspiration with a statement of existing principles, not unlike Joel Feinberg's "manifesto sense" of a right. J. Feinberg, *Social Philosophy* 67 (1973). I derive some support for this view from the similarity between the largely enforceable American Constitution and the many largely unenforceable international treaties, declarations, and conventions dealing with human rights. Learned Hand, of course, treated this manifesto sense as virtually the sole function of some constitutional provisions. L. Hand, *The Bill of Rights* 33–34 (1958).

13. One of the purposes of a metaphor is to get us to think in different ways, to block intentionally some of our routine thought processes. See, e.g., I. Hungerland, *Poetic Discourse* 127 (1958); Black, "Metaphor," in *Models and Metaphors* 25 (1962). It seems to me quite likely that this process is at least one of the implicit purposes of the Constitution, but proving that hypothesis is beyond the purview of this essay.

14. Fear of the possible results of judicial interpretation may explain a large part of this aversion. It has been 114 years since any very broad language was added to the Constitution (the ratification of the Fourteenth Amendment), and the rough road travelled by both the Equal Rights Amendment and the various proposed "right to life" amendments suggests that we may never again add a constitutional provision of similar openness. Quite possibly, it is only a fortunate historical accident that aggressive judicial review arose only after the enactment of those constitutional provisions which now occupy most of the Supreme Court's time. Perhaps such active review has, for all practical purposes, foreclosed the possibility of ever again achieving the consensus necessary to add similar provisions to the Constitution.

15. See generally Dellinger, "The Recurring Question of the 'Limited' Constitutional Convention," 88 *Yale L.J.* 1623 (1979); Dellinger, "Who Controls a Constitutional Convention?—A Response," 1979 *Duke L.J.* 999; Fordham, "Some Observations upon Uneasy American Federalism," 58 *N.C.L. Rev.* 289 (1980); Gunther, "The Convention Method of Amending the United States Constitution," 14 *Ga. L. Rev.* 1 (1979); Tribe, "Issues Raised by Requesting Congress to Call a Constitutional Convention to Propose a Balanced Budget Amendment," 10 *Pac. L.J.* 627 (1979); Van Alstyne, "Does Article V Restrict the States to Calling Unlimited Conventions Only?—A Letter to a Colleague," 1978 *Duke L.J.* 1295; Van Alstyne, "The Limited Constitutional Convention—The Recurring Answer," 1979 *Duke L.J.* 985; Note, "Good Intentions, New Inventions, and Article V Constitutional Conventions," 58 *Tex. L. Rev.* 131 (1979). The implicit theme of most of the recent literature, which has attracted an all-star lineup of constitutional scholars, is that an unlimited convention is fraught with danger.

16. See sup. note 3. A pervasive problem in attempting to generalize about constitutional language is that constitutional language is hardly uniform in degree of generality, in purpose, or in historical origin. This recognition of the diversity of constitutional language is most prominently associated with Justice Frankfurter. See, e.g., Malinski v. New York, 324 U.S. 401, 414–15 (1945). See generally H. Thomas, *Felix Frankfurter: Scholar on the Bench* 127–47 (1960).

17. 17 C.F.R. § 240.10b-5(a) (1981).

18. 15 U.S.C. § 1 (1976).

19. Note, for example, the intermingling of examples from both constitutional and statutory interpretation in E. Levi, *An Introduction to Legal Reasoning* (1949).

20. "When did you stop beating your wife?" contains a prototypical presupposition in that it presupposes, but does not assert, that you have a wife and that you have beaten her. Presuppositions are not asserted to be true or false, but undergird the thought and language of people. See also J. Austin, *Words* 48–52; J. Searle, *Speech Acts* (1969). See generally Strawson, "On Referring," 59 *Mind* 320 (1950).

21. Hart, "Definition and Theory," 37. See note 5 sup.

22. This notion is embodied in Hart's theory of the "internal" point of view. H.L.A. Hart, *The Concept of Law* 54–60, 84–88, 97–107, 138–44.

23. See J. Searle, *Speech Acts* 33–42, 184–87. See also Harris, "Do Performatives Still Exist?" (Paper presented at the Pacific Division of the American Philosophical Association, March 1980) (copy on file at *UCLA Law Review*).

24. On contextual definition, see J. Austin, *Words*; J. Searle, *Speech Acts* 20; L. Wittgenstein, *Philosophical Investigations*; Frankena, "Some Aspects of Language," in *Language, Thought & Culture* 121–23 (P. Henle, ed. 1958); Ryle, "Ordinary Language," in *Ordinary Language* 24 (V. Chappell, ed. 1964). For a somewhat controversial application of the notion of contextual definition to the problem of obscenity, see Schauer, "Speech and 'Speech'— Obscenity and 'Obscenity': An Exercise in the Interpretation of Constitutional Language," 67 *Geo. L.J.* 899 (1979).

25. There has been surprisingly little discussion of technical language in the philosophical literature, but one noteworthy source is Caton, "Introduction" to *Philosophy and Ordinary Language* v (C. Caton, ed. 1963).

26. See generally Morrison, "Technical Language (and the Law)," 10 *Colonial Law.* 18 (1980).

27. The nature of the ratification process makes the search for original intent in constitutional adjudication especially problematic. Are the states presumed to have ratified the intent of the drafters as well as the language those drafters wrote? What if legislative history from state legislatures shows that different states ratified for different reasons? What if the intent of the drafters is unavailable to the states? Given the nature of my conclusions, I need not attempt to answer these very troubling questions, but they cannot be avoided by any theory that is tied to original intent.

Even if we put the Whose intent? question aside, we must still address two different questions. The first is, What results would the drafters have intended had they been confronted with the problems and context of today's world? This question seems largely unanswerable, inviting the most speculative kind of historical psychoanalysis. This formulation of the issue has, however, attracted a substantial following. See, e.g., L. Lusky, *By What Right?* 21 (1975); Murphy, Book Review, 87 *Yale L.J.* 1770 (1978).

The other question that could be asked is, What results did the drafters specifically intend? This question is, at least, one that is possible to answer, although much of this essay contends that it is still the wrong question. This question is at the heart of the much-discussed theories of Raoul Berger. R. Berger, *Government by Judiciary: The Transformation of the Fourteenth Amendment* (1977). The assumption that clear or unmistakable intent, as evidenced in historical documents, is the exact equivalent of a textual statement to that effect is central to Berger's thesis. Ibid., p. 368; Berger, "A Political Scientist as Constitutional Lawyer: A Reply to Louis Fisher," 41 *Ohio St. L.J.* 162–63, 167 (1980). See also Oregon v. Mitchell, 400 U.S. 112, 203 (1970) (Harlan, J., concurring and dissenting in part); Harper v. Virginia Board of Elections, 383 U.S. 663, 677–78 (1966) (Black, J., dissenting); West Coast Hotel Co. v. Parrish, 300 U.S. 379, 402–3 (1937) (Sutherland, J., dissenting). Among current members of the Supreme Court, Justice Rehnquist most clearly subscribes to the view that original intent is dispositive. See, e.g., Trimble v. Gordon, 430 U.S. 762, 777—86 (1977) (Rehnquist, J., dissenting); Sugarman v. Dougall, 413 U.S. 634, 649–64 (1973) (Rehnquist, J., dissenting in *Sugarman* and also in *In re* Griffiths, 413 U.S. 717 (1973)). Because, as should be apparent from all of this essay, I disagree with Berger's assumption as to what is the proper question, I have no need to deal with the issue of whether Berger's own answers to his question are even correct. It is certainly not abundantly clear that they are. See, e.g., Murphy, Book Review 1754–60.

28. See Palko v. Connecticut, 302 U.S. 319 (1937); Murray's Lessee v. Hoboken Land & Improvement Co., 59 U.S. (18 How.) 272 (1856).

29. See Sniadach v. Family Finance Corp., 395 U.S. 337, 344–51 (1969) (Black, J. dissenting); Ownbey v. Morgan, 256 U.S. 94 (1921).

30. Patterson v. Colorado, 205 U.S. 454 (1907), is the Supreme Court's most explicit statement of the now-repudiated "prior restraints only" interpretation of the First Amendment (Idem at 462). For references to other historical exclusions, see, e.g., Roth v. United States, 354 U.S. 476 (1957); *Ex parte* Jackson, 96 U.S. 727 (1877); L. Levy, *Legacy of Suppression: Freedom of Speech and Press in Early American History* (1960).

31. See note 27 sup.

32. "The provisions of the Federal Constitution, undoubtedly, are pliable in the sense that in appropriate cases they have the capacity of bringing within their grasp every new condition which falls within their meaning. But, their meaning is changeless; it is only their application which is extensible." Home Bldg. & Loan Assn. v. Blaisdell, 290 U.S. 398, 451 (1934) (Sutherland, J., dissenting) (footnote omitted). See also Village of Euclid v. Ambler Realty Co., 272 U.S. 365, 387 (1926) (Sutherland, J.); 1 T. Cooley, *Constitutional Limitations* 124 (8th ed. 1927).

This distinction parallels the philosopher's related distinctions between connotation and denotation, and intention and extension. See W. Alston, *Philosophy of Language* 17 n.8 (1964); J.S. Mill, *A System of Logic* (8th ed. 1904); W. Salmon, *Logic* 122–29 (2d ed. 1973). See also J. Hospers, An Introduction to Philosophical Analysis 40–54 (2d ed. 1967). The distinction also parallels those between sense and reference. See Frege, "On Sense and Reference," in *Translations from the Philosophical Writings of Gottlob Frege* 58 (P. Geach and M. Black, eds. 1952) ("Sense" and "reference" are the generally accepted English translations of Frege's *"Sinn"* and *"Bedeutung"*). But, not wishing to carry more philosophical baggage than I must, I will stick to a distinction between the meaning of a rule and the instances of its application.

33. "[A] principle to be vital must be capable of wider application than the mischief which gave it birth." Weems v. United States, 217 U.S. 349, 373 (1910), quoted in Gregg v. Georgia, 428 U.S. 153, 171 (1976) (opinion of Stewart, J. joined by Powell and Stevens, JJ.).

34. See Munzer and Nickel, "Does the Constitution Mean What It Always Meant?"

1031; Bridwell, Book Review 914–15. On generality as part of the nature of law, see H.L.A. Hart, *The Concept of Law* 20–23, 234.

35. Cf. United States v. Seeger, 380 U.S. 163 (1965) (broad extension of concept of religion for purposes of statutory exemption from conscription for conscientious objectors). But cf. Wisconsin v. Yoder, 406 U.S. 205 (1972) (emphasis on the historical legitimacy of the Amish church).

36. See Munzer and Nickel, "Does the Constitution Mean What It Always Meant?" 1– 31. This seems to have been Justice Sutherland's point. See note 32 sup.

Whether there is a shift in meaning may depend on why a particular provision is in the Constitution. The narrower the reason, the more likely it is that a new application will be beyond the scope of that reason and will therefore constitute a shift of meaning. Conversely, the broader the reason taken to justify the provision in the text, the more likely it is that subsequent applications will still be within the scope of that reason, and therefore not represent a change of meaning.

37. See note 34 sup. But if you define the first meaning differently, then the application may involve no shift.

38. See Craig v. Boren, 429 U.S. 190 (1976).

39. See Graham v. Richardson, 403 U.S. 365 (1971).

40. See Levy v. Louisiana, 391 U.S. 68 (1968).

41. See San Antonio Indep. School Dist. v. Rodriguez, 411 U.S. 1 (1973) (rejecting strict scrutiny).

42. See A. Meiklejohn, *Free Speech and Its Relation to Self-Government* (1948), reprinted in A. Meiklejohn, *Political Freedom: The Constitutional Powers of the People* (1960); BeVier, "The First Amendment and Political Speech: An Inquiry into the Substance and Limits of Principle," 30 *Stan. L. Rev.* 299 (1978); Bork, "Neutral Principles and Some First Amendment Problems," 47 *Ind. L.J.* 1 (1971); Meiklejohn, "The First Amendment Is an Absolute," 1961 *Sup. Ct. Rev.* 245.

43. Virginia State Bd. of Pharmacy v. Virginia Citizens Consumer Council, Inc., 425 U.S. 748 (1976).

44. Linmark Associates, Inc. v. Township of Willingboro, 431 U.S. 85 (1977).

45. See, e.g., Bridwell, Book Review 34; Lusky, " 'Government By Judiciary': What Price Legitimacy?" 6 *Hastings Const. L.Q.* 403 (1979); Munzer and Nickel, 1030–33; Murphy, "Does the Constitution Mean What It Always Meant?" 27; Nathanson, Book Review, 56 *Tex. L. Rev.* 579 (1978); Perry, Book Review, 78 *Colum. L. Rev.* 685 (1978). Although it is possible that we have ignored the relevance of history and original intent (see Monaghan, *The Constitution* 117), it seems that we have more often succumbed to the error of ignoring Joseph Story's admonition that "Nothing but the text itself was adopted by the people." 1 J. Story, *Commentaries on the Constitution of the United States* 300 (4th ed. 1873).

46. See note 3 sup.

47. R. Dworkin, *Taking Rights Seriously* 133; Dworkin, "The Forum of Principle," 56 *N.Y.U. L. Rev.* 469 (1981).

48. J. H. Ely, *Democracy* 1; Ely, "The Wages of Crying Wolf: A Comment on Roe v. Wade," 82 *Yale L.J.* 920 (1973).

49. "[T]he most important datum bearing on what was intended is the constitutional language itself." J.H. Ely, *Democracy* 16.

50. This is implicit in any view that treats "unmistakable intention" as being equivalent to text. See note 27 sup. The difficult question occurs, however, when the text and the legislative history are in some way inconsistent. On this point, the canons of interpretation are not helpful, because one canon suggests that we look at the legislative history only when the text is unclear, and another says that we can look at legislative history to reject a textual statement inconsistent with that history. Compare Caminetti v. United States, 242 U.S. 470, 490 (1917), with United Steelworkers v. Weber, 443 U.S. 193, 201–2 (1979). See

generally, Note, "Intent, Clear Statements, and the Common Law: Statutory Interpretation in the Supreme Court," 95 *Harv. L. Rev.* 892 (1982).

It is unfortunately common for commentators to conflate textual and historical approaches to constitutional interpretation. See, e.g., Bork, "Neutral Principles" 8; Grey, "Unwritten Constitution" 712–13; Perry, "Interpretivism, Freedom of Expression, and Equal Protection," 42 *Ohio St. L.J.* 280–81 (1981). The two approaches are, however, fundamentally different. See Bobbitt, "Constitutional Fate," 58 *Tex. L. Rev.* 707 (1980). See also Alexander, "Modern Equal Protection Theories".

51. J. Story, *Commentaries* 300; Chafee, "The Disorderly Conduct of Words," 41 *Colum. L. Rev.* 399–402 (1941); Linde, "Judges, Critics, and the Realist Tradition," 82 *Yale L.J.* 254 (1972). See also Chevigny, "Philosophy of Language and Free Expression," 55 *N.Y.U. L. Rev.* 174 (1980).

52. "If, however, it were proved by twenty bishops that either party, when he used the words, intended something else than the usual meaning which the law imposes upon them, he would still be held, unless there were some mutual mistake, or something else of the sort." Hotchkiss v. National City Bank of New York, 200 F. 287, 293 (S.D.N.Y. 1911) (Hand, L., J.).

53. See, e.g., Ricketts v. Pennsylvania Ry. Co., 153 F.2d 757 (2d Cir. 1946) (Frank, J., concurring). See also Mansfield v. Hodgdon, 147 Mass. 304, 17 N.E. 544 (1888); Embry v. Hargadine, McKittrick Dry Goods Co., 127 Mo. App. 383, 105 S.W. 777 (1907); Smith v. Hughes, 6 Q.B. 597 (1871). See generally A. Corbin, 1 *Corbin on Contracts* § 106 (1963); A. Corbin, 3 *Corbin on Contracts* § 539, at 82 (1963); L. Simpson, *Handbook of the Law of Contracts* 10 (2d ed. 1965).

Corbin maintains that it is an "illusion" that words have meaning independent of those who use them (1 *Corbin on Contracts* § 106, at 474). Were it not for that "illusion," however, we would have no way of understanding each other. This is the whole point of any theory of meaning that stresses language as a rule-governed form of behavior. See, e.g., J. Searle, *Speech Acts* 33–50; B. Harrison, *An Introduction to the Philosophy of Language* 165–258 (1979).

Moreover, Corbin's critique of a strictly objective view exposes an important ambiguity in our use of the term *objective*. To the extent that *objective* suggests certainty or precision, then Corbin's criticism is well taken. But if *objective* suggests only that we interpret on the basis of external factors, including the conventions of language, but excluding the intentions of the language user, then a theory can be objective without making any claim of precision or certainty. It is the latter sense of *objective* that is at the heart of the objective theory of contracts and also at the heart of the theory of constitutional interpretation suggested in this essay.

54. See, e.g., Lorentz v. R.K.O. Radio Pictures, Inc., 155 F.2d 84, 87 (9th Cir. 1946), *cert. denied,* 329 U.S. 727 (1946); Lyman v. New England Newspaper Pub. Co., 286 Mass. 258, 260, 190 N.E. 542, 543 (1934); Roberts v. Camden, 103 Eng. Rep. 508, 509 (K.B. 1807). See generally W. Odgers, *A Digest of the Law of Libel and Slander* § 93, at 144 (2d ed. 1887); W. Prosser, *Handbook of the Law of Torts* § 111, at 747 (4th ed. 1971).

55. In Gibbons v. Ogden, 22 U.S. (9 Wheat.) 1 (1824), John Marshall noted that those who ratified the Constitution "must be understood . . . to have intended what they have said" (idem at 188).

56. See Frankfurter, "Some Reflections on the Reading of Statutes," 47 *Colum. L. Rev.* 538–39 (1947). See generally P. Brest, *Processes of Constitutional Decisionmaking: Cases and Materials* 31–44 (1975).

57. P. Jones, *Philosophy and the Novel* 183–84 (1975). The dispute between the "intentionalists" and the "anti-intentionalists" is prominent in contemporary philosophy of literary criticism. The dispute is described and fully documented in P. Juhl, *Interpretation: An Essay in the Philosophy of Literary Criticism* (1980). Juhl himself is an intentionalist. There is much in the corpus of writing about literary interpretation that is of great importance to the constitutional theorist, both for intentionalists and anti-intentionalists like myself.

58. P. Jones, *Philosophy and the Novel* 183–84. See also S. Cavell, *Must We Mean What We Say?* 32 (1969).

59. Perhaps the characteristic feature of a code is that it is perfectly translatable into some language. Natural languages, however, arising in the context of particular cultures, are not necessarily perfectly translatable into other natural languages. See W. Quine, *Word and Object* (1960).

60. See generally P. Jones, *Philosophy and the Novel* 182–99; J. Searle, *Speech Acts*; J. Searle, *Expression and Meaning: Studies in the Theory of Speech Acts* (1979). For a more intention-oriented theory of meaning, see Grice, "Meaning," 377; Grice, "Utterer's Meaning and Intentions," 78 *Phil. Rev.* 147 (1969). A more sophisticated version is found in S. Schiffer, *Meaning* (1972).

61. See note 7 sup.

62. The term "literalism" is ambiguous, because it is unclear where the literal meaning of the term at issue comes from. In one sense, every textually oriented theory, including this one, is a version of literalism. But we more commonly equate literalism with the ordinary language definition of constitutional terms, or with the notion that the text provides clear answers to all of our problems. In this sense, literalism shares both the characteristics and the flaws of what we usually refer to as "formalism" or "conceptualism." See H.L.A. Hart, *The Concept of Law* 126; J. Stone, *The Province and Function of Law* 149–65 (1946); Hart, "Problems of Philosophy of Law" 270. On the distinction between literalism and interpretivism, see Grey, "Unwritten Constitution" 703, 706 n.9.

63. In addition to the authorities cited sup. note 63, see Stone, "Ratiocination" 466, 472.

64. On purpose-oriented interpretation, see Fuller, "Positivism and Fidelity to Law—A Reply to Professor Hart," 71 *Harv. L. Rev.* 630 (1958). See also sup. note 56 and accompanying text.

65. See P. Jones, *Philosophy and the Novel* 183–84, 194–95; Frankfurter, "Some Reflections".

66. Whether there is a distinction between ethics and metaethics (between substantive ethical principles and the methodology of ethical inquiry) is by no means clear, because some metaethical views, particularly versions of relativism and subjectivism, may tend to collapse the distinction. But the distinction serves tolerably well for my present purposes.

67. R. Dworkin, *Taking Rights Seriously* 131–49.

68. Ibid., p. 149.

69. I do not mean to take Dworkin to task for this one word. The rest of his essay, as well as Dworkin's use of the word *connection* in the same sentence, cautions us against taking Dworkin's metaphor as an argument.

70. J. Murphy, "Cruel and Unusual Punishments," in *Retribution, Justice, and Therapy* 223–49 (1979).

71. Ibid., p. 223.

72. The quoted sentence is hardly crucial to Murphy's fine analysis of the problem of punishment, and in that sense I suppose I am being unfair. But the sentence is there, and it provides a concise statement of a position that has at times surfaced in constitutional theory. See, e.g., Thomas Grey's description of a now "moribund" first form of noninterpretivist review in Grey, "Origins," 844 n.8 (1978). For a powerful critique of theories that strive for congruence between constitutional law and "correct" moral theory, see Monaghan, "Our Perfect Constitution," 56 *N.Y.U. L. Rev.* 353 (1981).

73. Without getting too deeply into the issue of the meaning and scope of judicial discretion here, I use formal authorization to refer to a norm that grants authority without specifying the substantive standards or constraints for the exercise of that authority. See Paulson, "Material and Formal Authorisation in Kelsen's Pure Theory," 39 *Cambridge L.J.* 172 (1980).

74. U.S. Const. amend. VII. My unargued assumption that this provision has little moral content derives some support from the fact that it remains one of the few provisions of the Bill of Rights that has not been incorporated by the Fourteenth Amendment. See

Melancon v. McKeithen, 345 F. Supp. 1025 (E.D. La.), *aff'd sub nom*. Hill V. McKeithen, 409 U.S. 943 (1972).

75. See, e.g., D. Richards, *The Moral Criticism of Law* 51–54 (1977); Richards, "Constitutional Privacy, The Right to Die and the Meaning of Life: A Moral Analysis," 22 *Wm. & Mary L. Rev.* 327 (1981) [hereafter "Constitutional Privacy"]; Richards, "Human Rights"; Richards, "Sexual Autonomy and the Constitutional Right to Privacy: A Case Study in Human Rights and the Unwritten Constitution," 30 *Hastings L.J.* 957 (1979); Richards, "Unnatural Acts and the Constitutional Right to Privacy: A Moral Theory," 45 *Fordham L. Rev.* 1281 (1977). For Richards, "the concept of human rights" is his "unwritten constitution" (Richards, supra note 1, at 300–301), and it is this concept that he proceeds to use for the decision of particular cases. Richards acknowledges that there may be different conceptions of that concept, but that is not inconsistent with the theory that there is, for a particular analyst at a particular time, one unitary constitutional theory, and that is the methodology with which I take issue.

76. J.H. Ely, *Democracy and Distrust*. I have heard Professor Ely's theory of the Constitution described as "one big equal protection clause." His theory is far richer and more complex than that, but it is still one theory. For a quite different critique of unitary constitutional theories, including Ely's, see Gerety, Book Review, 42 *U. Pitt. L. Rev.* 35 (1980).

77. Dworkin's general theory of adjudication is similarly both unitary and reconstructive in that he would have judges construct the unifying theory that provides "the best justification . . . for the body of propositions of law already shown to be true . . ." Dworkin, "No Right Answer?" in *Law, Morality, and Society: Essays in Honour of H.L.A. Hart* 82 (P. Hacker and J. Raz, eds. 1977). See also R. Dworkin, *Taking Rights Seriously* 81–130. Dworkin, however, explicitly recognizes the underdetermination problem discussed in the text (Idem, pp. 64–68). See Alexander and Bayles, "Hercules or Proteus? The Many Theses of Ronald Dworkin," 5 *Soc. Theory & Prac.* 267 (1980). It is questionable whether Dworkin's solution is really a solution (idem). In any event, there is much in his theory that would provide support for any particular/general theorist.

78. The right to privacy, see Griswold v. Connecticut, 381 U.S. 479 (1965), and the right to travel, see Shapiro v. Thompson, 394 U.S. 618 (1969), are perhaps the most prominent of these gaps.

79. The methodology under discussion here was most notable in Griswold v. Connecticut, 381 U.S. 479 (1965). In that case, the Court used specific particulars, embodied in the First, Third, Fourth, and Fifth Amendments, to construct a right to privacy and then applied that constructed right to the issue (contraception) at hand. See D. Richards, *The Moral Criticism of Law* 81–109.

80. See J. H. Ely, *Democracy and Distrust* 177–79.

81. Thus, Richards talks about various specific rights being generated by the right of privacy. See, e.g., Richards, "Constitutional Privacy".

82. See L. Wittgenstein, *Tractatus Logico-Philosophicus* (D. Pears and B. McGuinness, trans. 1961). I do not claim to be using Wittgenstein's ladder metaphor for the same purpose for which he used it.

83. See A. Bickel, *The Least Dangerous Branch* 63 (1962); A. Bickel, *The Morality of Consent* 25–30 (1975); Munzer and Nickel, "Does the Constitution Mean What It Always Meant?"; Richards, "Human Rights."

84. Griswold did not generate nearly the avalanche of scholarly criticism that befell Roe v. Wade, 410 U.S. 113 (1973). See, e.g., J. H. Ely, "Wages of Crying Wolf" 15, 66; Epstein, "Substantive Due Process by Any Other Name: The Abortion Cases," 1973 *Sup. Ct. Rev.* 159. Part of the explanation might be that the statute at issue in Griswold was substantially more ridiculous than that in Roe. The more likely explanation, however, is that the reliance on specific textual provisions, rather than on general liberty/due process considerations, made Griswold seem more palatable.

85. The *loci classici* for the underdetermination thesis are P. Duhem, *The Aim and Structure of Physical Theory* (P. Wiener, trans. 1954); W. Quine, *From a Logical Point of View* (2d ed. 1961); W. Quine, *Word and Object*.

86. One practical, rather than strictly logical, objection to the underdetermination thesis is that a large enough number of observations will cause "convergence" toward only one theory. See M. Hesse, *Revolutions and Reconstructions in the Philosophy of Science* viii (1980). This seems to be the point implicit in Dworkin's references to "density." Dworkin, "No Right Answer" 83–84. Apart from the fact that the convergence thesis itself has some logical difficulties (M. Hesse, idem p. viii-x), it seems plain to me that the constitutional text is hardly dense enough to rebut the problem of underdetermination in reference to constructing a theory from the text.

87. See, e.g., C. Glymour, *Theory and Evidence* (1980); M. Hesse, *Revolutions and Reconstructions*; M. Hesse, *The Structure of Scientific Inference* (1974); T. Kuhn, *The Structure of Scientific Revolutions* (2d ed. 1970).

88. See Rader, "Fact, Theory, and Literary Explanation," 1 *Critical Inquiry* 245 (1974).

89. See generally R. Atkinson, *Knowledge and Explanation in History* (1978); R. Martin, *Historical Explanation: Re-enactment and Practical Inference* (1977).

90. Even though the actual theory constructed will not, in my view, be textually mandated, the process of theory construction still aids in assuring principled adjudication. Thus, theory construction serves methodological goals of the legal system that are independent of the substance of the theory. See Golding, "Principled Decision-Making and the Supreme Court," 63 *Colum. L. Rev.* 35 (1963); Greenawalt, "The Enduring Significance of Neutral Principles," 78 *Colum L. Rev.* 982 (1978).

91. In this sense, "values" incorporates not only particular views about particular subjects, but also the experiences and training of the selector. Imagine an automobile accident observed by a surgeon, a tort lawyer, and an automotive engineer. If we asked each of them the question, What happened? we would get fundamentally different answers which varied in the particular facts reported and the language used to describe the reported facts.

92. See generally P. Achinstein, *Concepts of Science: A Philosophical Analysis* (1968); M. Hesse, *Revolutions and Reconstructions*; K. Popper, *Unended Quest* 52 (1976) ("There is no such thing as a perception except in the context of interests and expectations . . .").

93. The story of the blind men and the elephant suggests just how easy it is to generalize on the basis of preselected and incomplete versions of the evidence. Saxe, "The Blind Men and the Elephant: A Hindoo Fable," in *Story Poems* 267 (L. Untermeyer's rev. ed. 1961).

94. J. H. Ely, *Democracy and Distrust* 87–101.

95. See R. Dworkin, *Taking Rights Seriously*; D. Richards, *The Moral Criticism of Law*.

96. Art. I, § 10; amend. III; amend. IV; amend. V; amend. XIV.

97. Even if all of the text is used, the weighting is selective. It is a mistake to assume that even "equal" weighting would be value-neutral, because the notion of equality is dependent upon the context. How would we react to a constitutional law casebook that devoted as much space to the Third and Twenty-third amendments as it did to the First and Fourteenth?

98. See notes 75–76 sup. For Professor Dworkin the principle is that of "equal concern and respect." Dworkin, "Liberalism," in *Public and Private Morality* 126 (S. Hampshire, ed. 1978).

99. See A. Meiklejohn, *Free Speech*.

100. On universalization, compare R. Hare, *Freedom and Reason* 7–50 (1963) to Schwartz, "Against Universality," 78 *J. Phil.* 127 (1981).

101. There are, in fact, two kinds of unitary theories. One kind involves only one ultimate principle, such as Dworkin's principle of "equal concern and respect." See note 98 sup. Other theories have two or more principles, but incorporate theories that relate those principles to each other in a priority relationship. See, e.g., J. Rawls, *A Theory of Justice* (1971). The distinction is therefore best expressed in terms of the complexity of the single ultimate principle.

102. Ibid., pp. 34–53.

103. D. Richards, *A Theory of Reasons for Action* (1971).

104. Dworkin, "Liberalism."

105. A. Gewirth, *Reason and Morality* (1978) ("Principle of Generic Consistency").

106. Perhaps the foremost pluralist of modern times is Isaiah Berlin. Berlin's most important works are collected in I. Berlin, *Against the Current: Essays in the History of Ideas* (H. Hardy, ed. 1980); I. Berlin, Concepts and Categories: Philosophical Essays (H. Hardy, ed. 1979); I. Berlin, *Four Essays on Liberty* (1969); I. Berlin, *Russian Thinkers* (H. Hardy and A. Kelly, eds. 1978). See also B. Williams, *Problems of the Self* 166–86 (1973); Feinberg, "Rawls and Intuitionism," in *Reading Rawls: Critical Studies on Rawls' "A Theory of Justice"* 108 (N. Daniels, ed. 1975); Williams, "Conflicts of Values," in *The Idea of Freedom: Essays in Honour of Isaiah Berlin* 221 (A. Ryan, ed. 1979). See generally B. Barry, *Political Argument* (1965); R. Brandt, *Ethical Theory* (1959); H.L.A. Hart, *Punishment and Responsibility* (1968).

107. The relation of coherence is stronger than the relation of consistency. Two propositions, such as "It is snowing today" and "Napoleon lost at Waterloo" may be consistent with each other, although not possessing the relation of mutual entailment implicit in the idea of coherence. See generally A. Woozley, *Theory of Knowledge* 129–75 (1949). A claim of coherence in any normative philosophy—moral, political, or legal—is a claim that in some way all of the norms of the system "fit together." Thus, coherence requires consistency, but the reverse is not true. I am now in the process of developing a fuller analysis and explication of the notion of coherence in the philosophy of law, and my remarks here are a specific and tentative embodiment of this larger project.

108. J. Rawls, *Theory of Justice* 34–40.

109. Ibid. See also B. Barry, *The Liberal Theory of Justice* 5–6 (1973).

110. Rawls concedes, however, that the desirability of having conflict-resolving higher principles is not *eo ipso* evidence of their existence. J. Rawls, *Theory of Justice* 39.

111. Because *intuitionism* has been used to refer to a method of identifying moral values rather than the relation among them (and in this sense Rawls, Richards, Dworkin, and Gewirth may all be intuitionists), Rawls's terminology is a trifle misleading. It has been suggested that *pluralism* would be a better appellation, as a plurality of values is used. B. Barry, *Liberal Theory of Justice* 6.

112. I use "coherence theorist" to refer to anyone who holds that there is one ultimate system of moral values, whether they be monists like Dworkin or priority-ranked pluralists like Rawls. See note 101 sup.

113. See Monaghan, "Our Perfect Constitution," 56 *N.Y.U. L. Rev.* 353, 371 (1981).

114. R. Dworkin, *Taking Rights Seriously* 134–37; Dworkin, "The Forum of Principle," 56 *N.Y.U. L. Rev.* 469 (1981). See also J. Rawls, *Theory of Justice* 10. For commentary on the distinction, see Munzer and Nickel, "Does the Constitution Mean What It Always Meant?" 1037–41; Saphire, "Professor Richards' Unwritten Constitution of Human Rights: Some Preliminary Observations," 4 *U. Dayton L. Rev.* 305 (1979). See also D. Richards, *The Moral Criticism of Law*, 44–56.

115. This is so, except to the extent that changes in meaning (different conceptions) are built into what Dworkin means by a concept. R. Dworkin, *Taking Rights Seriously* 134–37. In this sense, the meaning of a concept never changes, but this is only because in another sense the concept itself has no meaning apart from some conception of it. The real problem is that there is an inevitable tension between open concepts and most traditional theories of meaning. See generally M. Weitz, *The Opening Mind* 25–48 (1977).

116. R. Dworkin, *Taking Rights Seriously* 134–37.

117. Ibid.

118. I use the word "something" deliberately, because there is a long tradition of philosophical debate about just what concepts are, some claiming they are words of a particular sort, some claiming they are mental images, and so on. See generally M. Weitz, *Opening Mind* 3–24; N. Campbell, *Foundations of Science* 45 (1957).

119. Gallie, "Essentially Contested Concepts," 56 *Proc. Aristotelian Soc.* 167 (1955). See

also W.B. Gallie, *Philosophy and the Historical Understanding* (1964). For commentary, see Kekes, "Essentially Contested Concepts: a Reconsideration," 10 *Phil. & Rhetoric* 71 (1977); Garver, "Rhetoric and Essentially Contested Arguments," 11 *Phil. & Rhetoric* 156 (1978). See also Booth, " 'Preserving the Exemplar' or, How Not to Dig Our Own Graves," 3 *J. Critical Inquiry* 407 (1977); McIntyre, "The Essential Contestability of Some Social Concepts," 84 *Ethics* 1 (1973). Also useful is C. Stevenson, "Persuasive Definitions," in *Facts and Values* 32 (1963).

120. R. Dworkin, *Taking Rights Seriously* 103.

121. Gallie, "Essentially Contested Concepts" 178–79.

122. Ibid., pp. 176–86. Munzer and Nickel are cautious about taking up the question of the ultimate validity of the concept/conception distinction and presumably are equally cautious about Gallie's original notion of essentially contested concepts. Munzer and Nickel, "Does the Constitution Mean What It Always Meant?" 1039 n. 46.

123. Gallie, "Essentially Contested Concepts" 176–79.

124. The standard of being unattainable is important, although neglected by Gallie, for if the exemplar were attainable there would be little to contest. The question would only be whether one had attained identity in all respects with the exemplar, in which case the concept would apply—or had not, in which case the concept would not apply. But if the exemplar is unattainable, then we can argue about which features are necessary in order for the concept to apply.

125. L. Wittgenstein, *Philosophical Investigations* §§ 65–72 (G. Anscombe, trans.; 3d ed. 1958). Wittgenstein's famous example is that of games. Ibid. § 66.

126. Ibid.

127. See G. Pitcher, *The Philosophy of Wittgenstein* 215–27 (1964); Chandler, "Three Types of Classes," 3 *Am. Phil. Q.* 77 (1966). Hart has claimed that all legal terms could fit into the core and fringe characterization. Hart, "Scandinavian Realism," 1959 *Cambridge L. J.* 239–40. This seems mistaken, however, because it ignores the existence of terms, such as family-resemblance terms, that do not have a single core.

128. R. Dworkin, *Taking Rights Seriously* 136 n.l.

129. See note 30 sup.

130. See, e.g., Baker, "Scope of the First Amendment Freedom of Speech," 25 *UCLA L. Rev.* 964 (1978). The focus is similar in Richards, "Free Speech and Obscenity Law: Toward a Moral Theory of the First Amendment," 123 *U. Pa. L. Rev.* 45 (1974).

131. Most of the existing literature is in the philosophy of science, although the point has much more universal application. See generally P. Achinstein, *Concepts of Science* 157–201 (1968); N. Hanson, *Patterns of Discovery* (1958); C. Hempel, *Philosophy of Natural Science* 75 (1966); G. Ryle, *Dilemmas* 90–91 (1956). Philosophers of science refer to theory-ladenness in reference both to terms of this type and to observation (see note 91 sup. and accompanying text), but it is important to keep the two ideas distinct.

132. For a discussion of the theories to which these terms refer, see generally P. Achinstein, *Concepts of Science* 180–83; N. Hanson, *Patterns* 60.

133. See notes 27–65 and accompanying text sup.

134. See notes 46–49 and accompanying text sup.

135. P. Jones, *Philosophy and the Novel* 182. See also S. Barker, *The Elements of Logic* 7 (3d ed. 1980). The notion of commitment in this sense is central in the writings of John Searle. See J. Searle, *Speech Acts*. For an interesting application, see Finnis, "Scepticism, Self-Refutation, and the Good of Truth," in *Law, Morality, and Society: Essays in Honour of H.L.A. Hart* 247 (P. Hacker and J. Raz, eds. 1977).

136. "*Explication*, when not simply a synonym for 'explanation,' is the process whereby a hitherto imprecise notion is given a formal definition, and so made suitable for use in formal work. The definition does not claim to be synonymous with the original notion, since it is avowedly making it more precise." A. Lacey, *A Dictionary of Philosophy* 66 (1976). The idea of explication is usually attributed to Carnap. R. Carnap, *Meaning and Necessity* 7–8

(2d ed. 1956). See also W. Quine, *Word and Object* 258–59. I am using "explication" in a slightly looser sense. We explicate when we work out a theory, and when we explicate we put something in, rather than just pulling something out.

137. See Hesse, "Theory and Value in the Social Sciences," in *Action and Interpretation* 1–2 (C. Hookway and P. Pettit, eds. 1978). See also P. Feyerabend, *Against Method* 66 (1975). Whether there is or can be a value-free or theory-free observation language has been one of the perennial problems in the philosophy of science.

138. See G. Anscombe and P. Geach, *Three Philosophers* 5–63 (1961).

139. See J. Hospers, *An Introduction to Philosophical Analysis* 184–86.

140. "[O]ne must always specify the theory with respect to which a given term is or is not 'theory-laden' " (P. Achinstein, *Concepts of Science* 183). Although we often talk, especially in the context of constitutional theory, about vague or general terms, it is important to remember that vagueness is relative as well, and the degree of vagueness will depend on the particular context in which a term is used and the particular purposes for which it would or would not be vague. See I. Scheffler, *Beyond the Letter: A Philosophical Inquiry into Ambiguity, Vagueness and Metaphor in Language* 49–50 (1979).

141. This is at the heart of the assertion that scientific theories can be falsified, but not verified. K. Popper, *Conjectures and Refutations* (1963); K. Popper, *The Logic of Scientific Discovery* (1959).

142. In one sense, of course, the more we know of what a term does not mean, the more we know of what it *does* mean. But the point is that our ability to exclude some possibilities is relatively independent of how many possibilities remain.

143. One might point out in response that I *do* know what "shirt collar" means, and that is all I need to know that it is different from the theory of relativity. But I could make the same assertion about knowing that there is a difference between the theory of relativity and the Rule in Shelley's Case, although pace Professor Michelman, I could no more tell you what the Rule in Shelley's Case is than I could tell you what the theory of relativity is.

144. H. Kelsen, *Pure Theory of Law*, p. 245.

145. See Tinker v. Des Moines Indep. Community School Dist., 393 U.S. 503 (1969).

146. See Schauer, "Speech and 'Speech' " 906–7; Schauer, "Categories and the First Amendment: A Play in Three Acts," 34 *Vand. L. Rev.* 265 (1981).

147. The Court's Eleventh Amendment doctrine represents perhaps the most direct repudiation of plain language to be found anywhere in constitutional law. See Monaco v. Mississippi, 292 U.S. 313 (1934); Hans v. Louisiana, 134 U.S. 1 (1890).

148. For this point and the examples, I am indebted to Philip Devine.

149. W. Quine, *Word and Object* 3. Neurath used the metaphor to illustrate the progress of science.

150. This seems to be part of the thrust of Munzer and Nickel's "ancestral relation" ("Does the Constitution Mean What It Always Meant?" 1054). Although the premises and conclusions are different, there are important parallels with the dialectic process described by Michael Perry ("Noninterpretive Review in Human Rights Cases: A Functional Justification," 56 *N.Y.U. L. Rev.* 278 (1981)). See also Jones, "The Brooding Omnipresence of Constitutional Law," 4 *Vt. L. Rev.* 1 (1979); Monaghan, "Professor Jones and the Constitution," 4 *Vt. L. Rev.* 87 (1979); Monaghan, "Taking Supreme Court Opinions Seriously," 39 *Md. L. Rev.* 1 (1979).

151. The statement in the text is, to some extent, true even for "intentionalist" theories (see Rader, "Fact, Theory") but is even more true for "nonintentionalist" theories. See Fish, "Facts and Fictions: A Reply to Ralph Rader," 1 *Critical Inquiry* 883 (1975). See also note 58 sup.

152. See text accompanying notes 75–90 sup.

153. I draw the term "clause-bound" from J. H. Ely, *Democracy and Distrust*. Ely uses the term to refer to interpretation that views constitutional provisions as (*a*) self-contained units and (*b*) capable of interpretation on the basis of the language and the legislative histo-

ry alone (ibid., pp. 12–13). Ely's theory substitutes his view of the underlying theme of the entire document (which he gets from the document itself) for both (*a*) and (*b*). I describe my suggestions as horizontally clause-bound because I accept (*a*) more or less, but reject (*b*). Underlying my idea is the assumption that if we stick moderately close to (*a*) we can reject (*b*) without suffering most of the dangers of noninterpretivism that Ely properly identified.

154. See text accompanying note 148 sup.

155. See text accompanying notes 153–54 sup.

156. See note 75 and accompanying text sup.

157. See note 27 sup.

158. See, e.g., Van Alstyne, "The Fourteenth Amendment, The 'Right' to Vote, and the Understanding of the Thirty-Ninth Congress," 1965 *Sup. Ct. Rev.* 33.

159. One reason that literal and historical approaches tend to be conjoined (see sup. note 50), is that the meaning of words changes over time. Without the historical supplement, most literal approaches would be far less concrete than the literalist usually desires. Although I cannot explore the issue fully here, I am inclined to argue that language change is one of the conventions accepted by a user of language, especially one who puts language into an authoritative text. This argument touches more deeply on the very nature of law than is appropriate here.

160. "Historically oriented critics seem curiously reluctant to follow the lead of most historians, who expect to reinterpret the past and its works for each generation." P. Jones, *Philosophy and the Novel* 185. See generally Passmore, "The Objectivity of History," in *The Philosophy of History* 145 (P. Gardiner, ed. 1974).

161. "[C]ertainty generally is illusion, and repose is not the destiny of mankind." Holmes, "The Path of Law," 10 *Harv. L. Rev.* 466 (1897). See also J. Frank, *Law and the Modern Mind* (1930).

162. Ibid.

Law as Literature

1. C. Langdell, *A Selection of Cases on the Law of Contracts* vii (2d ed. 1879), quoted in Stevens, "Two Cheers for 1870: The American Law School," in 5 *Perspectives in American History* 435–36 (1971).

2. Address by Christopher Langdell, Harvard Law School Association Meeting (5 November, 1886), quoted in Stevens, "Two Cheers," 436 n. 50.

3. See H.L.A. Hart, *The Concept of Law* (1961).

4. Marbury v. Madison, 5 U.S. (1 Cranch) 137, 178 (1803).

5. Idem at 175–76 (emphasis added). Marshall goes on to say, "To what purpose are powers limited, and to what purpose is that limitation committed to writing, if these limits may, at any time, be passed by those intended to be restrained?" (idem). Marshall, however, undercut (dare one say "deconstructed"?) his argument in Marbury when he decided McCulloch v. Maryland, 17 U.S. (4 Wheat.) 316 (1819). So far are words from having obvious meanings that Marshall reminds us that "[s]uch is the character of human language, that no word conveys to the mind, in all situations, one single definite idea; and nothing is more common than to use words in a figurative sense" (idem at 414). And the "written-ness" of the Constitution becomes a far more complicated issue once one supplements the textualism of Marbury with the "texturalism" of McCulloch: "There is no express provision for the case, but the claim has been sustained on a principle which so entirely pervades the constitution, is so intermixed with the materials which compose it, so interwoven with its web, so blended with its texture, as to be incapable of being separated from it without rendering it into shreds" (idem at 426). See Levinson "Judicial Review and the Problem of the Comprehensible Constitution" (Book Review), 59 *Texas L. Rev.* 397–98 (1981). Indeed, the very multiplicity (if not promiscuity) of Marshall's approaches to constitutional interpretation (see P. Brest and S. Levinson, *Process of Constitutional Decisionmaking* 114 (2d ed.

1982)), calls into question whether interpretation for Marshall (or for anyone else) ever transcended a desire to achieve specific political results.

6. *New York Times*, 3 March, 1982 p. A18, col. 4 (emphasis added); see also Broder, "Assault on Constitution," *Dallas Times Herald*, 17 March, 1982 p. A29.

7. I became especially aware of this difference in modes of discourse during a sojourn in Great Britain in the fall of 1979, when the Thatcher government put before Parliament several bills regarding rights of non-native-born Englishpersons that struck me (and many others) as racist in the extreme. Many letter writers pointed out the evils of the bills, but none claimed that the proposals violated the English constitution, since, of course, that notion—in its Marbury sense—makes no sense within the English language. The description of Great Britain and the United States as two countries separated by a common language never seemed more apt, for the two countries speak two entirely different constitutional languages, even if the words used sometimes seem deceptively similar.

8. See Levinson, "Judicial Review" 418.

9. J. Culler *Structuralist Poetics* 134 (1975).

10. R. Barthes, *Writing Degree Zero* 19–20 (A. Lavers and C. Smith, trans. 1978).

11. *Oxford English Dictionary* s.v. "sentimental."

12. Abrams, "How to Do Things with Texts," 45 *Partisan Rev.* 566 (1979). I owe my familiarity with this comment to Richard Rorty. See R. Rorty, "Nineteenth-Century Idealism and Twentieth-Century Textualism," in *Consequences of Pragmatism* 139 (1982), reprinted from 64 *Monist* 155 (1981).

13. The best short treatment of these disputes is Culler, "Issues in Contemporary American Critical Debate," in *American Criticism in the Poststructuralist Age* 1–18 (I. Konigsberg, ed. 1981). A very illuminating book-length study is F. Lentricchia, *After the New Criticism* (1980). The commonality of some of the problems of law and literary analysis is touched on in Abraham, "Three Fallacies of Interpretation: A Comment on Precedent and Judicial Decision," 23 *Ariz. L. Rev.* 771 (1981); Abraham, "Statutory Interpretation and Literary Theory: Some Common Concerns of an Unlikely Pair," 32 *Rutgers L. Rev.* 676 (1980), reprinted in this volume; Michaels, Against Formalism: The Autonomous Text in Legal and Literary Interpretation," 1 *Poetics Today* 23 (1979), reprinted with minor changes as Michaels, "Against Formalism: Chickens and Rocks," in *The State of the Language* 410 (1980), reprinted in this volume; and Yeazell, "Convention, Fiction, and Law," 13 *New Literary Hist.* 89 (1981).

14. M. Robertson, "Language as Hero in Post-Modern Formalist Fiction" 180 (1979) (Ph.D. diss., University of Wisconsin). I am greatly indebted to this thesis (and its author) for many of the ideas contained in this essay.

15. Brest, "The Misconceived Quest for the Original Understanding," 60 *B.U.L. Rev.* 234 (1980), reprinted above. Brest, of course, is not unique in his perception. See, e.g., Sandalow, "Judicial Protection of Minorities," 75 *Mich. L. Rev.* 1183 (1977) ("[T]he evolving content of constitutional law is not controlled, or even significantly guided, by the Constitution, understood as an historical document"). And Michael Perry emphasizes that "[v]irtually all of modern constitutional decision-making by the [Supreme] Court—at least that part of it pertaining to questions of 'human rights,' [i.e., the rights individuals have, or ought to have, against government] . . . must be understood as a species of policymaking, in which the Court decides, ultimately without reference to any value judgment constitutionalized by the framers, which values among competing values shall prevail and how those values shall be implemented" (*The Constitution, The Courts, and Human Rights* 2 (1982)). Perry tries to defend this policy-making role in his book.

16. One certainly does not have to be an academic in order to repudiate one or another of these approaches. See, for example, Justice Traynor's opinion in Pacific Gas & Elec. Co. v. G.W. Thomas Drayage & Ry. Co., 442 P.2d 641 (1968), concerning the application of the parol evidence rule. Traynor dismisses "a judicial belief in the possibility of perfect verbal expression" as "a remnant of a primitive faith in the inherent potency and inherent meaning of words" (idem at 643–44).

If words had absolute and constant references, it might be possible to discover contractual intention in the words themselves and in the manner in which they were arranged. Words, however, do not have absolute and constant referents . . . . The meaning of particular words or groups of words varies with the ". . . verbal context and surrounding circumstances and purposes in view of the linguistic education and experience of their users and their hearers or readers (not excluding judges) . . . . A word has no meaning apart from these factors; much less does it have an objective meaning, one true meaning." [idem. at 644–45, quoting Corbin, "The Interpretation of Words and the Parol Evidence Rule," 50 *Cornell L.Q.* 187 (1965)].

It is clear that the parol evidence rule is philosophically indefensible. See also Michaels, "Against Formalism."

Traynor does, however, seem to retain faith in the ability to ascertain satisfactorily the context of any given speech act. As we become ever more aware, though, of the myriad difficulties standing in the way of contextual understanding (see, e.g., C. Geertz, *The Interpretation of Cultures* (1973)), the threat of chaos looms ever larger. See the remarkable review by Gordon Wood, "Star-Spangled History," *New York Review of Books*, 12 August, 1982, pp. 4–9, for a thoroughgoing attack on the possibility of continuing to write traditional narrative history, which relies for its cogency on the ability to embed events (and words) within a specific linear story. To the extent that cases are themselves narrative structures, there is disturbing relevance to the dilemma sketched by Wood. See also note 58 inf.

It is not surprising that judges are ultimately limited in their skepticisms, at least so long as they continue to engage in their responsible tasks of judging. Academics, being irresponsible (and often socially marginal), are freer to follow ideas out to their most destructive limits.

17. Monaghan, "Our Perfect Constitution," 56 *N.Y.U.L. Rev.* 382 (1981). Like Raoul Berger (see R. Berger, *Government by Judiciary* 412–13 (1977)), Monaghan does not really counsel turning back the clock by instantly overruling all putatively misdecided cases. Both offer what might uncharitably be regarded as an "adverse possession" approach to constitutional interpretation, whereby precedents that should at one time have been properly overruled (as wrongly decided) become entitled to recognition as authoritative after the passage of enough time and after the citizenry has come to rely on them. Neither offers the slightest guidance for recognizing the terms of such possession. To be fair, no other theorist of precedent does any better. Perhaps the central difference between law and literature is the lack in the latter of the notion of stare decisis.

18. See Cover, Book Review, *New Republic*, 14 January, 1978 p. 26 (reviewing R. Berger, *Government by Judiciary* (1977)). See also M. Perry, *The Constitution* 75 ("I prefer to let the framers sleep. Just as the framers, in their day, judged by their lights, so must we, in our day, judge by ours").

19. See Brest, "Misconceived Quest" 214–15.

20. See E. Hirsch, *Validty in Interpretation* 123 and n.53 (1967); see also E. Hirsch, *The Aims of Interpretation* 1–13 (1976).

21. R. Rorty, "Nineteenth-Centruy Idealism" 152.

22. Ibid., pp. 151–52.

23. Ibid., p. 152 (emphasis in original).

24. See Levinson, "Judicial Review," for an extended review of J. Ely, *Democracy and Distrust* (1980).

25. Fleming, "A Critique of John Hart Ely's Quest for the Ultimate Constitutional Interpretivism of Representative Democracy" (Book Review), 80 *Mich. L. Rev.* 634 (1982).

26. See C. Black, *Structure and Relationship in Constitutional Law* (1969).

27. R. Rorty, "Ninteenth-Century Idealism" 152 (emphasis in original).

28. S. Fish, *Is There a Text in This Class?* 327 (1980); cf. Marcel Duchamp's statement, "It is the Observers who make the pictures," quoted in M. Caws, *The Eye in the Text: Essays on Perception, Mannerist to Modern* 135 (1981). See generally the valuable anthologies *Reader-Response Criticism: From Formalism to Post-Structuralism* (J. Thompkins, ed. 1980); *The Reader*

in the Text: Essays on Audience and Interpretation (S. Suleiman and I. Crosman, eds. 1980). An excellent recent study is S. Mailloux, *Interpretive Conventions: The Reader in the Study of American Fiction* (1982).

29. S. Fish, *Is There a Text?* 43. For vigorous criticism of Fish and other radical literary critics, see Crews, "Criticism without Constraint," *Commentary*, January 1982, p. 65.

30. S. Fish, *Is There a Text?* 94. Professor Graff argues that the depiction of the controversy itself has ideological implications. Fish's statement might well be assessed against what Graff calls a "rhetorical scorecard":

Bad	Good
representation	creation
text as determinate object	text as open, indeterminate "invitation"
boundaries and constraints	voyages into the unforeseen
docility, habit	risk
truth as correspondence	truth as invention, fiction
meaning as "product"	meaning as "process"

G. Graff, *Literature against Itself: Literary Ideas in Modern Society* 23 (1979).

31. S. Fish, *Is There a Text?* 94. It occurs to me, as I dutifully footnote Fish's statement, that the act of footnoting is itself a bow toward the notion of objective knowledge, for I am purporting, even as I describe Fish's reader-response theories, to be giving you (the reader) an "accurate" rendition of those theories. Indeed, the point of footnotes, especially if "cite-checked" by law review editors, is to suggest that the proof of my accuracy is that you would arrive at the same conclusions by reading the same material.

This generates an obvious, albeit important, paradox, one only made worse because I of course also expect you to grasp "my" argument and to be able to state it correctly (as Graff basically does), even if you (like Graff) reject it. I suppose, therefore, that I can be accused of being one of those "newreaders" who introduce their "own interpretive strategy when reading someone else's text, but tacitly rely[ing] on communal norms when undertaking to communicate the methods and results of [their] interpretations to [their] own readers" (ibid., p. 303 (quoting Abrams, "How to Do Things with Texts" 587)). A similar point is made in Hirsch's review of H. Gadamer, *Wahrheit und Methode* (1960), reprinted in E. Hirsch, *Validity in Interpretation* 245 (1967); see also Graff's "Politics, Language, Deconstruction, Lies, and the Reflexive Fallacy: A Rejoinder to W.J.T. Mitchell," *Salmagundi*, Winter-Spring 1980, p. 78.

Professor Graff is correct in his own contribution to this Symposium when he notes that I do on occasion use the word "correct" to refer to an interpretation (see Graff, *"Keep off the Grass, Drop Dead* and Other Indeterminacies: A Response to Sanford Levinson," in this volume), so that I cannot be the arch-indeterminist that I sometimes appear to be. I am not sure how far apart he and I actually are, for there is relatively little in his response that I genuinely disagree with. I do agree, as does Fish for that matter, that our ordinary speech acts are full of meanings instantly grasped by listeners, given the standard contexts in which they occur. I would further agree that the Constitution is not entirely incomprehensible, that, e.g., the president must take office on 20 January (U.S. Const. amend. XX, § 1). There are circumstances in which this might be problematic (what if Congress changed the calendar year?), but it would be perverse to say that the ordinary reader would not be expected to give a single response to the question, When does a newly elected president take office? (Nor do I disagree with the Fifth Circuit that it was "quite incredible" to argue that ".82165" is not the equivalent of "82.165%." Oil & Gas Futures, Inc. of Texas v. Andrus, 610 F.2d 287, 288 (5th Cir. 1980), *reversing* [!] an unreported decision by the Hornorable Finis E. Cowan of the United States District Court for the Southern District of Texas. Yet (presumably) competent lawyers and a (presumably) competent judge did not find even this proposition compelling.)

The problem, of course, is that constitutional litigation almost never concerns such clauses. Professor Graff recognizes the multiplicity of ambiguity that *can*, even if not *must*, be present in literary or legal texts. He seems to chide me for emphasizing power, rather than authority, in resolving conflicting interpretations, but this seems to be the principal explanation for why one legal result, rather than its equally plausible (indeed, on occasion more plausible) alternative, is imposed on the parties. Even here, I will quickly concede that courts and other constitutional interpreters operate within constraints. That is the importance of Fish's own distinction between "on-the-wall" and "off-the-wall" arguments; but the point is that whatever constraints exist are not constant over time.

Finally, I agree with Professor Graff that the alternative to determinacy (certainty) is not an anything-goes indeterminacy. However, especially from the perspective of the losers in a necessarily coercive legal system, a court decision that remains even within the ambit of "on-the-wall" arguments may appear to be arbitrary (though not "whimsical"), given the presence of other available arguments that would have generated more palatable results.

32. See Levinson, "The Democratic Faith of Felix Frankfurter," 25 *Stan L. Rev.* 434 (1972) (author's student Note). No single citation, of course, can support the assertion that *disinterested* was Frankfurter's favorite word, but I challenge any reader of Frankfurter's prose to name a more oft-used and emotionally charged word in his vocabulary. (Proper nouns like Holmes or the Harvard Law School do not count.)

33. S. Fish, *Is There a Text?* 94. *Personal*, incidentally, is a tricky word in this context, for Fish, like most structuralists and poststructuralists, rejects the meaningfulness of genuinely individualistic idiosyncracies, and instead emphasizes the inevitable membership of such "individuals" in communities of shared discourses which, indeed, ultimately supply any person's own sense of self. Ibid., pp. 338–55.

34. See, e.g., H. Bloom, *A Map of Misreading* (1975).

35. F. Nietzsche, *On the Genealogy of Morals* 77 (W. Kaufmann, trans. 1967) (emphasis in original).

36. S. Fish, *Is There a Text?* 338–71.

37. See R. Dworkin, *Taking Rights Seriously* 279–90 (1977); Levinson, "Taking Law Seriously: Reflections on 'Thinking Like a Lawyer,' " Book Review, 30 *Stan. L. Rev.* 1071 (1978) (reviewing Dworkin).

38. See T. Kuhn, *The Structure of Scientific Revolutions* (2d ed. 1970).

39. S. Fish, *Is There a Text?* 356–57.

40. For the importance of the "mirroring" image, see R. Rorty, *Philosophy and the Mirror of Nature* (1979). Rorty's basic mission is the criticism of the possibility of mirroring.

41. R. Rorty, "Nineteenth-Century Idealism" 151.

42. E. Hirsch, *The Aims of Interpretation* 20 (1976).

43. Cover, Book Review 27.

44. See P. Bobbitt, *Constitutional Fate* (1982), for an extraordinarily subtle survey of various modes of constitutional argumentation. A shorter version of the book was published as Bobbitt, "Constitutional Fate," 58 *Texas L. Rev.* 695 (1981), and excerpts from the book are reprinted below.

45. See R. Rorty, *Mirror of Nature* 389.

46. This seems to be the approach taken by some of the most fruitful practitioners of "critical legal studies." See, e.g., M. Horwitz, *The Transformation of American Law, 1780–1860* (1977); M. Tushnet, *The American Law of Slavery 1810–1860* (1981).

47. Dred Scott v. Sandford, 60 U.S. (19 How.) 393 (1856).

48. 198 U.S. 45 (1905). There is obviously not space here to consider in depth the complexity of our responses to these two cases. One might begin, though, by asking whether Taney's or Peckham's arguments in the two cases are really "off-the-wall" in terms of conventions of American legal discourse; it seems clear that the answer is no.

49. J. Culler, *Structuralist Poetics* 113–238.

50. Indeed, it is not even clear that material emanating from a court can, except by stipulation, by described as "legal writing." See, e.g., Flood v. Kuhn, 407 U.S. 258, 260–64 (1972) (Justice Blackmun's ode to baseball).

51. S. Fish, *Is There a Text?* 322. One notes again the linkage between Fish and

Duchamp, one of whose most famous artistic achievements was the transformation of a urinal into art by the mere act of placing it in a museum. We might have our individual favorite candidates for transforming dubious arguments into law through the aegis of placing them in a judicial opinion.

Indeed, yet further theoretical questions are suggested by the text of the paragraph to which this footnote is addressed. Consider, for example, the problem of parody, an extraordinarily sophisticated literary construction which depends for its force on the competence of the reader to know the "proper" or "conventional" style that serves as the background to the foreground of the parody itself. See J. Culler, *Structuralist Poetics* 152–54; Culler, "Convention and Meaning: Derrida and Austin," 13 *New Literary Hist.* 15, 22 (1981). The 15 May 1978 issue of the *New Yorker* featured, among its offerings, "Supreme Court Roundup," one example of which is the report of a First Amendment decision in which "the Court ruled unanimously in favor of a twelve-year-old plaintiff who sought damages on account of being denied the chance to audition" for a movie. "The Court's opinion, written by Chief Justice Happ, argued that exclusion of the little girl was 'rotten, beastly, a crying shame—really makes the Court sick.' The case was not decided, as had been expected, on the ground of sex discrimination; rather, the Justices invoked the First Amendment's guarantee of freedom of expression. The court thus affirmed for the first time the constitutional right to a screen test" (Geng, "Supreme Court Roundup," *New Yorker* 15 May 1978, p. 31) This is clearly parody, right? But then what is the genre of, say, Justice Douglas's opinion for the majority in Griswold v. Connecticut, 381 U.S. 479 (1965) ("the specific guarantees in the Bill of Rights have penumbras, formed by emanations from those guarantees that help give them life and substance"), or of Justice Brennan's description of "the give-and-take negotiation common in plea bargaining between the prosecution and the defense, which arguably possess relatively equal bargaining power," Parker v. North Carolina, 397 U.S. 790, 809 (1970), quoted approvingly in Bordenkircher v. Hayes, 434 U.S. 357, 362 (1978). And consider Justice Stevens's remark in Young v. American Mini Theatres, 427 U.S. 50 (1976), that "few of us would march our sons and daughters off to war to preserve the citizen's right to see 'Specified Sexual Activities' exhibited in the theaters of our choice" (idem at 70). Justice Stevens's "marching-off-to-war" standard garnered only three additional votes; perhaps the replacement of the dissenting Justice Stewart by Justice O'Connor will enable it to receive the fifth vote necessary to enshrine it in our constitutional litany as a certifiably serious approach to constitutional analysis.

One of the general problems facing so-called postmodernist writers is the impossibility of satirizing patterns of ordinary life and talk which themselves are bizarre. See, e.g., the work of Donald Barthelme. Or, as Calvin Trillin has put it, "Someone who writes what has been officially labeled a 'humor column' about the American scene lives in constant danger of being blindsided by the truth" (*Uncivil Liberties* 2 (1982)). One sometimes wonders about the genre status not only of certain judicial opinions, but also of scholarly articles purporting to analyze them. See, e.g., Michelman, "States' Rights and States' Roles: Permutations of 'Sovereignty' in *National League of Cities* v. *Usery*," 86 *Yale L.J.* 1165 (1977) (arguing that Justice Rehnquist's majority opinion requires states to provide essential services to their citizens); Tribe, "Unraveling *National League of Cities*," 90 *Harv. L. Rev.* 1065 (1977). For general reviews of the status of so-called constitutional scholarship, see Tushnet, "Legal Scholarship: Its Causes and Cures," 90 *Yale L.J.* 1205 (1981); "Tushnet, Truth, Justice, and the American Way: An Interpretation of Public Law Scholarship in the Seventies," 57 *Texas L. Rev.* 1307 (1979).

Perhaps the best response to the issues raised in this footnote is to say that one should have a good sense of humor if teaching constitutional law these days, but this response works, of course, only if one has attained enough ironic distance so as not to care about the implications for living beings of the material analyzed.

52. Indeed, is *this* essay legal writing? If it is not, then why was it published in the *Texas Law Review*?

53. See, e.g., J. Culler, *Structuralist Poetics* 258; see also J. Culler, *The Pursuit of Signs: Semiotics, Literature, Deconstruction* 210 (1981) ("Literary Theory in the Graduate Program").

54. See text accompanying note 9.

55. For descriptions of the MacCabe controversy, see "Unquiet Flow the Dons," *News-*

week, 16 February 1981, pp. 95–96; "Controversy at Cambridge," *Times Literary Supplement*, 30 January 1981, 112. The *TLS* also published an interesting symposium sparked by the MacCabe flap, "Modern Literary Theory: Its Place in Teaching," *Times Literary Supplement*, 6 February 1981, p. 135, with contributions by George Steiner, John Bayley, Denis Donoghue, C.J.E. Ball, L.C. Knights, Malcolm Bowie, Malcolm Bradbury, and Roger Scruton.

56. For all of the alleged emphasis on cases in American legal education, there is little systematic attention paid to what, beyond agreement with the teacher's own emphasis, constitutes "legal competence." Perhaps the most notorious example of the lack of reflection concerning case reading is the bland assumption transmitted to generations of law students that cases can be "briefed." Exactly how it is that one distills "essence of case" from the full opinion, or why it was that the writer thought it necessary to write as fully as he or she did, is not usually brought to the student's attention.

57. See Fiss and Krauthammer, "The Rehnquist Court," *New Republic*, 10 March 1982, p. 14.

58. See Marbury v. Madison, 5 U.S. (1 Cranch) 137 (1803) (presentation and construction of § 13 of the Judiciary Act of 1789).

59. See McCulloch v. Maryland, 17 U.S. (4 Wheat.) 316 (1819) (invocation of American nationalism).

60. M. Farrand, 1 *Records of the Federal Convention* 262 (1937) (speech of 16 June 1787, Yates transcription).

61. *The Federalist* no. 40, 265–66 (J. Madison) (J. Cooke, ed. 1961) (emphasis in original). Compare Madison's argument with Lincoln's defense of his policy of military arrests and suspension of habeas corpus:

> The constitution contemplates the question as likely to occur for decision, but it does not expressly declare who is to decide it. By necessary implication, when Rebellion or Invasion comes, the decision is to be made, from time to time; and I think the man whom, for the time, the people have, under the constitution, made the commander-in-chief, of their Army and Navy, is the man who holds the power, and bears the responsibility of making it. If he uses the power justly, the same people will probably justify him; if he abuses it, he is in their hands, to be dealt with by all the modes they have reserved to themselves in the constitution. [*The Political Thought of Abraham Lincoln* 262 (R. Current, ed. 1967)]

There is a similarity between these arguments and the one made by Richard Nixon in his interview with David Frost:

> Mr. Frost: So what in a sense you're saying is that there are certain situations . . . where the President can decide that it's in the best interests of the nation or something, and do something illegal.
> Mr. Nixon: Well, when the President does it, that means that it is not illegal.
> Mr. Frost: By definition.
> Mr. Nixon: Exactly. Exactly. If the President, for example, approves something because of the national security, or in this case because of a threat to internal peace and order of significant magnitude, then the President's decision in that instance is one that enables those who carry it out, to carry it out without violating a law. Otherwise they're in an impossible position.

Transcript of Frost-Nixon Interview, *New York Times*, 20 May 1977 p. A16, col. 5.

Paradoxically, it may be that what most differentiates Nixon from the founders and Lincoln, beyond obvious differences in their breadth of vision, is his unwillingness to submit his deeds to the populace for their approbation. There is a public quality to the acts of Marshall and the others that is wholly lacking in those of Nixon, as revealed by the very term cover-up.

62. Since writing the statement in the text, I have benefited from an important article by Knapp and Michaels, "Against Theory," 8 *Critical Inquiry* 723 (1982), which attacks similar arguments in S. Fish, *Is There a Text?* 367–69. Briefly, the authors argue that a statement like "There are as many plausible readings of the United States Constitution as there are versions of *Hamlet*" implies knowledge about the underlying nature of reality, whereas the general argument of Fish (and of this essay) is that we can never have confidence that we

have such knowledge. Furthermore, they note that neither Fish nor any other critic, whether literary or legal, could actually live by such a view, since stands are constantly taken in the confidence, merited or not, that one's own views are indeed better than the alternatives. See Knapp and Michaels, ibid., pp. 738–41. Indeed, I have written that Buckley v. Valeo, 424 U.S. 1 (1976), is "perhaps the worst decision . . . in the past forty years" (Levinson, "Judicial Review" 415). Such an assertion clearly entails at least a momentary rejection of the view that all constitutional approaches are equal, though I remain troubled as to how one could ever genuinely establish the superiority of any given constitutional theory.

Professor Fish himself, in his reply to this essay, emphasizes the degree to which we make judgments regardless of (some of) the implications of the antirealist philosophy he endorses, though I do not know if he would concede the legitimacy of Knapp and Michaels's general argument. In any event, "Against Theory" promises to provoke an important debate among literary theorists which will have obvious relevance for legal analysts. See also note 85 inf. (I am grateful to Gerald Graff and Steven Mailloux for calling my attention to the Knapp and Michaels essay and for emphasizing its implications for the argument of this essay.)

Professor Bobbitt's inquiry, *Constitutional Fate*, is also highly relevant to the question of the intersection of theory and practice, since he finds our theories in our practices, rather than *underlying* them as a foundation.

One might, incidentally, be tempted to avoid the whole set of dilemmas raised in this chapter by taking refuge in a simple "the Constitution is what the Court says it is" argument. Putting aside the usual responses to this argument (Who or what authorizes the Court to say what the Constitution is?), there is an equally fundamental problem in relying on judicial precedent. Even if we ignore the fact that the Court itself does not feel bound by its own precedents, so that it regularly overturns them, there remains the question of how one figures out what a precedent means, and that of course brings us quickly back to the central problem of this chapter. See, for example, Deutsch, "Harvard's View of the Supreme Court: A Response," 57 *Texas L. Rev.* 1445 (1979), which emphasizes "that our society is forced to live with an awareness of the *essentially uncertain nature* of the precedent contained in a judicial opinion" (p. 1454; emphasis added). Thus Deutsch argues that "[t]he reading of a holding as not only unintended," but as something contrary to the intent of the opinion's author, is a permissible one, since a later Court might so construe the earlier holding, and the meaning of a precedent is what is held by that later Court" (ibid., p. 1453).

63. Fiss, "Objectivity and Interpretation," 34 *Stan. L. Rev.* 739 (1982).

64. Ibid., p. 763.

65. Fiss, "The Supreme Court, 1978 Term—Foreword: The Forms of Justice," 93 *Harv. L. Rev.* 1 (1979).

66. Ibid., p. 51.

67. Ibid., p. 57.

68. Ibid., p. 58. (emphasis added).

69. Fiss, "Objectivity and Interpretation" 755.

70. See Levinson, "Taking Law Seriously."

71. Fiss, "Objectivity and Interpretation" 743.

72. Ibid., p. 753. For an example of that form, see Monaghan, "Our Perfect Constitution."

73. See Brest, "Misconceived Quest."

74. Fiss, "Objectivity and Interpretation" 753.

75. Ibid., p. 754.

76. Ibid.

77. Ibid., p. 755.

78. Ibid., p. 744.

79. Ibid.

80. Ibid., p. 745.

81. Ibid.

82. Indeed, the full title of Fish's book is *Is There a Text in This Class? The Authority of Interpretive Communities*.

83. See T. Kuhn, *The Essential Tension: Selected Studies in Scientific Tradition and Change* (1977); T. Kuhn, *Structure of Scientific Revolutions*.

84. Rorty, too, draws on Kuhn as an ally in his attack on the meaningfulness of seeking conceptions that "mirror nature." See R. Rorty, *Mirror of Nature* 322–42.

85. In fairness to Fiss, I should note that he does not specifically endorse a correspondence theory of truth and, indeed, he specifically recognizes the participation of a reader-judge in bestowing meaning upon textual materials. "The idea of objective interpretation accommodates *the creative role of the reader*" ("Objectivity and Interpretation" 744; emphasis added). Yet Fiss's article is replete with the tension generated by the joint embrace of creativity and objectivity.

The implications of Kuhn's thought for resolution of this tension are themselves the subject of an important scholarly debate. To be a critic of Kuhn does not seem to require a commitment to a correspondence (or context-independent) notion of truth, nor, apparently, does being a supporter entail commitment to radical indeterminacy. See e.g., H. Putnam, *Reason, Truth and History* 113–19 (1981) (presenting criticisms of Kuhn within the context of a larger argument criticizing correspondence theories). Nonetheless it is clear that Kuhn has been most warmly embraced by critics of the notion of objectivity (and, beyond that, even of rationality), and that any theory which emphasizes the relevance of interpretive communities must confront the difficult sociological tasks of accounting for their composition and relationship to one another. See Brest, "Interpretation and Interest," 34 *Stan. L. Rev.* 765 (1982) (comments on Fiss). See the Fall 1982 (vol. 9) issue of *Critical Inquiry* dealing with the politics of interpretation.

86. Fiss, "Objectivity and Interpretation" 747.

87. Ibid., p. 755.

88. Levinson, " 'The Constitution' in American Civil Religion," 1979 *Sup. Ct. Rev.* 123, 132.

89. Fiss and Krauthammer, "Rehnquist Court."

90. Ibid., p. 15. I confess myself mystified, incidentally, by what it means to say that "society" (rather than the Court) is or is not prepared to abandon a precedent, since the only relevant evidence we have is the Court's behavior. That behavior may indeed be based on its assessment of what society would tolerate, but it is also possible that a judge's attitude toward a precedent would be based on internal legal considerations, leading to a vote to overturn a (putatively mistaken) precedent even though society generally endorses the extraconstitutional decision.

91. Ibid., p. 16.

92. See, e.g., First Nat'l Bank v. Bellotti, 435 U.S. 765, 823 (1978) (Rehnquist, J., dissenting) (rejecting equal application of First Amendment standards to state and national government).

93. Fiss and Krauthammer discuss Pennhurst State School v. Halderman, 457 U.S. 1 (1981), and National League of Cities v. Usery, 426 U.S. 833 (1976). They also mention Rizzo v. Goode, 423 U.S. 362 (1976), which severely limited the power of federal courts to impose effective remedies on state agencies. In *Rizzo* "a small percentage" of members of the Philadelphia police department had been found by a lower court to have systematically deprived people of their constitutional rights. Council of Organizations on Philadelphia Police Accountability and Responsibility v. Rizzo, 357 F. Supp. 1289, 1318 (E.D. Pa. 1973), *aff'd in part and rev'd in part sub nom.* Goode v. Rizzo, 506 F.2d 542 (3rd Cir. 1974), *rev'd*, 423 U.S. 362 (1976).

94. See National League of Cities v. Usery, 426 U.S. 833, 845–52 (1976) (arguing that

Congress cannot infringe on a state's sovereign power and that imposition of minimum wage laws on municipalities infringes on essential sovereign functions).

95. Fiss and Krauthammer, "Rehnquist Court" 18, 20.

96. See Rehnquist, "The Notion of a Living Constitution," *Texas L. Rev.* 693 (1976).

97. See Brest, "Misconceived Quest."

98. Fiss and Krauthammer, "Rehnquist Court" 20.

99. Ibid.

100. Ibid. But see Benedict, "Preserving Federalism: Reconstruction and the Waite Court," 1978 *Sup. Ct.* Rev. 47–48 (footnotes omitted):

> Historians now recognize that every Reconstruction-era effort to protect the rights of citizens was tempered by the fundamental conviction that federalism required that the day-to-day protection of the citizen had to remain the duty of the States . . . . As to the permanent protections for Americans' rights, despite arguments to the contrary by those modern legal scholars who write in the tradition of a new nationalism, all the evidence of the congressional discussions, the ratification debates, and the public controversy indicates that Republicans intended the States to retain primary jurisdiction over citizens' rights. They attempted to write into the Constitution an obligation that antislavery theorists already believed incumbent on the States: the requirement that they protect all citizens equally in fundamental human rights. They did not intend the national government to replace the States in fulfilling that obligation.

Benedict builds on the important book by Harold Hyman, *A More Perfect Union* (1973).

101. Fiss and Krauthammer, "Rehnquist Court" 20.

102. Brown v. Board of Educ., 347 U.S. 483 (1954).

103. Plessy v. Ferguson, 163 U.S. 537 (1896).

104. Fiss and Krauthammer, "Rehnquist Court" 20 (footnotes added).

105. See text accompanying notes 71–77 sup.

106. Now Judge Bork of the Court of Appeals for the District of Columbia.

107. Now Judge Winter of the Court of Appeals for the Second Circuit.

108. Now Judge Posner of the Court of Appeals for the Seventh Circuit.

109. See Levinson, "Taking Law Seriously" 1083–84, for a critique of Dworkin on this point. See also J. Ely, *Democracy and Distrust* 43–72 (1980), for a comprehensive attack on the "fundamental values" approach that Fiss in fact is defending.

110. B. Hammond *Banks and Politics in America* 120 (1957). See also Paul Bator's reminder that "the Constitution itself contains a multiplicity of various sorts of values, many in tension with each other: process values as well as substantive values, structural and institutional values as well as those embodying individual rights" ("The State Courts and Federal Constitutional Litigation," 22 *Wm. & Mary L. Rev.* 605, 633 (1981)). Indeed, Professor Bator argues eloquently for the desirability of a role for state court participation in constitutional adjudication precisely in terms of the ability of state judges to recognize values that federal judges are prone to overlook. In contrast to an argument which assumes "that the Constitution contains only one or two *sorts* of values: typically, those which protect the individual from the power of the state, and those which assure the superiority of federal to state law," Bator presents a different view: "But the Constitution contains other sorts of values as well. It gives the federal government powers, but also enacts limitations on those powers. *The limitations, too, count as setting forth constitutional values.* Will the federal judge be more sensitive than the state judge in insuring that these values are complied with? Whose institutional 'set' is likely to make one more sensitive to the values underlying the tenth amendment? . . . Why don't these sorts of issues even seem to count?" (ibid., pp. 631–32; emphasis in original). Though I suspect I share more of Fiss's political values than I do those of Professor Bator, I have little hesitation in saying that I think Bator presents a more plausible view of the Constitution. That view, however, offers no guidance as to the dilemmas generated by recognizing the multiplicity (and contradictions) of constitutional values.

Resolving the dialectical tension, of course, is a central dilemma. See, for example, Tushnet, "Darkness on the Edge of Town: The Contributions of John Hart Ely to Constitutional Theory," 89 *Yale L.J.* 1037 (1980), for an argument that value conflict cannot be resolved within the framework of traditional liberal constitutionalism. See also the remarkable article by Frank Easterbrook, "Ways of Criticizing the Court," 95 *Harv. L. Rev.* 802, 811–31 (1982), which demonstrates by the use of social choice theory the extreme unlikelihood (indeed, impossibility, given the most likely empirical conditions) of the existence of a procedure for legal decision-making adequate to generate "definitive" decisions over time by the Supreme Court (let alone by the community at large). Easterbrook's article is a major challenge to those who look to the Supreme Court for clear articulation of basic legal precepts, especially if one accepts the proposition that there are at least three values contending in Hammond's "dialectical arena." Whether or not Easterbrook is accurately described as a "nihilist," his conclusions are in their own way every bit as hopeless as any in Tushnet's writings or the instant essay.

111. Testa v. Katt, 330 U.S. 386, 390 (1947).

112. 1 A. de Tocqueville, *Democracy in America* 290 (Vintage ed. 1945). It should be noted that Tocqueville specifically stressed the tendency of a political question to be "resolved, sooner or later, into a judicial question" (ibid.). For the importance of the emphasis on the judiciary as institutional resolver, see Levinson, "Fidelity to Law and the Assessment of Political Activity," 27 *Stan. L. Rev.* 1190–91 (1975).

113. Fiss, "Objectivity and Interpretation" 763.

114. R. Rorty, "Nineteenth-Century Idealism" 157.

115. Ibid. Indeed, responding to an earlier version of the present essay, Rorty wrote, "I confess that I tremble at the thought of Barthian readings in law schools . . . . I suspect that civilization reposes on a lot of people who take the normal practices of the discipline with full 'realistic' seriousness. However, I should like to think that a pragmatist's understanding of knowledge and community would be, in the end, compatible with normal inquiry—the practitioners of such inquiry reserving their irony for after-hours" (Letter from Richard Rorty to author (28 April 1981) (copy on file with the *Texas Law Review*)). It is not clear, then, what Rorty's stance would be to those who would attempt to make his own thought central to their regular daily work.

116. See text accompanying note 109 sup.

117. See, e.g., S. 158, 97th Cong., 1st Sess. ("Human Life" bill) (1981); S. 481, 97th Cong., 1st Sess. (1981) (depriving federal courts of jurisdiction over cases regarding voluntary prayers in public schools).

118. R. Rilke, *Duino Elegies and the Sonnets to Orpheus* 105 (A. Poulin, trans. 1975) (Sonnets to Orpheus, First Series, No. 11).

119. Grant Gilmore has noted the existence in an earlier generation of "nihilist" individuals who were led by their own arguments to eschew writing itself. See G. Gilmore, *The Ages of American Law* 80–81 (1977) (discussing Wesley Sturges). Although the peculiar traditions of law schools in regard to tenure have meant that there have always been a relatively high number of nonwriters on law school faculties (see Ackerman, "The Marketplace of Ideas," 90 *Yale L.J.* 1132–35 (1981)), it may be that at least some of the failure to write is based on a conviction of having "nothing to say" in the profoundest sense of that term. It is not a coincidence, I suspect, that a substantial amount of the writing of scholars Fiss would be likely to view as "nihilists" is in the area of legal history and, more particularly, the ideological analysis of legal thought, whether expressed in cases, classic legal writings, or the work-product of scholars. In addition to the works cited sup. note 46, see, e.g., Gordon, "Historicism in Legal Scholarship," 90 *Yale L.J.* 1017 (1981); Katz, "Studies in Boundary Theory: Three Essays in Adjudication and Politics," 28 *Buffalo L. Rev.* 383 (1979); D. Kennedy, "The Rise and Fall of Classical Legal Thought 1850–1940" (1976) (unpublished manuscript); Kennedy, "The Structure of Blackstone's Commentaries," 28 *Buffalo L. Rev.* 209 (1979); Schlegel, "American Legal Realism and Empirical Social Science: From the Yale Experience," 28 *Buffalo L. Rev.* 459 (1979); Schlegel, "American Legal Realism and Emperical Social Science: The Singular Case of Underhill Moore," 29 *Buffalo L. Rev.* 195 (1980). This

(greatly truncated) list belies any genuine notion that persons alienated from a traditional stance of reverence (or even respect) for law have nothing to say. But it is fair to say that no one who defines his or her task as the search for "certain principles or doctrines" (see text accompanying note 3), is prepared to listen. Few today would admit that they *are* engaged in such a search, for all of us portray ourselves as postrealists, focusing on "policies" underlying the law. But see Gordon, Book Review, 1974 *Wis. L. Rev.* 1216 (reviewing G. Gilmore, *The Death of Contract* (1974)), for an analysis of the desiccated nature of the so-called policy analysis that occurs in American law schools.

120. W. Whitman, "Democratic Vistas," in *Walt Whitman: Poetry and Prose* 992–93 (Library of America ed. 1982).

121. See Leff, "Unspeakable Ethics, Unnatural Law," 1979 *Duke L.J.* 1249:
All I can say is this: it looks as if we are all we have. Given what we know about ourselves and each other, this is an extraordinarily unappetizing prospect; looking around the world, it appears that if all men are brothers, the ruling model is Cain and Abel. Neither reason, nor love, nor even terror, seems to have worked to make us "good," and worse than that, there is no reason why anything should. Only if ethics were something unspeakable by us, could law be unnatural, and therefore unchallengeable. As things now stand, everything is up for grabs.
Nevertheless:
Napalming babies is bad.
Starving the poor is wicked.
Buying and selling each other is depraved.
Those who stood up to and died resisting Hitler, Stalin, Amin, and Pol Pot—and General Custer too—have earned salvation.
Those who acquiesced deserve to be damned.
There is in the world such a thing as evil.
[All together now:] Sez who?
God help us.

Keep Off the Grass

1. Levinson, "Law as Literature," 60 *Texas L. Rev.* 373 (1982).

2. See Levinson, "Law," 35 *Amer. Q.* 191 (1983).

3. Levinson, "Law as Literature" 385.

4. Ibid., p. 391 & n.64.

5. Ibid., p. 388.

6. Ibid., p. 386.

7. This quotation is from an earlier draft of Professor Levinson's article, ibid.; and, although it is not in the final version of that article, Professor Levinson acknowledges that the quotation accurately reflects his views.

8. See J. Searle, *Expression and Meaning: Studies in the Theory of Speech Acts* 117–36 (1979); Grice, "Utterer's Meaning and Intentions," 78 *Phil. Rev.* 147 (1969).

9. The large element of redundancy in any communication is what tends to prevent our getting far with such mistakes and forces us to try more workable interpretive hypotheses. One just would not get very far in processing the sadistic text according to antisadistic conventions of morality.

10. Note 7 sup.

11. Ibid., p. 385.

12. Ibid., pp. 388–89 (emphasis added).

On the Use and Abuse of Nietzsche

1. In the fuller essay from which most of these lines have emerged, I treat the relationship between postmodernist hermeneutics and reactionary political behavior in the specific case of Heidegger. See my "Text into Theory: A Literary Approach to the Constitution," 20 *Georgia L. Rev.* 946–67 (1986). In those pages, I also discuss Paul de Man's treatment of Heidegger's Holderlin essays, where de Man found (and rearticulated) the prolegomenon for deconstructionist theory (ibid., pp. 949–50). I have elsewhere begun to discuss the question of de Man's misreadings of Nietzsche (particularly in the "Rhetoric of Persuasion" essay in *Allegories of Reading* 125–29 (New Haven: Yale University Press, 1979) and tentatively to link these with the political and cultural environment in which de Man lived and wrote. See my "De Man Missing Nietzsche: 'Hinzugedichtet' Revisited," proceedings of Nietzsche seminar, International Association for Philosophy and Literature (Lawrence, Kansas, 1–2 May 1987).

2. Hendrik Birus, "Nietzsche's Concept of Interpretation," in 3 *Texte: Revue de critique et de théorie littéraire* 87 (1984).

3. See Weisberg, *The Failure of the Word* (New Haven: Yale University Press, 1984), Introduction and Part One.

4. Cited in Birus, "Nietzsche's Concept," p. 90.

5. See *On the Genealogy of Morals*, Preface, Aphorism 8 (F. Golffing, trans. New York: Anchor, 1956).

6. See my "Text Into Theory," pp. 962–76.

7. *Genealogy*, Essay II, Aphorism 12.

8. Sanford Levinson, "Law as Literature," 60 *Tex. L. Rev.* 385 (1982), reprinted in this volume.

9. Ibid.

10. Ibid., p. 389.

11. See Sarah Kofman, *Nietzsche et la métaphore* (1972), pp. 67–74, where she purports to discuss the Nietzschean approach to justice yet fails even to cite the most important aphorism on the subject. See text at note 13. No wonder that Kofman, in perhaps the single most incorrect statement she makes, concludes that the will to power is "fundamentally unjust" (ibid., p. 53).

12. I elsewhere discuss the distinction perceivable in Nietzsche between written texts, which may be privileged as "*Stoffe*," and concepts, which are more diaphanous and more correctly subject to fanciful reinterpretations.

13. *Genealogy of Morals*, Essay II, Aphorism 11. I am using the Golffing translation, with certain modifications. This is the aphorism that, strangely, has not hitherto been cited by analysts such as Levinson and Kofman, who purport to deal centrally with the Nietzschean concepts of text and justice.

14. See Weisberg, *The Failure of the Word* 16–20.

15. Nietzsche equates the contemporary practice of German law with the illness of ressentiment: " 'We alone,' they say, 'are the good, the just, we alone the Men of Good Will' . . . . Among them are vindictive characters aplenty, disguised as judges, who carry the word *justice* in their mouths like a poisonous spittle and go always with pursed lips, ready to spit on all who do not look discontent, on all who go cheerfully about their business" (*Genealogy*, Aphorism 14).

16. Cited in Birus, "Nietzsche's Concept," p. 91.

17. For a discussion of the positive Nietzschean notion of *constraint*, see my "Text Into Theory."

18. Fish, *Is There a Text in This Class?* (1980).

19. Hartman, *Saving the Text: Literature/Derrida/Philosophy* xxi-xxii (1981).

20. See Gadamer, *Truth and Method* 236 (1960; trans. N.Y. Seabury, 1975):
> All correct interpretation must be on guard against arbitrary fancies and the limitations imposed by imperceptible habits of thought and direct its gaze "on the things themselves" (which, in the case of the literary critic, are meaningful texts, which themselves are concerned with objects). It is clear that to let the object take over this way is not a matter for the interpreter of a single decision, but is the "first, last and constant task." For it is necessary to keep one's gaze fixed on the thing throughout all the distractions that the interpreter will constantly experience in the process and which originate in himself.

21. I am influenced primarily by the early Lukacs, in his pre-Marxist *The Theory of the Novel* (1920 trans. Cambridge, Mass.: M.I.T. Press, 1971), and his later *Studies in European Realism* (1953 trans. New York: Grosset & Dunlap, 1964); my analyses of the novel are tied theoretically to those of the Russian formalist school of the 1920s, particularly Shklovski and Eikhenbaum (see *Russian Formalist Criticism* (L. Lemon and M. Reis, eds. 1965)). I am also strongly influenced by R. Barthes, *Essais Critiques* (Paris: Seuil, 1964).

22. No one has convinced me that what an author says should be irrelevant to understanding a work; however, my main interest is in what he or she says about interpretation itself.

23. For the development of ideas expressed in this part of the essay, see my "Law in and As Literature: Self-Generated Meaning in the 'Procedural Novel,' " forthcoming in Koelb and Noakes, eds., *The Comparative Perspective on Literature* (Ithaca: Cornell University Press, 1988).

24. See part III.

25. See Gary Wills, *Explaining America* 16, 66, 251 (1981).

26. Clinton Rossiter, ed., *The Federalist* 229 (New York: Signet, 1961).

27. Rossiter, ed., *Federalist* 201.

28. Ibid.; see also *The Federalist* no. 78, p. 466, Hamilton's famous "manifest tenor of the Constitution."

29. *U.S. Const.*, art. 1 section 7, cl. 2.

30. Henry Monaghan, "Our Perfect Constitution," 56 *N.Y.U. L. Rev.* 382 (1981).

31. Professor Walter Benn Michaels takes the converse position from my own. For him the text does carry the *meaning* intended by its authors, but this can only be discovered by a reader who wants to find it there, so it cannot be seen as a constraint on interpretation. Michaels thus at once posits the theoretical mandate to seek meaning (not interpretive theory) from a text's author and the inevitable subjectivism of that quest. Michaels, "Response to Perry and Simon," 58 *S. Cal. L. Rev.* 675 (1985).

32. There is only a brief mention in Ferrand, ed., 2 *Records of the Federal Convention of 1787*, 302 (1937).

33. Michael Perry, *The Constitution, The Courts and Human Rights* 19 (1982).

34. Ibid., pp. 101–2.

35. John Ely, *Democracy and Distrust* (1980).

36. See McGowan v. Maryland, 366 U.S. 420 at 452 n. 22 (1961).

37. The structure of the debates at the Constitutional Convention indicates such a secular purpose. Clearly, that constitutive group in particular needed a day of rest, not so much for religious as for "cooling off" or even private political purposes. A recent history of the convention makes clear that Sundays were often used to negotiate crucial compromises. See C. Collier and C. Collier, *Decision in Philadelphia* 94–95 (New York: Random House, 1986). Might not this experience have served as the litmus test justifying the constitutionalization of the concept? Indeed, the meager reference to the parenthetical in the debates indicates that the Framers switched from "seven days" to the present formulation; their own experience may have attested to the wisdom of lengthening negotiation periods and allowing a day (or two) of quasi-political "rest" to intercede.

38. Paul Brest, "The Misconceived Quest for the Original Understanding," 60 *B.U. L. Rev.* 204 (1980), reprinted in this volume.

39. Ibid., p. 220.

40. See Raoul Berger, "Paul Brest's Brief for an Imperial Judiciary," 40 *Md. L. Rev.* 1 (1981).

41. Brest, "The Misconceived Quest," pp. 220–21.

42. Recently compiled demographic data tends to contradict the idea that death was experienced, or conceptualized, more publicly in colonial days. For an overwhelmingly rural, if not isolated, population, it must have been at least as private, and probably a more cruel and horrifying, phenomenon as for us today. See Collier and Collier, *Decision in Phila- delphia,* pp. 16–24, n. 69. But this does not—or should not—compel us to accept (as the colonialists did) the constitutionality of the death penalty.

43. See, e.g., Trop v. Dulles, 356 U.S. 86 (1958); Weems v. U.S., 217 U.S. 349 (1910).

44. Brest, "The Misconceived Quest", p. 226.

45. I believe that, apart from the preamble, the parenthetical may be unique in this respect.

46. *The Federalist* no. 31, p. 193.

47. The cases fall into two categories. First are cases testing the language against non- covered situations that arguably increase or decrease the number of days given a president to return a bill. See, e.g., Wright v. United States, 302 U.S. 583 (1938) (temporary recess does not prevent return of bill to an appropriate agent of the originating House, within the stated time frame); the *Pocket Veto* case, 279 U.S. 655 (1929) (but a full intersession adjourn- ment within eight days, Sundays excluded, of the House presentation of a bill to the presi- dent prevents the return of a bill within the stated time frame); Kennedy v. Sampson, 511 F.2d 430 (D.C. Cir. 1974) (Christmas recess does not prevent return of the bill within the stated period). Second are cases employing the parenthetical to suggest a religious vision, incorporated by the Framers into the Constitution. See, e.g. Holy Trinity Church v. United States, 143 U.S. 457, 470 (1891) (Such words "affirm and reaffirm that this is a religious nation"); Doremus v. Board of Education, 7 N.J. Super. 442, 71 A.2d 732 (allowing public school reading of at least five verses daily from the Old Testament and daily readings of the Lord's Prayer, *aff'd.* 5 N.J. 435, 75 A.2d 880 (1950).

48. *The Federalist* nos. 72, 73, pp. 433, 442.

49. Wills observes that this elitism was almost as pronounced in Madison as it was in Hamilton. Wills, *Explaining America* 196.

50. *The Federalist* no. 48, p. 311.

51. *The Federalist* no. 71, pp. 432–33.

52. The phrase is Cardozo's in "The Growth of the Law," *Selected Writings of Benjamin Nathan Cardozo* 225 (M. Hall, ed,; New York: Bender, 1975).

Following the Rules Laid Down

1. H. Wechsler, *Principles, Politics, and Fundamental Law* 21 (1961). What senators have in mind when they ask about applying, not making, law is a corollary of this thesis—that a judge must remain faithful to the body of law within which he or she works by following the principles previously established, rather than constantly reshaping them to fit his or her preferences in the case at hand.

2. J. Ely, *Democracy and Distrust* 1 (1980).

3. Any summary description of the classical liberal view—the liberalism of Hobbes, Locke, and Mill and that of Dworkin and Rawls—must be a caricature. The description in text is supported by A. Gutmann, *Liberal Equality* (1980); D. Manning, *Liberalism* (1976); Bell, "Models and Reality in Economic Discourse," *Pub. Interest* 46 (special issue 1980); see also

Dworkin, "Liberalism," in *Public and Private Morality* 127–29 (S. Hampshire, ed. 1978) (deriving a similar view as the essence of contemporary political liberalism).

Liberalism, neutral principles, and interpretivism are regularly associated, but it is not important to my argument to decide whether they are mutually entailed. Each provides the others with metaphors that come to pervade all three theories (see D. Manning, ibid., pp. 9–30 (characterizing liberalism)); thus, a challenge to the accustomed way of talking about politics, meaning, or history will be felt as a challenge to the way of talking about the others as well.

4. See Leff, "Unspeakable Ethics, Unnatural Law," 1979 *Duke L. J.* 1242.

5. L. Levy, *Freedom of Speech and Press in Early American History: Legacy of Suppression* ix (Torchbook ed. 1963).

6. L. Marx, *The Machine in the Garden: Technology and the Pastoral Ideal in America* 220–21 (1964).

7. The best presentation of this view for those accustomed to Anglo-American styles of philosophical writing is R. Collingwood, *The Idea of History* (1956). Collingwood goes far along the way to the conclusions that I draw here, but he does not quite state them openly. Jürgen Habermas and Hans-Georg Gadamer have explored aspects of the hermeneutical tradition using a different style of philosophical writing. For summaries, see A Giddens, *Central Problems in Social Theory* 175–77 (1979); A. Giddens, *New Rules of Sociological Method* 54–65 (1976); R. Keat, *The Politics of Social Theory: Habermas, Freud, and the Critique of Positivism* 202–3 (1981); T. McCarthy, *The Critical Theory of Jürgen Habermas* 162–239 (1978). For a lawyer's perspective, see Abraham, "Statutory Interpretation and Literary Theory: Some Common Concerns of an Unlikely Pair," 32 *Rutgers L. Rev.* 676 (1979), reprinted in this volume; Abraham, "Three Fallacies of Interpretation: A Comment on Precedent and Judicial Decision," 23 *Ariz. L. Rev.* 771 (1981).

Though I do not believe that fashions in historical scholarship necessarily move in the direction of truth, I think it worth noting that contemporary historical scholarship finds in the hermeneutical tradition an understanding of the enterprise better than what previously prevailed. See Woodward, "A Short History of American History," *New York Times,* 8 August 1982, § 7 (Book Review), 14; cf. Kurland, "Curia Regis: Some Comments on the Divine Right of Kings and Courts 'To Say What The Law Is,' " 23 *Ariz. L. Rev.* 581, 584, 595 (1981) (assessing hermeneutical literary criticism as a style of constitutional interpretation).

8. R. Keat, *Politics of Social Theory* 7.

9. 274 U.S. 357, 372 (1927) (Brandeis, J., concurring).

10. Ibid., pp. 375–76. In a footnote to this passage, Justice Brandeis quotes Jefferson on the value of free public discussion (375 n. 2).

11. 347 U.S. 483, 492–93 (1954).

12. H. Wechsler, *Principles* 46–47.

13. Gordon, "Historicism in Legal Scholarship," 90 *Yale L.J.* 1021 (1981) (footnotes omitted).

14. I must, however, note the obvious ethnocentricity of this statement. Clearly, the history of kingship in Central Africa (see J. Vansina, *Kingdoms of the Savannah* (1966)), is as much a part of our past as is the history of the Constitution.

15. Wechsler, "Toward Neutral Principles of Constitutional Law," 73 *Harv. L. Rev.* 15.

16. Perry, "Why the Supreme Court Was Plainly Wrong in the Hyde Amendment Case: A Brief Comment on Harris v. McRae," 32 *Stan. L. Rev.* 1113.

17. 410 U.S. 113 (1973).

18. Harris v. McRae, 448 U.S. 297 (1980).

19. Perry, "Why the Supreme Court Was Wrong" 1120.

20. Ibid., pp. 1115–16.

21. Ibid., p. 1117; see Westen, "Correspondence," 33 *Stan. L. Rev.* 1188 (1981).

22. Perry, "Why the Supreme Court Was Wrong" 1116–17.

23. Perry rejects the "counterexample" of Brandenburg v. Ohio, 395 U.S. 444 (1969), in which the Court protected certain kinds of advocacy from criminal prosecution even though it acknowledges that states could "take [other] action predicated on the view that such advocacy is morally objectionable" ("Why the Supreme Court Was Wrong" 1118). He argues that the advocacy in *Brandenburg* is protected in order to avoid a chilling effect on truly protected speech (ibid., p. 1119). Thus, *Brandenburg's* real protection is given to "interests *distinct from*" the interest in advocating unlawful activity (ibid.). The same argument can be developed in the abortion context, however, and in fact in any other context as well. Consider the narrow principle that government may not predicate actions on the view that abortions are immoral in cases in which the woman has not consented to the sexual contact that caused her pregnancy. Roe v. Wade might then be defended on the ground that governmental inquiries into whether consent had been given, particularly in light of the obvious controversy over what consent might mean, would intrude on an independent interest in informational privacy. Because refusal to fund abortions does not intrude on that interest, such refusal is permissible on this interpretation of Roe.

24. 433 U.S. 584 (1977); see Westen, "Correspondence" 1188.

25. The first principle requires us to distinguish between laws criminalizing the abortion decision and those criminalizing theft, so that we can explain why the state is not injecting itself into the abortion decision when it prosecutes a poor woman—a Jeanne Valjean—who steals money to pay for an abortion. The second requires us to explain why the special protection is great enough to prohibit criminalization but is not enough, for example, to prohibit a requirement that parents of some minors be informed of their daughters' decisions to have abortions. See H.L. v. Matheson, 450 U.S. 398 (1981).

26. 381 U.S. 479 (1965).

27. 268 U.S. 510 (1925).

28. 262 U.S. 390 (1923).

29. Idem at 401.

30. C. Black, *Decision according to Law* 81 (1981); see also ibid., pp. 21–24 (metaphorical evocation of delicate logic of law); see Sandalow, "Constitutional Interpretation," 79 *Mich. L. Rev.* 1033 (1981) (tracing delicate balance between faithfulness to the constitutional text and accommodation to the needs of the time).

31. C. Black, "According to Law" 82.

32. 410 U.S. 113 (1973).

33. Roe v. Wade, 410 U.S. at 153.

34. Ely, "The Wages of Crying Wolf: A Comment on *Roe* v. *Wade*," 82 *Yale L. J.* 929–30 (1973).

35. Roe v. Wade, 410 U.S. at 209 (Douglas, J., concurring).

36. Dworkin observes that a person asked to add one chapter "in the best possible way" to a collaborative novel-in-progress faces limits similar to those that precedents place on judges. Dworkin, " 'Natural' Law Revisited," 34 *U. Fla. L. Rev.* 167 (1982). He fails to appreciate that, by disrupting our expectations about what fits best, the creative author may force us both to reinterpret all that has gone before and to expand our understanding of what a "novel" is.

37. Tushnet, Book Review, 78 *Mich. L. Rev.* 696–98 (1980).

Against Formalism: Chickens and Rocks

1. G. Hartman, "Beyond Formalism," *Beyond Formalism* 42 (1966).

2. S. Sontag, "Against Interpretation," *Against Interpretation* 12 (1966).

3. W.K. Wimsatt, "Genesis: An Argument Resumed," *Day of the Leopards* 26 (1968).

4. Hotchkiss v. National City Bank, 200 F287, 293 (S.D.N.Y. 1911).

5. O.W. Holmes, "The Path of Law," *Collected Legal Papers* 178 (1920).

6. A.L. Corbin, "The Interpretation of Words and the Parol Evidence Rule," 50 *Cornell L.Q.* 164 (1965).

7. Ibid., p. 171

8. Ibid.

9. Corbin, *A Comprehensive Treatise on the Rules of Contract Law* 357 (1960).

10. Corbin, "Interpretation" 171.

11. W.K. Wimsatt and M. Beardsley, "The Intentional Fallacy" (1946), in Wimsatt, *The Verbal Icon* 18 (1967).

12. E.D. Hirsch, "Objective Interpretation" [1960], *Validity in Interpretation* 216 (1967).

13. Ibid., pp. 239–40.

14. E.A. Farnsworth, " 'Meaning' in the Law of Contracts," 76 *Yale L.J. 965 (1967).*

15. P. de Man, *Blindness and Insight* 111 (1971).

Objectivity and Interpretation

1. See Taylor, "Interpretation and the Sciences of Man," 25 *Rev. Metaphysics* 3 (1971); see also Taylor, "Understanding in Human Science," 34 *Rev. Metaphysics* 25 (1980).

2. C. Geertz, *Negara: The Theatre State in Nineteenth-Century Bali* (1980) [hereafter *Negara*]; see also C. Geertz, "Deep Play: Notes on the Balinese Cockfight," in *The Interpretation of Cultures* 412 (1973).

3. See, e.g., Brest, "The Fundamental Rights Controversy: The Essential Contradictions of Normative Constitutional Scholarship," 90 *Yale L.J.* 1063 (1981); Levinson, "Law as Literature," 60 *Tex. L. Rev.* (1982) (reprinted in this volume); see also Walzer, "Philosophy and Democracy," 9 *Pol. Theory* 379 (1981). Following the 1980 national elections and the overwhelming victory of the Right, the affection for politics, which many thought belonged to elections, was conferred on the party caucus. See, e.g., Walzer, "Democracy vs. Elections," *New Republic*, 3 & 10 January 1981, p. 17.

4. See Ackerman, Book Review, *Daedalus* (Winter 1974), p. 119 (reviewing J. Frank, *Law and the Modern Mind* (1930)).

5. 347 U.S. 483 (1954).

6. 377 U.S. 533 (1964).

7. 376 U.S. 254 (1964).

8. 372 U.S. 335 (1963).

9. See, e.g., H. Bloom et al., *Deconstruction and Criticism* (1979). For a spirited review of this book, revealing the many strands within the deconstruction movement, see Donoghue, "Deconstructing Deconstruction" (Book Review), *New York Review of Books*, 12 June 1980, p. 37. For the more philosophic aspirations of deconstructionism, see J. Derrida, *Of Grammatology* (G.C. Spivak, trans. 1976).

10. See, e.g., J. Ely, *Democracy and Distrust: A Theory of Judicial Review* (1980). Professor Grey also understands interpretation in this narrow fashion. See Grey, "Origins of the Unwritten Constitution: Fundamental Law in American Revolutionary Thought," 30 *Stan. L. Rev.* 843 (1978); Grey, "Do We Have an Unwritten Constitution?" 27 *Stan. L. Rev.* 703 (1975).

11. I. Berlin, "Two Concepts of Liberty," in *Four Essays on Liberty* 118 (1969).

12. The bounded or relativistic quality of the interpretive method is suggested by the idea of the hermeneutical circle, which denotes the parameters within which an interpretation achieves its validity and is based on the assumption that, at some point, an interpretation must make an intuitive appeal to common understandings. The idea of the hermeneutical circle is discussed in Taylor, "Interpretation and the Sciences of Man," pp.

6–13, and vividly described by Geertz, *Negara*, p. 103, as "a dialectical tacking." David Hoy draws a parallel between the idea of the hermeneutical circle and John Rawls's notion of reflective equilibrium. See Hoy, "Hermeneutics," 47 *Soc. Research* 666 (1980).

13. See T. Kuhn, *The Essential Tension* (1977); T. Kuhn, *The Structure of Scientific Revolutions* (2d ed., enlarged 1970).

14. Taylor, "Understanding in Human Science," pp. 33–37.

15. The phrase belongs to Justice Holmes, Southern Pacific Co. v. Jensen, 244 U.S. 205, 222 (1916) (dissenting opinion) ("The common law is not a brooding omnipresence in the sky, but the articulate voice of some sovereign . . . ."), and is often used to mock the idea of objectivity.

16. See note 9 sup. and accompanying text.

17. See S. Fish, *Is There a Text in This Class?* (1980). Professor Fish acknowledges the creative relationship between reader and text, but sees the reader as a member of an interpretive community whose institutions shape or structure his view of the world. He argues that those who happen to share the same values and thus belong to the same interpretive community can judge the correctness of an interpretation, though the standards may change as the community does. The question for literature, however, is whether the interpretive community possesses the necessary authority to confer on what I have called the disciplining rules. For an illuminating review of this important book, see Graff, "Culture and Anarchy" (Book Review), *New Republic*, 14 February 1981, p. 36.

18. Gunther, "Too Much a Battle with Straw Men?" (Book Review), *Wall Street Journal*, 25 November 1977, p. 4, col. 4 (reviewing R. Berger, *Government by Judiciary* (1977)).

19. See generally Brest, "The Misconceived Quest for the Original Understanding," 60 *B.U.L. Rev.* 204 (1980), reprinted in this volume.

20. 163 U.S. 537 (1896).

21. L. Wittgenstein, *On Certainty* §§ 74, 156 (G. Anscombe and G. von Wright, eds.; D. Paul and G. Anscombe, trans. 1969).

22. 1 A. de Tocqueville, *Democracy in America* 123–32 (London 1838).

23. This tradition is explored in the articles of Professor Grey, referred to in note 10 sup., and also in R. Cover, *Justice Accused: Antislavery and the Judicial Process* (1975).

24. See *The Constitution a Pro-Slavery Compact* (W. Phillips, ed.; 2d ed., enlarged 1845) (W. Phillips, ed.; 1st ed. 1844) (*The Anti-Slavery Examiner* no. 11).

25. See C. Beard, *An Economic Interpretation of the Constitution of the United States* (1913).

26. This is the essential insight of Professor Lon Fuller and his attempt to reformulate the natural law tradition in procedural terms. See L. Fuller, *The Morality of Law* (rev. ed. 1969).

27. J. Rawls, *A Theory of Justice* (1971). A similar vision is found in Thomas Nagel's image of the individual struggling to stand outside himself and the world, as a way of achieving an objective perspective. See T. Nagel, "Subjective and Objective," in *Mortal Questions* 196 (1979).

28. J. Austin, *The Province of Jurisprudence Determined* (1832); see also Holmes, "The Path of the Law," 10 *Harv. L. Rev.* 457 (1897).

29. See generally *Bayonets in the Streets* (R. Higham, ed. 1969). The history of the efforts to desegregate the University of Mississippi is also detailed in United States v. Barnett, 330 F.2d 369 (5th Cir. 1963).

30. H.L.A. Hart, *The Concept of Law* (1961).

31. H. Kelsen, *General Theory of Law and State* (1945).

32. 369 U.S. 186 (1962).

33. This is part of the folklore of the Supreme Court and thus found its way into B. Woodward and S. Armstrong, *The Brethren* 176 (1979).

34. 358 U.S. 1 (1958).

35. Brown v. Board of Educ., 349 U.S. 294 (1955).

36. See Plessy v. Ferguson, 163 U.S. 537, 551–52 (1896).

37. See Milliken v. Bradley, 418 U.S. 717 (1974).

Fish v. Fiss

1. Fiss, "Objectivity and Interpretation," 34 *Stan. L. Rev.* 739 (1982), reprinted in this volume.

2. Ibid.

3. Ibid., p. 744.

4. Not that I am accepting this characterization of reader and text; it is just that I am proceeding within the assumptions of Fiss's model so that I can more effectively challenge it in all its aspects.

5. I refer to the distinction, assumed by many historians, between a *text* as something that requires interpretation and a *document* as something that wears its meaning on its face and therefore can be used to stabilize the meaning of a text. My argument, of course, is that there is no such thing as a document in that sense.

6. Fiss, "Objectivity" 744.

7. Ibid.

8. Ibid., p. 747.

9. Ibid.

10. Ibid.

11. Cf. Michaels, "Is there a Politics of Interpretation?" in *The Politics of Interpretation* 337–39 (W.J.T. Mitchell, ed. 1983) (directing a similar argument at a thesis offered by Ronald Dworkin).

12. It is sometimes the strategy of those who have been forced to acknowledge that all facts are contextual to posit context itself as a new fact or set of facts that can serve as a constraint, but the perception of context is no less contextually determined than the facts that context determines in turn. See, e.g., Fish, "With the Compliments of the Author: Reflections on Austin and Derrida," 8 *Critical Inquiry* 693, 708 (1982).

13. The requirement of explicitness can, in the strong sense, never be met, since it is the requirement that a piece of language declare its own meaning and thus be impervious to the distorting work performed by interpreters. It is my contention that language is always apprehended within a set of interpretive assumptions, and that the form in which a sentence appears is always an interpreted or "read" form, which means that it can always be read again. For the full argument, see S. Fish, *Is There a Text in This Class?* 281–84 (1980); Fish, "With the Compliments" 703–4.

14. T.S. Kuhn, *The Structure of Scientific Revolutions* 46 (2d ed. 1970).

15. Ibid., p. 191.

16. Ibid., p. 47.

17. I make this point in a more extended way in Fish, "Working on the Chain Gang: Interpretation in the Law and in Literary Criticism," in Mitchell, ed., *The Politics of Interpretation* 271–86.

18. Levinson, "Law as Literature," 60 *Texas L. Rev.* 392–402 (1982), reprinted in this volume.

19. When I use phrases like "without reflection" and "immediately and obviously" I do not mean to preclude self-conscious deliberation on the part of situated agents; it is just that such deliberations always occur within ways of thinking that are themselves the ground of consciousness, not its object.

20. Fiss, "Objectivity" 762.

21. S. Fish, "Is There a Text in This Class?" 281–84.

22. Cf. Whitney v. California, 274 U.S. 357, 376 (1927) (Brandeis, J., concurring) ("Men feared witches and burnt women").

23. See, e.g. R. Berger, *Government by Judiciary* (1977).

24. See, e.g., J.H. Ely, *Democracy and Distrust* (1980).

25. See, e.g., L. Tribe, *American Constitutional Law* 452 (1978).

26. On this point see S. Fish, "Is There a Text in This Class?" 342–49, where a similar argument is made in relation to the practices of literary criticism.

27. Fiss, "Objectivity" 749.

28. Ibid.

29. Ibid.

30. Ibid., p. 741.

31. Ibid., p. 757.

32. Ibid., p. 756.

33. Ibid.

34. Ibid., p. 757.

35. Ibid.

36. This is a familiar distinction in the literature and is central to the argument of S. Toulmin, *Human Understanding* (1972). For a critique of that argument, see Fish, "Anti-Professionalism," in 17 *New Literary History* 89 (1985).

37. Fiss, "Objectivity" 754.

38. Ibid., p. 759.

39. This may seem to be reinstating the distinction between inside and outside considerations, but any consideration that finds its way into the process of legal inquiry has been recharacterized as a legal consideration and has therefore become "inside."

40. Fiss, "Objectivity" 763.

41. On this point see S. Fish, "With the Compliments" 331–37; Fish, "Working on the Chain Gang" 276–79.

42. Fiss, "Objectivity" 763.

43. Ibid., p. 746.

44. There is a large issue to be considered here, the issue of the consequences of theory in general. It is my position that theory has no consequences, at least on the level claimed for it by its practitioners. Rather than standing in a relationship of precedence and governance to practice, theory is (when it happens to be a feature of an enterprise) a form of practice whose consequences (if there are any) are unpredictable and no different in kind from the consequences of any form of practice. Both those who fear theory and those who identify it with salvation make the mistake of conceiving of it as a special kind of activity, one that stands apart from the practices it would ground and direct. If there were a theory so special, it would have nothing to say to practice at all; and, on the other hand, a theory that does speak meaningfully to practice is simply an item in the landscape of practices. See Fish, "Consequences," in *Against Theory* 106–31 (W. J. T. Mitchell, ed. 1985).

45. Fiss, "Objectivity" 750.

The Poetics of Legal Interpretation

1. This distinction is first broached in "The Model of Rules I," in R. Dworkin, *Taking Rights Seriously* 22–23 (1978).

2. "How Law is Like Literature" is a reworking of an earlier essay, Dworkin, "Law as Interpretation," 9 *Critical Inquiry* 179 (September 1982), and was reprinted in *The Politics of*

Interpretation 249 (W. Mitchell, ed. 1983) [hereafter *Politics*] with a companion piece, Fish, "Working on the Chain Gang," in *Politics*, p. 271. *The Politics of Interpretation* included a second essay by Dworkin, "My Reply to Stanley Fish (and Walter Benn Michaels): Please Don't Talk about Objectivity Any More," in *Politics*, p. 287 [hereafter Dworkin, "My Reply"], which is also included in *A Matter of Principle* in revised form as "On Interpretation and Objectivity" (p. 167). A further essay by Fish, "Wrong Again," appeared in 62 *Tex. L. Rev.* 299 (1983). Dworkin replied to it in the last essay in the series, "Not Really" [hereafter Dworkin, "Not Really"]; however, he omitted this last essay from the present collection. In this chapter, I include arguments made from omitted sections of "My Reply," and "Not Really." In such cases, I cite the original publication, or an unpublished manuscript circulated by Dworkin.

3. See note 19 inf. and accompanying text.

4. Theory dependence is the view that meaning depends entirely upon the general theory or governing values that structure what an interpreter "sees."

5. R. Dworkin, *Taking Rights Seriously* 14–15.

6. Ibid, pp. 31–39, 87–88.

7. The contrast between the certainty that external verification promises and the uncertainty that theory dependence absorbs can be depicted by using one of external verification's favorite metaphors, the "furniture of the universe." This phrase suggests that theories must try to describe the nature of a reality that is as undeniable as a piece of furniture is, if one bumps into it while walking across a room. The table's position does not depend on where one thinks it is; and if one makes a mistake about it, one bangs one's shins. Theory dependence posits an altogether different relation to the piece of furniture. If one were a furniture-maker, one would construct a chair according to what one valued about chairs. One's chair might share only certain characteristics with other people's chairs; indeed, some other people might deny that one's chair *was* a chair. If one cared at all about other people—our interpretive community—one would begin a debate in which the crux of the matter would be the contending values for chair-making and for chair interpretation.

8. See R. Dworkin, *Taking Rights Seriously* 331–38.

9. Dworkin, "My Reply" 289.

10. However, even among the interpreters themselves, the persistence of skeptical critiques and frequent changes of minds offer countervailing evidence of the uncertainty of such internal judgment. It is a commonplace of law that judges come to results and then look for convincing—if hypocritical—reasons. This commonplace suggests either that people often find themselves coming to the "right" answer, and only then searching for rationales; or that people fail Dworkin's second test, which is to observe a correspondence between their own processes of interpretation and those of others. In any event, it raises troubling questions about what the testimony of interpreters is on this score.

11. P. de Man, *Blindness and Insight* 102–11 (1971). One does not have to reach de Man's radically skeptical views to be troubled by what he and Derrida would call the duplicity of language—its deception and its doubleness—which undermine the univocality of interpretation.

12. An intentionalist interpretation is one which organizes textuality as the place where an author's intentions are represented in language and which posits interpretation as a process of deriving, according to the relevant aesthetic/political morality values, what that intention "is," and hence, what the text "means."

13. As it happens, originalism is currently used to buttress a conservative political morality; and its advocates cite the intention of the Framers in their campaign to curtail what they call the Supreme Court's impermissible lawmaking, as if interpretation of these intentions, once made, self-evidently barred subsequent rethinking.

14. The *Southern California Law Review* devoted two issues of Volume 58 (1985) to an Interpretation Symposium on these controversial matters. Included were Fiss, "Conventionalism," 58 *S. Cal. L. Rev.* 177 (1985); Hoy, "Interpreting the Law: Hermeneutical and

Poststructuralist Perspectives," 58 *S. Cal. L. Rev.* 135 (1985); Levinson, "What Do Lawyers Know (And What Do They Do with Their Knowledge)? Comments on Schauer and Moore," 58 *S. Cal. L. Rev.* 441 (1985); Moore, "A Natural Law Theory of Interpretation," 58 *S. Cal. L. Rev.* 227 (1985); Perry, "The Authority of Text, Tradition and Reason: A Theory of Constitutional 'Interpretation' " 58 *S. Cal. L. Rev.* 551 (1985); Richards, "Interpretation and Historiography," 58 *S. Cal. L. Rev.* 489 (1985); Schauer, "Easy Cases," 58 *S. Cal. L. Rev.* 399 (1985); Simon, "The Authority of the Constitution and its Meaning: A Preface to a Theory of Constitutional Interpretation," 58 *S. Cal. L. Rev.* 603 (1985); as well as others.

15. Dworkin does not explicitly make this argument. However, I take it to be the subtext of his position. Otherwise his hostility to intentionalism (pp. 154–58), which he bases on the flimsiest grounds, seems inexplicable.

16. Advocacy of originalist interpretation can be traced in its recent history to R. Berger, *Government by Judiciary: The Transformation of the Fourteenth Amendment* (1977); A. Bickel, *The Least Dangerous Branch* (1962); Bickel, "The Original Understanding and the Segregation Decision," 69 *Harv. L. Rev.* 1 (1955); and Monaghan, "Our Perfect Constitution," 56 *N.Y.U. L. Rev.* 353 (1981). For writings by nonoriginalists, see J. Ely, *Democracy and Distrust* (1980); M. Perry, *The Constitution, the Courts, and Human Rights* (1982); Brest, "The Misconceived Quest for the Original Understanding," 60 *B.U.L. Rev.* 204 (1980), reprinted in this volume; Simon, "The Authority of the Framers of the Constitution: Can Originalist Interpretation Be Justified?" 73 *Cal. L. Rev.* 1482 (1985).

17. Even the most recent debates have stumbled over the idea that somehow one must either adhere to the social arrangements that the intentions of the Framers put into practice—or did not repeal—or declare oneself a noninterpretivist. For its advocates, the beauty of the originalist conception is the constraint it places on the power of the judiciary to rearrange social conditions to conform more perfectly to a conception of justice, a power that originalists believe should rest only with the legislative branch.

18. He seems to have in mind, perhaps among others, E. Hirsch, *The Aims of Interpretation* (1976). Dworkin ignores arguments about author's intention put forward by Stanley Fish and Walter Benn Michaels. See note 2 sup. In their work, intention has a theoretical power and flexibility that Dworkin altogether fails to acknowledge.

19. In Dworkin, "Not Really," part of an increasingly acrimonious exchange with Fish, he parried some of Fish's intentionalist arguments with the suggestion that Fish was saying the following: "[A] plausible interpretation must describe a point or theme or reading such that someone who intended to produce a work of the kind so described might have created the work being interpreted. I agree, which is why I said that asking about the intentions of an imagined author might be a useful way to put the question of interpretation."

20. Dworkin, "My Reply" 309.

21. See text accompanying notes 3–4 sup.

22. The equation between utterance meaning and textual meaning is not uncontroversial. For a very cogent argument on this point, see Fish, "With the Compliments of the Author: Reflections on Austin and Derrida," 8 *Critical Inquiry* 693 (1982).

23. In fact, such events are so common in "ordinary conversation" that the phrase "she heard what she wanted to hear" stands idiomatically for a kind of misinterpretation. However, the distinction the phrase inscribes will be meaningless under Dworkin's regime, unless what is "real," as opposed to what is "imagined," is brought to bear.

24. An example of such criticism is the unsigned review of *Northanger Abbey* and *Persuasion* by Richard Whateley in 24 *Critical Rev.* 352–76 (1821).

25. See M. Mudrick, *Jane Austen: Irony as Defense and Discovery* 1 (1952); Harding, "Regulated Hatred: An Aspect of the Work of Jane Austen," 8 *Scrutiny* 346–55 (1940).

26. See A. Duckworth, *The Improvement of the Estate: A Study of Jane Austen's Novels* 2 (1971); M. Mudrick, *Jane Austen* 155–78; Tanner, "In Between—Anne Elliot Marries a Sailor and Charlotte Heywood Goes to the Seaside," in *Jane Austen in a Social Context* 180 (D. Monaghan, ed. 1981).

27. See Auerbach, "O Brave New World: Evolution and Revolution in *Persuasion*," 112

Eng. Literary Hist. 112 (1972); Monaghan, "Jane Austen and the Position of Women," in *Jane Austen in a Social Context* 105.

28. Dworkin's political morality hypothesis implies that a text is read according to substantive values that are held prior to any particular reading. This is not to say that any reading will not necessarily involve a set of questions about how a text fits into a complex system of such values. However, the values themselves are there before the reading. Formal values, on the other hand, cannot be stated before the reading except trivially (as, for example, noting that we start on the first page and stop where the text notes "the end").

29. Perhaps the most familiar example of this phenomenon is the famous Carolene Products footnote, United States v. Carolene Prods. Co., 304 U.S. 144, 152 n.4 (1938).

30. For example, the critic Jerome McGann calls attention to the strange fact that for both W.H. Auden's "September, 1939" and M. Moore's "Poetry," quite distinct texts have been circulating simultaneously, each included in different collections and anthologies. He further argues that even for critics ignorant of the multiple texts of the poems, these texts are "felt" in the interpretations, because of the impact they have had on the poem's critical history. See J. McGann, *The Beauty of Inflections* 86–87 (1985).

31. Plays, often altered significantly in different productions, might occupy the other end of the spectrum. An example is the current production of *Wild Honey*, an unfinished Chekhov play substantially rewritten (and finished) for Broadway by Michael Frayn.

32. For instance, the canonical text of Keats's "La Belle Dame Sans Merci" was established in 1848 in *Life, Letters, and Literary Remains of John Keats* 268 (R. Milnes, ed. 1848). "La Belle Dame" had been published only once during Keats's lifetime: in 1819, in a literary magazine called *The Indicator*. However, the *Life* used another text of the poem, from the papers of one of its editors, which differed substantially from *The Indicator* text. Jerome McGann believes that the choice of text—which in this instance involved the changing of many "words" within *The Indicator* text—was affected by the editors' misogyny and naive romanticism. However, the arguments for the text were always couched in aesthetic terms. In creating a "definitive" text, editors change words of the text that "make no sense" or that are not as "good" as words on another text of the same poem, according to their idea of the effects the author must have intended—in this case to produce "beauty." See J. McGann, *Beauty of Inflections* 32–45.

33. Dworkin concedes that authorial intention is dispositive when it comes to word meanings; yet despite this, he claims that authorial intentions are not important when it comes to the meaning of the work as a whole (p. 155). Yet this concession gives away the game. Through word meaning, authorial intention insinuates itself into every aspect of interpretation. Indeed, the distinction between the meanings of words in the texts and meaning of the work as a whole is an artificial one. An interpretation will derive its view of meaning "as a whole" from certain critical passages, where the identification of word meaning will constitute the crux of the interpretive act.

34. See Knapp and Michaels, "Against Theory," in *Against Theory* 11–30 (W. J. T. Mitchell, ed. 1985) for a detailed argument for this point.

35. In "The Authority of Text," p. 564, Michael Perry suggests that if the author's intention is to be identified with "interpretation," constitutional scholars should do something else, for example, construe the Constitution "as the symbolization of the fundamental, constitutive aspirations of the political tradition." In the absence of any argument about how such construction of a symbol would be different from reading (or interpreting) a text, Perry seems simply to be changing terminology. In that case, all the arguments still apply. If he means construing a symbol in ordinary language, his project seems profoundly irrationalist.

36. Of course, it is difficult to assess the degree of intertextual influence. I earlier characterized "On Interpretation and Objectivity" as a "later version" of an essay, "My Reply to Stanley Fish . . . ." See note 2 sup. Yet Dworkin himself calls it a "new essay" that "draws on material" from "My Reply" (p. 408). This is a nontrivial distinction, having to do with how far one can attribute arguments fielded in "My Reply" to the present Dworkin.

If these are versions of the same essay, its passages in the earlier version might have greater bearing on the arguments being presented in the later one. Of course, it is possible that in omitting these passages, Dworkin meant to signal that he no longer held to them. Even if they were different essays, arguments about the degree to which the omitted material revealed Dworkin's underlying assumptions would still have to be made.

In analyzing Dworkin, I have made an ad hoc decision about whether to consider these texts versions of one text, as well as deciding what it would mean, in a revision, that a significant argument was cut out. It is only fair to point out that such decisions would be likely to depend on whether the deleted material is consistent with the view that I (or any interpreter) have deemed "the best interpretation."

It cannot be too strongly emphasized that numberless subtle questions of formal structure are sized up according to the requirements of the substantive arguments. I hope that my saying so does not cast me as an irrationalist. Nor do I mean to cast suspicion on my motives. I think I have good arguments for my view. However, there simply are no hard and fast rules, even when we act in good faith. The needs of the arguments that we are disposed to make will be a powerful interest, converting the available substance in perfect good faith into fodder for formal arguments and the available formal structure into fodder for substantive arguments.

37. This raises the question of the importance we place on contemporaneous reports by the Framers on their views of what they had done. Here, it is important to distinguish between a Framer's intention and his interpretation of his intention. Typically, constitutional scholars use the word "understanding" as a synonym for "intention," so that if a Framer seemed to "understand" that the Constitution would permit some activity, this means that the activity was permitted "according to the Framers' intentions." However, an understanding, in this sense, is simply an interpretation of what the intention was. It is not the intention itself. Moreover, a Framer's interpretation of his intention is not dispositive, although it may yield important clues. Nor does any single intention tell later interpreters how to aggregate the several intentions of the Framers, or those of the community that adopted their text. Moreover, the Framers could have no idea of the purposes for which later interpretation would be done. For further discussion of this point, see notes 40–41 inf. and accompanying text.

Dworkin sees, but misunderstands this problem. He gives the example of John Fowles's claim that his idea of what he meant by his novel *The French Lieutenant's Woman* changed after he saw the movie. At this, Dworkin points out that Fowles's intention had not changed as a result of the change in Fowles's view of his own meaning. Thus, Dworkin believes that author's intentions cannot be the same as the meaning of the text. The point is that what Fowles had in each case was an interpretation of his intention; and this interpretation was his view of what his intention had been. Fowles's "intention" had not changed, but his interpretation, thus his view of it, had (pp. 156–57).

38. Dworkin, "My Reply" 311–12.

39. There are conflicting impulses in Derridean deconstruction. Derrida in certain moods understands the "center" and the "truth" as functions that must and will continually be reinscribed in every interpretation. At such moments, free play seems to signify only the ceaseless displacement of one interpretation by another. In other moods, free play seems to invade every interpretation in a way that denies legitimacy to the gesture of its inscription of a center. For the more radically skeptical Derrida on the problem of communication and interpretation, see J. Derrida, "Signature Evénement Contexte," in *Marges de la Philosophie* 365 (1972). For an essay in which the two impulses strive with and against each other, see Derrida, "Structure, Sign, and Play in the Discourse of Human Sciences," in *The Structuralist Controversy: The Languages of Criticism and the Sciences of Man* 264–65 (R. Macksey and E. Donato, eds. 1972) [hereafter Derrida, "Structure"].

> There are thus two interpretations of interpretation, of structure, of sign, of freeplay. The one seeks to decipher, dreams of deciphering, a truth or an origin which is free from freeplay and from the order of the sign, and lives like an exile the necessity of interpretation. The other, which is no longer turned toward the origin, affirms freeplay and tries to pass beyond man and humanism, the name man being the name of that being who, throughout the history of metaphysics or of ontotheology—in other words, through the history of all his history—has

dreamed of full presence, the reassuring foundation, the origin and the end of the game. [Ibid.]

40. Free play is an enervating enough game for literary critics. In the realm of law, it is positively annihilating. Perhaps more than any discipline, law dreams of "the reassuring foundation . . . the end of the game" (Derrida, "Structure" 265).

41. Dworkin suggests a procedure similar to the first part of my answer; but he believes that it refutes the intentionalist argument. He says, "I might add that no compelling argument has yet been produced . . . in favor of deferring to a delegate's more concrete intentions, and that this is of major importance in arguments about whether the 'original intention' of the Framers requires abolishing, for example, racial discrimination or capital punishment" (p. 164). If no argument has been produced in favor of deferring to a delegate's concrete intentions, then the problem of intention does not present hard problems; it still always must be decided. Moreover, it seems clear that whether such arguments have been mentioned, they clearly underlie the originalist position. Dworkin's chain novel specifically countenances, incidentally, the notion that later interpretations of prior law will find the meaning that had always been there, even though they articulate it for the first time. Otherwise, individuals will have been retroactively subject to new law, and the legitimacy of Dworkin's system would be severely undermined. In this sense, even if the argument for concrete intention has not been articulated in those terms, it clearly is operating.

42. See also W. Shakespeare, *Othello*, III.iii.360 in *The Riverside Shakespeare* (H. Baker, ed. 1974). *Othello* is another play turning on the problem of proof. Its action, ironically, depends, contrary to Hamlet's, on Othello's impulsiveness, his speed in avenging the "wrong," despite an absence of proof.

43. Yet the play-within-the-play is subject to many interpretations. Indeed, it can be read as a veiled threat against Claudius himself, and Claudius's exit as the uproar of a man who suddenly fears that his life is in danger.

An Essay in the Deconstruction of Contract Doctrine

1. For a recent compelling account of the lawyer as storyteller, see Lopez, "Lay Lawyering," 32 *UCLA L. Rev.* 1 (1984).

2. For some incisive observations about the peculiar nature of *legal* stories, see Llewellyn, "What Price Contract?—An essay in Perspective," 40 *Yale L.J.* 705, 720–24 (1931).

3. If we lawyers create this world of story, then we may legitimately ask how we could ever transcend our own limitations to see the limitations of our creation. The answer must be that the stories we tell only partly constrain us. Lawyers and would-be lawyers can and do learn to set off their "professional" stories from their "personal" stories; in this sense, at least, some competing viewpoints are available to all of us. A fruitful comparison is provided by the work of Carol Gilligan, who writes of the two different voices that members of our society tend to use to formulate and resolve moral dilemmas. Both voices are generally available to each individual, but individuals differ dramatically in the extent to which they use each voice, and different types of situation may provoke the use of one voice rather than the other (C. Gilligan, *In a Different Voice* (1982)).

In addition, those who dominate the legal forum only incompletely dictate the range of legitimate stories. There is therefore some room for those who speak in a different voice, and who can use that voice to critique the dominant one.

4. I am using the word *doctrine* here in an expansive sense. I mean by it not just the bare-bones articulation of rules, as in "silence cannot generally constitute assent," or the text of a *Restatement* provision, but instead the rules as applied by judges and elaborated by commentators. A judicial opinion is therefore an instance of "doctrine," as are the commentary and illustrations that accompany each *Restatement* provision.

5. I have chosen these dualities because they are a familiar part of the discourse of contract doctrine. Since the nineteenth century, contract doctrine has conceived of itself as being about intention and not regulation, and therefore as private and not public. The

Second Restatement has expressed its preference for objective rather than subjective standards of interpretation by subordinating intent to manifestation. A long-standing debate over the nature of consideration asks whether the requirement is one of form or of substance.

Precisely because these concepts are familiar and much used, I am relying on my readers sharing at least a rough sense of what the terms convey, and how they are employed. This frees me from the task of having to offer initial definitions. Instead, I can ask my readers to explore with me the range of meaning and use of these key concepts as my analysis develops. Indeed, the provision of tidy definitions would be fundamentally incompatible with my project, which demonstrates that each pole of a duality is best understood and defined in relation to its opposite, and in fact depends upon an (unavailable) prior understanding of its opposite.

The dualities are also connected to one another by the problems of power and knowledge, in a fashion which their conceptual differentiation falsifies. Within our current doctrinal framework, the shift from intent to manifestation, as I will show, is most easily viewed as a shift from private to public from the perspective of knowledge. The shift from substance to form is most easily viewed as a similar shift from private to public from the perspective of knowledge but can be seen as a shift from public to private from the perspective of power. All this is the subject of my story.

6. *Restatement (Second) of Contracts* (1979) [hereafter *Restatement (Second)*]. Unless otherwise indicated, references in the text to the *Restatement,* are to the *Restatement (Second) of Contracts.*

I present what should be understood to be a flattened, synchronic picture of the *Second Restatement*'s current signification. This picture is the reality for most students of contract, who come to the subject with little or no appreciation for its history, or for the role of the Restatements in that history. To them the *Second Restatement* speaks with the authority of a single, not a divided, voice; and its provisions are taken to announce the best articulated wisdom we can muster on the various topics within its scope. This is indeed one of the claims the *Second Restatement* makes, and for students it is likely to be unmitigated by the sophisticated understanding of differing perspectives which allows teachers to excuse evidence of internal inconsistency. Perhaps most importantly, the "frozen" picture of the *Second Restatement* that I paint allows us all, teachers and students, to face more directly the question whether any group, unanimous or divided, *could* have produced the internally consistent document the *Second Restatement* turns out not to be.

7. I have found recent cases to be of particular use in the classroom. They give students the experience of using their own understanding of how their society works today as a basis for critiquing a judicial product. Otherwise students seem all too ready to assume that their lack of historical information prevents them from judging a result which, if it were contemporary, would instinctively appall them. A contemporary decision denying relief to a woman who lived with a man for twenty years, raised his children, helped set him up in business, and then was abandoned by him is harder for students to distance themselves from than, for example, the plight of Sister Antillico, related in Kirksey v. Kirksey, 8 Ala. 131 (1845).

8. F. Kessler and G. Gilmore, *Contracts: Cases and Materials* (2d ed., 1970) (1st ed., 1953) [hereafter Kessler & Gilmore].

9. Unfortunately the book has one severe limitation: it is now desperately out of date, the most recent edition having been published in 1970. At one level any such concern is trivial, given how many contract casebooks give pride of place to nineteenth-century cases, how much of doctrine is essentially the same now as then. But it does mean that the Uniform Sales Act receives undue prominence, while the *Uniform Commercial Code* and interpretive cases get short shrift; and the *Second Restatement* appears only as a ghost on the horizon, making marginal appearances through extant Tentative Drafts. I have resolved this problem, for my teaching purposes, by relying heavily on the *Second Restatement* as a separate source, and by adding recent cases in a number of places, to demonstrate current variations on doctrinal manipulation.

10. For the origins of this critique, see K. Marx, "On the Jewish Question," in *Early Writings* 1 (T. Bottmore, trans. 1963). Early legal work in this genre could be said to include

the writings of Commons, Hale, Felix and Morris Cohen, and Kessler. Later exponents are those working under the loose umbrella of "critical legal studies," with the first significant contribution perhaps being Kennedy, "Form and Substance in Private Law Adjudication," 89 *Harv. L. Rev.* 1685 (1976).

11. For a critical account of this liberal conception in a nonlegal context, see C. Mac-Pherson, *The Political Theory of Possessive Individualism* 1-4, 263-77 (1962). For an account in the context of legal consciousness, see Mensch, "The History of Mainstream Legal Thought," in *The Politics of Law: A Progressive Critique* 23-26 (D. Kairys, ed. 1982) [hereafter *The Politics of Law*].

12. It is crucial to understand that the critique is not espousing consistency or clarity or determinacy as its values; rather it seeks to reveal how the liberal system fails to live up to its expectations of itself. The flaw is measured against internal, not external, standards. This method of attack is frequently countered by an assertion that any "adult" understanding of the system includes the recognition that there will be "hard cases," and that clarity and consistency and determinacy are not universally attainable. The response to this argument must be, as I hope this chapter demonstrates, first, that the problems extend beyond the "hard case," and second, that a system that devotes so much rhetoric to disguising indeterminacy, rather than frankly acknowledging it, forfeits the claim to adulthood.

13. To take concrete examples from work that has explored this difficulty: To what extent do we imagine that people should have regard only for their own interests, and to what extent do we imagine that people should have regard for the interests of others? See Kennedy, "Form and Substance" 1713–37. To what extent do we think that people should be free to act, even if the consequences are injurious to others, and to what extent should people instead be protected against the consequences of others' activity? See Singer, "The Legal Rights Debate in Analytical Jurisprudence from Bentham to Hohfeld," 1982 *Wisc. L. Rev.* 980–84. Our difficulties with the boundary between self and other are reiterated in our inability definitively to know what is or is not in our interests, and to define what counts as injury.

14. In "Form and Substance," Kennedy frames his discussion around individualism and altruism, rule and principle (pp. 1685–87). Singer, in "The Legal Rights Debate," centers his analysis on the distinction between self-regarding and other-regarding behavior (p. 980); Feinman, in "Critical Approaches for Contract Law," 80 *UCLA L. Rev.* 838–47 (1983), uses individualism and collectivism as his organizing categories.

15. See Gordon, "New Developments in Legal Theory," in *The Politics of Law* 284–89.

16. Three helpful introductions are J. Culler, *On Deconstruction: Theory and Criticism after Structuralism* (1982); C. Norris, *Deconstruction: Theory and Practice* (1982); *Structuralism and Since: From Lévi-Strauss to Derrida* (J. Sturrock, ed. 1979).

17. For an introduction, see generally Culler, "Jacques Derrida," in *Structuralism and Since* 154; Spivak, "Translator's Preface" to J. Derrida, *Of Grammatology* ix (G. Spivak, trans. 1976).

18. See, e.g., Frug, "The Ideology of Bureaucracy in American Law," 97 *Harv. L. Rev.* 1277–96 (1984); David Kennedy, "International Legal Structures" (1984) (unpublished manuscript on file with author).

19. J. Derrida, *Of Grammatology* 144.

20. Ibid. An example of the dynamic of the dangerous supplement is contract doctrine's stressing of objective interpretations of contractual intent over subjective ones, invoking both the difficulty of assessing subjective intent, and the loss of predictability, stability, certainty, and security that reliance on subjective intent would produce. Yet subjective intent retains a tolerated supplemental position in contract doctrine, being invoked quite explicitly to resolve certain doctrinal problems. An examination of the way in which subjective intent is used as supplement reveals that even as the adherence to objectivity is designed to banish the unreliable subjective, that very objectivity is in fact sustained only by its claim to incorporate and represent the subjective. Because the subjective it purports to represent is unknowable, however, the privileged objective loses its claim to dominance. The lesson of subjective intent as supplement is that the problem of knowledge, which

the dominant voice of doctrine purports to resolve by recourse to objective standards, has not in fact been contained. By assuring us that problems of understanding arise only in the realm of the subjective, doctrine "defers" or "displaces" the problem of knowledge, puts it over to some other place where it will not threaten to sabotage the project at hand.

For an illustration of the dynamic of the dangerous supplement in Derrida's own writing, see his treatment of speech and writing in Rousseau's work, *Of Grammatology* 141–64. For an illustration based on conventional understandings of the relationship between law and society, see Frug, "Ideology of Bureaucracy" 1288–89.

21. Derrida has described the possibilities that would exist in such a world: "[E]verything becomes possible against the language-police; for example 'literatures' or 'revolutions' that as yet have no model. Everything is possible except for an exhaustive typology that would claim to limit the owners of graft or fiction by and within an analytical logic of distinction, opposition, and classification in genus and species" ("Limited Inc.," 2 *Glyph* 243 (1977)).

22. The strands of feminist theory that have most influenced my thinking are the psychoanalytic work represented by N. Chodorow, *The Reproduction of Mothering: Psychoanalysis and the Sociology of Gender* (1978) and D. Dinnerstein, *The Mermaid and the Minotaur: Sexual Arrangements and Human Malaise* (1976); the work in literary theory exemplified by J. Culler, *On Deconstruction* 43–64; J. Fetterley, *The Resisting Reader* xi–xxvi (1978); and S. Gilbert and S. Gubar, *The Madwoman in the Attic* 3–104 (1979); and the work of radical French feminists collected in *New French Feminisms* (E. Marks and I. de Courtivron, eds. 1981) and described in Stanton, "Language and Revolution: The Franco-American Dis-Connection," in *The Future of Difference* 73 (H. Eisenstein and A. Jardine, eds. 1980). Powerful examples of feminism brought to bear on legal materials and legal theory include MacKinnon, "Feminism, Marxism, Method, and the State: An Agenda for Theory," 7 *Signs: J. of Women in Culture & Soc.* 515 (1982); MacKinnon, "Feminism, Marxism, Method, and the State: Toward Feminist Jurisprudence," 8 *Signs: J. of Women in Culture & Soc.* 635 (1983); Olsen, "The Family and the Market: A Study of Ideology and Legal Reform," 96 *Harv. L. Rev.* 1497 (1983).

I use the word *aspire* to reflect that the search for an external perspective must be conducted with the awareness that we are always problematically implicated in the dominant discourse from which we wish to extricate ourselves. "Feminism criticizes this male totality without an account of our capacity to do so, or to imagine or realize a more whole truth. Feminism affirms women's point of view by revealing, criticizing and explaining its impossibility." MacKinnon, "Feminism, Marxism, Method, and the State: Toward Feminist Jurisprudence" 637.

23. It therefore seems unnecessary, for the purposes of this chapter, to choose among these critiques, although when it comes to looking behind and beyond doctrine to ask what is perpetrated through it, my own first commitment is to assess how women are viewed and treated in legal contexts.

24.
> Anything we know is outside
> of rational expression. Do we know
> anything? No, of course we don't.
> What we know is not true and what is true
> is beyond our knowing; knowing is not the point.
> But we are aware of something and, in that sense,
> we know. . . .
> [W. Bronk, "Rational Expression," in *Life*
> *Supports: New and Collected Poems* 210 (1982)]

25. The work of Foucault offers a highly relevant model, in its intricate examination of the relationship between knowledge and power, or the *"régime du savoir,"* as it operates in the development of both social institutions and disciplines of learning, and their interaction. See, e.g., M. Foucault, *The History of Sexuality* (1978); Foucault, "Afterword: The Subject and Power," in H. Dreyfus and P. Rabinow, *Michel Foucault: Beyond Structuralism and Hermeneutics* 208 (1982). On the methodology of "thick description," see C. Geertz, *The Interpretation of Cultures* 3–30 (1973) (discussing use of this technique in anthropological

research to produce ethnographic descriptions that advance interpretive rather than scientific theory of culture).

26. To borrow from Kessler: "The freedom of contract dogma is the real hero or villain in the drama . . . but it prefers to remain in the safety of the background if possible, leaving the actual fighting to consideration and to the host of other satellites—all of which is very often confusion to the audience which vaguely senses the unreality of the atmosphere" [Kessler, "Contracts of Adhesion—Some Thoughts about Freedom of Contract," 43 *Colum. L. Rev.* 639 (1943)].

27. See, e.g., P. Atiyah, *The Rise and Fall of Freedom of Contract* 405–8 (1979) (tracing the emergence of will theory in late eighteenth and early nineteenth centuries).

28. "[W]hen both parties will the same thing, and each communicates his will to the other, with a mutual engagement to carry it into effect, then (and not till then) an agreement or contract between the two is constituted." Haynes v. Haynes, 1 Dr. & Sm. 426, 433, 62 Eng. Rep. 442, 445 (1861).

29. See, e.g., Dickinson v. Dodds, 2 Ch. D. 463 (1876); Raffles v. Wichelhaus, 2 Hurl. & C. 906, 159 Eng. Rep. 375 (Ex. 1864), and the discussion of these cases in G. Gilmore, *The Death of Contract* 28–29, 35–42 (1974).

30. See, e.g., P. Atiyah, *Rise and Fall* 407–8; Cohen, "The Basis of Contract," 46 *Harv. L. Rev.* 575–78 (1933); Feinman, "Critical Approaches" 831–32.

31. "There is no contract without assent, but once the objective manifestations of assent are present, their author is bound." Kessler, "Contracts of Adhesion" 630. "The thing which characterizes the law of contracts and conveyances is that in this field forms are deliberately used, and are intended to be so used, by the parties whose acts are to be judged by the law." Fuller, "Consideration and Form," 41 *Colum. L. Rev.* 799, 801 (1941). Fuller also suggests that autonomy is dependent upon "security of transactions," and that "security of transactions" is by-and-large guaranteed by objective interpretation, even though objective interpretation may defeat party intention in particular instances. Ibid., p. 808.

32. "Contractualism in the law, that is, the view that in an ideally desirable system of law all obligation would arise only out of the will of the individual contracting freely, rests not only on the will theory of contract but also on the political doctrine that all restraint is evil and that the government is best which governs least. This in turn is connected with the classical economic optimism that there is a sort of preestablished harmony between the good of all and the pursuit by each of his own selfish economic gain" (Cohen, "Basis of Contract" 558).

33. Ibid., p. 562. See also Feinman, "Critical Approaches" 834.

34. Jerome Frank is an exception, in that he did consistently focus on the problematic relationship between subjective and objective in the area of contractual interpretation. On occasion, he stresses the vagaries of competing idiosyncratic subjectivities, as, for example, in Zell v. American Seating Co., 138 F.2d 641, 647 (2d Cir. 1943), *rev'd*, 322 U.S. 709 (1944) (*per curiam*), reprinted in Kessler and Gilmore, *Contracts* 679. See text accompanying note 110 inf. Elsewhere, he suggests the possibility for a more systematic imposition of cultural norms. See, e.g., J. Frank, *Courts on Trial: Myth and Reality in American Justice* 309 (1969).

35. See, e.g., *Restatement (Second)* § 4 comments a & b.

36. 29 Pa. 465 (1857). The case is reprinted in Kessler and Gilmore, *Contracts* 120. In this account I am indebted to Duncan Kennedy, who discusses the emergence of the modern concept of quasi contract in "The Rise and Fall of Classical Legal Thought: 1850–1940," 19–24 (chap. 4) (1975) (unpublished manuscript on file with author).

37. The suit also involved repayment of a loan, but that aspect is not treated here.

38. *Hertzog*, 29 Pa. at 465.

39. Idem at 466.

40. Idem at 467; see also *Restatement (Second)*, § 4 comments a & b (presenting parallel modern treatment of different types of contracts).

41. *Hertzog*, 29 Pa. at 467.

42. See idem (quoting 2 W. Blackstone, *Commentaries* *443).

43. 29 Pa. at 467.

44. Idem at 468 (emphasis in original).

45. Idem.

46. Idem at 467.

47. Idem.

48. Idem (emphasis added).

49. Idem at 468.

50. Idem at 470.

51. See idem at 467 (quoting 2 W. Blackstone, *Commentaries* at *443).

52. 26 Pa. at 468.

53. Idem at 469. Judge Lowrie wrote, "If we find, as ascertained circumstances, that a stranger has been in the employment of another, we immediately infer a contract of hiring, because the principles of individuality and self-interest, common to human nature, and therefore the customs of society, require this inference" (idem).

54. Idem. "But if we find a son in the employment of his father," Lowrie writes, "we do not infer a contract of hiring, because the principle of family affection is sufficient to account for the family association, and does not demand the inference of a contract" (idem).

Actually Lowrie goes further in his analysis of father-son employment. On the one hand, it demeans sons to put them in the legal position of hired servants, when they are characteristically much superior. On the other, the son who fails to strike out on his own is a burden to his father; the father supports such a son because he "lack[s] the energy and independence necessary for such a course," not because the father desires to employ him (idem). On this reading the son is inferior to the hired servant.

55. Idem.

56. Idem.

57. Idem at 470–71.

58. Idem at 471.

59. Costigan, "Implied-in-Fact Contracts and Mutual Assent," 33 *Harv. L. Rev.* 376 (1920).

60. Ibid., p. 383.

61. Ibid. pp. 384–85; see also Whittier, "The *Restatement of Contracts* and Mutual Assent," 17 *Calif. L. Rev.* 450–51 (1929) (role of custom and common understanding in implication (in fact) of promises).

62. Costigan, "Implied-in-Fact Contracts" 378.

63. Ibid., p. 390.

64. He suggests that his earlier discussion of Vickery v. Ritchie, 202 Mass. 247, 88 N.E. 835 (1909), reprinted in Kessler and Gilmore, *Contracts* 139, has "foreshadowed" this demonstration (Costigan, "Implied-in-Fact Contracts" 390). It has not. Later in the article, he refers back to the earlier discussion and he claims that "the real nature of the primary right . . . was contractual" (ibid., p. 400 n.37). It is not clear why.

65. See Part 1A. sup.

66. Cohen, "Basis of Contracts" 577.

67. Ibid., p. 589. Fuller is elaborating a similar idea when he details the "channeling function" of consideration. Fuller, "Consideration and Form" 801–3.

68. "[W]hile this objection has become familiar," Cohen writes, "it has not been very effective. The force of the old ideas, embodied in the traditional language, has not always

been overcome even by those who like Langdell and Salmond profess to recognize the fictional element in the will theory" ("Basis of Contracts" 75).

69. Thus, the promise "may be stated in words either oral or written, or may be inferred wholly or partly from conduct." *Restatement (Second)*, § 4. Comment a elaborates: "Contracts are often spoken of as express or implied. The distinction involves, however, no difference in legal effects, but lies merely in the mode of manifesting assent. Just as assent may be manifested by words or other conduct, sometimes including silence, so intention to make a promise may be manifested in language or by implication from other circumstances, including course of dealing or usage of trade or course of performance" (ibid.).

See also ibid. § 19 comment a (assent may be manifested in words or in acts, with no distinction as to effect of promise).

70. Ibid. § 4 comment b.

71. "Quasi-contracts have often been called implied contracts or contracts implied in law; but, unlike true contracts, quasi-contracts are not based on the apparent intention of the parties to undertake the performances in question, nor are they promises. They are obligations created by law for reasons of justice. Such obligations were ordinarily enforced at common law in the same form of action (assumpsit) that was appropriate to true contracts, and some confusion with reference to the nature of quasi-contracts has been caused thereby" (ibid.).

72. Ibid.

73. See *Restatement of Restitution: Quasi Contracts and Constructive Trusts* (1937).

74. *Restatement (Second)*, § 4 comment b.

75. Ibid.

76. Ibid. § 19 comment a.

77. Ibid.

78. Ibid.

79. The *Second Restatement* provides an example apparently intended to provide further reassurance. See ibid. § 19 comment a, illustration 1. The example involves a claim "against a decedent's estate for services rendered"—the *Hertzog* situation (ibid. § 19 comment a). Because one of the parties to the relationship is dead, his "words" are unavailable as evidence; because of the Dead Man's Statute, words exchanged between the parties are probably also inadmissable. Conduct and circumstance are therefore peculiarly preponderant as evidence of whether "services were rendered gratuitously" (ibid.). The carefully delimited parameters of the hypothetical convey a message: only in exceptional circumstances do courts risk crossing the line between enforcing private agreement and imposing external obligations; "publicness" will not invade the area of the express contract.

80. See Kessler and Gilmore, *Contracts* 116–19.

81. Ibid., p. 117.

82. Ibid. (quoting T. Parsons, *The Structure of Social Action* 311 (1949)).

83. Kessler and Gilmore, *Contracts* 117.

84. Ibid., p. 118 (quoting J. Clark, *Social Control of Business* 100 (2d ed. 1939)). In support of this proposition, Kessler and Gilmore cite Home Bldg. & Loan Ass'n v. Blaisdell, 290 U.S. 398 (1934). See Kessler and Gilmore, *Contracts* 118.

85. Kessler and Gilmore, *Contracts* 118.

86. Ibid., p. 119.

87. Ibid.

88. Ibid.

89. Ibid.

90. Ibid.

91. See Kessler and Gilmore, *Contracts* 35–38.

92. G. Gilmore, *Death of Contract* 41–44; see notes 103–5 inf. and accompanying text.

93. See, e.g., Costigan, "Implied-in-Fact Contracts"; Whittier, "Restatement" 442–44.

94. *Restatement (Second)*, § 2(1).

95. Ibid. § 2(1) comment b.

96. Ibid. § 2(1).

97. Ibid. § 18.

98. See Farnsworth, " 'Meaning' in the Law of Contracts," 76 *Yale L.J.* 943–45 (1967). This subjective theory of formation was firmly established by the end of the eighteenth century. See, e.g., Adams v. Lindsell, 106 Eng. Rep. 250 (K.B. 1818), reprinted in Kessler and Gilmore, *Contracts* 268; Cooke v. Oxley, 100 Eng. Rep. 785 (K.B. 1790), reprinted in Kessler and Gilmore, *Contracts* 239; Williston, "Freedom of Contract," 6 *Cornell L.Q.* 368 (1921).

99. Farnsworth, "Meaning" 945. Gilmore stresses the extent to which residual reliance on the subjective "meeting of the minds" standard continued to characterize such later cases as Raffles v. Wichelhaus, 159 Eng. Rep. 375 (Ex. 1864), reprinted in Kessler and Gilmore, *Contracts* 709, and Dickinson v. Dodds, 2 Ch. D. 463 (Ch. Div'l Ct. 1876), reprinted in Kessler and Gilmore, *Contracts* 240. G. Gilmore, *Death of Contract* 35–44.

100. Holmes, "The Theory of Legal Interpretation," 12 *Harv. L. Rev.* 417 (1899).

101. Ibid., p. 417.

102. Ibid., pp. 417–18.

103. See *Raffles*, 159 Eng. Rep. 375.

104. See Holmes, "Theory of Legal Interpretation" 417–18. As Gilmore comments, "The magician who could 'objectify' *Raffles v. Wichelhaus* . . . could, the need arising, objectify anything. But why bother?" (*Death of Contract* 41).

105. 1 S. Williston, *Law of Contracts* § 95 (3d ed. 1957), reprinted in Kessler and Gilmore, *Contracts* 707.

106. Hotchkiss v. National City Bank, 200 F. 287, 293 (S.D.N.Y. 1911), aff'd, 201 F. 664 (2d Cir. 1912), aff'd, 231 U.S. 50 (1913), reprinted in Kessler and Gilmore, *Contracts* 707.
By making bishops his oracles, Hand has fudged the issue of how they would show that their divination of intent was the correct one; if they were mere humans with no special access to higher authority, we might imagine that they too would have to rely on manifestations. This would change the nature of the exercise from a simple privileging of manifestation (and disregard for intent) to an exercise in which certain manifestations were given priority over others by a standard other than that of intent. The parol evidence rule is a perfect example of this. Williston's objectivism turns out to have very specific implications for the application of that rule, but they are implications that depend not just on the privileging of manifestation over intent, but also the privileging of some manifestations over others. See text accompanying notes 130–54 inf. (treatment of parol evidence rule).

107. Ricketts v. Pennsylvania R.R., 153 F.2d 757, 761 (2d Cir. 1946) (Frank, J., concurring). Judge Frank's concurrence is excerpted in Kessler and Gilmore, *Contracts* 707.

108. "[I]n part at least, advocacy of the 'objective' standard in contracts appears to have represented a desire for legal symmetry, legal uniformity, a desire seemingly prompted by aesthetic impulses." *Ricketts*, 153 F.2d at 761 (Frank, J., concurring) (citation omitted).

109. These arguments suggest, first, that for most people there is no coercion in imposing an external standard on their behavior, since that standard is one they have already internalized and, second, that even when the external standard has not already been internalized, it can be, without notable cost, and indeed with advantage. The first argument assumes that law follows fact, the second that fact follows law.

110. Zell v. American Seating Co., 138 F.2d 641, 647 (2d Cir. 1943), rev'd, 322 U.S. 709 (1944) (per curiam), reprinted in Kessler and Gilmore, *Contracts* 679.

111. *Ricketts*, 153 F.2d at 761 (Frank, J., concurring).

112. 94 Vt. 345, 111 A. 343 (1920).

113. Idem at 347–48, 111 A. at 344.

114. Idem at 348, 111 A. at 344.

115. Idem, 111 A. at 344–45.

116. Idem, 111 A. at 345.

117. Idem.

118. Idem (citation omitted).

119. Idem at 349, 111 A. at 345.

120. Idem at 348, 111 A. at 345.

121. Justice Powers's fervor for the rule is further demonstrated by his refusal to consider the evidence as demonstrating what time would be reasonable under the circumstances, because the parties had not offered it on that basis (idem at 349, 111 A. at 345), and his *assumption* that the oral conversations referred to took place before the written contract was executed, despite the silence of the record on that point (idem).

122. Powers does stress the primacy of the "rule" (idem at 348, 111 A. at 344), as well as the fact that it would be "illogical and wrong" to decide otherwise (idem at 348, 111 A. at 345).

A nice counterpoint is provided by Garden Plaza Corp. v. S.S. Kresge Co., 78 N.J. Super. 485, 189 A.2d 448 (N.J. Super. Ct. App. Div. 1963): "[E]xperience teaches that language is so poor an instrument for communication or expression of intent that ordinarily all surrounding circumstances and conditions must be examined before there is any trustworthy assurance of derivation of contractual intent, even by reasonable judges of ordinary intelligence, from any given set of words which the parties have committed to paper as their contract" (idem at 496, 189 A.2d at 454). The judge justifies the fullest consideration of "surrounding and antecedent circumstances and negotiations" (idem). If "intent" has thus been raised to primacy, however, the necessity for a residual commitment to "manifestation" finds expression in the limitation—exactly converse to Powers's statement of the exception to *his* version of the rule—that the court's interpretation must be "one 'which the written words will bear' " (idem at 497, 189 A.2d at 455 (quoting Deerhurst Estates v. Meadow Homes, Inc., 64 N.J. Super. 134, 149, 165 A.2d 543, 551 [N.J. Super. Ct. App. Div. 1960])).

123. I have already identified the first version as a "fact leading law" argument, and the second as a "law leading fact" argument. See note 109 sup. For an illustration of the two themes conflated to provide a perfectly circular argument, see Baron Alderson's opinion in Hadley v. Baxendale, 9 Ex. 341, 355, 156 Eng. Rep. 145, 151 (1854), reprinted in Kessler and Gilmore, *Contracts* 1023.

124. Section 203 reads:
> In the interpretation of a promise or agreement or a term thereof, the following standards of preference are generally applicable:
> (a) an interpretation which gives a reasonable, lawful, and effective meaning to all the terms is preferred to an interpretation which leaves a part unreasonable, unlawful, or of no effect;
> (b) express terms are given greater weight than course of performance, course of dealing, and usage of trade, course of performance is given greater weight than course of dealing or usage of trade, and course of dealing is given greater weight than usage of trade;
> (c) specific terms and exact terms are given greater weight than general language;
> (d) separately negotiated or added terms are given greater weight than standardized terms or other terms not separately negotiated [*Restatement (Second)*, § 203].

125. Ibid. § 203 comment a (emphasis added).

126. Ibid.

127. Ibid.

128. Cf. ibid. § 154, which, in the area of mistake, provides just such a candid expression of the limitations of the rule formulated.

129. Ibid. § 203 comment a.

130. See ibid. § 209.

131. See ibid.

132. See, e.g., ibid. §§ 215–16.

133. E.g., Corbin, "The Parol Evidence Rule," 53 *Yale L.J.* 603, 609–10 (1944).

134. On the use of external evidence to show that a writing is integrated, see *Restatement (Second)*, § 209 comment c. Such evidence is admissible even when the writing *purports* to announce its integrated nature: "Written contracts, signed by both parties, may include an explicit declaration that there are no other agreements between the parties, but such a declaration may not be conclusive" (§ 209 comment b). On the use of external evidence to show whether the writing is a complete or only a partial integration, and whether collateral agreements exist, see ibid. § 210. "[A] writing cannot of itself prove its own completeness . . . " (ibid. § 210 comment b).

135. Ibid. § 212. As § 212 comment b explains, "[M]eaning can almost never be plain except in a context."

136. Ibid. §§ 214, 217. Section 214 provides that "evidence of prior or contemporaneous agreements and negotiations" is available for the purpose of establishing "illegality, fraud, duress, mistake, lack of consideration, or other invalidating cause." Section 217 excludes orally agreed-upon conditions to a written agreement from the ambit of the integrated agreement.

137. Cf. Hurst v. Lake & Co., 141 Or. 306, 315, 16 P.2d 627, 630 (1932), reprinted in Kessler and Gilmore, *Contracts* 673 (evidence of custom should not be excluded, even though instrument is nonambiguous on its face).

138. See text accompanying notes 124–29 sup.

139. "Whether a writing has been adopted as an integrated agreement is a question of fact to be determined in accordance with all relevant evidence" (*Restatement (Second)*, § 209 comment c).

140. "[W]ide latitude must be allowed for inquiry into circumstances bearing on the intention of the parties" (ibid. § 210 comment b).

141. "Writings do not prove themselves; ordinarily, if there is dispute, there must be testimony that there was a signature or other manifestation of assent" (ibid. § 214 comment a).

142. Ironically enough, this increased reliance on procedural devices is allied, as already suggested, with an increased concern for the protection of party intent. It further corresponds to what is commonly described as a shift from viewing the parol evidence rule as a "rule of evidence" to viewing it as a "rule of substantive law."

143. *Restatement (Second)*, § 209(3) provides that the apparently complete writing "is taken to be an integrated agreement unless it is established by other evidence that the writing did not constitute a final expression."

144. "[A]fter the transaction has been shown in all its length and breadth, the words of an integrated agreement remain the most important evidence of intention" (ibid. § 212 comment b).

145. Ibid. § 209.

146. Ibid. § 210.

147. Ibid. §§ 212–18.

148. Ibid. § 213 comment a.

149. Ibid. § 214 comment a.

150. Ibid. §§ 209(2), 210(3).

151. Ibid. § 209 comment c.

152. Ibid. § 212(2). The commentary elaborates that this reservation of interpretive authority to the judge "has the effect of limiting the power of the trier of fact to exercise a

dispensing power in the guise of a finding of fact, and thus contributes to the stability and predictability of contractual relations" (ibid. § 212 comment d).

153. See also Garden State Plaza Corp. v. S.S. Kresge Co., 78 N.J. Super. 485, 189 A.2d 448 (1963).

154. *Restatement (Second)*, § 212 comment d; see also note 141 sup. and accompanying text (discussing *Restatement*'s conception of proof needed to validate a writing).

155. *Restatement (Second)*, § 19.

156. Ibid. § 69. Section 69(1) provides that "[w]here an offeree fails to reply to an offer, his silence and inaction operate as an acceptance in the following cases only." Section 69(1) comment a confirms that "[a]cceptance by silence is exceptional."

157. The same is true of the "plain meaning" rule classically used to prohibit the use of external evidence in interpreting the integrated agreement unless the contractual language was ambiguous. Under that rule, an unambiguous dictionary definition could replace the actual significance intended by the parties.

158. Ibid. § 69 comment a.

159. Ibid.

160. It is worth noting the way in which the language "silently takes offered benefits" jars with the category "silence and inaction" of which it is supposed to be an example. Inaction here has been transmuted into "action" on the basis of a judgment that the offeree has "benefited." The instability of the terms is thereby illuminated. This is an illustration of the maxim that could be said to haunt this whole discussion: action, and sometimes inaction, speaks louder than words.

161. Ibid. § 69(1)(a) (emphasis added).

162. Ibid. § 69(1)(b)-(c) (emphasis added).

163. The Supreme Court of Illinois in Hewitt v. Hewitt, 77 Ill. 2d 49, 394 N.E.2d 1204 (1979), used the traditional argument that policy in this area should be left to the legislature—that the judiciary should stay out of "public policy in the domestic relations field." (idem at 61, 394 N.E.2d at 1209 (citations omitted)). The appeals court doubted the validity of the distinction between intervention and nonintervention, or "public" enforcement of the agreement, and "private" nonenforcement:
> [A]lthough the courts proclaim that they will have nothing to do with such matters, the proclamation in itself establishes, as to the parties involved, an effective and binding rule of law which tends to operate purely by accident or perhaps by reason of the cunning, anticipatory designs of just one of the parties.
> [Hewitt v. Hewitt, 62 Ill. App. 3d 861, 867, 380 N.E.2d 454, 459 (quoting West v. Knowles, 50 Wash. 2d 311, 316, 311 P.2d 689, 693 (1957)].

164. The appeals court in *Hewitt* thought that not enforcing agreements of this sort would encourage the income-producing party to avoid marriage, and favor the cunning. The supreme court said: "We cannot confidently say that judicial recognition of property rights between unmarried cohabitants will not make that alternative to marriage more attractive by allowing the parties to engage in such relationships with greater security." *Hewitt*, 77 Ill. 2d at 61–62, 394 N.E.2d at 1209.

165. Justice Tobriner does this consistently in his opinion in Marvin v. Marvin, 18 Cal. 3d 660, 557 P.2d 106, 134 Cal. Rptr. 815 (1976).

166. See, e.g., Cropsey v. Sweeney, 27 Barb. 310, 314–15 (N.Y. App. Div. 1858) ("[H]er long, devoted, faithful love, and services, as a *wife* and *mother*, will not permit us to say that she is legally entitled to receive pay for those services *as a servant*.") (emphasis in original); Roberts v. Roberts, 64 Wyo. 433, 450, 196 P.2d 361, 367 (1948) (" '[T]he relationship as husband and wife negative[s] that of master and servant . . . . ' ") (citation to Stewart v. Waterman, 97 Vt. 408, 414, 123 A. 524, 526 (1924), in Willis v. Willis, 48 Wyo. 403, 437, 49 P.2d 670, 681 (1935)).

167. "The law would do injustice to the plaintiff herself, by implying a promise to pay

for these services; and respect for the plaintiff herself, as well as for the law, compels us to [deny her relief]." Cropsey v. Sweeney, 27 Barb. at 315.

168. "From plaintiff's own lips and from her own petition, the court was informed that she and the defendant lived together or cohabited together without the benefit of marriage and in this court's judgment she 'committed iniquity' and the court concludes that her action 'arises out of an immoral transaction.' " Roach v. Buttons, 6 Fam. L. Rep. (BNA) 2355 (Tenn. Ch. Ct. 29 February 1980) (quoting Q. Pomeroy, *A Treatise on Equity Jurisdiction* §§ 397–404, at 737–61 (4th ed. 1918)). That her partner has equally participated in immoral conduct but is rewarded by a decision not to enforce the agreement is simply irrelevant. See, e.g., Kinnison v. Kinnison, 627 P.2d 594, 596, 599 (Wyo. 1981) (Rooney, J., dissenting).

169. See, e.g., Vallera v. Vallera, 21 Cal. 2d 681, 685, 134 P.2d 761, 763 (1948) (where woman denied maintenance and share of property acquired in man's name during relationship, "[e]quitable considerations arising from the reasonable expectation of the continuation of benefits attending the status of marriage entered into in good faith are not present"); Roach v. Buttons, 6 Fam. L. Rep. (BNA) 2355 (Tenn. Ch. Ct. 29 February 1980) ("[M]arriage is a legal state or legal relationship between two persons of the opposite sex and, as aforesaid, certain mutual benefits flow one to the other as a result of the marriage contract. . . . If plaintiff had married defendant, these rights and benefits would have been hers, but she entered into a relationship that is not sanctioned by Natural or Divine Law").

170. See, e.g., Baker v. Baker, 222 Minn. 169, 171–72, 23 N.W.2d 582, 583–84 (1946) ("Where the arrangement under which the parties lived together was a meretricious one, the court will grant no relief, . . . [I]n such a situation, there is no implied obligation on the part of the man to compensate the woman for household services rendered by her") (citations omitted).

171. This suggestion arises out of the notion that the relationship is one equally chosen and therefore equally avoidable. The Illinois Supreme Court in Hewitt v. Hewitt, 77 Ill. 2d at 58, 394 N.E.2d at 1207, questions whether "legal rights closely resembling those arising from conventional marriages, can be acquired by those who deliberately choose to enter into what have heretofore been commonly referred to as illicit or meretricious relationships . . . ." See also Roach v. Buttons, 6 Fam. L. Rep. (BNA) at 2355 ("[S]he voluntarily and with her eyes open entered into an illicit relationship . . . ."); Kinnison v. Kinnison, 627 P.2d 594, 597 (Wyo. 1981) (Rooney, J., dissenting):

> [T]he plain fact exists that both parties have assumed a relationship that is recognizable in law, morals and public policy only if the legal requirements for such relationship are met. For either of them to ask the courts to disregard this fact but sanction an aspect flowing from such relationship is impertinent.

172. For a court to enforce a cohabitation agreement would be "but another failure by the court to maintain the standards and principles upon which our society and nation were founded and which are essential to their successful continuance." Kinnison v. Kinnison, 627 P.2d at 597 (Rooney, J., dissenting). Justice Underwood, for the Supreme Court of Illinois in *Hewitt*, 77 Ill. 2d at 58, 394 N.E.2d at 1207–8, uses rhetorical questions to suggest a parade of horribles: "Will the fact [of enforcement] . . . encourage formation of such relationships and weaken marriage as the foundation of our family-based society? . . . And still more importantly: what of the children born of such relationships? . . . What of the sociological and psychological effects on them of that type of environment?"

173. XI S. Freud, "A Special Type of Choice of Object Made by Men," in *The Standard Edition of the Complete Psychological Works of Sigmund Freud* 165 (J. Strachey trans. & ed., 1957); XI S. Freud, "On the Universal Tendency to Debasement in the Sphere of Love," ibid., p. 179.

174. See, e.g., A. Dworkin, *Woman Hating* (1974).

175. Ibid., see especially 31–46, 118–50.

176. C. Gilligan note 3 sup., at 24–63 ("Images of Relationship").

177. N. Chodorow, note 22 sup.; D. Dinnerstein, note 22 sup.

178. It may not be possible, ultimately, to "transcend" the kinds of categories our current ways of thinking and imagining condemn us to use in order to make sense of our

experience. But being self-conscious about the particular set of categories inhering in particular doctrine may at least enable us to expand our repertoire, and enlarge the number of concrete alternatives available to us in this context, even while recognizing the limits of our culture.

Interpreting the Law

1. This history of the effects and reception of works and their interpretations is what Gadamer labels *Wirkungsgeschichte*, and the awareness of the earlier interpretations and their importance for the present interpretation is called *wirkungsgeschichtliches Bewusstsein* (a phase I shall translate hereafter as "hermeneutical awareness.")

2. R. Berger, *Government by Judiciary* 300 (1977), cited in M. Perry, *The Constitution, the Courts, and Human Rights* 68 (1982).

3. G. Wills, *Inventing America: Jefferson's Declaration of Independence* 259 (1978), cited in M. Perry, *The Constitution* 62.

4. J. Ely, *Democracy and Distrust: A Theory of Judicial Review* 60–63 (1980).

5. 438 U.S. 265 (1977).

6. J. Ely, *Democracy and Distrust* 62.

7. Ibid., p. 63.

8. Gadamer explicates his phrase "connection with the tradition" as follows: "Changing the established forms is no less a kind of connection with the tradition than defending the established forms. Tradition exists only in constant alteration. 'To gain a connection' with the tradition is a formulation intended to call attention to an experience whereby our plans and wishes are always in advance of reality, and are, so to speak, even without connection with reality. What then becomes important is to mediate between desirable anticipations and practicable possibilities, between sheer wishes and genuine intentions—that is, to imagine the anticipations in the substance of reality." "Replik," in *Hermeneutik und Ideologiekritik* 307 (1971)

9. J. Ely, *Democracy and Distrust* 63.

10. T. McCarthy, *The Critical Theory of Jürgen Habermas* 332 (1978).

11. For a discussion of the early exchanges between Habermas and Gadamer, see D. Hoy, *The Critical Circle: Literature, History, and Philosophical Hermeneutics* 117–28 (1978).

12. J. Habermas, 1 *Theorie des Kommunikativen Handelns* 194 (1981).

13. J. Habermas, *Legitimation Crisis* 89 (1975) (emphasis in original).

14. Ibid., p. 87.

15. J. Habermas, "A Reply to My Critics," in *Habermas: Critical Debates* 251 (J. Thompson and D. Held, eds. 1982) (emphasis in original).

16. Ibid., p. 113.

17. I owe this point to Harvard philosopher Thomas Scanlon, who made it in a discussion of the differences between his own contractualist moral philosophy and Habermas's theory.

18. Fiss, "Objectivity and Interpretation," 34 *Stan. L. Rev.* 740 (1982), reprinted in this volume.

19. Ibid., p. 741 and n. 9.

20. Ibid.

21. Ibid., p. 762.

22. See Hoy, "Deciding Derrida," 4 *London Review of Books* 3 (18 February to 3 March 1982); Hoy, "Derrida," in *The Return of Grand Theory in the Human Sciences* (Q. Skinner, ed. 1985).

23. The "hermeneutic circle" is the claim that understanding the text as a whole de-

pends on understanding its parts, but that the parts cannot be understood independently of the whole. Using the metaphor of the circle then forces hermeneutic theorists to argue lamely that this circle is not a logically vicious one, but simply an unavoidable feature of all understanding. The metaphor of the circle thus creates its own problems, which can be obviated by changing the metaphor to that of weighing or balancing. Besides, the metaphor of balancing seems more natural in the context of legal interpretation, given the classical image of the scales of justice. In either case, the point is that reading must account for *both* (1) the complexity of the parts of the text, and (2) the sense of the text as a whole.

24. See J. Rawls, *A Theory of Justice* 20–21, 48–51 (1971); Hoy, "Hermeneutics," 47 *Soc. Research* 666 (1980).

25. For a reply to this objection, see Unger, "The Critical Legal Studies Movement," 96 *Harv. L. Rev.* 563, 586 (1983).

26. Ibid., p. 564.

27. Ibid., p. 565.

28. Ibid., p. 566.

29. Ibid., pp. 570–71.

30. See G. Hegel, *Philosophy of Right* 1–36 (1952).

31. Unger, "Critical Legal Studies Movement" 565.

32. Ibid., p. 584.

33. Ibid., p. 602.

34. Dworkin, "Law As Interpretation," in *The Politics of Interpretation* 269 (W. Mitchell, ed. 1983).

35. Dworkin, "Law As Interpretation" 270.

36. Unger, "Critical Legal Studies Movement" 576.

37. Ibid., p. 577.

38. Dworkin, "Law As Interpretation" 269.

39. Unger, "Critical Legal Studies Movement" 578.

Section III Introduction

1. Chaim Perelman, "The New Rhetoric: A Theory of Practical Reasoning," in *The Great Ideas Today: 1970* 281 (1970).

2. Ch. Perelman and L. Olbrechts-Tyteca, *The New Rhetoric: A Treatise on Argumentation* (trans. John Wilkinson and Purcell Weaver, 1969). Also see Ch. Perelman, *The Realm of Rhetoric* (trans. William Kluback, 1982).

3. Perelman, "The New Rhetoric" 284.

4. Chaim Perelman, "Opinions and Truth," in Perelman, *The Idea of Justice and the Problem of Argument* 125, 131 (1963).

5. C[haim] Pe[relman], "Rhetoric in Philosophy: The New Rhetoric," in *Encyclopaedia Britannica* (15th ed. 1983), vol. 15, p. 803.

6. Perelman, "Rhetoric in Philosophy" 805; "The New Rhetoric" 285–86. For more extensive discussion of the "universal audience," see Perelman and Olbrechts-Tyteca, *The New Rhetoric*, sections 6–9.

7. Perelman, "Rhetoric in Philosophy" 805; Perelman and Olbrechts-Tyteca, *The New Rhetoric* 33.

8. Cf. the passing references to American pragmatism in Perelman, "The New Rhetoric" 306–7, and "Rhetoric in Philosophy" 805.

9. Ch. Perelman, "Justice and Justification," trans. Susan Rubin, in Perelman, *Justice, Law, and Argument: Essays on Moral and Legal Reasoning* 61 (1980).

10. Perelman, "The New Rhetoric" 304. For further discussion of good reasons in argumentation, see Karl Wallace, "The Substance of Rhetoric: Good Reasons," 49 *Quarterly Journal of Speech* 239–49 (1963), and Wayne C. Booth, *Modern Dogma and the Rhetoric of Assent* (1974).

11. For recent discussions, see Richard Rorty, *Consequences of Pragmatism (Essays: 1972–1980)* (1982), and Saul Kripke, *Wittgenstein on Rules and Private Language* (1983).

12. Perelman, "Opinions and Truth" 133.

Rhetorical Hermeneutics

1. National Aeronautics and Space Act of 1958, Public Law 85–568, Title I, §102, 29 July 1958, 72 Stat. 426; Robert Cooper, Director of the Defense Advanced Research Projects Agency, quoted in Frank Greve, "Pentagon Research Retains Vision of 'Winning' N-war," *Miami Herald*, 27 March 1983, sec. D. p. 4.

2. This answer is only implicit in the most popular forms of American deconstruction— what Richard Rorty calls "weak textualism"—whose practitioners "think that they have now found the true method for analyzing literary works because they have now found the fundamental problematic with which these works deal" (Rorty, *Consequences of Pragmatism: Essays, 1972–1980*, 153 [Minneapolis, 1982] and see Rorty, "Deconstruction and Circumvention," 11 *Critical Inquiry* 2, 19–20 (September 1984). Cf. J. Hillis Miller: "The readings of deconstructive criticism are not the willful imposition by a subjectivity of theory on the texts but are coerced by the texts themselves" ("Theory and Practice: Response to Vincent Leitch," 6 *Critical Inquiry* 611 (Summer 1980)).

3. E. D. Hirsch, Jr., "Objective Interpretation" [1960], *Validity in Interpretation* 212 (New Haven, Conn., 1967).

4. Ibid., p. 209.

5. In this essay "conventions" refers to *instances of shared practices*. See the discussion in my *Interpretive Conventions: The Reader in the Study of American Fiction* 126–39 (Ithaca, N.Y., 1982).

6. Monroe C. Beardsley and W. K. Wimsatt, Jr., "The Affective Fallacy" [1949], in Wimsatt, *The Verbal Icon: Studies in the Meaning of Poetry* 21 (Lexington, Ky., 1954).

7. Beardsley, *Aesthetics: Problems in the Philosophy of Criticism* 403, 49 (New York, 1958).

8. Beardsley, "Textual Meaning and Authorial Meaning," 1 *Genre* 181 (July 1968).

9. Beardsley, *The Possibility of Criticism* 37 (Detroit, 1970), hereafter *PC*.

10. Beardsley, "Intentions and Interpretations: A Fallacy Revived," *The Aesthetic Point of View: Selected Essays* 195 (Michael J. Wreen and Donald M. Callen, eds., Ithaca, N.Y., 1982). The central texts on conventions and speech acts are J. L. Austin, *How to Do Things with Words* (New York, 1962), and John R. Searle, *Speech Acts: An Essay in the Philosophy of Language* (Cambridge, 1969).

11. See, e.g., the comments on "literary competence" in Beardsley, *Aesthetics: Problems in the Philosophy of Criticism* li (2d ed. Indianapolis, 1981); and Beardsley, "The Philosophy of Literature," in *Aesthetics: A Critical Anthology* 329–33 (George Dickie and R. J. Sclafani, eds., New York, 1977).

12. Stanley Fish, "Interpreting the *Variorum*" [1976], in Fish, *Is There a Text in This Class?: The Authority of Interpretive Communities* 171 (Cambridge, Mass., 1980).

13. Jonathan Culler, *Structuralist Poetics: Structuralism, Linguistics, and the Study of Literature* 113 (Ithaca, N.Y., 1975).

14. Ibid., p. 126. For a more extreme example of idealist conventionalism, see my *Interpretive Conventions* 192–207.

15. Culler, "Convention and Meaning: Derrida and Austin," 13 *New Literary History* 30 n. 12 (Autumn 1981); hereafter "CM." This essay was revised and incorporated into Culler, *On Deconstruction: Theory and Criticism after Structuralism* (Ithaca, N.Y., 1982); hereafter *OD*.

16. See Harold Garfinkel, *Studies in Ethnomethodology* 24–31 (Englewood Cliffs, N.J., 1967); and Hubert L. Dreyfus, *What Computers Can't Do: The Limits of Artificial Intelligence* 256–71 (rev. ed., New York, 1979).

17. On the first option, see Walter Benn Michaels, "Philosophy in Kinkanja: Eliot's Pragmatism," 8 *Glyph* 184–85 (1981); on the second, see Dreyfus, *What Computers Can't Do* 289. For further discussion of context as an explanatory concept, see my "Convention and Context," 14 *New Literary History* 399–407 (Winter 1983).

18. See Fish, *Is There a Text?* 277–84, and Fish, "With the Compliments of the Author: Reflections on Austin and Derrida," 8 *Critical Inquiry* 693–721 (Summer 1982). In this analysis I have followed Dreyfus, Fish, and others in using "context" and "situation" interchangeably. For a suggestive discussion of evaluation related to my analysis of interpretation, see Barbara Hernstein Smith, "Contingencies of Value," 10 *Critical Inquiry* 1–35 (September 1982).

19. See the discussion of Wolfgang Iser's phenomenological theory of reading in my *Interpretive Conventions* 49–56.

20. Steven Knapp and Michaels, "Against Theory," 8 *Critical Inquiry* 723 (Summer 1982).

21. See Knapp and Michaels, "Against Theory" 724–30. See also, in 9 *Critical Inquiry* (June 1983), Hirsch's rebuttal in his "Against Theory?" 743–47, and Knapp and Michaels's response in their "A Reply to Our Critics" 795–99.

22. For further arguments along these lines, see my "Truth or Consequences: On Being Against Theory," 9 *Critical Inquiry* 763–66 (June 1983). I should note that Knapp and Michaels come close to addressing my methodological point here when they argue that "nothing in the claim that authorial intention is the necessary object of interpretation tells us anything at all about what should count as evidence for determining the content of any particular intention" ("Reply to Our Critics," 796). True enough, for a theory that simply makes claims about the relation of intention and meaning—but what intentionalist theory stops there? For example, assuming that texts with intentions can be corrupted, textual-biographical critics claim that a valid interpretation must reconstruct the author's composing process, and thus they are consistent with their theory in advocating the close examination of manuscript stages and biographical evidence in the act of interpretation. Here methodological consequences follow logically from an intentionalist theory. See Hershel Parker, *Flawed Texts and Verbal Icons: Literary Authority in American Fiction* (Evanston, Ill., 1984).

23. Fish, "Fear of Fish: A Reply to Walter Davis," 10 *Critical Inquiry* 705 (June 1984).

24. See Fish, *Is There a Text?* 356–70, and "Fear of Fish" 701–3. Also, cf. Thomas S. Kuhn, *The Structure of Scientific Revolutions* 152–59 and 198–206 (2d ed., Chicago, 1970). On "argument fields" and related concepts, see Charles Arthur Willard, *Argumentation and the Social Grounds of Knowledge* (University, Ala., 1983), esp. pp. 5–11 and 89–91.

25. This distinction is nicely elaborated in Rorty, *Philosophy and the Mirror of Nature* 5–6 (Princeton, N.J., 1979).

26. Relevant here is the intersection of Hans-Georg Gadamer's hermeneutics with Chaim Perelman's rhetoric. Cf. Gadamer's analysis of tradition and interpretation throughout his *Truth and Method* (Garrett Barden and John Cumming, trans. and ed., New York, 1975), e.g., pp. 250–51, and the analysis of tradition and argumentation in Perelman and Lucie Olbrechts-Tyteca, *The New Rhetoric: A Treatise on Argumentation* (John Wilkinson and Purcell Weaver, trans.; Notre Dame, Ind., 1969), e.g., pp. 464–65. See also Fish, "Short People Got No Reason to Live: Reading Irony," 112 *Daedalus* 175–91 (Winter 1983) and Adena Rosmarin, "Hermeneutics versus Erotics: Shakespeare's *Sonnets* and Interpretive History," 100 *PMLA* 20–37 (January 1985).

27. Some of the more interesting studies along these lines have been done by the Group for Research on Institutions and Professionalism in literary study (GRIP), sponsored by the Society for Critical Exchange. The work of Michel Foucault stands behind my own and many other recent inquiries into criticism's institutional politics. Foucault's archaeology reveals the "relations between discursive formations and non-discursive domains" such

as institutions, while his genealogies trace the history of "the effective formation of discourse" within institutions, "the field of the non-discursive social" (*The Archaeology of Knowledge and the Discourse on Language* 162 (A. M. Sheridan Smith, trans., New York, 1972); "The Order of Discourse," trans. Ian McLeod, in *Untying the Text: A Post-Structuralist Reader* 71 (Robert Young, ed., Boston, 1981); and "The Eye of Power," trans. Colin Gordon, *Power/Knowledge: Selected Interviews and Other Writings, 1972–1977*, 198 (Gordon, ed., New York, 1980). More specifically, we might say that an institution "includes both the material forms and mechanisms of production, distribution and consumption *and* the ideological rules, norms, conventions and practices which condition the reception, comprehension and application of discourse" (Leitch, "Institutional History and Cultural Hermeneutics," 2 *Critical Texts* 7 [July 1984]; Leitch acknowledges his debt to Foucault on p. 10 n. 2). On the relation of rhetorical or discursive practices to a cultural background of nondiscursive practices, see Dreyfus and Paul Rabinow, *Michel Foucault: Beyond Structuralism and Hermeneutics*, (2d ed. Berkeley and Los Angeles, 1983).

28. Wimsatt and Cleanth Brooks, *Literary Criticism: A Short History* ix, vii–viii (New York, 1957).

29. Richard Ohmann, *English in America: A Radical View of the Profession* 4 (New York, 1976); and see John Fekete, *The Critical Twilight: Explorations in the Ideology of Anglo-American Literary Theory from Eliot to McLuhan* (London, 1977). See also Terry Eagleton, *Literary Theory: An Introduction* 47–53 (Minneapolis, 1983). For related histories of literary studies in other countries, see Brian Doyle, "The Hidden History of English Studies," in *Re-Reading English* (Peter Widdowson, ed., London, 1982), and Peter Uwe Hohendahl, *The Institution of Criticism* (Ithaca, N.Y. 1982).

30. Fekete, *Critical Twilight* 49.

31. See Fekete, *Critical Twilight* 49. Fekete does go on to say that "the New Criticism introduced a technicism and an accommodation with science, and it mercilessly attacked and destroyed left-wing aesthetic forms, including the totally reformist forms of historiographic or sociological criticism" (p. 49).

32. For a recent general history, see *The Organization of Knowledge in Modern America, 1860–1920* (Alexandra Oleson and John Voss, eds., Baltimore, 1979).

33. See William Riley Parker, "Where Do English Departments Come From?" *College English* 339–51 (February 1967); Arthur W. Applebee, *Tradition and Reform in the Teaching of English: A History* 25–28 (Urbana, Ill., 1974); and Phyllis Franklin, "English Studies: The World of Scholarship in 1883," 99 *PMLA* 356–70 (May 1984).

34. Applebee, *Tradition and Reform* 25–26.

35. For details of the conflict between criticism and scholarship in American literary study, see Franklin, "English Studies in America: Reflections on the Development of a Discipline," 30 *American Quarterly* 21–38 (Spring 1978); Grant Webster, *The Republic of Letters: A History of Postwar American Literary Opinion* 113–16 (Baltimore, 1979); and William E. Cain, *The Crisis in Criticism: Theory, Literature, and Reform in English Studies* 95–101 (Baltimore, 1984).

36. John Crowe Ransom, *The New Criticism* 281 (Norfolk, Conn., 1941). In chap. 1 Ransom works out his distinction between science and poetry in a critique of I. A. Richards's parallel distinction between two uses of language proposed in his *Principles of Literary Criticism* (New York, 1925).

37. Ransom, "Criticism, Inc.," *The World's Body* 329 (New York, 1938).

38. Frederick A. Pottle, *The Idiom of Poetry* (Ithaca, N.Y., 1941), quoted in Brooks, "Criticism, History, and Critical Relativism," *The Well Wrought Urn: Studies in the Structure of Poetry* 207 (New York, 1947); hereafter "CHCR."

39. Stephen Toulmin, "From Form to Function: Philosophy and History of Science in the 1950s and Now," 106 *Daedalus* 159 (Summer 1977).

40. Ohmann, *English in America* 239–40. See Magali Sarfatti Larson, *The Rise of Professionalism: A Sociological Analysis* (Berkeley and Los Angeles, 1977), esp. chaps. 4 and 12, and Dietrich Rueschemeyer, "Professional Autonomy and the Social Control of Expertise," in

The Sociology of the Professions: Lawyers, Doctors, and Others, 38–58 (Robert Dingwall and Philip Lewis, eds., New York, 1983).

41. For useful discussions of this New Critical legacy, see Frank Lentricchia, *After the New Criticism* (Chicago, 1980); Jane P. Tompkins, "The Reader in History: The Changing Shape of Literary Response," *Reader-Response Criticism: From Formalism to Post-Structuralism* 201–32 (Baltimore, 1980); Gerald Graff, "Who Killed Criticism?" 49 *American Scholar* 337–55 (Summer 1980); Culler, "Beyond Interpretation," *The Pursuit of Signs: Semiotics, Literature, Deconstruction* 3–17 (Ithaca, N.Y., 1981); Cain, "The Institutionalization of the New Criticism," *Crisis in Criticism* 104–21; and Edward W. Said, *The World, the Text, and the Critic* 140–77 (Cambridge, Mass., 1983).

42. See esp. recent work by Eagleton: *Walter Benjamin; or, Toward a Revolutionary Criticism* 101–13 (London, 1981); "Wittgenstein's Friends," 135 *New Left Review* 64–90 (September–October, 1982); and *Literary Theory* 204–14. See also Said, "Opponents, Audiences, Constituencies, and Community," 9 *Critical Inquiry* 1–26 (September 1982), and Robert Wess, "Notes toward a Marxist Rhetoric," 28 *Bucknell Review*, no. 2, 126–48 (1983).

43. Lentricchia (discussing Kenneth Burke's fable of history), *Criticism and Social Change* 160 (Chicago, 1983). For a general discussion of the cultural conversation, see my "Reading *Huckleberry Finn*: The Rhetoric of Performed Ideology," in *New Essays on Adventures of Huckleberry Finn* (Louis J. Budd, ed., New York, 1985).

Constitutional Fate

1. 347 U.S 483 (1954).

2. L. Hand, *The Bill of Rights* (1958).

3. 410 U.S. 113 (1973).

4. See, e.g., L. Hand, *The Bill of Rights*; A. Bickel, *The Least Dangerous Branch* (1962); C. Black, *The People and the Court* (1960); Wechsler, "Toward Neutral Principles of Constitutional Law," 73 *Harv. L. Rev.* 1 (1959); Deutsch, "Neutrality, Legitimacy, and the Supreme Court: Some Intersections between Law and Political Science," 20 *Stan. L. Rev.* 169 (1968); Grey, "Do We Have an Unwritten Constitution?" 27 *Stan. L. Rev.* 703 (1975); R. Berger, *Government by Judiciary* (1977); Wellington, "Common Law Rules and Constitutional Double Standards: Some Notes on Adjudication," 83 *Yale L. J.* 221 (1973); J. H. Ely, *Democracy and Distrust* (1980); Monaghan, "Constitutional Adjudication: The Who and the When," 82 *Yale L. J.* 1363 (1973).

5. On what individual justices have said, see, e.g., T. R. Powell, *Vagaries and Varieties in Constitutional Interpretation* (1956), p. 21, quoting a speech by Mr. Justice Holmes: "I do not think the United States would come to an end if we lost our power to declare an act of Congress void. I do think the Union would be imperiled if we could not make that declaration as to the laws of several states."

6. C. Black, *The People and the Court* 6 (1960).

7. J. Butzner, *Constitutional Chaff* 147 (1941).

8. A. Bickel, *The Least Dangerous Branch* (1962).

9. See U.C.C. § 2-209 (9th ed. 1978), comment 2: "[M]odifications . . . must meet the test of good faith imposed by this Act. The effective use of bad faith to escape performance on the original contract is barred, and the extortion of a 'modification' without legitimate commercial reason is ineffective. . . ."

10. "[N]o society can make a perpetual constitution. . . . The earth belongs always to the living generation. . . . They are masters too of their own persons, and consequently may govern them as they please. But persons and property make the sum of the objects of government. The constitution and the laws of their predecessors extinguished them in their natural course with those whose gave them being. This could preserve that being till it ceased to be itself, and no longer. Every constitution then, and every law, naturally expires. . . . If it be enforced longer, it is an act of force and not of right." Letter from Thomas

Jefferson to James Madison (5 September 1789), reprinted in Julian Boyd, ed., 15 *The Papers of Thomas Jefferson* 345–96 (Princeton: Princeton University Press, 1958).

11. Compare J. Rawls, *A Theory of Justice* (1971).

12. L. Fuller, "Positivism and Fidelity to Law—A Reply to Professor Hart," 71 *Harv. L. Rev.* 138 (1958).

13. See discussion in Berger, *Government by Judiciary* 118–119.

14. Home Building & Loan Ass'n. v. Blaisdell, 290 U.S. 398, 453 (1933) (Sutherland, J. dissenting).

15. It was to maintain this distinction that Justice Story wrote, "Is the sense of the Constitution to be ascertained, not by its own text, but by the 'probable meaning' to be gathered by conjectures from scattered documents . . . ? Is the Constitution of the United States to be the only instrument, which is not to be interpreted by what is written, but by probable guesses, aside from the text?" J. Story, 1 *Commentaries on the Constitution of the United States* (1st ed., Boston, 1833), § 405, p. 390, n. 1.

16. Although even as to this list, I should like to observe that at the time of my preparation of the Dougherty Lectures, and their publication, no typology of listing these five types *as argument* was in use. I include in this statement trivial variations that retain the definitions I have identified.

17. Moore v. City of East Cleveland, 431 U.S 494 (1977).

18. Village of Belle Terre v. Boraas, 416 U.S. 1 (1974).

19. Moore v. City of East Cleveland, 431 U.S 494, 503 (1977) (footnote omitted).

20. Ibid. at 504–5 (footnote omitted).

21. L. Tribe *American Constitutional Law* 990 (1978) (emphasis in original).

22. Ibid., p. 990, note 30.

23. G. Harman, *The Nature of Morality* (1977).

24. See Kuhn, "Logic of Discovery or Psychology of Research," in *Criticism and the Growth of Knowledge* 1 (I. Lakatos and A. Musgrave, eds. 1970).

25. A. de Tocqueville, *Democracy in America* 248 (J. Mayer and M. Lerner, eds. (1966).

26. See, e.g., H. Bloom, *The Anxiety of Influence* (1973); W. J. Bate, *The Burden of the Past and the English Poet* (1970).

27. See, e.g., G. Calabresi, *The Cost of Accidents* (1970); Calabresi, "Transaction Costs, Resource Allocation and Liability Rules: A Comment," 11 *J. Law Econ.* 67 (1968); Calabresi, "The Decision for Accidents: An Approach to Nonfault Allocation of Costs," 78 *Harv. L. Review* 713 (1965).

28. N. Goodman, *Ways of Worldmaking* 20 (1978).

29. Thucydides, *History of the Peloponnesian War* (T. Hobbes, trans., D.Grene, ed. 1959).

30. G. Calabresi and P. Bobbitt, *Tragic Choices* 195–99 (1978).

31. N. Bohr, "Discussion with Einstein on Epistemological Problems in Atomic Physics," in *Atomic Physics and Human Knowledge* 66 (1958).

32. U.S Const., Art. 1, § 6.

33. K. Llewellyn, *The Common Law Tradition: Deciding Appeals* (1960).

34. Dodd, "Congress and the Quest for Power," in *Discovery* 8–11 (Univ. of Texas Publication) (1979).

35. R. Pinto, *Des Juges Qui Ne Gouvernement pas: Opinions Dissidentes à la Cour Supreme des Etats-Unis, 1900–1933* (1934).

36. I quote from the paraphrase of Pinto's article by yet another political scientist, C. Ct. Haines, who shares this perspective. See Haines, "Judicial Review of Acts of Congress and the Need for Constitutional Reform," 45 *Yale L. J.* 816, 852 (1936).

37. See Goodman, *Ways of Worldmaking*.

38. Llewellyn, "The Constitution as an Institution," 34 *Colum. L. Rev.* 1, 39 (1934).

39. Ibid., p. 40.

40. W. Arrowsmith, "The Criticism of Greek Tragedy," in *Tragedy: Vision and Form* 342 (W. Corrigan, ed. 1965).

41. The *New Yorker*, 25 October 1941, p. 15.

42. J. B. Thayer, *Legal Essays* 1 (1908); originally in 7 *Harv. L. Rev.* 129.

43. R. Fogelin, *Wittgenstein* (1976).

44. Paraphrasing Holmes, who said, "Constitutional law, like other moral contrivances, has to take some chances." T. R. Powell, "The Logic and Rhetoric of Constitutional Law," in *Essays in Constitutional Law* 88, 89 (R. McCloskey, ed. 1957).

45. Lecture by Professor John Archibald Wheeler, 9 February 1979, University of Texas.

The Fate of the Constitution

1. "Symposium: Law and Literature," 60 *Texas L. Rev.* 373 (1982).

2. White "The Text, Interpretation, and Critical Standards," 60 *Texas L. Rev.* 579 (1982).

3. Ibid., p. 572.

4. Ibid.

5. Ibid.

6. Ibid., p. 573.

7. Ibid., pp. 573–74.

8. Ibid., p. 579 (emphasis in original).

9. Levinson, "Law as Literature," 60 *Texas L. Rev.* 381 (1982) (quoting S. Fish, *Is There a Text In This Class?* 327 (1980).

10. Ibid., p. 383.

11. R. Rorty, *Philosophy and the Mirror of Nature* 161 (1979).

12. P. Bobbitt, *Constitutional Fate: Theory of the Constitution* 245 (1982) [hereafter cited by page number only].

13. P. 245.

14. P. 245.

15. P. 245.

16. Pp. 243–44.

17. P. 245.

18. P. 7.

19. P. 94.

20. Pp. 247–48.

21. P. 211.

22. P. 248.

23. P. 7.

24. P. 11 (quoting Rhode Island v. Massachusetts, 37 U.S. (12 Pet.) 657, 721 (1838)).

25. P. 13.

26. P. 61.

27. P. 63.

28. As Bobbitt uses the term, "ethical arguments are not *moral* arguments. Ethical constitutional arguments do not claim that a particular solution is right or wrong in any sense

larger than that the solution comports with the sort of people we are and the means we have chosen to solve political and customary constitutional problems" (pp. 94–95 (emphasis in original)).

29. P. 94.

30. P. 96.

31. P. 132.

32. P. 163.

33. P. 136.

34. P. 222.

35. P. 242.

36. P. 249.

37. P. 235.

38. P. 245.

39. P. 57.

40. P. 61.

41. Ibid.

42. A. Bickel, *The Least Dangerous Branch* 39 (1962).

43. Levinson, "Law as Literature" 378.

44. For a more detailed exposition of this argument, see Knapp and Michaels, "Against Theory," 9 *Critical Inquiry* 723 (1982).

45. Levinson, "Law as Literature" 379.

46. P. 166.

Judicial Criticism

1. Olmstead v. United States, 277 U.S. 438 (1928), *overruled,* Katz v. United States, 389 U.S. 347 (1967).

2. J.B. White, *When Words Lose Their Meaning* (1984).

3. *Olmstead,* 277 U.S. at 40.

4. See generally Goldman v. United States, 316 U.S. 129 (1942) (admitting evidence obtained by placing a microphone against a common wall), *overruled,* Katz v. United States, 389 U.S. 347 (1967); Silverman v. United States, 365 U.S. 505 (1961) (a slight physical intrusion in placing microphone on wall was "an actual intrusion into a constitutionally protected area"); Katz v. United States, 389 U.S. 347 (1967) (bugging a defendant in a telephone booth "violated the privacy upon which he justifiably relied while using the telephone booth"); Rawlings v. Kentucky, 448 U.S. 98 (1980) (no expectation of privacy in the purse of an acquaintance).

5. See, e.g., United States v. Knotts, 460 U.S. 276 (1983) (monitoring of beeper signals did not invade any legitimate expectation of privacy).

6. See, e.g., Cardwell v. Lewis, 417 U.S. 583 (1974) (no expectation of privacy infringed when paint scrapings were taken from the exterior of a vehicle left in a public parking lot).

7. See, e.g., Davis v. Mississippi, 394 U.S. 721 (1969) (fingerprints obtained during defendant's illegal detention were a product of that detention and could not be admitted into evidence); Schmerber v. California, 384 U.S. 757 (1966) (taking blood sample was permissible); Terry v. Ohio, 392 U.S. 1 (1968) (no violation of the Fourth Amendment when a police officer conducted a limited search for weapons where the officer had reasonable grounds to believe that the individual searched was armed and dangerous).

8. See, e.g., United States v. Miller, 425 U.S. 435 (1976) (bank accounts and other bank transactions not protected by the Fourth Amendment).

9. See, e.g., United States v. Place, 462 U.S. 696 (1983) (trained canines sniffing luggage located in a public place held not a search); United States v. White, 401 U.S. 745 (1971) (tape recording made by undercover agent did not invade the defendant's expectation of privacy).

10. U.S. Const. amend. IV.

11. *Olmstead*, 277 U.S. at 464.

12. Idem at 438, 478 (Brandeis, J., dissenting).

13. See Silverthorne Lumber Co. v. United States, 251 U.S. 385 (1920) (when information is obtained by unconstitutional search and seizure, the Fourth Amendment protects the recipient from subsequent compulsory production of the information).

14. Gouled v. United States, 255 U.S. 298, 305-6 (1920) (when a representative of the government by "stealth, or through social acquaintance, or in the guise of a business call" enters the house or office of a person suspected of a crime, his subsequent seizure of a suspect's papers violates the Fourth Amendment).

15. *Olmstead*, 277 U.S. at 463.

16. Idem at 455–56.

17. Idem at 457.

18. Taft's summary of the cases dealing with the Fourth Amendment since Boyd v. United States, 116 U.S. 616 (1886), are, as I said above, descriptive and conclusory. His apparent aim—as it is with respect to the language of the Fourth Amendment, too—is that you instantly see that *this* has nothing to do with *that*.

His treatment of the defendant's claim that the criminality of the government's conduct requires exclusion of the evidence is of a piece with the rest. He simply subsumes it under a common-law rule of evidence, that admissibility is not affected by illegality. This move, the conclusory reduction of the constitutional to the merely evidentiary, is similar in structure to his definition of the Constitution and of his own role. He defines the common-law rule, then says "the common law rule must apply in the case at bar." *Olmstead*, 277 U.S. at 468. But he gives no reason why it "must."

19. This would, of course, require considerable skill. Consider, for example, the comprehensiveness of Taft's summary of a statute, made in his description of the *Boyd* case:

> The fifth section of the Act of June 22, 1874, provided that in cases not criminal under the revenue laws, the United States Attorney, whenever he thought an invoice, belonging to the defendant, would tend to prove any allegations made by the United States, might by a written motion describing the invoice and setting forth the allegation which he expected to prove, secure a notice from the court to the defendant to produce the invoice, and if the defendant refuses to produce it, the allegation stated in the motion should be taken as confessed, but if produced, the United States Attorney should be permitted, under the direction of the court, to make an examination of the invoice, and might offer the same in evidence. [*Olmstead*, 277 U.S. at 458]

20. Adamson v. California, 332 U.S. 46, 68 (1947) (Black, J., dissenting) (all of the guarantees specified in the Bill of Rights are incorporated in the Fourteenth Amendment); Griswold v. Connecticut, 381 U.S. 479, 507 (1965) (Black, J., dissenting) (only those rights explicitly protected by a specific Bill of Rights provision are protected by the Fourteenth Amendment).

21. *Olmstead*, 277 U.S. at 455.

22. Idem at 471 (Brandeis, J., dissenting).

23. Idem at 471–72.

24. Of course he does this in apparent confidence that he can persuade us that his view on this question is right, but this confidence may in fact be misplaced. To raise such a question is to start a conversation which may result in one's own refutation.

25. *Olmstead*, 277 U.S. at 472 (Brandeis, J., dissenting) (quoting McCulloch v. Maryland, 17 U.S. (4 Wheat.) 316, 407 (1819)).

26. *Olmstead*, 277 U.S. at 472 (Brandeis, J., dissenting).

27. Idem (quoting Euclid v. Ambler Realty Co., 272 U.S. 365, 387 (1926)).

28. 217 U.S. 349 (1910).

29. *Olmstead*, 277 U.S. at 472–73 (Brandeis, J., dissenting) (quoting *Weems*, 217 U.S. at 373).

30. *Olmstead*, 277 U.S. at 473 (Brandeis, J., dissenting).

31. Idem.

32. Idem at 474.

33. Idem.

34. 116 U.S. 616 (1886).

35. 96 U.S. 727 (1877) (letters and sealed packages in the mail can be opened only under warrant).

36. *Olmstead*, 277 U.S. at 475 (Brandeis, J., dissenting).

37. Idem at 477–78.

38. Idem at 478.

39. Compare here the way poets and other writers often give plain or ordinary speech a new freshness and power by locating it in a complicated context. See, for example, my discussion of Swift and Johnson in chapters 5 and 6 of *When Words Lose Their Meaning*, or better, read George Herbert's poem, "Jordan (I)," in *George Herbert and the Seventeenth-Century Religious Poets* 25 (M.A. Di Cesare, ed. 1978).

Taft in a sense claims that the Constitution is simply written in the vernacular, that there is nothing special about this language at all. But his simplicities are not embedded in a justifying complexity, and the result, as I suggest above, is an opinion of hidden authoritarianism.

40. *Olmstead*, 277 U.S. at 482 (Brandeis, J., dissenting).

41. Idem at 483.

42. Idem.

43. Idem at 485.

44. See, e.g., Griswold v. Connecticut, 381 U.S. 479 (1965); Henry v. United States, 361 U.S. 98 (1959).

45. 389 U.S. 347 (1967).

46. Idem at 351.

Index

Page numbers in italics indicate authors' contributions to this volume.

144–45, 159–60, 189, 210, 321–22, 328, 380, 449n.153
Ethical argument, 367–372

Farnsworth, E. Allan, 223–24
Fekete, John, 356–57
Fish, Stanley, 112–13, 160–61, 163–64, 182, 185, *251–68*, 276, 349, 353, 383
Fiss, Owen, 87, 88, 166–72, *229–49*, 251–68, 329–30
Formalism, 37, 42, 117, 133–*225 passim*, 277–82. *See also* Parol evidence rule
Foucault, Michel, 327
Fourteenth Amendment, "privileges and immunities" clause of, 6–7
Frank, Jerome, 305, 479n.34
Frankfurter, Felix, 32
Fried, Charles, *45–51*
Frigaliment Importing Company v. *B.N.S. International Sales Corporation*, 217–18

Gadamer, Hans-Georg, 83, 185–86, 319–25, 327–28
Gallie, W. B., 147
Geertz, Clifford, 229
Gilmore, Grant, 287, 300–301, 460n.119
Gordon, Robert, 202
Graff, Gerald, xiii, 112, 172, *175–80*, 453n.31
Grey, Thomas, 27
Grice, H. P., 177
Griswold v. *Connecticut*, 208, 210, 373, 445n.79

Habermas, Jurgen, 319, 323–29, 330
Hamilton, Alexander, 188, 191, 192
Hamlet, 284
Hancher, Michael, *101–14*
Hand, Learned, 46, 216, 305
Harris v. *McRae*, 205
Hart, H. L. A., 117, 127, 134, 135–36, 242
Hart, Henry, 121, 122, 123
Hartman, Geoffrey, 185, 215
Hawkins, F. Vaughan, 105, 106
Hayden v. *Hoadley*, 305–6
Hegel, G. W. F., 331, 335, 336
Heidegger, Martin, 185, 205, 325
Hermeneutics, ix–xiii, 37–42, 83–84, 199–203, 310–38, 341, 345–63
Hertzog v. *Hertzog*, 293–97
Hirsch, E.D., ix, 42, *55–68*, 125, 128, 159, 162, 221–22, 346, 347, 353
Historical argument, 366
Hobbes, Thomas, 193–94, 195
Holmes, Oliver Wendell, 217, 293, 302, 304
Holy Scripture, 61
Hoy, David Couzens, *319–38*

Hughes, Charles Evans, 91
Humpty-Dumpty, 56, 80

"Incorporation" of Bill of Rights against states, 6–9, 20–21, 85, 92, 94
In re will of Rowland, 107, 111
Intentionalism, 37–41, 45–129 *passim*, 137–40, 158–59, 198–99, 275–77, 282–84, 301–6, 389–91, 471n.12. *See also* "Jurisprudence of original intention"
"Intentional fallacy," 37–39, 40–41, 59–62, 102, 103, 128, 215–16, 221
Interpretation of Constitution. *See* Constitution of the United States, interpretation of
"Interpretivism," 193, 195–203

Jackson, Andrew, 97
Jefferson, Thomas, 29, 192
Johnson, Barbara, xi
Judicial craft, 209–11
"Jurisprudence of original intention," 6, 9, 15–16, 29, 31–32, 48, 49–51. *See also* Intentionalism

Kammen, Michael, 3
Kelsen, Hans, 242
Kessler, Friedrich, 285, 287, 300–301
Knapp, Steven, 352–54
Krauthammer, Charles, 169–70
Kripke, Saul, 63, 65, 66
Kuhn, Thomas, 168, 234, 255–56

"La Belle Dame Sans Merci" (Keats), 473n.32
Lane, Jessica, *269–284*
Langdell, Christopher Columbus, 155–66
Legal positivism, 240, 242–43
Levinson, Sanford, 111, 112, *155–73*, 175–80, 182–83, 185, 257, 383–84, 391
Levy, Leonard, 197
Lewis, David, 63, 65, 66
Lieber, Francis, ix
Llewellyn, Karl, 376–77
Locke, John, 105, 194, 195
"London" (Blake), 59–60, 67

MacCabe, Colin, 164, 180
Madison, James, 17, 29, 97–100, 165, 188
Mailloux, Steven, *345–63*
Marbury v. *Madison*, 27, 69, 85, 195–96
Marshall, John, 6, 27, 28, 31, 69, 70–71, 80, 156, 164–65, 183, 196, 379, 402
Martin, Philip, 53
Marx, Leo, 198–99
McCulloch v. *Maryland*, 71, 80–81, 379
Meese, Edwin, 5–6, 8–9, *25–33*
Meyer v. *Nebraska*, 208, 373